The Blackwell Companion to Judaism

Blackwell Companions to Religion

The Blackwell Companions to Religion series presents a collection of the most recent scholarship and knowledge about world religions. Each volume draws together newly commissioned essays by distinguished authors in the field, and is presented in a style which is accessible to undergraduate students, as well as scholars and the interested general reader. These volumes approach the subject in a creative and forward-thinking style, providing a forum in which leading scholars in the field can make their views and research available to a wider audience.

Published

The Blackwell Companion to Judaism
Edited by Jacob Neusner and Alan J. Avery-Peck

Forthcoming

The Blackwell Companion to Political Theology
Edited by William T. Cavanaugh and Peter Scott

The Blackwell Companion to Sociology of Religion
Edited by Richard K. Fenn

The Blackwell Companion to Hinduism
Edited by Gavin Flood

The Blackwell Companion to Religious Ethics
Edited by Charles Hallisey and William Schweiker

The Blackwell Companion to the Old Testament
Edited by Leo G. Perdue

The Blackwell Companion to Postmodern Theology
Edited by Graham Ward

The Blackwell Companion to Judaism

Edited by

Jacob Neusner
Bard Colllege

Alan J. Avery-Peck
College of the Holy Cross

Copyright © Blackwell Publishers Ltd 2000
Editorial matter and arrangement copyright © Jacob Neusner
and Alan J. Avery-Peck 2000

First published 2000

2 4 6 8 10 9 7 5 3 1

Blackwell Publishers Ltd
108 Cowley Road
Oxford OX4 1JF
UK

Blackwell Publishers Inc.
350 Main Street
Malden, Massachusetts 02148
USA

British Library Cataloguing in Publication Data

A CIP catalogue record for this book is available from the
British Library.

Library of Congress Cataloging-in-Publication Data

The Blackwell companion to Judaism / edited by Jacob Neusner and Alan J. Avery-Peck.
    p.   cm. — (Blackwell companions to religion)
  Includes bibliographical references and index.
  ISBN 1–57718–058–5 (alk. paper)
    1. Judaism.   I. Neusner, Jacob, 1932–   II. Avery-Peck, Alan J. (Alan Jeffery),
  1952–   III. Series.

  BM42.B54   2000
  296—dc21   00-021874

Desk editor: Anthony Grahame

Typeset in 10.5 on 12.5 pt Photina
by Graphicraft Limited, Hong Kong
Printed in Great Britain by Biddles Ltd, Guildford

This book is printed on acid-free paper.

Contents

Contributors

Jacob Neusner, Ph.D., Columbia University, is Religion and Research Professor of Theology at Bard College, Annandale-on-Hudson, New York. He is a Life Member of Clare Hall, Cambridge University and Member of the Institute for Advanced Study in Princeton, New Jersey. He holds sixteen honorary degrees and academic medals.

Alan J. Avery-Peck is Kraft–Hiatt Professor of Judaic Studies at the College of the Holy Cross, Worcester, Massachusetts. He has written broadly on Judaism in the first six centuries CE. Along with Jacob Neusner and William S. Green, he is co-editor of *The Encyclopaedia of Judaism* (Leiden: E. J. Brill, and New York: Continuum, 1999).

David H. Aaron is Professor of Bible and History of Interpretation at Hebrew Union College–Jewish Institute of Religion, Cincinnati. His publications are in the fields of Biblical and Rabbinic Literature, often with a focus on the transformations of myth and literary motifs.

Judith R. Baskin is Professor and Chair of the Department of Judaic Studies at the University at Albany, State University of New York. Her publications include *Pharaoh's Counsellors: Job, Jethro and Balaam in Rabbinic and Patristic Tradition* (1983) and the edited collections, *Jewish Women in Historical Perspective* (1991; 2nd edn., 1998) and *Women of the Word: Jewish Women and Jewish Writing* (1994).

S. Daniel Breslauer is Professor of Religious Studies at the University of Kansas, Lawrence, Kansas, where he has taught since 1978. His major field of research is modern Jewish thought, and he most recently has published *Toward a Jewish (M)Orality: Speaking of a Postmodern Jewish Ethics* (Greenwood Press, 1998) and *The Seductiveness of Jewish Myth: Challenge or Response* (SUNY, 1997).

Benjamin Brown is lecturer in Jewish Thought at Beit Morasha of Jerusalem and, since 1997, at the Hebrew University of Jerusalem. In 1999–2000, he is also guest-lecturer at Tel Aviv University. He has published several articles on Orthodox Judaism.

David R. Carr is Professor of History at the University of South Florida in Tampa, Florida.

Bruce D. Chilton is Bernard Iddings Bell Professor of Religion at Bard College and Rector of the Church of St. John the Evangelist. His publications include *God in Strength. Jesus' Announcement of the Kingdom: Studien zum Neuen Testament und seiner Umwelt 1* (Freistadt: Plöchl, 1979), *The Isaiah Targum. Introduction, Translation, Apparatus, and Notes: The Aramaic Bible 11* (Wilmington: Glazier, and Edinburgh: Clark, 1987), and *Pure Kingdom. Jesus' Vision of God: Studying the Historical Jesus 1* (Eerdmans: Grand Rapids, and London: SPCK, 1996). With Jacob Neusner, he is also the author of *Jewish–Christian Debates. God, Kingdom, Messiah* (Minneapolis: Fortress, 1998).

M. Herbert Danzger is Professor of Sociology at Lehman College CUNY and at the Graduate Center CUNY. His earlier work on community power structure, conflict, and social movements was supported by NIMH and NSF and published in the *American Sociological Review* and elsewhere. His studies of "return" to Jewish traditionalism benefited from two academic years in Israel, first at Bar-Ilan University as senior lecturer and then at the Hebrew University of Jerusalem as Fulbright Professor. A portion of his studies of "return" is described in *Returning to Tradition* (New Haven: Yale University Press, 1989).

Philip R. Davies is Professor of Biblical Studies at the University of Sheffield and founder and editor of the *Journal for the Study of the Old Testament*. His major interest lies in the Dead Sea Scrolls, on which he has written five books and numerous articles. He is also the author of *In Search of Ancient Israel* (Sheffield, 1992) and *Scribes and Schools: The Canonization of the Hebrew Scriptures* (Nashville, 1998).

Elliot N. Dorff is Rector and Professor of Philosophy at the University of Judaism in Los Angeles. He serves as Vice Chair of the Conservative Movement's Committee on Jewish Law and Standards, for which he has written a number of responsa on moral issues. His books include *Contemporary Jewish Ethics and Morality: A Reader* (edited with Louis Newman; New York: Oxford, 1995) and *Matters of Life and Death: A Jewish Approach to Modern Medical Ethics* (Philadelphia: Jewish Publication Society, 1998).

Daniel J. Elazar (1934–1999) was Professor of Political Science at Temple University, Philadelphia, and Senator N. M. Paterson Professor Emeritus of Intergovernmental Relations at Bar-Ilan University, Israel, and the founder and editor of the *Jewish Political Studies Review* and president of the Jerusalem Center for Public Affairs. He was the author or editor of over seventy books including a four-volume study of the *Covenant Tradition in Politics* (Transaction, 1995–1998), as well as *Community and Polity*, *The Jewish Polity*, and *People and Polity*, a trilogy on Jewish political and community organization from earliest times to the present.

Neil Gillman is the Aaron Rabinowitz and Simon H. Rifkind Professor of Jewish Philosophy at the Jewish Theological Seminary in New York. He is the author of *Sacred Fragments: Recovering Theology for the Modern Jew* and of *The Death of Death: Resurrection and Immortality in Jewish Thought*. He is currently working on a book-length study of images of God in Jewish literature.

Daniel Gordis is Director of the Jerusalem Fellows Program at the Mandel School in Jerusalem. He is author of *God Was Not in the Fire: The Search for a Spiritual Judaism* (1995), *Does the World Need the Jews? Rethinking Chosenness and American Jewish Identity* (1997), and most recently *Becoming a Jewish Parent: How to Explore Spirituality and Tradition with Your Children* (1999).

Yosef Gorny teaches modern Jewish history at Tel Aviv University and presently is Head of the Chaim Weizmann Institute for Research in the History of Zionism. His main publications in English are: *The British Labour Movement and Zionism 1917–1948* (London: Frank Cass, 1983), *Zionism and the Arabs 1882–1948: A Study of Ideology* (Oxford: Oxford University Press, 1987), and *The State of Israel in Jewish Public Thought: The Quest for Collective Identity* (London and New York: Macmillan and New York University Press, 1994). He has recently completed for publication the book *Between Auschwitz and Jerusalem: The Holocaust and the State of Israel as Components of Jewish Identity*.

William Scott Green is Professor of Religion, Philip S. Bernstein Professor of Judaic Studies, and Dean of the College at the University of Rochester.

Dana Evan Kaplan is a research fellow at the Center for Jewish Studies at the University of Wisconsin–Milwaukee and is associate rabbi at Congregation Emanu–El B'ne Jeshurun. He is editor of the forthcoming *Conflicting Visions: Contemporary Debates in Reform Judaism* (Routledge) and author of *The Jewish Community in South Africa during the Mandela Era* (forthcoming), *American Reform Judaism Today* (forthcoming), and *Conversion to Judaism in 19th Century America* (forthcoming).

Paul Mendes-Flohr is Professor of Jewish Thought at the Hebrew University of Jerusalem.

Frederick J. Murphy is Professor of Religious Studies at the College of the Holy Cross, Worcester, Massachusetts. His research interests are New Testament and late Second Temple Judaism and his publications include *The Structure and Meaning of Second Baruch*; *The Religious World of Jesus: An Introduction to Second Temple Palestinian Judaism*; *Pseudo-Philo: Rewriting the Bible*; and *Fallen Is Babylon: The Revelation to John*.

Sara Reguer teaches in the Department of Jewish Studies of Brooklyn College of the City University of New York.

Jeffrey K. Salkin is senior rabbi of The Community Synagogue, Port Washington, New York. He holds a Doctor of Ministry degree from Princeton Theological Seminary and is author of several books on popular theology, including *Being God's Partner: How to Find the Hidden Link between Spirituality and Your Work* (Jewish Lights). His most recent book is *Searching for My Brother: Jewish Men in a Gentile World* (Putnam).

Guenter Stemberger teaches at the University of Vienna, where he holds the chair of Jewish Studies. His main fields of research and teaching are Rabbinic Literature and the history of the Jews in the pre-Islamic period. His books in English translation are *Introduction to the Talmud and Midrash* (2nd edition, Edinburgh: T&T Clark, 1996), *Jewish Contemporaries of Jesus* (Minneapolis: Augsburg Fortress Press, 1995), and *Jews and Christians in the Holy Land. Palestine in the Fourth Century* (Edinburgh: T&T Clark, 1999).

Marvin A. Sweeney is Professor of Hebrew Bible at the Claremont School of Theology and Professor of Religion at the Claremont Graduate University, Claremont, California. He is author of *Isaiah 1–39, with an Introduction to Prophetic Literature* (Grand Rapids and Cambridge: Eerdmans, 1996); *King Josiah of Judah: The Lost Messiah of Israel* (Oxford and New York: Oxford University Press, 2000); and *The Book of the Twelve Prophets* (Berit Olam; Collegeville: Liturgical/ Michael Glazier, 2000). He is editor of the *Review of Biblical Literature* and co-editor of the *Forms of the Old Testament Literature* commentary series.

Tzvee Zahavy has taught at the University of Minnesota, the University of California, Berkeley, and the College of William and Mary. His publications include *The Traditions of Eleazar Ben Azariah* (Scholars Press), *The Mishnaic Law of Blessings and Prayers: Tractate Berakhot* (Scholars Press, 1987), *The Talmud of the Land of Israel: Tractate Berakhot* (University of Chicago Press, 1989), *Studies in Jewish Prayer* (University Press of America, 1990), and *The Talmud of Babylonia: Tractate Hullin* (Scholars Press, 1992–4).

Preface

The *Companion to Judaism* affords perspective on Judaism, its history, doctrines, divisions, and contemporary condition. The work systematically organizes and places into context the history of Judaism from ancient through modern times, identifies and expounds some of Judaism's principal doctrines, introduces the more important forms of modern and contemporary Judaism, and takes up topics of special interest in contemporary Judaic life. In this way, it identifies the focal points of an ancient and contemporary religion, defining a context in which diverse texts and facts of Judaism fit and make sense. Readers thus gain a view of the whole even as they encounter each of Judaism's important parts.

The essays provide perspective on dates and facts, the details of a complex religion. Readers thus will learn the facts of Judaism and its history even as they place these facts in the larger setting of Judaic theology, religious practice, and evolving social order. Not only so, but issues of acute contemporary concern – involving constructive theology and ethics, politics, and feminism – are addressed. Since Judaism is identified with a particular ethnic group (a "people"), chapters take up secular forms of being Jewish ("Jewishness") and Zionism alongside the contemporary trend of the reversion of Jews to the practice of Judaism as a religion. Through this wide range of significant topics, we guide those curious about the past and present of a vital religious tradition, one that, over time, has exercised influence far beyond its own rather modest community.

The essays in this *Companion* expound the topics, and the selections in the associated *Blackwell Reader in Judaism* illustrate important points with primary sources, complementing the exposition. In this way, we both talk about Judaism and let Judaism speak for itself in its own mode of formulating and expressing its convictions. Most important, in both the essays and the readings, all of the authors, experts in their fields, address a broad audience, assuming an interest in the subject but no prior knowledge. We present not academic essays for specialists but introductions and expositions for any literate person interested in our subject. Moreover, the authors do not take partisan or sectarian positions upon Judaism or its history, theology, and social expressions. They only build upon the consensus of contemporary learning.

The organization and selection of the topics deserves note. It goes without saying that we are able to cover only the more important topics, doctrines, movements, and problems. We should be the first to concede that other equally significant subjects could find a place in these pages. But, while the four principal parts of this book could have included other topics, we should affirm that those to which we have assigned priority would belong in any account of Judaism. These are the main topics that any portrayal of Judaism, its history, doctrines, and movements, must include, ranging from an account of Judaism's authoritative writings, to which all the faithful refer, to the main theological ideas and, for the contemporary period, the most important movements.

The first three parts of the *Companion* describe Judaism from two angles, the historical and the theological. These chapters deal with the definition of Judaism – exactly what are we talking about when we speak of that religion? – and its formative history, from Scripture up to and including modern times. Part I narrates the history of Judaism from its formative age, in dialogue with the Hebrew Scriptures, through the complex and diverse world of Second Temple times, to the ultimate emergence of the Rabbinic Judaism of the Talmudic period as the normative system. We deal with the history and literature of that Judaism and then turn to the relationships of Judaism with Christianity in both religions' formative age, and of Judaism with Christianity and Judaism with Islam in medieval times. In that same historical unit, we examine the relationship between Judaism and philosophy as conceived in the ancient world and depict Judaism's approach to concrete religious life with God, as that life of piety was shaped in the Talmudic period and has continued to be followed by the faithful to our own day.

God, Torah, and Israel define the principal parts of Judaic theology in the Rabbinic writings of classical and medieval times, and, in Part II, these topics are set forth as they take shape in the principal documents of the ancient rabbis: the Mishnah, Midrash, and Talmuds. Recognizing today's broad interest in the messiah-theme of Judaism, we include an exposition of that matter, and, finally, we call attention to the way in which a religion makes its statement through the media of culture, not only through theological categories. Hence, how the Hebrew language embodies the theological doctrine of normative Judaism, representing a set of religious choices of formidable cultural consequence, is spelled out.

Among many Judaic religious systems of modern and contemporary times, three dominate and so form the foundation of Part III: Reform Judaism, the first and most important Judaism of modernity, Orthodox Judaism in its western, integrationist mode, and Conservative Judaism. Modernity presented a new set of political and cultural questions to which these Judaisms responded, each in its own coherent and systematic manner. These are to be compared both to one another and to the classical Rabbinic Judaism to which all make constant reference. At the same time, while, like God, Torah, and Israel, these Judaisms are principal, they do not encompass all of the interesting constructions that have responded to issues of the social order of the nineteenth and twentieth century. Among other twentieth-century Judaisms, we chose the most acutely contemporary of them all, generally called "New Age Judaism," different in its media of expression from Orthodox, Reform, and Conservative Judaism, quite separate from the Rabbinic tradition that sustains the Judaic systems of modernity, and intensely interesting in its own right.

For our survey of contemporary issues of Judaism, Part IV, we chose the four issues we deem of most acute relevance to religious life today: ethics, feminism, politics, and constructive theology. In Judaism, these are the topics on which systematic thought, mediating between the received tradition and contemporary sensibility, distinguishes itself. So far as religious thinking does not merely recapitulate the received tradition but proposes to contribute to it, it is in these four areas that, as the twenty-first century commences, the world of living Judaism focuses its attention.

Three other special topics find their place, not only because of their importance to the Jews as a group but also by reason of their pertinence to the religion, Judaism. The first is secular Jewishness, the definition of ways of "being Jewish" or of identifying as a Jew on other than religious foundations. In some ways, secular Jewishness takes over the theological heritage of Judaism and translates it into the building blocks of culture. In other ways, secular Jewishness proposes to form a social culture out of the traits of Jews as an ethnic community. The importance of secular Jewishness for the study of Judaism lies in the influence that the secular reading of the religious tradition exercises within the framework of the faith, especially in Reform, Conservative, and New Age Judaisms. The second of the special topics is Zionism, which is the movement of national liberation of the Jewish people, regarded as "a people, one people," which brought about the creation of the State of Israel. Zionism both draws heavily upon the Judaic religious tradition and profoundly influences the life of the faith as it is practiced both in the State of Israel and in the diaspora. Hence it demands an important position in any account of Judaism today.

We conclude with the one chapter that combines an interest in religion and theology with a concern for the social group, "the Jews." In the recent past throughout the world of Jewry, a "return" to Judaism has marked a renewal of the faith for Jews formerly divorced therefrom. The interplay of the ethnic group and the religious tradition is worked out in the phenomenon of reversion. A religion that, at the advent of modern times, seemed to face a gloomy future turns out to exercise remarkable power, through the medium of the Torah, to lead to God people who presented unlikely candidates for religious practice or belief. The return of Jews to Judaism marks the conclusion of modernity. But what now is going to happen, we do not pretend to know.

Here, then, is our approach to making sense of the diverse and exotic data of an ancient and enduring faith. While, in these essays, readers will find guidance to pursue further a variety of critical issues, we are the first to point to areas treated only tangentially if at all. For the history of Judaism, we should like to have said a great deal more about the theology of Rabbinic Judaism as well as its liturgical and mystical life. Among the principal doctrines of Judaism we should have gladly accommodated besides God, Torah, Israel, and messiah, the matters of theological anthropology and theodicy, sin and atonement, and above all, the theology of history that for holy Israel made sense of all that happened. And we should have been glad to include a chapter on the mystical doctrines of the Kabbalah as well as on the social movements produced thereby. We should have been pleased to describe the actual practice of Judaism in the various countries in which the religion flourishes, first of all, in the State of Israel, the USA and Canada, and western Europe. In this way the theory of systematic thought would have taken on practicality in the realization of that theory by the various national communities of Jews, whether in France or in South Africa or in Russia. And it goes without saying that the special topics, taken up in constructive essays, could have multiplied many times over.

Happily, these and numerous other topics that we could not treat here are set forth in large, systematic essays, comparable to those in the present *Companion*, in the three volumes and 1,800 pages of the *Encyclopaedia of Judaism* (Leiden: E. J. Brill, 1999) edited by the editors of these books together with William Scott Green. The twenty-seven topics treated here are augmented by more than a hundred others. So we have done our best to present Judaism in a comprehensive and responsible manner.

The editors express their gratification at working with the fine staff of Blackwell Publishers, which proposed the project and cooperated at every stage in the work of organizing, editing, and bringing to realization this rather complex project. The editors and production managers of the firm reached a high standard of professionalism and made the work a real pleasure.

Professor Avery-Peck expresses his thanks to the College of the Holy Cross, and Professor Neusner his to Bard College, for sustaining their academic careers and making possible all that they do.

The two editors also point with thanks and pride to the contributors of the essays in the *Companion*. They gave us their best work. They accepted our requests for revision (often: concision!) and reorganization. They met deadlines responsibly. And they are the ones who in the end realized the project; we could not have done it without each of them. They never disappointed us, and they always kept their promises. Anyone who has ever contemplated undertaking a project comparable to this one will appreciate the weight of those well-earned compliments.

Jacob Neusner
Bard College

Alan J. Avery-Peck
College of the Holy Cross

PART I

The History of Judaism

CHAPTER 1
Defining Judaism

Jacob Neusner

Religion as an Account of the Social Order

Judaism is a religion, so we begin by asking what we mean when we define religion in general and one religion in particular. In general, people treat religion as a set of beliefs about God, and such a philosophical definition sets forth what a religion believes. A definition of Judaism, therefore, would begin with the statement that Judaism believes God is one, unique, and concerned for us and our actions, thus, "ethical monotheism." But the philosophical definition leaves out much that religion accomplishes within the social order. Religion transcends matters of belief, because it shapes behavior. Religion accounts for the life of the social group that professes that religion. So a definition of propositions and practices without close attention to their social context in the everyday world proves necessary but insufficient. Religion matters for several reasons. First, religion is public, it is social, something people do together, but what people believe tells us only about what individuals think or are supposed to think. Second, religion governs what we do, telling us who we are and how we should live, while what people believe tells us only about attitudes. Religion therefore encompasses not only beliefs or attitudes – matters of mind and intellect – but also actions and conduct. Above all, religion is something that a well-defined group of people does together.

Religion combines belief or attitude, world-view, which we may call "ethos," and also behavior or way of life or right action, which we may call in a broad and loose sense, "ethics." But because religion forms the basis of life of people otherwise unrelated to one another and not only or mainly families, it must be seen as an account of a social entity or a social group, for instance, a church or a holy people or a nation. In that sense, religion explains the social world made up by people who believe certain things in common and act in certain aspects of their lives in common, and so religion accounts for the social entity, which we may call, for the sake of symmetry, ethnos. These three things together – ethos, ethics, and ethnos – define religion, which forms the foundation of the life of many social entities in humanity. Indeed, only when we understand that religion does its work in the social world, then we can begin to grasp why religion is the single most powerful social force in the life and politics of the world today, as in nearly the whole of recorded history. That definition of religion as public and communal serves especially well when we come to Judaism, which, as we shall see, frames its entire message in the setting of the life of a group that calls itself "Israel," meaning, as we shall see, the heirs of the holy people of whom the Hebrew Scriptures or "Old Testament" speak.

A religious system – way of life, world-view, theory of the social entity that lives by the one and believes in the other – identifies an urgent and ongoing question facing a given social group and provides an answer that for the faithful is self-evidently valid. That is why to study any vital religion is to address a striking example of how people explain to themselves, by appeal to God's will or word or works, who they are as a social entity. Religion as a powerful force in human society and culture is realized in society, not only or mainly in theology; religion works through the social entity that embodies that religion. Religions form social entities – "churches" or "peoples" or "holy nations" or monasteries or communities – that, in the concrete, constitute the "us," as against "the nations" or merely "them." And religions carefully explain, in deeds and in words, who that "us" is – and they do it every day. To see religion in this way is to take religion seriously as a way of realizing, in classic documents, a large conception of the social order.

Ethnic and Religious, Jewish and Judaic

Judaism is identified as the religion of the Jews, that is, a religion of an ethnic group. But that identification brings confusion, for not all Jews practice Judaism or any other religion. Hence the beliefs and practices, if any, of Jews do not by themselves form data for the description of Judaism. Not only so, but while Judaism is practiced in communities, called synagogues or congregations, Jewish ethnic identification is formulated by individuals, large numbers of whom by reason of intermarriage may accept multiple components to their ethnic identity. Hence public consensus of congregations of Jews who practice Judaism defines the faith, but private opinion of isolated individuals, part of no community of Judaism, does not. For we cannot describe the religion, Judaism, if we are constantly confronted with the confusion created by the routine claim, "But I'm Jewish and I don't believe that" – or "I'm Jewish and I'm not religious at all." Now the importance of recognizing the social character of a religion, its power to explain a particular group's life, comes to the fore: when it comes to describing a religion in its own integrity, there is no "I" but only a "we."

We therefore distinguish Jews' opinions as individuals from the system of Judaism as a coherent statement – way of life, world-view, theory of the social entity, "Israel." The ethnic group does not define the religious system. We cannot study Judaism if we identify the history of the Jews with the history of Judaism, just as we cannot study Judaism if we regard the faith as a set of ideas quite divorced from the life of the people who hold those ideas. All Judaists – those who practice the religion, Judaism – are Jews, but not all Jews are Judaists. That is to say, all those who practice the religion, Judaism, by definition fall into the ethnic group, the Jews, but not all members of the ethnic group practice Judaism.

Public Religion versus Personal Religiosity: What is at stake in distinguishing Judaic religion from Jewish ethnicity?

When ethnic attitudes are confused with religious doctrines, the opinion of a given Jew, based on secular opinion or merely personal considerations and not in dialogue with the holy books of Judaism, is taken to speak for the religion, Judaism. But, in fact, the holy books of Judaism and the great body of believers may not hold such a view at all. Some simple examples make the point. Some Jews may declare themselves atheists. But Judaism teaches that one, unique God created the world and gave the Torah. Other Jews may not believe in the resurrection of the dead. But Judaic worship, whether Orthodox or Reform (matters we shall consider much later), affirms that God raises the dead and "keeps faith with those that sleep in the dust."

A public opinion poll might produce broad Jewish consensus in favor of abortion. Judaism, the religion, in its classical formulation condemns abortion from the fortieth day after conception. So many Jews regard "Judaism" as the foundation for liberal opinion, even quoting verses of Scripture to prove their point. But among the faithful considerable debate takes place on whether Judaism is conservative or liberal, or even whether these contemporary political categories apply at all. Because of these simple facts, the confusion of the ethnic and the religious must be addressed head on. Otherwise, a representation of Judaism based on its classical sources and on the contemporary practice of Judaism in synagogues by the faithful will conflict with the impressions we gain from everyday life.

Judaism, the religion, in North America, Europe, Latin America, the South Pacific and South Africa, finds itself wrapped around by Jewishness, the ethnic identity of persons who derive from Jewish parents and deem "being Jewish" to bear meaning in their familial and social life and cultural world. In considering the facts of Judaism that the world about us presents, therefore, we have always to remember that the Jews form a community, only part of which practices Judaism. Some may even join synagogues and attend public worship mainly to be with other Jews, not to engage in public worship. They may wish to utilize the synagogue to raise their children "as Jews," while in their homes they practice no form of Judaism. A key institution of Judaism, the Sabbath, is praised by a secular thinker in these words: "More than Israel has kept the Sabbath, the Sabbath has kept Israel." That is, the Sabbath is treated as instrumental, Israel the secular group as principal. But in Judaism, the Sabbath is a holy day, sanctified by Israel, the holy people, and not a means for some ethnic goal of self-preservation.

To explain the mixture of ethnic and religious, a simple case serves for illustration. The word "Israel" today generally refers to the overseas political nation, the State of Israel. When people say, "I am going to Israel," they mean a trip to Tel Aviv or Jerusalem, and when they speak of Israeli policy or issues, they assume they refer to a nation-state. But the word "Israel" in Scripture and in the canonical writings of the religion, Judaism, speaks of the holy community that God has called forth through Abraham and Sarah, to which God has given the Torah ("teaching") at Mount Sinai, of which the Psalmist speaks when he says, "The One who keeps Israel does not slumber or sleep." The Psalmists and the Prophets, the sages of Judaism in all ages, the prayers that Judaism teaches, all use the word "Israel" to mean "the holy community." "Israel" in Judaism forms the counterpart to "the Church, the mystical body of Christ" in Christianity. Today "Israel" in synagogue worship speaks of that holy community, but "Israel" in Jewish community affairs means "the State of Israel."

That example of the confusion of this-worldly nation with holy community by no means ends matters. In the Jewish world outside of the State of Israel, Jews form a community, and some Jews (also) practice Judaism. To enter the Jewish community, which is secular and ethnic, a gentile adopts the religion, Judaism; his or her children are then accepted as native-born Jews, without distinction, and are able to marry other Jews without conversion. So the ethnic community opens its doors not by reason of outsiders' adopting the markers of ethnicity, the food or the association or the music, but by reason of adopting what is not ethnic but religious. And to leave the Jewish community, which is ethnic, one takes the door of faith. Here comes a further, but not unimportant, complication. While not all Jews practice Judaism, in the iron-consensus among contemporary Jews, Jews who practice Christianity cease to be part of the ethnic Jewish community, while those who practice Buddhism remain within. The upshot is that the ethnic and the religious in the world of the Jews present confusion.

Judaisms and Judaism

When we deal with Judaism, we pay close attention to the various groups of Jews who do practice the religion they call Judaism – while respecting the differences that separate these groups from one another. This requires that we learn how to respect the plurality of Judaic religious systems and speak of Judaisms, not Judaism, or "a Judaism" when we mean a specific Judaic religious system. But it also necessitates a clear statement of what holds all Judaisms together as Judaism and also differentiates all Judaisms from any and all other religions.

The change in our normal way of speaking – Judaism to Judaisms – will prove less jarring when we remember that, while we speak of Christianity, we ordinarily mean, a particular Christian religious system. Christianity encompasses a remarkably diverse set of religious systems, which share some qualities in common – belief in Jesus Christ – but which differ deeply especially about matters on which they at first glance concur: who, exactly, was, and is, Jesus Christ? No one imagines that by describing a single common denominator we define one unitary religion; Catholic, Protestant, and Orthodox, Methodist, Mormon, and Lutheran – each is comprised by clearly-delineated groups of Christians, all of them with their respective systems of belief and behavior. Just as from the very beginning, when Peter and Paul contended about absolutely fundamental issues of faith, the world has known Christianities, but no single Christianity, so the world has known, and today recognizes, diverse Judaisms, but no single Judaism.

If we were studying Christianity, we would differentiate Catholic from Protestant, noting that Italian, Hispanic, German, and Irish Catholics practice a common religion but differ on ethnic grounds; so when studying Judaism we differentiate one Judaism from another, noting that the ethnic group, the Jews, also thrives partly concentric with, but partly beyond, the circles of the faithful. But now we have to ask, what holds all Judaisms together and permits us to speak of not only Judaisms but Judaism? To answer that question, we have to consider another way of viewing religion, and that is, as a set of responses to a single ecological circumstance. Here is where the ethnic and the religious, the Jewish and the Judaic, come together, and it also is where Judaisms meet and become Judaism.

The Ecology of Religion

Ecology is concerned with the interrelationships of organisms and their environments. By "ecology of . . ." I mean the study of the interrelationship between the religious world a group constructs for itself and the social and political world in which that same group lives. I refer to the interplay between a particular religious system's way of viewing the world and living life, and the historical, social, and especially political situation of the people who view the world and live life in accord with the teachings of their religion. The Jewish people form a very small group, spread over many countries. One fact of Jews' natural environment is that they form a distinct group in diverse societies. A second is that they constitute solely a community of fate and, for many, of faith, but that alone, in that they have few shared social or cultural traits. A third is that they do not form a single political entity. A fourth is that they look back upon a very long and in some ways exceptionally painful history. The Holocaust – the murder of millions of Jews in Europe in German death-factories – has intensified Jews' sense of themselves as a persecuted group and obscured the long history of stable and secure life that they have enjoyed in various times and places, a thousand years in Poland, for example, and long centuries in much of the Muslim world. But Scripture itself presents its account of the people of Israel as the story of disaster and destruction.

A world-view suited to the Jews' social ecology must make sense of all of these facts, taking account of their unimportance and explaining their importance. It must explain the continuing life of the group, which in significant ways marks the group as different from others and persuades people that their forming a distinct and distinctive community is valuable and worth carrying on. The interplay between the political, social, and historical life of the Jews and their conceptions of themselves in this world and the next – that is, their world-view, contained in their canon, their way of life, explained by the teleology of the system, and the symbolic structure that encompasses the two and stands for the whole all at once and all together – these define the focus for an inquiry into the ecology of the religion at hand, that is, the ecology of a Judaism.

Indeed, what holds all Judaic religious systems together can be identified. It is a single ecology, made up of two components: first, the permanent and ubiquitous appeal to the Torah, that is, the Five Books of Moses (Genesis, Exodus, Leviticus, Numbers, and Deuteronomy), and, second, the inquiry into the Torah to make sense of the diverse circumstances of various groups, all of them identifying with the "Israel" of whom the Torah speaks – and all of them small, weak, scattered, and concerned with their status as a small minority, wherever they are (including, in our own time, the Jewish state – The State of Israel in the Land of Israel – which in its time and place is small, weak, and uncertain). These two then – an ongoing reference to a single holy writing, and a permanent social situation – define the eco-system in which any Judaism must take shape.

The Ecology of Judaism: What holds the whole together

We cannot reduce all Judaisms to a single common denominator. But we can point to traits that will characterize a Judaism and no other religious system. These are more than a few. One idea predominates in nearly all Judaic religious systems, the conception that the Jews are in exile but have the hope of coming home to their own land, which is the Land of Israel (a.k.a. Palestine). The original reading of the Jews' existence as exile and return derives from the Pentateuch, the Five Books of Moses, which were composed as we now have them (out of earlier materials, to be sure) in the aftermath of the destruction of the Temple in 586 BCE. In response to the exile to Babylonia, the experience selected and addressed by the authorship of the document is that of exile and restoration. But that framing of events into the pattern at hand represents an act of powerful imagination and interpretation. That experience taught lessons people claimed to learn out of the events they had chosen and, in the Pentateuch, which took shape in 450 BCE when some Jews returned from Babylonia to Jerusalem, for their history: *the life of the group is uncertain, subject to conditions and stipulations. Nothing is set and given, all things a gift: land and life itself. But what actually did happen in that uncertain world – exile but then restoration – marked the group as special, different, select.*

There were other ways of seeing things, and the Pentateuchal picture was no more compelling than any other. Those Jews who did not go into exile and those who did not "come home" had no reason to take the view of matters that characterized the authorship of Scripture. The life of the group need not have appeared more uncertain, more subject to contingency and stipulation, than the life of any other group. The land did not require the vision that imparted to it the enchantment, the personality, that, in Scripture, it received: "The land will vomit you out as it did those who were here before you." And the adventitious circumstance of Iranian imperial policy – a political happenstance – did not have to be recast into return. So nothing in the system of Scripture – exile for a reason, return as redemption – followed necessarily and logically. Everything was invented: interpreted.

That experience of the uncertainty of the life of the group in the century or so from the destruction of the First Temple of Jerusalem by the Babylonians in 586 to the building of the Second Temple of Jerusalem by the Jews who, with Persian permission and sponsorship, returned from exile, formed the paradigm. With the promulgation of the "Torah of Moses" under the sponsorship of Ezra, the Persians' viceroy, at ca. 450 BCE, all future Israels would then refer to that formative experience as it had been set down and preserved as the norm for Israel in the mythic terms of that "original" Israel, the Israel not of Genesis and Sinai and ending at the moment of entry into the promised land, but the "Israel" of the families that recorded as the rule and the norm the story of both the exile and the return. In that minority genealogy, that story of exile and return, alienation and remission, imposed on the received stories of pre-exilic Israel and adumbrated time and again in the Five Books of Moses and addressed by the framers of that document in their work overall, we find that paradigmatic statement in which every Judaism, from then to now, found its structure and deep syntax of social existence, the grammar of its intelligible message.

No Judaism recapitulates any other, and none stands in a linear and incremental relationship with any prior one. But all Judaisms recapitulate that single paradigmatic experience of the Torah of "Moses," the authorship that reflected on the meaning of the events of 586–450 selected for the composition of history and therefore interpretation. That experience (in theological terms) rehearsed the conditional moral existence of sin and punishment, suffering and atonement and reconciliation, and (in social terms) the uncertain and always conditional national destiny of disintegration and renewal of the group. That moment captured within the Five Books of Moses, that is to say, the judgment of the generation of the return to Zion, led by Ezra, about its extraordinary experience of exile and return, would inform the attitude and viewpoint of all the Israels beyond.

Let me now spell out this theory accounting for the character and definition of all of the diverse Judaisms that have taken shape since the destruction of the First Temple of Jerusalem in 586 and the return to Zion, the building of the Second Temple of Jerusalem, and writing down of the Torah, a process complete in 450 BCE. Since the formative pattern imposed that perpetual, self-conscious uncertainty, treating the life of the group as conditional and discontinuous, Jews have asked themselves who they are and invented Judaisms to answer that question.

Accordingly, on account of the definitive paradigm affecting their group-life in various contexts, no circumstances have permitted Jews to take for granted their existence as a group. Looking back on Scripture and its message, Jews have ordinarily treated as special, subject to conditions and therefore uncertain, what (in their view) other groups enjoyed as unconditional and simply given. Why the paradigm renewed itself is clear: this particular view of matters generated expectations that could not be met, hence created resentment – and then provided comfort and hope that made possible coping with that resentment. To state my thesis with appropriate emphasis: *Promising what could not be delivered, then providing solace for the consequent disappointment, the system at hand precipitated in age succeeding age the very conditions necessary for its own replication.*

There have been many Judaisms, each with its indicative symbol and generative paradigm, each pronouncing its world-view and prescribing its way of life and identifying the particular Israel that, in its view, is Israel, bearer of the original promise of God. But each Judaism retells in its own way and with its distinctive emphases the tale of the Five Books of Moses, the story of a no-people that becomes a people, that has what it gets only on condition, and that can lose it all by virtue of its own sin. That is an unsettling story for a social group to tell of itself, because it imposes acute self-consciousness, chronic insecurity, upon what should be the level plane and firm foundation of society. That is to say, the collection of diverse materials joined into a single tale on the occasion of the original exile and restoration because of the repetition in age succeeding age, also precipitates the recapitulation of the interior experience of exile and restoration – always because of sin and atonement.

So it is the Pentateuch that shaped the imagination of Jews wherever they lived, and it is their social condition as a small and scattered group that made the question raised by the Pentateuchal narrative urgent, and it is the power of the Pentateuch both to ask but also to answer the question, that made the answer compelling whenever and wherever Jews (that is to say, "Israel") lived. Now that we have formulated a theory of the history of Judaism, from the beginning to the present day, let us turn from the historical and contemporary context of the Judaic religious system to its contents. Judaism sets forth the way of Torah – God's teaching.

The History of Judaism: Brief definitions

The approach we work out here requires us to describe not Judaism as a whole – all the Judaisms of all times and all places set forth through the common denominator that holds them together – but *a Judaism*, that is to say, a single religious system. Such a system will be composed of three elements: a world-view, a way of life, and a social group that, in the here and now, embodies the whole. The world-view explains the life of the group, ordinarily referring to God's creation, the revelation of the Torah, the goal and end of the group's life in the end of time. The way of life defines what is special about the life of the group. The social group, in a single place and time, then forms the living witness and testimony to the system as a whole and finds in the system ample explanation for its very being. That is *a Judaism*.

Social Entity, Way of Life, World-view: Ethnos, ethics, ethos

How shall we know when we have a Judaism? The answer to that question draws us to the data – the facts – we must locate and describe, analyze, and interpret. The first requirement is to find a group of Jews who see themselves as "Israel," that is, the Jewish People who form the family and children of Abraham, Isaac, Jacob, Sarah, Rebecca, Leah, and Rachel, the founding fathers and mothers. That same group must tell us that it uniquely constitutes "Israel," not *an* Israel, the descriptive term we use.

The second requirement is to identify the forms through which that distinct group expresses its world-view. Ordinarily, we find that expression in writing, so we turn to the authoritative holy books that the group studies and deems God-given, that is, the group's Torah or statement of God's revelation to Israel. Since we use the word Torah to mean biblical books, starting with the Five Books of Moses, we must remind ourselves that the contents of the Torah have varied from one Judaism to the next. Some groups regard as holy what other groups reject or ignore. A more suitable word than Torah, therefore, is canon, meaning the collection of authoritative writings. The canon contains much of the group's world-view and describes its way of life. We of course err if we treat as our sole source of facts only what is in writing.

A group expresses its world-view in many ways, through dance, drama, rite and ritual; through art and symbol; through politics and ongoing institutions of society; through where it lives, what it eats, what it wears, what language it speaks, and the opposites of all these: what it will not eat, where it will not live. Synagogue architecture and art bear profound messages, powerful visible messages. The life-cycle, from birth through death, the definition of time and the rhythm of the day, the week, the month and the year – all of these testify to the world-view and the way of life of the social group that, all together, all at once, constitutes a Judaism.

In the long history of the Jews, groups of people who regarded themselves as "Israel," that is, groups of Jews, have framed many Judaisms. What permits us to make sense of the history of these Judaisms is the fact that, over time, we are able to identify periods in which a number of Judaisms competed, and other times in which a single Judaism predominated. The historical perspective therefore permits us to sort out the Judaisms that have flourished, keeping each by itself for the purpose of description, analysis, and interpretation, and also to hold the Judaisms together in a single continuum, over time and space, of the whole of which, all together and all at once, we can make sense. By recognizing that a given Judaism came into existence at a time in which Judaisms competed, and by understanding that, at another point, a single Judaism defined the Jews' way of life, world-view, and social existence as a distinct entity, we may understand how the diverse facts – writings, theologies, definitions of what matters in the everyday life, doctrines of the end of time and the purpose of life – fit together, when they cohere, or do not fit together, when, in fact, they prove discrete.

Diverse Histories of Jews – the history of Judaism

In studying about the history of Judaism, we concentrate not on the Jews as an ethnic group, but on the Judaic religious systems that various groups in diverse times and places have set forth as an account of the social world that diverse ethnic groups, all of them regarding themselves as "Jewish," or as "Israel," have adopted. The Jews as a people have not had a single, unitary, and continuous history. They have lived in many places, centuries here, centuries there, and what happened in one place rarely coincided with what happened in some other place. When Jews in the Iberian peninsula flourished, those in other parts of western Europe, for example, England, France, and Germany, perished; when, in 1492, the Spanish and Portuguese governments expelled Muslims and Jews, Jews in Poland and in the Turkish empire flourished. Only rarely did the histories of many distinct and different communities of Jews coincide, for example, in the horror of the mass extermination of European Jews between 1933 and 1945 in Germany and German-occupied Europe.

But if the ethnic group proves too diverse and distinct to treat as whole and harmonious (except as a matter of theology in the conception of Israel, God's first love, or as a matter of ideology in the conception that the Jews form a people, one people), we can treat as a coherent whole, harmonious and unitary, the history of the Judaic religious system, or Judaism. Let me specify the periods of the history of Judaism. I see four: first, an age of diversity, then an era of definition, third, a time of essential cogency, and, finally, a new age of diversity.

The Five Facts that Define the History of Judaism

Since the definition rests on historical facts of the life of Israel, the Jewish people, I have to list the facts of political history that mark off everything else. Here are those facts out of the histories of various groups of Jews, in diverse times and places, that govern the history of the Jews and also of Judaism from the beginning to the present.

586 BCE: The destruction of the First Temple in Jerusalem by the Babylonians

The ancient Israelites, living in what they called the Land of Israel, produced Scriptures that reached their present form in the aftermath of the destruction of their capital city and Temple. Whatever happened before that time was reworked in the light of that event and the meaning imputed to it by authors who lived afterward. All Judaisms, from 586 forward, appeal to the writings produced in the aftermath of the destruction of the First Temple. Therefore we must regard the destruction of that Temple as the date that marks the beginning of the formation of Judaism(s).

70 CE: The destruction of the Second Temple in Jerusalem by the Romans

The Jews' leaders – the political classes and priesthood – after 586 were taken to Babylonia, the homeland of their conquerors, where they settled down. A generation later, Babylonia fell under the rule of the Persians, who permitted Jews to return to their ancient homeland. A small number did so, where they rebuilt the Temple and produced the Hebrew Scriptures. The Second Temple of Jerusalem lasted from about 500 BCE to 70 CE, when the Romans – by that time ruling the entire Middle East, including the Land of Israel, mainly through their own friends and allies, put down a Jewish rebellion and, in the war, destroyed Jerusalem again. The second destruction proved final and marked the beginning of the Jews' history as a political entity defined in social and religious terms, but not in territorial ones. That is, the Jews formed a distinct religious–social group, but all of them did not live in any one place, and there were some of them living nearly everywhere in the West, within the lands of Christendom and Islam alike.

640 CE: The conquest of the Near and Middle East and North Africa by the Muslims

The definition of the world in which the Jews would live was completed when the main outlines of western civilization had been worked out. These encompassed Christendom, in western Europe and in eastern Europe, inclusive of the world west of the Urals in Russia, and Islam, in command of North Africa and the Near and Middle East, and, in later times, destined to conquer India and much of the Far East, Malaysia, and Indonesia in particular, as well as sub-Saharan Africa. During this long period of time, the Jews in Christendom and Islam alike ordinarily enjoyed the status of a tolerated but subordinated minority and were free to practice their religion and sustain their separate group existence. Of still greater importance, both Christianity and Islam affirmed the divine origin of the Jews' holy book, the Torah, and acknowledged the special status, among the nations, of Israel, the Jewish people.

1787 or 1789: The American Constitution or the French Revolution

The American Constitution in the USA and the French Revolution in western Europe marked the beginning of an age in which political change reshaped the world in which the West, including Western Jewries, lived. Politics became essentially secular, and political institutions no longer acknowledged supernatural claims of special status accorded either to a church or to a religious community. The individual person, rather than the social group, formed the focus of politics. In the case of the Jews, the turning meant that the Jews would be received as individuals and given rights equal to those of all others, at the same time that "Israel" as a holy people and community no longer would enjoy special status and recognition.

1933–1948: The destruction of the Jews in Europe ("the Holocaust") and the creation of the State of Israel

In 1933 Germany chose the National Socialist Party to govern. A principal doctrine of that party was that various groups among humanity, called races, possess traits that are inherent in the genes and that are passed on through time: racial characteristics. Some races have good traits, others, bad, and the worst of all of these "races" are the Jews. To save humanity from this dreadful "curse," all of the Jews of the world have to be murdered ("exterminated") and this will constitute "the final solution of the Jewish problem." This racist doctrine, broadly held in Europe and elsewhere, during World War II, from 1939 to 1945, led to the murder of nearly six million European Jews. In the aftermath of World War II, seeking a home for the remnants who had survived, the United Nations voted, in 1947, to create a Jewish and an Arab state in what was then Palestine. The Jewish state came into being on May 15, 1948, as the State of Israel. These events defined an entirely new ecology for Judaism. On the one side, the problem of evil was restated with great intensity. On the other, the social and political life of the Jews was entirely redefined. The issue of "exile and return," paramount at the outset, was framed with fresh urgency, but with a new resolution. The formation of the State of Israel in the aftermath of the Holocaust opened a new chapter in the history of Judaism, but the story that that chapter will tell is not yet clear to any observer.

The Four Principal Periods in the History of Judaism

The history of Judaism is the story of how diverse Judaisms gave way to a single Judaism, which predominated for a long time but, in the modern age, both broke up into derivative Judaisms and also lost its commanding position as the single, defining force in the life of the Jews as a social group. Here we consider the history of Judaism as a whole. In later units we return to important chapters in that history, examined in detail, though our emphasis is on modern times. Seen whole, the history of Judaism the religion divides into four principal periods, as follows:

The first age of diversity	ca. 500 BCE to 70 CE
The age of definition	ca. 70 CE to 640 CE
The age of cogency	ca. 640 CE to ca. 1800
The second age of diversity	ca. 1800 to the present

The first age of diversity begins with the writing down, in more or less their present form, of the Scriptures of ancient Israel, beginning with the Five Books of Moses. Drawing upon writings and oral traditions of the period before the destruction of the First Temple of Jerusalem, in 586, the authorship of the surviving leadership of that Temple and court, the priests, produced most of the books we now know as the Hebrew Bible ("Old Testament," or "Tanakh"), specifically, the Pentateuch or Five Books of Moses, the prophetic writings from Joshua and Judges through Samuel and Kings, and Isaiah, Jeremiah, Ezekiel, and the twelve smaller books of prophetic writings; and some of the other Scriptures as well. During this same period a number of diverse groups of Jews, living in the Land of Israel as well as in Babylonia, to the east, and in Alexandria, in Egypt, to the west, took over these writings and interpreted them in diverse ways. Hence during the period from the formation of the Torah-book to the destruction of the second Temple, there were many Judaisms.

The destruction of Jerusalem in 586 BCE produced a crisis of faith, because ordinary folk supposed that the god of the conquerors had conquered the God of Israel. Israelite prophets saw matters otherwise. Israel had been punished for her sins, and it was God who had carried out the punishment. God was not conquered but vindicated. The pagans were merely his instruments. God could, moreover, be served anywhere, not only in the holy and promised Land of Israel. Israel in Babylonian exile continued the cult of the Lord through worship, psalms, and festivals; the synagogue, a place where God was worshiped without sacrifice, took shape. The Sabbath became Israel's sanctuary, the seventh day of rest and sanctification for God. When, for political reasons, the Persians chose to restore Jewry to Palestine and many returned (ca. 500 BCE), the Jews were not surprised, for they had been led by prophecy to expect that with the expiation of sin through suffering and atonement, God would once more show mercy and bring them homeward. The prophets' message was authenticated by historical events.

In the early years of the Second Temple (ca. 450 BCE), Ezra, the priest-scribe, came from Babylonia to Palestine and brought with him the Torah-book, the collection of ancient scrolls of law, prophecy, and narrative. Jews resolved to make the Torah the basis of national life. The Torah was publicly read on New Year's Day in 444 BCE, and those assembled pledged to keep it. Oral traditions, explanations, instructions on how to keep the law, and exegeses of Scripture were needed along with the canonical Scriptures, to apply the law to changing conditions of everyday life. A period of creative interpretation of the written Torah began, one that has yet to come to conclusion in the history of Judaism. From that time forward, the history of Judaism became the history of the inter-pretation of Torah and its message for each successive age.

The age of definition, beginning with the destruction of the Second Temple in 70 CE, saw the diverse Judaisms of the preceding period give way, over a long period of time, to a single Judaism.

The formative generations of Rabbinic Judaism – the next period before us – drew upon more than the ancient Hebrew Scriptures. They flowed out of particular groups in the world of Judaism that read these Scriptures in a par-ticular way and that had a distinctive approach to the religious life of the com-munity of Israel. There were three main components of the religious life of the Jews in the last two centuries BCE and the first century CE to which we must pay attention. These components, not mutually exclusive, were (1) the priests, with their commitment to the Temple of Jerusalem and its sacred offerings and to governance of the people of Israel in accord with the orderly world created by and flowing out of the Temple; (2) the scribes, with their commitment to the ancient Scriptures and their capacity to interpret and apply these Scriptures to the diverse conditions of the life of the people (later on, the heirs of the scribes would gain the honorific title of "rabbi," which was not distinctive to their group of Jews or even to the Jews); and (3) the messianic Zealots, who believed that God would rule the Jews when foreign rulers had been driven out of the Holy Land. Obviously, these three components were talking about different things to different people.

Of these three groups, one predominated in the shaping of events in the first century CE, and the other two fused thereafter. The messianic Zealots until the destruction of the Temple of Jerusalem in 70 CE were the most powerful force in the history of the Jews. For they precipitated the single most important event of the time, the war fought against Rome from 66 to 73 CE, climaxed by the fall of Jerusalem in 70 CE. And the messianic Zealots must have remained paramount for another three generations, since the next major event in the history of the Jews was yet a second, and still more disastrous, holy and messianic war against Rome, fought under the leadership of Ben Kosiba (also called *Bar Kokhba*, the Star's Son) from 132 to 135 CE. That war surely was a mass uprising, which tells us that a large part of the population was attracted to the Zealots' way of thinking.

The other two groups – the priests and the scribes – with their interest in continuity, order, and regularity lost out both times. The priests of the Temple saw the destruction of their sanctuary in 70 CE and realized after 135 CE that it would not be rebuilt for a long time. The scribes who taught Scriptures and administered their law witnessed the upheavals of society and the destruction of the social order that war inevitably brings in its aftermath. While both groups doubtless shared in the messianic hopes, they most certainly could not have sympathized with the policies and disastrous programs of the messianic Zealots.

The religion that emerged – called Rabbinic because of its authorities' title; normative or classical because of its later paramount position; "the Judaism of the dual Torah" because of its generative myth – was the system worked out by the sages who, after 70, developed a Judaism that was linked to Scripture but enriched by an autonomous corpus of additional holy writings. This Judaism is marked by its doctrine of the dual media by which the Torah was formulated and transmitted, in writing on the one side, in formulation and transmission by memory, hence, orally, on the other. The doctrine of the dual Torah, written and oral, then defined the canon of Judaism.

The written Torah encompassed pretty much the same books that the world at large knows as the Old Testament. The oral Torah added the writings of the sages, beginning with the Mishnah, a philosophical law code produced at ca. 200 CE, two massive commentaries on the Mishnah, the two Talmuds, one produced in the Land of Israel and called the Yerushalmi, or Jerusalem Talmud, ca. 400 CE, the other in Babylonian and called the Bavli, or Talmud of Babylonia, ca. 600 CE. In that same age, alongside Mishnah-commentary, systematic work on Scripture yielded works organized around particular books of the written Torah, parallel to works organized around particular tractates of the Mishnah. These encompassed Sifra, to the book of Leviticus, Sifre, to Numbers, another Sifre, to Deuteronomy, works containing statements attributed to the same authorities who stand behind the Mishnah, to be dated sometime between 200 and 400, as well as Genesis Rabbah and Leviticus Rabbah, discursive works on themes in Genesis and Leviticus, edited between 400 and 450, Pesiqta deRab Kahana, a profoundly eschatological treatment of topics in Pentateuchal writings, of about 450, and similar works. These writings all together, organized around, first, the Mishnah, and then, Scripture, comprised the first works of the oral Torah. That is to say, the teachings of the sages, originally formulated and transmitted in memory, were the written down contents of the oral Torah that God had revealed – so the system maintained – to Moses at Sinai. During the age of definition, that Judaism of the dual Torah reached its literary statement and authoritative expression.

The age of cogency is characterized by the predominance, from the far West in Morocco, to Iran and India, and from Egypt to England, of the Judaism of the dual Torah. During this long period, the principal question facing Jews was how to explain the success of the successor-religions, Christianity and Islam, which claimed to replace the Judaism of Sinai with a new testament, on the one side, or a final and perfect prophecy, on the other. Both religions affirmed but then claimed to succeed Judaism, and the Judaism of the dual Torah enjoyed success, among Jews, in making sense of the then-subordinated status of the enduring people and faith of Sinai. While during this long period heresies took shape, the beliefs of the new systems responded to the structure of the established one, so that a principal doctrine, for example, the doctrine of the dual Torah, written and oral, or of the messiah as a faithful sage, would take shape in opposition to the authoritative doctrines of the Judaism of the dual Torah.

The age of cogency ran into the nineteenth century. That does not mean there were no other Judaic systems, including heresies, which selected a "false doctrine" by defining in a way different from the Judaism of the dual Torah a category emerging in that Judaism. It means, rather, that the Judaism of the dual Torah set the standard, absorbing into itself and its structure many powerful movements, such as philosophy, on the one side, and mysticism (called Qabbalah), on the other, finding strength in both of them. The philosopher thus defended the way of life and world-view of the Judaism of the dual Torah, and the mystic observed the faith defined by that same way of life as the vehicle for gaining his or her own mystical experience.

Of course philosophers of Judaism raised and dealt with questions in ways essentially separate from the established and accepted Rabbinic ways of thinking about religious issues. Still these philosophers of Judaism not only lived in accord with the Rabbinic way of life; all of them were entirely literate in the Talmud and related literature, and many of the greatest philosophers were also great Talmudists. The same is to be said of the mystics. Their ideas about the inner character of God, their quest for a fully realized experience of union with the presence of God in the world, their particular doctrines, with no basis in the talmudic literature produced by the early rabbis, and their intense spirituality, were all thoroughly "rabbinized" – that is, brought into conformity with the lessons and way of life taught by the Talmud. In the end, Rabbinic Judaism received extraordinary reinforcement from the spiritual resources generated by the mystic quest.

Both philosophy and mysticism found their way into the center of Rabbinic Judaism. Both of them were shaped by minds that, to begin with, were infused with the content and spirit of Rabbinic Judaism. So when we see the Judaism of the dual Torah as cogent for nineteen centuries, it is not because the system remained intact and unchanged, but because it was forever able to take within itself, treat as part of its system of values and beliefs, a wide variety of new concepts and customs. This is an amazingly long time for something so volatile as a religion to have remained essentially stable and to have endured without profound shifts in symbolic structure, ritual life, or modes of social organization for the religious community. The Judaism that predominated during that long period and that has continued to flourish in the nineteenth and twentieth centuries thus bears names familiar from the period of its inception: *Rabbinic* because of the nature of its principal authorities, who are rabbis; *talmudic* because of the name of its chief authoritative document after the Hebrew Scriptures, which is the Talmud; *classical* because of its basic quality of endurance and prominence; or, simply, *Judaism* because no other important alternative was explored by Jews.

The second age of diversity is marked not by the breaking apart of the received system but by the development of competing systems of Judaism as well as of entirely secular systems that, for millions of Jews, took the place of Judaism, the religion. In this period, new Judaisms came into being that entirely ignored the categories and doctrines of the received system, responding not to its concerns but to other issues altogether. Now the principal question addressed by new systems concerned matters other than those found urgent by the Judaism of the dual Torah, with its powerful explanation of the Jews' status in the divine economy. The particular points of stress, the self-evident answers to urgent questions, came at the interstices of individual life. Specifically, Jews now needed to explain to themselves how as individuals, able to make free choices on their own, they found a place, also, within the commanded realm of the holy way of life and world-view of the Torah of Judaism. The issue again was political, but it concerned not the group but the individual. Judaisms produced in modern times answered the urgent question of individual citizenship, just as the Judaism of the long period of Christian and Muslim hegemony in Europe, Africa, and western Asia had taken up the (then equally pressing) question of a subordinated, but in its own view, holy society's standing and status as Israel in Islam or in Christendom. Reform Judaism marks the first of the new Judaisms, responsive to the issues of political change that confronted European, and then North American Jews who wished to practice Judaism (or a Judaism); Orthodox Judaism in its integrationist mode, maintaining that Jews could both keep the Torah and live among gentiles, formed a pointed response; and Conservative Judaism took a mediating position, agreeing with Reform that change in response to political challenge was legitimate, agreeing with Orthodoxy that change should be moderate and take place within the disciplines of the revealed torah.

The contemporary age has produced Judaic religious systems that fall outside of the framework of the received Torah and do not privilege the Pentateuch and its narrative and law. In addition, the same age witnesses the formation of ethnic Jewish ideologies, which explain the existence of the Jews as a group ("people") without appeal to God's revelation but rather by reference to the continuing history and shared culture of that group. At the present time, the vast majority of Jews who practice Judaism – Orthodox, whether segregationist or integrationist, Conservative, Reform, Reconstructionist – concur on the enduring authority of the Torah and refer for its interpretation to the Rabbinic tradition, read variously to be sure. But most of that same majority regards the Jews as an ethnic group (in Europe and North and Latin America) or a nation (in the state of Israel) and, all together, as a people, and, as ever, that complicates the study of Judaism.

CHAPTER 2
The Religious World of Ancient Israel to 586 BCE

Marvin A. Sweeney

Judaism traces its origins to the people of ancient Israel and Judah and their relationship with God, who is identified throughout Jewish tradition by the ineffable name YHWH. The Hebrew Bible, known to Jews as the Tanakh and to Christians as the Old Testament, constitutes the fundamental presentation of the origins and early history of the people of Israel from the creation of the world through the period of restoration following the Babylonian exile in 587/ 586 BCE. Whereas Christian versions of the Old Testament, which include the books of 1–2 Maccabees either as part of the Old Testament itself or as part of the Apocrypha, trace the history of Israel through the so-called Hasmonean period in the second and first centuries BCE, the Jewish Tanakh concludes the presentation of Israel's history in the Persian period during the fifth or fourth centuries BCE with the books of Ezra–Nehemiah and Esther.

The Biblical Account of the Origins and Early History of Israel

The Hebrew Bible presents Israel as a distinctive, holy people or nation in relation to YHWH. Following the creation of the world according to the book of Genesis, various problems arose in the relationship between the newly-created human beings and YHWH that resulted in Adam's and Eve's expulsion from the Garden of Eden, the near-destruction of the world by flood, and the scattering of nations as a result of the building of the Tower of Babel. YHWH therefore decided to establish Israel as a distinctive people through whom divine "instruction" or "Torah" might be revealed in order to bring knowledge of God or holiness, morality, order, and peace to a chaotic world. In order to accomplish this goal, YHWH established a special relationship or covenant with Abraham, in which YHWH promised to make Abraham into a great nation in the land of Israel in return for Abraham's adherence to YHWH as the only God and to YHWH's commandments (Gen. 15).

When Abraham's wife Sarah gave birth to their son, Isaac, the covenant continued through him and his descendants. Jacob, the son of Isaac and Rebecca, was renamed Israel to represent his status as the eponymous ancestor of the nation Israel when YHWH continued the covenant with him (Gen. 35). Jacob in turn fathered twelve sons and a daughter with his wives, Leah and Rachel, and their handmaidens, Zilpah and Bilhah. The twelve sons – Reuben, Simeon, Judah, Levi, Issachar, Zebulun, Gad, Asher, Dan, Naphtali, Joseph, and Benjamin – then became the ancestors of the twelve tribes that formed the nation Israel. Levi eventually became a priestly tribe without its own land, but Joseph's sons, Ephraim and Manasseh, were adopted by Jacob to become the ancestors of tribes in Israel in place of their father (Gen. 48).

Whereas the book of Genesis focuses on the ancestors of the nation Israel, the books of Exodus, Leviticus, and Numbers present the formative experience of the nation in the Exodus from Egypt, the revelation of YHWH's Torah at Mt. Sinai (or Horeb), and the period of wandering in the wilderness of Sinai prior to their entry into the promised land of Canaan or Israel. Following Israel's movement to Egypt during the time of Joseph, the Egyptians enslaved the people of Israel. In order to deliver Israel from Egyptian bondage, YHWH instructed Moses, a Levite living in the Sinai wilderness who was raised as an Egyptian prince, to return to Egypt and demand the release of his people from the Egyptian Pharaoh or king. When the Pharaoh refused, YHWH released a series of ten plagues, culminating in the deaths of the Egyptian firstborn. When Pharaoh relented, the people of Israel departed from Egypt and came to the Red Sea. Pharaoh changed his mind and brought his soldiers and chariots to the Red Sea in order to stop Israel's escape. With Israel trapped between the Red Sea and Pharaoh's chariots, Moses called upon YHWH to divide the Red Sea, allowing the people of Israel to cross on dry land to the Sinai wilderness. When the Egyptians attempted to pursue, the waters of the Red Sea closed over them so that Israel was miraculously delivered by YHWH. Following the Exodus from Egypt, YHWH revealed divine Torah to the people through Moses at Mt. Sinai, and for the next forty years the people traveled through the wilderness at Sinai until it was time to enter the promised land.

According to the book of Deuteronomy, immediately prior to his own death and the people's entry into the promised land, Moses repeated YHWH's Torah to Israel. The purpose, of course, was to remind the people of their covenant with YHWH as they took possession of the land. Under the leadership of Moses' successor, Joshua, the people of Israel conquered the land in three very swift campaigns (Josh. 1–12) and then divided the land among the twelve tribes (Josh. 13–23). YHWH's involvement is evident throughout, as various miracles, such as the collapse of the walls of Jericho (Josh. 6) or the sun that stood still at Gibeon (Josh. 10), enabled the people to take full possession of the land. At the conclusion of the campaign and division of the land, Joshua reiterated the people's responsibilities to YHWH in a renewed covenant at the city of Shechem (Josh. 24).

The books of Judges, 1–2 Samuel, and 1–2 Kings present Israel's history in the land itself from the time following the conquest until the Babylonian exile. The book of Judges presents the period prior to the rise of the Israelite monarchy as a time at which there was no continuous central leadership in Israel. As the tribes were threatened by various enemies, individual rulers known as Judges, such as Ehud, Deborah, Gideon, and others, arose to defend Israel, but no successors were appointed at the death of the judge until such time as a new threat materialized. At the end of Judges and the beginning of 1 Samuel, it is clear that Israel needed a monarch, as the Philistines and other enemies increasingly posed a threat to Israel's security and existence. The prophet Samuel anointed Saul ben Kish from the tribe of Benjamin as the first king over Israel, with the expectation that he would deliver Israel from its enemies (1 Sam. 9:1–10:16). It became evident, however, that Saul was inadequate to the task, as he was never able decisively to defeat the Philistines. In addition, 1 Samuel maintains that Saul suffered from an "evil spirit" from YHWH and spent a great deal of his time attempting to kill his armor-bearer and son-in-law, David ben Jesse of the tribe of Judah, whom he perceived to be a rival for the throne (1 Sam. 18).

Following Saul's death at the hands of the Philistines, 2 Samuel relates David's rise to power as king over all Israel. Upon defeating the Philistines, David captured the city of Jerusalem and made it his capital (2 Sam. 5). He brought to Jerusalem the ark of the covenant, the symbol of YHWH's presence among the people during the time of the wilderness wanderings, thereby establishing the city as the holy center in Israel for the worship of YHWH (2 Sam. 6). David went on to establish a large empire that included all the central hill country of Israel and Judah, the land of the Philistines along the Mediterranean coast, the lands east of the Jordan River, and Aram (ancient Syria). According to 2 Sam. 7, YHWH promised David an eternal dynasty in Jerusalem, and David's son Solomon later built the Temple in Jerusalem to house the ark of the covenant and to serve as the central sanctuary of the nation Israel (1 Kgs. 6–8). The presentation of Solomon's reign in 1 Kgs. 1–11 represents the apex of ancient Israel's history according to the Hebrew Bible. The twelve tribes were united under the rule of YHWH's chosen monarch, the nation was secure from threat by enemies, and the Temple in Jerusalem served as the center of worship for the entire people.

The remainder of 1–2 Kings presents the dissolution of this great kingdom over the course of some four hundred years. Although Solomon ruled over a magnificent kingdom as the chosen monarch of YHWH, 1 Kings maintains that he abused his rule by forcing the people of Israel to work on various state building projects and that he allowed pagan religious practices to flourish in Jerusalem as a result of his devotion to his many foreign wives. Following Solomon's death, the ten northern tribes revolted against his son Rehoboam, and established Jeroboam ben Nebat of Ephraim as king over a newly constituted northern kingdom of Israel (1 Kgs. 12). Judah and Benjamin were left to Rehoboam and the Davidic dynasty based in Jerusalem.

Despite portraying YHWH's sanction for the revolt, 1–2 Kings is unrelenting in its criticism of the northern kings. 1 Kgs. 12 presents Jeroboam's decision at the outset of his reign to set up golden calves at Dan and Beth El, which would serve as idolatrous sanctuaries and turn the people away from the worship of YHWH. 1–2 Kings maintains that all the northern kings were as evil as Jeroboam and argues that the idolatry of the northern monarchs resulted some two hundred years later in the Assyrian empire's destruction of northern Israel. The southern kingdom of Judah escaped destruction by the Assyrians, and, under the rule of King Josiah, attempted to purify the worship of the people of Israel (2 Kgs. 22–23). Nevertheless, 2 Kgs. 21:10–15 maintains that the sins of Josiah's grandfather, Manasseh, were so great that YHWH decided to destroy Jerusalem and the Temple. Josiah was killed by the Egyptians, and the city of Jerusalem and the Temple were destroyed twenty-two years later by the invading Babylonian empire. As a result of the Babylonian destruction, many Judeans were sent into exile to Babylonia, and the kingdom of Judah ceased to exist as an independent state.

Historical Background

The biblical account of the origins and early history of ancient Israel is a heavily theologized narrative that asserts YHWH's actions as the primary cause for Israel's existence and experience in the ancient world. Some contend that the biblical narrative is therefore a work of fiction that need not be taken seriously as history. For instance, names such as Abraham, Moses, David, or Solomon are not attested until long after the periods in which they were supposed to have lived. Still a great deal of evidence from archeology and ancient Near Eastern texts provides historical background for the basic outlines of the biblical narratives. Like any work of history, the biblical narrative employs its own historiographical perspectives, and it has its own important points to make. Specifically, it offers a reflection on the history of Israel and Judah that attempts to explain the origins of Israel as an effort by God to bring order into the world, and the Babylonian exile as an act of divine punishment. In order to understand the Hebrew Bible's presentation of Israel's history, it is important to understand the historical foundation on which it is based.

The nation of Israel was a relative late-comer to the land of Canaan. Although Canaan was the site for some of the world's oldest inhabited cities – Jericho, for example, dates back to 9000 BCE – Israel emerged as an independent state only in the tenth century BCE. The origins of Israel, however, may be traced back as far as the beginning of the Middle Bronze I and II Ages in 2300–2000 and 2000–1550 BCE respectively. During these periods, Semitic-speaking, semi-nomadic peoples known in Mesopotamian sources as the Ammuru, "westerners," began to move in from the regions of the Arabian desert to the west of Sumeria or Babylonia into the settled regions of the so-called "Fertile Crescent," which extended from the region watered by the Tigris and Euphrates rivers in Mesopotamia or modern Iraq, through Syria and eastern Turkey, and south into the land of Canaan or modern Israel. The Ammuru or Amorites created the earliest Babylonian kingdoms, which incorporated the earlier Sumerian city-states, and some maintain that their influence extended into upper Syria and the western regions of Canaan as well. Sites that are important to the later history of Israel, such as Hebron, Shechem, Shiloh, and Beth El, appear to have been founded during these periods, whereas others, such as Dan, Megiddo, Beth Shean, and Jerusalem, appear to have been founded in earlier periods. Although the Amorites are generally regarded with suspicion in the Hebrew Bible (see Gen. 15:16; Josh. 24:15), some see this period as the so-called "Patriarchal" or "Ancestral" Age of Abraham and Sarah and their descendants.

Another potential antecedent to the people of Israel may be found in the Late Bronze Age, 1550–1200 BCE, when other groups of semi-nomadic peoples known in ancient Near Eastern records as the Habiru or Apiru began to move into the land of Canaan from the desert regions to the east. Some have attempted to equate the Akkadian term Habiru with the Hebrew term 'Ibri (Hebrew), but the linguistic arguments are not entirely compelling. The term itself appears to serve in Akkadian as a designation for barbarians who stood outside of settled civilization, which would correspond roughly to Abraham's status in Gen. 14:13, where he is called a Hebrew. Canaan during this period was constituted as a conglomeration of separate city-states that were subservient to Egypt. The Amarna letters, written during this period by the various Canaanite city-state rulers to their Egyptian overlords, constantly mention the role of the Habiru in relation to the conflicts that broke out among the city-states. The rulers of Megiddo and Jerusalem in particular complain of the threat posed to them by the alliance between King Lubayu of Shechem and the Habiru. Shechem, of course, was the site of important Israelite covenant ceremonies at the time of Moses (Deut. 27) and Joshua (Josh. 24). Egyptian records during this period speak of Habiru/Apiru slaves. A victory stele by Pharaoh Merneptah (reigned 1224–1216 BCE) contains the first reference to Israel, which is represented in the hieroglyphs as a landless, nomadic group.

The beginning of the Iron Age in 1200–1000 BCE saw a great deal of conflict in the land of Israel, particularly in the border regions between the central hill country of Ephraim and Judah that served as the homeland of Israel, equivalent to the modern West Bank, and the low-lying coastal plain that served as the homeland of the Philistines. The Philistines are generally identified with the so-called Sea Peoples who attempted to invade Egypt in the twelfth century BCE and settled into the coastal plain of Israel after they were defeated by the Egyptians. The Sea Peoples came originally from the Greek islands and are believed to have destroyed the Hittite empire of Asia Minor prior to their attempted invasion of Egypt. Some identify them with the Homeric Greeks who conquered Troy. They first brought iron to ancient Canaan and used their expertise to build weapons and to organize an alliance among their five principal cities: Ashdod, Ashkelon, Gaza, Ekron, and Gath. The goal apparently was the domination of the trade routes through Canaan, and the evidence of conflict at the borders of the coastal plain and the hill country indicates an early conflict between the Philistines and the less advanced inhabitants of the hill country, whom many identify as early Israelites.

The period of conflict ended in approximately 1000 BCE, which corresponds to the beginning of the Davidic–Solomonic empire as represented in the Hebrew Bible. Archeological evidence from this period points to a great deal of urban building. The major cities in Israel are constructed with strong casemate walls, a double wall that may be filled in with dirt and debris for greater strength in a time of emergency. The so-called Solomonic gate, a well-protected, six-chamber gate with three heavy doors, appeared throughout Israel's major cities, including Megiddo, Gezer, Hazor, Lachish, and others. A variety of major buildings were constructed in these cities and in Jerusalem as well. Although the site of the Jerusalem Temple cannot be excavated because of the sanctity of the site in Judaism and the presence of Islam's Dome of the Rock, the description of the three-chambered Temple of Solomon in 1 Kgs. 6–8 represents the typical construction of contemporary temples (and royal palaces) in ancient Phoenicia and Syria.

There are no ancient accounts of the revolt of northern Israel against the royal House of David, but subsequent Assyrian and Babylonian records acknowledge that the kingdoms of Israel and Judah stood as separate states from the ninth through the eighth centuries BCE. Assyrian records testify to successive invasions of the region by Tiglath-Pileser III at the time of the Syro-Ephraimite War in 735–732, which first saw the subjugation of Israel and Judah to Assyria (reigned 745–727 BCE; see 2 Kgs. 15–16; Is. 7; 17); by Shalmanezer V and Sargon II, who destroyed the northern kingdom of Israel and exiled many of its inhabitants in 721–720 BCE (reigned 727–721 and 720–705 BCE respectively, see 2 Kgs. 17; Is. 8–10); and by Sennacherib, who invaded Judah and besieged Jerusalem in 701 BCE (reigned 705–681 BCE; see 2 Kgs. 18–20; Is. 36–39). Archeological evidence points to massive devastation in Israel and Judah during this period as well. The decline of Assyria following the death of Assurbanipal in 627 BCE and the fall of Assur and Nineveh in 614 and 612 respectively provides the background for King Josiah's attempts at the restoration of Judah (reigned 639–609 BCE). Again, Babylonian records recount Nebuchadnezzar's successive campaigns against Judah (reigned 605–562 BCE), and archeological evidence demonstrates the overwhelming destruction that Judah suffered during this period.

Of course, neither ancient Near Eastern records nor archeological investigation can ever confirm or deny God's involvement in the history of Israel and Judah. That is, after all, an assertion of religious faith rather than of empirically demonstrable science. Nevertheless, such evidence does confirm the basic framework of Israel's and Judah's history as presented in the Hebrew Bible, and it points to an understanding of the reasons why such history was written. History is written not only to chronicle the past but to provide a basis for understanding the present and for making decisions concerning the future. In this respect, the narrative histories of Genesis through Kings must be understood as an effort on the part of the writers to assert YHWH's relationship with Israel and Judah and to argue that to a certain extent YHWH controlled historical events. According to the Hebrew Bible, YHWH acted to form Israel, redeem Israel from Egyptian bondage, grant to Israel the promised land, and to punish Israel with exile for failure to observe divine expectations. At the same time, such history points to restoration and an interest in learning from the past in order to construct a better future. The Hebrew Bible does not end with the Babylonian exile; in both its Jewish and Christian forms, it ends in the period when the post-exilic restoration had already taken place. The account of Israel's history from creation to the Babylonian exile is not simply an attempt to write the epitaph of a defeated people. Instead, it constitutes guidance for Jews who sought to restore Israel in the period following the Babylonian exile.

The Role of State and Temple in Israel's Religious Life

As noted above, the biblical account of the origins and early history of Israel emphasizes YHWH's covenant with Abraham and his descendants and the Exodus from Egypt and traditions related to Moses as the foundational events of the nation Israel. Both of these events are therefore of prime importance in considering the religious and national self-identity of the people of Israel. Although they play prominent roles in Israel's self-understanding, the survey of Israel's historical background provides little basis to confirm either event. This does not mean that Abraham and Moses are not historical figures; it simply means that both are the products of Israelite tradition regardless of their historical character. The presentation of each must therefore be considered in relation to the major Israelite institutions that were primarily involved in the transmission of Israelite tradition and the formation of Israelite national and religious self-identity, i.e., the monarchy and the Temple.

Because of the American separation of Church and State, modern North American readers are accustomed to thinking of religion and politics as different spheres of life. Nevertheless, it is important to recognize that throughout world history, the interests of state and religion are closely intertwined so that the rulers of state frequently establish, support, and shape religious institutions and religious institutions in turn frequently legitimize, support, and shape state institutions. Thus, the rise of Confucianism as a state religion in China coincides with the rise of the Han dynasty (206 BCE–220 CE); Buddhism was established in India by the Maurya dynasty that first unified the south Asian sub-continent in the third century BCE; Christianity became the religion of the Roman Empire in the fourth century CE; and Islam grew into prominence together with the rise of the Ummayid dynasty in the seventh and eighth centuries CE. Similar phenomena are well known in the ancient Near East as the Egyptian Pharaohs ruled Egypt with the support of the priests of Amon-Re and the Babylonian monarchs ruled with the support of the priests of Marduk.

Much the same may be observed in the interrelationship of the ruling House of David in Israel and Judah and the Temple in Jerusalem. Although Saul was the first king of Israel, David was the first monarch to successfully unify the nation and establish a secure ruling dynasty, at least over the tribe of Judah. David's success may be attributed to a number of factors. He was a military and political genius who was able to forge alliances, both within and outside of Israel, so that he could gain the support necessary to defeat Israel's enemies and to establish himself as the sole legitimate ruling monarch of the nation. Key to his success, however, was his selection of Jerusalem as his political and religious capital.

Although we think of Israel as a combination of twelve tribes, a close reading of 2 Sam. 1–7 indicates that Israel was actually divided into two major parts during David's early reign, i.e., the northern tribes of Israel who were ruled by Saul's son Eshbaal (known as Ish-boshet, "man of shame," in 2 Sam. 2–4; cf., 1 Chr. 8:33; 9:39, which name him Eshbaal, "man of Baal"), and the southern tribe of Judah ruled by David at Hebron. There was civil war between the two parts of Israel for some seven years until, after the deaths of Eshbaal and his commander Abner, David was able to unite all of the tribes of Israel under his own rule. In order to avoid the perception that he favored either his own tribe, Judah, or the far more powerful northern tribes, David chose to establish his capital in Jerusalem, a Jebusite city situated in the territory of Benjamin at the boundary between Judah and the northern tribes. Jerusalem could be considered neutral ground, and when David used his own mercenaries to capture the city, neither Judah nor the northern tribes could claim that the city belonged to them. When David had secured Jerusalem, he brought the ark of the covenant, which represented the presence of YHWH among the people, to the city from its prior location in Kiryat Yearim. David thereby established Jerusalem as both his political and religious capital for ruling the entire nation of Israel.

The rise of David as king over all Israel and his selection of Jerusalem as his political and religious capital plays a foundational role in the conceptualization and development of ancient Israelite religion because it establishes a close interrelationship between the Davidic kings and YHWH. This interrelationship is evident in YHWH's promise of an eternal dynasty to David immediately after David brings the ark of the covenant to Jerusalem in 2 Sam. 6. According to 2 Sam. 7, David had thought to build a "house" or Temple for YHWH once he had become king, but the prophet Nathan came to David and declared that YHWH did not desire a "house." Instead, YHWH would build a "house," i.e., a dynasty, for David so that his descendants would rule forever in Jerusalem. David never built the "house," or Temple, for YHWH in Jerusalem, but his son Solomon did and thereby established the Davidic monarchy and the Jerusalem Temple as the two primary institutions of ancient Israel or Judah. In short, the

House of David established and supported the Jerusalem Temple of YHWH, and YHWH established and supported the House of David.

The close interrelationship between the House of David and YHWH is evident in the Psalms, which were apparently sung as liturgical hymns in the Jerusalem Temple. 1 Chr. 16, for example, relates the psalm sung at the time that David established the ark in Jerusalem. The psalm draws upon Pss. 105, 95, and 106 to thank and praise YHWH for all the wonderful things YHWH had done for Israel, such as making a covenant with Israel through Abraham, Isaac, and Jacob, and defending Israel from the various threats posed by its enemies. Although the House of David is not mentioned in this version of the psalm, others are much more explicit. Ps. 132, for example, rehearses David's efforts to provide a dwelling place for YHWH and the ark of the covenant. Declaring YHWH's choice of Zion as the site for the ark, the psalm reiterates YHWH's oath to David that his sons will sit upon David's throne in perpetuity. Ps. 89 likewise declares YHWH's eternal steadfast love for David and the promise of an eternal dynasty and relates the Davidic promise to traditions concerning YHWH's creation of the world and defeat of the forces of chaos, so that the House of David emerges as a fundamental element of the creation of the cosmos. Ps. 110 declares the king in Zion to be a priest forever according to the order of Melchizedek, and Ps. 2 declares the Davidic king to be the son of YHWH in Zion whom YHWH will defend from attacks by the kings of the earth. Pss. 46, 47, and 48 in turn declare YHWH as the king of the nations and the God of Abraham and Jacob who will defend the holy habitation in Mount Zion from the nations. When Solomon dedicated the Temple in Jerusalem, he highlighted YHWH's promise to the House of David and YHWH's role in bringing rain and fertility to the land and world at large.

Indeed, the preceding examples demonstrate the close interrelationship between the House of David and YHWH in Zion, and they point to the cosmic dimensions of the Jerusalem Temple as the center of all creation. According to Ezek. 43:14, the sacrificial altar of the Temple was the "bosom of the earth" and thereby represented the role of the Temple as the site where creation took place, both in the Temple liturgy and in the Israelite conception of the cosmos. Various psalms therefore celebrate YHWH's role as creator of the universe. Ps. 33, for example, reiterates YHWH's creation of the heavens and the earth from the depths of the sea, and Ps. 8 emphasizes YHWH's creation of human beings and their dominion over the creatures of the earth. Ps. 19 points to YHWH's establishment of a tent in the heavens, much like the tent that housed the ark in Jerusalem prior to the construction of the Temple, and the "instruction" or Torah of YHWH that brings righteousness to the world. Ps. 104 portrays YHWH in relation to the sun and recounts YHWH's creation of the winds, springs, animals, plants, light, seasons, etc., that testify to YHWH's wisdom and capacity to bring bounty and order to the world.

The conceptualization of the Temple in Jerusalem as the home of YHWH and the center of creation also influences the narrative traditions of creation and Israel's early history. The description of the Temple as built by Solomon in

1 Kgs. 6–7 highlights the decorative lilywork, pomegranates, cherubim, lions, and palm trees that symbolized the Temple's identification with the Garden of Eden as presented in Gen. 2–3. The two pillars that stood at the Temple entrance, Jachin and Boaz, symbolized the foundations of the earth on which creation is based. The molten sea, which was set outside the Temple on the backs of twelve cast oxen, symbolized the sea from which creation proceeded. The Temple lampstands with their seven branches for lights represented both the light of creation and the trees of the Garden of Eden. Later tradition regarded the high priest in the Temple as a symbolic representation of Adam in the Garden of Eden. The spring Gihon, which provided water for the city of Jerusalem (2 Chr. 33:14) and was where Solomon was anointed king (1 Kgs. 1:33, 38, 45), is identified in Gen. 2:13 as one of the rivers that emerged from the Garden of Eden to water the world (see also Ezek. 47:1).

Temple symbolism also appears in relation to the traditions concerning the Exodus from Egypt, revelation at Sinai, and wilderness wanderings, especially since many of the motifs from these traditions are related to those of creation and YHWH's kingship over the world. Indeed, the Exodus is also well represented in the Psalms, such as Pss. 78, 105, and 106, which were sung in the Temple to recount YHWH's acts of deliverance on behalf of Israel. But the Exodus narratives themselves are also heavily influenced by Temple symbolism. The narratives in Exod. 7–13 concerning the ten plagues against Egypt, such as the Nile's turning to blood, the frogs, the gnats, thunder and hail, locusts, darkness, etc., demonstrate YHWH's control of the natural forces of creation. The tenth plague in particular, the death of the firstborn, is related to the Israelite practice of bringing the first fruits of the harvest and flock for sacrifice to the Temple in Jerusalem. Indeed, YHWH's statement in Exod. 13:2, "consecrate to me all the firstborn; whatever is the first to open the womb among the Israelites, of human beings and animals, is mine," draws upon the laws concerning the requirement to sacrifice the firstborn to YHWH at the Temple, such as Exod. 34:19, "All that first opens the womb is mine, all your male livestock, the firstborn of cow and sheep. The firstborn of a donkey you shall redeem with a lamb . . . all the firstborn of your sons you shall redeem."

Likewise, the account of the crossing of the Red Sea, Exod. 14–15, emphasizes the emergence of dry land from the sea (Exod. 14:22, 15:8), much like the creation of dry land in Gen. 1, and states that the people have been redeemed so that they might come to YHWH's sanctuary and acknowledge that "YHWH will reign forever and ever" (Exod. 15:17–18). The purification of the priests in the water of the previously mentioned molten sea outside the entrance to the Temple similarly symbolizes Israel's entry into the Red Sea at the time of the deliverance from Egypt. The symbolism of Mt. Sinai, from which YHWH revealed Torah to Israel through the Levitical priest Moses, recalls the symbolism of Mt. Zion, from which YHWH revealed Torah through the priests to Israel and to the world at large (Pss. 19, 94, 119; Is. 2:2–4; Mic. 4:1–5). The creation of the tabernacle and the ark of the covenant in the wilderness to represent YHWH's presence among the people points ultimately to the creation of the Temple once

Israel took possession of the land. Indeed, the prior representation of YHWH's presence as a pillar of fire and smoke employs the symbolism of the Temple altar in operation as the offerings of the people were consumed in fire and smoke. As many scholars have noted, the language pertaining to the building of the tabernacle and YHWH's settling into it in Exod. 35–40 draws upon the language of Gen. 2:1–3, which describes YHWH's rest from creation at the first Shabbat or Sabbath, so that the building of the tabernacle (and ultimately of the Temple) symbolizes the completion of creation.

The conceptualization of the Temple as the center of creation also legitimized its role as the source for YHWH's instructions or laws that governed the life of the people. Many have noted that the ten commandments in Exod. 20 and Deut. 5 provide a summation of the basic principles that governed the laws of ancient Israel in both the cultic and the social spheres. Thus, the commands concerning the exclusive worship of YHWH, the prohibition of idolatry, the use of YHWH's holy name, and observance of the Sabbath define the basic spheres of holiness in Israelite religious life. Likewise, the commands to honor one's parents and the prohibitions against murder, adultery, theft, false witness in court, and coveting that which belongs to one's neighbor provide the basic foundations for order in Israel's social life. The balance of the laws in Exodus, Leviticus, Numbers, and Deuteronomy elaborate on these basic principles extensively.

The religious laws of the Hebrew Bible emphasize the Temple as the sacred center of the Israelite state as well as of creation at large. As the holy center of Israel and the universe, the Temple represented the stability of both the cosmos and the nation through its system of festivals that established and maintained the relationship between YHWH and the people of Israel. Fundamental to the system is the weekly Sabbath, which Jews call by its Hebrew name, Shabbat, in which all normal work ceases, so that the people can celebrate YHWH's creation of the world each week and resanctify themselves for the week ahead. In addition to Shabbat are the three major pilgrimage festivals, Pesach (Passover), Shavuot (Weeks), and Sukkot (Booths, Tabernacles), in which all Israelite men were required to come to YHWH's Temple to present the first fruits of their seasonal crops and the firstborn of their flocks and herds.

Insofar as each festival commemorates both an event in Israel's sacred history and a stage in the seasonal agricultural cycle, the festivals reinforce Israel's identity as the chosen people of YHWH and provided a means by which the Temple could collect the one-tenth of the produce of the crops and livestock of the land. In this respect, the festivals constituted the basis of a system of state taxation that was sacralized and legitimized by the Temple to support the state at large. Thus Pesach commemorates YHWH's redemption of Israel from Egyptian bondage, and it also marks the beginning of the grain harvest in the land of Israel following the first planting season in the spring. Shavuot, counted as seven weeks or forty-nine days following the festival of Pesach, commemorates the revelation of YHWH's Torah at Mt. Sinai and the conclusion of the grain harvest in the early summer season. Sukkot commemorates the period of wilderness wandering in which the people lived in tents, but it also marks the grape and olive harvest, when the harvesters dwell in sukkot – temporary booths. In addition, Sukkot marks the beginning of the rainy fall season in the land of Israel, with its promise of future growth for the following year. Sukkot closes the agricultural year and marks the time when the full harvest of the season is known. It is therefore an appropriate time to celebrate YHWH's sovereignty and to rededicate oneself to YHWH's service.

The observance of the New Year, Rosh ha-Shanah, on the first day of the seventh month, and of the Day of Atonement, Yom Kippur, on the tenth day of the seventh month is therefore closely tied to the seven-day festival of Sukkot beginning on the fifteenth day of the seventh month. The former celebrates YHWH's role as sovereign of creation and the latter provides a time for repentance from wrongdoing at a time when the year is to begin again. Both present an opportunity to renew one's sense of loyalty to YHWH and to the Israelite state and Temple that represent YHWH to the people. Detailed laws concerning the celebration of the festivals, the sacrifices pertaining to them, and the conduct of the priests appear in Exod. 23:14–19; 34:17–26, Lev. 23, Num. 15–19, 28–29, and Deut. 14:1–16:17. The laws concerning the building of altars appear in Exod. 20:22–26 and Deut. 12. Those concerned with the building of the wilderness tabernacle (and thus of the Temple), its furnishings, and the accoutrements of its priests appear in Exod. 25–30 and 35–40.

In addition to the sacred laws, the Temple served as the source for laws governing the social life of the people. Extensive laws concerning issues of murder, personal injury, property transfer, property damage, marriage, rape, debt, inheritance, etc., appear in Exod. 21–24, 34; Lev. 18–20; Num. 27, 30–36; and Deut. 16–26. Thus, Exod. 22:28 forbids cursing God or a prince, i.e., the monarch, among the people. Deut. 19:1–13 establishes cities of refuge where one may go for protection from death in the event of justified manslaughter. The rule of an "eye for an eye" in Exod. 21:18–27, Lev. 24:10–23, and Deut. 19:21 establishes principles by which compensation is decided in cases of manslaughter and personal injury. Exod. 21:28–36 employs the example of an ox that gores, to establish principles for deciding cases of property damage, and Exod. 21:37–22:14 defines other areas of restitution for damaged or stolen property. Lev. 18 and 20 define the principles for proper marriages, i.e., those that avoid incest and other issues. Exod. 22:15–16 defines the terms of marriage for a man who seduces a virgin, and Deut. 22:13–29 regulates cases of adultery and rape. Exod. 21:1–11 and Deut. 15:1–18 regulate the terms by which a man or woman may serve as a slave, i.e., they may work as a slave for a defined period of time in order to pay back a debt. The levirate law in Deut. 25:5–10 establishes a procedure by which a brother may father a son and legal heir for his dead brother through the widow, and Num. 27:1–11 and 36:1–12 establish regulations by which women may inherit their father's estate when no male heirs exist. Other areas of Israelite social life are addressed as well, but these examples demonstrate the importance of divine authority in establishing laws that promoted order in the social life of ancient Israel and thus supported a stable state or monarchy.

Although the monarch is rarely mentioned in the narrative and laws of the Pentateuch, it is important to note that the conceptualization of the Davidic covenant and the Temple priesthood does influence the presentation of Abraham's covenant with YHWH in Gen. 12–25. When YHWH declares to Abraham in Gen. 15 that he will become a great nation, Abram/Abraham responds that he has no son. YHWH reiterates the divine oath that Abram will indeed have a son who will succeed him and continue the covenant, which corresponds to YHWH's promise to David in 2 Sam. 7, Pss. 89 and 132, etc., that his sons will rule eternally. YHWH's everlasting promise to Abraham is reiterated in Gen. 17:4–8 at the time Abraham was circumcised as a sign of his adherence to YHWH. YHWH's promise to Abram of the land that his descendants will inherit in Gen. 15:18–21, "from the river of Egypt to the great river, the river Euphrates," corresponds to the furthest extent of the Davidic empire as represented in 2 Sam. 8 (cf., Num. 34; Ezek. 47:13–20). Others have noted Abraham's close association with the city of Hebron, David's first capital, especially since Abraham is buried there (Gen. 25:7–11). Abraham also acknowledged God and paid a tithe at Salem, generally identified as Jerusalem, before the priest-king Melchizedek in Gen. 14:17–24 (cf., Ps. 110). Abraham's near sacrifice of Isaac took place at Mt. Moriah, which is also identified as the site of the future Temple (2 Chr. 3:1). Insofar as the traditions concerning Abraham begin the Hebrew Bible's presentation of Israel's history, it would appear that the interests of the Davidic dynasty and the Jerusalem Temple are signaled at the outset through the figure of Abraham.

The Prophets and National Crises in Israel and Judah

The preceding discussion demonstrates the fundamental role the Davidic monarchy and the Jerusalem Temple played in shaping ancient Judah's religious life and national self-identity. The northern monarchies and temples undoubtedly played a very similar role in the northern kingdom of Israel, but very little literary material from the northern kingdom appears in the Hebrew Bible. The Hebrew Bible is basically the product of Judean authors, and their perspectives shape our understanding of both the southern kingdom of Judah and the northern kingdom of Israel. Even when biblical writings originated in the north, e.g., the book of the northern prophet Hosea or the Jacob traditions of Genesis, they apparently were edited and given their final literary form in the south and therefore reflect Judean influence.

The preceding discussion also demonstrates that the religious and national outlook of ancient Judah was based in the belief that YHWH had chosen Jerusalem and the House of David and that YHWH had made an eternal covenant that would guarantee the security of both. But the people of Israel founded their nation during the twelfth–tenth centuries BCE at a time when the major world powers, Egypt to the south and the northern powers of Asia Minor and Mesopotamia, were relatively weak and unable to exert much influence in the land of Israel as they had done in the past. By the late-tenth and ninth centuries BCE, this situation began to change, as Egypt and Assyria made increasing efforts to extend their power beyond their own borders so that they might control the lucrative trade routes through the land of Israel that had made Solomon's empire so powerful and wealthy. The Egyptians apparently had a hand in supporting the revolt of the northern tribes of Israel against Solomon's son Rehoboam in 922 BCE. Pharaoh Shishak (Shoshenq I, 931–910 BCE) had given sanctuary to Jeroboam ben Nebat when he was forced to flee Israel after inciting revolt against Solomon (1 Kgs. 11:26–40), and after the northern revolt Shishak invaded Israel and stripped the Jerusalem Temple of Solomon's gold shields (1 Kgs. 14:25–28). Likewise, Assyrian records indicate that King Ahab of Israel joined a coalition of small states led by Aram in 853 BCE to stop the Assyrian king Shalmanezer III from an attempted invasion of Aram and Israel. Although both Israel and Judah suffered setbacks during this period, nothing fundamentally challenged the expectation that YHWH would protect the people of Israel.

By the late-eighth century BCE, however, this situation began to change as the Assyrian empire, led by Tiglath-Pileser III and his successors, grew stronger and ultimately conquered much of the ancient Near East, including Israel and Judah. During the Syro-Ephraimitic War of 735–732 BCE when Israel and Aram allied against Judah in an attempt to force it into an anti-Assyrian coalition, Tiglath-Pileser III destroyed Aram and subjugated Israel in an attempt to support the Judean monarch Ahaz (2 Kgs. 16; Is. 7). By 921/920 BCE, Shalmanezer V and Sargon II destroyed the kingdom of Israel when it revolted against Assyrian rule and deported major portions of the surviving Israelite population to other lands within the Assyrian empire (2 Kgs. 17). In 701 BCE, Sennacherib invaded Judah when King Hezekiah attempted a similar revolt in conjunction with Babylonia. Although the Assyrians overran Judah (2 Kgs. 18–20; Is. 36–39), Hezekiah remained on the throne and Judah continued as an Assyrian vassal through much of the seventh century BCE. Following an attempted restoration by the Judean monarch Josiah in the late-seventh century, Babylonia ultimately emerged as the ruler of Judah. When Judah revolted against Babylonia in the early-sixth century, Babylon destroyed Jerusalem and the Temple of Solomon in 587/586 BCE and carried major elements of the Judean population into exile. The Judean kingdom of David came to an end.

Naturally, the Assyrian invasions of the eighth and seventh centuries BCE and the Babylonian invasions of the sixth century BCE posed a fundamental challenge to Israelite religion in that they pointed to the possibility that YHWH either would not or could not protect the people of Israel. This prompted some major rethinking of the principles of Israelite religion on the part of the prophets, who began to argue that the Assyrian invasions represented punishment brought upon the people by YHWH because the people had failed to observe the terms of the relationship between themselves and YHWH. The prophets of Israel and Judah were hardly a unique phenomenon in the ancient Near Eastern world; prophets were known in many cultures as oracle-givers and priests who communicated the will of the gods to monarchs and the people at large. But in presenting their understanding of the significance of the Assyrian and later Babylonian and Persian empires, the prophets of ancient Israel and Judah provided the means by which Judah at least would survive the crisis and lay the foundations for Judaism during the period of the Babylonian exile and beyond, when the continuity of the Davidic monarchy and an autonomous Judean state could no longer be assured.

All of the prophets who presented a critique of ancient Israelite or Judean society and religion during this period drew upon their own individual perspectives and understanding of tradition, and each pointed to ways in which the people could reform themselves and thus conform to the will of YHWH. Amos, for example, was a Judean farmer from Tekoa during the mid-eighth century who was forced to bring his offerings to the northern sanctuary at Beth El during a period when Judah was allied as a vassal to the more powerful northern Israel. In his view, the northern monarch Jeroboam ben Joash (Jeroboam II; 2 Kgs. 14) was corrupt in that he did not show enough concern for the poor of the people of Israel and Judah as required by Israelite laws that made provision for the poor (see Amos 2:6–16, 7:10–17; Exod. 21–23). Amos therefore argued that Jeroboam II must die and that the sanctuary at Beth El must be destroyed. As he was a Judean, Amos's view of righteous kingship lay in the restoration of Davidic rule over all of the twelve tribes, as it had been in the days of David and Solomon (Amos 9:11–15).

The prophet Hosea, who lived in the northern kingdom shortly after the time of Amos, likewise condemned the northern monarchy for its alliance with Assyria. In Hosea's view, Jeroboam II and the monarchs of the house of Jehu had acted like an unfaithful wife who abandoned her husband to pursue other lovers, because they had allied the nation with Assyria and Egypt rather than with Aram, from where Israel's ancestors had come (see Hos. 12:1–15). In portraying Israel as his own wife, Gomer, whom he accused of adultery (Hos. 1–2), Hosea offered the possibility of a reconciliation, i.e., just as Hosea could accept his wife's return (Hos. 3), so YHWH could accept the return of Israel (Hos. 14). Of course, in its present form, such a return also means a return to the rule of the House of David (Hos. 3:5). Hosea's book was apparently brought south and edited in Judah after Israel was destroyed by the Assyrians.

When the Assyrian empire threatened Israel and Judah, southern prophets began to respond in similar fashion. The prophet Isaiah ben Amoz, for example, argued that the destruction of the northern kingdom of Israel represented YHWH's judgment against the north, but that YHWH would continue to protect Judah if King Ahaz would trust in the Davidic promise. At the time of the Israelite and Aramean invasion of Judah in 735–734 BCE, Isaiah counseled Ahaz not to seek outside help from Assyria, but to trust in YHWH and the defenses of Jerusalem: "If you will not believe, surely you will not be established" (Is. 7:9). When Ahaz refused Isaiah's advice and turned to Assyria, Isaiah condemned Ahaz as a faithless monarch and argued that the Assyrians would indeed subjugate Judah – which they did (see Is. 7–8). For his own part, Isaiah looked forward to the time when a righteous Davidic monarch would arise, who would trust in YHWH's promise and who would restore righteous Davidic rule over all of Israel (see Is. 8:16–9:6, 11:1–16, 32:1–20).

The prophet Micah viewed things somewhat differently. As a resident of Moresheth-Gath at the border between Philistia and Judah, Micah saw his village destroyed in Sennacherib's invasion of 701 BCE and fled as a refugee to Jerusalem, which was placed under siege. In his view, the experience of Israel would be a model for that of Judah, i.e., Jerusalem would be destroyed because its rulers had made foolish decisions, such as, to revolt against Assyria, without considering their impact upon the people (see Mic. 1–3). Jerusalem and Judah would be restored when its rulers learned the basic principles of justice as a result of YHWH's punishment (Mic. 6).

Unlike northern Israel, Judah survived the Assyrian onslaught. When the Assyrian empire fell in the latter half of the seventh century BCE, Judah enjoyed a brief period of potential resurgence under King Josiah (639–609 BCE) who apparently saw his reign as a fulfillment of earlier prophecies of restoration. But when Josiah was killed by Pharaoh Necho at Megiddo in 609 BCE (2 Kgs. 23:28–30), Judah again fell under the domination of foreign powers, first Egypt and then Babylonia. The Davidic tradition of security for Jerusalem and Judah continued to exert a great deal of influence among the people and prompted several unsuccessful attempts to revolt against Babylonian rule.

The viewpoint of the prophet Isaiah was especially influential, as indicated by the appearance of the prophet Hannaniah, who argued like Isaiah that YHWH would protect Judah and that the Babylonians would be driven away in a short period of time (see Jer. 27–28). But the prophet Jeremiah, an Elide priest who traced his ancestral roots to the pre-monarchic temple at Shiloh (see 1 Sam. 1–3), did not share this view. His perspective was that of a Levite like Moses, who looked to YHWH's Torah or instruction as the basis for the nation's future (cf., Deut. 28–30). Although he was apparently an early supporter of Josiah's Torah-based program of national restoration (see Jer. 2:1–4:4; 2 Kgs. 22–23), the premature death of Josiah convinced him that Judah would suffer much like Israel. He therefore declared Hannaniah to be a false prophet, and that it was the will of YHWH that Judah submit to Babylon. In his Temple sermon in Jer. 7, Jeremiah argued that the Temple would not guarantee Judah's security; after all, his ancestral temple at Shiloh had been destroyed, and the Jerusalem Temple could suffer a similar fate. Instead, adherence to YHWH's Torah, such as some of the ten commandments, cited in his speech, was what YHWH required. Jeremiah was put on trial for his remarks and nearly executed (Jer. 26), but, much to his own dismay, his words came true when the Babylonians destroyed Jerusalem and the Temple in 587/586 BCE. Nevertheless, Jeremiah did not see a full end to the people but spoke of their future restoration, when YHWH's Torah would be placed in the heart of the people and they would return to Jerusalem and the land of Israel.

Although the restoration of Jerusalem and the Temple would take place only in the early Persian period, after the Babylonian empire had been conquered and incorporated into the Persian empire, the pre-exilic prophets of Israel and Judah developed the theological basis by which YHWH's covenant with the people could be maintained despite the destruction of the northern kingdom of Israel, the Jerusalem Temple, and the Davidic monarchy.

Bibliography

Hallo, William W., and William Kelly Simpson, *The Ancient Near East: A History* (New York, 1971).

Levenson, Jon D., *Sinai and Zion: An Entry into the Jewish Bible* (Minneapolis, Chicago, New York, 1985).

Mazar, Amihai, *Archaeology of the Land of the Bible, 10,000–586* BCE (New York, 1990).

Miller, J. Maxwell, and John H. Hayes, *A History of Ancient Israel and Judah* (Philadelphia, 1986).

Smith, Mark S., *The Early History of God: YHWH and the Other Deities in Ancient Israel* (San Francisco, 1990).

Sweeney, Marvin A., *King Josiah of Judah: The Lost Messiah of Israel* (New York and Oxford, 2000).

West, James King, *Introduction to the Old Testament* (Second edition: New York, 1981).

CHAPTER 3
Judaism and the Hebrew Scriptures

Philip R. Davies

Among most Christians and Muslims (as well as a number of Jews), Judaism is seen as a religion of the Bible. It is often stated that the Christians took over the "Old Testament" from the Jews; while the Qur'an retells many biblical stories, and both Christians and Jews are called the "people of the book" in Islam. But is Judaism a "biblical religion"? In other words, did it derive from Scripture or is it essentially based on the contents of Scripture? For those who like short answers, that answer is that Judaism is (and was) *not* in either sense strictly a "biblical religion." But the qualifications to that answer are numerous. Like most interesting and important questions, this one has no easy answer, and, indeed, deserves the famous response: "It depends what you mean by . . ." A proper answer really does depend partly on how we define both "Judaism" and "Bible."

In fact, the origins and history of Judaism and its scriptures (not necessarily "the Bible")[1] are closely entwined. The Jewish people possessed a literary canon during the Second Temple period. How and when precisely this canon developed is not really important, but almost certainly it grew out of the professional activities of the Judean scribal class and scribal communities under the Persians and Greeks (i.e., from the sixth century BCE onwards).[2] Its major components were historical, legal, prophetic and didactic writings. Many, but not all, of these genres have parallels in the cultures of the ancient Near East and among the Greeks.[3] The planting in the Levant of Greek culture (which was not entirely unknown even before the Persian period) through the conquests of Alexander, the creation of Greek kingdoms, founding of Greek cities and colonization by Greeks led in Judah, as elsewhere, to cultural reactions among the recipients designed to accommodate or resist the new forms of social and political life that were now being offered. This complex process should not be oversimplified, but among the Judeans five major threads in this process of negotiation with Hellenism can be identified. These were antiquity, language, education, religion, and identity, and, of course, they were interconnected. They can now be very briefly sketched.

The Greeks were characteristically interested in ethnography, in the origins of those peoples with whom they came into contact.[4] Such an interest was not, of course, alien to the peoples of the ancient Near East, either, but in the collision of Greek and Levantine cultures the question of which was the more ancient became of interest to both sides (Hellenism is, of course, the result of a fusion of aspects of both cultures). Egyptians, Babylonians, Phoenicians, and Jews all produced, during the period of the Hellenistic monarchies (end of fourth century– mid-first century BCE), works of history asserting their most ancient origins.[5] All of these were written in Greek, except for those composed or edited in Judah, which were in Hebrew. We do have fragments of Jewish histories written in Greek, and from the first century CE the completely preserved *Jewish Antiquities* of Josephus. But in Judah, a tiny part of first the Ptolemaic and then the Seleucid kingdom before nearly a century of Hasmonean independence, this history was in Hebrew, and, while it was translated into Greek at some stage, its original composition in Hebrew signifies the important fact that the Judeans of Palestine remained firmly devoted to Hebrew as their native language, despite using not Hebrew but Aramaic and Greek for their everyday discourse. This particular form of resistance to Hellenism is extremely important to note and to try and explain.

Education was, according to most scholars of the subject, the major instrument by which Hellenism spread and took hold. Already, thanks to various changes begun under the Persians and continued by the Hellenistic kingdoms, literacy had spread beyond the scribal classes, and the new Hellenistic forms of political and social life required greater literacy. Use of the Greek language and literacy led, among the Hellenized subjects and (in the case of independent cities) citizens of the Levant, to familiarity with Greek literature and with it the values that Homer, Herodotus, Thucydides, Euripides, and other works of the Greek and Hellenistic canon imparted. Education, then, was a major factor in the absorption of Hellenism and would necessarily be a factor in any resistance to it.

The place of religion in Greek political life among the Greeks was different in some important respects from the Levant, where priesthood and powerful temple cults, even temple-states, were common and where kingship and religion were closely intertwined. Greek religion was not, however, typically expressed through politics, and, during the Hellenistic age, religion became more humanistic and less theistic, though to generalize about the development of religion in the Hellenistic kingdoms and the succeeding Greco-Roman period is unwise. But the role of philosophy and its alliance to science marks off a clear separation from religion in the Greek way of life and thought, in contrast to the more public role of religion and its inseparability from science in the traditional forms of life of the ancient Near East.

These factors so far discussed (and certainly oversimplified) all contribute to a sense of individual and social identity, or ethnicity. The Judeans, under the

Persians, Ptolemies and, at first, Seleucids, had been either encouraged or permitted to live according to their "ancestral laws" or customs. Since the Jerusalem Temple and its priesthood increasingly dominated the political and religious thought and the social behavior of Judeans, what would later, under the Seleucids, become identified as "Judaism" has an intrinsically religious character. It is important to note this apparently obvious fact, for it is not so obvious as to need no explanation. Indeed, the Greeks tended to regard Judaism as a philosophy. The basis of Judean autonomy and identity was felt to lie in religion.

Moreover, the relative isolation and the small size of the province of Judah encouraged what Greek–Egyptian writers such as Hecataeus and Manetho (early third century BCE) observed as a high degree of segregation from their neighbors. The geographic–political location of Judah also meant that little or no colonization took place in the wake of Alexander's arrival, and no Greek cities were built in its territory or even immediately on its borders. The encounter between Hellenism and Judea, then, exhibits a number of unique features. Scholarly dispute continues over whether Palestine was "Hellenized" or the Jews of Judah[6] and their culture remained largely impervious to most aspects of Hellenism. The truth is that Judeans did absorb a great deal of Hellenism but also resisted it. The pattern of relationships is a complicated one (as it was also in the diaspora).[7]

An important motif in this pattern is the interlude of Judean independence. The tensions that Hellenism induced in Judean society over the role of the priesthood and Temple in social, political and economic life, and the struggle for power between the dominant priestly dynasty and other priestly and non-priestly interests, resulted in a war both within Judean society and between certain Judean groups and the Seleucid king Antiochus IV (the so-called "Maccabean revolt"). The outcome of this struggle was the establishment of a native dynasty that combined both secular and priestly functions (adopting at times the titles of both king and high priest in one person) and also carried out, while increasingly displaying the trappings of Hellenistic monarchy and features of Hellenistic culture, a program of nationalistic conquest and internal unification. Under a native dynasty, the question of the political forms of Judean (we can now also say "Jewish") life had to be addressed: the regulation of the Temple and cult and adoption of a calendar and appropriate festival days. It is clear that these issues were not, and probably never had been, matters of universal agreement. The idea of a unified "Judaism" from, say, the early Persian period, is not tenable. Indeed, the notion is probably anachronistic: "Judaism" as an idea, and thence as a problem, is a Hellenistic phenomenon, encouraged also by the social and political structures of the Roman Empire.

The Hasmoneans, therefore, having gained power over a divided society by the judicious use of alliances between groups, found themselves confronting both internal and external pressures. Among the measures they took were the promotion of "Judaism" as the way of life to which their rule, over an enlarged territory (including all of Palestine, including Idumea, Galilee and parts of Transjordan), gave political expression. This involved adjudication between

Pharisees and Sadducees over matters of religion, in which allegiance shifted from ruler to ruler. It also seems that use of the language of Hebrew was encouraged, lest, perhaps, the Greek language, trailing Greek education and Greek literary classics in its wake, overcome the tradition of cultural autonomy that Judeans revered. It seems hard to doubt that some system of education that was Judean, rather than Greek, must also have been encouraged. There is evidence that education in the Hebrew classics had already been long established: the Jerusalem scribe ben Sira (ca. 200 BCE) had a school of his own. But it is likely the Hasmoneans promoted a greater knowledge of Hebrew literature, meaning the "classic" works of the Scribal canon, and some other popular writings.

Now we turn again to scriptures. The determination of a "canon," an official collection of books and a fixed text of these books (no doubt centered on a Jerusalem library that must have existed in earlier times), can be most plausibly traced to the Hasmonean period, in which a number of related measures were designed to instill a national identity that was commensurate with political independence, a Hellenistic environment, and an essentially religious culture. At this time, then, both Judaism (Juda-ism) and its scriptures came into existence in a formal and related manner. This statement is not intended to deny that prior to this time there existed a Judean culture or a literary tradition: merely that these two now acquire a formal identity as "Judaism" and a fixed set of holy books that numbers twenty-two (as Josephus counts them) or twenty-four (as 4 Ezra reckons). The discrepancy in numbering does not alter the fact that both sources agree that the number is fixed and put it at about the same.

Rabbis and Holy Books

The relationship between "Judaism" and "Bible" must nevertheless be taken further than the Second Temple period. The political triumphs of Judah and Judaism in the mid-second – mid-first centuries BCE that did so much to establish both Judaism and its scriptures ran fairly quickly into collapse as the power of Rome overshadowed the Hellenistic kingdoms, including the territory of Judah, and, indeed, nearly all Jews in the ancient world fell under its regime (a few lived under the Parthians). But the legacy of Judaism and the scriptures persisted strongly, especially in Judea: indeed, the power of both is evident in the suicidal attempt to revolt against Roman hegemony that lost first the Jerusalem Temple and then possession of the territory of Judea itself. The regime that emerged from the ruins of this destruction brought a new definition of Judaism and a new relationship with the inherited scriptural canon. For in attempting to unite "Judaism" as they united and enlarged the land of Judah, the Hasmoneans had in effect also divided it, for there was already a long legacy of dissent within the religious life of Judah, however much it clustered around the Temple cult. To this, the civil war that had in turn brought about the measures of Antiochus IV to suppress the practice of Judean religion in 167 BCE had added great bitterness.

For it would not be fair to say that the so-called "Hellenizers" saw themselves as traitors to Judaism: rather, they espoused a different agenda for Judaism (and one that was very largely followed in many parts of the diaspora). The measures of the Hasmoneans, in their promotion of both a certain kind of "Judaism" and a life-style that was increasingly seen as degenerate and divisive, created new divisions and sects, such as those described in the scrolls from Qumran. The emergence of Christianity (whatever kind of Jew Jesus of Nazareth may have been, a matter of perennial dispute) is merely one symptom of the highly fissiparous nature of Palestinian Judaism in the first century CE.

The political and religious frustrations left by the Hasmoneans, and controlled with considerable, though by no means total, success by Herod, brought an end to most forms of Judaism and the creation of a new religious system, which has remained to this day the basis for the religion of Judaism: that of the rabbis.

The relationship of the rabbis to the scriptures is a complex one. First, their Judaism undoubtedly has its roots in categories that derive from the written Mosaic law (the Pentateuch, the "Torah"). For example, the covenantal theory of Israelite religion expressed in Deuteronomy strongly influenced the way in which the rabbis framed their understanding of the relationship between Israel and its god. Equally influential, and more so in practice, was the system of holiness expressed particularly in the book of Leviticus. The category of holiness was to form the basis of Rabbinic theology. Without the instruments of sanctification that the cult and priesthood had once provided, holiness was to be achieved through other means: deeds of obedience, prayer, observance of holy times, and objects, regulation of diet, study of the law.

The role of the *scriptures* in the Rabbinic system must be carefully distinguished from the role of *Torah*, especially since Torah and Scripture overlap. In my opinion, the canon of Scripture was not created by the rabbis and not intrinsically part of their system. This was inherited: but it did fit ideally into the categories the rabbis were developing, among which holiness was the most important. Hence, the rabbis regarded the books of Scripture in a rather material way, prescribing them to be holy *objects*. Like everything else in the entire universe, literature was divided into the categories of holiness and unholiness. There were books that "defiled the hands" and those that did not. The defiling books were holy and could not be handled as secular literature could. This sense of the physical holiness of books that were now literally "sacred" has been not only preserved in Judaism but conveyed into various forms of Christianity and indeed into Western culture (where witnesses in a court of law may swear with a hand on the Bible). Accordingly, the preparation of scriptural scrolls is an important matter and has been subject to strict regulation in Judaism (the advent of print has, of course, had a major impact on this). Even here, though, there is a clear difference of hierarchy between scrolls of Torah and other scriptural literature: the degree of holiness of Torah is in practice, if not in theory, higher (see below).

What precisely made a book "defile the hands"? This was never seriously debated by the rabbis. To be sure, there are records of discussions about whether or not certain books "defile the hands." Esther, the Song of Songs, and Ecclesiastes fall into this category. These scrolls may have been mentioned because of a feeling that the content of a scriptural book is a criterion for its holiness. Esther does not include the name of God, Ecclesiastes is somewhat skeptical in its view of divine interest in humans, and the Song of Songs has no explicit religious message unless allegorized and seems to condone unmarried sex. Alternatively, the fact that these three belong to a collection of scrolls used at Jewish festivals may form part of the explanation (or the remedy?). But these Rabbinic discussions (if they were real and not constructed) do not reflect any serious debate about the *nature* of a scriptural canon. Nor is the famous "council of Jamnia," if it occurred, likely to have made any determination about a scriptural canon. This is not to say that the rabbis did not have either a term, or a use, for scriptures. They called Scripture *miqra* (which means, indeed, "Scripture") and especially in their midrashic writing exploited the full range of scriptural writings in the belief that it constitutes a single and coherent piece of divine discourse that in principle explains itself. Yet "Scripture" itself does not constitute a "pillar" of Rabbinic Judaism in the way that the Bible does for Christianity or the Qur'an for Islam. Judaism is not a religion of the scriptures, but a religion of Torah – not quite the same thing.

The Rabbinic system did operate with a concept of *written law*. The five books of Moses clearly function in a way that the scriptures as a whole do not. These books (strictly, scrolls) are read in an annual cycle, and the scrolls of Torah are housed in the synagogue in the place that symbolically represents the site of the ark in the First Temple (the ark was, of course, where the original tablets of the law were said to have been placed). Excerpts of prophetic books (called *haftarot*; sing.: *haftarah*) are assigned to each section (*seder*) of the reading from the law. As referred to earlier, five scrolls (Song of Songs, Ruth, Lamentations, Ecclesiastes, Esther) are read on festival days. But certain parts of Scripture are not read at all.

We shall see presently that the Rabbinic midrashim nevertheless exploit the whole range of scriptural books, being quite prepared to make use of a canon that had been inherited and indeed to regard it as a single voice. For reasons that lie beyond the scope of this essay, the rabbis found it proper to locate the expression of the divine will in written texts; for them, charismatic authority, a "voice from heaven" (called a *bat qol*, lit. "daughter of a voice"), which in effect legitimated individual authority, was wrong. God had spoken, Moses (and others) had written, and it was necessary only to study and understand. The "only" is perhaps misleading: it was a duty and a privilege to study. But it was Torah that was preeminently studied. And since Torah is the essence of Rabbinic Judaism, all Scripture became Torah. This statement is true not only in the sense that the scriptures can sometimes be loosely referred to as "torah," but in that the *meaning* of the entire scriptures is Torah. The prophets and other books are commentaries on or explanations or elucidations of Torah. Just as the scriptural *books* were all subject to the category "holiness," so their *content* was taken to be, essentially, Torah.

The Origin of the Jewish Scriptures

For over a hundred years the agenda of historical-critical biblical scholarship has been directed at discovering the processes by which its literature came into being. The main motivation for this quest has been the importance of history for our modern understanding of the social world. In secular terms this means that phenomena were thought to be best understood in the light of their *origins*; while in the arena of theology the rediscovery of archaeological remains in Palestine prompted a return to viewing much of the Bible as history and, according to the influential "Biblical Theology" movement, to reducing the essence of the Old Testament (for this movement was a Christian enterprise) to a witness of historical acts. The idea of the Old Testament as primarily a historical record is one of a series of ways in which, throughout history, Christianity has tried to comprehend the relevance of this first part of its canon to the New Testament.

Historical-critical methods quickly challenged the Bible's own view of the history of Israel, as source-criticism of the Pentateuch led to Julias Wellhausen's famous inversion of the historical/canonical order in which the Mosaic law came first, so that now prophecy *preceded* law, and natural religion "ritualism." Christianity could then view the Jewish law as a falling away from the essential revelation of God to the chosen people and instate Christ as the true representative of Old Testament prophetic religion.

In the last few decades, a reaction again this historical emphasis has set in on two fronts: on the level of literary criticism, synchronic methods have risen to challenge diachronic ones, while on the theological level, approaches to the Old Testament that stress its *canonical* function have emerged. According to the latter, the canon of the Bible is more than the sum total of its parts, and the history of the formation of that canon, as a whole and in its parts, answers to a theological witness: the "believing community" or "community of faith" that stands for ancient Israel has continually shaped the contents of its canon in a way that reflects its ongoing experiences and produced a canon that has the authority of that witness.

The two tendencies just described pull in different directions. For the historical critic, the canon of the Old Testament/Hebrew scriptures is the outcome of a concluding part of a historical process, an act that put an authoritative seal on a collection of literatures that had accumulated over centuries. It would, according to this view, be anachronistic to speak of "canon" or "bible" before the time in which such a collection became functional as such. For the "canonical" approach, on the other hand, canon is a process and inseparable from the history of the literature. (In Platonic terms, canon is the form underlying the matter and superior to it.) The history of the literature itself is shaped by a "canonical intention" according to the hermeneutics of Brevard Childs.

Between these two approaches lies a crucial difference, as it seems to me, over a definition of "Scripture." In the classical languages (including Hebrew), the terms (*scriptura, graphe, miqra*) mean "writing, literature," although in both

Judaism and Christianity they have acquired the restricted sense of canonized writings, the sense in which we nowadays use the word in English. From the perspective of the historical critic, the *contents* of the Hebrew Bible are the literature of ancient Israel, accumulated for whatever purposes. They can therefore be addressed in a secular way as documentary evidence of the society of ancient Israel. On this view, it would be incorrect to say that the Hebrew Bible was "written by Jews": rather, one would say it was written by Israelites or Judeans.

For the canon(ical) critics, the literature of ancient Israel never can be secularized in this way as mere historical sources; rather they are faith-documents, a canon on the way to completion. While Childs, in particular, tries to retain some connection between these writings and the history of Israel, most of those scholars who follow his approach disregard historical questions – and rightly so, on their terms, for on this view the secular history of ancient Israel is of little relevance to the theological importance of the canon. Only the *canonized* history matters. As to whether the canon was developed by Israel, Judah or "the Jews," the question is not of great importance to this approach, since what is perceived here is a continuity of *theological* development (and one that Christian critics see continuing into the Church). The theological value of this approach is to underline a continuity between the community behind the Old Testament (acknowledged as Jewish) and Christian communities. It is not only confessional, but Christian, and implicitly disowns the rather different appropriation of the Scripture in Judaism, in which the continuity of the people of "Israel" is central.

We shall see presently that in the Judaism of the Second Temple both perspectives just discussed are reflected: for some writers the scriptures are an ahistorical (or transhistorical) revelation about the nature of God and human-ity, whether or not encoded and in need of decipherment, while for others the scriptures are essentially a *history* of divine dealings with Israel and of various responses to this divine treatment. The rabbis, quite characteristically, inherited and used both perspectives, though the ahistorical tendency is undoubtedly the more prominent as they sought always to make the scriptures speak to the contemporary Israel and pursued a program of transforming the relics of change-able history into ahistorical (and so permanent) values and categories.

The view that has been argued in the first part of this essay is that *from a purely historical point of view*, there is an element of truth (and of error) in both perspectives. The production of the writings in the Jewish scriptural canon is due, as is increasingly acknowledged, largely to a small class of Judeans writing in the Persian (and in some cases, the Hellenistic) period. That these scribes (for these alone had the literacy, authority, motivation, and access to relevant materials) used earlier sources is very probable in some cases but questionable in others. The motivation has much to do with the historical situation: it simply cannot be said that these persons set about compiling a set of scriptures, or a Bible. A religious canon was not the original intention; merely the eventual outcome.

The historical reasons for the creation of a literary corpus that was to become a canon are, in my opinion, as follows. The reconstitution of a province of Judah (Yehud) by the Persians involved the cooperation of the indigenous population (farmers, aristocrats, priests), those moved or moving back from Mesopotamia to settle (farmers, priests, merchants, scribes), and elements of neighboring populations that had settled in the territory during the sixth century. From this small, diverse and not entirely compatible population a society was to be created, basically around a temple and a monotheistic cult. In the absence of a monarch, the scribal class served not only the function of administering and tax-collecting on behalf of the Persians but also of creating the kind of propaganda text that under a monarchy would be required. But these texts were not royal inscriptions, victory pillars, law codes, monumental inscriptions, or the like. The scribes aimed to (re)create a shared history in a monarchic world, a world that had been full of promise but also ended in divine displeasure. These writings united the present through the past and argued for the status quo, while hinting at a better future. The importance of a constitution expressed through laws and of the indispensability of a temple cult emerges clearly – but not necessarily at a stroke. The process (which can in some way be compared to the "canonical process" of Childs) continued until it culminated in "Judaism." These texts were not composed for the purpose of dissemination among the population, though the contents did over time achieve this: rather they were an intellectual, cultural exercise among the literate and their patrons. Scribes, as a class, sought to understand and classify all knowledge, and the classification of the inhabitants of Judah, and the past, were proper objects of scribal research, speculation and writing.

The essential point, then, is that many of these scriptural writings were composed as part of an exercise in self-definition, in a conscious attempt to invent an "Israel" that had an ancient history, a constitution, a land, and a wisdom ethic. It is therefore legitimate to see in the Pentateuch not only various accounts of the ideal society (compare Numbers, Leviticus, and Deuteronomy for quite different visions), but an "official" history that draws these together, attaches them to the name of a great lawgiver, and embeds them in a history that takes the society/people of Israel from the creation of the world to its life under the great world empires of first Assyria, then Babylonia, then Persia, and finally Greece.

That the history told in the books of Moses is largely unreal, as modern scholarship has discovered, is irrelevant to its purpose, which is to define an Israel that can be perceived as a reality by its rulers and then, no doubt, exported to the remainder of the population, at least in outline, through the organs of oral exchange (market, city square, public assembly, etc.). In the same way, that the books of the prophets contain much that no prophet ever uttered (and also, in a few cases, that is attributed to prophets that never existed) is equally irrelevant – indeed, it does not matter whether there ever was a discrete institution such as "prophecy" in Israel or Judah, rather than a variety of forms of intermediation. That David and Solomon did not do (much less write) what was attributed to them does not matter either, for the attachment of these stories, psalms, and proverbs to legendary figures of the past is, for ancient societies, perfectly natural.

The origin of the Jewish scriptures, then, cannot be explained in terms of a history that the scriptures themselves have produced, for that history is not a real history at all, and to try and interpret it as such means to miss the very essence of what these writings are trying to do: create an Israel through writing about the past (Genesis to Kings) or the present (the wisdom literature), or the future (some of the prophetic writings).

How these writings came together, as individual scrolls or as multi-scroll works, it will never be possible to show exactly. It is clear that by the late Second Temple period, Torah was recognized as a discrete (Mosaic) canon, to which other collections were added. These were collectively known as "Prophets," though the title "Psalms" was used for a collection of supposedly Davidic compositions. The latest stage in the formation of the Jewish scriptural canon saw "Prophets" formalized as a collection of three large and twelve small scrolls, and the term "Writings" used of all the remainder. The ultimately tripartite nature of the scriptural canon is probably of little if any significance. Of more importance is the process by which the contents of the classic works of Hebrew literature (for this is what a "canon" is) came to be adopted as an agenda for living as a Judean/Jew. Why, in other words, did Judaism assume the guise of a religion and therefore its writings the role of a religious canon? This process, the historical context of which has been sketched above, can now be looked at.

Scriptures in Pre-Rabbinic Judaism

The nature of canon formation is that writings *become* classic by being quoted, alluded to, imitated, because of their exemplary value or excellence or subject matter. It is therefore not surprising that one can find, already within canonized writings, cases of reference in later works to earlier ones.[8] To call this phenomenon "inner-biblical exegesis," as Fishbane does,[9] is rather misleading, since "biblical" is anachronistic and "exegesis" suggests the establishment of a formal canon and a subsequent relationship between that canon and commentary upon it. It may be more helpful to consider instead a process by which familiarity with a certain body of literature formed part of the education of the professionally literate class of scribes, much as Homer functioned among the Greeks. The analogy with Homer is fairly apt, since in the Hellenistic era Homer was indeed subjected to formal commentary, having become canonized in a formal sense.

Thus, we can see that by the third century BCE the scholars of Jerusalem would be studying the Hebrew classics (among others?). Jeshua ben Sira of Jerusalem wrote (in Hebrew) as follows:

> . . . he who devotes himself
> to the study of the law of the Most High
> will seek out the wisdom of all the ancients
> and will be concerned with prophecies;
> he will preserve the discourse of notable men
> and penetrate the subtleties of parables;
> he will seek out the hidden meanings of proverbs
> and be at home with the obscurities of parables . . .
> If the great Lord is willing
> he will be filled with the spirit of understanding
> he will pour forth words of wisdom
> and give thanks to the Lord in prayer.
> He will direct his counsel and knowledge aright,
> and meditate on his secrets.
> He will reveal instruction in his teaching
> and will glory in the law of the Lord's covenant
>
> (39.1–3, 6–8)

One can see also from Ps. 1 that "meditating on the law" was recommended as a way to piety and blessedness, while Hos. 14:10 shows that at some stage (we cannot tell when this gloss was added) the prophetic scrolls were also seen as reading *for the wise*. Only a little later than ben Sira, the writer of Dan. 9:2 has the hero looking through the scrolls and finding a statement in Jeremiah.

What is quite interesting in these examples is the notion that somehow the contents of the scriptures require elucidation and thus study and not merely reading. Ben Sira refers to "hidden meanings" and "obscurities"; Daniel has to learn that Jeremiah's seventy years means seventy years times seven; and quite possibly Hosea has to be read allegorically too.

The idea that ancient writings contain important information is common to the ancient Near East and the Greek philosophers. But already in the instances just quoted we can detect that Judeans were reading for philosophical–religious ends, to instill piety. This connection between reading, study and piety is central to Rabbinic Judaism and, of course, has persisted in an attenuated form in the function of Bible reading among Christians ever since.

But a contrary hermeneutic is simultaneously at work, for ben Sira also shows a quite literal appreciation of the scriptures as offering a historical record of the past. In chapters 44–50, he provides a eulogy of famous people, drawn from the contents of Genesis–Kings and Nehemiah (not Ezra). He may well not have the contents of these scrolls exactly as we now know them, but he is aware of the story that they cumulatively tell. This understanding of the scriptures as historical records is represented, as we shall see, even more strongly by Flavius Josephus in the first century CE. That ben Sira treats the "ancient writings" of the Judeans in such different ways warns us against being too simplistic in modeling Jewish attitudes toward what they came to regard as their "scriptures." In fact, there seems to have been a fairly wide range of possibilities for understanding and using these writings during the last centuries of the Second Temple period. Since they offer us the most extensive material, let us take the Dead Sea Scrolls, Josephus, and Philo for examples within that range.

Scriptures in the Dead Sea Scrolls

Just how typical the Scrolls are of the understanding and use of scriptures in late Second Temple Judaism is impossible to say and much disputed. But the degree to which the groups represented in these documents were steeped in the scriptural language and literature is extremely high and reflected in several genres, from copies of scriptural scrolls (about 25 percent of the total) through phylacteries, legal interpretations, paraphrases, and expansions to commentaries, and even to pseudepigrapha assigned to scriptural figures. Scriptural language is also reflected in many of the wisdom and liturgical compositions. It is tempting (and not at all implausible) to suggest that the authors of these scrolls are direct successors of those who wrote the scriptural literature, who themselves built on the works they knew and read, both making allusions to earlier works and editing and rewriting them (e.g., the relationship of the books of Chronicles to Kings). The authors of the Scrolls show a great familiarity with the language and content of the scriptural books, which they sometimes comment on exegetically, but sometimes also treat quite freely.

On the theory offered earlier, the Scrolls come from a period in which there was already a Hasmonean canon of "official" Judean/Jewish writings, though it cannot be concluded that the writers of these scrolls, who were not sympathetic to the ruling priestly establishment, necessarily adhered to the definition of that canon exactly. For instance, they almost certainly regarded works attributed to Enoch, and the book of Jubilees, as "scriptural." But whether, indeed, they had strictly defined limits to their canon we cannot tell. Such limits, as has been argued, had never been contemplated before the Hasmonean era.

The manner in which the writers of the Scrolls read the scriptures corresponds fairly well to those categories we shall encounter in the Rabbinic literature: halakhic, haggadic, and paraphrase (i.e., Mishnah, Midrash, Targum). Brief examples of each category can be given here. As examples of halakhic treatment there are several texts in which biblical laws are interpreted – and in such a way that shows they were practiced – differently from the interpretation of other Jews. The *Damascus Document* 5:7–11 is an instance:

> And people take as a wife the daughter of their brother and the daughter of their sister. Yet Moses said, "Do not have intercourse with your mother's sister, for she is a blood-relation of your mother" [Lev. 18:13]. The law of incest is written in the masculine gender, but applies to females also, and so [prohibits] the daughter of a brother who has intercourse with the brother of her father, for he is a blood relation.

Here is a vigorous demonstration that the scriptural law, not always being unambiguous, required not only exegesis, but exegesis based on a principle (masculine gender can mean common gender). A little earlier (4:20–5:1) a strict rule of "one wife per lifetime" (and hence a ban on remarriage) is imposed, on the grounds not only that God created one male and one female, according to Gen. 1:27 (an argument that is also attributed to Jesus, Matt. 19:3–19), but also that Noah only took pairs of animals (and humans) into the ark (Gen. 6–9).

The *Damascus Document* speaks of the community it represents as being in possession of the true law, as revealed to its founder by God. It contrasts the "public" and the "hidden" law, the former being the scriptural Torah, the latter its own law. However, no new rulings (apart from disciplinary measures that may not have been regarded as divine law) are presented as examples of "hidden" law. We find this "hidden" law rather in *interpretations* of scriptures such as the one just quoted, and, perhaps, also in the observance of a calendar different from that followed by the Temple (which subsequently remained normative). But the idea of a *twofold revelation of law* is important as a precursor of the Rabbinic theory of written and oral Torah.

Mention must also be made of the *Temple Scroll* (11QT), an arrangement of scriptural laws, *with other laws added*, whose purpose is not entirely clear, but which may have been an attempt to create a statement of law as understood by the authors that was in principle scriptural, and in practice their very own. One of the significant features of this collection is that scriptural passages referring to God in the third person are converted into first-person statements, making the divine authorship of the law quite unambiguous. But by this means, the Temple Scroll almost certainly also offers itself as a divinely-inspired document. That itself is an indication of an important, if gradual, development in both Judaism and Christianity toward the view that the scriptures were of divine authorship (see below).[10]

As an example of *Midrash* (by which for this purpose I mean non-halakhic interpretation, though "Midrash" can mean *any* interpretation), let me take two instances. The first is the commentary (*pesher*) on Habakkuk (1QpHab). Here the text of chapters 1–2 is lemmatized and each lemma given an esoteric and atomized interpretation, divorced from context (literary or historical) and subjected to what appear to be arbitrary equations by which figures in Habakkuk designate characters of the recent past. The prophetic text functions as a sequence of divinely-revealed cryptic statements, which require a divinely-inspired decoding, as the commentary itself explains (1QpHab 7:1–5):

> And God told Habakkuk to write that which was to happen to the final generation, but he did not reveal to him when time would come to an end. And as for the statement "He who reads it may run," its interpretation refers to the Teacher of Righteousness, to whom God revealed all the mysteries of his servants the prophets.

The *pesharim* (there are several) are primarily concerned with identifying recent events as being those foretold in Scripture, employing a technique found in the Gospel of Matthew's story of Jesus' birth and in parts of the gospel passion narratives. This view of ancient sayings as containing hidden wisdom, including prognostication of future events, was also fashionable in the Greco-Roman period; it was not exclusive to Jews.

However, another Qumran Midrash illustrates a quite different technique of scriptural interpretation, in which phrases from various scriptural scrolls, including those included in the law, prophets, and other-writings sections of the Jewish canon, are combined into a coherent argument about the end of world history. The importance of this technique is that it already implies, as the rabbis were to accept, that all of Scripture forms a single discourse, with different scriptural texts mutually illuminating each other. The meaning of a passage in one scroll may thus be elucidated by a passage in another. Accordingly, Lev. 25:13 and Deut. 15:2 are first cited to present the release of slaves and debts; Is. 61:1 is then cited, which also speaks of the release of prisoners, and is taken to refer to a jubilee year. Since debts to God take the form of sins, and these are atoned for on behalf of all Israel every year by the High Priest at the Day of Atonement, the agent of this final release of debts to God will be the heavenly High Priest on the final day of atonement in history. Through further citations of texts from Psalms and Daniel, this heavenly figure is identified as Melchizedek, who will appear "at the end of the tenth jubilee," i.e., after 490 or 500 years from the start of the calendar (which is the destruction of the Temple and the beginning of the Babylonian exile). A similar technique is used in other Qumran texts, such as the Florilegium (4QFlor).

It is already apparent from the Qumran scrolls that their authors regarded scriptures as messages from God and did not place much emphasis on the distinction between a divine and a divinely-inspired author. The fundamental turn in the Jewish understanding of its scriptures, noticeable in a comparison of the Scrolls with ben Sira, is that Scripture is now divine in origin. Thus, for instance, the law of Moses is the divine Torah, and the words of the prophets are God's revelation about the secrets of the future.

Scripture in Josephus

The view of Scripture exhibited in the Qumran scrolls just discussed does not, however, represent a monolithic shift among Jews, only a movement that is perceptible in certain circles. At the end of the century following the majority of the Scrolls (first century BCE), the Jewish historian Josephus Flavius, writing for a Greek-speaking and pro-Roman audience, regards the scriptures essentially as a record of the great achievements of the Jewish people. The law was given by Moses, the greatest of all lawgivers; David and Solomon were among the greatest rulers in antiquity; the prophets were reliable recorders of history. It is, of course, true that Josephus has particular interest in utilizing the scriptures in this way, since his wish is to portray, defend, and even glorify the people whom he may have felt he had personally betrayed by becoming a client of the Roman emperor. But it remains nevertheless true that the view of scriptures as human products, however inspired by God, remained a valid one, even while the contemporary work called 4 Ezra tells of Ezra's dictating under divine inspiration the lost books of Scripture as well as seventy other secret books, after their destruction by the Babylonians at the time of the destruction of Jerusalem and the exile.

Scripture in Philo

The writings of Philo of Alexandria, from the first half of the first century CE, represent a synthesis between laws and narratives from the books of Moses and Greek philosophical ideas, particularly Stoic and Platonic. While Philo's particular achievement is unique, attempts to fuse Greek and Jewish "philosophies" were quite common among the many Jews living in a Hellenistic environment, as the majority of them did. Alexandria, of course, contained a large number of Jews but was also a center of Greek scholarship.

Though he has been treated as a philosopher, Philo is essentially an exegete, and he uses philosophical ideas quite eclectically. The two most important of these ideas are the Stoic technique of allegory and the Platonic theory of forms. The Stoic method of reading ancient religious narratives such as myths was to treat them as having an inner philosophical meaning that required discovery; while Plato had taught that everything in the material world is an imperfect imitation of its archetype in the eternal world of Forms. Humans themselves consisted of a perishable material body and a soul (the "form") that was immortal, originating in, and destined to return to the world of Forms. The Platonic tradition of philosophy proposed that the highest human faculty was reason, and the lowest were those most closely related to the body, namely the senses. The Stoics themselves also believed in the virtue of controlling the senses through reason, mastering pain and passion.

Philo seems to have accepted the literal meaning of the biblical laws, but only the unlearned mind would treat them in a purely literal way, solely as acts to be performed; the wise would understand them, like the biblical stories, to have a deeper, philosophical meaning. Typically, while the literal meaning of the laws and narratives concerns the material, sensual world, the deeper (and true) meaning addresses the mind, the eternal part of the human being. Moses, the lawgiver, thus becomes the greatest of the world's philosophers.

In distinguishing between literal and allegorical meanings, Philo's technique is reminiscent of that of the Qumran *pesharim*, which also find a hidden meaning behind the literal sense. But the resemblance ends there. Behind Philo lies an entire world of Judaism coming to terms with Greek philosophical categories and exploiting them in the development of an understanding of the scriptures as the finest expressions of universal truth.

Scriptures in Rabbinic Judaism

The earliest of the great Rabbinic compilations, the Mishnah, was developed after the first revolt against Rome (66–73 CE) and written down in its final form early in the third century CE. With the loss of the Temple, cult, and later, land, the law was to become the focus of Jewish life as the rabbis conceived it, and the Mishnah is a systematic exposition of that law, to which we give the name halakhah. The agenda of the Mishnaic system followed closely that of the Pharisees, who had been a lay group promoting personal sanctity, especially at table and in tithing. But it also inherited priestly and scribal elements and was thus able to fuse from the disparate Judaisms of the era before the destruction of the Temple a religion that could, despite the radical context of its formation, claim to be continuous with everything that went before. In this religion, holiness and knowledge of Torah were paramount principles.

But the Mishnah does not take the form of a commentary on scriptural laws. It simply makes its statements. Its six divisions do, of course, as a whole express much of the content and categories of the Torah, but according to its own arrangement, which tries to cover systematically all aspects of Jewish domestic and public life: food, sex, marriage, festivals. It also describes the now inoperative Temple cult, which is part of the life of an ideal Israel living in its own land. But of course Israel is, at the time, largely *not* living in its land. Rabbinic Judaism is a religion of diaspora.

The substantial lack of any explicit support from Scripture in the Mishnah led to the impression that it constituted an autonomous authority and this in turn created a problem for its status in relation to Scripture, especially the Mosaic law. This problem was solved by means of a theory of two Torahs, the written and the oral, with the Mishnah representing the latter. According to the Mishnah tractate Abot (probably the last of the Mishnah's sixty-three chapters to be composed), Moses received, as well as a written, also an *oral* Law from Sinai, and transmitted it through Joshua, the Elders, prophets, sages, and so on up to the rabbis. Of course, the claim was never intended as a *historical* truth, but rather, what for the rabbis was a *theological* truth: that their Mishnah is a completion of the written law; the two are parts of one whole, and the authority of the Mishnah is equal to that of the books of Moses.

In speaking in the name of Moses, the rabbis were, however, hardly innovating, for the scribes, who had been acquiring an increasingly religious authority as interpreters of Scripture and authorities on Jewish law, were recognized as "sitting in the seat of Moses" in Matt. 23:2; and this viewpoint is echoed elsewhere in the Gospels, which may well be reflecting the behavior of the rabbis.

But despite the theory of a dual torah, the Mishnah could not be regarded as of *equal* authority to Scripture, or the rabbis be compared to Moses. The Babylonian Talmud, the final great work of Rabbinic Judaism, completed by the sixth century, is organized as a commentary on the Mishnah, but also represents an attempt to link the Mishnah more closely to Scripture, giving it explicit Mosaic justification. A number of Rabbinic commentaries on scriptural law were written between the time of the Mishnah and that of the Talmud. These are known as the "Tannaitic midrashim" (rabbis who lived during the time of compilation of the Mishnah were called *tannaim*) and comprise Mekhilta on Exodus, Sifra on Leviticus, and Sifre on Numbers and Deuteronomy. They also testify to a concern to ground Rabbinic halakhah in scriptural law.[11]

The halakhic program of the rabbis became necessary, of course, precisely because the books of Moses had *not* been written to present a legal system, for the collections of laws they contained were generally included to illustrate or exemplify the character and life of an ideal Israel or to elaborate a legal theory. Where ancient practices were mentioned, they were separated from their original social context. However, the Rabbinic theory held – as had already long been maintained by Jews – that in these laws God revealed his will to Israel, and Israel's duty was to obey that will, despite the fact that Scripture does not provide a complete exposition of it. An excellent example is the keeping of Sabbath. There are two formulations of the command (Exod. 20:8 and Deut. 5:12), and they are not identical in wording. What *is* meant by "remembering" (Exodus) or "observing" (Deuteronomy) the Sabbath? How does one keep it holy? What qualifies as "work"? Again, there is only one passage in the whole of the Torah dealing with divorce (Deut. 24:1–4). How can one extract an entire process from one prescription? The Mishnah expressed its system largely through statements unsupported by Scripture. But when this system needed that support, it became necessary to explore both the statements of Scripture *and the underlying logic that generated them.* Unlike the writers of the Qumran *pesher* who claimed divine inspiration, or Philo, who worked from philosophical premises, the rabbis adopted a rational system that accepted categorically the premise that Scripture, correctly studied, and understood, explained itself. A set of exegetical principles (called *middot*, lit.: "measures") permitted one text to be explained on the basis of other texts, through linguistic or topical associations. Whether or not these rules were regularly and systematically applied (and they were not), the principle was important: the true meaning of Scripture (which, of course, it was accepted that the Mishnah had correctly, but incompletely formulated) could be found in Scripture itself.

Scripture and Mishnah were thus combined through midrashim and through the Babylonian Talmud. For that reason, scriptures in Judaism do not enjoy the same preeminence or autonomy that they do in Protestant Christianity: in Rabbinic Judaism, they have already been given a more complete and explicit form. Accordingly, in Judaism the scriptural canon is not, as in Christianity, a closed system. The Torah in Judaism is in theory always incomplete, always capable of fuller exposition. In a certain sense, it is always provisional. Rabbinic exegesis has, perhaps on this account, generally exhibited a much greater freedom and creativity towards the scriptures.

There is a further important difference between the Jewish and Christian treatment of Scripture. Because for the rabbis *Torah* and not *Scripture* as a whole is the key to the Rabbinic system, the scriptures as a whole need to be related to Torah in some way. But not all Scripture is halakhic. The primary concern of the rabbis was the development of halakhah, and, as just noted, the earliest Rabbinic midrashim are on Exodus–Deuteronomy. But toward the end of the Talmudic period there emerged in literary form a different genre of Midrash.

The Great Midrash (*Midrash Rabbah*), dates from about the fifth century CE (and perhaps onwards), and its character is not halakhic but *haggadic* ("homiletic"). It deals with the five books of Moses together with the five festival scrolls (Song of Songs–Esther). But the aim of haggadah is to retell (sometimes quite creatively) the scriptural story to solve an apparent problem in the story line or to derive a moral teaching. The structure of the Midrash Rabbah is simple, but the hermeneutic quite complex. It conforms much more to what we are now familiar with as a scriptural commentary. Each small section of text is treated to several exegeses – like the Mishnah and Talmud, each one is characteristically attached to the name of a rabbi – and there is a constant invocation of texts from other scriptural books to illuminate that verse. Two important principles are at work here: one is that the meaning of Scripture cannot be exhausted, for true meaning is not to be reached by limitation or exclusion of all options (as was necessarily the case in halakhic Midrash) but by recognizing and celebrating the multivocality of Scripture. The rediscovery by modern literary critics of this feature of literary texts is certainly not new, nor a dislike of the concern with the historical meaning of texts. The other principles, we have mentioned earlier: that Scripture explains itself, that the scriptural book is not a boundary. In both of these principles the Rabbinic midrashim differ from modern commentaries.

They also differ in one other way. Rabbinic Midrash is directed at the present, for the scriptures are texts for all time. Thus, for example, when Genesis Rabbah deals with Esau/Edom, the brother of Jacob/Israel, it is, according to Neusner, addressing the fraternal (but inimical) relationships between Christianity and Judaism at the time when Christianity was the official religion of the Roman Empire. But the individual exegeses collected in these midrashim are also thought to stem from Rabbinic sermons (and perhaps even school discourses) that point in turn to a tradition of homiletic teaching that undergirded the development of the halakhic program and make the point that Rabbinic Judaism emphasized the importance of motivation, of intention, as much as (in some cases, more than) they did conformity with practice.

The final genre of Rabbinic literature to be mentioned is the Targum. Targum (lit.: "translation") designates an Aramaic version of a scriptural book. The genre has an interesting history, reaching back well before the rabbis. To begin with, its roots are manifold. First, there are examples from Qumran of translations into Aramaic of the books of Job and Leviticus. These translations appear to be literal. Their purpose is not clear: were they intended for the use of non-Hebrew speakers? Possibly, but how many Jews unable to read Hebrew would be interested in the contents of Leviticus? The translation of the scriptures into Greek is a different case, since large communities of Jews lived in Greek environments where Hebrew was not preserved. But, second, there are also examples at Qumran of scriptural paraphrases, which both amend and amplify the scriptural text and demonstrate the extent to which, at least for the purpose of haggadah, the *textual form* of the biblical story was not paramount. (One might suggest that just as the law was not completely expressed in Scripture, neither was [hi]story.)

The targumic tradition incorporates elements of both translation and amplification. Whatever the purpose of the Qumran targums, the targumic tradition of Rabbinic Judaism probably begins in the custom of reading in the synagogue. As explained earlier, the Torah was read sequentially throughout each year and was accompanied, in the Aramaic-speaking world between the Mediterranean and the Tigris, by an Aramaic rendering. Eventually these translations, which would hardly have been standardized at first, were cast into written forms, several of which are extant. These are the Targum Yerushalmi (also known as Pseudo-Jonathan), Targum Neofiti, the Fragmentary Targum, and Targum Onkelos. Fragments of other targums have also been found in the Cairo Geniza, a medieval archive rediscovered at the end of the nineteenth century.

Over the dating and sequence of these targums there is great dispute. Some scholars assign all or parts of the first two to the early centuries of the Christian era; others recognize the possibility of early traditions but regard the literary compositions as later. This debate is best avoided here, because, although it is important for determining the antiquity of certain exegeses, the arguments are complex and often speculative. There is also a dispute over whether one can speak of a "Palestinian Targum," of which there are different written recensions, in the singular, or, rather, of a Targum *tradition* that spawned several literary targums. Here the latter position is preferable. But regardless of these issues, the main lines of development of the tradition can probably be agreed upon.

Many scholars accept the principle that the targums in their earliest phase tended to be quite paraphrastic, often introducing extra material, offering explanations, and making theological corrections. This characteristic is preserved most in what are called the "Palestinian Targums," stemming from before the time when the center of Rabbinic study moved to Babylonia (fourth century CE). These comprise Neofiti and the Fragmentary Targum. The Yerushalmi or Pseudo-Jonathan represents a Babylonian recension, and so does Onkelos. Of all these, it is Onkelos that was adopted by the rabbis as the "official" Targum; and this choice may have to do with the fact that it is the least expansive, being the closest of all to a straight translation.

There are references in other Rabbinic literature both to the practice of reading Aramaic translations in the synagogue and to the correct principles of translation. It seems, in fact, that from about the second or third centuries CE, the rabbis took an interest in bringing some conformity within the Targum tradition and also in restricting its freedom with the scriptural text. But the rabbis did not invent the Targum tradition, and targums are "Rabbinic literature" only in this sense, that they were subject to Rabbinic influence and only under this influence was Targum adopted into Rabbinic Judaism. Rabbinic influence on the targums may also have increased over time due to the fact that Rabbinic discourse in Babylonia, at least, took place in Aramaic rather than in Hebrew (and hence Aramaic is the predominant language of the non-Mishnaic part of the Talmud).

The Pentateuchal targums are by far the most important. Perhaps because other scriptures were not read as a whole in the synagogue, their targums are relatively later and in origin literary. There is a single official Targum to the Prophets, called Targum Jonathan (because it was wrongly assigned to Jonathan ben Uzziel, a rabbi of the second century CE), of uncertain date, while various targums to the Writings (excluding Ezra, Nehemiah, and Daniel, which already contain some Aramaic) are mostly medieval. These are perhaps not part of a Targum tradition as such but imitations of the established genre.

Conclusion

The relationship of Judaism to scriptures, examined above, falls into distinct phases. The origins and function of the scriptural writings are still a matter of guesswork, but from the late Second Temple period, and decisively under the Hasmoneans, Jews look to their scriptures as a validation of their identity, which assumes an essentially religious character. With the loss of Temple and land, the Torah assumes a central place, and under the rabbis scriptures are integrated into a system of twofold Torah.

Unfortunately, there is no space here to explore other aspects of Jewish use of Scripture, including a magnificent array of medieval commentators, who both affirmed and challenged Rabbinic exegesis, and Rashi who sought to combine both. One important feature of Rashi's interpretation (although he did not invent it) is the distinction between *peshat* ("plain meaning") and *derash* ("derived meaning"). It is also important to point out that rationalistic and philosophical interpretation of Scripture was developed by Jewish commentators in a way not matched in the Christian West (which drew upon this exegesis in no small way) until centuries later.

The ways in which the scriptures are interpreted from the Hellenistic period onwards are varied, from the exactitude of halakhic exegesis to the invention of homiletic Midrash, from atomistic to pan-scriptural. If there is one abiding characteristic of Jewish use of Scripture, however, it is the desire always to make it contemporary. For this reason, both halakhic and haggadic forms of interpretation have a certain open-endedness that can be contrasted with the post-Reformation exegesis in which the doctrine of a "plain meaning" of Scripture has elevated a narrow, literal, and historical mode of interpretation. The modern interest in both literary and canonical forms of criticism is in many respects (and this has been acknowledged) a revival of the Rabbinic perspective on the multivocal, problematic, and always contemporary possibilities of Scripture.

Notes

1   Since Jews did not adopt the codex (our "book") for scriptural texts until well into the Middle Ages and, indeed, not long before printing came to the West, the Jewish "Bible" was preserved in the form of scrolls of individual books and collections of books.

2 For a fuller version of the treatment here of the growth of the Jewish scriptural canon, see my *Scribes and Schools. The Canonization of the Hebrew Scriptures*.

3 The major exception is the scrolls of prophetic writings. While individual prophetic sayings are found elsewhere, such large collections as Isaiah and Jeremiah are unparalleled.

4 That impulse is perhaps the chief motivation for Herodotus's *Histories*.

5 Berossus, Manetho, Philo Byblos, and the Jewish books of Genesis – Kings.

6 The terms "Judean" and "Jewish" are not quite interchangeable in my own usage, although in Greek they are indistinguishable. Basically, Judaism is a philosophy or religion belonging to those who claimed membership of the *ethnos* of "Judeans." In Hebrew usage of the period (and since), "Jewish" is conveyed by the use of the term "Israel." The majority of Jews in the Greco-Roman period were not Judean, i.e., were not born or did not live in Judah.

7 See the excellent study by John M. G. Barclay, *Jews in the Mediterranean Diaspora from Alexander to Trajan (323 BCE–117 CE)* (Edinburgh, 1996).

8 The possibility that some such quotations are contemporary must also be accepted, though to discuss this possibility involves a discussion of authorship that is beyond the scope of this essay.

9 Michael Fishbane, *Biblical Interpretation in Ancient Israel* (Oxford, 1985).

10 Note that according to the statement attributed to Jesus in Matt. 19:7–8, it was Moses, not God, who issued the law permitting divorce, a command against the will of God! That the emphasis in the Gospels on Mosaic, not divine, authorship reflects Christian bias is of course quite likely. But it was not a viewpoint expressed exclusively by Christians.

11 There is no halakhic Midrash on Genesis because it contains no laws.

Bibliography

Bowker, John, *The Targums and Rabbinic Literature* (Cambridge, 1969).

Davies, Philip R., *In Search of Ancient Israel: A Study in Biblical Origins* (Sheffield, 1992).

Davies, Philip R., *Scribes and Schools. The Canonization of the Hebrew Scriptures* (Louisville, 1998).

Fishbane, Michael, *Biblical Interpretation in Ancient Israel* (Oxford, 1985).

Green, W. S., "The Hebrew Scriptures in Rabbinic Judaism," in Jacob Neusner, *Rabbinic Judaism: Structure and System* (Minneapolis, 1995), pp. 31–44.

Mulder, M. J., ed., *Miqra* (Assen and Philadelphia, 1988).

Neusner, Jacob, *Judaism: The Evidence of the Mishnah* (Chicago, 1981).

Neusner, Jacob, "Rabbinic Judaism: History and Hermeneutics," in Jacob Neusner, ed., *Judaism in Late Antiquity* (Leiden, 1995), vol. 2, pp. 161–225.

Neusner, Jacob, *Midrash in Context. Exegeses in Formative Judaism* (Philadelphia, 1983).

Patte, Daniel, *Early Jewish Hermeneutic in Palestine* (Missoula, 1975).

Ulrich, Eugene, "The Canonical Process, Textual Criticism, and Later Stages in the Composition of the Bible," in M. Fishbane, E. Tov, and W. W. Fields, eds., *Sha'arei Talmon* (Winona Lake, 1992), pp. 267–91.

Ulrich, Eugene, "The Bible in the Making," in Eugene Ulrich and J. C. VanderKam, eds., *The Community of the Renewed Covenant* (Notre Dame, 1994), pp. 77–93.

CHAPTER 4
Second Temple Judaism

Frederick J. Murphy

The Second Temple period begins with the rebuilding of the Temple in 520–515 BCE and ends with its destruction in 70 CE. It was a time of momentous change in Judaism and of remarkable richness for Jewish literature, thought, and religion. The entire Hebrew Bible was written or assembled at this time, as was a large corpus of extra-canonical literature in Hebrew, Aramaic, and Greek. The Temple in Jerusalem, destroyed by the Babylonians in 587 BCE, was rebuilt and was the center of Jewish religion. The diaspora flourished in many important places such as Alexandria, Rome, Antioch, the cities of western Asia Minor, and Mesopotamia. The varieties of Judaism during this period were the soil from which Rabbinic Judaism and Christianity grew.

It is legitimate to treat the Second Temple period as a unit because it differed in significant ways from what preceded and what followed it. The most obvious way in which the period differed from the monarchical period is that there was no longer a native king ruling in Judah. Judah was now incorporated into the Persian empire. This subordinate status characterized Israel during most of the Second Temple period. The Second Temple was destroyed by the Romans in 70 CE, and in 135 CE the Jews were banned from Jerusalem except for visits on the Day of Atonement. This led to major changes in the religion and polity of Israel and ultimately to the ascendancy of Rabbinic Judaism.

Because of the absence of the monarchy, the high priesthood assumed a greater importance in the Second Temple period than it had before that time, and the Temple was even more central to the life of the people than before. Judah was now a temple-state, a province centered on and controlled by its temple-establishment. At various times, the priest was advised by a council that consisted of the most prominent of Judah's citizens, priests and laymen. A term applied to this body is "sanhedrin," a Greek word meaning "council." The period was marked by conflicts between different groups of Jews and even between factions within the priesthood, and those conflicts often led to negative judgments on the temple and its priests.

Circumcision and Sabbath received renewed emphasis in the post-exilic era as signs of Israel's close relation with God, which defined them as a people. In the absence of temple and land, the exiles turned to these portable symbols for their self-identity. The claim that the institution of synagogues originated during the exile is plausible, but evidence is lacking. It is clear that synagogues occupied an increasingly important role in Judaism as the Second Temple period progressed. The written Torah came into being in the Second Temple period, and by the end of the period there was a collection of sacred texts that were becoming a fixed canon. Jews living abroad, generally known as the diaspora (a Greek word meaning "dispersion"), became important in the Second Temple period. Since there was no native monarchy and the reality of Israel's existence did not match the hopes preserved in its traditions, messianic expectations surfaced from time to time.

The Second Temple period falls into three main parts – the Persian period (539 BCE–333 BCE), the Hellenistic period (333 BCE–63 BCE), and the Roman period (63 BCE–70 CE) – each defined by whichever foreign power was dominating Israel at the time.

The Persian Period

The Persian period begins with Cyrus's conquest of Babylon in 539 BCE. Israel benefited from his policy of allowing captive peoples to return home and to reestablish their native cults. The author of Isaiah 40–55 was so delighted with Cyrus's policy that he declared him God's messiah (Is. 45:1). This section concentrates on three pivotal events: the rebuilding of the Temple, the mission of Ezra, and the mission of Nehemiah.

Cyrus's decree allowing the Jews to return to the land of Israel is considered the end of the Babylonian exile. The idea that all Israel was exiled by the Babylonians and that their return to Judah signified Israel's restoration in the land is rooted in the biblical sources but can be misleading. The picture masks Judaism's diversity. Many Judahites never went into exile, and many who did, never returned. The Babylonians deported those most likely to cause further trouble – political and religious leaders, those influential in society – as well as those with valuable skills. They left a population in Palestine to till the land. When the Persians allowed the exiles to return about fifty years later, many did not do so. The Jewish community that remained in Babylonia continued to influence Judahite Jews throughout the Persian period. The Temple rebuilt by the returned exiles became the religious and symbolic center of worldwide Judaism for the next six hundred years.

The general picture of Judah under Persia is of a province that accepted its subordinate status. This laid the groundwork for a pattern of coexistence with overlords that characterized much of the Second Temple period.

The main sources for the Persian period are the books of Ezra and Nehemiah. Ezra begins with a decree of Cyrus allowing the exiles to return to Judah under the leadership of Sheshbazzar and rebuild the Temple (Ezra 1:2–4). Ezra claims that 42,360 persons returned to Judah, among whom were Zerubbabel and Joshua (Ezra 2). The number of returnees is doubtlessly exaggerated. Israel had settled into exile, and there is evidence that some Jews prospered. The prospect of going back to a land devastated by war and neglect, a land most had never seen, was not attractive to many.

Ezra 5:14 says that Cyrus made Sheshbazzar governor, implying that Judah was constituted as an independent province of the Persian empire. Since no other governor is mentioned until the second half of the fifth century, some think that the region was administered by Samaria in the intervening time. Sheshbazzar is said to have laid the foundation for the Second Temple (Ezra 5:16), but little seems to have come from the effort, since almost twenty years later the Temple still lay in ruins.

In the second year of King Darius I of Persia (520 BCE), the prophets Haggai and Zechariah began to insist that the Temple be rebuilt. Haggai saw a rebuilt Temple and a functioning cult as necessary for the fertility of the land. The picture of God's people gathered around his cultic presence in the midst of his chosen land was a priestly ideal that took on renewed meaning in the restored community. It was at the Temple that the covenant between God and people was maintained. There the people offered to God the sacrifices he demanded, and there they effected the atonement that made possible the continuation of God's relation with Israel despite human sin.

At this time Zerubbabel and Joshua take an active role in Ezra's story, so they probably did not return in 539, but just before 520 BCE. Joshua was high priest in the restored community, and Zerubbabel was its non-priestly leader. Zechariah 4 is a visionary representation of this dual leadership in which Joshua and Zerubbabel are both presented as messiahs. In Ezra 3, Zerubbabel lays the Temple foundation, and the Temple is finished in 515 BCE (Ezra 6:15). There are hints in Haggai and Zechariah that some held messianic hopes for Zerubbabel, perhaps when Darius I struggled to consolidate his power in the early years of his reign (522–486 BCE). Since Zerubbabel later drops out of the picture, the Persians may have deposed him. Zechariah 6 assigns royal traits to Joshua, indicating the increased importance of the high priesthood in the absence of a king. It is possible that the text originally referred to Zerubbabel as king and was edited to refer to Joshua after Zerubbabel left the scene.

In Ezra 4:1–5, Yahwists who are natives of Judah and Samaria attempt to join the returned exiles in the rebuilding of the Temple but are rebuffed. They then oppose the building, unsuccessfully. The attitude of the returnees matches the exclusivistic outlook apparent elsewhere in Ezra and Nehemiah. The assumption of the book of Ezra is that those who returned were the true Israel and that unless one joined them and conformed to their understanding of the Torah, one was cut off from the people. This is expressed ritually when Passover is celebrated shortly after the return: "It was eaten by the people of Israel who had returned from the exile, and also by all who had joined them and separated themselves from the pollutions of the nations of the land to worship the LORD, the God of Israel" (6:21). Those wishing to join the returned exiles would have to accept their interpretation of God's law, and those who did not would be considered impure. The use of cultic categories of pure and impure to regulate social contact becomes typical of the Second Temple period. Exilic Jews dominated Jews in Judah because they had Persian support. This pattern repeats itself later in the careers of Ezra and Nehemiah.

Besides tensions between the returned exiles and those who never went into exile, there were internal disagreements in the restored community. Isaiah 65 (late sixth century) is especially noteworthy in that it implies the existence of a group alienated from the priestly establishment, which expected God's intervention to set things right. This foreshadows similar hopes of other groups later in the period (see also Malachi).

Ezra and Nehemiah were Jews who came to Israel with commissions from the Persian court. The books of Ezra and Nehemiah imply that Ezra came to Judah from the exile before Nehemiah did and that their work overlapped somewhat, but it is more likely that they were not in Judah at the same time and that Nehemiah came first, in 445 BCE. Ezra probably came in 398 BCE, but the issue is disputed. Both came to a community with a functioning cultic establishment at the center of a Jewish community, and both sought to reform that community according to a specific interpretation of Torah.

Ezra 7 contains what claims to be Ezra's commission from the Persian king Artaxerxes. The king tells Ezra, "You are sent by the king and his seven counselors to make inquiries about Judah and Jerusalem according to the law of your God, which is in your hand" (7:14). He is told to teach the law (Torah) to Judah's inhabitants, a law that binds them under pain of confiscation of goods, banishment, and even death (7:26). Ezra is to set up a judicial system to enforce both God's law and Persian law. He is also to bring the king's support for the Jerusalem cult. Ezra is not called "governor." He is a priest of illustrious ancestry (Ezra 7:1–5), but he is never portrayed as performing priestly service in the Temple. In fact, he seems to operate independently of the Temple establishment. Most importantly, Ezra is a scribe, skilled in God's law, in great favor both with the Persian king and with God.

The precise identity of the law that Ezra brought to the restored community has been debated. The Hebrew word for it is *torah*, usually translated as "law" but originally meaning something closer to "instruction." Throughout most of the pre-exilic period, the word referred not to a written code but to priestly rulings. But the Bible tells the story of a book of law discovered in the Temple at the end of the seventh century BCE that furnished the basis for a reform by King Josiah (2 Kgs. 22:8–23:27). Most scholars identify that book with some form of Deuteronomy and consider it an important landmark in the formation of a scriptural canon. The biblical history of pre-exilic Israel was written using principles of Deuteronomy as interpretive guides (Joshua, Judges, 1–2 Samuel, and 1–2 Kings). Those principles included strict monotheism, seeing Jerusalem as the only legitimate place for God's Temple, condemnation of mixed marriages, and adherence to a written Torah in some form.

Ezra came to the land of Israel with, as the Persian emperor says, "the law of your God, which is in your hand." Many think Ezra's law consisted essentially of the first five books of the Bible, the "Torah" proper. Ezra's main reform was against mixed marriages. He believed strongly that intermarriage made proper observance of Torah difficult, if not impossible. Close relations with polytheistic inhabitants of the land had always been a means by which Israel was influenced by its neighbors. It was primarily from a later point of view that such influence was viewed so negatively. Devotion to foreign gods was seen as responsible even for the exile itself. Ezra's view reflected that of the Jewish community living in Babylonia, which had to maintain clear social boundaries in order to survive. That view was not shared by all Jews in the land of Israel, since Ezra found many, including priests and Levites (Ezra 10:18–24), who had married foreign women and had children by them. All were forced to give up their gentile wives and renounce their children in order to belong to the community now reformed by Ezra. Separation from the nations was seen as necessary to maintain loyalty to the one God.

Certain broad conclusions can be drawn from Ezra's story. When Judahites returned from the exile under the aegis of the Persian crown, they determined the shape of the restored community. They did so on the basis of their understanding of their traditions, customs, and institutions developed during the exile. Ezra's mission marked a new stage in this process. He was a Jewish agent of the Persian crown who reformed Judahite society on the basis of a written Torah. This was simultaneously a strengthening of Persian control of Judah and a religious reform. The written Torah eventually became the foundation on which other groups could challenge the priestly establishment and each other. The Torah was considered God's word to Israel revealed to Moses on Sinai. It enshrined the covenant. A key feature of the Second Temple period and beyond became conflicting interpretations of the Torah. Such emphasis on the Torah ultimately made it possible to construct a Judaism in the absence of Temple and cultic establishment after 70 CE.

Most of the book named after Nehemiah consists of his personal memoirs. He was cupbearer to the Persian king, a position of prominence and trust. The king appointed him governor of Judah in 445, a post that he held until 433, later returning to Judah for an unspecified period. He rebuilt Jerusalem's walls despite the opposition of its neighbors. Ranged in opposition to Nehemiah were an alliance of the Samaritan priestly elite, well-to-do Jewish inhabitants of the region east of the Jordan, and some of the Judahite elite, including members of the Jerusalem priestly establishment. They may have opposed Nehemiah for fear of a shift in power relations in the region. Nehemiah sought to strengthen Jerusalem's autonomy, reinforce its Levites (a lower-level category of priests), ban mixed marriages, and strengthen Sabbath observance. Noteworthy is his effort to institute land reform, probably on the basis of ancient Israelite law decreeing that land should remain within families (Neh. 5; see Lev. 25). Nehemiah's mission demonstrates the close relationship between religion, economics, and politics in ancient Israel. Although Nehemiah had the power of the Persian crown behind him, his account of his second trip to Judah shows that not all of his reforms were successful (Neh. 13:4–31).

A key feature of Second Temple Judaism was the importance of the diaspora, Jews living outside the land of Israel. The most important group of Judahites living abroad in the Persian period was in Babylon, but there were also Jews in Egypt. Some of those who rebelled against Babylon in the sixth century BCE fled to Egypt. There was a Jewish military colony in upper Egypt, on an island called Elephantine. This group left Aramaic papyri from the fifth century BCE that give a picture of Yahwists with little concept of the profound reforms of Judaism being carried on in Judah by the returning exiles. Jews in Elephantine had their own temple, indicating that the insistence that there should be only one temple to Yahweh was unknown to them. One letter in the collection is from the Persian king Darius I, authorizing the colony to celebrate the feast of unleavened bread, implying that the feast had not previously been celebrated. The Elephantine papyri remind us that ancient Judaism was always more varied than is known from extant evidence and that the emerging structures in Babylonia and Judah do not tell the whole story. Nonetheless, there was widespread and deep dedication in the diaspora to Jerusalem and its Temple, which, along with the Torah, symbolized God's relationship with Israel.

Persian influence on Jewish religion is fully visible only in the Hellenistic period. This topic is difficult because the sources for Persian religion are late, and it is not easy to decide which features go back to the time Persia ruled Israel. There is also a question about whether any given development in Judaism is a result of internal dynamics or of outside influence. Ideas often attributed to Persian influence include resurrection from the dead, eschatology, hell, angelology, demonology, periodization of history, and the dualistic concept that there are forces of light and of darkness at odds with each other in the universe.

The Hellenistic Period

The word "Hellenistic" and derivatives come from the Greek words *Hellas* meaning "Greece" and *hellenizo* meaning "to imitate the Greeks." To be Hellenized means to be heavily influenced by Greek language and culture. The Hellenistic period commences with the beginning of Alexander the Great's conquest of the Persian empire (333 BCE) and extends to the Roman conquest of the eastern Mediterranean. Since Palestine came under Roman rule in 63 BCE, for our purposes the Hellenistic period stretches from 333 to 63 BCE.

Alexander the Great was from Macedonia, an area just north of Greece, which was already Hellenized in his time. He united the Greek city-states and then conquered the entire Persian empire, dying in 323 BCE. Although there had been some interaction between Greece and lands to the east before Alexander, that interaction now increased exponentially. The center of Greek life and culture was the city, and Alexander's activity in founding new cities and rechartering old ones helped to Hellenize the conquered areas. Such Greek cities had Greek civic institutions and enjoyed some autonomy, although their authority was severely limited by kings and emperors. Native populations, particularly the upper classes, began to adopt the language and customs of their new overlords. Culture, including its religious elements, took on an international aspect. The cultures that evolved in specific areas resulted from interaction between native cultures and the wider, heavily Greek culture.

When Alexander died, his successors struggled over control of his vast empire. To the north of Palestine, Seleucus founded a dynasty, the Seleucids, that ruled in Syria. To the south, Ptolemy founded the dynasty of the Ptolemies, who ruled Egypt from Alexandria, a city founded by Alexander. Both dynasties claimed Palestine. In 301, Alexander's successors divided his empire, giving Palestine to the Seleucids, but the Ptolemies had already occupied the area and refused to relinquish it. There followed a century of conflict, until Palestine was finally seized by the Seleucids in 200 BCE. Close relations between Palestine and Egypt during Ptolemaic rule led to the increase of Jewish communities in Egypt. An important Jewish community developed in Alexandria, home to the famous Jewish philosopher Philo. It is clear from events in the next century that Hellenism made significant cultural inroads among Jews during the third century BCE, which would have been most apparent among the upper classes.

Relations between the Ptolemies and the inhabitants of Palestine were fairly peaceful, although the earliest extant Jewish apocalypses date from this time. Apocalypses are a literary form in which a revelation is given to a human seer through a supernatural figure, disclosing information about the heavenly world and about the future. Many apocalypses express dissatisfaction with the present state of affairs and look forward to a time when the world will be constituted in a way deemed proper by the apocalyptic authors. The precipitating factor in the formation of the apocalyptic genre may have been the dislocations caused by the new world order after Alexander. One Jewish apocalypse, the *Book of the Watchers* (1 Enoch 1–36), seems to attribute the wars of Alexander's successors and their dynasties to demonic forces and rebellious angels. Apocalypses helped Jews reconcile their traditions, in which the almighty God had chosen them, with their everyday experience, in which they were subject to foreigners.

When Antiochus III took Palestine from the Ptolemies, he contributed to the growth of the Jewish diaspora by transferring a large number of Jewish families from Palestine to parts of Asia Minor as military colonies, a common way of controlling conquered territories. In these areas and throughout the diaspora, Jews formed semi-autonomous communities governed by their own laws and customs.

When Antiochus III captured Palestine, he allowed the Jews to continue to live by their ancestral laws, the Mosaic Torah. The political structure continued to be the temple-state, administered by the high priest in Jerusalem. There Israel had access to God through the cult. For a quarter of a century, things continued much as they had under the Ptolemies.

In 175 BCE, Jason, brother of the ruling high priest, Onias III, offered Antiochus IV, the reigning Seleucid, a sum of money if he would award him the high priesthood. Antiochus agreed. To a Seleucid king, awarding a priesthood for financial considerations would be normal. For the Jews, it violated the custom that a high priest held his office for life. Jason offered Antiochus additional money if the king would charter Jerusalem as a Greek city, with its own gymnasium and body of citizens. Antiochus agreed to this as well. This is usually called the "Hellenistic Reform." In one version of events, Onias fled to Egypt where he built a temple at Leontopolis.

Events of the next few decades were complicated, but the essential facts can be laid out quickly before we return to some of them in more detail. Jason was high priest for three years. Menelaus then outbid Jason for the post and was installed by Antiochus IV. Jason fled to an area east of the Jordan. While Antiochus was in Egypt on a military campaign, a rumor arose in Judah that he had been killed. At this news, Jason besieged Jerusalem. Antiochus advanced against the city, and Jason fled and died soon after. Antiochus took punitive measures against the city. He founded a citadel in Jerusalem, the Akra, where he stationed Syrian troops. He also outlawed the practice of Judaism and enjoined brutal punishments against those who circumcised their children, kept copies of the Torah, or refused to participate in pagan religious rites. He set up a pagan altar on the altar of sacrifice in the Temple, a terrible defilement of that sacred object.

Antiochus's persecution of Judaism provoked a revolt led by a priestly family headed by Mattathias, who had five sons. One of them, Judah, was nicknamed in Hebrew "the hammer," from which the name "Maccabees" comes, a name then applied to the entire family. When they later claimed royal status, they were called the "Hasmoneans." In the books of the Maccabees, they are presented as heroes of the Torah, a family chosen by God to defend divine law and the Jerusalem Temple. Although they began their careers in opposition to the Hellenization sponsored by Antiochus, over the next century they became ever more Hellenized themselves. The family was joined in the revolt by other Jews, but not all had exactly the same agenda. A group that receives special mention in the books of the Maccabees is the Hasidim, a Hebrew term meaning "pious ones." It is not clear to what extent the Hasidim were a consistent group. They may have been a loose coalition of Jews opposed to what they saw as erosion of the Torah.

The fortunes of the Maccabean revolt over the next two decades depended on the circumstances of the Seleucids, who dissipated their energy and resources in conflicts between rival claimants to the throne. In 164 BCE, Judah recaptured Jerusalem and cleansed the Temple. The Maccabean victory and rededication of the Temple is commemorated in the feast of Hanukkah, a word meaning "dedication."

Revolution was not the only available option in responding to the crisis under Antiochus IV. The book of Daniel, the only apocalypse in the Hebrew Bible, advocated not military resistance but faithful waiting for God to intervene (see also the *Testament of Moses*). However, another apocalypse from the time, the *Animal Apocalypse* (1 Enoch 85–90), had a more positive view of the revolt and saw the Maccabees as God's agents.

In 152 BCE, Jonathan was appointed high priest by a Seleucid ruler. The Hasmoneans were priests, but they were not Zadokites, the traditional high priestly family. When Jonathan died in 142 BCE, he was succeeded by his brother Simon. Simon was granted the power to mint his own coins, which amounted to granting Judah independence. That same year, Simon succeeded in expelling the Seleucid garrison from the Akra, a move that was both symbolic and substantive in overthrowing Seleucid hegemony. 1 Macc. 14 contains a declaration by the priests, elders, and people of Judah proclaiming Simon leader and high priest and allowing him to wear royal apparel "until a trustworthy prophet should arise" (14:41). This qualification may indicate that although the Hasmoneans were accepted as kings and high priests, there was a consciousness that things were not as they should be. It is possible that there were some supporters of Hasmonean rule who thought that God would eventually restore the Davidic monarchy and the Zadokite high priesthood.

Simon's son John Hyrcanus ruled from 135 to 104 BCE. He took advantage of infighting among the Seleucids to extend his rule to Idumea, the area south of Judah named after Israel's traditional enemies the Edomites. Josephus tells us that he forced the Idumeans to convert to Judaism. John also took Samaria and is said to have destroyed the Samaritan temple at Shechem. This exacerbated tensions between Jews and Samaritans, a group that traced its origins to the northern kingdom of Israel, but whom Judeans thought of as foreigners and not valid members of the covenant (see 2 Kgs. 17:24–41).

In 104 BCE, John was succeeded by his son Aristobulus I, who ruled for less than a year. His significance lies in the fact that he was the first Hasmonean to claim the title of king. Since the Hasmoneans were not of Davidic lineage, some Jews would have been troubled by this move. He was called "Philhellene," a name indicating his support for Greek culture. Aristobulus is a Greek name, as is the name Hyrcanus, another indicator of the degree to which Hellenism had penetrated the Hasmonean dynasty.

Alexander Jannaeus ruled from 103 to 76 BCE. His reign was marked by expansion of Hasmonean territory and by internal conflicts. Alexander suffered a six-year insurrection against his reign. Among his enemies were the Pharisees. In 76 BCE, Alexander was succeeded by his wife Alexandra Salome. She appointed her son Hyrcanus II high priest. Her other son, Aristobulus II, was not satisfied with being subordinate to his brother, but he made no move until his mother's death. Josephus credits Alexandra with strengthening the army and living in peace with surrounding powers.

When Alexandra died in 67 BCE, the ambitious Aristobulus II moved against his brother. Hyrcanus fled, leaving Jerusalem to Aristobulus. An Idumean named Antipater now enters the story. His father had governed Idumea for Alexander Jannaeus. In 63 BCE, Antipater convinced Hyrcanus to attack Aristobulus in Jerusalem. Meanwhile, the Roman general Pompey was in Syria, extending Roman control over the region. All factions sent representatives to him. Pompey ultimately set up Hyrcanus as high priest. Thus began Roman rule of Judah, to be discussed in the next section of this chapter. This ended almost a century

of Jewish independence, during which the Hasmoneans won for themselves
a kingdom even larger than that of David and Solomon.

Judaism and Hellenism

Much discussion has centered around the interaction between Hellenism and
Judaism. Some of the discussion assumes that Hellenism and Torah are incompatible, and to the degree that Judaism was Hellenized, to that extent it ceased
to be Judaism. A more accurate picture would be more complex and nuanced.
Jason probably wanted Judah to take its place in the contemporary world
without surrendering dedication to God, abrogating God's constitution for
Israel, or defiling the Jerusalem Temple. If monotheism and the centrality of
Torah were guarded, there was still much room for accommodation. To this
end, Jason made Jerusalem a Greek city. Some scholars detect elements of
class struggle, where the upper class wished to Hellenize and the lower classes
were more conservative, but there were also disagreements within the upper
class on these issues.

The idea in 1 Maccabees that Antiochus's persecution was simply the whim
of a self-indulgent ruler can be dismissed as tendentious. Antiochus acted
according to the logic of the ruling classes of the time. It is also unlikely that, as
2 Maccabees claims, he decided to make all of his subjects abandon their local
customs and adopt Greek ways in order to unite his empire. Such an unprecedented policy would have had the opposite of its intended effect. Antiochus IV
faced conflict within Judah that needed to be resolved. His decision to outlaw
Judaism may have been related to his efforts to bring the area under tighter
control. He may have seen the civil struggles in Judah as related to Torah, and
he may have wanted to remove it as a source of conflict. Whatever his intentions, the persecution did not serve to pacify Judah but to ignite it, for many
Jews thought it their sacred obligation to fight to the death for Torah.

The Maccabean struggle, even after it issued in independence for Judah,
did not mark the end of Hellenistic influence in the region. Judaism was now
Hellenistic for better or worse, and one must speak of degrees of Hellenistic
influence on Jewish society, religion, literature, and so on. Nor can a simple
contrast be made between Jews living in the Greek-speaking diaspora in places
like Alexandria in Egypt and Jewish inhabitants of Judah. The Jews of the
diaspora may have been more open to Greek ways, but Palestinian Jews were
also part of the Hellenistic world.

Qumran

The groups into which Josephus divides Palestinian Jews – Pharisees, Sadducees,
the fourth philosophy, and Essenes – may have originated in the Hellenistic
period, specifically in the second century BCE. Our main sources for the first
two groups are Josephus, the New Testament, and Rabbinic literature. We defer

treatment of them and of the fourth philosophy to the end of the next section and treat the Essenes here.

The Essenes are spoken of by Philo, Josephus, and Pliny the elder, a Roman writer, and they are usually identified with the inhabitants of a small community whose ruins, called Qumran, are visible today near the northwestern corner of the Dead Sea. Beginning in 1947, a collection of ancient scrolls, now called the Dead Sea Scrolls, was discovered in caves near Qumran. Most scholars connect the scrolls with the ruins. The library consists of three main categories of literature – biblical texts, texts by a sect or sects connected with the community at Qumran, and other non-biblical documents, some known from other sources. The piecing together of Essene history and religion is extremely complicated and is the subject of a great deal of current debate, some of it quite heated. The method here will be to follow a fairly mainstream reconstruction, with the caution that most elements of any reconstruction can be challenged.

The community at Qumran probably originated in a group that arose in opposition to the Hasmoneans. Traces of the original conflict can be found in the scrolls, especially where the Teacher of Righteousness, the founder of the sect, is portrayed as being locked in a struggle with a figure or figures called the "Wicked Priest" and the "Liar." Since the scrolls emphasize the Zadokite identity of the priests at Qumran, it is possible that one source of dissatisfaction for the group was the assumption of the high priesthood by the Hasmoneans, who were not Zadokites. Another contentious issue between the people of Qumran and the Jerusalem establishment was the calendar, a topic of great importance for the determination of feast days. The sect followed a solar calendar, as does a non-biblical document from the first half of the second century BCE that was popular at Qumran, *Jubilees*. Jerusalem may have used a lunar calendar or a calendar combining lunar and solar determinations. One scroll (MMT) enumerates other legal issues on which the sect disagreed with the Jerusalem establishment.

Under the direction of the Teacher of Righteousness, the sect found in Scripture what it considered prophecies of its own beginnings and history. The Teacher claimed that God had revealed to him divine mysteries, including the proper interpretation of Torah. Supported by their biblical interpretation, members of the sect withdrew to the shores of the Dead Sea where they kept the Torah according to their own strict interpretations and waited for God to intervene in history on their behalf. Some texts indicate that at least for some part of their history the sectarians did not frequent the Temple, believing it defiled. Deprived of the use of the cultic institutions to relate to God and to effect atonement, they conceived of their own community as the place of purity on earth where God's angels were present. The community's observance of the law and its prayer were seen as atoning and substituting for the Temple sacrifices. Such a situation would be ended after the great battle, with God, the good angels, and the Qumran community on one side, and Satan, the wicked Jews, and the gentiles on the other, at the conclusion of which, members of the sect would be vindicated and possess Jerusalem as the true priestly Israel.

The conception of a single community with a single history is simplified. The community lasted from the early Hasmonean period until the settlement at Qumran was destroyed by the Romans in 68 CE. Some of the scrolls, the Damascus Document in particular, picture members of the sect living in villages throughout Palestine, marrying and in close contact with non-Essene Jews and even gentiles, while other scrolls, especially the Community Rule, assume a more isolated setting, such as that at Qumran, where the community was male and celibate. At any given time, there may have been different sorts of Essenes, and, over time, communities may have changed, merged, or split.

The Diaspora

Although Palestinian Judaism was part of the Hellenistic world, Hellenization may have been more extensive in the diaspora. Although it is not possible here to trace the differences between the Jewish homeland and diaspora in detail, it must be kept in mind that the story of Judaism at this time is much more than the story of Palestinian Jews. Several significant topics can be mentioned here. First, synagogues were significant in the diaspora, since Jews there were so far from the Temple in Jerusalem. By the first century CE, synagogues became significant in Palestine as well. In the synagogues, God's Torah was studied and interpreted, and prayer became an increasingly valuable way of relating to God. Second, the translation of the Jewish scriptures into Greek probably took place in the diaspora, where most Jews did not know Hebrew. The Torah proper, the Pentateuch, was probably translated in Egypt in the third century BCE. Third, liberal attitudes toward outsiders were common among diaspora Jews. For example, one collection of Jewish oracles written in Egypt, the third book of Sibylline Oracles, thought that God would raise a messianic figure from the line of the Ptolemies. Fourth, ancient Judaism was part of Hellenistic culture, and this is especially apparent in the diaspora. An excellent example is the philosopher Philo, who, while remaining faithful to Judaism and the Torah, interpreted it with the aid of the philosophy of his day, particularly Middle Platonism. Another example is Ezekiel the Tragedian, who retold biblical stories in the form of Greek tragedy.

The Roman Period: 63 BCE to 66 CE

The main source for the Roman period is the Jewish historian Josephus. He was born to a priestly family in Judea around 37 CE. He participated in the war against the Romans, was captured by them, and, at the conclusion of the war, went to Rome and spent the rest of his life under the patronage of the Flavians, the imperial family that ruled from 69 to 96 CE. The Roman period of Israel's history began when Pompey intervened in a Hasmonean power struggle in

63 BCE, ultimately setting up Hyrcanus as high priest. The Romans used the Idumean Antipater and his sons to help them administer Judea and environs and even made them Roman citizens. Antipater's son Herod, later to be known as "Herod the Great," took responsibility for Galilee in 48 BCE and proved himself an able administrator and skillful soldier. These early decades of Roman rule in Judea corresponded to a chaotic period in internal Roman politics, a period that included the two triumvirates. Herod showed great skill both in making himself useful to important Romans and in ingratiating himself with the winners of Rome's struggles. In 40 BCE, the Romans appointed him king. Herod ruled until his death in 4 BCE.

Herod had an ambivalent relationship with the Hasmoneans. He tried marrying into the family, but suspecting conspiracies he eventually killed his wife, Mariamne, and their two sons. Over time, he brought in new high priestly families from Egypt and Babylonia to assume the high priesthood. In so doing, he continued the control over the high priesthood that the Romans had initiated. Josephus, who claims Hasmonean ancestry, depicts the reign of Herod as dominated by terror and repression, sustained by an efficient secret police and brutal punishments. Herod deprived the Sanhedrin of any real power.

Whatever the judgment about Herod's repressiveness, he did manage to maintain his kingdom in relative peace throughout his reign. The Romans gradually added territories to his authority until his kingdom was again comparable in size to that of the Hasmoneans. He undertook a substantial building program through which he promoted his relationship with both his Jewish and non-Jewish subjects. In Jerusalem, Herod's greatest accomplishment was the rebuilding of the Temple on a grand scale. He built or reinforced a series of fortresses, including Masada, on top of high cliffs just west of the northern tip of the Dead Sea, and Antonia (named after Marc Antony), a fortress overlooking the Temple.

When Herod died, his son Archelaus took over Judea. Disturbances broke out in various sections of the country. The Romans decided to confirm Archelaus in office, but with the title of "ethnarch," "leader of the people," rather than "king." Further, they reduced his territory, giving part of it to two other sons of Herod. Herod Antipas received Galilee and Perea (an area east of the Jordan), and Philip received territories to the north and east of the Sea of Galilee, each receiving the title "tetrarch."

The uprisings at Herod's death had messianic overtones, for some felt that God would use this moment to liberate Israel from foreign bondage. The Jewish rebels enjoyed initial success against Roman forces in the area, but then the Syrian governor, Varus, came south and crushed the rebellion mercilessly, destroying cities such as Sepphoris in Galilee, crucifying thousands of the rebels and selling many into slavery. The "War of Varus" went a long way toward discouraging rebellion in Judea for the next seventy years.

After ten years even the Romans were dissatisfied with Archelaus. They deposed and banished him (6 CE), instituting direct Roman rule through a Roman administrator called a prefect (more popularly called a governor). Direct Roman rule meant direct taxation. This required a census, conducted in 6 CE.

Censuses had always been sensitive issues in Israelite and Jewish history, for they signified a kind of ownership of the people that belonged to God alone (see 2 Sam. 24). Judas the Galilean and Zadok the Pharisee declared a tax revolt, claiming that God alone was king of the Jews. The revolt was not violent or well organized, and the Romans crushed it easily. A passage in Josephus has been taken to mean that Judas and Zadok founded a revolutionary movement, often called the Zealots, that operated underground between the tax revolt in 6 CE and the outbreak of war sixty years later. Recent scholarship has shown this to be false. Josephus means only that the idea that God's kingship should mean freedom from foreign kings caused much disturbance and bloodshed throughout the first century. The Zealots as an organized group did not come into being until 68 CE.

Although there was now a Roman administrator in Judea, the Romans still governed as much as possible through the local elites. The Sanhedrin and high priesthood regained some of the authority they had before Herod's rule. The Romans again assumed the right to appoint the high priest.

Pontius Pilate administered Judea from 26 to 36 CE. This was during the reign of Tiberius (14–37 CE). Pilate is perhaps the best example of a succession of Roman administrators who were insensitive to Jewish concerns. He began his administration by bringing Roman military standards bearing the emperor's images into Jerusalem. Torah forbids human images. Popular protests forced him to withdraw them. He also hung golden shields dedicated to the emperor in Herod's palace in Jerusalem. Again he relented under pressure. He then took money from the Temple treasury to repair an aqueduct bringing water into Jerusalem. This provoked Jewish ire, but this time Pilate did not back down, using violence to overcome the resistance. Finally, Pilate did something to which even the Romans took exception. The Samaritans gathered together to ascend their sacred mountain, Mount Gerizim, allegedly to find the Temple vessels Moses hid there according to Samaritan tradition. Pilate took this to be a potentially seditious act, for it could have meant that the Samaritans expected God to intervene, eject the Roman forces, and allow for the rebuilding of the Samaritan temple. He attacked the Samaritans and killed many of them. Pilate's Roman superiors apparently thought that he used excessive force, so Tiberius removed him from office.

Roman insensitivity toward Palestinian Jews seems on the whole to have been due to neglect and ignorance rather than outright antipathy. In the diaspora, the Jews usually lived according to their own laws and customs, even when that meant exemption from military service. There was even a sizeable Jewish community in Rome. Some Romans had mixed feelings about their presence there, but they felt that way about other foreign groups, too. The Jews were expelled from Rome in 139 BCE, 19 CE, and 39 CE, but each time they returned shortly afterward.

Many of the Herodian family spent time in Rome, either as hostages, a common form of control of client kingdoms, or for education and political grooming. Agrippa I, grandson of Herod the Great, spent much time with the imperial family. He was for years on the island of Capri with Tiberius, and there he became friendly with Gaius, nicknamed Caligula. When Tiberius died in 37 CE, Caligula ascended the throne. Agrippa I fared well during Caligula's reign. In 37 CE, the territory formerly under the control of Philip, who died in 34 CE, was awarded to Agrippa, and he was given the title of king. In 39 CE, Herod Antipas was deposed and his territory added to Agrippa's kingdom.

During Gaius's reign a conflict erupted in Alexandria between its Jewish and gentile inhabitants. The Jews as a group were not citizens of Alexandria, but there was a vibrant Jewish population there who lived according to their own laws. They wanted to become citizens. A pogrom against the Jews occurred in 38 CE. Both sides in the Alexandrian conflict appealed to Gaius. The Jewish philosopher Philo was a member of the Jewish delegation and recorded his experiences in *Legatio ad Gaium*. He charges that Gaius was hostile to Judaism and that Gaius claimed to be divine, an affront to the one true God.

In 40 CE, Caligula demanded that a statue of himself be installed in the Jerusalem Temple. Some attribute this to madness, while others see it as an expression of annoyance toward a group that caused him trouble in Alexandria and perhaps elsewhere. Still others think that Caligula wished to confront Jewish refusal to worship him. He was assassinated before the statue was erected, and in any case he may already have been persuaded to relent by Agrippa I.

The new emperor, Claudius, denied Alexandrian Jews citizenship but reaffirmed their permission to regulate their own affairs. Agrippa received Judea and Samaria from Claudius, and now his kingdom was comparable in size to his grandfather Herod's. When Agrippa died in 44 CE, Claudius made his kingdom a Roman province. The next two decades saw deteriorating relations between Rome and the Palestinian Jews, as well as between different factions among the Jews.

The governor Fadus (44–46 CE) fought banditry, and he suppressed a movement under a prophet-like figure named Theudas who went to the east of the Jordan, claiming that God would split the Jordan as he had for Joshua when Israel first captured the land of Canaan. This had obvious overtones of political liberation. The next governor was an Alexandrian Jew, Tiberius Julius Alexander (46–48 CE), son of Alexander, alabarch of Alexandria, and nephew of Philo. Later he became prefect of Egypt (66–70 CE), and was also the Roman general Titus' chief of staff during the siege of Jerusalem (70 CE). Philo claims that he had abandoned the Jewish religion. He crucified two rebels who were sons of Judas the Galilean. Under the third governor, Cumanus (48–52 CE), there were several disturbances. A Roman soldier made a rude gesture during Temple festival ceremonies, causing an uproar in which many were killed. In another incident, Romans were attacked while traveling near Jewish villages. Cumanus held the villages responsible. One of the soldiers sent to the villages tore a Torah scroll, prompting an indignant response from the population. Cumanus had the man executed to quiet the disturbance. In yet another incident, Samaritans killed Jews traveling through Samaria to a religious festival in Jerusalem. When Cumanus would not respond, Jewish bandits did, leading to further fighting.

The Syrian governor sent Cumanus and his military tribune to Rome along with delegations of Jews and Samaritans. The Jews were vindicated and Cumanus was removed from office.

The administrations of these three governors show problems with Roman rule in Jewish Palestine at this time. Conflicts were the more potent when they involved Roman disrespect for Torah and Temple. Armed resistance to Roman rule, although still sporadic and limited, was now on the rise. Banditry, which can be an early form of violent political action, was increasing. Roman administrators were not equal to the task of dealing with complex and volatile situations. Under the next governor, Felix (52–60 CE), resistance spread. He crushed the movement of an Egyptian Jew who was a prophet-like figure similar to Theudas. This man gathered his followers on the Mount of Olives and expected God to bring down Jerusalem's walls as he had those of Jericho when Joshua was invading the land. Felix also captured the Jewish bandit Eleazar.

Another form of violence arose during this time. A group called the Sicarii, named after the short dagger (*sica*) they used, pursued a program of assassination and kidnapping. Their victims were the Jewish aristocracy. They considered these their enemies, both because they cooperated with Rome and because they themselves were perceived as oppressors. This shows that there was an element of class conflict in the mounting tensions. This is confirmed by the fact that one of the first acts of the rebels once the war broke out was to burn debt records.

The 60s witnessed a quick descent into all-out warfare. Josephus reports widespread banditry and armed resistance. There were three governors during this period – Festus (60–62 CE), Albinus (62–64 CE), and Florus (64–66 CE). Agrippa II, son of Agrippa I, tried to smooth these relations several times and had some limited success. Relations between Florus and the Judeans reached such a low that he crucified many of them. An important factor apparent in Florus's administration was the tension between Jewish and gentile segments of the population in some areas. This was particularly acute in Caesarea. It was there that the precipitating events of the war occurred. Tensions mounted until fighting broke out, exacerbating Jewish–gentile tensions elsewhere as well.

The War Against Rome

Finally, in 66 CE, Eleazar, captain of the Temple, stopped the Temple sacrifices offered on behalf of Rome. Such sacrifices were an important way to demonstrate Jewish loyalty to Rome, since Jews could not participate in the imperial cult because of their monotheism. The Roman garrison in Jerusalem was promised safe passage when they surrendered but were then slaughtered. The Syrian governor Cestius Gallus responded rapidly by taking Galilee and the port of Joppa, and laying siege to Jerusalem, but he then withdrew, suffering many casualties. The withdrawal gave the Jews time to organize and prepare for the coming war. As events turned out, they would have been luckier if they had been defeated quickly.

The causes of the Jewish revolution against Rome were many. Roman maladministration played a key role, particularly as it related to Jewish religion. Class conflict was also present. Sacred traditions of national liberation (for example, the Exodus) and native kingship (messianic hopes) could well have fueled Jewish hopes. Clashes between the Jewish and gentile inhabitants of Palestine were important at least as precipitating factors for the violence. The fractured nature of the Jewish ruling class also made Jewish society more volatile and may have given some members of the aristocracy motives for desiring war.

Much of the rest of the war featured Jewish infighting. Early on, the Sicarii leader Menahem came with his followers from Masada with messianic claims. He was killed and the Sicarii were driven back to their stronghold. In 68 CE, the population that had been driven before Vespasian's advance, some of them perhaps Jewish bandits, entered Jerusalem and formed the group called the Zealots. They killed the current high priest and appointed their own, from a valid family but from a lower class. This indicates their acceptance of priesthood, cult, and Temple as central to Judaism, but it also shows their opposition to the ruling priests. In this way, the Zealots were similar to the Essenes. Idumean forces at first allied with the Zealots and then opposed them. Vespasian, perhaps because he hoped the Jewish infighting would do his work for him, did not attack Jerusalem directly, but besieged it.

In 68 CE, Nero was assassinated. The following year saw three emperors, none of whom lasted long. Finally, the legions in Egypt, Palestine, and along the Danube acclaimed Vespasian as emperor. He placed the war in the hands of his son Titus.

In 70 CE, Jerusalem fell and was destroyed. The Temple was also destroyed, after a thousand years of existence interrupted only by its destruction in 587 BCE by the Babylonians. This was a tragedy of epic proportions for Judaism, and throughout history Jews have mourned this loss. The Sicarii in Masada held out a few years more, but the seemingly impregnable fortress also fell to the Romans. Its last defenders committed suicide. Some of the Sicarii went to Egypt and beyond that to Cyrene, attempting to foment resistance to Roman rule there as well, but the Jews of those areas did not support them.

Not much is known about the decades immediately following Jerusalem's destruction. The Romans converted the annual tax paid by the empire's Jews to maintain the Temple into a poll tax benefiting the Roman treasury. In another form of response, several apocalypses were written that tried to come to grips with the destruction (4 Ezra, 2 Baruch, the Apocalypse of Abraham). Pharisees, priests, and scribes gathered in Jamnia (Yavneh) to piece together Judaism's future. This coalition was the seed that eventually grew into Rabbinic Judaism. There were later revolts in the diaspora under the emperor Trajan (97–115), but they were put down and Judaism was not made to suffer worldwide sanctions on their account. Palestinian Jews revolted again under Hadrian in 132 CE and were defeated in 135 CE.

Pharisees, Sadducees, and the Fourth Philosophy

Josephus, we recall, sees the main Jewish groups as the Pharisees, Sadducees, "fourth philosophy," and the Essenes, whom we already have examined. Some Essenes may have participated in the war against Rome. The settlement at Qumran was destroyed in 68 CE.

Josephus says that the fourth philosophy believed the same things as the Pharisees, except that they adopted the radical stance against foreign rule espoused by Judas the Galilean. They probably did not constitute a consistent group as did the other three.

The Pharisees left no documents that can be attributed to them with certainty. The main sources for the Pharisees are Josephus, the New Testament, and the Rabbinic literature. Each source has biases and relates only those things that fit its interests. The most consistent trait mentioned by all sources is their knowledge of the Torah and their interpreting of it in specific ways that set them apart.

In his summary of the beliefs of the Jewish "philosophies," Josephus says that the Pharisees were the most accurate interpreters of the laws (Torah), that they believed in a balance between fate and freewill, and that they believed in an afterlife. They first appear during the reign of John Hyrcanus I and are active in politics (135–105 BCE). Josephus says that John Hyrcanus at first adhered to rulings of the Pharisees, until a prominent Pharisee criticized him for holding the offices of both civil ruler and high priest. John then turned to the rivals of the Pharisees, the Sadducees, as his counselors, and the Pharisees lost their political clout.

Josephus claims that there was strong hostility between the Pharisees and Alexander Jannaeus. When his wife became queen, the Pharisees played a major role as her advisors. Herod undermined the political influence of the Pharisees, as he did that of the Hasmoneans and others. The Pharisees are for the most part absent from Josephus' accounts of Jewish history between the reign of Herod and the outbreak of the war. He says nothing about them as a group during the war, although certain prominent Pharisees did play a role as members of the Sanhedrin. Their lack of prominence in Josephus' account of this period may be due to their reduced role in politics, Josephus' main interest.

In the New Testament, the Pharisees are stereotyped as opponents of Jesus. Their particular interests are in ritual purity, especially as concerns tithing and eating. They also were strict observers of the Sabbath. They are presented as believing in resurrection of the body, an idea first clearly attested in the book of Daniel (165 BCE).

In Rabbinic literature, the Pharisees are interested in basically the same sorts of things as in the New Testament. The overall aim of their program was to introduce into daily life, purity rules for raising and eating food, rules that in Torah are meant only for the priests. In so doing, they marked off one's family table as holy, as were the Temple and altar.

It is possible that the Pharisees, active in politics from the time of John Hyrcanus to that of Alexandra Salome, turned to pious domestic interests, particularly with respect to the raising and tithing of crops and the eating of food (things that they could control even when stripped of political power), when faced with Herod's opposition. The famous leader Hillel may have had something to do with this shift in emphasis. But their major role in the reconstruction of Judaism after the disaster of 70 CE attests to their readiness to participate in Judaism's public side. Their agenda of applying Temple purity rules to everyday life and thus fulfilling Torah in a way that was both continuous and discontinuous with the Temple cult became a feature of Judaism after the destruction in 70 CE.

The Sadducees also left no documents behind. As in the case of the Pharisees, the main sources for the Sadducees are Josephus, the New Testament, and Rabbinic literature. Josephus and the New Testament present them as a group within Jerusalem's ruling class, associated with the chief priests. Both sources see them as conservative, Josephus saying that they accepted nothing not written in the laws, and the New Testament claiming that they refused to believe in resurrection, angels, and spirits, the Pharisees believing in all three. Josephus contrasts the Sadducees unfavorably with the Pharisees and says that they were part of the upper class, whereas the Pharisees were closer to the people and had great influence over them. Josephus may say some of what he does because he wished to promote the Pharisees as leaders of Judaism after 70 CE. The Rabbinic literature is mainly interested in disputes between the Pharisees and the Sadducees over legal issues, and it consistently takes the side of the Pharisees.

Another group is the scribes. In the New Testament they are unified in opposition to Jesus. This picture is unrealistic. Scribes were in the first instance members of a profession. Each group had its own scribes, and scribes could be found in many layers of society. Scribes were not a single group with a single outlook.

The New Testament gives the impression that the career of Jesus and the movement he founded were the major events in Judaism in the first century. This is an assessment colored by Christian perspectives. Seen in its context in Second Temple Judaism, the Jesus movement is not of great significance. Jesus led a non-violent reform movement with eschatological overtones within Judaism, and this brought him into conflict with Jewish leaders who saw him as a threat to public order and their own authority. That the Romans also saw Jesus as a political threat is shown by the fact that they executed him, and did it in a way appropriate for political offenders – crucifixion. While Jesus was alive, his movement stayed entirely within Judaism. When he died, there were disputes over the role of Torah in the movement, which were exacerbated by the admission of more and more gentiles. As time went on, beliefs about Jesus became problematic for Jews and probably some Jewish Christians. Gradually, and at different rates in different places, Christianity became separate from Judaism.

After the Second Temple period and up to the present, the story of Israel is primarily the story of Rabbinic Judaism. This transformation did not happen overnight. The reinventing of Judaism began in the aftermath of the war, when Pharisees, scribes, and some priests started to address the problem of how Judaism was to continue without a homeland and without the Temple and cult.

Conclusion

The Second Temple period was an extremely fertile and active time for Judaism. Second Temple Judaism was very diverse, but what united all Jews in this time was monotheism, the belief that Jews had a special relationship with God originating in the covenant of Sinai and expressed in the Mosaic Torah, and dedication to the Temple in Jerusalem and to the holy land. While the Temple stood, it was a visible center for Jews everywhere, a symbol of God's relation with Israel, and a means of maintaining the covenant. Its fall was devastating. Rather than succumb to despair and conclude that God had abandoned his people, Pharisees, scribes, and some priests began to build a Judaism based on Torah without temple, city, and land. Traditional interpretations of Torah continued to develop and eventually achieved the authority of the Torah itself. Those interpretations were eventually called the Oral Torah, written down in Mishnah and the Babylonian and Palestinian Talmuds. But the Temple had not been forgotten. Cultic laws, symbols, and concepts continued to be central to the interpretation of Torah and to the way Israel thought of its relation to God and its place in the world.

CHAPTER 5

The Formation of Rabbinic Judaism, 70–640 CE

Guenter Stemberger

Beginnings at Yavneh

When the Roman troops under Titus destroyed Jerusalem and its Temple after four years of war in 70 CE it must have been clear to all Jewish contemporaries that something very important had happened; but they certainly could not know how definitive the demise of the Temple and its priesthood was to be. According to Rabbinic legend (B. Git. 56a–b), Yohanan ben Zakkai left the city when it was still under siege and was brought before the Roman commander Vespasian, who granted him permission to settle in Yavneh and to teach the Torah there. This story may be considered the foundation legend of the Rabbinic movement.

It is almost impossible to reconstruct what really happened. It is most likely that Yavneh was a kind of internment camp for Roman prisoners of war. There, Yohanan assembled a group of like-minded people to study Torah. In order to meet as a study-group, they may have needed some permission, but this certainly was not an official Roman authorization of the Rabbinic movement that was to arise from these beginnings. Roman authorization may have been needed later when the Rabbinic group was to assume some kind of national leadership; but this was still a long way ahead. Only decades, even centuries, afterwards, these small beginnings at Yavneh could be recognized as the foundation of a lasting and important development.

It is common to speak of Pharisaic–Rabbinic Judaism. This presupposes that the rabbis were the legitimate heirs to the Pharisees and continued their movement personally and ideologically. Yohanan ben Zakkai himself may not have been a Pharisee (see M. Yad. 4:7, where Yohanan seems to disassociate himself from the Pharisees), and the agenda of the early rabbis certainly was not predominantly Pharisaic, although main elements of Pharisaic tradition – a certain form of halakhah, belief in the resurrection, oral Torah – did become important in rabbinism, too. Priests and scribes seem to have played an important role, probably other groups as well, so that one may even speak of a great coalition of all those educated Jews willing and prepared to reorganize Jewish life for a period without Temple and sacrifices.

It has frequently been argued that the emerging new movement almost immediately took over the leadership of the Jewish people and was considered the legitimate heir to the national institutions from before 70. Thus, e.g., E. Schürer's account from the beginning of this century was taken over unchanged in the revised English edition of 1973:

> The Pharisees and the Rabbis entered into the heritage of the Sadducees and the priests. They were excellently prepared for this role, for they had been pressing for leadership during the last two centuries. Now, at one stroke, they acquired sole supremacy, as the factors which had stood in their way sank into insignificance . . . These scholars . . . now constituted, more exclusively and unrestrictedly than ever before, the nation's supreme authority . . . No external compulsion was needed. Whatever was laid down by the distinguished teachers was accepted as valid by the devout without further ado.[1]

There are numerous points indicating that this idealized picture, which is derived from much later gaonic and medieval texts, has little to do with reality. Rabbinic texts themselves frequently hint at the strong opposition rabbis met even in a much later period; legal texts dating from the late first and early second century CE, found in the Desert of Judah, do not correspond with Rabbinic legislation; most important, the outbreak of the Second Jewish Revolt under Bar Kokhba demonstrates that the rabbis had been absolutely unable to hand on to the people their own understanding of history and to hold it back from this revolt; even one of their leaders, Aqiba, is said to have acclaimed Bar Kokhba as the awaited messiah (Y. Ta. 4:8, 68d).

A New Start in Galilee

After the Bar Kokhba revolt (132–135 CE) and some years of legal restrictions ("persecution" – i.e., the temporary withdrawal of privileges granted to the Jews in the Roman Empire that had enabled them to live according to their own traditions), Jewish life and the Rabbinic movement had to be renewed; but now Galilee was to become the center, since many Jewish communities in Judea had been destroyed during the war. Usha replaced Yavneh as the center of the surviving rabbis; subsequently the center moved to Bet Shearim, later to Sepphoris, and finally to Tiberias. Already in Yavneh, Rabban Gamaliel had taken over from Yohanan ben Zakkai the leadership of the young movement; Gamaliel's son Simeon eventually became the rabbis' leader in Galilee, and Judah, who succeeded his father Simeon as the leader of the Rabbinic school, seems to have been the first "patriarch," recognized by the Roman authorities as the representative of the Palestinian Jews. With the redaction of the Mishnah – the foundational document of Rabbinic Judaism – at around 200, he also represented the quintessential rabbi, frequently cited with only that word, without additional name or other title. His descendants were recognized as patriarchs until the early fifth century, and, indeed, laws of the Theodosian Code from the second half of the fourth century demonstrate how greatly they were honored by the Roman authorities. In 415 CE, however, the patriarch Gamaliel VI was officially reprimanded for overstepping his privileges (Cod. Theod. 16,8,22), and the next thing we learn about the patriarch in official texts is a law of 429 CE (Cod. Theod. 16,8,29), which declares the office no longer existing and its income confiscated by the state.

By that time, however, the Rabbinic movement had learned to get along without the leadership of the patriarch, who, already in the second half of the third century, had become too busy with official duties to act as a leading member of the Rabbinic scholarly community. But the patriarchs, starting with Judah ha-Nasi (the Prince), increasingly tried to influence the general Jewish population with Rabbinic ideals and thus always sought to employ rabbis (or at least their favorites among them) not only at their court (which traditionally, but without real historical basis, has been understood as successor to the Sanhedrin in the period of the Temple), but also to place them in leadership positions in Jewish towns and villages: rabbis became increasingly interested in the running of schools, synagogues, and local courts, all things the rabbis of the founding generations had tried to avoid. This was the beginning of the long journey of the rabbis to spiritual leadership of the Jewish community.

As to the internal structure of the movement, the recruitment of new members and their education, we are not really well informed. Where the initial members of the Yavneh group were educated, we can only guess: some will have studied in priestly institutions, others in Pharisaic or scribal schools; but what these "schools" really looked like, we do not know. In Yavneh, the study-groups of the early masters must have served to train newcomers as well; whether the school became a well-established institution with admission requirements and a fixed curriculum is unknown. There were certainly other centers, for instance, Lydda or Bene Beraq, where individual rabbis trained their own disciples, especially their own sons. The aim of the course of study was to become able to live according to Rabbinic standards, to contribute to the development of halakhic learning, to give halakhic advice, and to train new disciples. It was not only an intellectual training leading to a certain level of knowledge regarding the Torah and the traditions connected with it; it also implied a personal discipleship, living together and serving the master in order to get accustomed to a life of Torah.

A special problem concerns the procedure by which a student was declared to have finished his studies and to have become a full member of the Rabbinic group. The traditional answer is that the disciple was included in the chain of tradition through the ceremony of *semikhah*, the "laying on" of the hands by his master or the patriarch, with or without the consent of the Sanhedrin. The main evidence for this ceremony is M. San. 4:3–4 and Y. San. 1:2, 19a. These texts speak of the appointment of Rabbinic students to membership in a *bet din* (Rabbinic court) or to certain concrete functions, but it is not fully clear that here the *semikhah* implies a general life-long qualification and makes the one upon whom it was bestowed an essential link in the chain of tradition.

For this reason, some scholars now doubt completely that there ever was a rite of *semikhah* equivalent to "ordination." It is a fact that too many Rabbinic texts have been read in a too systematic way; a thorough reexamination of all the texts in some way connected with this question or formerly adduced for the traditional concept of *semikhah* is urgently required. But even now, it may be stated that *semikhah*, whatever importance it may have had in the early Rabbinic movement, later on, probably already in the third century, lost this importance and must have been replaced by some other form of declaring the disciple of the rabbis an independent teacher of the Torah.

How did the rabbis finance their living? At least in the beginning, they rejected the idea that they might use their knowledge of Torah as "a spade" to make a living (M. Abot 4:5). Many of those who kept strictly to this idea had to be men of means; others relied on menial work or some trade in order to earn their living (quite a number of rabbis are named by their profession; this, however, is not a certain indication that they themselves still exercised this profession), or had to offer their services as scribes. At least from the third century onwards, a number among them tried to be employed in the service of the local communities, being paid for their services as teachers, etc., or relying on the munificence of the richer members: the rabbis insisted that the study of the Torah had replaced the service in the Temple; whatever was formerly due to those working for the maintenance of the Temple and its cult should now be given to the Torah scholars.

The Rabbinic Movement in Babylonia

The Rabbinic movement seems to have started in Babylonia in the context of the Bar Kokhba revolt. Students of Aqiba as well as of Ishmael, the two leading Palestinian rabbis of the period, fled during the revolt to Babylonia and brought there the earliest expression of Rabbinic thought. When the war and the difficult years afterwards were ended, not all returned to the land of Israel; some at least remained and continued to develop there the Rabbinic expression of Torah-scholarship and piety. There seems to have been a continuous exchange between the Rabbinic scholars of Palestine and Babylonia; several Babylonians, among them the well-known rabbi known simply as Rab, are said to have studied in the land of Israel before returning to Babylonia; others – the so-called *nahote*

– frequently traveled between the two countries for professional reasons and furthered a continuous exchange of traditions.

It seems that already at a very early stage of the Rabbinic movement in Babylonia, rabbis were well connected to the court of the exilarch, the representative of the Jewish population in Babylonia before the Parthian government. We do not know when exactly the institution of the exilarchate began – medieval tradition links it to the time of the Babylonian exile and establishes an uninterrupted chain of exilarchs descending from the members of the House of David deported to Babylonia after the fall of the First Temple; modern scholarship – mainly J. Neusner – has suggested that the institution was installed as a consequence of the fall of Jerusalem and the Temple in the revolt against Rome, as an attempt to secure the loyalty of Babylonian Jews. This is a useful suggestion but remains an educated guess; there are no sources that suggest the existence of this institution before the second half of the second century – and even if it existed at that time, it was immediately endangered by the change of power from the rather feudal regime of the Parthians to the more centralized government of the Sassanians at the beginning of the third century. Mar Samuel (according to later tradition, he died in 254) is generally credited with the "historical compromise" of the Jewish population with the Sassanian government along the principle of *dina de-malkhuta dina* – "the law of the state is valid law" (B. B.Q. 113a) and accepted as long as it does not interfere with vital religious concerns of the Jews; this principle became the guideline for all Jewish existence in the diaspora.

The Babylonian rabbis seem to have found a cordial welcome in the autonomous administration of the exilarch within a territory of mainly Jewish population; thus, they could apply their views of halakhah in practical life at a period when their Palestinian counterparts still had very little influence on the daily life of the common Jewish people. If this was really the case and affected a larger group of Babylonian rabbis, it must certainly have influenced their outlook on halakhah and its relationship with legal traditions older than the imported Rabbinic rules. But here again, we are on very unstable ground if we want to reconstruct the history of the early Babylonian rabbinate.

As to the training of Babylonian rabbis, quite a number of students continued to migrate to the land of Israel to study there. But the great majority must have preferred to stay at home and to study with local masters. Gaonic tradition has it that already in the early third century two great Rabbinic academies were established – Sura and Nehardea; with the latter replaced by Pumbedita after it was destroyed by Odenat in 259. But modern research has made quite clear that the gaonic picture retrojects the circumstance of the gaonic period into the early history of the Rabbinic movement. In the early period, there were no real academic institutions in Babylonia, only small groups of disciples who gathered around an individual master, after whose death they were dispersed in search of a new master. In spite of the employment possibilities offered by the institutions of the exilarchate, the training of young rabbis did not much differ from that of their colleagues in Palestine. It was based on the study of the Mishnah and the Bible, trying to fit the Palestinian traditions to local customs, regional law, and differing economic conditions in Babylonia.

The Rabbis and the Diaspora

It is frequently assumed that from the very beginning, the Rabbinic leadership was recognized not only in their Palestinian and Babylonian centers but in the diaspora as well. In reality, we have only a few indications of how rabbis related to some centers of the diaspora. In tannaitic and later texts, we read that some rabbis traveled to Rome, including Mattia ben Heresh, who is said to have had a yeshivah there in the early second century (B. San. 32b). Some have seen this as a full-fledged Rabbinic institution; but the very few Rabbinic references to Mattia do not support this hypothesis. It may be that rabbis who visited the capital of the Empire for other reasons used the occasion to acquaint Jews at Rome with their halakhic views; but later on, Rome gets completely out of sight in the Rabbinic sources. What is known about the Jewish communities of Rome (there does not seem to have been a central organization, but a number of synagogues independent from each other) is derived almost exclusively from inscriptions in the catacombs (mostly third to fourth century). The information gathered from them is too rudimentary to inform us much about the religious beliefs and way of life of Roman Jews. A few of the deceased are called "student of the law" (*nomomathes*) or "teacher of the law" (*nomodidaskalos*); this might be comparable to rabbis; but the title rabbi never occurs. Apart from words like *shalom* or *amen*, Hebrew is not used. We may wonder if Roman Jews could have found a common language with visitors from Palestine and if they ever heard of developments like the redaction of the Mishnah.

The situation changes only much later, when Rome was no longer the center of Italian Jews, but most evidence comes from southern Italy, mainly Venosa. There is a funerary inscription mentioning "two apostles and two rabbis" (*duo apostuli et duo rebbites*) speaking the dirges at the burial of a Jewish girl (early sixth century). These may have been rabbis coming from Palestine, the apostuli emissaries of the school at Tiberias, trying to raise funds for the institution. But these are only guesses. We have to wait until the early ninth century to find the first unequivocal trace of knowledge of Rabbinic culture in Italy: a tombstone, discovered only a few years ago, written in Hebrew and using for the eulogy of the dead, phrases from B. Ber. 17a and 58b. This is the first known attestation of knowledge of the Talmud outside of the Rabbinic centers.

Given the vicinity of the Palestinian homeland to Asia Minor, early influence of the rabbis is more likely there. Rabbinic texts frequently mention visits of rabbis to Asia (or more concretely, Cilicia or Cappadocia); Meir is said to have visited and to have written an Esther scroll for a community that did not have one (T. Meg. 2:5). If there is any historical value to this story, we may deduce from it that the Rabbinic practice of reading the book of Esther at Purim was not followed there and that Meir tried to introduce it. Two Palestinian rabbis, Yudan and Samuel, are called Cappadocians. The Palestinian patriarchs tried to extend their influence to Asia Minor and sent there special envoys to visit Jewish communities and to collect money for their institutions. Comes Joseph, about whom we learn from Epiphanius, is said to have been such an envoy before his conversion to Christianity in the time of Constantine.

Other evidence that has been adduced is an inscription from the synagogue of Sardes, inserted around 500 CE in the very center of the synagogue floor. It refers to the vow of a certain "Samoe, priest and teacher of wisdom" (*sophodidaskalos*). This man has been understood as a Palestinian envoy who tried to conform the community to Rabbinic standards. But this must remain as uncertain (perhaps even unlikely) as the Rabbinic interpretation of the long inscription from Aphrodisias (late third or fourth century), which lists many people, Jews as well as proselytes and God-fearers, who contributed to the *patella*, most probably a charitable institution of the community, a soup kitchen or something similar. The editors of this inscription tried to link the institution to the Rabbinic *tamhui* and to see the *dekania philomathon* mentioned in the inscription as a study group along Rabbinic lines. Much in this interpretation of the inscription is open to doubt; there is nothing in it to prove knowledge or influence of Rabbinic teaching in Palestine, although the names in the list might point to an increasing consciousness of Jewish tradition (a number of people have biblical names whereas their fathers still have Greek names without any Jewish connotation).

More weight may be given to a legal document, Justinian's 46th novella from 553 CE that, upon Jewish request, interferes with Jewish liturgy, especially the reading of the Bible in the synagogue. Some Jews insist on the Hebrew reading of Scripture in the Sabbath service whereas others want to keep the readings (only?) in Greek. The emperor recommends the use of the Septuagint, but allows the use of other Greek versions, too, and, by the way, suggests that Jewish communities in the Empire use their respective languages. The same text attacks the use of *deuterosis* in the liturgy. Since this term sometimes is used as a literal translation of Mishnah, the "repetition" of the Law of Moses, many authors believe that the emperor speaks here against the teaching of Rabbinic tradition in the diaspora communities. It is not clear, however, what the term in the law precisely refers to, except that it is an extra-biblical Jewish tradition. The term itself is probably derived from the writings of the Church Fathers (Eusebius and others); but its use does not prove what exactly the lawgiver had in mind nor that the Mishnah or even the (Palestinian) Talmud was at that time already known in Asia Minor. Against other interpretations of this law, I do not think that it may be used as a proof of growing Rabbinic influence in these communities.

The Formation of Rabbinic Theology – The Tannaitic period

Before 70, one can roughly speak of two basic forms of Judaism: the Temple-centered Jewish religion of the land of Israel, more exactly of Judea, and the Scripture-orientated Judaism of the diaspora (including Galilee, which in many respects shared the characteristics of the diaspora). This, of course, much over-simplifies a situation in which there were many overlaps between Palestine and the diaspora and in which, in neither Palestine nor the diaspora, can we suppose uniform expressions of Judaism; but it indicates the most important centers of gravity. The rabbis transformed Palestinian Judaism into a profoundly biblical religion; but they did not just copy what already existed in the diaspora. Their special contribution was the theology of the Dual Torah that affected all fields of their religious thinking.

Within the system, there is, of course, a continuous change and development. In a schematic way, Jacob Neusner has characterized it as the move from philo-sophy through religion to theology. This certainly goes a long way in explain-ing the main emphases of the different stages of Rabbinic thought, especially if one wants to characterize the main features of the principal documents of each of the three stages.

The clearest case can be made for the founding document of Rabbinic Judaism, the Mishnah. Traditionally, it is seen as the all-encompassing religious law code, the halakhic system of the rabbis of the first two centuries of our era. This is certainly correct in part; this understanding covers one important aspect of the document and the impact it has had on all future development of the halakhah. But it is not the whole picture. Looking more closely at the document, we not only see that more than half of the rules contained in the Mishnah could not be practiced at the time of its redaction, because there was no longer a Temple, a Jewish state, or a possibility of enforcing the civil law, etc. We also see that most of the rules are not so much concerned with normal cases of daily life but with the gray zones of definitions: what cases can be thought of that are at the utmost extremes of certain possibilities, what, e.g., is the absolute minimum of meaning-ful work that may be considered a violation of Sabbath rest (one of the answers, M. Shab. 7:3: writing two letters, the minimum necessary for meaningful com-munication)? To a large extent, the Mishnah explores the borderlines of defini-tions and the halakhic consequences connected therewith. It thus offers a perfectionist classification of the whole existing world, in many regards a utopian world-order. That much of this agenda is defined by philosophic premises seems clear. It is, of course, not philosophy for philosophy's sake. Charting the map of the existing world, one also wants to draw out the basic patterns of the world created by God and to show how Israel is expected to live in accordance with this plan, what deviates from this ideal order, and how such deviations are to be remedied.

It would certainly miss the mentality of the early rabbis if we thought that this map of the world is the whole of their enterprise and their religiosity. They, of course, pray, have a more personal relationship with God than is to be discovered in the code of the Mishnah; they are occupied with central religious concerns outside the world of halakhah; they are certainly also most interested in the Bible, the reading of which is regulated for the first time within Tractate Megillah. But all this does not define the shape of the Mishnah as such.

Much is not explicitly mentioned in the Mishnah but presupposed as general knowledge. Thus, for example, the Mishnah does not offer full texts of prayers; it includes mainly what is disputed and has to be clarified. Even more striking, the Mishnah does not define its relationship with the Bible. It states that all sacred writings defile the hands, including the book of Canticles, but that there is no agreement with regard to Ecclesiastes (M. Yad. 3:2–5). Here again, only disputed cases are explicitly named, and no list of the books belonging to the Holy Scriptures is given; this is regarded as generally known. Thus one can decree without further precision that he who says that the Torah does not come from heaven, but also he who reads in outside (heretical) books, has no share in the world to come (M. San. 10:1).

One saying in the Mishnah explicitly explains how its statements relate to the Torah (M. Hag. 1:8; translation: J. Neusner):

> The absolution of vows hovers in the air, for it has nothing [in the Torah] upon which to depend.
> The laws of the Sabbath, festal offerings, and sacrilege – lo, they are like mountains hanging by a string, for they have little Scripture for many laws.
> Laws concerning civil litigations, the sacrificial cult, things to be kept cultically clean, sources of cultic uncleanness, and prohibited consanguineous marriages have much on which to depend.
> And both these and those [equally] are the essentials of the Torah.

Apart from this general statement, the Mishnah never explicitly deals with the question of how its laws are derived from the written Torah; biblical quotations are rarely given as proof texts (such biblical texts have frequently been added in the later manuscript tradition).

The Tosefta, the somewhat later companion to the Mishnah, adds many biblical texts in order to make the biblical foundation of the mishnaic rules and world-view explicit. The halakhic Midrashim (Mekhilta to Exodus, Sifra to Leviticus, Sifre to Numbers and Deuteronomy) go much further. These writings, which at least in their earliest strata seem to have been worked out in the same period as the Mishnah, may be considered the exegetical foundation of many rulings presented there without biblical reference. Many of the same rabbis who contributed to the Mishnah were also engaged in the interpretation of the biblical text. The redactors of the Mishnah decided to present their work as standing on its own and in relative independence from the Bible. This decision has to be respected and must be taken into account when we try to understand the Mishnah. The philosophical mode of thought of the Mishnah is closely connected with this decision. Still, one should not lose sight of the enormous exegetical program of largely the same rabbis. Together, these two lines of work form the intellectual and spiritual context of the early Rabbinic period.

The Classical Period of the Amoraim in Palestine

The Rabbinic thinking of this second period is expressed through its most important literary products, the Palestinian Talmud (Yerushalmi) and the classical Midrashim (mainly Midrash Rabbah on Genesis, Leviticus, and Lamentations, as well as the earliest homiletical Midrash, Pesiqta deRab Kahana, but also a number of slightly later Midrashim). These voluminous writings, reaching their closure in the fifth century, are witness to the enormous creativity of the rabbis of the 150 to 200 years following the redaction and inner-Rabbinic general acceptance of the Mishnah.

Jacob Neusner has defined this period of Rabbinic thinking as the period of religion, because in contrast with the Mishnah's mode of deriving rules from the observation of the natural world in order to build its philosophical system of religion, the Yerushalmi continuously and explicitly appeals to a corpus of truths deemed to be revealed by God. While, as is already clear, even for the description of the attitudes of the earlier period, I prefer not to see a strict separation from what we find in the halakhic Midrashim, it is certainly a fact that the constant and explicit appeal to revealed knowledge becomes much more dominant now and can be considered essential for this period.

What characterizes the developments of these centuries? There are three lines that seem of the greatest importance: (1) The effort to transform a philosophically based, in large measure utopian, halakhah into rules of everyday-life. (2) The full development of a theology of the Dual Torah, including the bridging of the gap between Mishnah and halakhic Midrash. (3) The efforts to develop a theology of history.

The first point, the transformation of the *halakhic doctrine*, is intimately connected with the increased efforts of the rabbis to transform the normal Jewish population according to their own ideals. We already mentioned the growing involvement of the rabbis in matters of local schools and courts and in the life of the synagogue. The halakhah of the Mishnah, in many respects theoretical and utopian, had to be adapted to this purpose. When the Palestinian rabbis started to comment on the Mishnah, they certainly addressed the whole corpus. But in the outcome, the last two of six orders of the Mishnah received no gemara (with the single exception of part of tractate Niddah). Omitted were the laws concerning the sacrifices in the Temple and those concerning ritual purity, both immense areas of law that could not be put into practice in the absence of a Temple and while the land was occupied by heathens. It is not only that the land was deemed, to a large extent, impure, but also that, again because of the absence of the Temple, for many sources of impurity there simply were no longer means of purification. The omission of a full commentary on tractate Hullin, in the fifth order of the Mishnah, which treats the complex field of *kashrut*, later became a foundation of Babylonian teachers' attack on Palestinian tradition; these laws were certainly studied and applied in daily life in Israel in the period of the Amoraim, but perhaps not so systematically developed as in Babylonia.

As to the second point, it has already been mentioned that the Tosefta and even more so the Yerushalmi provided, for the laws of the Mishnah, biblical proof texts and tried to base the laws on the written Torah. Even more important is the systematic effort to develop a theology of the dual Torah, the written and the oral Torah as two branches of the same revelation to Moses on Sinai. The best-known expression of this effort is found in tractate Abot, a later addition to the Mishnah. It starts with the statement that Moses received not just "the Torah," that is, the Pentateuch, but Torah as such, i.e., not limited to its written expression, from Sinai, and handed it on in an unbroken succession to Joshua, the elders, and so on until the Rabbinic masters of the second century. What is written in the Mishnah and has no evident basis in the Bible is therefore nevertheless part of the Torah revealed to Moses on Sinai. The tractate thus becomes an apology for the Mishnah and its mode of teaching. In a second stage, this oral Torah has to be united with the written Torah; the proof texts added to mishnaic halakhot go a long way in dealing with this problem and in demonstrating that the written and oral Torah are essentially the same revelation.

In a period in which Judaism had to share the text of the written Torah with Christianity, which had taken it (in the form of the Septuagint) as part of its Jewish heritage, the oral Torah became the essential mark of the true people of God, distinguishing them from all who knew only the written Torah. The Torah as a whole is viewed as the basic principle of the world; it was created before the world and served in the world's creation as God's tool; from the time of creation, everything is directed towards Torah's revelation on Sinai, the culmination of creation. Being the principle of all existence, the Torah is offered to all nations, but only Israel accepts it and thus becomes God's partner in the perfection of the world. Even more so, the sage who studies the Torah and decides the halakhah according to his understanding of it takes part in the revelatory character of the Torah and contributes to the development and expansion of the oral Torah. The Torah, its study and realization in daily life, is Israel's means of sanctification and transformation and thus the only way to salvation.

The third point to be addressed is the Rabbinic understanding of history. The Mishnah presents a rather timeless picture of the universe. There are hints that laws had to be changed because of changes in society (*taqqanot*), but God's plan in history is hardly a topic. The destruction of the Temple should have been a central problem (and it certainly was), but it is not dealt with in the Mishnah. The closest the Mishnah comes to speaking about this problem is the end of tractate Sotah, which – at least for its larger part – may not be part of the original Mishnah (most of it is not discussed in the Gemara of Sotah, neither in the Yerushalmi nor in the Babli, but is quoted and commented upon as a baraita, an extra-mishnaic tradition, in tractate Sanhedrin).

One of the fears expressed in this end of Sotah is that the empire will be converted to *minut*, heresy, here most probably to be understood as Christianity. If this understanding is correct, the text certainly is not an anticipation of future developments foreseeable already at the end of the second century, but probably a reaction to the conversion of Constantine to Christianity and its consequences. This topic is dealt with, although never quite directly, in the Yerushalmi and in Bereshit Rabbah. Following the lead of the book of Daniel, they commonly presuppose a periodization of history among four empires – Babylonia, Media, Greece, and Edom (= Rome). Rome destroyed the Temple; but Rome itself will come to an end when the final period of history begins, Israel's period, the time of the messiah when the Temple will be rebuilt.

The Third Period: The final stages of the Babli

The Babylonian Talmud comes at the end of centuries of development, taking up whatever its redactors found useful in the Palestinian tradition and bringing it to its culmination. According to Jacob Neusner, the Babli is the first document of Judaism to turn out a theology, that is, the conscious reflection on the bases of Jewish religion and a persistent effort conceptually to explain and reconstruct the received tradition. The Babli also brings to perfection the union of the mishnaic mode of thought with its foundation in the interpretation of Scripture; there is no longer a separation of Talmud and Midrash: the Babli unites both in its pages. What distinguishes the Babli from its predecessor, the Talmud of the Land of Israel, or Yerushalmi, is not only this systematic union of the two main disciplines of Rabbinic thinking in one single document but also the conscious effort to show the essential unity and harmony of earlier Rabbinic thinking. What is new and unique in the Babli, is – in the words of Jacob Neusner:[2]

> the Talmud's insistence on showing how contending authorities (meaning, of course, positions in conflict) in fact harmonize, saying the same thing in different ways, for example, or differing about points that are, in fact, distinct. That persistent interest in limiting difference and extending consensus forms a principal plank in the document's program . . . while the Yerushalmi is satisfied to lay out differences of opinion, as a matter of information, the Babli wishes to analyze for the possibility of concurrence among superficially differing opinions. That is not a mere hermeneutical preference. It is critical to the Babli's most profound quest, which is for the point in its search for the abstraction at which discrete principles come together in shared premises, and premises in a point common to them all.

This search for unity dominates the Babli mainly in its latest layers, the mostly anonymous stratum of the talmudic teachers from the sixth century onward (the Savoraim); it tries to draw together the different strands of tradition and to deal with this Rabbinic tradition using the same hermeneutical principles that

had been applied to the Bible by the Palestinian rabbis: There are no real contradictions and no superfluous repetitions in the teaching of the Bible; but, the
later Babylonian rabbis insist, the same is true with regard to the teachings of
the Mishnah, the *Baraitot*, and the earliest generations of Amoraim. There are
not just different traditions; tradition as such forms a unity and is an essential
element of the dual Torah.

The Transformation of the People of Israel according to the Rabbinic Ideal

We have very little real evidence to trace the history of growing Rabbinic influence on the general Jewish population in both Rabbinic centers, and even less
in the diaspora. With regard to the land of Israel, we have already mentioned
the increasing efforts of the rabbis since the third century to influence the life of
the synagogue by participating in and contributing to the services as teachers,
experts in the liturgy, and preachers. The texts also speak of a growing participation of rabbis in communal services, as local judges and as *parnassim*
in charitable institutions. How successful were the rabbis in their efforts?

Rabbinic sources may always be suspected to depict the situation according
to the wishful thinking of the rabbis and with their own group as the dominating force of Jewish life. There certainly was a growing acceptance of Rabbinic
ideas because of the continuing efforts of the rabbis; but if we look for hard
evidence, we may point only to non-Jewish references for Rabbinic interpretations of the Bible and other teachings. Christian scholars in Palestine like
Eusebius and most importantly Jerome did have access to a considerable amount
of Rabbinic teaching. It may be taken for granted that they learned all this not
through direct contact with the leading rabbis but indirectly, from Christians
who still frequented synagogues and listened there to the sermons, as Christian
writers complain, and from simple Jews with whom Christians were in regular
contact in the market-place and in daily life. That this channel of information
functioned may be evidence of the fact that at least some Rabbinic teachings
had become general Jewish knowledge.

Archaeological excavations of synagogues in Israel provide another source
of information. It is noteworthy that up to the end of the Byzantine period and
beyond, the excavated synagogues hardly document any Rabbinic influence. Of
course, we may point to the growing centrality of the Torah and its ark, which,
beginning in the fourth century, received a fixed place in the apse and was
permanently placed in ever more artistic Torah shrines (instead of being brought
in during the service); this may be due to Rabbinic influence. But accepting this
point, one is even more amazed at the growing acceptance of figurative art in
the synagogue and the illustration of biblical scenes on the mosaic floors (e.g.,
the sacrifice of Isaac in Bet Alfa and Sepphoris, David with the weapons of
Goliath, and the messianic peace in Meroth).

As stated in the Yerushalmi, in the days of Yohanan, the Jews started painting the walls (of their synagogues?), and in the days of Abun, they started laying figurative mosaics, and the rabbis did not stop them (Y. A.Z. 3:3, 42d; the second part is not to be found in the traditional text, but is documented in a manuscript from the Genizah of Cairo). The rabbis did not react because they had no power to do so, not because they favored this development. Equally interesting is the fact that among the many inscriptions found in synagogue excavations, none mentions a rabbi known to us from Rabbinic literature. Whenever somebody is called rabbi in these inscriptions, it is a popular way of referring to respected people and nothing specific for the Rabbinic movement. Thus during the whole period of Roman and Byzantine rule, we have only indirect evidence for the growing influence of the rabbis among the Jewish population.

In Babylonia, as already mentioned, rabbis working in the service of the exilarch had direct access to and a certain influence on the common Jewish population. But here, again, Rabbinic thinking became more widespread only over a long period. The institution of the *pirqa* ("chapter"), attested from the fourth century, a public lecture before a larger audience including simple lay people and, at least since Gaonic times, held regularly on the Sabbath in the synagogues of the Rabbinic academies, certainly greatly contributed to the spread of the Rabbinic mentality among the common people. Another institution, the *kallah*, equally attested since the fourth century, was directed at people with some Rabbinic education. Twice a year, they could gather for a whole month to review and update their Rabbinic knowledge. In this way, a strong and permanent network was created that guaranteed the growing presence of rabbinically trained people able to carry this knowledge into ever more Jewish communities. Thus we may assume that by the time the Babli attained its (almost) final shape in the eighth century, the Rabbinic form of Judaism had already a relatively strong hold on the common Jewish people in Babylonia. Babylonian rabbis, who already in an earlier period had tried to make their teachings acceptable among Palestinian rabbis, now made every effort to impose their Talmud on the Jewish community of the land of Israel. They argued that the Yerushalmi lacked an authoritative treatment of such important spheres of halakhah as the laws of *kashrut* and that in other fields, too, it was far from perfect, because its rabbis continuously had suffered persecutions by the Roman government, which prevented sufficient dedication to the study of the Torah. Whatever was acceptable in the Yerushalmi had been taken over by the Babylonians, who had known and examined all earlier tradition; their own Talmud – so the argument proceeds – thus contained everything in the most perfect and valuable form and should therefore replace the Yerushalmi as well.

Most important is the evidence from the diaspora. It has already been mentioned that Justinian's novella 46 of the year 553 is not a clear indication of Rabbinic influence in Asia Minor and that a funerary inscription from Venosa (about 800 CE) is the first clear evidence of the knowledge of a text from the Babli in the western diaspora. At about the same time, the first Rabbinic scholars settled in northern Africa. Still in the ninth century, a Rabbinic school was founded in Kairouan, where, in the tenth century, the first non-Babylonian commentaries on the Babli were composed; this same community asked the Rabbinic leaders in Baghdad for clear information about the origins of Rabbinic literature: The Babylonian answer was the famous Letter of Sherira Gaon (987 CE), the first extensive account of the historical development of Rabbinic doctrine and the major Rabbinic writings. The permanent contacts between this African community (and soon other communities in North Africa and in Spain, as well) and the Rabbinic center in Baghdad were decisive for the development of Rabbinic thinking and the growth of Rabbinic influence in these new centers of Judaism.

After the decline of the Gaonic academies in Baghdad in the first half of the eleventh century, these new centers were able to continue on their own, becoming centers of a Jewish life already fully impregnated by Rabbinic thought and spirituality. At the same time, Jewish communities in southern Italy, formerly in the sphere of Palestinian influence, also started to accept Babylonian doctrines; from there, the Rabbinic mode of thought and life spread to the north, to Ashkenaz (Germany and northwestern France). Here, the Rabbinic way of life got hold of the life of the Jewish communities even more than in Spain; there, the intellectual talents and interests were always divided between the study of Rabbinic texts and traditions and the rich intellectual life of the Arabic culture and philosophy; but in Ashkenaz, Jews found little attraction in the rather backward and exclusively Christian cultural life of their surroundings. Thus they were almost completely limited to their own traditions and dedicated much of their time and energies to the study of Rabbinic texts and to the application of them to their daily life.

The real triumph of Rabbinic Judaism thus came about not in its original centers but in the North African and European diaspora communities. The last texts of the Rabbinic corpus – the first half of Exodus Rabbah, the first half of Numbers Rabbah as well as some minor late midrashim – in fact were redacted in Europe. Here, the Rabbinic heritage found a fertile ground, the ideal surroundings for the future development of Jewish communities based on the theology and halakhah of their Palestinian and Babylonian ancestors. The final success of Rabbinic Judaism was achieved not at home, but in North Africa and Europe, where the Babli received its most influential halakhic compendium in the work of Alfasi and its definitive early commentary at the hands of Rashi, thus becoming the basis of daily Jewish life.

Notes

1   E. Schürer, *The History of the Jewish People in the Age of Jesus Christ*, revised and edited by G. Vermes and F. Millar (Edinburgh, 1973), vol. 1, pp. 524–5.

2   Jacob Neusner, *Judaism States Its Theology. The Talmudic Re-Presentation* (Atlanta, 1993), pp. 59f.

CHAPTER 6
The Canon of Rabbinic Judaism

Jacob Neusner

Defining the Canon

Since in antiquity, as in modern times, diverse sets of books have been defined as the canon of one Judaism or another, we recognize that no single, unitary, linear "Judaism" ever existed. Quite to the contrary, a variety of Judaic systems, comprising a way of life, world-view, and definition of a social entity, an "Israel," have flourished. Comparison of one Judaic system with another shows that all of them are freestanding. Each one appeals to its distinctive symbolic structure, explains itself by invoking its particular myth, sets forth its indicative way of life, accounts for its way of life by appealing to its own world-view. The Judaic system revealed by Philo side by side with the one preserved in the Essene library found at the Dead Sea, or the Judaic system presented by the ancient rabbis with the Judaic system defined by the Pentateuchal editors in the fifth century BCE, makes the point quite clear. Harmonizing all of the diverse Judaisms into a single Judaism imposes a theological construct upon diverse and discrete historical facts. Since (except in the theological context) there never has been a single, "orthodox," unitary and harmonious "Judaism," against which all "heterodox" or "heretical" Judaisms have to be judged, we recognize that each Judaism is to be described in its own terms, meaning, in the context of its literature or other enduring evidences. Here we deal with the canon of the Judaism that became normative and remains paramount, Rabbinic Judaism.

The canon of that Judaism, also called the Judaism of the dual Torah, which took shape in the first seven centuries CE, encompasses the Hebrew Scriptures (a.k.a., "the Old Testament") and the Rabbinic writings from the Mishnah, ca. 200 CE, through the Talmud of Babylonia, ca. 600 CE. In the Judaism of the dual Torah, the Torah is set forth and preserved in three media, (1) a book, the Hebrew Scriptures, (2) a memorized oral tradition, first written down in the

Mishnah and other ancient documents, and (3) stories that exemplify the model of a sage who embodies in the here and now the paradigm of Moses, called a rabbi. Other Judaic systems identified other holy books, in addition to Scripture, for their canon. The canon of Rabbinic Judaism is only one distinct and autonomous corpus of writings; other Judaisms defined their own canons in accord with their systems' requirements. Each canon then recapitulated its system and no other.

The Traits of a Canonical Writing in Rabbinic Judaism

A simple definition follows from what has been said. Rabbinic literature is the corpus of writing produced in the first seven centuries CE by sages who claimed to stand in the chain of tradition from Sinai and uniquely to possess the oral part of the Torah, revealed by God to Moses at Sinai for oral formulation and oral transmission, in addition to the written part of the Torah possessed by all Israel. Among the many, diverse documents produced by Jews in late antiquity, the first seven centuries CE, only a small group coheres and forms a distinctive corpus, called "Rabbinic literature." Three traits together suffice to distinguish Rabbinic literature from all other Jewish (ethnic) and Judaic (religious) writing of that age:

1   These writings of law and exegesis, revered as holy books, copiously cite the Hebrew Scriptures of ancient Israel ("written Torah").
2   They acknowledge the authority and even the existence of no other Judaic (or gentile) books but the ancient Israelite Scriptures.
3   These writings promiscuously and ubiquitously cite sayings attributed to named authorities, unique to those books themselves, most of them bearing the title "rabbi."

Other writings of Jews, for example, Josephus, to begin with do not claim to set forth religious systems or to form holy books. Other Judaic writings ordinarily qualify under the first plank of the definition, and the same is to be said for Christian counterparts. The second element in the definition excludes all Christian documents. The third dismisses all writings of all Judaisms other than the one of the dual Torah. Other Judaisms' writings cite Scriptural heroes or refer to a particular authority; none except those of this Judaism sets forth, as does every Rabbinic document, extensive accounts of what a large number of diverse authorities say, let alone disputes among them. "Rabbinic" is therefore an appropriate qualifier for this Judaism, since what distinguishes it from all others is the character of its authorities (the matter of title being a mere detail) and the myth that accounts for its distinctive character.

Any book out of Judaic antiquity that exhibits these three traits – focus upon law and exegesis of the Hebrew Scriptures, exclusion of all prior tradition except for Scripture, and appealing to named sages called rabbis – falls into the category of Rabbinic literature. All other Jewish writings in varying proportions exhibit the first trait, and some the second as well, but none all three. It goes without saying that no named authority in any Rabbinic writing, except for scriptural ones, occurs in any other Judaic document in antiquity (excluding Gamaliel in Acts), or in another Jewish one either (excluding Simeon b. Gamaliel in Josephus's histories).

The Components of the Rabbinic Canon

Rabbinic literature is divided into two large parts, each part formed as a commentary to a received part of the Torah, one oral, the other written. The written part requires no attention here: it is simply Scripture (Hebrew: "the written Torah," TaNaKH, for Torah, Nebi'im, Ketubim). The oral part begins with the Mishnah, a philosophical law code that reached closure at the end of the second century. Promulgated under the sponsorship of the Roman-appointed Jewish authority of the land of Israel ("Palestine"), Judah the Patriarch, the Mishnah formed the first document of Rabbinic literature and therefore of the Judaic system, "Rabbinic Judaism," or "the Judaism of the dual Torah," that took shape in this period. The attributed statements of its authorities, named sages or rabbis called Tannaites ("repeaters," "memorizers," for the form in which the sayings were formulated and transmitted), enjoyed the standing of traditions beginning at Sinai. Numerous anonymous sayings, alongside the attributed ones and bearing upon the same controverted questions, appear as well.

The Mishnah and the Exegetical Tradition of the Oral Torah

Comprising six divisions, dealing with agriculture, holy seasons, women and family affairs, civil law and politics, everyday offerings, and cultic purity, the Mishnah served as the written code of the patriarch's administration in the land of Israel, and of that of his counterpart, the exilarch, in Iranian-ruled Babylonia as well. Alongside the Mishnah's compilation of sages' sayings into well-crafted divisions, tractates, and chapters, other sayings of the same authorities circulated, some of them finding their way, marked as deriving from Tannaite authority, into subsequent documents, the Tosefta and the two Talmuds:

1   The Tosefta, a compilation of supplementary sayings organized around nearly the whole of the Mishnah as citation and gloss, secondary paraphrase, and freestanding complement thereto, of no determinate date but probably concluded about a century after the closure of the Mishnah, hence ca. 300;
2   The Talmud of the Land of Israel, which reached closure in ca. 400, a commentary to most of the tractates of the Mishnah's first four divisions;

3   The Talmud of Babylonia, concluded in ca. 600, providing a sustained exegesis to most of the tractates of the Mishnah's second through fifth divisions.

The Tosefta's materials occasionally form the basis for exegetical compositions in the two Talmuds, but the second Talmud's framers know nothing about the compositions of the prior Talmud, even though they frequently do cite sayings attributed to authorities of the land of Israel as much as of Babylonia. So the line of the exegesis and extension of the Mishnah extends in an inverted Y, through the Tosefta, to the two, autonomous Talmuds.

$$\begin{bmatrix} \text{Mishnah} \\ \text{Tosefta} \end{bmatrix}$$

Talmud of the Land of Israel   Talmud of Babylonia
        (Yerushalmi)   (Babli)

Scripture and the Exegetical Tradition of the Written Torah

Parts of the written Torah attracted sustained commentary as well, and, altogether, these commentaries, called Midrash-compilations, form the counter-part to the writings of Mishnah-exegesis. It should be noted that both Talmuds, in addition, contain large composites of Midrash-exegesis, but they are not organized around books or large selections of Scripture. The part of Rabbinic literature that takes Scripture, rather than the Mishnah, as its organizing structure covers the Pentateuchal books of Exodus, Leviticus, Numbers, and Deuteronomy, and some of the writings important in synagogue liturgy, particularly Ruth, Esther, Lamentations, and Song of Songs, all read on special occasions in the sacred calendar. Numbering for late antiquity twelve compilations in all, the earliest compilations of exegesis, called Midrash, were produced in the third century, the latest in the sixth or seventh.

Sages and the Exemplary Torah

There is a third type of writing in Rabbinic literature, which concerns teachings of sages on theological and moral questions. This comprises a very small, free-standing corpus, tractate Abot ("the fathers," or founders) and Abot deRabbi Nathan ("the fathers according to Rabbi Nathan"). The former collects sayings of sages, and the latter contributes in addition stories about them. But the bulk of Rabbinic literature consists of works of exegesis of the Mishnah and Scripture, which is to say, the principal documents of the Torah, oral and written respectively. But throughout the documents of the oral Torah also are collected compositions and large compilations that are devoted to the sayings and exemplary deeds of named sages. No documents took shape out of that kind of writing, which, nonetheless, was abundant.

Mishnah and Midrash, *Halakhah* and *Aggadah*

Viewed as a whole, therefore, we see that the stream of exegesis of the Mishnah and exploration of its themes of law and philosophy flowed side by side with exegesis of Scripture. Since the Mishnah concerns itself with normative rules of behavior, it and the documents of exegesis flowing from it ordinarily are comprised of discussion of matters of law, or, in Hebrew, *halakhah*. Much of the exegesis of Scripture in the Midrash-compilations concerns itself with norms of belief, right attitude, virtue, and proper motivation. Encased in narrative form, these teachings of an ethical and moral character are called *aggadah*, or lore.

Midrash-exegesis of Israelite Scripture in no way was particular to the Rabbinic literature. To the contrary, the exegesis of the Hebrew Scriptures had defined a convention of all systems of Judaism from before the conclusion of Scripture itself; no one, including the sages who stand behind Rabbinic literature, began anywhere but in the encounter with the written Torah. But collecting and organizing documents of exegeses of Scripture in a systematic way developed in a quite distinct circumstance.

For Rabbinic literature, the circumstance was defined by the requirement of Mishnah-exegesis. The Mishnah's character itself defined a principal task of Scripture-exegesis. Standing by itself, providing few proof texts of Scripture to back up its rules, the Mishnah bore no explanation of why the people of Israel should obey its rules. Brought into relationship to Scripture, by contrast, the Mishnah gained access to the source of authority by definition operative in Israel, the Jewish people. Accordingly, the work of relating the Mishnah's rules to those of Scripture got under way alongside the formation of the Mishnah's rules themselves. It follows that explanations of the sense of the document, including its authority and sources, would draw attention to the written part of the Torah.

Exegetical Discourse and the Pentateuch

One important dimension, therefore, of the earliest documents of Scripture-exegesis, the Midrash-compilations that deal with Leviticus, Numbers, and Deuteronomy, measures the distance between the Mishnah and Scripture and aims to close it. The question is persistently addressed in analyzing Scripture: precisely how does a rule of the Mishnah relate to, or rest upon, a rule of Scripture? That question demanded an answer, so that the status of the Mishnah's rules, and, right alongside, of the Mishnah itself, could find a clear definition.

Collecting and arranging exegeses of Scripture as these related to passages of the Mishnah first reached literary form in Sifra, to Leviticus, and in two books, both called Sifre, one to Numbers, the other Deuteronomy. All three compositions accomplished much else. For, even at that early stage, exegeses of passages of Scripture in their own context and not only for the sake of Mishnah-exegesis attracted attention. But a principal motif in all three books concerned the issue of Mishnah–Scripture relationships.

A second, still more fruitful path in formulating Midrash-clarifications of Scripture also emerged from the labor of Mishnah-exegesis. As the work of Mishnah-exegesis got under way, in the third century, exegetes of the Mishnah and others alongside undertook a parallel labor. They took an interest in reading Scripture in the way in which they were reading the Mishnah itself. That is to say, they began to work through verses of Scripture word for word, phrase for phrase, line for line – just as the exegetes of the Mishnah pursued the interpretation and explanation of that document. And, as people began to collect and organize comments in accord with the order of sentences and paragraphs of the Mishnah, they found the stimulation to collect and organize comments on clauses and verses of Scripture. This kind of verse-by-verse exegetical work got under way in the Sifra and the two Sifres, but reached fulfillment in Genesis Rabbah, which presents a line-for-line reading of the book of Genesis. Characteristic of the narrowly-exegetical phase of Midrash-compilation is the absence of a single, governing proposition running through the details. It is not possible, for example, to state the main point, expressed through countless cases, in Sifra or Sifre to Deuteronomy.

From Exegesis to Proposition

A further group of Midrash-compilations altogether transcends the limits of formal exegesis. Beyond these two modes of exegesis – search for the sources of the Mishnah in Scripture, line-by-line reading of Scripture as of the Mishnah – lies yet a third, an approach we may call "writing with Scripture," meaning, using verses of Scripture in a context established by a propositional program independent of Scripture itself. To understand it, we have to know how the first of the two Talmuds read the Mishnah. The Yerushalmi's authors not only explained phrases or sentences of the Mishnah in the manner of Mishnah- and Scripture-exegetes. They also investigated the principles and large-scale conceptual problems of the document and of the law given only in cases in the Mishnah itself. That is to say, they dealt not alone with a given topic, a subject and its rule, the cases that yield the rule, but with an encompassing problem, a principle and its implications for a number of topics and rules.

This far more discursive and philosophical mode of thought produced for Mishnah-exegesis sustained essays on principles cutting across specific rules. Predictably, this same intellectual work extended from the Mishnah to Scripture. Exegesis of Scripture beyond that focused on words, phrases, and sentences produced discursive essays on great principles or problems of theology and morality. Discursive exegesis is represented, to begin with, in Leviticus Rabbah, a document that reached closure, people generally suppose, sometime after Genesis Rabbah, ca. 450, and that marked the shift from verse-by-verse to syllogistic reading of Scripture. It was continued in Pesiqta deRab Kahana, organized around themes pertinent to various holy days through the liturgical year, and Pesiqta Rabbati, a derivative and imitative work.

Typical of discursive exegesis of Scripture, Leviticus Rabbah presents not phrase-by-phrase systematic exegeses of verses in the book of Leviticus, but a set of thirty-seven topical essays. These essays, syllogistic in purpose, take the form of citations and comments on verses of Scripture to be sure. But the compositions range widely over the far reaches of the Hebrew Scriptures while focusing narrowly upon a given theme. They moreover make quite distinctive points about that theme. Their essays constitute compositions, not merely composites. Whether devoted to God's favor to the poor and humble or to the dangers of drunkenness, the essays, exegetical in form, discursive in character, correspond to the equivalent, legal essays, amply represented in the Yerushalmi. The framers of Pesiqta deRab Kahana carried forward a still more abstract and discursive mode of discourse, one in which verses of Scripture play a subordinated role to the framing of an implicit syllogism, which predominates throughout, both formally and in argument.

Writing with Scripture reached its climax in the theological Midrash-compilations formed at the end of the development of Rabbinic literature. A fusion of the two approaches to Midrash-exegesis, the verse-by-verse amplification of successive chapters of Scripture and the syllogistic presentation of propositions, arguments, and proofs deriving from the facts of Scripture, was accomplished in the third body of Midrash-compilations: Ruth Rabbah, Esther Rabbah Part I, Lamentations Rabbah, and Song of Songs Rabbah. Here we find the verse-by-verse reading of scriptural books. But at the same time, a highly propositional program governs the exegesis, each of the compilations meaning to prove a single, fundamental theological point through the accumulation of detailed comments.

Halakhah and Aggadah, Mishnah and Midrash in a Single Definitive Document

The Talmud of Babylonia, or Babli, which was the final document of Rabbinic literature, also formed the climax and conclusion of the entire canon and defined this Judaism from its time to the present. The Talmud of Babylonia forms the conclusion and the summary of Rabbinic literature, the most important document of the entire collection. One of its principal traits is the fusion of Mishnah- and Scripture-exegesis in a single compilation. The authors of units of discourse collected in the Talmud of Babylonia drew together the two, up-to-then distinct, modes of organizing thought, either around the Mishnah or around Scripture. They treated both Torahs, oral and written, as equally available in the work of organizing large-scale exercises of sustained inquiry. So we find in the Babli a systematic treatment of some tractates of the Mishnah. And within the same aggregates of discourse, we also find (in somewhat smaller proportion to be sure, roughly 60 percent to roughly 40 percent in a sample made of three tractates) a second principle of organizing and redaction. That principle dictates that ideas be laid out in line with verses of Scripture, themselves dealt with in cogent sequence, one by one, just as the Mishnah's sentences and paragraphs come under analysis, in cogent order and one by one.

Dating Rabbinic Documents

While we have no exact dates for the closure of any of the documents of Rabbinic literature – all the dates we have are mere guesses – we have solid grounds on setting them forth in the following sequence: (1) Mishnah, then Tosefta, (2) Yerushalmi, (3) Babli for the exegetical writings on the Mishnah; and the three corresponding, and successive groups – (1) Sifra and the two Sifres, (2) Leviticus Rabbah, Pesiqta deRab Kahana, Pesiqta Rabbati, then (3) Ruth Rabbah, Esther Rabbah Part One, Lamentations Rabbah, and Song of Songs Rabbah – for the exegetical writings on Scripture. The basis in the case of the sequence from the Mishnah is citation by one compilation of another, in which case the cited document is to be dated prior to the document that does the citing. The basis in the case of the sequence from Scripture is less certain; we assign a post-Mishnah date to Sifra and the two Sifres because of the large-scale citation of the former in the latter. The rest of the sequence given here rests upon presently-accepted and conventional dates and therefore cannot be regarded as final.

Study of the history of Rabbinic Judaism through the literature just now set forth must proceed document by document, in the sequence presently established for their respective dates of closure. In such a study of documentary sequences, for example, how a given topic or theme is set forth in one writing after another, we learn the order in which ideas came to expression in the canon. We therefore commence at the Mishnah, the starting point of the originally-oral part of the canon. We proceed systematically to work our way through tractate Abot, the Mishnah's first apologetic, then the Tosefta, the Yerushalmi, and the Babli at the end. Along the same lines, the sequence of Midrash-compilations is to be examined and the results, if possible, correlated with those of the Mishnah and its companions. In tracing the order in which ideas make their appearance, we ask about the components in sequence so far as we can trace the sequence. The traits of documents govern, and the boundaries that separate one from another also distinguish sayings from one another. The upshot is the study of the documents one by one, with emphasis on their distinguishing traits. When properly analyzed data are in hand, the work of forming of the facts a coherent historical account of the whole may get under way.

The Mishnah

The Mishnah is a philosophical law code, covering topics of both a theoretical and practical character. It was produced in about 200 CE under the sponsorship of Judah, Patriarch (*nasi*) or ethnic ruler of the Jews of the land of Israel. It comprises sixty-two tractates, divided by topics among six divisions, as follows:

1   Agriculture (Zeraim): Berakhot (Blessings); Peah (the corner of the field); Demai (doubtfully tithed produce); Kilayim (mixed seeds); Shebiit (the seventh year); Terumot (heave-offering or priestly rations); Maaserot (tithes); Maaser Sheni (second tithe); Hallah (dough offering); Orlah (produce of trees in the first three years after planting, which may not be eaten); and Bikkurim (first fruits).

2   Appointed Times (Moed): Shabbat (the Sabbath); Erubin (the fictive fusion meal or boundary); Pesahim (Passover); Sheqalim (the Temple tax); Yoma (the Day of Atonement); Sukkah (the festival of Tabernacles); Besah (the preparation of food on the festivals and Sabbath); Rosh Hashanah (the New Year); Taanit (fast days); Megillah (Purim); Moed Qatan (the intermediate days of the festivals of Passover and Tabernacles); Hagigah (the festal offering).

3   Women (Nashim): Yebamot (the levirate widow); Ketubot (the marriage contract); Nedarim (vows); Nazir (the special vow of the Nazirite); Sotah (the wife accused of adultery); Gittin (writs of divorce); Qiddushin (betrothal).

4   Damages or civil law (Neziqin): Baba Qamma, Baba Mesia, Baba Batra (civil law, covering damages and torts, then correct conduct of business, labor, and real estate transactions); Sanhedrin (institutions of government; criminal penalties); Makkot (flogging); Shabuot (oaths); Eduyyot (a collection arranged on other than topical lines); Horayot (rules governing improper conduct of civil authorities).

5   Holy Things (Qodashim): Zebahim (everyday animal offerings); Menahot (meal offerings); Hullin (animals slaughtered for secular purposes); Bekhorot (firstlings); Arakhin (vows of valuation); Temurah (vows of exchange of a beast for an already consecrated beast); Keritot (penalty of extirpation or premature death); Meilah (sacrilege); Tamid (the daily whole offering); Middot (the layout of the Temple building); Qinnim (how to deal with bird offerings designated for a given purpose and then mixed up).

6   Purity (Tohorot): Kelim (susceptibility of utensils to uncleanness); Ohalot (transmission of corpse-uncleanness in the tent of a corpse); Negaim (the uncleanness described at Lev. 13–14); Parah (the preparation of purification-water); Tohorot (problems of doubt in connection with matters of cleanness); Miqvaot (immersion-pools); Niddah (menstrual uncleanness); Makhshirin (rendering susceptible to uncleanness produce that is dry and so not susceptible);

Zabim (the uncleanness covered at Lev. 15); Tebul-Yom (the uncleanness of one who has immersed on that self-same day and awaits sunset for completion of the purification rites); Yadayim (the uncleanness of hands); Uqsin (the uncleanness transmitted through what is connected to unclean produce).

In volume, the sixth division covers approximately a quarter of the entire document. Topics of interest to the priesthood and the Temple, such as priestly fees, conduct of the cult on holy days, conduct of the cult on ordinary days and management and upkeep of the Temple, and the rules of cultic cleanness, predominate in the first, second, fifth, and sixth divisions. Rules governing the social order form the bulk of the third and fourth. Of these tractates, only Eduyyot is organized along other than topical lines, collecting sayings on diverse subjects attributed to particular authorities. The Mishnah as printed today always includes Abot (sayings of the sages), but that document reached closure about a generation later than the Mishnah. While it serves as its initial apologetic, it does not conform to the formal, rhetorical, or logical traits characteristic of the Mishnah overall.

The stress of the Mishnah throughout on the priestly caste and the Temple cult points to the document's principal concern, which centered upon sanctification, understood as the correct arrangement of all things, each in its proper category, each called by its rightful name, just as in creation as portrayed in the Priestly document at Gen. 1:1–2:4, and just as with the cult itself as set forth in Leviticus. Further, the thousands of rules and cases (with sages' disputes thereon) that comprise the document, upon close reading turn out to express in concrete language abstract principles of hierarchical classification. These define the document's method and mark it as a philosophical work. Not only so, but a variety of specific, recurrent concerns, for example, the relationship of being to becoming, actual to potential, the principles of economics, the politics, correspond point by point to comparable ones in Greco-Roman philosophy, particularly Aristotle's tradition. This stress on proper order and right rule and the formulation of a philosophy, politics, and economics, within the principles of natural history set forth by Aristotle, explains why the Mishnah makes a statement to be classified as philosophy, concerning the order of the natural world in its correspondence with the supernatural world.

The Talmuds

We come now to the two Talmuds, the Talmud of the Land of Israel, ca. 400 CE, and the Talmud of Babylonia, ca. 600 CE. Since the second of the two forms the definitive statement of the Judaism of the dual Torah and defines the curriculum of Torah-study in the centers in which the Torah is studied as God's word and will for Israel, we do well to begin by considering the purpose that these documents were meant to serve. In a word, the Talmuds propose to state in writing the basic rules of the social order and to show us how to discover the right rule, based on the principles God has made known in the Torah, for the affairs of everyday life. The Talmuds are documents full of debates on erudite and esoteric questions. But in the debates about fine points of law, ritual, and theology, "our sages of blessed memory" formulated through concrete examples the rules of right thinking and accurate formulation in words, of God's will for the here and now. For they held that the Torah is given to purify the hearts of humanity and that what God really wants is the heart. But there, in the center of life, in the streets and homes of the holy community, Israel, what does that mean? It is through close and careful thinking about little things that "our sages" brought the Torah's great principles into the everyday world of ordinary people. The media of language, logic, and law express the message of the Torah of Sinai. The Talmuds show us how, for the purposes of portraying the entirety of the social order, its culture and its politics alike, people write in signals an account of their modes of thought and how these are to be replicated any time and anywhere.

First, to define matters: a talmud – generically defined – is a sustained, systematic amplification and analysis of passages of the Mishnah and other teachings alongside the Mishnah, inclusive of the Tosefta, that are accorded the status of Tannaite authority. Of the genus, talmud, there are two species, the Tosefta, on the one side, the two Talmuds, on the other. These further divide into the Talmud of the Land of Israel ("the Yerushalmi") and the Talmud of Babylonia ("the Babli"). The former treats the first four divisions of the Mishnah; the latter, the second through the fifth; each is independent of the other, the two meeting only at parts of the Mishnah and sharing, further, some sayings attributed to authorities after the Mishnah; but these the documents' respective authorships read each in its own way.

The genus, talmud, as a source of information in clarification of the Mishnah was established by the Tosefta; but there information was left inert, the Tosefta's framers knowing nothing of dialectics (other than what they found on rare occasion in the Mishnah itself). What characterizes the other species of talmud, the one that encompasses the two Talmuds, is the transformation of information into principle, the systematic formation of argument, the transformation of facts, the raw materials of analytical inquiry, through the modes of thought of applied reason and practical logic, into systemic truth.

The sub-species of the species formed of the two Talmuds must be differentiated. What the first Talmud contributed was the definition of a talmud in which received facts ("traditions") were treated as active and consequential, requiring analysis and deep thought. The second Talmud transformed thought into argument, subordinating fact to the fully-realized processes of dialectical argument and reasoning. So the three talmuds in sequence expanded the definition of the genus, talmud, each adding an important component of that definition.

Both Talmuds – strictly-speaking the Yerushalmi, the Babli – are formed into commentaries to some of the same passages of the Mishnah (tractates in the divisions of Appointed Times, Women, and Damages, but not in Agriculture or

Holy Things; neither Talmud takes up Purities, except for tractate Niddah). Both are laid out in the same way, that is, as ad hoc treatments of phrases or even whole paragraphs of the Mishnah; the two Talmuds are identical in form, species of a genus. The two Talmuds defined Mishnah-commentary in a distinctive way, through their active program of supplying not merely information but guidance on its meaning: a program of inquiry, a set of consequential issues, in place of mere information. That program would be fully realized only in the second, and last, of the two Talmuds.

But both Talmuds in common exhibit definitive traits as well. Specifically they share the program of harmonizing one rule or principle with another. Both, furthermore, propose to uncover the scriptural foundation of the Mishnah's rules. In common therefore they undertake the sustained demonstration of the theology of the Torah: its perfection, on the one side, its unity (oral and written), on the other. Because of that fact, we may properly speak of "the Talmuds," since both do one thing, though the second does another in addition.

To begin with, the two Talmuds look alike. That is because both comment on the same prior text, the Mishnah. Both take up a few sentences of that prior text and paraphrase and analyze them. Both ask the same questions, for example clarifying the language of the Mishnah, identifying the scriptural foundations of the Mishnah's rules, comparing the Mishnah's rules with those of the Tosefta or other texts of Tannaite status, that is, presented with attributions solely to names that occur also in the Mishnah or Tosefta. They furthermore are comparable because they organize their materials in the same way. They take up pretty much the same topical agenda, in common selecting some divisions of the Mishnah and ignoring others, agreeing in particular to treat the matters of everyday practice, as distinct from theory, covered by Mishnah's divisions of Appointed Times, Women, and Damages. Both documents moreover are made up of already-available compositions and composites, which we may identify, in each document, by reference to the same literary traits or indications of completion prior to inclusion in the Talmuds. So they exhibit traits of shared literary policy.

In both, moreover, we find not only the same received document, the Mishnah, but occasionally also citations of, and allusions to, the same supplementary collection to the Mishnah, the Tosefta, and also a further kind of saying, one bearing the marks of formalization and memorization that serve to classify it as authoritative ("Tannaite") but external to the composition of the Mishnah and the compilation of the Tosefta. The points of coincidence are more than formal, therefore, since both Talmuds cite the same Mishnah-tractates, at some points the same Tosefta-passages, and also, from time to time, the same external Tannaite formulations.

Not only are the two Talmuds alike, but in their canonical context, the two Talmuds also are different from all other documents of the Judaism of the dual Torah in the formative age. First of all, among Mishnah-centered writings in the canon – the Tosefta, Sifra, the two Sifres, the Babli and the Yerushalmi – only the two Talmuds conduct sustained analytical inquiries over a broad range of problems. The Tosefta is not an analytical document; we have to supply the missing analytical program (as the authors of the two Talmuds, but particularly the Babli, themselves discovered early on). Sifra treats the Mishnah in only a single aspect, while the two Talmuds cover that aspect generously, along with a far more elaborate program. They pursue no encompassing exegetical program. So the two Talmuds are unique in context.

Both Talmuds invariably do to the Mishnah one of these four things, and each of these procedures will ordinarily be expressed in patterned language. It suffices here to classify the types of patterns:

1   text criticism;
2   exegesis of the meaning of the Mishnah, including glosses and amplifications;
3   addition of Scriptural proof-texts of the Mishnah's central propositions; and
4   harmonization of one Mishnah passage with another such passage or with a statement of Tosefta.

Each of these types of compositions follows a well-defined form, so that, if we were given only an account in abstract terms of the arrangement of subject and predicate or a simple account of the selection of citation language (e.g., "as it is said," "our rabbis have taught") we could readily predict the purpose of the composition or composite. So formal traits accompany the purpose of the commentary-compositions and other compositions and composites and permit differentiation one type from another.

The first two of the four procedures remain wholly within the narrow frame of the Mishnah-passage subject to discussion. Therefore, in the natural order of things, what the two Talmuds will find interesting in a given Mishnah-passage will respond to the same facts and commonly will do so in much the same way. The second pair takes an essentially independent stance *vis-à-vis* the Mishnah pericope at hand. Part of the rhetorical convention of the Talmuds governs the order in which types of compositions – Mishnah-text-criticism, exegesis, Scriptural proof-texts, and the like – are set forth. Ordinarily, the order for both Talmuds is the same as given above. While both Talmuds conform to complex and distinctive rhetorical programs, what makes them different from all other documents of Rabbinic literature is not only rhetoric but logic.

Midrash: The earlier compilations

The word *midrash*, translated "exegesis," presents confusion, since it is routinely used to convey three distinct, if related, meanings. If people say "the *midrash* says," they may mean to refer to:

1   a distinctive *process* of interpretation of a particular text, thus, the hermeneutic;

2   a particular compilation of the results of that process, thus, a book that is the composite of a set of exegeses; or

3   a concrete unit of the working of that process, of scriptural exegesis, thus the write-up of the process of interpretation as it applies to a single verse, the exegetical composition on a particular verse (or group of verses).

It follows that for clear speech the word *midrash*, standing by itself, bears no meaning. Let us consider the three distinct usages.

1   The word *midrash* refers to the processes of scriptural exegesis carried on by diverse groups of Jews from the time of ancient Israel to nearly the present day. Thus people say, "He produced a *midrash* on the verse," meaning, "an exegesis." A more extreme usage produces, "Life is a *midrash* on Scripture," meaning that what happens in the everyday world imparts meaning or significance to biblical stories and admonitions. It is difficult to specify what the word *midrash* in Hebrew expresses that the word *exegesis* in English does not. It follows that just how "exegesis" in English differs from *midrash* in Hebrew is not self-evident. Nor is there any reason that the Hebrew will serve better than the more familiar English.

2   The word *midrash* further stands for a compilation of scriptural exegeses, as in "That *midrash* deals with the book of Joshua." In that sentence, *midrash* refers to a compilation of exegeses, hence the statement means, "That compilation of exegeses deals with the book of Joshua." *Compilation* or composite in the present context clearly serves more accurately to convey meaning than *midrash*. That is why in this Introduction we speak of Midrash-compilation, as in "the Midrash-compilation on Exodus . . ."

3   The word *midrash*, finally, stands for the written-out result of a process of scriptural exegesis, that is to say, a composition (e.g., a paragraph with a beginning, middle, and end, in which a completed thought is laid forth), resulting from the process of *midrash*. In this setting *a midrash* refers to a paragraph or a unit of exegetical exposition, in which a verse of the Hebrew Scriptures is subjected to some form of exegesis or other. In this usage one may say, "Let me now cite the *midrash*," meaning, a particular passage of exegesis, a paragraph or other completed whole unit of exegetical thought, a composition that provides an exegesis of a particular verse. We use the word composition in this sense, that is, Midrash-composition, the particular presentation of a given passage.

Types of Midrash-Compilations

Midrash-compilations are classified on the basis of their relationship to Scripture and distinctive use of verses of Scripture. In the Midrash-compilations of Rabbinic literature, verses of Scripture serve not merely to prove but to instruct.

Israelite Scripture constituted not merely a source of validation but a powerful instrument of profound inquiry. The framers of the various Midrash-compilations set forth propositions of their own, yet in dialogue with Scripture. Scripture raised questions, set forth premises of discourse and argument, supplied facts, and constituted that faithful record of the facts, rules, and meaning of humanity's, and Israel's, history that, for natural philosophy, derived from the facts of physics or astronomy.

Whether or not a midrashic statement in fact accorded with the position of Scripture on a given point, or merely repeated the simple and obvious sense of Scripture, or found ample support in proof-texts – none of these considerations bears material consequence. These authorships made use of Scripture, but they did so by making selections, shaping a distinctive idiom of discourse in so doing. True, verses of Scripture provided facts; they supplied proofs of propositions much as data of natural science proved propositions of natural philosophy. Writing with Scripture meant appealing to the facts that Scripture provided to prove propositions that the authorships at hand wished to prove, forming with Scripture the systems these writers proposed to construct.

Classifications of relationships to Scripture are three:

1   The first mode of relationship is to develop an anthology on a theme, showing that a verse of the Israelite Scriptures illustrates a theme, providing *information* on a given subject. The theme then imposes cogency on facts, which are deemed to illuminate aspects of that theme. Such a statement constitutes a topical anthology. But the materials in such an anthology do not, all together, add up to a statement that transcends detail, pointing toward a conclusion beyond themselves. They rather comprise a series of facts, e.g., fact 1, fact 2, fact 3. But put together, these three facts do not yield yet another one, nor do they point toward a proposition beyond themselves. They generate no generalization, prove no point, propose no proposition. This use of Scripture is most prominent in Mekhilta Attributed to R. Ishmael, though even there the number of topical anthologies is not formidable.

2   A second mode of relationship suggests that a verse of the Israelite Scriptures defines a *problem* on its own, in its own determinate limits and terms. In the setting of a document, the problem will be identified and addressed because it is systemically active. That is not at all common in Mekhilta Attributed to R. Ishmael, while Sifra, for its part, takes a keen interest in verses and their meanings. Yet in doing so, its authorship weaves a filigree of holy words over a polished surface of very hard wood: a wood of its own hewing and shaping and polishing. Our sense is that, in this literature, recurrent allusions to verses of Scripture form an aesthetic surface rather than a philosophical foundation.

3   Yet a third mode utilizes Scripture in the formation and expression of *an independent proposition*, autonomous of the theme or even the facts contained within – proved by – Scripture. This approach characterizes the relationship between Scripture and Sifra, which is not extra-scriptural but meta-scriptural. Scripture in this function is systemically essential yet monumentally irrelevant.

Sifra in that way addresses and disposes of Scripture by rewriting it in ways of Sifra's authorship's design. That is the wonder of this marvelous writing: its courage, its brilliance, its originality, above all, its stubbornness.

The routine relationship to Scripture is indicated when the focus of interest is on the exegesis of Scripture. In the earlier Midrash-compilations, Mekhilta Attributed to R. Ishmael, as well as in Sifra and Sifre to Deuteronomy, we have composites of materials that find cogency solely in the words of a given verse of Scripture but in no other way. These materials string together, upon the necklace of words or phrases of a verse, diverse comments; the comments do not fit together or point to any broader conclusion; they do not address a single theme or form an anthology. Cogency derives from the (external) verse that is cited; intelligibility begins – and ends – in that verse and is accomplished by the amplification of the verse's contents. Without the verse before us, the words that follow form gibberish. But reading the words as amplifications of a sense contained within the cited verse, we can make good sense of them.

Midrash: The later compilations

While Mekhilta Attributed to R. Ishmael, Sifra, and Sifre to Numbers, like the Mishnah, cover many topics and yield no prominent propositional program but only implicit principles of thought, the second and later set of Midrash-compilations, produced in the fifth and sixth centuries (ca. 450–600 CE), form highly propositional statements. The first of the group, Genesis Rabbah, makes the same point many times and sets forth a coherent and original account of the book of Genesis. The next set, Leviticus Rabbah, Pesiqta deRab Kahana, and Pesiqta Rabbati, provide well-argued syllogistic arguments, entirely leaving behind the structure of verse-by-verse exposition. Generally thought to have been closed ("redacted") in ca. 400–450 CE, sometime after the Talmud of the Land of Israel had been redacted, Genesis Rabbah transforms the book of Genesis from a genealogy and family history of Abraham, Isaac, Jacob, then Joseph, into a book of the laws of history and rules of the salvation of Israel: the deeds of the founders become omens and signs for the final generations.

Genesis Rabbah

In Genesis Rabbah, the entire narrative of Genesis is so formed as to point toward the sacred history of Israel, the Jewish people: its slavery and redemption; its coming Temple in Jerusalem; its exile and salvation at the end of time – the whole a paradigm of exile and return. In the rereading by the authorship of Genesis Rabbah, Genesis proclaims the prophetic message that the world's creation commenced a single, straight line of significant events, that is to say, history, leading in the end to the salvation of Israel and, through Israel, of all humanity. The single most important proposition of Genesis Rabbah is that, in the story of the beginnings of creation, humanity, and Israel, we find the message of the meaning and end of the life of the Jewish people in the here and now of the fifth century. The deeds of the founders supply signals for the children about what is going to come in the future. So the biography of Abraham, Isaac, and Jacob also constitutes a protracted account of the history of Israel later on.

Leviticus Rabbah

In Leviticus Rabbah, we find the interest in verse succeeding verse has waned, while the proposition comes to the fore as the dominant organizing motif throughout. With Genesis Rabbah, the Sifra's and Sifre's mode of exegesis of verses and their components, one by one in sequence, comes to its conclusion and a new approach commences. The mixed character of Genesis Rabbah, joining propositional to exegetical rhetoric in order to make points of both general intelligibility and also very specific and concrete amplification of detail, marks a transitional moment in the workings of Midrash. Exactly what did the framers of Leviticus Rabbah learn when they opened the book of Leviticus? When they read the rules of sanctification of the priesthood, they heard the message of the salvation of all Israel. Leviticus became the story of how Israel, purified from social sin and sanctified, would be saved.

Pesiqta deRab Kahana

A compilation of twenty-eight propositional discourses, Pesiqta deRab Kahana ("Chapters attributed to R. Kahana") innovates because it appeals for its themes and lections to the liturgical calendar rather than to a Pentateuchal book. Pesiqta deRab Kahana marks a stunning innovation in Midrash-compilation, because it abandons the pretense that fixed associative connections derive solely from Scripture. Rather, the document follows the synagogal lections. The text that governs the organization of Pesiqta deRab Kahana thus comprises a liturgical occasion of the synagogue, which tells our authorship what topic it wishes to take up, and therefore also what verses of Scripture (if any) prove suitable to that topic and its exposition. The topical program of the document thus may be defined very simply: expositions of themes dictated by special Sabbaths or festivals and their lections.

It follows that, unlike Genesis Rabbah and Leviticus Rabbah, the document focuses upon the life of the synagogue. Its framers set forth propositions in the manner of the authorship of Leviticus Rabbah. But these are framed by appeal not only to the rules governing the holy society, as in Leviticus Rabbah, but also to the principal events of Israel's history, celebrated in the worship of the synagogue. What we do not find in this Midrash-compilation is exposition of

Pentateuchal or prophetic passages, verse by verse; the basis chosen by our authorship for organizing and setting forth its propositions is the character and theme of holy days and their special synagogue Torah-lections. That is, all of the selected base verses upon which the *parashiyyot* or chapters are built, Pentateuchal or prophetic, are identified with synagogal lections for specified holy days, special Sabbaths, or festivals.

Song of Songs Rabbah

The Song of Songs, called in the Christian Bible "the Song of Solomon" – both referring to the opening line, "The Song of Songs, which is Solomon's" – finds a place in the Torah because the collection of love-songs is understood to speak about the relationship between God and Israel. The intent of the compilers of Song of Songs Rabbah is to justify that reading. What this means is that Midrash-exegesis turns to everyday experience – the love of husband and wife – for a metaphor of God's love for Israel and Israel's love for God. Then, when Solomon's song says, "O that you would kiss me with the kisses of your mouth! For your love is better than wine" (Song 1:2), the sages think of how God kissed Israel. Reading the Song of Songs as a metaphor, the Judaic sages state in a systematic and orderly way their entire structure and system.

Ruth Rabbah

Like the other Midrash-compilations of its class, Ruth Rabbah makes one paramount point through numerous exegetical details. It concerns the outsider who becomes the principal, the messiah out of Moab, and this miracle is accomplished through mastery of the Torah. Sages impose upon the whole their distinctive message, which is the priority of the Torah, the extraordinary power of the Torah to join the opposites – messiah, utter outsider – into a single figure, and to accomplish this union of opposites through a woman. The femininity of Ruth seems to me to be as critical to the whole as her Moabite origin: the two modes of the (from the Israelite perspective) abnormal, outsider as against Israelite, woman as against man, therefore are invoked, and both for the same purpose, to show how, through the Torah, all things become one. That is the message of the document, and, seen whole, the principal message, to which all other messages prove peripheral.

Lamentations Rabbah (Eikha Rabbati)

The theme of Lamentations Rabbati is Israel's relationship with God, and the message concerning that theme is that the stipulative covenant still and always governs that relationship. Therefore everything that happens to Israel makes sense and bears meaning; and Israel is not helpless before its fate but controls its own destiny. This is the one and whole message of this compilation, and it is the only message that is repeated throughout; everything else proves secondary and derivative of the fundamental proposition that the destruction of the Temple in Jerusalem in 70 CE – as much as in 586 BCE – proves the enduring validity of the covenant, its rules and its promise of redemption. Lamentations Rabbah's is a covenantal theology, in which Israel and God have mutually and reciprocally agreed to bind themselves to a common Torah; the rules of the relationship are such that an infraction triggers its penalty willy-nilly; but obedience to the Torah likewise brings its reward, in the context envisaged by our compilers, the reward of redemption. The compilation sets forth a single message, which is reworked in only a few ways: Israel suffers because of sin, God will respond to Israel's atonement, on the one side, and loyalty to the covenant in the Torah, on the other. And when Israel has attained the merit that accrues through the Torah, God will redeem Israel. That is the simple, rock-hard and repeated message of this rather protracted reading of the book of Lamentations. Still, Lamentations Rabbah proves nearly as much a commentary in the narrowest sense – verse by verse amplification, paraphrase, exposition – as it is a compilation in the working definition of this inquiry of mine.

CHAPTER 7
Judaism and Christianity in the Formative Age

Bruce D. Chilton

From its outset in the movement of Jesus, generated by his program for the eschatological renewal of Israel in his focus on God's kingdom, Christianity understood itself within the terms of reference of Israel. Consequently, its identity as a form of Judaism was systemic, and its treatment of Judaism – by Jews and by non-Jews – was a predictable result. That result is attested as late as the collection of Jesus' sayings called "Q" and the letters of Paul. By the turn of the first century CE, however, and particularly in the Epistle to the Hebrews, Christianity's center of gravity was so thoroughly christological, even when it spoke in terms of Judaic institutions, that a claim effectively to replace Judaism had become a characteristic feature. That theological revolution, more than any demographic shift, marks the emergence of Christianity as a religion distinct from Judaism.

But the separation of Christianity from Judaism by no means represented the end of argument. On the contrary, now began the persistent expositions, on the part of theologians such as Justin and Clement, of how the Jewish understanding of Scripture was faulty. Those arguments were mounted on a philosophical basis, but even they pale in comparison with the supreme assurance of an Aphrahat, for whom the christological reading of Scripture was susceptible of exegetical demonstration, and not only commendable on the strength of philosophical conviction.

The triumphalism that in modern discussion has been associated with the Emperor Constantine was more the product of the theological confidence of theologians such as Aphrahat. They infused Christianity with the ambition to account for the whole of reality, not to permit spirit to be conceived of as alien to the human world. Just that project was taken up, under the favorable conditions Constantine introduced, by Eusebius and Augustine in the fields of political theory and history. By this point, Judaism – in the mind of Christian theology – had not only been replaced and successfully disputed but put in the position of a voice of fruitless opposition to the activity of God both in Scripture and in the world. The intellectual foundation for developments during the Middle Ages was therefore very near to completion.

Jesus

The position of Jesus within Christianity is unique, because it was a firm conviction of his movement from the outset that God's own activity was inherent in what he was doing. The dynamic quality of transcendence in Jesus' teaching is evident in a famous saying from the source known as "Q" (Matt. 12:28; Luke 11:20):

> If I by the spirit of God cast out demons,
> then the kingdom of God has arrived upon you.

Luke's version of the saying prefers "finger of God" to "spirit of God"; the change both alludes back to the "finger of God" by which Moses worked wonders in Egypt (Exod. 8:19) and avoids equating the power of exorcism with the spirit of God, such as Christians understood was available in baptism. In this case Matthew gives the more accurate version of "Q," but the meaning is evident in both Gospels. Jesus saw the removal of unclean spirits in response to his activity as a clear indication that God's kingdom had arrived or come (*phthano* in Greek, from *meta'* in Aramaic) upon those who witnessed his activity.

Jesus' understanding of the kingdom was that God was personally active on behalf of his people. For that reason, he thought of it as being revealed along distinct coordinates.[1] The kingdom is near in terms of its final disclosure (its eschatology), while in terms of its impact on the world (its transcendence), the kingdom has arrived. That arrival is limited, and so there is no question of all the eschatological promises being realized wholly in the present. But to qualify the arrival of the kingdom as limited in no sense denies the reality of God's rule. After all, even an eschatological hope conceives of what is to come as already existent in heaven. And Jesus' saying about the kingdom and his exorcisms maintains that the kingdom is not only real but a matter of what occurs in the experience of his hearers. Along its transcendent coordinate, the kingdom arrives in a local, sporadic, but intense occurrence, so as to clear away demons. The removal of their influence makes a place which is to be like every place, because it is where God rules.

Because Jesus' own activity is the particular occasion of the kingdom here ("If I by the spirit of God . . ."), an implicit Christology is involved. The unspoken assertion is that his exorcisms are effective of the kingdom in a way that others' are not. The link between Jesus and the kingdom becomes explicit in a saying from the Gospel according to Thomas (saying 82):

> Who is near to me is near to the fire,
> and who is far from me is far from the kingdom.

The imagery of fire was prominent within Jesus' teaching (in this case, see Luke 12:49), and serves to evoke the connection in his mind between the local, dynamic incursion of the kingdom (the fire) and the permanence of God's triumph (the kingdom itself).

Allowance must be made in Thomas, just as in the canonical Gospels, for the influence of later theologies upon the text as it stands. The famous incident of Thomas' doubt of Jesus' resurrection in John 20:24–29 shows that, at the time John was written (around 100 CE in Ephesus), its community was aware of a tradition of dialogue between Thomas and the risen Jesus. That tradition was later developed, with much borrowing from the canonical Gospels, and composed in Edessa ca. 160 CE. The ascetic emphasis of Christianity in Edessa was a profound influence upon Thomas; a central saying (saying 22), for example, stipulates that one must be neither male nor female in order to enter the kingdom. A denial of sexuality is manifest. The ascetic version of Thomas was then expanded in Egypt under the influence of Gnosticism and rendered into Coptic by the fourth century. By that stage, even the prophets of Israel could be dismissed as voices of "the dead" (saying 52): such a denigration of the Hebrew Scriptures was routine among many Gnostic groups.

Even after one has allowed for the influences of Egyptian Gnosticism and Syrian asceticism, there is a further complication in assessing the sayings of Thomas as statements of Jesus during the period of his public activity. Thomas conveys what it explicitly calls sayings of the risen Jesus (or "living Jesus," as the first statement in the document calls him): the generative point of the tradition is Jesus' encounter with Judas Thomas after the resurrection. That encounter may well be seen to have been consistent with Jesus' teaching before he was crucified, since that was a principal claim inherent within the faith that Jesus had been raised from the dead. But Thomas does not set itself up in relation to the sources of the historical Jesus in the way that the Synoptic Gospels do.

The reference to the fire and the kingdom in saying 82 is not inherently ascetic or Gnostic, but it could be explained as an example of how Jesus was understood to speak by those who experienced him as risen from the dead. After all, he had said, "Everyone shall be salted with fire" (Mark 9:49); saying 82 might be seen as a further application of the imagery of fire, in the context of the resurrection. At the same time, in its implicit Christology, as distinct from the explicit status Christians commonly attributed to Jesus, the saying commends itself as authentic. It stands side by side with the saying from "Q" in asserting the dynamic incursion of the kingdom as a promise of its universal scope. Whether in exorcised demons or scarifying fire, the kingdom is portrayed as an intense intervention of God which is not to be contained. There is an affinity between the two images, in that both involve the necessity of purity. The removal of an unclean spirit establishes a person as pure; the story of the legion of demons illustrates that motif unforgettably (see Matt. 8:28–34, Mark 5:1–20,

Luke 8:26–39). Similarly, the purity of sacrifice within the covenant with Israel is marked by the presence of salt in what is offered by fire (see Lev. 2:13). Just as breaking the power of one demon dethrones them all, so the fire of the kingdom is uncontainable. Both images involve an intense manifestation of power which, once manifested, is not to be limited.

"Q" and Paul

Recent discussion of the source known as "Q" has brought about a wide agreement that at least some of the sayings within it were circulated a few years after the crucifixion, around 35 CE. David Catchpole, in his critical study,[2] understands the "confrontational sense" of such statements as John the Baptist's claim that God could raise up children for Abraham from stones in order to replace those of Israel who refused to repent (Luke 3:8); but he does not adequately allow for the distance from Israel such a threat implies.

Q is best seen as evolving in two distinct stages. In the first, Jesus' teaching was arranged in the form of a mishnah by his disciples. They took up a ministry in Jesus' name that was addressed to Israel at large after the resurrection. The mishnaic form of Q was preserved orally in Aramaic and explained how the twelve were to discharge their mission. It included instructions to Jesus' disciples, a strategy of love to overcome resistance, paradigms to illustrate the kingdom, threats directed toward enemies, and a reference to John the Baptist that would serve as a transition to baptism in the name of Jesus. As specified, that is probably the original, mishnaic order of Q. It is the order that accords with Q's purpose within the mission to Israel.

At the second stage, Q's order was changed to become quasi-biographical, in accordance with the order of the Petrine teaching reflected in the Synoptic Gospels. At that stage, for example, material concerning John the Baptist was moved to the beginning, and the story of Jesus' temptations (Luke 4:1–13) was added in order to make the transition to an unequivocal focus upon Jesus rather than John. The final redaction of Q probably took place a decade after the mishnaic stage of Q was composed, probably in Syria, an environment in which both Aramaic and Greek were spoken. In that environment, tensions between Jesus' movement and received definitions of Israel had grown evident; but it took Paul, two decades later, to turn that confrontation into a new definition of Israel itself.

Paul wrote a letter to a group of churches in the northern part of Asia Minor (present-day Turkey) sometime around 53 CE. He was writing to communities in Galatia he himself had founded, where Christians were embroiled in a deep and (to his mind) destructive controversy. As Paul sees the matter (in chapter 2 of Galatians), he had established the practice of common fellowship at meals, including eucharistic meals, in churches he founded. Such fellowship of course included Jews who became Christians, signaling their acceptance of Jesus' teaching by being baptized. But it also – and increasingly – saw the participation of non-Jews who had been baptized, but not circumcised. Paul won the agreement of Christian leaders in Jerusalem that circumcision should not be required of non-Jewish members of his church (Gal. 2:1–10). The remarkable and early agreement that Jews and non-Jews could be included in the movement established a radical principle of inclusion. But it also brought about one of the greatest controversies within the early Church. Paul's version of events is the best available (in Gal. 2, seconded by Acts 15). At Antioch, Jews and non-Jews who had been baptized joined in meals of fellowship together. According to Paul, Peter fell in with the practice, and Barnabas at least tolerated it (Gal. 2:11–13). Peter – whom Paul also calls "Cephas," the Aramaic original for the Greek *petros*, "rock" – was a founding apostle of the church in Jerusalem, whose nickname came from Jesus himself. Barnabas, a Levite from Cyprus, was a prominent, loyal recruit in Jerusalem, who enjoyed the trust of the apostles and mediated relations between them and Paul.

Paul's policy of including gentiles with Jews in meals, as well as in baptism, needed the support of authorities such as Peter and Barnabas, in order to prevail against the natural conservatism of those for whom such inclusion seemed a betrayal of the purity of Israel. When representatives of James arrived, James who was the brother of Jesus and the preeminent figure in the church in Jerusalem, that natural conservatism reasserted itself. Peter "separated himself," along with the rest of the Jews, and even Barnabas (Gal. 2:12–13). Jews and gentiles again maintained distinct fellowship at meals, and Paul accuses the leadership of his own movement of hypocrisy (Gal. 2:13).

The radical quality of Paul's position needs to be appreciated before his characteristic interpretation of Scripture may be understood. He was isolated from every other Christian Jew by his own account in Gal. 2:11–13: James, Peter, Barnabas, and "the rest of the Jews." His isolation required that he develop an alternative view of authority in order to justify his own practice. Within Galatians, Paul quickly articulates as authoritative the distinctive approach to Scripture that characterizes his writings as a whole.

Paul grounds his argument in a matter of widespread agreement: belief in Jesus Christ endows one with spirit. But he spins the consensus in the interest of his polemical point (Gal. 3:3): "Are you so foolish that, having begun with spirit, you will now end with flesh?" The unexpressed assumption is that the observance of purity, such as the emissaries of James insist upon, is a matter of "flesh," not "spirit." Of course, just that presumption is what separates Paul from James, as well as Peter, Barnabas, and "the rest of the Jews." What Paul requires in order to sustain his polemic is some convincing demonstration that faith is on the side of spirit, and observance on the side of flesh.

Paul finds what he needs in Scripture, in the example of Abraham. He says that when believers hear with faith, they are "just as Abraham, who believed in God, and it was reckoned to him as righteousness" (Gal. 3:6). The characterization of Abraham is taken from Gen. 15:5–6, when Abraham is promised that his descendants shall be as the stars of the heavens: his trust in what he is told makes him the father of faith, and in the course of the sacrifice he subsequently offers, God seals his promise as the solemn covenant to give the land that would be called Israel (Gen. 15:7–21).

Paul understands the role of Abraham as the patriarch of Judaism, but he argues that Abraham's faith, not his obedience to the law, made him righteous in the sight of God (Gal. 3:7): "Know, therefore, that those who are of faith are sons of Abraham." Paul was capable of remarkable elaborations of that theme, in Galatians and elsewhere, but the essential simplicity of the thought must not be overlooked. Abraham, for Paul, embodied a principle of believing that was best fulfilled by means of faith in and through Jesus Christ. Descent from Abraham, therefore, was a matter of belief, not a matter of genealogy. Scripture itself is held to attest a radically new definition of Israel, which challenges the received understanding of both Judaism and the Greco-Roman world.

Paul's use of Scripture is instrumental, because his point is more theological than exegetical (Gal. 3:26–29):

> For you are all sons of God through faith in Christ Jesus. For as many as were baptized into Christ, were clothed in Christ. There is neither Jew nor Greek, neither slave nor free, neither male nor female: for you are all one in Christ Jesus. And if you are of Christ, then you are Abraham's seed, heirs according to promise.

Once that is understood to be the central theme of Scripture, realized whenever one appropriates one's new identity in baptism, it becomes the point of interpretation to illustrate that theme.

For all that the documents of Israel's canon may vary, for all that their periods and perspectives differ, the documents attest a single truth on Paul's reading. What is said in the case of Abraham amounts to "the Scripture foreseeing that the gentiles would be righteous from faith" (Gal. 3:8). "Scripture" for Paul is what the documents finally mean, the ultimate significance in the light of which the interpretation of individual documents and passages unfolds. That is why it is natural for Paul to proceed from Christ to the passages at issue: the point of departure was the point at which one had arrived by means of baptism. And the end point was what Paul specifies at the close of Galatians (6:15–16):

> For there is neither circumcision nor foreskin, but new creation. And as many as behave by this standard, peace be on them and mercy, even upon the Israel of God.

The choice of Israel is God's response to the choice of faith, and that involves a radical new definition of the people of God.

Hebrews

The Epistle to the Hebrews has long stood as an enigma within the New Testament. "Who knows who wrote the epistle?" asked Origen in the third century; he answered the question himself, "God knows!"[3] But the enigma of Hebrews goes beyond the question of who wrote it; when and where it was written, and to whom, are also issues of lively debate.

It is natural to wish to answer such questions as clearly as possible, but it is even more vital not to permit them to obscure the essential clarity of Hebrews' contribution. B. F. Westcott, perhaps the greatest commentator in English on Hebrews, provides the key to why the epistle was accepted as canonical, doubts regarding its authorship aside: "no Book of the Bible is more completely recognized by universal consent as giving a divine view of the facts of the Gospel, full of lessons for all time, than the Epistle to the Hebrews."[4] "A divine view of the facts of the Gospel" is just what Hebrews purports to deliver, and by understanding its purpose and achievement, the epistle comes into a clear focus.

The epistle has been compared to a homily,[5] and calls itself a "word of exhortation" in 13:22. "Word" here (*logos*, as in John's Gospel) bears the meaning of "discourse," and the choice of diction declares Hebrews' homiletic intent. It is a sustained argument on the basis of authoritative tradition that intends to convince its readers and hearers to embrace a fresh position and an invigorated sense of purpose in the world. Hebrews engages in a series of scriptural identifications of Jesus: both Scripture (in the form of the Septuagint) and God's son are the authoritative point of departure.

Scripture is held to show that the son, and the son's announcement of salvation, are superior to the angels and their message (1:1–2:18, see especially 2:1–4). Jesus is also held to be superior to Moses and Joshua, who did not truly bring those who left Egypt into the rest promised by God (3:1–4:13). Having set up a general assertion of the son's superiority on the basis of Scripture, the author proceeds to his main theme (4:14):

> Having, then, a great high priest who has passed into the heavens, Jesus the son of God, let us hold the confession fast.

That statement is the key to the central argument of Hebrews and therefore to an understanding of the epistle.

Two terms of reference in the statement are used freshly and – on first acquaintance with the epistle – somewhat unexpectedly. Jesus, whom we have known as son, is now "great high priest." The term "high priest" is in fact used earlier, to speak of his having expiated sin (2:17), and in that role Jesus is also called the "apostle and high priest of our confession" (3:1). But now, in 4:14, Jesus is the "great high priest," whose position is heavenly. Now, too, the single confession of his heavenly location is the only means to obtain divine mercy.

Jesus' suffering is invoked again in 4:15 in order to make the link to what was said earlier, of Jesus' expiation. But then 4:16 spells out the ethical point of the entire epistle:

> Let us then draw near with assurance to the throne of grace, so that we might receive mercy and find grace in time of need.

With bold calculation, Jesus is presented as the unique means of access to God in the only sanctuary that matters, the divine throne in heaven. The portrayal of Jesus as great high priest, exalted in heaven, proves to be the center of the epistle (Heb. 4–7). At first, the argument may seem abstruse, turning as it does on Melchizedek, a relatively obscure figure in Gen. 14. In Genesis, Abram is met by Melchizedek after his defeat of the king of Elam. Melchizedek is identified as king of Salem, as priest of God Most High (Gen. 14:18). He brings bread and wine and blesses Abram; in return, Abram gives Melchizedek one tenth of what he has in hand after the victory (Gen. 14:18–20).

The author of Hebrews hammers out a principle and a corollary from this narrative. First, "It is beyond all dispute that the lesser is blessed by the greater" (Heb. 7:7). From that straightforward assertion, the superiority of Melchizedek to Levitical priests is deduced. Levi, the founding father of the priesthood, was still in Abram's loins at the time Abram paid his tithe to Melchizedek. In that sense, the Levitical priests who were to receive tithes were themselves tithed by the greater priest (Heb. 7:8–10).

The importance of Melchizedek to the author of Hebrews, of course, is that he resembles Jesus, the son of God. His very name means "king of righteousness," and he is also "king of peace," Salem. He does not bear a genealogy, and his birth and death are not recorded (Heb. 7:2b–4). In all these details, he adumbrates Jesus, true king of righteousness and peace, from a descent which is not priestly in a Levitical sense, of whom David prophesied in the Psalms, "You are a priest for ever, after the order of Melchizedek" (Heb. 7:11–25, citing Ps. 110:4 on several occasions; cf., 7:11, 15, 17, 21). Jesus is the guarantor by God's own promise of a better, everlasting covenant (Heb. 7:22). His surety is linked to Melchizedek's as clearly as the bread and wine that both of them use as the seal of God's promise and blessing.

The superiority of the better covenant is spelled out in what follows in Hebrews through chapter 9, again relying on the attachment to Jesus of God's promise in Ps. 110 (Heb. 7:28):

> For the law appoints men having weakness as high priests, but the word of the oath which is after the law appoints a son for ever perfected.

Perfection implies that daily offerings are beside the point. The son was perfect "once for all, when he offered himself up" (7:26–27). The author leaves nothing to implication: Moses' prescriptions for the sanctuary were a pale imitation of the heavenly sanctuary that Jesus has actually entered (8:1–6). Accordingly, the covenant mediated by Jesus is "better," the "second" replacing the "first," the "new" replacing what is now "obsolete" (8:6–13).

Chapter nine simply puts the cap on an already clear argument. It begins with the "first" covenant's regulations for sacrifice, involving the Temple in Jerusalem. Specific mention is made of the menorah, the table and presented bread in the holy place, with the holy of holies empty, but for the gold censer and the ark. The reference to the censer as being in the holy of holies fixes the point in time of which the author speaks: it can only be the Day of Atonement, when the high priest made his annual visit to that sanctum, censer in hand.

That precise moment is only specified in order to be fixed, frozen forever. For Hebrews, what was a fleeting movement in the case of the high priest was an eternal truth in the case of Jesus. The movement of ordinary priests, in and out of the holy place, the "first tabernacle" (9:6), while the high priest could only enter "the second tabernacle," the holy of holies (9:7), once a year, was designed by the spirit of God as a parable: the way into the holy of holies could not be revealed while the First Temple, the first tabernacle and its service, continued (9:8–10). That way could only be opened, after the Temple was destroyed, by Christ, who became high priest and passed through "the greater and more perfect tabernacle" of his body (9:11) by the power of his own blood (9:12) so that he could find eternal redemption in the sanctuary.

In the conception of Hebrews, the Temple on earth was a copy and shadow of the heavenly sanctuary, of which Moses had seen "types." A type (*tupos* in Greek) is an impress, a derived version of a reality (the anti-type). Moses had seen the very throne of God, which was then approximated on earth. That approximation is called the "first covenant" (9:1), but the heavenly sanctuary, into which Christ has entered (9:24), offers us a "new covenant" (9:15) that is the truth that has been palely reflected all along.

Jesus alone offers perfection, as "the pioneer and perfecter of our faith" (12:1–3). Divine vision, the sanctification to stand before God, is in Hebrews the goal of human life, and the only means to that is loyalty to Jesus as the great high priest. The sense of finality, of an ideal from which one must not defect, is deliberately emphasized (12:22–24):

> But you have come to Mount Zion and the city of the living God, the heavenly Jerusalem, and to myriads of angels in festal gathering, and to the assembly of first-born enrolled in heaven, and to a judge – God of all, and to the spirits of the just who are made perfect, and to Jesus the mediator of a new covenant, and to sprinkled blood which speaks better than the blood of Abel.

Jesus, the only mediator of perfection, provides access to that heavenly place that is the city of the faithful, the heart's only sanctuary.

The themes of Hebrews were to become the themes of catholic Christianity. The son of God would be understood as inherently and obviously superior to the angels, to Moses and Joshua, as the great high priest who alone provides access to the only sanctuary which matters. Framing a single confession of his heavenly location in relation to the divine throne was to require literally centuries of discussion within the Church, but the necessity of such a confession was axiomatic. Moses' prescriptions are shadows, imitations of the heavenly sanctuary which Jesus has actually entered. The Temple in Jerusalem has in Hebrews been replaced by a conception of the divine throne in heaven and the faithful congregation on earth, and Jesus' perfect sacrifice is the unique and perfect link between the two.

The author of Hebrews understands Israel as a thing of the past, the husk of the first, now antiquated, covenant. He says the word "Israel" just three times.

Twice in chapter 8, he refers to Israel, but simply as part of his quotation of Jer. 31:31–34, where to his mind a completely new covenant is promised (Heb. 8:8, 10). The point of that citation, as elaborated by the author, is that the new covenant makes the former covenant obsolete (8:13). Accordingly, when the author speaks of Israel in his own voice, it is simply to refer to "the sons of Israel" in the past, at the time of the Exodus from Egypt (11:22). Melchizedek is a positive, theological category. Israel is no longer, and remains only as a cautionary tale from history.

The ability of the author of Hebrews to relegate Israel to history is related to the insistence, from the outset of the Epistle, that the son's authority is greater than that of the Scripture. Once, God spoke in many and various ways through the prophets; now, at the end of days, he speaks to us by a son (Heb. 1:1, 2). The comparative judgment is reinforced, when the author observes that, if the word delivered by angels (that is, the Torah) carried with it retribution for transgression, we should attend much more to what we have heard concerning the son (Heb. 2:1–4). The implication of both statements is clear: Scripture is only authoritative to the extent that it attests the salvation mediated by the son (1:14, 2:3–4). The typology framed later in the epistle between Jesus and the Temple derives directly from the conviction of the prior authority of the son of God in relation to Scripture.

The dual revaluation, of Israel and Israel's Scripture, is what permits Hebrews to trace its theology of Christ's replacement of every major institution, every principal term of reference, within the Judaisms of its time. Before Hebrews, there were Christian Judaisms, in which Christ was in various ways conceived of as the key to the promises to Israel. There is a single center within the theology of Hebrews. It is not Christ with Moses, Christ with Temple, Christ with David, Christ with Abraham, Christ with Scripture, Christ with Israel. In the end, the center is not really even Christ with Melchizedek, because Melchizedek disappears in the glory of his heavenly archetype. Hebrews' theology proceeds from those earlier theologies, and it remains a Christian Judaism, in the sense that all of its vocabulary of salvation is drawn from the same Scriptures that were axiomatic within the earlier circles.[6] But the Christian Judaism of Hebrews is also and self-consciously a system of autonomous Christianity, because all that is Judaic is held to have been provisional upon the coming of the son, after which point it is no longer meaningful. Christ is the beginning, middle, and end of theology in Hebrews, just as he is the same yesterday, today, and forever (Heb. 13:8). Everything else is provisional – and expendable – within the consuming fire that is God (12:29).

Justin and Aphrahat

Justin Martyr was the theologian who articulated the doctrine of Jesus Christ as the *logos* of God most clearly from the perspective of Christianity, on the basis of the Gospel according to John. In 151 CE he addressed his *Apology* to the emperor himself, Antonius Pius. Such was his confidence that the "true philosophy" represented by Christ, attested in the Hebrew Scriptures, would triumph among the other options available at the time. Justin himself had been trained within some of those traditions, and by his Samaritan birth he could claim to represent something of the wisdom of the East. Somewhere between 162 and 168, however, Justin was martyred in Rome, a victim of the increasing hostility to Christianity under the reign of Marcus Aurelius.

Justin argued that the light of reason in people is put there by God and is to be equated with the Word of God incarnate in Jesus. His belief in the salvation of people as they actually are is attested by his attachment to millenarianism, the conviction that Christ would return to reign with his saints for a thousand years. That conviction, derived from Revelation 20, was fervently maintained by catholic Christians during the second century, in opposition to the abstract view of salvation that Gnosticism preferred.

In strictly religious terms, Christianity did not compete well within the second century. Greco-Roman preferences were for ancient faiths, and the movement centered on Jesus was incontrovertibly recent. Moreover, it could and often did appear to be subversive of the authority of the emperor. After all, Christians did not accept the imperial title of *divi filius* and actually applied it to their criminal rabbi. And he was a rabbi who was not a rabbi, because the recognized authorities of Judaism did not accept Christians as among their numbers. For such reasons, the persecution of Christianity had been an established policy of state for nearly a century by the time Justin wrote.

The Christianity Justin defended, however, was as much a philosophy as it was a religion. His claim was that the light of reason in humanity, which had already been indirectly available, became fully manifest in the case of Jesus Christ. Jesus, therefore, was the perfect sage, and Socrates as much as Isaiah was his prophet. In that sense, Christianity was as old as humanity; only its open manifestation was recent.

In order to make out his case, Justin used arguments previously employed by Philo of Alexandria, but on behalf of Judaism. Philo also identified the *logos*, the prophetic word articulated in Scripture, as the reason by which God created the world and animates humanity. (Unlike Justin, of course, Philo draws no conclusions about Jesus, his contemporary.) Philo even makes out the historical case that Moses was an influence on Plato (*De aeternitate mundi* 17–19), so that the extent to which Greek philosophy illuminates God's wisdom is quite derivative. Justin is actually bolder in his Platonism, in that his argument does not rely on such a historical argument but on the contention that in Jesus the primordial archetype of humanity and of the world itself, the *logos*, became accessible and knowable in a way it was not before.

A comparison between Philo and Justin shows the extent to which Judaism in the first century and Christianity in the second century relied upon the revival of Platonism to provide them with a way of expressing how their respective religions were philosophically the most appropriate. The Platonic picture of perfect intellectual models was their common axiom, invoked in Philo's rounded, elegant Greek and in Justin's controversial, rhetorical Greek. But the rabbis who reinvented Judaism during the second century did so, not on the basis of Platonism, but on grounds of a new intellectual contention. They held that the categories of purity established in their oral teaching as well as in Scripture were the very structures according to which God conducted the world. The Mishnah, the principal work of the rabbis, is less a book of law (for which it is commonly mistaken) than a science of the purity that God's humanity – that is, Israel – is to observe.

So complete was the Rabbinic commitment to systematic purity at the expense of Platonism that Philo's own work was not preserved within Judaism but only became known as a result of the work of Christian copyists. And the very philosophical idiom that the Rabbis turned from as a matter of survival, apologetic argument, was what Justin turned to, also as a matter of survival. Justin sets his *Dialogue with Trypho, A Jew* in the period after the revolt under Simon called bar Kokhba (*Dialogue*, chapter 1). Thematically, Justin disputes Trypho's conception of the permanent obligation of the law (chs. 1–47) and sees the purpose of scriptures in their witness to Christ's divinity (chs. 48–108), which justifies the acceptance of non-Jews within the Church (chs. 109–136). Trypho, that is, is portrayed as arguing that the systemic meaning of the Scriptures is the law, while Justin argues that their systemic meaning is Christ.

Justin describes his own development from Platonism to Christianity as a result of a conversation with an old man. The sage convinced him that the highest good Platonism can attain, the human soul, should not be confused with God himself, since the soul depends upon God for life (ch. 6). Knowledge of God depends rather upon the revelation of God's spirit (ch. 7). Here is a self-conscious Christianity, which distinguishes itself from Judaism and proclaims itself the true and only adequate philosophy. Justin's account of the truth of the *logos* depends – in a Pauline manner – upon two sources of revelation, each resonant with one another: the prophetic Scriptures that attest the Spirit and the wise reader who has been inspired by the Spirit.

In his *Dialogue*, Justin portrays Trypho as being limited to the immediate reference of Scripture, enslaved by its specification of laws. Justin is committed to a typological reading of Scripture, the Christian norm during the second century. The prophets were understood to represent "types" of Christ, impressions on their minds of the heavenly reality, God's own son. Trypho, by contrast, is portrayed as becoming lost in the immediate minutiae of the prophetic text. So prevalent was this understanding of Judaism, by the end of the century, that Christians such as Clement of Alexandria called any limitation to the immediate reference of Scripture (its "literal meaning") the "Jewish sense."

Aphrahat (ca. 300–ca. 350) represents the mounting intellectual confidence of Christianity in its claim to convey the underlying meaning of the Scriptures. Aphrahat's assurance is such that he does not support his perspective with recourse to a typological or philosophical argument. Rather, the correct arrangement of discrete texts, in their mutual relationships, is held to attest the truth of Christ. This reliance upon an exegetical, rather than a philosophical, demonstration of faith is characteristic of Syrian Christianity, in contrast to its Hellenistic counterpart. In form, this exegetical approach is the closest Christianity ever came to embracing the genre of argument used at Qumran, called *pesher*.[7] Syrian Christianity insisted that it understood Scripture within its own terms better than Rabbinic Judaism. That helps to explain why Aphrahat is so trenchant that he must write "a response to the Jews," because even their observation of the Torah causes them to act "unlawfully," that is, without reference to the stated meaning of Scripture as a whole.

Eusebius

The beginning of Christian history came with Eusebius (260–340), bishop of Caesarea. Through Pamphilus, his teacher and model, Eusebius had been deeply influenced by the thought of Origen. So before there was a consciously Christian history, there was an irony of history: from a basically non-historical perspective (Origen's Platonism) there was provided the first comprehensively historical account of the meaning of Christ. His prominence in the ecumenical Church at various councils from Nicea onward, as well as his friendship with Constantine, go a long way toward explaining why Eusebius should have made the contribution that makes him the Herodotus of ecclesiastical history.

As he attempted to express the startling breakthrough under Constantine, Eusebius portrayed the new emperor as chosen by God himself. The most famous result of his meditation on the significance of the new order is his *History of the Church*, a vitally important document that takes up the Christian story from the time of Christ. The settlement under Constantine is his goal, however, and his portrayal of the emperor is perhaps most vividly conveyed in his *Praise of Constantine*. After speaking of Christ the word of God which holds dominion over the whole world, Eusebius goes on to make a comparison with Constantine (*Praise of Constantine* 1.6), "Our Emperor, beloved of God, bearing a kind of image of the supreme rule as it were in imitation of the greater, directs the course of all things upon earth." Here the old Stoic idea of the rule of the emperor as commensurate with the divine rule is provided with a new substance: the emperor who obeys Christ, himself imitates Christ's glory. Eusebius was inclined to describe himself as moderately capable, and that may be an accurate assessment of him as a theologian and historian. But as a political theorist, he is one of the most influential thinkers in the West. He provided the basis upon which the Roman Empire could be presented as the Holy Roman Empire, and the grounds for claiming the divine rights of rulers. At the same time, his reference to the conditional nature of those rights, as dependent upon the imitation of Christ, has provided a basis upon which political revolution may be encouraged on religious grounds.

Part of Eusebius' argument was that Constantine restored the united form of the Empire that had been the ideal of Augustus. After a preface that sets out

Christ's divine and human natures, Eusebius carefully places Christ's birth during Augustus' reign, after the subjugation of Egypt (*History of the Church* 1.5). The pairing of Augustus and Christ, Christ and Constantine is therefore symmetrical and defines the scope of the work. The result is to present a theologically structured political history.

The extent of that history is determined by its political horizon, much as in the case of Eusebius' predecessors in classical history. Whether we think of Herodotus in his explanation of the Persian War, or of Thucydides in the case of the Peloponnesian War, the impetus of writing history seems to be the experience of political change and dislocation. The scope of such work would be extended by such writers as Polybius (the apologist for Rome) and Josephus (the apologist for Judaism), but the desire to learn from the past in the effort to construct a more politically viable present is evident throughout.

Most readers of Eusebius feel uncomfortable at his apology for Constantine. Although the form is political history, the substance seems embarrassingly like flattery. How could Eusebius so thoroughly fail to be critical, whether as historian or as theologian? As an historian, he knew that kings and their flatterers were transient; as a theologian in the line of Origen, he knew that perfection eluded human flesh. The key to this riddle lies in Eusebius' conviction that Christ was at work in Constantine's conversion (*History of the Church* 10.1):

> From that time on, a day bright and radiant, with no cloud overshadowing it, shone down with shafts of heavenly light on the churches of Christ throughout the world, nor was there any reluctance to grant even those outside our community the enjoyment, if not of equal blessings, at least of an effluence from and a share in the things that God had bestowed on us.

The sharp change from persecution and all it involved was as disorienting for Eusebius as the Peloponnesian War had been to Thucydides, and an explanation was demanded. In that explanation, ecclesiastical history was born: that is, not simply the anecdotes of experience, but a rational account of God's activity within human events. The sequence of flesh met the conviction of consequence of flesh (which was as well established as belief in the Incarnation itself), and history was the offspring.

The intervention in the case of Constantine and his colleague Licinius (who at first reigned with Constantine) was nothing less than the appointed plan of God within a definite sequence of events. Eusebius reminds the reader of the terrible tortures Christians had experienced, and then proceeds (*History of the Church* 10.4):

> But once again the Angel of the great counsel, God's great Commander-in-Chief, after the thoroughgoing training of which the greatest soldiers in his kingdom gave proof by their patience and endurance in all trials, appeared suddenly and thereby swept all that was hostile and inimical into oblivion and nothingness, so that its very existence was forgotten. But all that was near and dear to Him He advanced beyond glory in the sight of all, not men only but the heavenly powers as well – sun, moon, and stars, and the entire heaven and earth.

Only the language of apocalypse, of the sequenced revelation of God himself in Christ, can explain to Eusebius' satisfaction how the former agony can so quickly have been transformed into festivity. In Constantine, the promised future had begun, and there was no room for a return to the past.

The picture Eusebius draws of the contemporary scene might have been drawn from an apocalyptic work in Hellenistic dress (10.9, after the narrative of the removal of Licinius):

> Men had now lost all fear of their former oppressors; day after day they kept dazzling festival; light was everywhere, and men who once dared not look up greeted each other with smiling faces and shining eyes. They danced and sang in city and country alike, giving honor first to God our Sovereign Lord, as they had been instructed, and then to the pious emperor with his sons, so dear to God.

History for Eusebius was not just an account of the past, it was an apocalypse in reverse. His account was designed to set out the sequence of events that brought about the dawn of a new age. Long before Eusebius, Origen had written that Rome would prosper better by worshiping the true God than even the children of Israel had (*Against Celsus* 8.69). For Origen, the argument was hypothetical; for Eusebius, it had become a reality. The new unity of the Empire, under God, in Christ, and through the piety of the emperor himself, constituted for Eusebius a divine polity (*politeia* or *politeuma*), literally a breath away from paradise.[8]

Augustine

If Christian history was born under the pressure of success, its baptism of fire was the experience of an unimaginable failure. In 410 CE, Alaric sacked the city of Rome itself. That event was a stunning blow to the Empire generally, but it was a double blow to Latin Christianity. First, the pillage occurred while the Empire was Christian; two centuries before, Tertullian had argued that idolatry brought about disaster (see *Apologeticus* 41.1), and now Christianity could be said to do so. Second, Latin Christianity – especially in North Africa – had been particularly attracted to a millenarian eschatology. How could one explain that the triumphant end of history, announced by Eusebius and his followers, seemed to be reversed by the Goths?

The explanation of that dilemma occupied Augustine in his *City of God*, a work of twenty-three books, written between 413 and 426. From the outset, he sounds his theme, that the City of God is an eternal city that exists in the midst of the cities of men; those two cities are both mixed and at odds in this world, but they are to be separated by the final judgment (*City of God* 1.1). That essentially simple thesis is sustained through an account of Roman religion and Hellenistic philosophy, including Augustine's critical appreciation of Plato (books 1–10).

In the central section of his work, Augustine sets out his case within a discussion of truly global history, from the story of the creation in Genesis. From the fall of the angels, which Augustine associates with the separation of light and darkness in Gen. 1:4, he speaks of the striving between good and evil. But the distinction between those two is involved with the will of certain angels, not with any intrinsic wickedness (*City of God* 11.33). People, too, are disordered in their desire, rather than in their creation by God (*City of God* 12.8).

The difference between the will God intends for his creatures and the will they actually evince attests the freedom involved in divine creation. But the effect of perverted will, whether angelic or human, is to establish two antithetical regimes (*City of God* 14.28):

> So two loves have constituted two cities – the earthly is formed by love of self even to contempt of God, the heavenly by love of God even to contempt of self. For the one glories in herself, the other in the Lord. The one seeks glory from man; for the other God, the witness of the conscience, is the greatest glory . . . In the one the lust for power prevails, both in her own rulers and in the nations she subdues; in the other all serve each other in charity, governors by taking thought for all and subjects by obeying.

By book 18, Augustine arrives at his own time and repeats that the two cities "alike enjoy temporal goods or suffer temporal ills, but differ in faith, in hope, in love, until they be separated by the final judgment and each receive its end, of which there is no end" (*City of God* 18.54).

That commits Augustine to speak of eschatological issues, which he does until the end of the work as a whole. It is in his discussion of eschatology that Augustine frames classic and orthodox responses to some of the most persistent questions of the Christian theology of his time. He adheres to the expectation of the resurrection of the flesh, not simply of the body (as had been the manner of Origen). In so doing, he refutes the Manichaean philosophy he accepted prior to his conversion to Christianity. In Manichaeanism, named after a Persian teacher of the third century named Mani, light and darkness are two eternal substances that struggle against one another, and they war over the creation they have both participated in making. As in the case of Gnosticism, on which it was dependent, Manichaeanism counseled a denial of the flesh. By his insistence on the resurrection of the flesh, Augustine revives the strong assertion of the extent of God's embrace of his own creation in the tradition of Irenaeus.

At the same time, Augustine sets a limit on the extent to which one might have recourse to Plato. Augustine had insisted with Plato against the Manichaeans that God was not a material substance, but transcendent. Similarly, evil became in his mind the denial of what proceeds from God (see *Confessions* 5.10.20). When it came to the creation of people, however, Augustine insisted against Platonic thought that no division between soul and flesh could be made (so *City of God* 22.12). Enfleshed humanity was the only genuine humanity, and God in Christ was engaged to raise those who were of the city of

God. Moreover, Augustine specifically refuted the contention of Porphyry (and Origen) that cycles of creation could be included within the entire scheme of salvation. For Augustine, the power of the resurrection within the world was already confirmed by the miracles wrought by Christ and his martyrs. He gives the example of the healings connected with the relics of St Stephen, recently transferred to Hippo (*City of God* 22.8).

Even now, in the power of the Catholic Church, God is represented on earth, and the present, Christian epoch (*Christiana tempora*) corresponds to the millennium promised in Rev. 20 (*City of God* 20.9). This age of dawning power, released in flesh by Jesus and conveyed by the Church, simply awaits the full transition into the city of God, complete with flesh itself. In his adherence to a kind of millenarianism and to the resurrection of the flesh in the Latin creed, Augustine is very much a product of North Africa and Italy, where he was active (chiefly as a teacher of rhetoric) prior to his conversion and his return to North Africa. But his *City of God* creates the greater frame, primordial and eschatological, within which history becomes a theological discipline. Here, he argues, is more than a lesson in how to avoid war and create order. And here there is certainly more than the superficial enthusiasm which comes of histories written by the winners. Rather, history for Augustine – and from Augustine – is the interplay of those two forces which determine the existence of every society, every person.

Augustine died in Hippo while the city was under siege by the Vandals. His passing, and the passing of his church and his city, was a curious witness to his *Christiana tempora*. But his conception that his history and every history reflected the struggle between the two cities prepared him and the global Church for that, and for much worse. He had turned back to the Eusebian model of history as apocalypse, and he took it even more seriously than Eusebius himself had. No apocalyptic seer ever promised an easy transition to the consuming reign of Christ, and on to that moment when God would be all in all (so 1 Cor. 15:28, which Augustine quotes). Smooth, unhampered progress is a model of history which only recommends itself to those in the line of Eusebius and (paradoxically) historians since the nineteenth century. If history is apocalyptic, because the times of the Church are millennial, then our flesh has indeed been blessed, but our history is equally dedicated to struggle.

The struggle, however, is not ultimately between good and evil, but between the love of God and the love of self. That is the key to Augustine's ceaseless, pastoral ministry, as well as to his remarkably broad intellectual horizon. In every time and in every place, there is the possibility that the city of God will be revealed and embraced; now, in the *Christiana tempora*, we at last know its name and can see the face of that love which would transform us all.

History after Augustine could be painted on canvasses of indeterminate size, because he established the quest to integrate the historical task with philosophical reflection. At the same time, in his *Confessions*, he established the genre of autobiography as an investigation of the dynamics of universal salvation within the life of the individual he knew best, himself. Written large in nations and written small in persons, history attested the outward-working and inward-working power of God, if only one's eyes could see with the love of God, and be freed of the blindness of self-love.

Conclusion

Jesus' movement, rooted firmly and without afterthought within early Judaism, emerged as an anticipation of the kingdom of God. But Christianity had developed by the second century to the extent that it was widely recognized as a different religion. A comparison of the stances of Jesus himself and of Justin makes that contrast apparent. Between those two, the sources of earliest Christianity attest a growing tension with Judaism as usually understood, and then an attempt to construct "Israel" as a definition of the people of God without regard to Jewish ancestry (see "Q" and "Paul"). The Epistle to the Hebrews marks the self-consciousness of early Christianity as a religion that supersedes Judaism, so that by the end of the second century, Clement of Alexandria could refer to the "Jewish sense" of Scripture as an inadequate reading. Once the fundamental category of salvation, "Israel" was now only a provisional indication of how God would relate to his people. That implication of Christianity's perspective was most clearly set out by Aphrahat in Persia. But it was under the particular conditions introduced by Constantine within the Roman Empire that Christianity invented global history as an account of universal soteriology. Eusebius and Augustine are the most notable contributors to that achievement.

Notes

1   For a fuller discussion, see Bruce Chilton, *Pure Kingdom. Jesus' Vision of God: Studying the Historical Jesus 1* (Grand Rapids and London, 1996).
2   David Catchpole, *The Quest for Q* (Edinburgh, 1993), pp. 77, 248.
3   Quoted in Eusebius' *History of the Church* 6.25.
4   B. F. Westcott, *The Epistle to the Hebrews* (London, 1909 [first published in 1889]), p. lxxi.
5   See William L. Lane, *Hebrews* (Dallas, 1991), pp. lxix–lxxxiv.
6   See Bruce Chilton and Jacob Neusner, *Judaism in the New Testament. Practices and Beliefs* (London and New York, 1995).
7   See Bruce Chilton, "Commenting on the Old Testament (with particular reference to the *pesharim*, Philo, and the Mekhilta)," in D. A. Carson and H. G. M. Williamson, eds., *It is Written: Scripture Citing Scripture, Essays in Honour of Barnabas Lindars* (Cambridge, 1988), pp. 122–40.
8   For the antecedents of Eusebius' thought in Irenaeus and Origen, see Bruce Chilton and Jacob Neusner, *Trading Places. The Intersecting Histories of Judaism and Christianity* (Cleveland, 1996), pp. 191–203.

Bibliography

Catchpole, David, *The Quest for Q* (Edinburgh, 1993).

Chilton, Bruce, "Commenting on the Old Testament (with particular reference to the *pesharim*, Philo, and the Mekhilta)," in D. A. Carson and H. G. M. Williamson, eds., *It is Written: Scripture Citing Scripture, Essays in Honour of Barnabas Lindars* (Cambridge, 1988), pp. 122–40.

Chilton, Bruce, and Jacob Neusner, *Judaism in the New Testament. Practices and Beliefs* (London and New York, 1995).

Chilton, Bruce, and Jacob Neusner, *Trading Places. The Intersecting Histories of Judaism and Christianity* (Cleveland, 1996).

Chilton, Bruce, *Pure Kingdom. Jesus' Vision of God: Studying the Historical Jesus 1* (Grand Rapids and London, 1996).

Lane, William L., *Hebrews* (Dallas, 1991).

CHAPTER 8
Judaism in the Muslim World

Sara Reguer

As the Muslim armies marched out of Arabia to conquer the Middle East and cross into Spain and Sicily, they introduced not only a new religion and political regime but, eventually, a new intellectual regime as well. The Jews, always sensitive to intellectual challenges, found that their own attitudes to Judaism were influenced by the Muslims' attitudes to Islam. This manifested itself in a variety of ways, even as, at the same time, they remained specifically Jewish.

Since the Islamic Empire was conceived to be a religious community, there was officially no place in it for non-believers. However, by special arrangement, those peoples who possessed a holy scripture were given, in return for a head tax (Jizya), the rights of domicile, personal safety, and the opportunity to earn a living. Their religious activities and institutions were their own concern, and, as long as they paid their taxes, the Muslim government left them alone to organize and control their internal affairs. This internal autonomy enabled the Jewish communities under Islam to continue a Jewish way of life and to cultivate Jewish learning and patterns of behavior that remained rooted in the Talmud.

The great Islamic imperial centers were 'Umayyad Spain, Abbasid Baghdad, and Fatimid Egypt, and the period of creativity stretched from the eighth to the thirteenth century. Then, as Muslim unity broke down, Jewish communities shrank. This was reversed in part with the arrival of Sephardic refugees and the expansion of Ottoman Turkish power, but only for a few centuries.

The Muslim conquerors recognized the older forms of Jewish leadership, especially the institution of the exilarch in Iraq, who shared his power with the heads of the two main seats of intellectual power, the academies of Sura and Pumbeditha, which had moved to Baghdad during the early Abbasid caliphate. Local communities ruled themselves, but major legal questions were directed to the geonim (heads of the academies), and their answers formed the basis for uniformity among the Jews. Questions were posed on legal matters, on interpretation of Talmudic passages, on theological issues, on current affairs, on historical problems, and on proper behavior. The extensive correspondence that was created as a result – referred to as the responsa literature – served as a means of instruction. A student who did not understand the meaning of an Aramaic phrase, did not follow the drift of a discussion, could not adduce the law, or questioned the implications of a view would inquire of the Gaon or refer to existing documents. Thus men of distant lands continued their education and in turn became teachers. The responsa were supplemented by the instruction acquired by the best students, who traveled from all over to study in the academies in Baghdad and then returned to their homes, which, eventually, became new centers of Jewish culture. The responsa existed alongside the traditional Talmudic literature, studied by students who came from all over the Muslim world to form one cultural Jewish world.

The Arabs brought with them a great respect and love of the Arabic language of the Qur'an. Their belief that Arabic was God's perfect language spurred Jews to study Hebrew to show that it was equally rich. Developments in Hebrew grammar paralleled the study of Arabic grammar, and this stress on language both opened a new path in the study of the Bible and instigated the birth of medieval Hebrew poetry. In an environment of Islam's sanctification of the Qur'an, from which all of its articles of faith and theology were derived, the Jews felt impelled to do the same with the Bible, to show that it was God's sole word and that its teachings were all-inclusive. Thus the Torah in particular became the focus of unprecedented attention. An outstanding example of a biblical commentator was the Spanish scholar Abraham ibn Ezra (1089–1164). Poet, grammarian, biblical commentator, philosopher, astronomer, and physician, he wandered from Spain through Italy, Provence, and northern France, spreading the Islamic approach to scholarship to other parts of Europe by translating works from Arabic into Hebrew. His introduction to his commentary on the Torah dismissed the four usual types of commentaries, arguing instead in favor of a focus on the literal meaning of the text, to be revealed using grammatical and etymological explanations. The result, which draws on ibn Ezra's personal experiences and insight into human nature, as well as on his metaphysical views, is encyclopedic, terse, and critical.

An even more powerful influence in the direct study of the Bible was the rise of the Karaite sect. On the fringes of Rabbinic Judaism arose a series of shadowy messianic figures who were quickly suppressed. More serious was the eighth-century challenge posed at the very center of Jewish life, Baghdad, by the man who had not been chosen to be exilarch, Anan ben David. His political rebellion had religious overtones, similar to the history of Shi'i Islam as it was started by Ali, son-in-law of the prophet Muhammad, who was not immediately chosen as his successor. Anan ben David labeled the Oral Law as man-made and claimed that Jews should seek legal guidance only from the text of the Bible. This movement, originally known as Ananism, raised serious questions about the Rabbinic rulings of the Talmud and the geonic responsa. Designed to uphold the Bible as the sole source of the law, in practice it contributed to the disintegration of the new movement, because every one had his own opinion as to what the text meant.

By the ninth century, the Karaite movement was a conglomeration of various anti-Rabbanite heresies. Consolidation then occurred under Benjamin ben Moses Nahawendi (ca. 830–860) who, influenced by Islamic and Rabbanite writing, provided a clear dogma and philosophy. In principle, the Bible is the sole source of Karaite creed and law. All religious precepts must derive directly from the Bible, based on the literal meaning of the text and the customary use of the words and context. Principles were established as norms for the determination of the law, for example, consensus of the community. Aside from the stand on Oral Law, Karaite creed does not differ in its essentials from that of Rabbanite Judaism, but it has no fixed number of commandments. The calendar, laws of marriage, precepts on ritual purity, circumcision, and dietary laws are severely interpreted. When Karaism began to spread rapidly to the masses, the geonim turned their own methodology against the Karaites. Led by Saadya Gaon, the counter-attack utilized the newest Rabbinic studies of the Bible and Hebrew language. At the end of the eleventh century, the Karaites, who, as part of their call for a return to Zion, had moved out of Iraq, were forced to leave the world of Islam for Byzantium.

In Spain in particular, wealthy Jews imitated the courts of Islamic civilization, where they became patrons of the arts. The most outstanding example of this is Hisdai ibn Shaprut (ca. 915–ca. 970), who entered the service of the 'Umayyad caliph 'Abd al-Rahman III (912–61) in Cordoba as a physician. He was appointed director of the customs department, a very important administrative and political position in the court. His diplomatic and scholarly skills led to his rise in influence in the caliphal court, and he was appointed leader of the Jews in Muslim Spain. Imitating the caliph, Hisdai supported Jewish scholars and intellectuals, such as Menahem ben Saruq, who was his long-time Hebrew secretary, until the poet Dunash ibn Labrat surpassed him. It was Hisdai who, in attempting to make Cordoba the true center of Jewish creativity instead of Baghdad, appointed the Italian refugee Moses ben Hanokh to the rabbinical seat there. This led to loosening the ties of Spanish Jews and Babylonia, with the former becoming as independent as the Spanish 'Umayyad caliphate was from the Abbasid court in Baghdad.

The "Golden Age" of Spanish Hebrew poetry, between the tenth and twelfth centuries, produced not just a poetry of frivolity and materialism – praise of a person, friendship, joyous occasions, sorrow, love, pleasures of wine, reflections on the world – but the poetry of profound religious feeling. Some of these poems would be included in Jewish liturgy. Strict metrical forms were adopted, and an elaborate scheme of rhythmic patterns evolved. The Hebrew language itself underwent a marked change, for example, with new plurals for nouns created and new words coined. The religious themes include Israel's plight, hopes, sinfulness, and pleas for God's mercy. The personal note of the Spanish Jewish poets is very obvious. Their religious lyrics and hymns are a direct expression of their feelings toward God. Among the most famous poets were Moses ibn Ezra (ca. 1055–ca. 1135), Solomon ibn Gabirol (1021–1153), Samuel ibn Nagrela (993–1056), and Judah Halevi (ca. 1075–1141). One of the most prolific poets, Moses ibn Ezra, wrote with beauty and versatility in his secular and sacred verse. His secular poems celebrate the joys of life, but he was most powerful in his meditations on life and death. His *selihot* (penitential prayers) are the most important of his piyyutim – liturgical poems – in which he focuses on introspection, meditation, penance, and contrition.

Solomon ibn Gabirol started composing outstanding poems as a youth, showing linguistic virtuosity and great knowledge of Biblical Hebrew. Using images and idioms from Arabic poetry, he created an original style. His secular poetry was composed in honor of his patrons. His nature poetry was very much influenced by Islamic culture, but his so-called "wisdom" poetry was very Jewish. His ethical poems deal with the transience of life and the worthlessness of bodily existence, as opposed to the eternal values of spiritual life and the immortality of the soul. His religious poetry raised medieval Jewish poetry to its highest point. Numerous poems have been preserved in both Ashkenazic and Sephardic prayer books.

Samuel ibn Nagrela, who rose to become vizier of Granada, was a statesman, poet, scholar, and military commander. His political career marks the highest achievement of a Jew in medieval Muslim Spain. In 1027, the Jews conferred on him the title of *nagid*, designating him head of the community. As a result of his long years on the battlefield, Samuel introduced the themes of war and battle into Hebrew poetry. Indeed, his poems reflect his multifaceted career and personality, and he wrote on all topics popular at the time. Still, many of his works were specifically Jewish.

Judah Halevi, probably the best known of all the Jewish poets from the world of Islam, wrote love poems, poems of eulogy and lament, personal lyric religious poetry, piyyutim, and songs of Zion. In his piyyutim, he combined the style of his time with ancient Hebrew style. In his lyric religious poetry, he expressed reverence for God, dread of sin, fear of judgment, and love and devotion to God. In his songs of Zion, he expressed the tension between the Jewish dream and the reality of diasporic Spain, concluding that there was no secure place for a Jew except in the land of Israel.

Within one hundred years after the Muslim conquest, the majority of the Jews of the Islamic world had adopted Arabic as their native language. This gave them access to the evolving philosophical thinking of the Arabs, who were profoundly affected by the classics of antiquity, newly translated from Greek or Syriac into Arabic. At the time Greek thinking was at its height, Jews had avoided it as pagan, fearing its influence. But with the passage of time and its reappearance as part of the monotheistic world of Islam, Greek philosophy was seen as a challenge to both Islam and Judaism. Saadya Gaon and Moses Maimonides used Greek philosophy and the medieval discourse on it to present Judaism as a rational body of beliefs, in imitation of contemporary Islamic theologian-philosophers. Not only Greek thinking was translated into Arabic, but also Greek medicine, physics, astronomy, and mathematics. In addition, Persian belles-lettres were translated, as were Hindu mathematics and astronomy. The Arabs may have been military and political victors, but they never regarded the civilization of those they conquered with contempt.

In imitation of the Islamic theologians, too, Jewish thinkers as well as some of the geonim of Baghdad began to codify and systematize Jewish law and special subjects within it. The goal was to state the law explicitly and make it more accessible. Logical organization and scientific exposition of Jewish law would also increase its intrinsic merit. The Aramaic and Hebrew *Sheiltot* of Rabbi Ahai, the *Halakhot Pesukot* of Rabbi Yehudai, and the *Halakhot Gedolot* of Simeon Kayyara, all composed in the eighth/ninth centuries, are examples of this. In the tenth century, a change took place, with the writers attaching introductions to their writings, including things like the purpose of the work, the principles governing the subject, and the distinction between general and specific rules. This is seen in the works of Saadya Gaon, Samuel ben Hofni, and Hai Gaon. Some, such as Maimonides, wrote philosophical introductions to their codes, or to Talmudic tractates, thus introducing a new stratum to Rabbinic writing. But not only the vocabulary of Islam finds its way into Jewish books; also the Arab practice of citing poetry, science, and philosophy became the general intellectual background of Judaism.

Considered the greatest scholar and author of the geonic period, Saadya Gaon was a leading protagonist in favor of Babylonian leadership over that of the Jerusalem academy. Arriving in Baghdad from Egypt in 922, he was appointed to the yeshiva of Pumbeditha, and, in 928, he became the head of the Sura academy. For years he was involved in major controversies, most of which were reconciled only at the end of his life. Saadya was a halakhist, philosopher, grammarian, translator, and liturgist. He was one of the creators of Rabbinic literature, the first to write "books" in the modern sense, with his monographic form assigning a separate book to each topic. He also set a standard pattern for these books, thus introducing systematic structure and logical order with lengthy, detailed introductions. He was the first to write halakhic works in Arabic.

Samuel ben Hofni (d. 1013), Gaon of Sura, was one of the most prolific writers of the period, following the pattern of Saadya, covering halakhah, biblical exegesis, philosophy, theology, and polemical writings. He wrote an introduction to the Talmud and a commentary to the Bible rooted mainly in talmudic-midrashic tradition and not grammar.

Hai ben Sherira (939–1038), Gaon of Pumbeditha for forty years, was a major molder of halakhah. In his writings he set out in detail his approach to the principles of faith and to the requirements of community leadership, drawing special attention to the duty of the *dayyanim* – judges – to guide the people and be responsible for their conduct. A man of his time, he, too, wrote poems, most of which are prayers, *selihot*, and piyyutim.

The most outstanding example of this period is Moses ben Maimon – Maimonides (1135–1204) – who imposed the stringent requirements of logic and the perfection of form on his halakhic writings. He made major contributions in the field of Jewish law as well as philosophy. First is his commentary on the Mishnah, for he regarded the Mishnah as the basic law code and the Gemara as commentary. In the long introduction, he summarizes the principle of revelation and tradition, determines how to judge acceptable and unacceptable prophets, describes the growth of oral law, discusses aggadic material, and explains the method of his work. He adds introductions to the other volumes of the Mishnah and to some smaller works as well, for example, dealing with human psychology in the preface to Abot. He also lists the thirteen essential beliefs, in a chapter in tractate Sanhedrin.

The second major contribution of Maimonides to the field of Jewish law is his fourteen-volume code, called Mishneh Torah, commonly known as Yad HaHazaqah – "The Mighty Hand," in which the numerical value of the word "hand" is fourteen. He lists the six hundred and thirteen commandments, grouping them into five logical categories, each based on a degree of obligation. The commandments are broken down into fourteen types, forming the fourteen books. He expected this work, together with study of the Torah, to provide a Jew with an adequate knowledge of the law. He wrote this work in Hebrew for he expected it to be one of the basic works on Judaism, which could only be written in the language of all Jews. It was his masterpiece.

Maimonides' third major contribution is in the field of philosophy. To introduce his philosophical work, we first examine briefly the contributions of the other outstanding Jewish philosophers, Saadya Gaon, who was a member of the Mu'tazilites (Kalam; literally, speech, discussion) school, which was of Islamic origin, Solomon ibn Gabirol, who was of the Neoplatonic school, and Judah Halevi.

As a philosopher, Saadya wrote in Arabic. His major work, known by the Hebrew title *Sefer ha-Emunot va-ha-De'ot*, generally translated as *The Book of Beliefs and Opinions*, placed Saadya in the school of the Mu'tazilites, but he was also influenced by Aristotle, Plato, and the Stoics. He wrote this partially as a polemical work, to give Jews spiritual guidance at a time of sectarianism and religious disputes. He attempted to reconcile the Bible with philosophy and reason with revelation.

Solomon ibn Gabirol's philosophic work, *Meqor Hayyim*, *The Source of Life*, was written in Arabic too, but is known better in the Latin translation, *Fons Vitae*. It is a dialogue between master and pupil (a popular Arab style), in which the master expounds his views on principles of matter and form. His philosophy is close to Neoplatonism, which was popular in medieval thought, but it has very Jewish overtones as well as Islamic Ismaili teachings. It expounds a complete philosophical–religious system lacking in Jewish content and terminology. Ibn Gabirol does not mention biblical persons or events and does not quote from the Bible, Talmud, or Midrash.

Judah Halevi's philosophy, contained in a single volume, is entitled *The Book of Argument and Proof in Defense of the Despised Faith*. Judah ibn Tibbon translated it from the original Arabic into Hebrew, yielding the better known Hebrew name, *Sefer Ha-Kuzari*. It is written against Aristotelianism as well as against Christianity and Islam. It is not a systematic treatise but an apologia structured around the literary framework of a discussion of the three monotheistic religions with the king of the Khazars, who wanted to convert to monotheism. Halevi thus compared these three religions, as well as Karaism and Aristotelianism, and proved the superiority of Judaism over all. He also explains Jewish suffering in exile, as evidence not of the inferiority of Judaism but of its superiority, for persecution allowed Jews publicly to sanctify the name of God. Halevi argued that Judaism's purpose will be understood at the time of deliverance, which will come when people perform the divine commandments by willingly submitting to divine authority. For reasons we shall see, this work thus became popular in the next phase of Jewish thinking, the popularization of Kabbalah.

Maimonides was an Aristotelian whose work "Guide for the Perplexed" answered the questions raised by the conflict between faith and reason. The huge success of the "Guide" shows how deep was the need among Jews to harmonize religion with the philosophical standards of reason, both assumed to be unimpeachable sources of truth. Still, there were Jews – including philosophers – who disagreed with this attempt at harmonizing faith and reason, feeling that faith was at a disadvantage. The Bible provided divine guidance and could not be compared with the mental processes of man. Judah Halevi wrote this way in his "Kuzari," for the ultimate objective was knowledge of God. Halevi's object was not to deny philosophy but to put it in its place. It was not reason but experience – the emotional experience a Jew derived from observing Judaism – that assured him that Judaism was the only true path.

Philosophy did not attract those interested in the contemplative rather than intellectual life. Bachya ibn Pakuda's ethical treatise, "The Duties of the Heart," describes an interest in the life of piety and meditation, in an inwardness of religious experience. He may or may not have been influenced by the Sufi trend in Islam, which emphasized the inner, contemplative side of religion.

Indeed, orthodoxy and traditionalism fought against Maimonides' philosophy, especially his views on immortality. From the thirteenth century on within Christianity, Islam and, notably, in the Jewish world there was a reaction against freedom of inquiry. Fatimid Egypt was committed to a defense of Islamic orthodoxy. At the same time, the Crusades and their offshoot, the Reconquista in Spain, led to an end of tolerance. The cultural climate thus was no longer propitious to rationalism. Pietism swept over the Muslim and Christian worlds.

Philosophy came to be replaced gradually by Kabbalah, a system of mystic, esoteric wisdom. All biblical texts, according to Kabbalah, have an inner sense that is their true meaning. In searching for answers to expulsion, suffering, and martyrdom, Jews turned more and more to Kabbalah, especially because – as the result of the teachings of Isaac Luria (1534–72) of Safed, a new Sephardic center, and his disciple Hayyim Vital – it was able to explain both exile and redemption.

Isaac Luria, known as HaAri or Rabbi Isaac Ashkenazi, engaged in traditional learning before embarking on his studies in mysticism and moving to Safed. He taught a circle of disciples, developing an original system of theoretical Kabbalah. While he wrote down little of his teaching, his chief disciple, Hayyim Vital, collected his works, as did other disciples. He became famous first because of his conduct and saintly qualities, then because of his teachings.

The structure of Lurianic mysticism is permeated with messianic tension and is implicit in his doctrine of *Tiqqun* (restitution or restoration of the inner and outer cosmos). The deeds of men are invested with mystical significance, geared toward rectifying the original blemish in the world, namely the existence of evil and impurity. It was not the role of the messiah to bring about redemption; rather, the task is imposed on the entire Jewish people, who will accomplish it through strict observance of the commandments and prayer. When this has taken place, the messiah's appearance is inevitable, for that is the consummation of the cosmic process. This gives an explanation for the existence of evil and impurity in the world. It also relates at every stage to the Jewish national and messianic mission. The teachings of Isaac Luria led to the popularization of Kabbalah, moving it out beyond the private teachings of earlier mysticism. It laid the groundwork for the explosion that took the form of the messianism of Shabbetai Zevi.

The sufferings of the Jews were many, but for the Iberian Jews, the focus was on the riots of 1391, which led to conversions or emigration, the Disputation at Tortosa (1413–14), which led to anti-Jewish decrees in Aragon, and the expulsion of the Jews from Spain and its colonies in 1492, followed by the expulsion from Portugal in 1497. The creation of a Converso sect added to the suffering and questioning. The paths of the expelled Sephardim led them to North Africa, Italy, the Lowlands, and the Ottoman Empire. After the initial difficulties of readjustment, the Sephardim, if they came in large enough numbers, imposed their form of Judaism and customs on the local communities. They also replanted the internal social divisions of Iberia, namely the small group of aristocrats, the larger group of the middle class, and the largest group of lower classes. The leaders and rabbis of the aristocracy imposed their views and guided the communities. But there was opposition to them, and this too was replanted in the Ottoman Empire.

The religious questions raised by the Iberian expulsions had never been answered. Add to this the suffering and religious questioning caused in the eastern Ashkenazic communities by the Chmielniczki-led Cossack pogroms of 1648–54 and the arrival of Ashkenazi refugees in the Ottoman Empire, and the groundwork was prepared for an explosion.

The Iberian exiles were tried and tested and full of messianic hope. So were the newly arrived Ashkenazim. The air was full of the newly popular mystical ideas of Isaac Luria, and large circles were convinced that the messianic age was at hand. Cosmic and human significance were given to the Exile, and the final redemption was believed to be imminent.

Shabbetai Zevi (1626–76) and his "prophet" Nathan of Gaza (1644–80) stepped into the historical limelight. Shabbetai Zevi became the center of the movement, but he would not have achieved it without the support and encouragement of Nathan of Gaza, who became his prophet and standard-bearer. In 1665, Shabbetai Zevi declared himself the messiah and swept the whole of Gaza with him. Nathan went with him to Jerusalem and to all proclaimed the need for mass repentance to facilitate the transition to redemption. Letters went out to wider circles of Jews calling for harsh penitence preparing for the End of Days. Shabbetai Zevi was an attractive man, whose charismatic personality drew the masses to his claim of being the messiah. He had periods of "illumination," during which he sang beautifully and fully believed in his messiah-hood; but these would be followed by periods of depression during which he behaved as an ascetic doing repentance. But it was the demands of Nathan for perfection and penance that awakened the ascetic zeal of the Jews. Nothing Shabbetai Zevi did could be wrong, even as he led a revolt against Jewish law.

Shabbetai Zevi traveled from Jerusalem to Aleppo, where many rabbis flocked to him, and then to Smyrna, his birthplace, where he performed "strange acts" and strongly impressed the Jewish community. Mass hysteria followed, trade and commerce stopped. The Turkish authorities received alarming reports, and when Shabbetai Zevi arrived in Istanbul in 1666, he was arrested. But his initial confinement added to the messianic fervor. In September 1666, the Turks finally gave him the choice of conversion or death. Agreeing to apostatize, Shabbetai Zevi took on the name Aziz Mehmed Effendi. This shocked the Jewish world to the core, but because of the depths of emotional commitment, it took a while before the movement dissipated. Official silence descended for years. The group that defended Shabbetai Zevi's apostasy rationalized his action, and this group either converted along with him or became heretical and sectarian Sabbateans. The Sabbatean movement brought the Jewish Middle Ages to a climactic crisis. The depression that set in among the Jews of the Ottoman Empire enabled the rabbis to regain control over their communities and impose conservative interpretations of Judaism on the masses.

The rabbis were aided by the availability of two codes, of which the first was written in the fourteenth century by Jacob ben Asher, and then, two hundred year later, the second was written by Joseph Caro. Jacob ben Asher's work, the *Sefer HaTurim*, omitted those laws that were in abeyance during the exile (e.g., Temple offerings) as well as any systematic presentation of a religious outlook or philosophy. It included both Sephardic and Ashkenazic views.

Joseph Caro (1488–1575), leading halakhist of Safed, composed his major work in the form of a commentary on *Sefer HaTurim* and called it *Bet Joseph*. It is encyclopedic in knowledge, thoroughly researched, and of superior critical insight. His aim, set out in his introduction, was to make order out of chaotic local customs by investigating each law and tracing it from the Talmud through each stage of its development, including divergent views, and arriving at a decisive ruling. He too confined himself to laws of practical application in his time. Yet his admiration for and dependence on Maimonides is clear, even though he did not base his commentary on the latter's code. In many situations where the legal ruling was unclear, he empirically accepted the majority opinion of Isaac Alfasi, Maimonides, and Asher ben Yechiel (father of Jacob ben Asher); yet he also made his own rulings stating that a contrary established custom was acceptable especially if more stringent.

In 1555, he wrote a summary of this commentary, called the *Shulhan Arukh* ("set table"). In succinct paragraphs, Caro stated a specific halakhah and its practical application. He followed the halakhic principle and customs of Sephardic sages. This brief digest was to serve as a memory refresher for the scholar and a book for young beginners.

The work of Joseph Caro became the practical guide to Jewish individual and communal life from the end of the sixteenth century onwards. The same thing happened in the Ashkenazic world with the commentary written by Moses Isserles on the *Shulhan Arukh*, giving Ashkenazic custom and interpretation; he called his work "Mappa," or tablecloth, to be placed on the Sephardic "set table."

Technical factors promoted the success of these works: the invention of the printing press enabled both works to be widely disseminated. The closer ties and increased communication within the diaspora also helped promote their popularity. The personal charisma and authority of Joseph Caro as well as the sanctity of Safed supplemented all this.

The depression of the Jews after the débâcle of the false messiah led to the decline of intellectual creativity on the part of the Jews within the world of Islam. By the late sixteenth century, the Ottoman Empire had already begun its prolonged process of decay. The era of vigorous sultans was over. New trade routes bypassed the Middle East, and the importation of cheap silver from the Americas led to a major economic decline. The border wars with European powers were lost, one after the other, and the Ottoman Empire thus shrank. With Ottoman Turkish stagnation came the stagnation of the Jews in the Islamic world. The poverty of the Jewish masses and the stranglehold of the conservative Rabbinic leadership continued into the modern age.

Modernization, starting in the nineteenth century, for most of the Jews of the Middle East, came from outside. The Damascus affair of 1840 with its blood libel brought Moses Montifiore of England and Adolphe Crémieux of France onto the scene, creating new ties between the Jewries. The desire on the part of western Jews, especially French Jews, to aid in the emancipation of the "Oriental" Jews led to the establishment of the Alliance Israélite Universelle, which, via modern education, would accomplish just that. Other groups were also active. However, the Jews of the world of Islam never went through the processes of enlightenment that led to Reform Judaism and disparagement of what came to be known as Orthodox Judaism. The central challenge, secularization, marginalized religion in social and individual life. Science seemed to enable the understanding of nature without the divine.

The Rabbinic class declined in part because talented sons now had the opportunity to get a western education and enter modern professions, an opportunity that had not been available to their father or grandfathers. This decline contributed to a decrease in cultural and literary output of halakhic works. Still, the rabbis responded to the challenges of modernity. Similar to their Muslim compatriots, the Jews did not attack rabbis as backward nor criticize halakhic Judaism as obscurantist, and movements that advocated abandonment of Rabbinic Judaism in favor of a new definition of Jewish identity did not develop in the Middle East. Islamic states continued to recognize personal status as the realm of the religious courts, and many rabbis in major cities came to be recognized as state functionaries.

In the absence of Jewish ideological attacks on Judaism or against Rabbinic authority, and in the context of increased political recognition of the status of office-bearing rabbis, the rabbis moved in the direction of reaching novel halakhic decisions in the face of the challenge of modernity. The Torah was eternal and its words had the capacity to yield multiple meanings appropriate even to modern times. This flexibility and dynamic attribute of halakhah leads to a positive regard for science and technology, support for integrating secular studies into a Jewish curriculum, and affirming some political values, like women's suffrage.

But the world of the Jews of Islam came to an end with the emergence of the State of Israel. Some Muslim countries expelled their Jews, other Jewish communities chose to self-destruct out of fear of the repercussions that would come with the attainment of political independence. Others, because of messianic yearnings, moved to Israel. The end of the twentieth century sees only small Jewish communities left in Morocco, Tunisia, Turkey, and Iran; most of the other Middle Eastern countries are empty of Jews, some after thousands of years of continuous history there. The future will tell what will happen to the Judaism of the Sephardic/Middle Eastern Jews as they find themselves outside the orbit of Islam in their new centers in Israel, the Americas, and Europe.

CHAPTER 9
Judaism in Christendom

David R. Carr

The relationship between Judaism and Christianity in the Middle Ages defies simple characterization. Christianity steadily advanced from being an obscure, Jewish sect to an "official religion" of the Roman Empire under Constantine to the overwhelmingly dominant religion of the medieval west. Judaism in the same period experienced uneven fortunes, alternately protected and persecuted by both secular and ecclesiastical authorities, welcomed and exiled, trusted and suspected. Yet, for all the divergence and difference, Christians and Jews had parallel experiences and ideals: martyrdom, mysticism, piety, ritualistic devotion, exegetical textual scholarship, philosophical inquiry, and a communal focus. A richly textured interplay – beneficial and detrimental – between these faiths and their followers shaped – for good and for evil – medieval culture.

Dispersion and Migration

Because the geographic locus of Jewish culture shifted repeatedly in the course of the Middle Ages, the core and periphery of that culture exhibited similar mobility. Beginning with the Assyrian diaspora (722 BCE), the dispersion of the Jews through both forced and voluntary migration continued through the Babylonian, Roman, and Muslim periods. By the last period, the center of Judaism had shifted from Palestine to Babylon. In the following centuries, westward migration increased, as did the relative cultural significance for Judaism of western Europe.

Fittingly, given their broad geographic distribution in the West, Jews used multiple languages. Hebrew continued as the language of religion, cultural creativity, and more. Continually influenced by local vernacular languages, Hebrew was frequently used in such mundane applications as loan agreements. Aramaic functioned as the common language of the Jews until their dispersal and certainly continued after that as a language of both religion and literature. Those who went West learned Latin and the local patois. Jews who remained within the Byzantine sphere continued to write and speak Greek. Those who came under Muslim control acquired Arabic. Jews spoke and wrote in, e.g., French and English as languages of commerce, but they also developed new, hybrid vernaculars: Judeo-Latin, Judeo-Greek, Judeo-Arabic, Judeo-Persian, Judeo-Italian, Judeo-French, Judeo-Provençal, Judeo-Spanish, and Judeo-German or Yiddish. While all of these were spoken, they were also employed in a wide variety of written works.

The Jewish presence in western Europe began in ancient times. As part of the Roman Empire, Jews had settled in Italy and the Mediterranean regions of Gaul and Iberia as imperial power waned and medieval culture emerged. Small settlements within Christian territories sprang up in Marseilles, Narbonne, Palermo, Apulia and Otranto. In these locales, the Jews held land and erected public buildings. By the late sixth century they had spread to Rome, Benevento, Gaeta, Ancona, Verona, and Lucca. At the same time, a Jewish community had been established at Lyons, and they had become evident in Rhineland areas at the end of the eighth century. While evidence for the period prior to the ninth century remains spotty, Jewish migrants from northern and central Italy, most notably from Lucca, settled in the Frankish territories on both sides of the Rhine.

The cultural core changed in concert with the migration of populations. Southern Italy flourished in the ninth and tenth centuries, Spain from the tenth to the twelfth, the Rhineland in the tenth and eleventh, Champagne and Paris in the twelfth, the Rhineland again in the first half of the thirteenth, and Rome in the late thirteenth and early fourteenth. Clearly persecution and exile account for some of the relocations, particularly the spread of Jewish communities into Germanic and Slavic territories in central and eastern Europe.

A variety of factors then contributed to the geographic mobility of the Jews in the early Middle Ages. In some instances, travel preserved familial connections. In the late sixth century, a certain Priscus returned from Francia to Spain for his son's wedding. In others, commerce dictated travel or relocation. In many others, however, volition disappeared. Forced conversions, such as those of Sicilian Jews under the Byzantines in 873 and 936, spurred migration to northern portions of Italy. Expulsions, such as that of 661 by the Lombard king Pertaric and that of 855 by the Carolingian Lothair who ruled Lombardy, dispersed Jewish populations both north and south. Lothair's father, Louis the Pious, and grandfather, Charlemagne, had actively encouraged Jews to migrate into their territories and welcomed Jewish scholars at the imperial court. Communities of Jews were established at Mainz, Worms, Regensburg, and Speyer from the mid-eighth to the late eleventh century. Moshe ben Kalonymos from Lucca, closely linked to the emergence of a distinct Ashkenazic culture, came into the Rhineland in the course of the tenth century. Now part of the Carolingian culture that linked the northern, Frankish territories with Italy, their commercial activities made them valuable to an economy otherwise dominated by the agrarian sector.

Jews did not appear in England prior to the Norman Conquest that brought them from northern France to the British Isles. Christian anti-Semitism – especially during the fervor of the crusades – and repeated instances of persecution and exile – whether prompted by piety, fear, or greed – account for much of the migratory movement: from North Africa to Muslim Spain, from Christian Spain to Muslim territories, from England to France, and from the Rhineland to central and eastern Europe. Some entertained and even realized notions of returning to Palestine.

Status and Occupation of Jews

While some evidence exists for Jews having been involved in agriculture in the early medieval West, clearly the greatest number of them functioned as long-distance merchants. Jews traded pagan slaves acquired at Verdun to Spanish Muslims. Gregory of Tours also portrays them – in unflattering terms – as physicians and creditors. In 638, the Sixth Toledo Council prohibited Christians from using Jewish physicians and from dining and bathing with Jews. Frankish monarchs, however, frequently attached Jewish physicians to their courts and used Jews as customs officials during the ninth century. Later, in the eleventh century, Gregory VII would complain to the king of Leon about Jewish customs officials. A handful of Jews rose to become familiars with the Merovingian and Carolingian kings. Priscus, despite refusing conversion, maintained a close relationship with Chilperic in the late sixth century and went about with a sword and armed retainers. (The weaponry did not prevent his assassination by a converted Jew.) Charlemagne's delegation to Harun al-Rashid in 801 had a Jew named Isaac among its number. Isaac purportedly returned from the caliph with an elephant to which the emperor became devoted.

More so than the Christian princes, Muslim rulers in Iberia rewarded well-educated Jews with substantial positions. Hisdai ibn Shaprut (ca. 915–ca. 970), a physician, served two caliphs at Cordoba as a diplomat, and was *nasi* (prince) of the Iberian Jews. His multiple functions enriched him and permitted him to become a patron of artists and scholars. The disintegration of the Cordoban caliphate did not impede talented Jews. Jewish courtiers such as Jekuthiel ibn Hasan (d. 1039) and Abraham ben Muhajir (d. ca. 1100) served the successor Muslim rulers. Samuel ha-Nagid (933–1055) served the Granadan ruler as its vizier, commanding the royal army, as well as being the *nasi*, a Talmudic scholar, a master poet, and a patron. He was succeeded as vizier by his son Jehoseph who was killed in the uprising of 1066, during which the Granadan Jewish community was destroyed. The political influence of the Jews slowly eroded from that moment.

But such exotic individuals aside, Jews in the medieval West might be artisans, such as the guild of armorers in Rome, viticulturalists, or even cartographers such as the Mallorcan Jewish Abraham Cresques (d. 1387) and his son Judah Cresques, who converted to Christianity. The great biblical scholar Samuel ben Meir (Rashbam, ca. 1080–1160) raised grapes and cattle. Other scholars earned their living as physicians. In the High Middle Ages, physicians were present in relatively small Jewish communities. Twelfth-century Norwich, for example, had two Jewish physicians, but they were outnumbered by the five rabbinical scholars there. Nonetheless, the great bulk of Jews in the medieval West spent their lives as merchants and moneylenders. The renewal of the charter of the Jews living at Speyer provides for merchants dealing in long-distance trade items used in cloth-dyeing and medicine. The Jews of both Sicily and Spain carried the same goods. The frequency of Jewish moneylenders in Christian communities stemmed from scriptural prohibitions of extracting interest – usury – from co-religionists.

Communities and Culture

Despite their commercial activities, the Jews appear to have become more insular. Jewish gravestones in Apulia employed both Latin and Hebrew in the seventh century but only Hebrew after that. Indeed, despite the travel of Jewish merchants, the connections between Levantine Jews and those of the West deteriorated, perhaps because of Muslim control, perhaps because of the necessity of creating local independence in the face of long and arduous travel and communication. Christian and Muslim pressures, whether spiritual, political, or economic, had broken the link between both Italian and Iberian Jews and those of Palestine by the ninth century. Despite the forced conversions or deaths of many of the Jews of southern Italy in the late eighth and early ninth century, the bulk of the Jewish population in Italy in the twelfth century resided in the south. Rome and Salerno held the largest communities, which came to exert a broader influence.

Strong Jewish communities existed in Iberia, particularly at Cordoba. The authority of the Babylonian geonim held sway in Iberia until the time of Hisdai ibn Shaprut, who realigned Cordoban Judaism with the Italian rabbinate. Hisdai brought Moses ben Hanokh from Italy to Spain where he became the *rav* (leading scholar) and the *rosh yeshiva* (master) of the Cordoban Talmudic academy (ca. 950). Moses was ably succeeded by his son, Hanokh ben Moses (d. 1014).

Religion and Its Practice

Medieval Judaism centered on the Torah (Pentateuch, Old Testament) and the law derived from this sacred scripture through *midrash* (exegesis). The Torah, believed to be written by God, contained law, but that demanded interpretation of meaning and application. By the beginning of the Middle Ages, two major centers of Jewish scholarship had developed, the Palestinian and the Babylonian. So too, two Talmuds. The Palestinian Talmud Yerushalmi had been completed by the mid-fourth century; the Babylonian Talmud Babli, which became most widely accepted, during the sixth century. In the course of the tenth century, Judaism in the East split into two major factions because of the differences between the rabbis of the Palestinian yeshiva at Tiberias and then at Jerusalem and the Babylonian geonim who headed the yeshivas at Sura, Pumbedita, and later at Baghdad. Palestinian authority had held sway throughout the Byzantine empire, while the Babylonian had applied to the Sassanid (or New Persian) empire. The split involved issues such as whose Talmud held authority, the calendar, if major holidays should be celebrated over one or two days, and whether the Torah should be read in annual or triennial cycles.

Technically, the Talmud, although recognized as an extra-scriptural source of law, functioned as philosophical discussion of the law rather than as a code. Hence, Rabbinic "legislation" continued from that point on throughout the medieval period. Codification of Jewish law became necessary as the rabbinical halakhic statements and responses (*teshuvot* or *responsa*) to queries (*she'elah* or *quaestiones*) multiplied. From the geonic period (sixth to eleventh century) onward, numerous codifications and collections appeared. In the late eighth century, the Aramaic *Halakhot Pesukot* ("Judicially-Determined Laws"), problematically attributed to Yehuday ben Nahman Gaon, informed Jews in the diaspora of the current laws that applied to them. A century later, Simon Kayyara compiled his more thorough *Halakhot Gedolot* ("Great Corpus of Laws").

Attempts at anything other than abridgements were absent until the late eleventh century. Then Isaac ben Jacob Alfasi (1013–1103; known as Rif, the acronym for *Rabbi Issac of Fez*) produced the *Sefer ha-Halakhot*. Essentially abridging the Talmud, it became known as *Talmud Katan* ("Little Talmud") and spread throughout the diaspora. While all of these codifications prompted commentaries, that of Moses ben Maimon (Maimonides, Rambam, 1135–1204) spurred controversy. His *Mishneh Torah* ("Repetition of the Torah") systematically stripped away the encumbrances of previous Talmudic and halakhic oral and written traditions. Organized according to subject matter, the *Mishneh Torah* was massive, comprehensive, and readily accessible, Because Maimonides had eliminated both conflicting opinions and references to earlier authorities, controversy ensued. While most subsequent codes followed his approach, the controversy prompted some in the twelfth and thirteenth centuries to return to the earlier style found in the more traditional Ashkenazic authorities.

A variety of scholars in the south of France and in Spain added to the genre of legal codes and commentary. Rabbi Menahem ben Solomon Meiri of Perpignan (1249–1316), who defended the study of philosophy, produced an introduction to the Talmud in the late thirteenth century, the *Bet ha-Behirah*. Introductions to the Talmud were also written by David of Estella in Provence ca. 1320, Issac de Lates, also of Provence, in 1372, and Menahem ben Aharon ben Zerah (ca. 1310–85) of Navarre in the same period. Already influenced by the earlier introduction of Italian approaches, fourteenth-century Spain received Ashkenazic traditions at the appointment of Asher ben Jehiel (Rosh, ca. 1250–1327) as rabbi of Toledo in 1305. A student of Rabbi Meir ben Barukh of

Rothenburg (d. 1293) and a tosafist, his clear, Talmud-based *responsa* established his reputation as a halakhic authority throughout the diaspora. His sons, Rabbi Judah ben Asher (1270–1349) and Rabbi Jacob ben Asher (ca. 1270–ca. 1343), strengthened their father's beginnings. However, Jacob's *Sefer ha-Turim* ("Book of Columns") returned to the broader Maimonidean approach, adding specific quotations and citations. Later, Joseph Caro (d. 1575) used the newer method in his *Shulhan Arukh*.

Unity and Diversity: Sephardic and Ashkenazic Judaism

Judaism in exile, lacking a centralizing authority, had split in two in the West. The Ashkenazic and Sephardic division, exemplified in the *Siddur* ("order of prayers," prayer book), stemmed from the devotion of the Italo-Ashkenazic scholars in Rome, specifically Judah ben Menahem, to the Palestinian rite, and the Sephardic to the Babylonian geonic prayers sent by Rabbi Amram bar Sheshna to the scattered communities throughout the diaspora. He dispatched the *Seder Rav Amram* to Spain in 860. The Palestinian authority, then, waned in the face of Babylonian polemics and correspondence. However, the geonic yeshivas themselves declined in the course of the eleventh century as distinctly separate Jewish cultures developed in the Muslim and Christian regions of the West.

Roman Judaism played a key role in the formation of Ashkenazic culture. The Kalonymos family had moved from Rome to Lucca after the expulsion of the Jews from Rome by Lothair in 855. From Lucca the Kalonymos migrated to Mainz by the mid-ninth century and brought with them the texts and scholarly traditions of Italian Jewry. In the early thirteenth century, Eleazar ben Judah of Worms (ca. 1165–ca. 1230), in his *Sefer ha-Roqeah* ("Book of the Perfumer"), credited the Kalonymides with shaping Ashkenazic practices such as atonement rituals and mystical prayer. Rome, however, continued to be regarded as authoritative by the Jews of Paris in the late twelfth century.

Explaining the Ashkenazic–Sephardic differences as exclusively the result of Palestinian–Babylonian ones, however, ignores more significant factors. The Sephardic culture resulted from the environment of Muslim culture and society encountered in North Africa and southern Spain. Ashkenazic culture, by contrast, developed in the Christian territories of the Rhineland and northern France. While both relied upon the Torah, the Babylonian Talmud, and fundamentally the same Rabbinic canon, their interpretations of these differed, as did their receptivity to gentile works.

Religious Leadership

As in any era, religion suffused the life of the Jew in the medieval West. The community as a whole practiced the religion but had within it the distinctly religious institutions of the synagogue and the rabbinate. Whatever social or administrative functions attached to these institutions were incidental to the religious ones. The synagogue provided the locus of public worship and religious ceremony. The rabbi interpreted and applied the law.

Knowledge of the law defined the position. Any Jew sufficiently versed in religious tradition might function as his own rabbi. The title of rabbi might refer to an officer appointed by the *Kehillah*, the community. But the title could also be bestowed upon scholars and "recognized halakhic authorities" who held no such appointment. Indeed, Rabbinic power showed a marked decline once the rite of ordination lost the official status it had in the Talmudic period. Those who demonstrated high levels of halakhic scholarship received the title of *morenu* ("our teacher"), which empowered them to hand down halakhic decisions (*responsa*) on significant cases. But, again, many who were not rabbis could pronounce such decisions: judges, heads of *yeshivot*, teachers, and preachers.

While rabbis then had a good deal of competition, they sought out the opinions of others and sometimes issued their decisions conditioned upon the concurrence of other authorities to avoid both pride and error. But even after the later development of a large body of literature and of codifications, such as the sixteenth-century *Shulhan Arukh*, the rabbinate survived.

Rabbis also had the responsibility to ensure that the members of the Jewish community conducted their lives according the law. An individual's misconduct elicited a public rabbinical reprimand and a recitation of applicable provision to educate the person. Later, sermons by scholars, who were not necessarily rabbis, performed a similar function for the community as a whole. Study at a *bet midrash* ("house of study") or *yeshiva* permitted both amateur and professional preachers to address the community. The professionals, retained by the community, were expected to instruct their listeners and exhort them to repentance at least twice a year. Sermons on *Shabbat ha-Gadol* ("the Great Sabbath"), just before Passover, and on *Shabbat Shuva* ("the Sabbath of Penitence"), between the New Year and the Day of Atonement, were expected. The emergence of such preachers, resident or itinerant, stemmed from a variety of causes ranging from the emergence of reforming sects and mystics to the growth of Jewish communities. Some were deemed threats to local authority, while others provided elevated entertainment.

Worship and Practice

Medieval Judaism emphasized the necessity for worship to be performed three times a day. Whether fixed by the Ashkenazic or Sephardic traditions, the prayers were to be performed in a *minyan*, a quorum, composed of at least ten males aged thirteen or over. The formal prayers were distinguished as either obligatory or *piyyutim*, which were liturgical. The ideal location for such prayer was the synagogue or a school. In smaller or legally hindered communities, however, private houses with a room devoted to an ark containing a Torah scroll had to suffice. Status within the community was signaled by seating within the synagogue, participation in the services, and the donation of religious items.

The practice of Judaism in the medieval West made substantial demands upon the individual to adhere to religious and social ideals. Following the halakhah could be expensive, demanding, and dangerous. Jews, who frequently needed protection, could wear no iron to synagogue. Laws also restricted commercial activities, such as trading in goods used by Christians in their worship and purchasing Christian-produced wine or meat.

Their devotion became most apparent when Jews were subjected to violence or forced conversions by Christians and Muslims. Under the Berber Almohads (1130–1269), who controlled Spain from 1150 until 1212, those Jews forced to convert to Islam observed their religion in secret and were consoled in this by the letters of Maimon ben Joseph (d. ca. 1165) and his son Maimonides. Early on in Christian territories, a Jew might receive a royal order to undergo baptism and still remain a practicing Jew. While coerced conversions had been a recurrent theme in the Christian West from the seventh century, the Crusades exacerbated the circumstances of the Jews. Acts of martyrdom (*Qiddush ha-Shem* or "The Sanctification of God's Name") cluster in the period from the late eleventh to the late twelfth century. At the end of the eleventh century in Mainz, Jews martyred themselves to avoid baptism. Toward the end of the next century, the Jews of York, clustered in a royal tower, committed mass suicide.

Religious Developments

Several of the developments in medieval Judaism present interesting parallels with Christianity in both orientation and chronology. As with Christian millenarianism, increasing numbers of Jews entertained messianic expectations for the immediate future. Likely stemming from the effects of the *Reconquista*, Jewish messianism erupted in Cordoba ca. 1110–15. With such leaders as Judah Halevi (ca. 1075–1141) expecting an apocalyptic end to Muslim rule in 1130, Passover that year found Jews throughout Spain and Morocco preparing for the messiah.

Sometimes prompted by millenarian and messianic expectations, Christian mysticism and piety grew steadily from the twelfth century. The hasidic movement also showed similarities to and chronological coincidence with Christian developments. The Hasidei Ashkenaz stemmed from the mystical traditions preserved and articulated by the Kalonymos family, which had been in Lucca prior to migrating to the Rhineland. The terrible fortunes of the Jews in that latter area on the occasion of the First Crusade led to the emergence of a pietism that stressed conformity to the halakhah. While traceable to practices among the Italian Jews in the eighth century, specifically hasidic sources date only from the late twelfth century. These *exempla*, however, perform a morally didactic function and not a historical one.

Among the leaders of these pietists stood Eleazar ben Judah of Worms (Rokeah, ca. 1165–ca. 1230) whose scholarship preserved the older traditions, and his relatives and contemporaries, Samuel ben Kalonymos the Elder ("the Pietist, the Holy, and the Prophet," fl. mid-twelfth century) and his son Judah ben Samuel, "the Pietist" (ca. 1149–1217), both instrumental in the creation of the *Sefer Hasidim* ("Book of the Pietists"). Judah also wrote *Sefer ha-Kavod* ("Book of Divine Glory," now lost), liturgical commentaries. Eleazar's *Sefer ha-Roqeah* ("Book of the Perfumer") combined the disparate subjects of personal piety and Ashkenazic customary law. The Rhenish Ordinances, signed by Eleazar and based upon pietistic principles, provided some political and religious uniformity to the Jews settled in the Rhineland.

As with the Christian mendicants and their followers, they combined a social awareness of the plight of the poor with a mystical and esoteric penchant. Their strain of mysticism, however, owed nothing to the Franciscans and drew upon earlier, Jewish sources. As with some of the Christian millenarians, they were elitist and at least suspected of antinomianism. The hasidim were to be judged only by the *Din Shamayim* – an unwritten Law of Heaven. These pietists, not unlike the Christian flagellists, took on something of the role of scapegoat by assuming the responsibility for the errors of all Jews. This prompted the criticism of such "sages" by authoritative rabbis. Solomon bar Samson portrayed them in his chronicle as poor leaders who issued evil halakhic responses. They, in turn, considered their rabbinical critics as insolent "jugglers."

The devotional ideals of the pietists, based upon perfectionist notions, resulted in curious practices. Exposing oneself to sin, resisting its temptation, and subsequently performing severe penance demonstrated the piety of the practitioner. The adoption of such procedures has been traced to the influence of Ahimaaz ben Paltiel's (1017–60) *Genealogy*. That work has also been viewed as the source of hasidic esoteric beliefs which included such disturbing, magical elements as the transformation and cannibalizing of children. At the same time, the pietists' renunciation of temporalities, serenity, and altruism contributed an attractiveness, seen in the presence of Jewish mystics in England in the second half of the twelfth century.

Kabbalism

A more esoteric mysticism emerged in Kabbalism. Devotees of Kabbalah – esoteric "tradition" – sprang up in twelfth-century Provence and filtered into Spain in the following century. The earliest, anonymous text, *Sefer ha-Bahir*, was followed by the *Sefer ha-Zohar* ("Book of Splendor"), written in Spain by 1286, which informed both Ashkenazic and Sephardic Jews searching for mystical union with God. Kabbalah gained a philosophical facet in the same period with Rabbi Moses de Leon's *Midrash ha-Ne'lam* ("The Hidden Midrash") (1275–80). Gnostic and Neoplatonic cosmologies combined with ecstatic goals in multiple Kabbalistic works in the fourteenth century. Its popularity spread to Germany and to Italy where several works were translated into Latin and influenced the thinking of fifteenth-century Christian humanists, among them Pico della Mirandola. Kabbalah, while more pervasive among the Ashkenazim than the Sephardim, came to suffuse western Judaism because of the increasing popularity of mysticism and the growing number of Kabbalistic schools.

Education

Ideally, a male Jew should study Torah whenever he is not devoting himself to physical needs or religious duties. In reality, such a life was led by only the great scholars. More commonly, a man established a set time for study and spent the bulk of his time tending to business. The more successful businessman might even support a scholar to fulfill the requirement by proxy. Nonetheless, the demands of scholarship and, more probably, business resulted in a comparatively high literacy rate among both males and females. Female literacy may be traced to the involvement of Jewish wives in commercial activities, sometimes to support a scholar-husband.

While the paucity of written religious texts points to memorization, the number of secular documents indicates advanced literacy. Ethical wills and letters frequently praised education, and the wills of English Jews include books. Betrothal contracts, deeds, chirographies were all written in Hebrew. While Jewish deeds lack the refinement of continental documents, they suggest that the signatories had written them. The documents of the English Jews also reveal literacy in both Latin and French. An elaborate royal requirement resulted in the emergence of a professional class of chirographers whose *archae* recorded in Hebrew the transactions of the Jewish merchants.

Perhaps since antiquity, but certainly from the twelfth century on, formal schooling began for boys at the age of five or six. The boy was wrapped by his father in a prayer shawl and brought to a teacher. The boy then read the Hebrew alphabet, verses of the Torah, and "May the Torah be my occupation." Each letter was then covered with honey, and all were licked off by the boy, who was then fed cakes and hard-boiled eggs with additional verses written upon them. Prior to this moment, fathers prepared their sons for school, drilling the boys with the alphabet and scriptural verses. Having acquired fundamental reading abilities by following the weekly reading of the Torah, they subsequently studied the Mishnah and the Talmud. In Spain, boys learned Hebrew grammar as they studied the Torah, but they might also have tutors in Arabic. While the instruction in the north might take place in French or German, neither language received formal study. Neither, apparently, did Latin.

Rabbis normally headed the *yeshivot* within the cities of the Ashkenazic Jews. The *rosh* (master) of a yeshiva might also stand as its *rav* (leading scholar). By the mid-tenth century, great rabbinical schools had been established in Italy at Rome, Venosa, and Oria, in Andalusia at Cordoba, and in the Rhineland, particularly at Mainz. The thirteenth-century students of Rabbi Meir ben Baruch of Rothenburg (d. 1293) studied, ate, and slept at his house.

Teachers might fall under the scrutiny of fathers, rabbis, and community officers. In the north, instruction might be private, with tutors instructing boys at either their house or the home of the pupil. However, the synagogue most commonly provided a room designated for teaching larger groups. While some communities shouldered the burden of the teacher's salary, in others the parents paid the teacher directly. Whether private or communal, teachers entered into contractual agreements.

Among Ashkenazic Jews, the Talmud received the greatest emphasis. In the tenth and eleventh centuries, students were read the text by the teacher. From the beginning of the twelfth century and the receipt of Rashi's (Solomon ben Isaac of Troyes, 1040–1105) commentary on the Talmud, Ashkenazic students had direct access to manuscript portions of the text. That prompted the development of fuller interchange between the students and the masters, spurring innovative interpretations and the development of the dialectic. All this added luster to the reputations of the various masters.

In contrast, Sephardic schools continued to emphasize the Torah as well as the liturgy and legal codes. Only the most advanced would study the Mishnaic and Talmudic texts. Their traditionalism gradually fell before the advancing *Reconquista*. From the twelfth century, advanced scholars in Aragon and Castile continued the curricular breadth developed in Muslim regions. Science, mathematics, philosophy, medicine, and music joined religious studies. In the early fourteenth century, a reaction set in against philosophy, and Ashkenazic Talmudic methods were brought to Toledo by the German Asher ben Jehiel. Still, not all abandoned the devotion to the Torah and grammar.

The international character of Judaism exerted profound influences. By the mid-ninth century, the Geonim of the Babylonian yeshiva communicated with both Iberia and Italy and became instrumental in determining the intellectual and educational character, especially in Italy. For the future development of Ashkenazic culture, the Italo-Judaic heritage was most influential. Numerous settlements within Italian cities ranging from Palermo in the south to Verona in the north became centers of Judaic learning, but the most significant was that at Lucca. The institutional framework of Ashkenazic Jewry had been established by the Lucchese family of the Kalonymos, particularly Meshullam ben Kalonymos (930–1005). As their followers migrated northward, they translated his authoritative structures into France and Germany, where scholars and communal leaders developed them. Patterns of academic leadership varied among the French and Rhenish communities, as well as between Sephardic and Ashkenazic ones. In twelfth-century Narbonne, the *nasi*, as leader of the community, also headed the schools there. The title, and apparently the function, had descended from the Kalonymos family. As the communities grew, new schools sprang up, often with recent migrants as their masters.

Mainz, for example, had scholars from places as distant as Anjou as its teachers. While five major Rabbinic families wielded authority in Mainz, Rabbi

Gershom ben Judah ("The Light of the Exile," ca. 960–1028) had dominant status. Under him, Talmudic learning centered on the thorough discussion between master and student. This exegetical technique became the standard didactic method within the schools. Rabbi Gershom maintained communication with rabbinical authorities in both Rome and Baghdad and transformed the nature of Rhenish Judaism through his legal decisions, *responsa*, exegesis of the Talmud, and his poetry. He grappled with crucial social issues facing the Jewish community, supporting monogamy, the consent of women to divorce, and the return to Judaism of those who had, volitionally or not, converted to Christianity.

The *yeshivot* of the Rhineland communities were small institutions, and so were the preparatory schools where the students began their academic life. Such size fitted the methods, facilitating the individual attention given by the teachers to their pupils. Although closely supervised, students were encouraged to challenge the interpretations set forth by the master and often did so in the glosses of their notebooks. Whether commenting on the simple meaning of the text (*peshat*) or engaging in broader inquiry (*drash*), such critical exegesis led to improved texts through increasingly thorough editing.

Certain scholars loomed as dominant authorities. In the late eleventh century, Rashi produced Talmudic and Biblical glosses widely known by both Jewish scholars and thirteenth-century Christian Hebraists. One grandson and disciple, Samuel ben Meir (Rashbam, ca. 1085–1175), completed his work, while the other, Jacob ben Meir (Rabbenu Tam, ca. 1100–71), a tosafist, attracted students, such as the Kievan Rabbi Moses, from great distances. Abraham ben Meir ibn Ezra also produced influential exegetical texts. The emergence of the tosafists (*tosafot* are additions or glosses upon texts) and their focus on the dialectic mirrored the methods of the Christian scholars, particularly of Roman law, in the High Middle Ages. Their critical method examined contradictory elements in the Talmud, sought the best texts, and offered both syntheses and new interpretations. The rapid spread of the tosafists' dialectic from France to Germany testified to its usefulness.

Cultural Mobility and Exchange

Judaism in the Christian West also incorporated educational and intellectual traditions developed under Muslim rule in both North Africa and Iberia. The development of that culture began at Qayrawan [Kairouan]. Of the "sages of Qayrawan," Isaac ben Solomon Israel (ca. 850–ca. 950) stands out as both the "Monarch of Medicine" and the "Father of Jewish Neoplatonism." Two yeshivas at Qayrawan emerged, both in the late tenth century. Jacob ben Nissim ibn Shahin (d. ca. 1006), a correspondent of the Babylonian Sherira ben Hanina Gaon (tenth century), founded one school and was succeeded by his son Nissim ben Jacob ben Nissim ibn Shahin (ca. 990–1062). Nissim, in addition to his Arabic commentary on the Talmud, established the model for didactic tales.

The other academy was begun by an immigrant from Italy, Hushei'el ben Elhanan (d. early eleventh century), who brought with him the rabbinical legal scholarship that had emerged in Italy. He was succeeded by his son Hananel ben Hushi'el (RaH, ca. 990–1055), whose commentary on the whole of the Babylonian Talmud was known throughout medieval Jewry.

When Bedouin invasions in the mid-eleventh century ended the preeminence but not the influence of Qayrawan, its scholars migrated westward. Isaac Alfasi (1013–1103), active first in Morocco and then in Spain, established new standards of Talmudic, halakhic scholarship with his *Sefer ha-Halakhot* ("Book of Laws"). Its authority would be supplanted only by Maimonides' code.

North African Judaism flowed into Iberia, and Jewish culture in Spain flourished under the patronage of leading Jewish courtiers of the Cordoban caliphate. These individuals greatly influenced the character of Iberian Judaism as it developed in Muslim and, later, Christian cultures. The disintegration of the Cordoban caliphate did not impede talented Jews. Jewish courtiers, among them Jekuthiel ibn Hasan (d. 1039) and Abraham ben Muhajir (d. ca. 1100), served the successor Muslim rulers. Samuel ha-Nagid became the Granadan vizier (1036–55) and commanded the royal army, as well as being the *nasi*, a Talmudic scholar, a master poet, and a patron. His son Joseph succeeded him as vizier but was killed in the uprising of 1066, which destroyed the Granadan Jewish community. The political influence of the Jews slowly eroded from that moment.

With the Almoravid conquest at the end of the eleventh century, Andalusian Jewish intellectuals such as the poet Moses ibn Ezra (d. post 1135) began migrating to Christian territories. Despite the loss of political power, however, Jewish culture thrived. The Talmudic scholars Isaac Alfasi (1013–1103) and his student Joseph ibn Migash (d. 1141) established the reputation of Lucena's yeshiva. The greatest of the medieval Hebrew poets, Judah ha-Levi (ca. 1075–1141), was also a philosopher and practiced medicine at Toledo until 1108 and the murder of his patron. He produced secular and religious poems, his "Songs of Zion," and *The Kuzari*, before his religious ideals led him to abandon Spain for Palestine in 1140. The intolerance of the Almohads toward any non-Muslim and the resulting forced conversions led Iberian Jews to flee both to Christian and to the more tolerant Muslim territories of the eastern Mediterranean litoral.

Between 1140 and 1230, Jewish culture in both North Africa and Spain eroded under the persecutions of the Almohad rulers. After their decline in 1230, Jewish culture in the North African kingdoms of Tunisia and Algeria, by fits and starts, was replenished by Sephardic refugees from Christian Iberia whose numbers swelled because of anti-Jewish uprisings in 1391 and the exile of 1492.

Texts and their Transmission

The transmission of texts to the West remains somewhat shrouded. Rabbi Natronai may have carried a copy of the Talmud into Italy toward the end of the eighth century, but the letter stating this was written a century later. Certainly Jewish texts had been making their way west for centuries before that as Jews had settled in Rome by the time of Julius Caesar. Indeed, one descendant of such a family, Nathan ben Yehiel (1035–ca. 1110), compiled a Talmudic dictionary, the *Baal he-Arukh*, at the beginning of the twelfth century. He had studied in Sicily, Babylonia, and Tunisia.

Italian Judaism itself had ties with both Palestinian and Babylonian traditions. The *Tana de-vei Eliyahu* (late ninth or early tenth century) drew upon Palestinian midrashic literature to present an integrated theory of history that progressed from creation to the messianic redemption. Despite their affinity with the Palestinian tradition, Babylonian influences increased, partly because of the superior texts emanating from that quarter and partly because of commercial travelers who transmitted questions and responses to and from the Gaon. The local merchants' agents between the West and Babylon copied these for their own communities. The geonic Rabbi Amram bar Sheshna's (d. ca. 875) *Siddur* was distributed to Jewish communities in the West and elsewhere in the ninth century. As late as the thirteenth century, however, Jewish scholars in Rome, particularly Judah ben Menahem (Judah Romano), relied more on the Palestinian model to guide the Italo-Ashkenazic rite.

Among the eastern texts was the anonymous "Order of the Tannaim and Amoraim" (late ninth century), incorporating the *Abot*, which recorded Judaic law from Moses to Rabbi Judah ha-Nasi (ca. 135–220), who compiled the Mishnah, and listing the succession of the Amoraim (Talmudic sages) and the Tannaim (Mishnaic sages). Later lists continued the succession of authorities: the Savoraim (successors of the Amoraim), the Geonim (successors of the Savoraim after the close of the Talmud), and the Rabbanim (who followed the Geonim). To such "historical" texts belongs the "Small Order of the World" (as opposed to the "Large" of Rabbi Yose), which traces geneaology from Adam to the descendants of David.

Poetry

Hebrew poetry, often coalescing religious with secular themes, emerged early in the medieval West. Rhymed inscriptions date from the late seventh century. More sustained creations were present in Apulia in the tenth century. The late ninth-century liturgical poetry of Shefatyah and Amittai ben Shefatyah of Oria (southern Italy) reveal an independent, western European Jewish culture. As had their father and grandfather before them, these *payyetanim* based their compositions on earlier, Palestinian piyyutim but developed a distinct style adopted by the Italo-Ashkenazic rites. Silano of Venosa's hymn, 'Enqat Mesaldekha, continues as a part of the Ashkenazic High Holy Days liturgy. Rome produced at least twelve religious poets by the end of the thirteenth century. Notable among them was Solomon the Babylonian, whose poems grapple with the themes of exile, hostility, forced conversions, and martyrdom. Poets also numbered among the Jewish writers in England. Meir the Poet, expelled in 1290, afterwards composed his works around the themes of persecutions, executions, and expulsions, but he also wrote an elegy on his teacher. Rabbi Shem Tov ben Isaac Ardutiel (Santob de Carrio'n) incorporated Jewish ethics into his *Proverbios morales*, written in both Hebrew and Spanish.

Chronicles

Among the more "secular" texts were the chronicles and books of remembrance. While persecutions and martyrdom dominated the "chronicles" of the Ashkenazic Jews, other chronicles presented chronologically and thematically broader portraits of Jewish society. *The Book of Josippon*, ascribed to Joseph ben Gurion (fl. first century) yet completed in 953 by a Jew of southern Italy or Sicily, used Josephus' *Jewish War* and *Antiquities* but extended the chronological scope to include early medieval Rome and southern Italy. Inventing "historical" details, Joseph placed the descendants of Esau among the founders of Rome. In Toledo in 1161, Abraham ben David ha-Levi (Abraham ibn Daud, ca. 1110–80) wrote the "Book of Tradition," a history of the Jews during the Second Temple period using *Josippon*, and, employing both Arabic and Latin sources, a history of Rome from the foundation of the city to the reign of the Visigoth Reccared in late sixth-century Spain. In the thirteenth century, an anonymous chronicle dealt with the persecutions of 1007, and Meir ben Simeon of Narbonne's *Milhemet Mitzvah* recounted more recent relations between the Jews and the church. Rabbi Menahem Meiri's (1249–1316) commentary on *Abot* depicted the fortunes of the Jews from the age of Moses to the late thirteenth century. The ritual book, *Zekher Zaddiq*, of Joseph ben Zaddiq of Spain contains a chapter which chronicles the history from creation to 1467. Such historical works, however, were rare in the Middle Ages, and their numbers increased only at the end of the era and during the early modern period. The great concern of Rabbinic scholars resided not in history *per se*, but in establishing and justifying their authority to interpret religious texts and oral traditions.

Forced conversions and massacres of entire communities by both Muslims and Christians begot creativity. Abraham ibn Ezra's (1089–1164) *Aha Yarad* ("Oh, There Descended") lamented Jewish martyrs during the Almohad persecutions. Joseph ben Judah ibn Aknin (1150–1220), a philosopher and refugee, vividly described those persecutions. Ashkenazic chronicles and books of remembrance or memorial books recorded the names of the Jews who had been slain or had committed suicide during outbreaks of anti-Semitism in various towns. Eliezer ben Nathan of Mainz's (ca. 1090–1170) *Chronicle*, Solomon bar Samson's *Chronicle*, and *The Narrative of the Old Persecutions* listed those who perished during the First Crusade. Both Eleazar of Worms and Ephraim of Bonn (1133–post 1196) in his *Sefer Zekhirah* ("The Book of Remembrance") accounted for the Jewish victims of the Second Crusade.

Polemics

Jewish texts, beyond those recounting their persecution, often assumed a polemical character. Biblical, midrashic, Mishnaic, and Talmudic literature often contained direct responses to Christian challenges. The Jewish criticism of Christianity began early, disparaging both Jesus and the subsequent religion. *Toledot Yeshu*, an early parody written in Hebrew, presented an unflattering biography of Jesus. Hebrew chronicles written during and after the Crusades not only blamed the Christians for their suffering but also denounced Christianity as idolatrous.

Polemical disputes more often hinged on exegesis. The method was common to both Christian and Jew, but the variant interpretations gradually increased the hostility between the two. For the Jew more so than the Christian, exegetical interpretation determined not only the religion but the society, its institutions, and its relation to external entities. The traditions of Rabbinic exegesis within Ashkenazic culture stemmed from the work of Meshullam ben Kalonymos and the successor rabbis such as Gershom ben Judah Machiri (ca. 960–1028). This scholarship drew on several traditions, predominantly Italian midrashic and Talmudic studies, but geonic (Babylonian) and even Karaitic influences were also present. Jews – and also Christians – had to grapple with the application of scripture emerging from an urban, commercial society to a predominantly agrarian, feudal one.

As Christian efforts to convert the Jews increased, Christian exegesis of Scripture became the target of criticism by the leading Jewish scholars: Rashi, his grandson, Samuel ben Meir (Rashbam, ca. 1085–ca. 1174), and Joseph Kara (b. ca. 1065), Rashi's student. As Christian polemicists increased their production in the twelfth century, so too did the defenders of Judaism. Joseph Kimhi (ca. 1105–ca. 1170), who had fled from the Almohad persecution, attacked Christianity in his *Book of the Covenant*. He criticized the messianic identification of Jesus and the concept of the Virgin Birth. He also defended the moneylending of the Jews, stating that they took no usury from their co-religionists. His contemporary, Jacob ben Reuven, wrote "Wars of the Lord" (ca. 1170), which criticized the biblical and logical validity of the doctrines of the trinity and incarnation. Curiously, one work from the late thirteenth century adopted the format of the Christian scholastics in a "summa" that employed a technique similar to Pierre Abailard's *sic et non*. The *Sefer Nitzahon Yashan* ("The Old Book of Polemic") took Christian exegesis to task by following Christian interpretations with Jewish responses.

The increasingly confrontational nature of Jewish works matched that of the Christians. Prior to the Crusades, Christian intellectuals, especially those who sought knowledge of Hebrew, looked upon the various genres of Rabbinic literature with less hostility. While this certainly continued among the scholastics well into the fourteenth century, the more common attitude changed toward the Rabbinic Judaism of the Christian era. Rather than being supplanted by

Christianity and withering away, Judaism continued to evolve. Rather than merely prefiguring Christianity as the Old Testament had, Talmudic literature presented a "heretical" interpretation of biblical literature. Increasingly, Jewish scholars were forced to defend the Talmud and associated literature in a number of public disputations and trials, most famously at Paris in 1240–42, Barcelona in 1263, and Tortosa in 1414–15. Maimonides, however, counseled greater toleration.

Disputations

The proliferation of Talmudic and Mishnaic literature in the West gave rise to a two-faceted attack. The more significant one came from a Christian church increasingly concerned about the persistence of the Jews under a Rabbinic Judaism based upon the Talmud. The second prong involved charges that the rabbis had corrupted a Torah-based religion through their Talmudic studies. Converted Jews led the attack, particularly Nicholas Donin in the early thirteenth century, Petrus (Pablo) Christiani in Barcelona in 1263, Peter Alfonsi in the early fourteenth, Jeronimo de Santa Fe in Tortosa in 1413–14, and Hermann of Cologne. Whether the accusations were made to kings or popes, Jews had to defend their positions. Rabbi Jehiel ben Joseph (d. 1268), a Parisian tosafist, proved inadequate to the task of defending the Talmud in 1240. The French king subsequently ordered twenty-four cartloads of the Talmud burned as blasphemous. Rabbi Moses ben Nahmanides (1194–1270) openly confronted Dominican accusers before the royal court at Barcelona in 1263. Nahmanides fled to Israel three years later. For the rest of the century, the Talmud was repeatedly condemned, confiscated, and burned throughout France. During these times the inquisitors and kings showed more zealotry than the popes, who displayed hesitance in condemning the Jewish texts. Indeed, after John XXII's temporary expulsion of Jews from his Avignon territory, nearly a century of calm relations ensued.

Philosophy

Works of philosophy also emerged. Shabbetai Donnolo (ca. 913–982), one of the first European Jews identified as a philosopher, traveled extensively and incorporated gnostic and mystical elements in his *Sefer Hakhmoni* ("Book of Enlightenment"). He was acquainted with a mystical tract, *The Book of Creation*, and Arab medicine prior to the adoption of Aristotelian approaches by the Muslims. Philosophy, however, presented the danger of assessing the veracity of other religions, a danger realized in early fourteenth-century Provence. Ashkenazic Jews avoided the threat by refusing to engage in philosophical examinations of Judaism. Italian, Iberian, and eastern Jews employed philosophy, but limited speculation. Spanish Jewish philosophers fell into two camps. The older, Andalusian sorts had been trained in Neoplatonic schools that led them to oppose the newer, Aristotelian trends of Christian Spain.

In the twelfth century Jewish Aristotelianism rose in response to the challenge of mystical Neoplatonism to Judaism. The Spaniard Abraham ben David ha-Levi ibn Daud (d. ca. 1180) employed a strict rationalism in his *The Exalted Faith*, which grappled with the dichotomies of religion and philosophy, faith and reason. Abraham also provided an addition to the *Book of Tradition* in 1161. Meir ben Todros ha-Levi Abulafia (ca. 1170–1244) in Spain and Maimonides had both made use of Muslim commentaries on Aristotle.

The best known and most profound Jewish philosopher of the period, Moses ben Maimon (Maimonides, Rambam, 1135–1204), employed Aristotelian methods. Medieval Jews regarded his commentaries on and introductions to works of religious law as authoritative. Best known of these were his Arabic commentary on Mishnah as well as his later work, the *Mishneh Torah*. The extreme rationalism he expressed in his philosophical work, however, prompted much controversy. Maimonides' *Moreh Nevukhim* (*Guide of the Perplexed*) scrutinized biblical passages and rejected literal interpretations of many accounts, prompting arguments between Jews of the rationalist and mystical approaches. Maimonides, however, sought to reconcile philosophy and religion. Contrary to the fears of his critics, he subordinated reason to revelation, much as Thomas Aquinas would in the following century. Exiled, Maimonides died in Cairo. His death did not silence his critics, particularly the pietists and Kabbalists. In the thirteenth and fourteenth centuries, Solomon ben Abraham of Montpellier, Abba Mari ben Moses ha Yarhi (Astruc of Lunel), and Asher ben Jehiel (Rosh, 1250–1327) inveighed against both the study of philosophy by young students and the rationalist interpretation of Jewish law.

In thirteenth-century Italy, Jacob ben Abba Mari Anatoli distanced himself from the Arabic works by relying on Michael Scot's recent translation from the Arabic of Averroes' commentary on *Metaphysics*. The two had met at the Sicilian court where Jacob served as physician to Frederick II. A bit later in the century, Judah Romano, in addition to writing a commentary on Maimonides' *Mishneh Torah*, translated into Hebrew various works by Boethius, Albertus Magnus, Alexander of Hales, and Giles of Rome. At the same time, Christian scholars and polemicists sought to learn Hebrew for access to Rabbinic works, the Torah, the Talmud, and Jewish philosophy. Agobard of Lyons and Rabanus Maurus in the ninth century and numerous Christian scholars in the twelfth and subsequent centuries sought out Rabbinic scriptural commentaries and midrashim. While most used these to further their polemics, Thomas Aquinas used Maimonides with appreciation. Christian scholars, however, took the risk of being condemned as "Judaizers."

Significant to the intellectual development of the entire West, Jewish translators at Toledo began rendering both Arabic and Hebrew texts into Latin. From the taking of the city by Alfonso VI in 1085, through the reign of Alfonso VII (1126–57), and into the thirteenth century, Jewish scholars made works of philosophy, medicine, and astronomy accessible to western Christians. In Barcelona, Rabbi Abraham bar Hiyya (d. ca. 1136) wrote treatises on mathematics and astronomy. Thirteenth-century Spain witnessed the productivity of such scholars as Moses ben Nahman (Nahmanides, Ramban, 1194–1270), Solomon ben Abraham Adret (Rashba, 1235–1310), Aaron ben Joseph ha-Levi (ca. 1235–1300), and Rabbi Yom Tov ben Abraham Ishbili (Asbili) of Seville (ca. 1250–1330).

Jewish literary productivity encompassed philosophy, biblical exegesis, poetry, elegies and dirges, ethics, grammar texts, mystical works, chronicles, epics, political theory, dialogues on ethics, manuals of behavior, sermons, midrash, memoirs, and even such adventures as Benjamin of Tudela's *Book of Travels* (ca. 1160–70). Some works incorporate multiple literary genres. Ahimaaz ben Paltiel's *Megillah Ahimaaz*, completed in 1054, is at once a family chronicle, a hagiography, and a geography. Most interestingly, he reveals the Babylonian influences upon Jewish culture in the south of Italy. The letters of merchants and purely commercial documents remain uncounted.

Conclusion

Judaism in the medieval West seems a tree clinging to a cliff. Infamously, Jews were repeatedly accused of killing Christian children in blood rituals, poisoning wells, profaning the host, acting as minions of the devil, and generally corrupting Christian society. Unfounded as the accusations were, and although they might originate among the lower classes, even kings gave them credence. Although exiled, reviled, massacred, and converted, medieval Jews managed to sustain and create thriving communities and cultures. Judaism did so because it drew upon multiple traditions and influences during the best and worst of days. Persian, Palestinian, and North African Judaism, filtered and not, flowing or seeping, affected the West. The West, Sephardic and Ashkenazic, absorbed these influences, transformed them in challenging circumstances, and created a rich heritage. The roots went deep, the trunk was gnarled, the foliage wondrous, and the seeds fruitful.

Bibliography

Cohen, Mark R., *Under Crescent and Cross: The Jews in the Middle Ages* (Princeton, 1994).
Jordan, William C., *The French Monarchy and the Jews: From Philip Augustus to the Last Capetians* (Philadelphia, 1989).
Katz, Jacob, *Exclusiveness and Tolerance: Studies in Jewish–Gentile Relations in Medieval and Modern Times* (Oxford, 1991).
Katz, Jacob, *Tradition and Crisis: Jewish Society at the End of the Middle Ages* (New York, 1993).

Marcus, Ivan, *Rituals of Childhood: Jewish Acculturation in Medieval Europe* (New Haven, 1996).

Sirat, Colette, *A History of Jewish Philosophy in the Middle Ages* (New York, 1990).

Stow, Kenneth R., *Alienated Minority: The Jews of Medieval Latin Europe* (Cambridge, MA, 1992).

Twersky, Isadore, ed., *Studies in Medieval Jewish History and Literature* (Cambridge, MA, 1979).

CHAPTER 10
Philosophy in Judaism: Two Stances

S. Daniel Breslauer

The Jewish historian Josephus Flavius (ca. 38–100 CE) in his defense of the Jews in his *Against Apion* offers several examples to demonstrate that philosophy has an exalted place in Judaism. He claims that, among the formative Greek thinkers, both Protagoras and Aristotle learned from the Jews. In this way he suggests that Judaism has a "natural" philosophy, inherent in itself, that has instructed even the most advanced of Greek thinkers. This point of view identifies Judaism and philosophy. True Judaism demonstrates its authenticity through its philosophical rigor.

This view suggests an exalted place of philosophy in Judaism, since philosophy uncovers authentic Jewish ideas. Another story related by Josephus, however, takes a different approach. This story reports that Aristotle once met with a certain Jewish scholar whom he described as one who had "become a Grecian, not only in his language, but also in his soul."[1] His thought, that is, had taken on the garb of the "soul of a Greek." That description suggests something alien about "philosophy," and many Jewish thinkers, although not Josephus, argue that adopting a Greek soul rather than a Jewish one betrays Judaic ideals. For these thinkers, philosophy must prove its benefit to Judaism rather than Judaism defend itself before philosophy.

Josephus clearly intended "philosophy" to refer to the thought of the Greeks. Other Jewish thinkers define philosophy differently. Nevertheless, the two ideas Josephus introduces – that Judaism and philosophy are essentially identical or that philosophy is alien to the soul of a Jew – remain the dominant strands in Jewish philosophical reflection. This chapter examines how Jews from the earliest to the most contemporary times have sought to balance what they thought of as Judaism with what they considered "philosophy." Each section introduces a historical period, briefly lists the major philosophical trends and thinkers of that age, and then focuses on a representative of each stance, one defending philosophy as natural in Judaism and the other finding philosophy an essential, but basically external, tool in understanding Judaism.

Philosophy in Ancient Judaism

Our first period is that of Josephus himself, in which philosophy was defined as he saw it – as Hellenic thought, the ideas of the pre-Socratics, of Socrates, of Plato, Aristotle, the Stoics, and their later followers. This period, beginning with the time of Alexander the Great (332 BCE) and extending through the completion of the Babylonian Talmud (c. 600 CE), reveals a wide variety of Jewish responses to Greek thought. Two foci help narrow our investigation of this lengthy period: the first is the Hellenism of the Jewish diaspora, particularly that found in Alexandria, Egypt, and the second is Rabbinic Judaism, in its centers of Yavneh and Usha. "Ancient" Judaism, understood this way, comprises two subsets or foci of study – Hellenization in the diaspora and rabbinism in the land of Israel.

These two foci share a common feature: they imbibed the thought and categories of Greek culture as disseminated by Alexander the Great and his successors. While scholars may debate "How much Greek in Roman Palestine?" they do not deny its presence or influence. Intellectual probity during this period required that a system of thought measure up to Greek standards. Yet how this was achieved differed radically in each of our two areas of study, with the difference reflected in a linguistic choice. The diaspora Jews chose to express themselves in Greek, while the Jews of the land of Israel championed Hebrew as the authentic Jewish language.

No better example of this difference exists than the responses each group gave to the Greek translation of the Hebrew Bible, the Septuagint. The central texts of Hellenistic diasporic thinking – the writings in the Apocrypha, especially the so-called *"Letter of Aristeas,"* Josephus, Philo of Alexandria, and the Jewish thinker Aristobulus as cited by Eusebius, all emphasize the benefit of having the Bible translated into Greek. Such a work enabled Jewish ideas to spread in the non-Jewish world, allowed all to discover the truth of philosophy, and testified to God's continuing acts of revelation and inspiration of Jewish teachers. The texts from the land of Israel are far more ambiguous. At best they acknowledge political reasons for the translation and for changes introduced into the Bible through that translation (B. Meg. 9a, Y. Meg. 1, 71d). At worst, they declare the day of the translation one of apostasy comparable to the worship of the Golden Calf, or a time in which darkness descends as punishment on the world (Masseket Soferim 1:7–10 and additions to Megillat Taanit). For the diaspora Jewish thinkers, Greek language and thought represent welcome tools for expounding and understanding Judaism.

Despite these differences, the two approaches to Judaism share much in common. Both maintain the Scripture demands interpretation. The text as literally read, for the Rabbinic tradition no less than for the Hellenistic diaspora, requires the insight of an interpreter and hermeneutic principles to yield its meaning. Both also agree that the unity of the divinity implies a unity of the cosmos. Despite the diversity and plurality of existence, Hellenistic Jewish theorists and their Judean counterparts maintained belief in a higher reality in which all apparently diverse entities find their unification. Finally, both affirm that Jewish life and practice serve to train a person in the proper habits and behavior necessary for a fulfilled existence. The categories of human virtue correspond, for diaspora Jews and Jews of the land of Israel alike, to the categories of Jewish religious living. The following sections focus first on the Alexandrian philosopher Philo and then on the Judean historian and thinker Flavius Josephus. While Josephus is not himself represented in the Rabbinic texts such as the Mishnah, Talmud, or midrashim, he makes references to the Jewish "sects," one of whom, the Pharisees, is usually understood as the predecessor of Rabbinic Judaism. Secondly, Josephus represents the Judean mentality in contrast to that of the Alexandrians and should be seen in the context of that environment. Like Rabbinic writers, he sees the Jewish soul as different from the Greek soul, although he interprets that soul as a philosophical one, a soul that needs no instruction from Greek thought.

Philo of Alexandria

Philo of Alexandria (whose dates are traditionally given as about 20 BCE to 50 CE) stands as the first in a long line of Jewish thinkers who harmonize biblical and Hellenic traditions.[2] The one episode in his life about which Philo informs his readers in any detail (his *Embassy to Gaius*) refers to events occurring between 39 and 41 CE and shows Philo defending the Jewish community of Alexandria before Gaius Caligula. Philo's communal spirit also demonstrates itself in his *Against Flaccus*, a polemic defending Jews against a Roman official in Egypt who persecuted them. From these writings it is clear that Philo was not immune to the historical pressures of his time. Yet while he clearly recognized the problems Jews faced and the dangers they endured, his thinking offers a positive view of a cultural and intellectual unity of Judaism and Hellenism.

His optimism was well grounded in the history of the Jews in Hellenistic Egypt. Jews had already lived in Alexandria for centuries. They enjoyed civil privileges and pointed to a charter that they said Alexander the Great himself had ratified. They viewed the Greek translation of the Bible as a miraculous sign of God's great works among them. Together with this cultural development there arose new ways of reading and understanding the biblical tradition. The church father and Christian historian Eusebius preserves the ideas of Aristobulus (second century BCE), who already used an allegorical method of showing the presence of Greek ideas in the Jewish teachings. Philo accepts both the method and the presuppositions of Aristobulus. He builds his thought on the idea that Judaism, by becoming familiar with Greek thought, has entered into a universal context. He declares that through the Septuagint, Jewish law is made known to all humanity. While nations usually reject the rules and customs of other nations, they all accept the teachings of Judaism that "attract and win the attention of all". Philo interprets Judaism as conveying a universal message; it transmits true philosophy and righteousness to all nations. It is on the basis of this universalism that Philo writes his books.

His first task, then, is showing that, despite the contrary appearance, the categories of the Hebrew Bible are really the same categories as those of Greek thought. He uses the allegorical method to show that while the Bible may seem to be a set of disconnected historical narratives (much like Homer's work in Greek literature), it in fact inculcates philosophical ideals. The stories and laws of the Bible are, for Philo, true on several levels. These levels correspond to the pragmatic virtues of wisdom and the intellectual virtues of a spiritual quest. The Bible only appears to be relating facts about events; it is, in fact, a pedagogy instructing the reader in the variety of Greek sciences for human living.

One of those intellectual sciences is cosmology, an understanding of the natural world, its evolution, and its causes. Plato had already provided a design and program to explain reality in his *Timaeus*. Philo accepts the general presuppositions of Plato's thought. The physical world emanates from a spiritual source through gradations of ever more concrete stages of existence. The Hebrew Bible, for Philo, allegorically alludes to this emanational system. God starts, he claims, with the creation of "the model of the world, perceptible only by intellect," and then proceeds with an incorporeal heaven and earth, incorporeal substances of "water," "light," and "air," and only after the completion of the incorporeal world "having its seat in the Divine Reason" was a corporeal world, "perceptible by the external senses," begun. This beginning, in its turn, leads to ever more corporeal concretizations of the divine plan.[3]

Such a scheme finds a place for the various Platonic entities that extend between our corporeal world and the purely intellectual realm of The Good. As a living link between these two, Philo posits a spiritual being, the Logos. This entity, designated by a Greek term meaning "Word" or "Reason," represents one link in a great chain of being. Some people recognize only that which their external senses show them; others recognize in the Logos the reigning power of the world; still others discover in the Logos the power which creates all things; finally, at the highest level, a person sees the Logos as part of an indivisible unity which is the Godhead itself. Philo emphasizes the importance of ascending this ladder of knowledge. The highest level occurs when a person not only *understands that* the Logos is identified with the One reality, but actually experiences that unity together with the Logos itself. Philo describes how such experiences have occurred to him.[4]

These very experiences, however, taught him the danger of too extreme a spirituality. He insists that the practice of Judaism includes a necessarily concrete and physical expression so as to purify the actual living person. Seclusion may lead one away from true thought, just as being with others may be beneficial. While the practice of circumcision, for example, teaches a sublime intellectual lesson – "the excision of pleasure and all passions, and the putting away of the impious conceit under which the mind supposed that it was capable of begetting by its own power" – the practice itself must not be rejected. Merely learning the philosophical lesson is not enough, for Philo contends "let us not on this account repeal the law laid down for circumcising."[5] On the basis of this view. Philo criticizes those Jews who think that because they understand the allegorical meaning of Judaic law they can dispense with its concrete performance. He insists on following such observances as Sabbath, circumcision, and Temple sacrifice. Without maintaining the practices, he avers, it is impossible to grasp the ideas to which they point. Jewish practice becomes, for Philo, justified as a means by which the Greek ideas he discovers in Judaism disclose their truth; bodily obedience to Torah law teaches the mind philosophy.

Philo, then, understands Judaism as the best pedagogy for teaching true philosophy. Through allegorical interpretation, he identifies the ideals and values of the Bible with Greek thought. He justifies Jewish observances as inherently philosophical and as indispensable for a philosophic life. In this way he defends Judaism, the true philosophy, as an exalted religious tradition worthy of emulation by Jew and non-Jew alike.

Flavius Josephus

Just as Philo addressed the questions of the interpretation of Torah, the unity of the cosmos, and the purpose of observing Jewish law, so too did Joseph ben Mattathias, better known as Flavius Josephus. Josephus, however, presented Jews as uniquely philosophical in their inherent being; the "garb" of Greek philosophy was alien to them, although the content was not. Unlike Philo, Josephus (38–100) was steeped in Judean Judaism. He took part in the great war against Rome (66–73) and is best known as a historian writing to correct the unfavorable impressions other historians had given of the Jews and their culture. His major works consist of *The Jewish War*, which describes the Jewish struggle for freedom that began under Antiochus IV (168 BCE) and culminated in the destruction of Jerusalem (73 CE); and his *Jewish Antiquities*, a review of biblical history into which he inserts evidence from Greek historians about ancient Jewish wisdom and knowledge; and several polemics against those who vilify the Jews, such as *Against Apion*, a defense of Jews and Judaism in response to anti-Semitic propaganda.

While maintaining that Jews have a long history of being philosophical, Josephus goes even further than Philo, arguing that the Greeks already recognized this aspect of Jewish philosophical inclination as inherent to Judaic culture. Josephus does not merely show that Jewish and Greek thought teach the same truths. He insists that native Jewish thought is intrinsically philosophical. Why then do the Jews have such a poor reputation among the philosophers and historians of Josephus's time? Josephus responds by charging that the Greeks are defective. Their culture, unlike that of the Jews, the Egyptians, or the Babylonians, lacks a true historical perspective. He contends "that they knew but little on any good foundation when they set to write, but rather wrote their histories from their own conjectures."[6] Confusion occurs when Greeks expect to find the same word and name used among the Jews as among the Greeks and condemn Jews for a lack that is, in actuality, only verbal and not substantial.[7]

Josephus continues his defense of Jewish thinking and philosophy by claiming that the ridicule directed at Jews merely reflects envy and historical accident. He claims that if the laws of Judaism had been proclaimed as some philosopher's *own* thinking, all men would admire them. These laws are both rational and humane.[8] But unlike Philo, Josephus does not allegorize the laws, considering them self-evidently clear and defensible. Indeed, he remarks that they are visible in their own nature and appear to teach not impiety but the truest piety in the world. They do not make men hate but, rather, encourage people to communicate with one another freely.[9]

Josephus goes beyond this defense of the natural piety of Jewish law. He asserts that even the divisions among Jews reflect philosophical theories. Thus the three Jewish sects he identified are distinguished by their different opinions concerning human actions.[10] This discussion, inserted into a political narrative on intrigues among rulers, generals, and pretenders to the throne, seems initially out of place. Why should Josephus interrupt his historical discussion with a definition of the philosophy of political sects? The answer seems to be his desire to stress that Jewish consciousness is basically philosophical, that even the Jews' political divisions are based on intellectual issues. The rationale for Jewish life is, for Josephus, intellectual and rational. There is no need for allegory and interpretation, since, in its essence, Judaism is a philosophical system.

Philosophy and Judaism in the Medieval Period

Neither Philo nor Josephus provided the model by which most Jews from 70 CE through the rise of Islam understood themselves. Even as Philo produced his allegorical explanation of Judaism that reconciled it to Greek thought and Josephus defended Judaism as inherently philosophical, rabbis in Judea created an alternative Judaic philosophy.[11] While, when judged by Greek theories, especially the principles of Aristotle, this Rabbinic system qualifies as philosophy, it was a different kind of "philosophy of Judaism" than that easily recognized by the Hellenistic tradition. Indeed, the principal writings of the Rabbinic system, the Mishnah, midrashim, and Talmud, tend to distance themselves from "philosophers," who are usually portrayed as skeptics, opponents of Jewish thought, or unbelievers. After Josephus and Philo, few Jews felt it imperative to present Judaism to the philosophical world or to present philosophy as inherent in Judaism.

The impetus for such self-representation reawakened only in the so-called "medieval" period. The idea of a "medieval" period in Judaism or in Jewish philosophy is borrowed from Christian periodization, which perceives an early period of Greek philosophy followed by a dark ages, emerging with the Renaissance into a new philosophical era. But this periodization misrepresents the Jewish experience, in which the so-called "Middle Ages" stretches from Saadia ben Joseph Al-Fayyumi (882–942) in the ninth century through Judah Moscato (1532–90) in the sixteenth. Saadia's position anticipates the general view – religious certainty corresponds with and does not contradict general knowledge. This may mean, as it does for Saadia, that the same truths are perceived by the senses, reason, and right tradition. It might also mean, as it does for Judah Halevi, that philosophy points beyond itself to the necessity of some truth that transcends reason. It could also entail, as Moses Maimonides thinks, that religious teaching supplies the necessary foundation for the discovery of philosophical truth. What these three different positions have in common is a recognition that reason and sense perception play a positive role in human learning and that religion can build on them or accept them without fear for its own validity.

Four distinct groupings mark Jewish philosophical thinking during this time span: one occurring under the Abbasid Califate in Iraq, a second occurring in Muslim Spain and North Africa, a third under Christian Spain, and a fourth in Italy during the Renaissance. Jewish thinkers in these groups used different languages – Arabic prevailing for the first two groups, Hebrew, Latin, and Italian in the last two groups. The styles of writing employed also differed, including philosophical and moral treatises, biblical commentaries, narrative and poetic literature, and sermonic writings. During the last three periods, Jewish thinkers pondered the nature of dogmas in Judaism and sought to establish authoritative creeds of belief and to justify the identification of certain principles as fundamental. While disagreeing as to the nature and scope of such dogmas, the philosophical enterprise of studying them occupied many Jewish thinkers.

These various activities and periods suggest a diversity that, while present, disguises a basic uniformity. In every case, Jewish and non-Jewish scholars engaged in lively conversation with one another – Muslim and Jewish philosophers studied each other's works, Christian thinkers referred to Jewish and Arabic philosophers, Christians sought Hebraic learning from their Jewish colleagues, and even disputations testify to inter-group interest in the thought of other religionists. Perhaps the best example of the common background among religionists of this period is found in the fate of the philosophical work by Solomon ibn Gabirol. Translated into Latin as *Fons Vitae*, the work was considered the product of either a Muslim or a Christian known as Avicebron. Only in the nineteenth century did Solomon Munk note the correspondence between this Latin work and the Hebrew epitome of Gabirol's *Meqor Hayyim* (both the Latin and Hebrew mean "Source of Life," a term taken from Ps. 36:10). That a Jewish philosopher could write in such a way that the work might be considered either Christian or Muslim demonstrates the commonality among philosophers of religion at that time.

The differences between the four groups of Jewish thinkers in the Middle Ages reflect the chronology of the period. While the dates given below are mostly approximate, they suggest the periodization of the four groups. Important thinkers among the first group are Saadia, Isaac Israeli (855–955), and several Karaite thinkers. Luminaries of the second period, often considered the "Golden Age" of Jewish philosophy, include the poets Solomon ben Judah ibn Gabirol

(1020–57) – also known by his Arabic name Abu Ayyub Sulayman ibn Yahya ibn Gabirol, and his Latin name, Avicebron – Moses Ibn Ezra (1055–1135), and Judah Halevi (1075–1141). The biblical commentators Abraham ibn Ezra (1089–1164) and David Kimchi (1160–1235) include important philosophical ideas in their work. Thinkers such as Abraham bar Hiyya (d. 1136), Abraham ben David Halevi (1110–80), known by the Arabic name ibn Daud, Bachya ben Joseph ibn Pakuda (1050–1120), Joseph ibn Zaddik (d. 1149), and Moses ben Maimon (1135–1204), called by his Latinized name, Maimonides, flourished during this time. The third period is dominated by the influence of and controversy over Maimonides. Important figures in the period include Hasdai Crescas (1340–1412), Joseph Albo (1380–1444), Levi ben Gershom (1288–1344), also called by his Latinate name Gersonides, and Simeon ben Zemah Duran (1361–1444). The final period, while centered on Italy with figures such as Elijah Delmedigo (1460–98), Isaac Abravanel (1437–1508), Isaac ben Moses Arama (1420–94), Judah Abravanel (1460–1523), also called Leon Ebreo, Joseph ibn Yahya (1496–1539), and Judah Moscato, includes some thinkers living elsewhere, such as Judah Loew ben Bezalel (1525–1609), known as the MaHaRaL of Prague.

Despite the differences between these periods and the thinkers associated with them, the term "Middle Ages" has a useful meaning. Before this period, Jewish thinkers like Philo or the authors of the Mishnah contended against a world in which polytheism dominated religious thought. After this period, enlightened philosophy no longer maintained a consensus of belief about the deity, revelation, and the cosmos. This period thus may be considered the "Golden Age" of religious philosophy. Jews lived in intellectual communities that accepted as truths beyond questioning the unity of the divine being, the fact of divine revelation and prophecy, and the interest of the divinity in human actions. While Muslim, Jewish, and Christian philosophers disagreed on which revelation was primary and which set of expectations truly reflected the divine will, they agreed on the need of philosophy to support those principles. When Christians in the Renaissance began to question this consensus, their Jewish colleagues remained recognizably "medieval" in retaining the old presuppositions as the basis of their thinking. The basic consensus among philosophers of religion emphasized that revelation does not provide a literal rendering of a divine word but rather conveys the basic principles of faith, that philosophical speculation establishes God's unity, and that religious legislation effects a social and political program that leads to the perfection of human society and human persons.

A common paradigm distinguishes between those thinkers of the Middle Ages who emphasized "reason" and those who emphasized "faith." The various controversies over the teachings of Moses Maimonides give plausibility to this dichotomy. Philosophers opposed what they considered the obscurantism of their opponents. Those who attacked Maimonides and his followers claimed that rationalism undermined faith. Yet this facile distinction is also misleading. Both those who supported philosophy as the means to understanding Judaism and those who used Judaism to criticize philosophy had as their main objective countering the possibility of Jews' being seduced away from Judaism.

This possibility faced Jewish thinkers in each of our four periods. Both Maimonides and Halevi, for example, sought to stem the abandonment of Jewish life by intellectuals of their times, but they did so differently, according to their different understandings of the place of philosophy within Judaism. Comparing their views on the creation of the world, for example, both agreed that the biblical story should be read not for its literal meaning but for the principles it enunciates: for instance, that a Creator freely created the world for a designated purpose. Both agree that creation, therefore, entails human responsibilities. Where they disagree, however, is on the importance of history. Maimonides does not deem it necessary to emphasize that creation occurs in time, that it begins a process that will culminate in a historical event. Halevi, by contrast, makes creation in time central, a difference that marks the distinction between those who use philosophy to defend Judaism and those who use Judaism to put philosophy in its rightful place. For the former, Judaism survives as an example of an eternal, rational truth. For the latter, Judaism exists as a unique historical expression that must bend philosophy so that it serves its needs. Whether the contending thinkers are Halevi and Maimonides (whose thought is examined below), Maimonideans and anti-Maimonideans in the thirteenth century, or rationalists and anti-rationalists in the fifteenth and sixteenth centuries, the distinction remains constant. By looking at two representatives from the Golden Age, we again expose the two ways of understanding Judaism and philosophy.

Judah Halevi on Judaism and Philosophy

Judah Halevi (1075–1141) stands as a touchstone for a fideist approach to philosophy in Judaism. His major work, *The Khuzari*, introduces a philosopher whose irrelevance to religion appears self-evident.[12] The philosopher then disappears for the rest of the book, present, perhaps, by being absent, but never engaged as a major protagonist. Those who followed Halevi's lead in making Judaism the criterion by which to judge philosophy are inevitably compared to him. Halevi's life experience underlines the unease he felt with philosophy. His life began in comparative security. Born in Muslim Toledo, he cultivated the intellectual skills of poetry, philosophy, and medicine. These skills are evident in his writings, which include secular, philosophical, and liturgical poetry, and a major philosophical treatise. After the Christian reconquest of Toledo, Halevi went to Andalusia to study. His stay in Cordoba was interrupted by the invasion of the militant Islamic revivalists, the Al-Moravids. Halevi began a life of travel, going from Cordoba to Lucena to Seville and back to Toledo and from thence to Castile and later to Cordoba again. His experience as a courtier taught him to distrust a life based on the patronage of others, yet he was fated to just such a life. It seems that he ended his life in Egypt, from whence he set forth to the land of Israel only to turn back, at least once.

This insecurity echoes in his major philosophical work, which takes the form of a dialogue. Historically, King Bulan of the Khazar people in Russia (ruled

786–809) converted to Judaism together with several of his nobility. This conversion most probably reflected social, economic, and political necessity for a kingdom composed mainly of Christians and Muslims. Yet Halevi turned this story into a narrative philosophical work, explicating the basis of Judaism as a rabbi elucidates it for a prospective convert, in this case, the King of the Khazars. Halevi creates a "utopia" in which Jewish arguments prevail against all alternatives. The book opens as the King of the Khazars has a dream telling him that while God approves of his pious intentions, he must still learn correct actions. The king summons a philosopher to instruct him, but the philosopher emphasizes intention over action, thus explicitly failing to answer the king's need. Throughout the rest of the book, philosophers are treated with condescension. Aristotle, for example, should be admired, since he labored without having a true tradition to guide him (*Khuzari* I:65); philosophers who know only general ideas about God are not to be blamed, for they lack revelation to teach them (IV:13).

The book continues as the king dismisses first a Christian scholastic and then a Muslim jurist. Only as a last resort does he turn to a Jew (the *haver*) who explains the principles of Judaism. He begins by insisting on the priority of history, of the Jewish experience, and then shows how this experience confirms Jewish claims without denying philosophical truth. Halevi reads the Bible for its basic principles, not as a literal dictation of the divine. When describing revelation, the Jew declares "Heaven forbid that I should assume what is against sense and reason!" (I:89). Yet while Halevi gives rational explanations for biblical texts and interprets their principles rather than their literal meaning, he insists on the primacy of Hebrew. He argues that "To Hebrew, however, belongs the first place, both as regards the nature of the languages, and as to fullness of meanings" (II:66). This suggests that even while the ideas of the Bible can be translated into rational terms, the essence of the Hebrew Bible surpasses philosophy.

The same duality holds true for the Jewish view of the divine. Halevi notes the two names the Bible uses for God, "Elohim" and "Adonai." The first embraces the rational and philosophic qualities derived from a definition of divinity. The philosophers do understand the nature of divine unity. Yet beyond this, divine power manifests itself in ways that philosophers cannot fathom. They lack revelation to enable them to experience the historical basis of religious claims (IV:11–16). The key consequence of this difference lies in its existential effect on the believer. Halevi emphasizes that the Jew who accepts revelation has a fear and knowledge of the divine that transcends intellectual perception. That transcendence explains the importance of Jewish law and practice. Of course Halevi admits that such practice leads to a well ordered human life. Using the analogy of the soul to a city – the influence of Plato's *Republic* IV:434–441 is clear – Halevi claims for Jewish law the ability to produce the well-balanced personality (III:3–5). At the same time, Halevi suggests an inherent power and significance in Jewish practices that goes beyond personal self-improvement. He claims there are "ordinations especially given to Israel as a corollary to the rational laws. Through this they received the advantage of the Divine Influence . . ." (II:48). Philosophical equilibrium by itself is not enough; philosophers need the addition of divinely given laws to become worthy of the influx of spiritual power.

Philosophy and Judaism in the Thought of Moses Maimonides

Moses Maimonides stands as the giant of medieval Jewish philosophy. His two major works, *The Guide for the Perplexed*, a philosophical treatise, and *The Mishneh Torah*, a legal compendium that not only follows a philosophical ordering of material but begins with a treatise devoted to the fundamental philosophical beliefs of Judaism, show how philosophy clarifies the truths of Judaism. What might appear to be superstitious or anthropomorphic elements in Jewish religion become, with the application of reason, understandable and acceptable.

Maimonides' life seems the opposite of Halevi's. Born in Cordoba, he experienced the fall of Cordoba in 1148 and began a life of wandering that led him to Fez and other parts of North Africa, until he settled finally in Fostat, old Cairo. In Cairo, under the Ayyubid Sultan Saladin, he became the virtual head of the Jewish community in Egypt. His son, in fact, inherited that position. Thus Maimonides completed his life in security, sure of his position and of his power in the Jewish community. He devoted his life in Egypt to philosophy, medicine, and Jewish communal life. This combination of talents gave him a political as well as intellectual prestige that made his thought particularly influential. Modern biographies offer several interpretations of Maimonides, some emphasizing his political sagacity, others his communal spirit, still others his ethical and moral vision, others his philosophical cunning. This variety of images of the philosopher from Fostat testifies to his ability to comprehend several positions, offices, and concerns. From his position of power, Maimonides was able to provide a philosophy of Judaism that would convince doubters concerning the rationality and acceptability of Jewish religion.

For Maimonides the first requirement for a true knowledge of Judaism was an understanding of the coded language of the Bible. The first section of his *Guide for the Perplexed* concerns the interpretation of biblical terms. When applied to God, such terms have only a linguistic relationship to the meanings they have when applied to human beings. Maimonides, that is, insists that anthropomorphic expressions in the Bible must be understood allusively and not literally. Thus he introduces the book by saying, "The first purpose of this Treatise is to explain the meanings of certain terms occurring in the books of prophecy" (I:1).[13] Scripture, then, must be made to yield its secrets to the philosophical reader. Yet this is not only a philosophical principle. Maimonides insists that the incorporeality of the divine must be taught to philosophers and non-philosophers alike. It is a principle of Judaism fit for the masses no less than the elite (I:31, 35). Maimonides thereby makes the Bible a fit text for intellectuals and Judaism a philosophically reputable faith.

One of the chief reasons for this approach is to remove the idea of anthropomorphism from the biblical text. Maimonides emphasizes the utter otherness of the divinity. God's unity implies that for God, unlike for creatures, change and division are impossible. One of Maimonides' most important ideas reflects this idea – his view of "negative attributes." Human beings, he claims, cannot definitively state what God is. They cannot know what it means to say that God "lives," "is powerful," or "is knowing." Instead, predicates of God must be understood to reject the negation of certain qualities. God cannot be "dead," "powerless," or "unknowing." This limitation on what human language can do instills humility in the philosopher. Philosophy must stop short of claiming to reveal truth; it only indicates the boundaries of knowledge. Such a stance reminds readers that Judaism presents a faith based on human limitations; it restrains a critique of Jewish belief based on philosophic arrogance.

That critique looks to the moral attitude of the human being. Maimonides interprets Jewish religious practices as a means to inculcate morality. That morality prepares a person for the life of the philosopher. "The Law as a whole," he comments, "aims at two things: the welfare of the soul and the welfare of the body" (III:27). Maimonides describes how the laws fulfill these functions in detail, rejecting the argument that giving the reasons for the commandments undermines their authority (III:31). Here again, Maimonides defends the philosophical validity of Jewish religion. Judaism proves its merit by the usefulness of its code of laws. When Maimonides arranges the laws according to their types, he again underlines the rationality of Judaism and demonstrates its validity.

Philosophy and Judaism: The modern period

Most historians agree that the modern period begins with the Enlightenment, but that term itself is subject to controversy and contention. If by "enlightenment" one follows Immanuel Kant, one of its foremost exponents, the period was distinguished by "critical" philosophy. If criticism marks the modern period, then Harry Wolfson was surely right to identify Baruch Spinoza (1632–77) as both the last of the medievals and, as Benedict de Spinoza, the first of the moderns. In his life and in his writings Spinoza undermined the foundations of medieval religious philosophy. He wrote as an outsider who could convert the language of faith – the Bible – into the more familiar language of philosophy – in the modern form that Descartes established. Spinoza sought to dethrone theology and replace it with philosophical rigor. Unlike the pre-moderns, he began with the assumption that the traditional language was incomprehensible, unclear, inadequate. The modern Jewish philosopher finds the original expression of Judaism, whether in the Bible, in the Talmud, or in medieval writings, unfamiliar, daunting, inaccessible. The new philosophic task begins by facing this alienation and making sense of it.

After that confrontation, the philosopher may either accept or reject the Judaism uncovered. Spinoza's approach gave the tradition a place in the history of human society. Jewish theology was, for him, a relic from a past civil society and no longer relevant. His verdict on Judaism reflects his personal history. One of the first native-born Jews of Amsterdam, Spinoza suffered excommunication from his community, misunderstanding from Jews and Christians alike, and offered a critical appraisal of all previous thought. His *Theological–Political Treatise* uses medieval definitions of the divine, of scripture, and of prophecy to undermine the methods and intentions of the medievals. His *Ethics* provides new definitions of philosophical conceptions that disguise the continuities of his underlying philosophical venture with those of the past through a radically new form.

Spinoza's critical thinking challenged modern Jewish philosophers to reconceive their views of revelation, divinity, and Jewish religion. Perhaps the best example of this influence is Moses Mendelssohn (1729–86), who self-consciously opposed "Spinozism." In reaction to Spinoza, he conceived of Judaism as "revealed legislation" rather than "revealed truth" and defended its civil usefulness. His translation and commentary on the Hebrew Bible reflects a modern rather than medieval consciousness. His fierce monotheism refuses to grant Spinoza a foothold. Yet on every page he writes, Spinoza's presence is felt.

Spinoza's critical approach dominates "modern" Judaism, but it also permeates what has come to be known as "postmodern" thinking. Nietzsche perceptively recognized his kinship to Spinoza. Both recognized the alienated, isolated life of the philosopher in modern times. Spinoza, almost in spite of himself, seems to recognize the constructive, creative power of philosophizing. He reads Scripture as he reads Nature, recognizing the impenetrable within that which is most intimate to us, acknowledging that the human mind seems to create its categories rather than derive them from the given. Spinoza's impact on Jewish thinking extends into postmodern no less than purely "modern" works.

Spinoza demands that the Bible be read on its own terms and criticizes Moses Maimonides for importing into his reading foreign ideas. Such a reading he characterizes as "harmful, unprofitable, and absurd."[14] Under his scrutiny, the Bible was forced to speak for itself, and he found it a political, not a philosophical, document. Modern Jewish exegetes like Martin Buber (1878–1965), Emmanuel Levinas (1906–95), and Franz Rosenzweig (1886–1929) take up the challenge he sets down. They too refuse to impose a meaning on the biblical text. The meanings that they hear in the Bible, however, differ dramatically from those that Spinoza thinks the text articulates.

Spinoza's famous dictum that *Deus sive Natura sive Substantia* – God is Nature is Substance – solves the problem of the unity of reality by identifying it as part of a single entity, called God. This move preserves a unified cosmos, but at the expense of a transnatural, transcendent divinity. Spinoza's identification of the divine and nature leads him to declare that the height of blasphemy is belief in divine intervention that reverses the laws of nature. He drives home this point in his discussion of miracles. If miracles refer to events that have no natural cause, then they are in direct opposition to God. To say that Nature cannot control reality is to say that God lacks control of the world, and that is heresy. Where the Bible appears to make such a claim, Spinoza argues, the passage must be judged spurious: anything found in Scripture that can be conclusively proven to contravene the laws of Nature, or that cannot possibly follow from them, must have been inserted by sacrilegious men (p. 134). Jewish thinkers have had to cope with this reintroduction of empirical evidence and pluralism into their thought.

Spinoza also challenges the adequacy of Jewish religious practice. He provides a purely utilitarian justification of Jewish ritual. The ceremonial law aims not at "blessedness" but rather at civil welfare (p. 113). Jewish law has a peculiar effectiveness to it. Spinoza claims that by virtue of the rite of circumcision alone, the Jewish people – had it not been emasculated by its historic conditions – would be able to regain its glory (p. 100). Yet Spinoza adds that such a revival seems unlikely. Jewish law no longer serves a useful purpose, because Jews no longer live in their own social or political state. Theoretically, Jewish law may one day become justifiable, but Spinoza's practical judgment is that Jews have no currently legitimate reason to maintain their religious practices.

Responses to Spinoza entail either accepting the limitations he imposes and finding a place – which he did not anticipate – for Judaism within them or rejecting the framework of philosophy as somehow an inadequate rendition of reality. Two thinkers seem to mark these alternatives best – Hermann Cohen (1842–1918), the neo-Kantian who, out of the sources of Judaism, reconstructed a Religion of Reason, and Emmanuel Levinas, the postmodernist thinker who "translates" from Hebraic thought into Hellenic language (while writing his books in French!). Their thought shows the two ways in which Judaism and philosophy contend in the modern period.

Hermann Cohen's View of Judaism and Philosophy

Hermann Cohen's thought has been judged as either a thoroughly Judaized philosophical system or a radical break with traditional Judaism's core belief. Which of these views is accepted does not alter Cohen's clearly philosophical orientation. His "Religion of Reason" is "Out of the Sources of Judaism," which means that modern philosophy provides the hermeneutic for understanding religion. Cohen, born in Coswig in 1842, began his higher studies at the Jewish Theological Seminary at Breslau but eventually decided upon a career in philosophy, studying at the University of Breslau, the University of Berlin, and receiving his doctorate from the University of Halle in 1865. He taught at the University of Marburg from 1873 to 1912, becoming renowned as an interpreter and expositor of Immanuel Kant and influencing what became known as the Marburg School of neo-Kantian thought. At the age of seventy, he left Marburg for Berlin and began applying his thought to religion in general and Judaism in particular.

Cohen's understanding of Judaism self-consciously opposes Spinoza's philosophy with that of a neo-Kantianism that justifies religious life. He approaches the Bible in a way that makes its meaning flexible, dynamic, and evolutionary. Rabbinic interpretation, he insists, does not represent arrogance but rather "the overflow of a critical self-consciousness" that transcends the locality of Palestine and the temporality of the biblical period.[15] This ability of Judaism to find in contemporary thought new keys to revelation legitimates Cohen's procedure of rereading classic texts to show their relevance to a Kantian understanding of reason and religion.

Cohen insists against Spinoza that identifying God with nature or substance misrepresents the personalized unity of all things. While Spinoza may solve his problem of unifying thought and extension, he does not solve the deeper problem of the duality between being and becoming: "The unity of substance may thereby be defined, but its uniqueness is abolished" (p. 45). The uniqueness of humanity, for Cohen's neo-Kantianism, lies in the ability to feel compassion, to think as a human person. This ethical dimension of human beings requires rooting in a divinity who makes such compassion possible. Spinoza's theories do not, so what they gain in unifying the cosmos, they lose by ignoring human uniqueness. Judaism's monotheism, Cohen claims, provides a better basis for positing cosmic unity than does Spinoza's.

Cohen rejects Spinoza's critique of Jewish practice no less than his opposition to Jewish monotheism. He begins by noting the absurdity of substituting a past religion for a more modern one: "The idea of replacing one religion by another makes no sense historically, for it contradicts the philosophy of history which has to ward off the idea of the absolute and has to investigate the share of reason in the various phenomena of culture" (p. 364). More than that, Spinoza has mistaken the specific rules of Jewish law for the idea of Jewish lawfulness itself. Lawfulness, the idea of Jewish practice, is "valid as the foundation of the moral world" and thus perseveres despite "Spinoza's polemic" that "has become the source of a fundamental misunderstanding of the Jewish religion" (pp. 331, 338). Because the ideas of Jewish practice and lawfulness rather than the specific practices themselves are central, Cohen justifies the modern transformation of those actions. "It would be superficial," he comments, " to think that in modern Judaism the power of the law is absolutely broken and destroyed" (p. 359). As an expression of a moral presupposition, law takes different forms while retaining the same function.

Emmanuel Levinas's Translation from Hebraic to Greek Thought

While Cohen uses the categories of Kantian philosophy to construct a defensible Judaism, Emmanuel Levinas, drawing on the insights of Franz Rosenzweig, Martin Heidegger, and Edmund Husserl, intimates a postmodern phenomenology of the Other that translates from Judaic concepts into the language of philosophy. Levinas, like Cohen, first gained recognition as a philosopher; Jean-Paul Sartre brought him to notoriety by acknowledging him as his instructor in phenomenology (the philosophical movement associated with Husserl in particular). In this way, like Cohen, Levinas represents the peculiarly modern perspective. Jews today approach the tradition "through the backdoor." They are more comfortable with general categories of thought than with the traditional sources of Judaism. They need someone to translate Judaism from its original modes and categories into the more familiar ones of general thought. Levinas was well suited to this task. Unlike Cohen, he never lost contact with Jewish sources or students and engaged in ongoing dialogue with the Jewish tradition.

Even Levinas's purely philosophical writing indicates his Judaic sensibility. He acknowledges his debt to Franz Rosenzweig as an "interruption" to an extended discussion of phenomenology. Rosenzweig provides the impetus to challenge "totality and eternity" in the name of the "other," of multiplicity and individuality rather than universalism. Levinas takes a stand within Judaism against the homogenization of philosophy. While, like Hermann Cohen, Levinas places the subject, the human being, at the center of thought, he does so not as an expression of universal philosophy but as a protest against such philosophy.

Levinas takes this stance because he sees his task as "translating" from Hebraic thought into Hellenistic, or western philosophical, categories. Greek, as he understands it, emphasizes "deciphering" demystification. It is "prose," whereas religious language is poetry. Jewish religion, he claims, always aims at such demythologization. It rationalizes what is being deciphered. This process, begun by the Talmudic rabbis and the Hellenistic Jewish philosophers at one and the same time, represents the philosophical impulse in Judaism, an impulse expressed in both the Septuagint and Talmud. The task of the Septuagint, he claims, is not complete – not only the Bible but the Talmud and all Jewish tradition awaits translation into philosophical terms. Like Hermann Cohen, then, he sees the Bible as teaching basic ideas, not merely literal truths. He struggles with the meaning in the Bible and Rabbinic literature, again like Cohen, to derive the significance of the texts anew. Unlike Cohen, however, he does not use philosophy as the guide to what the texts must mean. Instead his reflection on texts leads him to challenge philosophy, to put it to the test, to rebel against its imperialism and to augment it with ethical sensitivity.

This augmentation involves drawing attention to the unique and the individual. The cosmos has meaning not in its universalism but in its particular manifestations. The God of the universe, for Levinas as for Cohen, loves particulars. What summons us, what is the foundation of our reality, is the face of the Other. It is responsibility for the Other that creates both ethics and the idea of unity, the recognition that every article and every process holds its own uniqueness.[16] As with Cohen, so with Levinas, God ensures this freedom and responsibility. God does so as an Other "who sends me to serve my neighbor, to responsibility for him. God is personal insofar as He brings about interpersonal relations between myself and my neighbors."[17] Again, as with Cohen, it is the uniqueness of person that is essential. Unlike Cohen, however, Levinas takes the ethical Otherness of the divine as his point of departure, as a religious given in experience.

Levinas reflects on all Jewish living, the ethical dilemmas faced by Jews today, the ritual practices such as prayer that Jews observe, the difficulties faced by Judaism in a liberated world. Levinas begins with what he calls "The Judaism of the House of Prayer," this is, the Judaism of Psalms, a Judaism born out of the subject's experience and life. Yet he admits that this Judaism "has ceased to be transmittable. The old-fashioned Judaism is dying off, or is already dead." This tragedy leads him to translate Jewish religion into a new key, to present its rationality since "the Judaism of reason must take precedence over the Judaism of prayer; the Jew of the Talmud must take precedence over the Jew of the Psalms."[18]

This approach enables Levinas, like Cohen, to defend the concepts of Jewish practice even more than he does the detailed observances themselves. Levinas clearly observed traditional Jewish law, considered himself a halakhic Jew, and respected the legal prescriptions of Jewish Orthodoxy. He declares that "The whole of Jewish Law is commanded *today* even though Mount Sinai belongs to the past."[19] Yet he recognizes that that past needs a new translation into the present.

Among the needed transition is a shift from concern with what God does for human beings to the contribution humanity makes to God. With this in mind, Levinas claims that God needs prayer even more than the human participant in worship. Prayer makes no demands, but rather elevates the soul. Ritual such as prayer provides the divine with a means of bringing justice to the world.[20] As with Cohen, so too with Levinas, ethics infuses ritual with meaning. Levinas, however, comes to this exposition by beginning with the tradition and then translating it into philosophical terms. Cohen worked in the opposite way, asking what philosophy required of religion and then finding it in Judaism.

Conclusion

What is the relationship of philosophy and Judaism? The examples studied have three foci in common: an interpretation of scripture, a defense of the unity of reality, and a justification for Jewish practice. In the ancient period the problem was determining the categories by which to understand scripture, reality, and Jewish life. In the medieval period, Jewish thinkers sought to justify the particular religion of Judaism against competing monotheistic faiths; they needed to show that the Jewish approach to Scripture, the cosmos, and human virtue rivaled or surpassed that of other traditions. In the modern period, Jewish philosophy wrestled with naturalism and worked to establish the transcendence of Scripture, the transcendental unity of reality, and the evocative power of Jewish practice. In each period, however, Jewish thinkers divided over how to achieve their common goal. Some used the resources of philosophy as a hermeneutic to create a palatable Judaism. Others began with Judaism and resorted to philosophy only as a prop to support their claims. Perhaps the dialectic at work here was what the contemporary thinker Jacob Agus had in mind when declaring that the "mighty tensions within the soul" of western thought "were reflected faithfully and clearly in the currents and cross-currents of the historic stream of Judaism."[21]

Notes

1   Flavius Josephus, *The Complete Works of Josephus*, William Whiston, tr. (Edinburgh, 1960), pp. 614–15.
2   Citations are from Hans Lewy, ed., "Philo: Selections," in *Three Jewish Philosophers* (New York, 1965).
3   Ibid., pp. 53–4.
4   Ibid., pp. 38–9.
5   Ibid., p. 41.
6   Josephus, op. cit., p. 608.
7   Ibid., p. 622.
8   Ibid., p. 633.
9   Ibid., p. 636.
10 Ibid., p. 274.
11 See Jacob Neusner, *Judaism as Philosophy: The Method and Message of the Mishnah* (Columbia, 1991).
12 See Judah Halevi, *The Kuzari (Kitab Al Khazari): An Argument for the Faith of Israel*, Hartwig Hirschfeld, tr. (New York, 1954).
13 Moses Maimonides, *The Guide of the Perplexed*, Shlomo Pines, tr. (Chicago, 1963).
14 Baruch Spinoza, *Tractatus Theologico-Politicus*, Gebhardt Edition, 1925, Samuel Shirley, tr. (Leiden, 1989), p. 159.
15 Hermann Cohen, *The Religion of Reason: Out of the Sources of Judaism* (New York, 1971), p. 28. Page citations in the following discussion are to this work.
16 Emmanuel Levinas, *The Levinas Reader*, Seán Hand, ed. (Oxford, 1989), pp. 83, 87.
17 Emmanuel Levinas, *Outside the Subject* (Stanford, 1993), pp. 46–7.
18 Levinas, Emmanuel, *Difficult Freedom: Essays on Judaism*, Seán Hand, tr. (Baltimore, 1990), p. 271.
19 Ibid., p. 191.
20 Ibid., pp. 227–34.
21 Jacob Bernard Agus, *The Evolution of Jewish Thought: From Biblical Times to the Opening of the Modern Era* (New York, 1960), p. 6.

Bibliography

Agus, Jacob Bernard, *The Evolution of Jewish Thought: From Biblical Times to the Opening of the Modern Era* (New York, 1960).

Barzilay, Isaac E., *Between Reason and Faith: Anti-Rationalism in Italian Jewish Thought, 1250–1650* (The Hague, 1967).

Cohen, Richard A., *Elevations: The Height of the Good in Rosenzweig and Levinas* (Chicago, 1994).

Fackenheim, Emil L., *Jewish Philosophers and Jewish Philosophy* (Bloomington, 1996).

Frank, Daniel N. and Oliver Leaman, eds., *History of Jewish Philosophy* (London, 1997).

Levinas, Emmanuel, *The Levinas Reader*, Seán Hand, ed. (Oxford, 1989).

Levinas, Emmanuel, *Difficult Freedom: Essays on Judaism*, Seán Hand, tr. (Baltimore, 1990).

Moses Maimonides, *The Guide of the Perplexed*, Shlomo Pines, trans. (Chicago, 1963).

Norris, Christopher, *Spinoza and the Origins of Modern Critical Theory* (Oxford, 1991).

Seeskin, Kenneth, *Jewish Philosophy in a Secular Age* (Albany, 1990).

Sirat, Colette, *A History of Jewish Philosophy in the Middle Ages* (Cambridge, 1990).

Wolfson, Harry Austryn, *Studies in the History of Philosophy and Religion* I, Isadore Twersky and George H. Williams, eds. (Cambridge, 1973).

CHAPTER 11
Jewish Piety

Tzvee Zahavy

Piety means acting in one's personal life primarily in accord with religious principles and values. Ideally, piety fills the life of every practicing Jew and endows it with transcendent meaning. In all forms of Rabbinic Judaism, ancient and modern, piety of action overshadows philosophical faith at the central defining core of the religion. This article explores the daily, weekly, and annual routines of the pious Jew, the regular elements of life-cycle events and the transcendent meanings ascribed to these within the system of religion. The elements of the Rabbinic forms of piety are most commonly prevalent in Orthodox and Hasidic articulations of the religion. They are less prominent in Conservative Judaism and only selectively present in Reform and Reconstructionist systems of Judaism.

Early Rabbinic Piety

The rabbis of the second century CE emphasized distinctive groups of practices that differentiated their form of Judaism. Some scholars theorize that the rabbis chose to prescribe these practices as a means of maintaining spirituality after the loss of the Temple. The rabbis prescribed, for example, that each Jew recites one hundred blessings every day. The recitation of a blessing prior to the performance of many basic rituals imprints on them a mark of mystical piety. R. Meir (second century CE) spelled this out in his statement, "There is no man in Israel who does not perform one hundred commandments each day [and recite over them one hundred blessings]. . . . And there is no man in Israel who is not surrounded by [reminders of the] commandments: [Every person wears] phylacteries on his head, phylacteries on his arm, has a *mezuzah* on his door post and four fringes on his garment around him . . ." (T. Ber. 6:24–25).

In the Home

Rabbinic practices, especially those associated with prayer and blessings, relate strongly to rituals of the home, village, and fellowship. Rabbinic authorities expect all Jews to practice rituals from morning until night so that, from the first stirring every morning, the Jew begins his day with acts of religious significance. Hence, washing hands upon arising takes on a special meaning. The individual conducts the washing according to a simple but prescribed practice. Water is poured on the fingers of each hand up to the joint as specified by the masters. The inclusive Rabbinic vision of piety starts here and extends broadly to the individual throughout the activities of the day. Accordingly, religious observances are associated with even some bodily functions like elimination, not ordinarily linked to the realm of religious ritual. The rabbis said that one had to recite a blessing after the act as thanks for continued health. This imbues even a normally profane physical process with an aspect of piety.

Prayers

In Rabbinic Judaism, daily morning prayers are literally clothed in piety. The man puts on the *tallith* (prayer shawl) and *tefillin* (phylacteries) while reciting the respective blessings. Each pious male obtains and maintains these prized and essential objects of piety in accordance with the prescriptions of the rabbis and scribes. The man wears these objects to show compliance with the prescriptions of the verses of the Torah recited in the *Shema* (Deut. 6:4–9, 11:13–21, and, especially, Num. 15:37–41). Each knot on the four fringes of the *tallith* garment is tied in accord with age-old tradition. The *tefillin* are crafted of select leather, made into cubical containers to hold the small parchments of biblical paragraphs, written by trained scribes. The head-*tefillin* has to rest on the worshiper on the forehead between the eyes, neither too high on the head nor too low on the face. The leather strap that holds it in place has to be tied in accord with known custom. The wearer understands that the knot of leather that sits at the base of his skull represents the letter *yod*, the third letter of *Shaddai*, one of the divine names. On the leather box of the arm-*tefillin* is inscribed the letter *shin*. The wearer knows that the knot that holds it fast on his left biceps – opposite his heart – is a form of the letter *dalet*. Thus as he recites prayer, the Jew is bound head and heart to God, *Shaddai*. He wears these appurtenances each weekday from the time he reaches thirteen, the age of maturity, now commonly called the age of Bar Mitzvah. Obtaining a pair of *tefillin* from the scribe is the most significant overt sign of achieving adult membership in the Rabbinic community. The standard practice now is to wear the *tallith* and *tefillin* during the morning prayers and then remove them. However, to show extreme piety, some few virtuoso rabbis wore them all day as they sat immersed in the study of Torah.

An ordinary Jewish man can recite his prayers in a designated synagogue or study hall, in private at home, or in any orderly place. For optimal piety, he goes to the synagogue to pray with the *minyan*, the prayer quorum of ten adult Jews. The formalization of the synagogue as a standard communal institution took place over a span from the first century through the Middle Ages. The emphasis in Jewish custom and law was always on prayer in a public gathering of ten or more men, not on prayer in a specified building or designated place for gathering. This aspect of Rabbinic piety was thus defined mainly in terms of a societal association with a community of other Jews. The rabbis placed little emphasis on the need for sacred buildings to fulfill the spiritual needs of prayer.

Rabbinic piety centers on stability and repetition. On weekdays, Jews gather for the morning, afternoon, and evening prayers. Major elements of prayer are repeated with small variations at the three services. A person says the *Shema* in the morning and evening services; the *Amidah* (standing prayer of eighteen blessings) in the morning, afternoon, and evening services; the *alenu* (a sublime prayer proclaiming God king) to conclude all three. To these, on Monday, Thursday, and on festival and fast days, they add a morning Torah service to the public prayer, during which they read the first section of the seven-part Torah-lection that would be read on the coming Sabbath during morning worship. This focuses attention on the coming Sabbath celebration and gives the men gathered during the week an added opportunity to hear the inspiration of the words of Torah.

During the week, a fourth service, the additional prayer, called *Musaf*, is added to celebrate special days. On New moons, celebrants add several paragraphs to the regular services and read an appropriate passage from the Torah. They conclude the morning prayers with the recitation of the *Amidah* – the standing prayer of eighteen blessings – of the additional service. Likewise on holidays, modifications are made in the regular prayers and the additional *Musaf Amidah* is appended.

Evening prayers consist of the *Shema*, *Amidah*, and *Aleinu*. A widespread custom is to recite the *Shema* once more at bedtime. Many believe this added evocation of piety also protects the person who recited it from harm during the night.

Women's Piety

Women were not assigned an egalitarian role in traditional Rabbinic piety. In accord with the profile of Prov. 31:10–31, a woman was assigned a life of valor in support of her family. Piety for the woman in classical Judaism emphasized more her personal character as wife, mother, and homemaker and less her participation in public rituals of prayer and the synagogue. In many Jewish cultures through the course of history, women were not required or expected to attend the synagogue at all. One Rabbinic expression used to justify these choices was that, "The princess is honored inside (i.e., in the home, not the synagogue)."

For the traditional Jewish woman, developing good personal character is considered a process of piety. Shyness, kindness, and good-heartedness are singled out as desired traits. Modesty is a paramount virtue for the pious woman. The rabbis translate this expectation into formal custom. The pious woman has to dress in accord with the prevalent rules of modesty. The norms are more rigorous for a married woman. In most cultural settings of Rabbinic communities, the conventions require that she cover her hair with a hat, kerchief, or wig, cover her arms and legs with suitable clothing, and that she act in a humble and quiet manner. Ideally, to conform to the needs of piety, a woman's speech and conversation at all times is to be modest. The rabbis prohibit a married woman from any form of flirtation or any action that could be misconstrued as an invitation to licentiousness.

Several meaningful prayers are reserved as acts of piety predominantly for women. Saying special chapters from the book of Psalms, especially for the sick, is an act of piety more prevalent among women. Characteristically, lighting candles just before the onset of the Sabbath on Friday evening is a woman's act of piety on behalf of her entire household.

Rabbis gave serious attention to obligations and exemptions for women in all acts of piety and *mitzvot*. The rabbis distilled their concept down to a principle. They exempted women from all pious acts for the performance of which time was of the essence. Women thus are not expected to attend the synagogue and are not counted in the official quorum for public prayer. The common expectation is that women will not join with men in the professional study of Torah. With rare exceptions, they do not study alongside men in the yeshiva and are not ordained as rabbis.

The Pious Home

The woman's main role is to aid her husband in building a household in Israel. It is deemed a major act of piety to marry, raise children, and to maintain a pious family life. Simple rites of piety mark the life-cycle rites of passage in Rabbinic tradition. The wedding ceremony creates the pious state of matrimony in a few symbolic stages. At the betrothal, the woman is designated for marriage to her intended husband. In medieval and later times, the betrothal and wedding were combined into one event. Bride and groom often fasted and repented from wrongdoing on their wedding day, which some rabbis equated for the couple to Yom Kippur.

The writing of the *Ketubah* marks the matrimony. This Aramaic legal document is given to the wife to protect her interests within the marriage. The writ is often read aloud by a dignified rabbi during the wedding ceremony. At the brief ceremony, the groom places the ring on the bride's finger and recites, "Behold you are sanctified to me in accord with the laws of Moses and Israel." The presiding rabbi or distinguished members of the family or community recite the Seven Blessings. They contain allusions to the cosmic and mythic biblical accounts of the beginning and end of time, brought to bear to sanctify the present moment of piety. The concluding blessing declares, "Blessed art Thou Lord our God, King of the Universe, who created joy and happiness, bride and groom, gladness, jubilation, cheer and delight, love, friendship, harmony and fellowship." It continues, "Lord our God, soon may it be heard in the cities of Judah and the streets of Jerusalem the sounds of joy and happiness, bride and groom, exultation of grooms from their wedding canopy and of children from their joyous banquets." It concludes, "Blessed are you Lord our God who gladdens the groom with the bride."

The wedding is to be held out-of-doors under a canopy. Thus it is endowed with the cosmic symbolism of the heavens and a metaphor for the canopy of the new home. According to tradition, the Divine Presence comes down upon the canopy and angels of heaven cry out that it be God's will that the bride and groom rejoice with one another. After the ceremony, it is a common custom to break a glass, symbolizing both the fragility of the relationship and the sufferings of the Jewish people. The bride and groom then go briefly into a private room, to embody their intimacy. After the wedding feast, the couple continue to celebrate the marriage for one week, with special blessings and customs at every festive dinner.

Pious Relationships

A peaceful home and harmonious family life is a simple ideal for Rabbinic society. Those goals are elevated to acts of piety. In a proper relationship a pious husband has to make efforts to understand and cater to the needs of his wife, and to control his anger and his ego. The wife in turn has to strive continually to fulfill her roles within the family. Biblical models of loyalty, like that of Ruth, and bravery, like that of Esther, guide the actions of the pious woman. The rabbis said that sanctity resided in the correct union of partners.

Childbearing and rearing are imbued with elements of piety, making it incumbent upon both partners to provide a nurturing environment for their children. The obligation to educate one's children is also elevated to the level of an act of piety. The Talmud prescribes that a father has to teach his son Torah, a trade, and how to "swim," that is, survival skills and self-defense.

More so than in other religions, Rabbinic Judaism asserts that religious piety governs sexuality and intimacy between partners in a marriage. This area of piety is called "family purity." Couples are encouraged to observe the rules both by promises of merit and by threats of dire consequences both to those who violate them and to their offspring. Based on Lev. 18:19, the rabbis formalized a taboo against sexual relations at certain times during a woman's monthly menstrual cycle. A form of piety thereby governs the most intimate physical relations between husband and wife.

Intricate rituals govern the abstinence from intimacy of man and wife. During the wife's menstrual period, they may not touch each other casually, or at meals, or share the same bed. The separation is compared to a hedge of roses erected between lovers. Mastery of one's desires is considered a sure sign of piety. The rabbis taught that the laws of family purity assuredly would continually renew the love between husband and wife. After the prescribed period of abstinence during menstruation and seven clean days, the wife immerses herself in the specially constructed *mikvah*-bath, under the supervision of another woman, before she may resume intimacy with her husband. If there are uncertainties about the menstrual period, a rabbi is consulted to judge whether the emission requires additional abstinence. Traditionally, this was done through the anonymous submission of test cloths to the authority. Maimonides in the Middle Ages urged Jews to observe these laws, not based on fact or logic, but out of "the devotion of one's heart."

The rights and expectations of husband and wife are formulated into Rabbinic prescriptions for the pious to observe. Elements of a relationship, like love, devotion, and faithfulness, are not merely character traits to be admired. They are integral aspects of a pious life within the parameters of a marital relationship.

The Pious Household

Piety extends to nearly all aspects of life in the Rabbinic home. The symbolic *mezuzah* hangs on every doorway, sanctifying the space of the house and protecting its inhabitants. It contains passages from Deut. 6:4–9 and 11:13–21 written on parchment in twenty-two lines like that of the *tefillin*. The rabbis noted that the *mezuzah*, *tefillin*, and fringes of the prayer shawl remind a person of the need to be pious and they protect one from sin. A person has thirty days from the time of initial occupancy to affix a *mezuzah* to one's home.

Especially noteworthy is the extensive reach of practices of pervasive piety in the cuisine of the Rabbinic home governed by the laws of Kashrut. Kosher food categories and rules require constant attention to the sources and preparation of food in the household. Meats may only be obtained from a trusted butcher who would know that it was from a kosher species, a healthy animal, and that it was properly slaughtered and prepared. A Jew may not consume *treifa*, unfit meat.

The taboo against cooking milk and meat together necessitates that homes have two sets of utensils for preparation of meals. The theory behind this is that a pot or utensil absorbs the flavor when milk or meat is cooked in it and imparts that flavor to any milk or meat that is subsequently cooked in it. The complex details of maintaining separate utensils for dairy products and meat requires extensive Rabbinic guidance.

In kosher preparation, meat is soaked in water, carefully salted with coarse kosher salt, and washed to extract as much of the blood as possible. Specific veins are removed. Liver may be used only if cut, washed, salted, and broiled over a fire. Eggs with a spot of blood in them are forbidden. Vegetables must be carefully inspected for insects and worms that might render them unfit for consumption. Kosher consumption requires that milk and meat foods neither be prepared together nor eaten at the same meal. Rabbinic law requires also the immersion in a *mikvah* of new metal or glass cooking utensils before use.

Piety extends to baking as well. In an effort to perpetuate some of the rules of the Temple involving priestly dues, the rabbis symbolically extended the laws of dough offerings, tithes, and heave-offerings. When baking bread, it is necessary to separate *challah*, a small piece of dough that is burned rather than consumed. This serves as a memorial to the priestly dues that could no longer be brought to the Temple and as a sign of hope for the redemption of Israel and the restoration of the Temple service. Any bread dough made of wheat, barley, spelt, rye or oat flour is liable to this obligation.

Charitable giving to the poor naturally is motivated by piety. The rabbis recommended as an act of piety that a Jew donate a tithe of his income to charity, a memorial to the voluntary Levitical tithes of Israelite times. Much was written and preached about the piety of giving generously to charity. Maimonides, a medieval authority, extolled the virtues of anonymous donation as the most pious form of charity.

As noted, every occasion for eating is transformed by Rabbinic precept into a pious meal. Before partaking of bread, the pious Jew washes his hands and recites a blessing as symbols of the purity once associated with the priests entering the Temple to perform the sacred rites of the cult. In accord with the system developed in the Mishnah and Talmud, a pious Jew recites blessings and prayers before and after eating or drinking any food.

The rabbis determined that what constituted a full meal was the breaking of bread. The blessing recited over bread is, "Blessed art thou, O Lord our God, who brings forth bread from the earth." Once this is said, all foods eaten during the meal are subsumed, and no other blessings are recited. The full grace after meals is intoned after the meal. Rabbinic authorities also developed a system of blessings recited before eating specific foods and drinks outside the framework of a full meal. Special blessings are specified for vegetables, fruits, baked goods, wine, and drinks. Piety requires that one recite shorter blessings of thanksgiving after eating baked goods or individual foods.

Piety at meals creates a formal fellowship that is expressed in additional practices. At the completion of a formal meal in which bread has been eaten, one person is designated to invite the other diners to recite the grace together. Good table manners become a matter of piety as well.

Furthermore, a righteous Jew is to uphold the imperative of hospitality. To support this, the rabbis taught that one who engages in the kindness of welcoming guests emulates Abraham the patriarch. Opening one's house to the poor is the highest form of the piety of welcoming the stranger. Proper behavior toward animals is also expected as a matter of piety. Causing any suffering to an animal is a transgression. As a reminder of this imperative, one is not permitted to eat before feeding one's animals.

Part of the Rabbinic way of life is devotion to children. This started at the primary commandment that a father circumcise his son on the eighth day. This practice goes back to Abraham as the most ancient sign of the covenant between God and his chosen people. If the father cannot fulfill his role, he designates a professional *mohel* to carry out the rite. Most often the ceremony is an occasion for a public celebration and obligatory feast. All members of the community are expected to participate in the celebration. Members of the family and distinguished guests receive the honors of carrying and holding the infant before, during, and after the procedure. All the assembled guests bless the child that he might enter into a life of Torah, marriage, and good deeds. The child's name is then announced in public for the first time.

There was no formal ritual to mark the birth of a daughter. However, it became a common practice to name one's daughter in the synagogue after being called to the Torah on the Sabbath following the birth.

Another symbolic act harking back to Israelite times is the practice of redeeming one's first-born son from a priest (see Exod. 13:1–15 and Num. 3:11–13 and 44–48). Thirty-one days after the birth, the father symbolically exchanges with a priest five shekel coins, or their equivalent, for his son.

The caring roles of mother and father are demarcated clearly within the pious family structure. Caring for infants is thought to be the role of the mother. Discipline of children is evenly shared between mother and father. Education of the young up to a certain age is entrusted to the mother. An example of a Jewish lullaby captures the spirit of pious child rearing: "Run my son, run hard/ enter the house of your teacher/ Search and seek only in the Torah/ For her wealth is better than all wares." When old enough, boys are educated by the father or sent off to formal training with a rabbi or suitable teacher. Girls are afforded a less intensive education.

The bar mitzvah was a late development in Judaic ritual and piety. As discussed above, it is the occasion for boys to put on *tefillin* for the first time and to be called in public to read from the Torah. The bat mitzvah ceremony for girls was an even later practice. Some communities mark it with a celebration in the synagogue or, more commonly, by a public feast. Filial piety or honor of one's parents is a hallmark of all Jewish piety. Some rabbis expressed this in mystical terms. Rav Joseph, hearing his mother's footsteps approaching, would say, "I rise before the *shekhinah* (Divine Presence) that draws nigh."

Philosophical Meanings of Piety

Rabbinic sources rarely make philosophical generalizations about piety. From the perspective of Judaism, even the definition of the category or term "piety" is problematic. Piety is a classical category of western discourse regarding religious action and ethics (cf., Plato, Euthyphro) not a category drawn out of, or native to, classical Judaism. The premise of this chapter is that, for Rabbinic Judaism, piety implies living in accord with a faith in the validity and relevance of the dual Torah (written and oral) as taught and expanded by the rabbis. In this form of Judaism, piety endows everyday activities, decisions, and attitudes with special significance based on historical, mystical, and redemptive beliefs. Piety requires that Jews create and perform new practices based on the same.

The motives and goals of piety within the Judaic application lead to several outcomes: Piety leads to a life of sanctification – *qedushah* – in accord with the *Halakhah* – Jewish law. It leads to a life of awe, love, or fear of God. It results in submission to a higher power engendering a sense of creatureliness. It enables the believer to insure entry to paradise in the "World to Come" (i.e., the afterlife or heaven). Piety aids in bringing about the messianic era. On the most basic level, many believe that piety also results in material gain.

The high status of obligation and commandment within Judaism defines the nature of Judaic piety. Most Jewish acts of piety have official status so that they are incumbent upon the entire community of faith (*mitzvah*). God's command both compels the Jew to live a pious life and endows daily activities with transcendent meanings. Custom, *minhag*, by contrast, gives quasi-official status to pious practice. It is limited in time and place and less authoritative, but often this distinction is unrecognized in the life of a pious Jew.

Categories of Piety

The ultimate yardstick of piety is the *Zaddiq* – the righteous saint. How closely one adheres to the norms of ultimate piety indicates the righteousness of the individual. The righteous saints are those who we would call purely ethical, those who flourish as proper humans, and those who achieve true virtue.

Cognitive piety is a subset of the general category. Its highest form is the perpetual study of the Torah, the sources and authoritative basis of Judaic piety. The well-known epigram that expresses this notion asserts that, "The study of Torah is as important as all other acts of piety combined." Another dimension of this subset is "mind-piety," that is, the desirability of maintaining perpetually pure thoughts, of focusing one's thoughts on Torah at all times. Along these lines, the rabbis emphasized the centrality of meditation, prayer, and contemplation in the daily life of the Jew.

Body-piety is another aspect of the larger concern. Physical actions endowed with piety include bowing and other bodily postures; washing for extra-hygienic purposes; wearing proper clothing and appurtenances of pious living: *tzitzit* (fringes), *tefillin*, and yarmulke (hat); other forms of dress; and haircut, beard, or side locks. Naturally all aspects of sexuality can be included in this subset, as discussed above.

Synagogue piety is a third major area of the subject. Many acts associated with prayer in the synagogue define elements of this type of piety. Blowing and hearing the shofar at the New Year and shaking the lulav on the festival of Sukkot constitute two examples of this area. All acts of prayer come under this rubric.

Some modern, secular, attitudes appear to deflate the value of a life defined by piety. Apologists for piety argue that this denies one modality for fulfilling a basic human need: piety provides individuals with connections to the past and future, to heaven and earth, to family, and to community. The modern secular person bereft of piety lives a more lonely, detached life with less passion and devotion. Proponents of piety ask if the rise in secularization has been accompanied by an increase in happiness or by a decline in economic oppression or by psychological dysfunction. In addition, it needs to be explored whether constant piety and familiarity with the sacred indeed, as some have claimed, devalue the worshiper's relationship to the deity and render it rote and mechanical.

The believer–practitioner of the pious life emphasizes a main advantage afforded by the intimacy of piety. In the Judaic notion, God wants constant contact with the believer, akin to an obsessive love affair, renewed frequently by expected daily affirmations. Constant devotion to the divine provides the perpetual training and conditioning for that relationship. Piety invigorates with energy all the devotions of one's life, such as marriage, raising children, advancing one's vocation, and contributes to the vigor of one's community.

PART II
The Principal Doctrines of Judaism

CHAPTER 12

The Doctrine of Torah

Jacob Neusner

The word Torah stands for God's revelation to Moses at Sinai. It further refers to all authoritative teaching by sages, which enjoy the same status as God's revelation to Moses at Sinai. The religion that the world calls "Judaism" calls itself "Torah," for the outsider names the religion, but the faithful define it by their lives together. Holy Israel has always looked to the Torah to find God and what God is, does, and wants of humanity. The doctrine of Torah thus encompasses, among other much prized religious virtues and actions, study of the Torah as the highest priority of Judaism. Our problem is to discover what, exactly, the word Torah means in its setting in Judaism. A striking and unexpected usage proves also highly suggestive (B. Ber. 62a):

> *It has been taught on Tannaite authority:*
> Said R. Aqiba, "I once went after R. Joshua to the privy and I learned the three things from him: I learned that people defecate not on an east–west axis but on a north–south axis. I learned that one urinates not standing but sitting. And I learned that one wipes not with the right hand but with the left."
> Said Ben Azzai to him, "Do you behave so insolently toward your master?"
> He said to him, "It is a matter of Torah, which I need to learn."
> *It has been taught on Tannaite authority:*
> Ben Azzai says, "I once followed R. Aqiba into the privy, and I learned three things from him: I learned that people defecate not on an east–west axis but on a north–south axis. And I learned that people urinate not standing up but sitting down. And I learned that people wipe themselves not with the right hand but with the left."
> Said R. Judah to him, "Do you behave all that insolently toward your master?"
> He said to him, "It is a matter of Torah, which I need to learn."

[In Aramaic:] R. Kahana went and hid under Rab's bed. He heard [Rab and his wife] "conversing" and laughing and doing what comes naturally. He said to him, "It appears that Abba's mouth has never before tasted 'the dish.'"

He said, "Kahana, are you here! Get out! That's disgraceful!"

He said to him, "It is a matter of Torah, which I need to learn."

Here is a set of three curious stories that make the same jarring point: natural bodily processes, intimate chapters in the private life – both fall within the framework of Torah, which is to be taught by the sage and must be learned by the disciple. The details of the text need not detain us for long. The story shows us that "the Torah," referring to a specific set of authoritative Scriptures, has lost its definite article. It now refers to authoritative teachings by a sage, teachings deriving from tradition to which the sage in particular has access and affecting every detail of ordinary life. The doctrine of "Torah" in Judaism then refers not to canonical writings alone but to God's will for holy Israel in every dimension of the everyday.

Defining the Word Torah

What, exactly, do we mean by the word "Torah"? Torah means "teaching," and in Scripture refers to the teaching that God revealed to Moses at Mount Sinai. The most familiar referent of the word is the Five Books of Moses or Pentateuch, that is, Genesis, Exodus, Leviticus, Numbers, and Deuteronomy. "The Torah" may also refer to the entirety of the Hebrew Scriptures (called by Christianity, "the Old Testament"). But since Judaism maintains that at Sinai God revealed the Torah to Moses in two media, written and oral, with the written part corresponding to the Pentateuch, a further, oral part of the Torah is included in the meanings assigned to the word Torah. This oral part is held to encompass the teachings ultimately written down by the sages of the Torah in ancient times and is contained, in part, in the Mishnah, Talmud, and Midrash-compilations.

The definitive ritual of the religion outsiders call Judaism consists in studying the Torah. The form of study is meant to be public, engaging all Israel, which is why the centerpiece of synagogue worship is meant to be the proclamation of the Torah. Study-groups, where people read sacred texts, discuss them, and relate what they read to the world they know, form the ideal setting for Torah-study. In the classical tradition, moreover, study means discipleship, for study of Torah involves entering into a tradition that is preserved only in part in writing but in important measure also in memory, orally. Then the faithful learn Torah from experienced teachers of the Torah, and, in turn, they become teachers themselves. So for the people of the Torah, study of the Torah requires a shared and public encounter. One who studies Torah, according to the teachings thereof, becomes holy, like Moses, who is called "Moshe rabbenu," "Moses, our rabbi," and like God, in whose image humanity was made and whose

Torah provided the plan and the model for what God wanted of a humanity created in his image. In the system of Judaism found in the Torah, it is that image of God to which Israel should aspire, and to which the sage in fact conformed.

How Scripture became Torah

Let us now ask how the word Torah acquired its critical position within Judaism. For Judaism as we know it at the end of late antiquity reached its now familiar definition when "the Torah" lost its capital letter and definite article and ultimately became "torah." That is the sense of the stories with which we commenced. What for nearly a millennium had been a particular scroll or book thus came to serve as a symbol of an entire system. When a rabbi spoke of torah, he no longer meant only a particular object, a scroll and its contents. Now he used the word to encompass a distinctive and well-defined world-view and way of life. Torah came to stand for something one does. Knowledge of the Torah promised not merely information about what people were supposed to do, but ultimate redemption or salvation.

The Torah of Moses clearly occupied a critical place in all systems of Judaism from the closure of the Torah-book, the Pentateuch, in the time of Ezra onward. But in late antiquity, for one group alone the book developed into an abstract and encompassing symbol, so that in the Judaism that took shape in the formative age, the first seven centuries CE, everything was contained in that one thing. How so? When we speak of torah, in rabbinical literature of late antiquity, we no longer denote a particular book, on the one side, or the contents of such a book, on the other. Instead, we connote a broad range of clearly distinct categories of noun and verb, concrete fact and abstract relationship alike. "Torah" stands for a kind of human being. It connotes a social status and a sort of social group. It refers to a type of social relationship. It further denotes a legal status and differentiates among legal norms. As symbolic abstraction, the word encompasses things and persons, actions and status, points of social differentiation and legal and normative standing, as well as "revealed truth."

In all, the main points of insistence of the whole of Israel's life and history come to full symbolic expression in that single word. If people wanted to explain how they would be saved, they would use the word Torah. If they wished to sort out their parlous relationships with gentiles, they would use the world Torah. Torah stood for salvation and accounted for Israel's this-worldly condition and the hope, for both individual and nation alike, of life in the world to come. For the kind of Judaism under discussion, therefore, the word Torah stood for everything. The Torah symbolized the whole, at once and entire. When, therefore, we wish to describe the unfolding of the definitive doctrine of Judaism in its formative period, the first exercise consists in paying close attention to the meanings imputed to a single word.

Seven Meanings of the Word Torah

The several meanings of the word Torah require only brief explanation:

1 When the Torah refers to a particular thing, it is to a scroll containing divinely revealed words.
2 The Torah may further refer to revelation, not as an object but as a corpus of doctrine.
3 When one "does Torah" the disciple "studies" or "learns," and the master "teaches," Torah. Hence while the word Torah never appears as a verb, it does refer to an act.
4 The word also bears a quite separate sense, torah as category, classification, or corpus of rules, e.g., "the torah of driving a car" is a usage entirely acceptable to some documents. This generic usage of the word does occur.
5 The word Torah very commonly refers to a status, distinct from and above another status, as "teachings of Torah" as against "teachings of scribes." For the two Talmuds that distinction is absolutely critical to the entire hermeneutic enterprise. But it is important even in the Mishnah.
6 Obviously, no account of the meaning of the word Torah can ignore the distinction between the two Torahs, written and oral. It is important only in the secondary stages of the formation of the literature.
7 Finally, the word Torah refers to a source of salvation, often fully worked out in stories about how the individual and the nation will be saved through Torah. In general, the sense of the word "salvation" is not complicated. It is salvation in the way in which Deuteronomy and the Deuteronomic historians understand it: kings who do what God wants win battles, those who do not, lose. So too, people who study and do Torah are saved from sickness and death, and the way Israel can save itself from its condition of degradation also is through Torah.

This matter of status requires amplification. For it points to the very center of matters: knowledge of the Torah shapes conduct, and by one's conduct, a person shows precisely who he or she is. What difference does study of the Torah make within the community of holy Israel? The answer must surprise us, even after nearly two thousand years: the person who masters the Torah enjoys the highest status, even overtaking the status conferred by birth, wealth, caste, or class. The Mishnah places a high value upon studying the Torah and upon the status of the sage (M. Hor. 3:8).

> A priest takes precedence over a Levite, a Levite over an Israelite, an Israelite over a *mamzer* [one whose parents cannot legally marry by reason of consanguinity], a *mamzer* over a *Netin* [descendant of a Temple slave], a *Netin* over a proselyte, a proselyte over a freed slave.
> Under what circumstances?
> When all of them are equivalent.

But if the *mamzer* was a disciple of a sage and a high priest was an *am haares* [lacking all knowledge of the Torah], the *mamzer* who is a disciple of a sage takes precedence over a high priest who is an *am haares*.

The stakes prove very high when we realize that the kind of knowledge afforded by Torah-study – Talmud Torah – changes the status of the one who knows, moving that person from the lowest to the highest level of Israelite society. Here is a world in which a particular sort of knowledge corresponds to money in our own society.

The one premise of all that follows insists upon the transforming power of Torah-study. The Torah bears the power of gnostic learning, that is to say, learning that transforms the very being of the person who learns. What they learn, when the faithful study Torah, not only informs but changes them, affecting not only their mind but their heart and soul, their character. Here is a text that speaks of the change in supernatural terms, a change in the very meaning of family relationships for example (M. B.M. 2:11):

[If someone has to choose between seeking] what he has lost and what his father has lost, his own takes precedence.

. . . what he has lost and what his master has lost, his own takes precedence.

. . . what his father has lost and what his master has lost, that of his master takes precedence.

For his father brought him into this world.

But his master, who taught him wisdom, will bring him into the life of the world to come.

But if his father is a sage, that of his father takes precedence.

[If] his father and his master were carrying heavy burdens, he removes that of his master and afterward removes that of his father.

[If] his father and his master were taken captive, he ransoms his master, and afterward he ransoms his father.

But if his father is a sage, he ransoms his father, and afterward he ransoms his master.

Here is another surprising text: the natural father brings the child into this world, but the sage brings the disciple into the world beyond the natural, the world to come, life eternal. Once more, we confront a remarkable claim in behalf of Talmud Torah.

The Mishnah as the Nexus

The critical moment in the transformation of the concept of "Torah" to encompass matters vastly transcending the Hebrew Scriptures came when the Mishnah, a philosophical law code, was promulgated in ca. 200 CE under the sponsorship of Judah, patriarch of the Jews of the land of Israel. The document differed in every way from any prior writing Jews had valued. It made its statement in a kind of Hebrew of its own. It rarely cited verses of Scripture or in other ways aligned its rules and teachings with the Torah of Sinai. And yet, the document gained authority over Israel, both in the land of Israel and in Babylonia, and so its standing required an explanation.

Upon its closure, the Mishnah gained an exalted political status as the constitution of Jewish government of the land of Israel. Accordingly, the clerks who knew and applied its law had to explain the standing of that law, meaning its relationship to the law of the Torah. But the Mishnah provided no account of itself. Unlike biblical law codes, the Mishnah begins with no myth of its own origin. It ends with no doxology. Discourse commences in the middle of things and ends abruptly. What follows from such laconic mumbling is that the exact status of the document required definition entirely outside the framework of the document itself. The framers of the Mishnah gave no hint of the nature of their book, so the Mishnah reached the political world of Israel without a trace of self-conscious explanation or any theory of validation.

The one thing that is clear, alas, is negative. The framers of the Mishnah nowhere claim, implicitly or explicitly, that what they have written forms part of the Torah, enjoys the status of God's revelation to Moses at Sinai, or even systematically carries forward secondary exposition and application of what Moses wrote down in the wilderness. Later on, I think two hundred years beyond the closure of the Mishnah, the need to explain the standing and origin of the Mishnah led some to posit two things. First, God's revelation of the Torah at Sinai encompassed the Mishnah as much as Scripture. Second, the Mishnah was handed on through oral formulation and oral transmission from Sinai to the framers of the document as we have it. These two convictions, fully exposed in the ninth-century letter of Sherira, in fact emerge from the references of both Talmuds to the dual Torah. One part is in writing. The other was oral and now is in the Mishnah.

As for the Mishnah itself, it contains not a hint that anyone has heard any such tale. The earliest apologists for the Mishnah, represented in tractate Abot and the Tosefta alike, know nothing of the fully realized myth of the dual Torah of Sinai. It may be that the authors of those documents stood too close to the Mishnah to see the Mishnah's standing as a problem or to recognize the task of accounting for its origins. Certainly they never refer to the Mishnah as something out there, nor speak of the document as autonomous and complete. Only the two Talmuds reveal that conception – alongside their mythic explanation of where the document came from and why it should be obeyed. So the Yerushalmi marks the change. In any event, the absence of explicit expression of such a claim in behalf of the Mishnah requires little specification. It is just not there.

But the absence of an implicit claim demands explanation. When ancient Jews wanted to gain for their writings the status of revelation, of torah, or at least to link what they thought to what the Torah had said, they could do one of four things. They could sign the name of a holy man of old, for instance, Adam, Enoch, Ezra. They could imitate the Hebrew style of Scripture. They could claim that God had spoken to them. They could, at the very least, cite a verse of Scripture and impute to the cited passage their own opinion. These four methods – pseudepigraphy, stylistic imitation (hence, forgery), claim of direct revelation from God, and eisegesis – found no favor with the Mishnah's framers. They signed no name to their book. Their Hebrew was new in its syntax and morphology, completely unlike that of the Mosaic writings of the Pentateuch. They never claimed that God had anything to do with their opinions. They rarely cited a verse of Scripture as authority. It follows that, whatever the authors of the Mishnah said about their document, the implicit character of the book tells us that they did not claim God had dictated or even approved what they had to say. Why not? The framers simply ignored all the validating conventions of the world in which they lived. And, as I said, they failed to make explicit use of any others.

It follows that we do not know whether the Mishnah was supposed to be part of the Torah or to enjoy a clearly defined relationship to the existing Torah. We also do not know what else, if not the Torah, was meant to endow the Mishnah's laws with heavenly sanction. To state matters simply, we do not know what the framers of the Mishnah said they had made, nor do we know what the people who received and were supposed to obey the Mishnah thought they possessed.

A survey of the uses of the word Torah in the Mishnah, to be sure, provides us with an account of what the framers of the Mishnah, founders of what would emerge as Rabbinic Judaism, understood by that term. But it will not tell us how they related their own ideas to the Torah, nor shall we find a trace of evidence of that fully articulated way of life – the use of the word Torah to categorize and classify persons, places, things, relationships, all manner of abstractions – that we find fully exposed in some later redacted writings.

True, the Mishnah places a high value upon studying the Torah and upon the status of the sage. A "*mamzer*-disciple of a sage takes priority over a high-priest *am haares*," as at M. Hor. 3:8, noted above. But that judgment, distinctive though it is, cannot settle the question. All it shows is that the Mishnah pays due honor to the sage. But if the Mishnah does not claim to constitute part of the Torah, then what makes a sage a sage is not mastery of the Mishnah in particular. What we have in hand merely continues the established and familiar position of the wisdom writers of old. Wisdom is important. Knowledge of the Torah is definitive. But to maintain that position, one need hardly profess the fully articulated Torah-myth of Rabbinic Judaism. Proof of that fact, after all, is the character of the entire wisdom literature prior to the Mishnah itself.

So the issue is clearly drawn. It is not whether we find in the Mishnah exaggerated claims about the priority of the disciple of a sage. We do find such claims. The issue is whether we find in the Mishnah the assertion that whatever the sage has on the authority of his master goes back to Sinai. We seek a definitive view that what the sage says falls into the classification of Torah, just as what Scripture says constitutes Torah from God to Moses. That is what distinguishes wisdom from the Torah as it emerges in the context of Rabbinic

Judaism. To state the outcome in advance: we do not find the Torah in the Mishnah, and the Mishnah is not part of the Torah.

When the authors of the Mishnah surveyed the landscape of Israelite writings down to their own time, they saw only Sinai, that is, what we now know as Scripture. Based on the documents they cite or mention, we can say with certainty that they knew the Pentateuchal law. We may take for granted that they accepted as divine revelation also the Prophets and the Writings, to which they occasionally make reference. That they regarded as a single composition, that is, as revelation, the Torah, Prophets, and Writings appears from their references to the Torah, as a specific "book," and to a Torah-scroll. Accordingly, one important meaning associated with the word Torah was concrete in the extreme. The Torah was a particular book or sets of books, regarded as holy, revealed to Moses at Sinai. That fact presents no surprise, since the Torah-scroll(s) had existed, it is generally assumed, for many centuries before the closure of the Mishnah in 200.

What is surprising is that everything from the formation of the canon of the Torah to their own day seems to have proved null in their eyes. Between the Mishnah and Mount Sinai lay a vast, empty plain. From the perspective of the Torah-myth as they must have known it, from Moses and the prophets, to before Judah the Patriarch, lay a great wasteland. So the concrete and physical meaning attaching to the word Torah, that is the Torah, the Torah revealed by God to Moses at Mount Sinai (including the books of the Prophets and the Writings), bore a contrary implication. Beyond "The" Torah there was no torah. Besides the Pentateuch, Prophets, and Writings, not only did no physical scroll deserve veneration, but no corpus of writings demanded obedience. So the very limited sense in which the words "the Torah" were used passed a stern judgment upon everything else, all the other writings that we know circulated widely, in which other Jews alleged that God had spoken.

The range of the excluded possibilities that other Jews explored demands no survey. It includes everything, not only the Gospels (by 200 CE long since in the hands of outsiders), but secret books, history books, psalms, wisdom writings, rejected works of prophecy – everything excluded from any biblical canon by whoever determined there should be a canon. If the library of the Essenes at Qumran tells us what might have been, then we must regard as remarkably impoverished the (imaginary) library that would have served the authors of the Mishnah: The Book of Books, but nothing else. We seldom see so stern, so austere a vision of what commands the status of holy revelation among Judaisms over time. The tastes of the Mishnah's authors express a kind of literary iconoclasm, but with a difference. The literary icons did survive in the churches of Christendom. But in their own society and sacred setting, the judgment of Mishnah's authors would prevail from its time to ours. Nothing in the Judaisms of the heritage from the Hebrew Scripture's time to the Mishnah's day would survive the implacable rejection of the framers of the Mishnah, unless under Christian auspices or buried in caves. So when we take up that first and simplest meaning associated with the word Torah, "The Torah," we confront a stunning judgment: this and nothing else, this alone, the thing alone of its kind and no other thing of similar kind.

"Moses Received Torah from Sinai"

It is tractate Abot, added to the Mishnah about 250 CE, a generation after the Mishnah was promulgated, that presented a systematic account of the authority of the document, which rested on the position of its authorities in the chain of tradition from Sinai. Because its authorities possessed the oral tradition of Sinai, what they said – without proof-texts or other external marks of origin with Moses – enjoyed the standing of revelation, tradition of Sinai, and, it follows, the very concept of Torah underwent considerable expansion.

What we shall now see, in the opening chapter of tractate Abot, is that Moses forms the nexus. He is the master of the Torah – because he is the first disciple. God is the master, Moses the disciple, and, in the model of that same relationship, all those who come to serve as disciples, to study Torah, endow their teachers with the standing of Moses. Here is the whole story:

Tractate Abot presents the concept of "Torah" in a very specific way. It treats as a matter of Torah a saying of an authority who stands in the chain of tradition from Sinai. But what the sage says never is a citation of, or a comment upon, a verse of Scripture (the written Torah). Rather, the sage makes a saying of his own. Hence the authority of the Torah, that is, of Sinai, attaches to what sages teach on their own, and that is because the sage has mastered the tradition of Sinai and found a place within that tradition. Tractate Abot thus draws into the orbit of Torah-talk the names of authorities of the Mishnah. Not only so, but tractate Abot says a great deal about Torah-study.

What makes the statements important to us is simple. The claim that Torah-study produces direct encounter with God forms part of Abot's thesis about the Torah. That claim, by itself, will hardly have surprised Israelite writers of wisdom books over a span of many centuries, whether those assembled in the Essene commune at Qumran, on the one side, or those represented in the pages of Proverbs and in many of the Psalms, or even the circle of scribes and prophets who produced the book of Deuteronomy, in the time of Josiah, on the other.

A second glance at tractate Abot, however, produces a surprising fact. In Abot, Torah is instrumental. The figure of the sage, his ideals and conduct, by contrast, forms the goal, focus and center. To state matters simply: Abot regards study of Torah as what a sage does. The substance of Torah is what a sage says. That is so whether or not the saying relates to scriptural revelation. The content of the sayings attributed to sages endows those sayings with self-validating status. The sages usually do not quote verses of Scripture and explain them, nor do they speak in God's name. Yet, it is clear, sages talk Torah. What follows is that if a sage says something, what he says is Torah. More accurately, what he says falls into the classification of Torah. Accordingly, Abot treats Torah-learning as symptomatic, an indicator of the status of the sage, hence, as merely instrumental.

The simplest proof of that proposition lies in the recurrent formal structure of the document, the one thing the framers of the document never omit and always emphasize: (1) the name of the authority behind a saying, from Simeon the Righteous on downward, and (2) the connective-attributive "says." So what is important to the redactors is what they never have to tell us. Because a recognized sage makes a statement, what he says constitutes, in and of itself, a statement in the status of Torah. Let me set forth the opening statements of tractate Abot, so we shall see what "receiving" and "handing on" Torah consists of – that is to say, the contents of "Torah."

1:1   Moses received Torah at Sinai and handed it on to Joshua, Joshua to elders, and elders to prophets.
      And prophets handed it on to the men of the great assembly.
      They said three things:
      "Be prudent in judgment.
      "Raise up many disciples.
      "Make a fence for the Torah."

1:2   Simeon the Righteous was one of the last survivors of the great assembly.
      He would say: "On three things does the world stand:
      "On the Torah,
      "and on the Temple service,
      "and on deeds of loving-kindness."

1:3   Antigonos of Sokho received [the Torah] from Simeon the Righteous.
      He would say,
      "Do not be like servants who serve the master on condition of receiving a reward,
      "but [be] like servants who serve the master not on condition of receiving a reward.
      "And let the fear of Heaven be upon you."

1:4   Yose b. Yoezer of Seredah and Yose b. Yohanan of Jerusalem received [it] from them.
      Yose b. Yoezer says,
      "Let your house be a gathering place for sages.
      "And wallow in the dust of their feet.
      "And drink in their words with gusto."

1:5   Yose b. Yohanan of Jerusalem says,
      "Let your house be wide open.
      "And seat the poor at your table ['make them members of your household'].

"And don't talk too much with women."

(He spoke of a man's wife, all the more so is the rule to be applied to the wife of one's fellow. In this regard did sages say, "So long as a man talks too much with a woman, (1) he brings trouble on himself, (2) wastes time better spent on studying Torah, and (3) ends up an heir of Gehenna.")

1:6   Joshua b. Perahiah and Nittai the Arbelite received [it] from them.
Joshua b. Perahiah says,
"Set up a master for yourself.
"And get yourself a fellow disciple.
And give everybody the benefit of the doubt."

1:7   Nittai the Arbelite says,
"Keep away from a bad neighbor.
"And don't get involved with a wicked man.
And don't give up hope of retribution."

1:8   Judah b. Tabbai and Simeon b. Shatah received [it] from them.
Judah b. Tabbai says,
"Don't make yourself like one of those who make advocacy before judges [while you yourself are judging a case].
"And when the litigants stand before you, regard them as guilty.
"And when they leave you, regard them as acquitted (when they have accepted your judgment)."

1:9   Simeon b. Shatah says,
"Examine the witnesses with great care.
"And watch what you say,
"lest they learn from what you say how to lie."

To spell out what this means, let us look at the opening sentences. "Moses received Torah," and it reached "the Men of the Great Assembly." "The three things" those men said bear no resemblance to anything we find in written Scripture. They focus upon the life of sagacity – prudence, discipleship, a fence around the Torah. And, as we proceed, we find time and again that, while the word Torah stands for two things, divine revelation and the act of study of divine revelation, it produces a single effect, the transformation of unformed man into sage. Strikingly, few of the sayings appeal to Scripture for authority; what the sage says gains authority because the sage says it.

One climax of the list that commences with Moses at Sinai comes in Yohanan ben Zakkai's assertion that the purpose for which a man (an Israelite) was created was to study Torah, followed by his disciples' specifications of the most important things to be learned in the Torah. All of these pertain to the conduct of the sage; none appeals to a verse of Scripture for validation.

2:8   Rabban Yohanan b. Zakkai received [it] from Hillel and Shammai.
He would say,
"If you have learned much Torah, do not puff yourself up on that account, for it was for that purpose that you were created."
He had five disciples, and these are they: R. Eliezer b. Hyrcanus, R. Joshua b. Hananiah, R. Yose the priest, R. Simeon b. Netanel, and R. Eleazar b. Arakh.
He would list their good qualities:
R. Eliezer b. Hyrcanus: A plastered well, which does not lose a drop of water.
R. Joshua: Happy is the one who gave birth to him,
R. Yose: A pious man.
R. Simeon b. Netanel: A man who fears sin.
And R. Eleazar b. Arakh: A surging spring.
He would say, "If all the sages of Israel were on one side of the scale, and R. Eliezer b. Hyrcanus were on the other, he would outweigh all of them."
Abba Saul says in his name, "If all of the sages of Israel were on one side of the scale, and R. Eliezer b. Hyrcanus was also with them, and R. Eleazar [b. Arakh] were on the other side, he would outweigh all of them."

2:9   He said to them, "Go and see what is the straight path to which someone should stick."
R. Eliezer says, "A generous spirit."
R. Joshua says, "A good friend."
R. Yose says, "A good neighbor."
R. Simeon says, "Foresight."
R. Eleazar says, "Good will."
He said to them, "I prefer the opinion of R. Eleazar b. Arakh, because in what he says is included everything you say."
He said to them, "Go out and see what is the bad road, which someone should avoid."
R. Eliezer says, "Envy."
R. Joshua says, "A bad friend."
R. Yose says, "A bad neighbor."
R. Simeon says, "Defaulting on a loan."
(All the same is a loan owed to a human being and a loan owed to the Omnipresent, blessed be he, as it is said, The wicked borrows and does not pay back, but the righteous person deals graciously and hands over [what he owes; Ps. 37:21].)
R. Eleazar says, "Bad will."
He said to them, "I prefer the opinion of R. Eleazar b. Arakh, because in what he says is included everything you say."

We have to locate the document's focus not on Torah but on the life of sagacity (including, to be sure, Torah-study). But what defines and delimits Torah? It is the sage himself or herself. So we may simply state the tractate's definition of Torah: Torah is what a sage learns. Accordingly, the Mishnah contains Torah. It may well be thought to fall into the classification of Torah. But the reason, we recognize, is that authorities whose sayings are found in the Mishnah possess Torah from Sinai. What they say, we cannot overemphasize, is Torah. How do we know it? It is a fact validated by the association of what they say with their own names.

Now, clearly, when we speak of "Torah," we mean something other, more than Scripture alone. The Torah reaches us through a chain of tradition made up of masters and disciples, and in the Rabbinic writings, the relationship of disciple to master is portrayed as identical to the relationship between Moses and God, or between Aaron and Moses (B. Erub. 54b):

> *Our rabbis have taught on Tannaite authority:*
> What is the order of Mishnah-teaching? Moses learned it from the mouth of the All-powerful. Aaron came in, and Moses repeated his chapter to him, and Aaron went forth and sat at the left hand of Moses. His sons came in, and Moses repeated their chapter to them, and his sons went forth. Eleazar sat at the right of Moses, and Itamar at the left of Aaron . . .
> Then the elders entered, and Moses repeated for them their Mishnah-chapter. The elders went out. Then the whole people came in, and Moses repeated for them their Mishnah-chapter. So it came about that Aaron repeated the lesson four times, his sons three times, the elders two times, and all the people once.
> Then Moses went out, and Aaron repeated his chapter for them. Aaron went out. His sons repeated their chapter. His sons went out. The elders repeated their chapter. So it turned out that everybody repeated the same chapter four times.

Here is a different kind of portrait of imitation of God: what the pious imitate about God is the wording of teachings (which of course we are to carry out), and how the faithful encounter God is in the labor of using their minds. Studying Torah is not reading a book but forming a community with a teacher and fellow-students and transforming that community from this world to a realm in which God's presence comes to rest.

The point is simple. We have to locate the focus of tractate Abot not on Torah but on the life of sagacity (including, to be sure, Torah-study). But what defines and delimits Torah? It is the sage himself. So we may simply state the tractate's definition of Torah: Torah is what a sage learns. Accordingly, as stated above, the Mishnah contains Torah and may be considered to fall into the classification of Torah, that is, to constitute part of the revelation from Sinai. This is because the authorities whose statements are found in the Mishnah possess Torah exactly as it was revealed to Moses. What they say, therefore, is commensurate with the written revelation contained in Scripture, also understood to derive from Sinai.

So we miss the real issue when we ask Abot to explain for us the status of the Mishnah, or to provide a theory of a dual Torah. The principal point of insistence – the generative question – before the framers of Abot does not address the status of the Mishnah. And the instrumental status of the Torah, as well as of the Mishnah, lies in the net effect of their composition: the claim that through study of the Torah sages enter God's presence. So study of Torah serves a further goal, that of forming sages. The theory of Abot pertains to the religious standing and consequence of the learning of the sages. To be sure, a secondary effect of that theory endows with the status of revealed truth things sages say. But then, as I have stressed, it is because they say them, not because they have heard them in an endless chain back to Sinai. The fundament of truth is passed on through sagacity, not through already formulated and carefully memorized truths. That is why the single most important word in Abot also is the most common, the word "says."

At issue in Abot is not the Torah, but the authority of the sage. It is that standing that transforms a saying into a Torah-saying, or, to state matters more appropriately, that places a saying into the classification of the Torah. Abot then stands as the first document of the doctrine that the sage embodies the Torah and is a holy man, like Moses "our rabbi," in the likeness and image of God. The beginning is to claim that a saying falls into the category of Torah if a sage says it as Torah. The end will be to view the sage himself as Torah incarnate.

The Yerushalmi's Doctrine of the Torah

The Mishnah is held in the Talmud of the Land of Israel to be equivalent to Scripture (Y. Hor. 3:5). But the Mishnah is not called Torah. Still, once the Mishnah entered the status of Scripture, it would take but a short step to a theory of the Mishnah as part of the revelation at Sinai – hence, oral Torah. In the first Talmud, we find the first glimmerings of an effort to theorize in general, not merely in detail, about how specific teachings of Mishnah relate to specific teachings of Scripture. The citing of scriptural proof-texts for Mishnaic proposi-tions, after all, would not have caused much surprise to the framers of the Mishnah; they themselves included such passages, though not often. But what conception of the Torah underlies such initiatives, and how do the Yerushalmi's sages propose to explain the phenomenon of the Mishnah as a whole? The following passage gives us one statement. It refers to the assertion at M. Hag. 1:8D that the laws on cultic cleanness presented in the Mishnah rest on deep and solid foundations in the Scripture (Y. Hag. 1:7):

> The laws of the Sabbath [M. Hag. 1:8B]: R. Jonah said R. Hama bar Uqba raised the question [in reference to M. Hag. 1:8D's view that there are many verses of Scripture on cleanness], "And, lo, it is written only, 'Nevertheless a spring or a cistern holding water shall be clean; but whatever touches their carcass shall be unclean (Lev. 11:36). And from this verse you derive many laws. [So how can M. 8:8D say what it does about many verses for laws of cultic cleanness?]"
>
> R. Zeira in the name of R. Yohanan: "If a law comes to hand and you do not know its nature, do not discard it for another one, for, lo, many laws were stated to Moses at Sinai, and all of them have been embedded in the Mishnah."

The Mishnah now is claimed to contain statements made by God to Moses. Just how these statements found their way into the Mishnah, and which passages of the Mishnah contain them, we do not know. That is hardly important, given the fundamental assertion at hand. The passage proceeds to a further, and far more consequential, proposition. It asserts that part of the Torah was written down, and part was preserved in memory and transmitted orally. In context, that distinction must encompass the Mishnah, thus explaining its origin as part of the Torah. Here is a clear and unmistakable expression of the distinction between two forms in which a single Torah was revealed and handed on at Mount Sinai, part in writing, part orally.

While the passage below does not make use of the language "Torah-in-writing and Torah-by-memory," it does refer to "the written" and "the oral." Only when the passage reaches its climax does it break down into a number of categories – Scripture, Mishnah, Talmud, laws, lore. It there makes the additional point that everything comes from Moses at Sinai. So the fully articulated theory of two Torahs (not merely one Torah in two forms) does not reach final expression in this passage. The ultimate theory of Torah of formative Judaism is at hand here (Y. Hag. 1:7):

> R. Zeirah in the name of R. Eleazar: " 'Were I to write for him my laws by ten thousands, they would be regarded as a strange thing' (Hos. 8:12). Now is the greater part of the Torah written down? [Surely not. The oral part is much greater.] But more abundant are the matters that are derived by exegesis from the written [Torah] than those derived by exegesis from the oral [Torah]."
>
> And is that so?
>
> But more cherished are those matters that rest upon the written [Torah] than those that rest upon the oral [Torah].
>
> R. Haggai in the name of R. Samuel bar Nahman, "Some teachings were handed on orally, and some things were handed on in writing, and we do not know which of them is the more precious. But on the basis of that which is written, 'And the Lord said to Moses, Write these words; in accordance with these words I have made a covenant with you and with Israel' (Exod. 34:27), [we conclude] that the ones that are handed on orally are the more precious."
>
> R. Yohanan and R. Yudan b. R. Simeon: one said, "If you have kept what is preserved orally and also kept what is in writing, I shall make a covenant with you, and if not, I shall not make a covenant with you."
>
> The other said, "If you have kept what is preserved orally and you have kept what is preserved in writing, you shall receive a reward, and if not, you shall not receive a reward."
>
> [With reference to Deut. 9:10: "And on them was written according to all the words which the Lord spoke with you in the mount,"] said R. Joshua b. Levi, "He could have written, 'On them,' but wrote, 'And on them.' He could have written, 'All,' but wrote, 'According to all.' He could have written, 'Words,' but wrote 'The words.' [These then serve as three encompassing clauses, serving to include] Scripture, Mishnah, Talmud, laws, and lore. Even what an experienced student in the future is going to teach before his master already has been stated to Moses at Sinai."

What is the Scriptural basis for this view?

"There is no remembrance of former things, nor will there be any remembrance of later things yet to happen among those that come after" (Eccl. 1:11).

If someone says, "See, this is a new thing," his fellow will answer him, saying to him, "This has been around before us for a long time."

Here we have absolutely explicit evidence that people believed part of the Torah had been preserved not in writing but orally. Linking that part to the Mishnah remains a matter of implication. But it surely comes fairly close to the surface, when we are told that the Mishnah contains Torah-traditions revealed at Sinai. From that view it requires only a small step to the allegation that the Mishnah is part of the Torah, the oral part.

To define the category of the Torah as a source of salvation, as the Yerushalmi states matters, I point to a story that explicitly proposes that the Torah constitutes a source of salvation. In this story we shall see that because people observed the rules of the Torah, they expected to be saved. And if they did not observe, they accepted their punishment. So the Torah now stands for something more than revelation and a life of study, and (it goes without saying) the sage now appears as a holy, not merely a learned, man. This is because his knowledge of the Torah has transformed him. Accordingly, we deal with a category of stories and sayings about the Torah entirely different from what has gone before (Y. Ta. 3:8):

> As to Levi ben Sisi: troops came to his town. He took a scroll of the Torah and went up to the roof and said, "Lord of the ages! If a single word of this scroll of the Torah has been nullified [in our town], let them come up against us, and if not, let them go their way."
>
> Forthwith people went looking for the troops but did not find them [because they had gone their way].
>
> A disciple of his did the same thing, and his hand withered, but the troops went their way.
>
> A disciple of his disciple did the same thing. His hand did not wither, and they also did not go their way.
>
> This illustrates the following apophthegm: You can't insult an idiot, and dead skin does not feel the scalpel.

What is interesting here is how taxa into which the word Torah previously fell have been absorbed and superseded in a new taxon. The Torah is an object: "He took a scroll . . ." It also constitutes God's revelation to Israel: "If a single word . . ." The outcome of the revelation is to form an ongoing way of life, embodied in the sage himself: "A disciple of his did the same thing . . ." The sage plays an intimate part in the supernatural event: "His hand withered . . ." Now can we categorize this story as a statement that the Torah constitutes a particular object, or a source of divine revelation, or a way of life? Yes and no. The Torah here stands not only for the things we already have catalogued. It represents one more thing that takes in all the others. Torah is a source of salvation.

How so? The Torah stands for, or constitutes, the way in which the people Israel saves itself from marauders. This straightforward sense of salvation will not have surprised the author of Deuteronomy.

In the canonical documents up to the Yerushalmi, we look in vain for sayings or stories that fall into such a category. True, we may take for granted that everyone always believed that, in general, Israel would be saved by obedience to the Torah. That claim would not have surprised any Israelite writers from the first prophets down through the final redactors of the Pentateuch in the time of Ezra and onward through the next seven hundred years. But, in the Rabbinic corpus from the Mishnah forward, the specific and concrete assertion that by taking up the scroll of the Torah and standing on the roof of one's house, confronting God in heaven, a sage in particular could take action against the expected invasion – that kind of claim is not located, so far as I know, in any composition surveyed so far.

Still, we cannot claim that the belief that the Torah in the hands of the sage constituted a source of magical, supernatural, and hence salvific power, simply did not flourish prior, let us say, to ca. 400 CE. We cannot show it, hence we do not know it. All we can say with assurance is that no stories containing such a viewpoint appear in any Rabbinic document associated with the Mishnah. So what is critical here is not the generalized category – the genus – of conviction that the Torah serves as the source of Israel's salvation. It is the concrete assertion – the speciation of the genus – that in the hands of the sage and under conditions specified, the Torah may be utilized in pressing circumstances as Levi, his disciple, and the disciple of his disciple, used it. That is what is new.

To generalize: this stunningly new usage of Torah found in the Talmud of the Land of Israel emerges from a group of stories that treat the word Torah (whether scroll, contents, or act of study) as source and guarantor of salvation. Accordingly, evoking the word Torah forms the centerpiece of a theory of Israel's history, on the one side, and an account of the teleology of the entire system, on the other. Torah indeed has ceased to constitute a specific thing or even a category or classification when stories about studying the Torah yield not a judgment as to status (i.e., praise for the learned man) but promise for supernatural blessing now and salvation in time to come.

To the rabbis, the principal salvific deed was to "study Torah," by which they meant memorizing Torah-sayings by constant repetition, and, as the Talmud itself amply testifies (for some sages), profound analytic inquiry into the meaning of those sayings. The innovation now is that this act of "study of Torah" imparts supernatural power of a material character. For example, by repeating words of Torah, the sage could ward off the angel of death and accomplish other kinds of miracles as well. So Torah-formulas served as incantations. Mastery of Torah transformed the man engaged in Torah-learning into a supernatural figure, who could do things ordinary folk could not do. The category of "Torah" had already vastly expanded so that through transformation of the Torah from a concrete thing to a symbol, a Torah-scroll could be compared to a man of Torah, namely, a rabbi. Now, once the principle had been established, that salvation would come from keeping God's will in general, as Israelite holy men had insisted for so many centuries, it was a small step for rabbis to identify their particular corpus of learning, namely, the Mishnah and associated sayings, with God's will expressed in Scripture, the universally acknowledged medium of revelation.

The key to the first Talmud's theory of the Torah lies in its conception of the sage, to which that theory is subordinate. Once the sage reaches his full apotheosis as Torah incarnate, then, but only then, the Torah becomes (also) a source of salvation in the present concrete formulation of the matter. That is why we traced the doctrine of the Torah in the salvific process by elaborate citation of stories about sages, living Torahs, exercising the supernatural power of the Torah, and serving, like the Torah itself, to reveal God's will. Since the sage embodied the Torah and gave the Torah, the Torah naturally came to stand for the principal source of Israel's salvation, not merely a scroll, on the one side, or a source of revelation, on the other.

The Transformation of the Torah from Scroll to Symbol

The history of the symbolization of the Torah proceeds from its removal from the framework of material objects, even from the limitations of its own contents, to its transformation into something quite different and abstract, quite distinct from the document and its teachings. The Torah stands for this something more, specifically, when it comes to be identified with a living person, the sage, and endowed with those particular traits that the sage claimed for himself. While we cannot say that the process of symbolization leading to the pure abstraction at hand moved in easy stages, we may still point to the stations that had to be passed in sequence. The word Torah reached the apologists for the Mishnah in its long-established meanings: Torah-scroll, contents of the Torah-scroll. But even in the Mishnah itself, these meanings provoked a secondary development, status of Torah as distinct from other (lower) status, hence, Torah-teaching in contradistinction to scribal-teaching. With that small and simple step, the Torah ceased to denote only a concrete and material thing – a scroll and its contents. It now connoted an abstract matter of status. And once made abstract, the symbol entered a secondary history beyond all limits imposed by the concrete object, including its specific teachings, the Torah-scroll.

Tractate Abot stands at the beginning of this process. In the history of the word Torah as abstract symbol, a metaphor serving to sort out one abstract status from another regained concrete and material reality of a new order entirely. For the message of Abot, as we saw, was that the Torah served the sage. How so? The Torah indicated who was a sage and who was not. Accordingly, the apology of Abot for the Mishnah was that the Mishnah contained things sages had said. What sages said formed a chain of tradition extending back to Sinai. Hence it was equivalent to the Torah. The upshot is that words of sages enjoyed the status of the Torah. The small step beyond was to claim that what sages said was Torah, as much as what Scripture said was Torah. And, a further small step (and the steps need not have been taken separately or in the order here suggested) moved matters to the position that there were two forms in which the Torah reached Israel: one [Torah] in writing, the other [Torah] handed on orally, that is, in memory. The final step, fully revealed in the Talmud at hand, brought the conception of Torah to its logical conclusion: what the sage said was in the status of the Torah, was Torah, because the sage was Torah incarnate. So the abstract symbol now became concrete and material once more. We recognize the many, diverse ways in which the Talmud stated that conviction. Every passage in which knowledge of the Torah yields power over this world and the next, capacity to coerce to the sage's will the natural and supernatural worlds alike, rests upon the same viewpoint. The first Talmud's theory of the Torah carries us through several stages in the processes of the symbolization of the word Torah. Changed from something material and concrete into something abstract and beyond all metaphor, the word Torah finally emerged once more in a concrete aspect, now as the encompassing and universal mode of stating the whole doctrine, all at once, of Judaism in its formative age.

CHAPTER 13
The Doctrine of God

Alan J. Avery-Peck

Religious belief helps people make sense of the world in which they live and comprehend the experiences of their life, both what they face on an immediate, personal level and the larger historical occurrences that shape the life of a society and nation. In order to continue to make sense of changing social, political, economic, and international circumstances, religions tend to be flexible; theologies are written and rewritten to answer the specific questions posed by the conditions in each successive age. Religion, a human construct through which people lend meaning to and make sense of their lives, thus responds to the conditions of those lives. As changing circumstances render inherited truths and ways of life implausible or impractical, these truths, and the modes of living they engender, are recast.

This fact, a commonplace within the study of religions, explains the changing understandings of God and God's role in history evident in the emergence and growth of classical Judaism in the first six centuries CE. Comparing Rabbinic ideology with that implicit in the biblical Exodus story, we find a strikingly new theology of God and God's relationship to the people Israel. The rabbis did not deny that, as Scripture holds, God controls and manipulates history so as to reward and punish and that God ultimately will fulfill the covenantal promises made to the Israelite nation. But, in a period that did not witness miracles such as occurred in the Exodus, and writing at a time at which what actually occurred on the stage of human history did not portray God's immediate use of his power to protect the people, Talmudic rabbis developed a very different approach to understanding God's relationship to the world. Contrary to Scripture, Talmudic sages developed, on the one hand, an image of a God whose purposes are not always easily discerned or comprehended. And they suggested, on the other, that in all events God's intervention in human affairs was undesirable, either because such divine activity is inappropriately coercive, forcing people to embrace that which they should accept solely on faith, or because, through such actions, God settles issues that in fact were given to human determination. Certainly, Rabbinic sages accepted the biblical picture of an all-powerful deity who controls history and will ultimately fulfill the promises made to the Israelite nation. Yet, responding to the world in which they lived, they shifted their focus away from such perspectives, concentrating instead upon the role and importance of human activity in creating the world that God desires.

This dramatic shift from what is central in biblical ideology occurred in a period in which Jews no longer experienced such miracles as occurred in the biblical Exodus story. To the contrary, by the first centuries CE, what Jews endured on the stage of history hardly reflected the presence of an all-powerful God who assured the safety and prosperity of his chosen nation. At issue was not simply the long recognized fact that the evil do not always suffer and the righteous do not invariably flourish. This had already been expressed poignantly in the biblical book of Ecclesiastes. Rather, what the Israelites had experienced on the stage of history – loss of the Temple and promised land; later, the rise of Christianity as the official religion of the Roman Empire – will have suggested to many that, at least in the short run, contrary to what the weight of the biblical perspective had taught Israel to expect, God's actions were not reasonable and therefore could not be easily interpreted. In this setting, the rabbis shaped a new image of God, of how God behaves, and of what people should expect from God. This renewed understanding of God allowed Jews to make sense of the world in which they actually lived, a world that no longer reflected a God such as is described in the Exodus story and throughout the Bible's historical narrative.

The Exodus

The story of Egyptian bondage, the Exodus, and the events of Sinai comprise the most important narrative in the Hebrew Bible. With this story, we move from the lives of a small group of individuals – the Patriarchs and their families – to the events through which the Israelite nation is created and, in the covenant ceremony at Sinai, becomes finally and inextricably bonded to the God who created the world. These stories reveal the biblical understanding of how God took the Israelite people as his own and reached an agreement with them that would require God's continued devotion to and protection of the people, on the one side, and their exclusive relationship with God, marked by the observance of a detailed system of legal and theological precepts, on the other.

Central for our purposes is that, in the biblical depiction, the Israelites do not achieve knowledge of God through their own spiritual awakening or even as a result of God's simple and direct actions in responding to the circumstance in which the people find themselves. In the Exodus story, God does not neatly and quickly rescue the tribes of Israel from Egyptian bondage. Instead, God's power over nature and nations is highlighted: to promote God's purposes and desires,

God manipulates history, hardening Pharaoh's heart to prevent him from releasing the Jews while at the same time punishing him with increasingly harsh measures for failing to set the people free. God, according to Exodus, has little choice but to act as he does, not only to force the Egyptians to recognize his power, but, more important, to compel the Israelites themselves to accept God's sole sovereignty over the world. In the Bible's view, the manifestation of God's power is the appropriate, indeed, the only possible, foundation for acceptance of God.

While Exodus frequently refers to God's goal of forcing all people to recognize his power, the most comprehensive statement is at Exod. 10:1–2:

> Then the Lord said to Moses, "Go in to Pharaoh; for I have hardened his heart and the heart of his servants, that I may show these signs of mine among them, and that you may tell in the hearing of your son and of your son's son how I have made sport of the Egyptians and what signs I have done among them; that you may know that I am the Lord."

People are to recognize and accept God as a result of seeing what happens in history. Because God protects them and destroys their enemies, the Israelites are to accept as a continuing obligation the requirement that they follow God's will. This means that God is not to be found through an inner, spiritual awakening, a process that the book of Exodus, at least, seems to see as impossible. Recall God's appearing to Moses in the burning bush and describing Moses' mission. Moses responds that the people will not know who this God is; even knowing God's name is not enough. God answers by giving Moses "signs" to convince the nation that Moses indeed speaks for the powerful deity of the people's ancestors.

Absent a conception that the people can develop faith in God apart from God's saving acts, the Bible sees no problem with God's hardening of Pharaoh's heart and, ultimately, killing Egypt's first-born males, both those instrumental in the persecution and murder of Israelites and those, including mere children, who had no involvement at all: God's nature is to use history to prove his power and to show all nations his control over the entire world. So far as Scripture is concerned, whatever God does to accomplish this purpose is right and good. And it was, moreover, effective. God did what he said he would, and the people of Israel accordingly stood at the foot of Sinai, stating, "All that the Lord has spoken we shall do, and we shall be obedient" (Exod. 24:7).

The Exodus and the Biblical Theology of God

This attitude toward God's use of history is central in the Hebrew Bible as a whole. Outside of the book of Exodus' telling of the Exodus story, the Exodus theme is mentioned in Scripture approximately one hundred and twenty times, more than any other historical event or theological concept. While Scripture clearly encompasses other – even contrary – ideas, this is incontestable evidence of the Exodus' centrality in the religion of Israel. Most important, as Nahum Sarna phrases matters,[1] "from this preeminence flow certain consequential conceptions of God, of the relationship between God and Israel, of the meaning of history, and of the proper ordering of human associations":

1. "The Exodus negates any notion of an otiose deity and asserts the reality of a God who is intimately involved in the life of the world. He is the God of History in the sense that the coming into being of the people of Israel, their enslavement in Egypt, their liberation, and the events connected therewith are not fortuitous or the result of human endeavors, but the unfolding of the divine plan of history."

2. "The breaking of Egyptian resistance establishes God's absolute hegemony over history. History is the area of divine activity and thus is endowed with meaning."

3. "A major consequence of this is that the religion of Israel became embedded in a historical matrix. Its major institutions, its religious calendar, its rituals and observances have all been reinterpreted in terms of the Exodus and emptied of any theological associations with the rhythm of nature and the life of the soil . . ."

4. "Axiomatic if unexplicated is the idea that knowledge of God's qualities and of his demands on Israel can be acquired only insofar as God takes the initiative in revealing them."

In the biblical view, then, people come to know God, to recognize God's qualities, and to understand and follow God's demands on Israel and the world only insofar as God personally and directly takes the initiative to reveal them. Everything we know about God, in this approach, we know because God explicitly shows or tells us. Referring to Exod. 20:5–6 and 34:6–7, where God describes himself as compassionate and gracious, yet visiting the sins of the parents on the children, Sarna puts things as follows:

These descriptions are presented as God's self-revelation, not as the product of speculation or experience. The same idea that, to know God, man must depend on God's self-disclosure is implicit in Moses' request, "Let me know your ways" (Exod. 33:13), and it is inherent in the obligations of the covenant set forth in the Decalogue, which is portrayed as being the content of a great national theophany. It governs Israel's understanding of the law. All the legislative complexes of the Pentateuch are formulated as a series of divine commands to Israel, albeit mediated by Moses.

In the biblical picture, knowledge of and faith in God do not result from theological or philosophical speculation. Rather, such knowledge is given primarily in the theophany at Sinai, where God purposefully and directly dictated his will. But, in the biblical understanding, such revelation equally takes place in the events of history in general, seen as reflecting God's plans and purposes. Comparably, God's will is revealed in his speech to prophets, through whom God explains the meanings of and reasons for the events of history.

At the heart of Scripture's view thus is the idea that people come to know God only through God's own actions and speech. God makes himself known through displays of power that force people to accept his will. In this understanding, it is entirely appropriate that the covenant with Israel should emerge in the context of the destruction of the armies of Pharaoh and the mixed fear and joy of the people who, having just been brought out of Egyptian slavery, stand trembling at the foot of Sinai as Moses receives directly the word of God.

The Rabbinic Period

The roughly six-hundred-year Second Temple period, framed by the destruction of the First Temple (to be rebuilt ca. 520–515 BCE) and the Babylonian exile of 586 BCE, on the one side, and the destruction of the Second Temple in the course of the Jewish revolt again Rome in 66–73 CE, on the other, witnessed the appearance of diverse Judaisms – world-views and ways of life that people believed to represent God's will for the Jewish people and that competed with each other for each individual Jew's loyalty. Still, this period was unified by the advent at this time of broad social, religious, and political characteristics, the central feature of which was the new, and growing, polarity between Judaism's center, which, as in biblical times, remained Jerusalem, and the ever increasing plurality of areas of Jewish life in the diaspora. While Jews in this period continued to turn to Jerusalem as a spiritual center that represented Jewish unity, most of them now chose to live and worship far from the biblical Promised Land. Thus, even as the Temple and its cult continued as before to constitute the preeminent focus of Jewish religiosity, for most Jews, living far from Jerusalem, the Temple was no more than a distant ideal, a metaphor for Jewish peoplehood as they developed distinctive cultures in diverse areas far from the Holy Land.

Alongside the creation of the diaspora, a second pivotal feature of the Second Temple period was that, with the exception of a brief period of Hasmonean rule, from now on, even Jews who lived in the land of Israel would be governed by foreigners. To be sure, a gentile ruler might appoint a Jewish administrator to govern the Jews under Jewish law. But even such home-rule could not hide the reality of foreign domination or the fact that Jewish life was now to be shaped not by a distinctive Israelite culture but by the dominant culture of Hellenism, within which Jews in the land of Israel, just like those in the diaspora, made their lives. Even as Temple worship and limited governance under Jewish law continued, life for Jews even in the Holy Land was not what it had been before the Babylonian Exile. In this setting, Jews themselves began to recognize that biblical Judaism and the sacred history of the chosen people in the Promised Land had come to an end. This is explicit, for instance, in the Wisdom of Ben Sirah, composed in Jerusalem ca. 190 BCE, which lists the Persian Jewish governor Nehemiah, 538–532 BCE, as the last of the historical heroes of Judaism.

And yet, it appears to be primarily the Second Temple period's end point, the destruction of the Jerusalem Temple in 70 CE, followed by the Bar Kokhba

Revolt of 133–5 CE, that made clear that the Second Temple period's central features – diaspora, foreign domination, the growing irrelevance of the Temple-cult – would become permanent aspects of the Jewish condition. The *beginning* of the Second Temple period had taught Jews to live as Jews far from their national homeland. The *end* of this period made firm the message to which many had begun to respond even while the Temple stood: Jews would need now to worship God and practice Judaism without the priestly service and with no expectation of an immediate return of Israelite sovereignty over the land of Israel – no more prophecy, no more miracles, no more God-driven military victories.

These facts, not surprisingly, stand at the foundation of the Rabbinic Judaism that arises at the end of the Second Temple period and that, in the subsequent five hundred years, becomes the dominant mode of Judaism practiced by all Jews. This Judaism faced squarely the challenge presented by the reality of Jewish existence in the post-biblical period, a reality depicted forcefully by those events of the first centuries CE that led Jews carefully to evaluate who they were, what they believed, and how they would face an increasingly inhospitable world.

1   This Judaism was conceived in the period following the war with Rome that, in the first century, led to the destruction of the Jerusalem Temple.
2   The Rabbinic program for Judaism was shaped in the immediate aftermath of the devastating Bar Kokhba Revolt of the second century, which left as many as half a million Jews dead and which resulted in Jerusalem's being turned into a Roman colony, with a temple of Jupiter Capitolinus erected on the Temple Mount.
3   Rabbinic Judaism achieved its classical formulation and gained control over the Jewish nation as a whole in the fourth through sixth centuries, the period of the firm establishment of Christianity as the official religion of the Roman world.

Especially in the aftermath of the devastating Bar Kokhba Revolt, the political and religious realities created by the Second Temple period – diaspora, loss of sovereignty, the eventual destruction of the Temple – led Jews to evaluate afresh who they were, what they believed, and how they would face an increasingly inhospitable world. At the heart of the dominant response to these questions was the recognition prompted by the ruinous Bar Kokhba Revolt, the end point of five centuries of struggles to regain control of the Holy Land, that the Jewish people were not well served by following ambitious political leaders who insisted upon the use of military means to fulfill the biblical promise of a sovereign Jewish nation worshiping in a Jerusalem Temple. The preceding centuries of nationalistic revolts had ended in the almost complete destruction of Jewish life in the Promised Land. Jews were better off now accepting Roman domination and developing modes of piety independent of an active political nationalism.

The destruction of the Temple, the failed Bar Kokhba Revolt, and the ascent of Christianity potentially meant the end of the Jews' previous perception of their destiny as a great and holy nation – the chosen people. The destruction of the Temple meant that, as in the period of the Babylonian exile, the cult ceased operation. But this time, the failure of the Bar Kokhba Revolt meant that any expectation of the rebuilding of the Temple or of a return to the way things had been before was unrealistic. And the success of Christianity, with its claim to embody a new covenant, meant that even the notion of Israel's chosenness and unique relationship to God were subject to significant challenge.

In these ways, both the political and theological contexts in which Judaism existed had been dramatically altered. The Temple, for the Jews, the visible sign of God's presence and dominion, was gone; the cult, through which the people had acknowledged God's lordship and appealed to his mercies, had ceased; the land of Israel was now under foreign rule, with little hope for its return to Jewish sovereignty. As a result of these events, the nation lost the symbols of its power, the sign of its place within the family of nations, and the physical representation of its stature before God. Clearly, in the face of such historical developments, one central question concerned how the people could still be certain of their continuing covenantal relationship with the one who had created the world and who controlled all history. This issue indeed was phrased succinctly and emotionally shortly after the destruction of the Second Temple. The author of IV Ezra asked (3:32–34, 6:59):

> Have the deeds of Babylon been better than those of Zion? Has any other nation known You besides Zion? . . . If the world has indeed been created for our sakes, why do we not enter into possession of our world? How long shall this endure?

IV Ezra's question directly challenges inherited biblical beliefs about the way in which God carries out his will through the control of history. The Jews had known God and followed the path of Torah, and yet they had been dispossessed by nations who had not known God at all. How could this be?

While little evidence survives to describe how the Jewish people as a whole responded to this question, it is clear that the nation faced contradictory needs. On the one hand, the memory of the Temple and nationhood – of a God who could be depended upon to act in history – could not easily be erased. Any new direction would need to reflect the inherited attitudes. On the other hand, the devastating wars caused by the belief that God would fight on behalf of his people meant that new groups that followed quite different paths were most likely to succeed. As Sean Freyne phrases matters:[2]

> With the temple destroyed, those groups within Judaism who had taken their religious stance in relation to it were now totally deprived of any basis for their faith, and were consequently forced to rethink their position in regard to the temple and its meaning, or to find another way. We do not know how many of the religious leaders survived the catastrophe. Presumably they were not very many, given the civil strife, as well as the Roman siege and its aftermath. Subsequently we do hear of a group called "The holy congregation of Jerusalem," who in all probability attempted to retain their identity as Jerusalemites in exile, presumably

hoping for the rebuilding of the temple. There is also some evidence of people returning to the temple mount on pilgrimage even after the destruction. Clearly then, the memory of the temple could not be wiped away so easily, something underlined by the fact that the emperor Hadrian's desire to build a temple in honour of the head of the Roman Pantheon, Jupiter, in Jerusalem was a major contributory factor to the second Jewish revolt of 132–135 CE. Yet despite these scattered pieces of evidence, it is clear that the strand of Judaism that was least dependent on visible or political structures for its survival was likely to have been most successful, and it is in this respect that Pharisaism was best equipped to fill the breach.

Freyne correctly emphasizes the contradictory needs of the nation as it searched for new leadership. On the one hand, the memory of the Temple could not easily be erased, so that any new direction would need to reflect the historical reality of Judaism as a Temple-based religion. On the other hand, the cessation of the cult and the devastating wars caused by political motivations meant that new groups that did not depend upon prior political and cultic associations were most likely to succeed. In making this judgment, we obviously benefit from hindsight. For it is exactly such a group, the Rabbinic movement, that did succeed. At the same time, reflection upon the character of the group that successfully filled the breach left by the Temple's destruction suggests that Freyne has correctly assessed the larger situation of the Jewish people. The destruction of the Temple and the failed revolt under Bar Kokhba made clear what Josephus, by the year 90 CE, had argued: the Jewish people were not well served by following ambitious political leaders who insisted upon the use of military means to fulfill the biblical promise of a sovereign Israelite nation worshiping in its Temple in God's chosen city. It was preferable to accept Roman political domination and to develop modes of piety independent of priestly and nationalistic aspirations.

The Rabbinic Program

The Rabbinic plan for Judaism in the aftermath of the destruction of the Temple grew out of the conflicting interests just described. Under Rabbinic leadership, Judaism continued to be shaped by the model of the Temple-cult, and Jews continued to pray for the rebuilding of the Temple, the re-establishment of animal sacrifice, and renewed Israelite sovereignty, to be achieved, to be sure, through God's personal intervention in history. But these things were seen now as signifiers of the advent of the messianic age, as things that would happen at the end of time, not as aspects of this world, which could be expected to occur today or tomorrow.

This means that Rabbinic ideology entirely refocused the people's concerns, from the events of political history, which are, after all, far beyond the control of the individual, to events within the life and control of each person and family. What came to matter were the everyday details of life, the recurring actions that, day-in and day-out, define who we are and demarcate what is truly important to us. How do we relate to family and community? By what ethic do we carry out our business dealings? How do we acknowledge our debt to God, not only or primarily for the events of past history or the awaited future, but for the food we eat and for the wonders of the universe evidenced in the daily rising and setting of the sun?

By making such aspects of life the central focus of Judaism, rabbis assured that what the Temple had represented – an economy of the sacred – would be actualized in the life of the Jewish family and village. The people were to live as a nation of priests, eating their common food as though it were a sacrifice on the Temple's altar, seeing in their personal daily prayers and in their shared deeds of loving kindness a replacement for the sacrifices no longer offered. Certainly they understood this observance of a detailed system of ritual and communal law as directly affecting God, as leading God to act on their behalf. But, through the Rabbinic system, they were made to recognize that they should expect no quick, spectacular response as had occurred in the Exodus. A messiah would come, but only in some distant future. And, in light of the battles and bloodshed that were understood to come along with the messianic event, people should not even overly yearn to experience the messiah's arrival.

In this way, those who created Rabbinic Judaism responded to the critical theological problem of their day. God's presence and love of the people had always been represented in his deeds on behalf of the people. Insofar as such miracles apparently could no longer be expected, let alone depended upon, Jews needed to locate a new proof for the existence of God and a new explanation for how the people could be assured that their obligation to follow God's will remained, on the one hand, and that such faith would eventually be rewarded, on the other. They found this explanation in a new attitude toward God, an attitude phrased by Talmudic sages who argued not only that God's actions in history were beyond human comprehension but that an essential requirement of faith was that it be independent of God's action in history, that the people find God through their own inquiry and not depend upon divine proofs of God's power. Let us examine how these several ideas found expression in specific Talmudic texts.

God's Plan is Unclear

In the face of the experiences of the first centuries, the rabbis faced the question of how to understand God's intentions for the Israelite nation. If God indeed has authority over all that occurs, why does he not use that control to the benefit of the Chosen People? B. Men. 29b answers this question by asserting that, while God indeed has absolute control, the reasons for his use of his power in one way and not another are beyond human comprehension. God does what God does simply because God has determined to act in that way and not another. Humans cannot expect to make sense of what happens in history.

A   Said R. Judah said Rab, "At the time that Moses went up on high, he found the Holy One in session, affixing crowns to the letters [of the Torah]. He said to him, 'Lord of the universe, who is stopping you [from regarding the Torah as perfect without these crowns]?'

B   "He said to him, 'There is a man who will arrive at the end of many generations, and Aqiba b. Joseph is his name, who will interpret on the basis of each point of the crowns heaps and heaps of laws.'

C   "He said to him, 'Lord of the Universe, show him to me.'

D   "He said to him, 'Turn around.'

E   "[Moses] went and took a seat at the end of eight rows, but he could not grasp what the people were saying. He felt faint. But when the discourse reached a certain matter, and the disciples said [to Aqiba], 'My lord, how do you know this?' and he answered, 'It is a law given to Moses from Sinai,' [Moses] regained his composure.

F   "[Moses] went and came before the Holy One. He said before him, 'Lord of the Universe, How come you have someone like that and yet you give the Torah through me?'

G   "He said to him, 'Silence! That is how I have determined it.'

H   "[Moses] said to him, 'Lord of the Universe, you have shown me his Torah, now show me his reward.'

I   "He said to him, 'Turn around.'

J   "[Moses] turned around and saw [Aqiba's] flesh being weighed out at the butcher-stalls in the market.

K   "He said to him, 'Lord of the Universe, 'Such is Torah, such is the reward?'

L   "He said to him, 'Silence! That is how I have determined it.' "

Moses confronts God and is shown an image of the future, both of the great Torah scholar Aqiba's knowledge and of his death as a martyr. When Moses asks why God has worked things out in this way, God demurs: "That is how I have determined it."

In the understanding of this passage, while God indeed controls history, his actions are unintelligible to people, and even God, if asked, may be unwilling – or unable – to articulate a cogent plan. This means that, unlike the biblical Exodus story would have it, people cannot depend upon what they see happening in the world around them as a foundation for faith or for deciding whether or not to accept the covenant. What happens to them on the stage of human existence is not even a gauge of whether or not they are righteously following God's will: Aqiba is learned and pious, and yet (like the nation as a whole) he suffers. The stage of human events thus has no humanly discernible meaning, cannot be interpreted as a path to God or God's will. People will need to choose and retain faith on other grounds.

The passage points to another new idea about God, for it holds that, rather than leading armies or dictating the law from Mt. Sinai, God prepares and studies Torah in an academic setting similar to that which the rabbis themselves created. Most important in this image is that God does not himself even determine or control the meaning of his own revelation. God draws crowns on the letters of the Torah but does not know what their meaning ultimately will be. God certainly has not dictated the entirety of the law's meaning to Moses, who, as a result, is awestruck when he sees the image of a sage, Aqiba, determining the meaning of the crowns and hence fixing the content and nature of God's revelation. Strikingly, though Aqiba is the first to know what the crowns God has drawn signify, his statements have the status of laws given by God to Moses at Sinai, God's own teachings in God's own words. The biblical view so carefully described by Sarna, that all knowledge of God depends upon God's self-revelation, thus is here rejected. The rabbis propose, rather, that through their own study of Torah, people come not only to comprehend God and God's will but even to shape that will, to reveal that which was unknown even to God, but which is part of the divine will and, as an aspect of Torah, represents God's original intention at the time of creation.

It bears noting that ideas such as are expressed here are not totally absent from the Hebrew Scriptures. Though overshadowed by the more prominent attitude of the Exodus narrative and Prophetic books, the Wisdom literature emphasizes human experience, reasoning, morality, teaching, and learning. It focuses upon the relationship between master and disciple, and its goal is that people make the best possible use of the worldly resources available to them. The Wisdom authors see this focus upon knowledge and correct behavior as the path to finding out about God and to creating a just world. As in the passage we just reviewed, concomitant to this emphasis on the human foundation of all experience and learning, the Wisdom authors de-emphasize the role of God and suggest that humans are incapable of discerning God's plan or explaining God's actions. As God declares to Job out of the whirlwind and as Ecclesiastes expresses through the idea that the brevity of human life makes it impossible to conceive of God's overall plan, humans simply cannot comprehend why God does what God does.[3] Without arguing for a direct link between these similar approaches to understanding God, it is suggestive that both emerged in watershed periods of Jewish history, in which the inherited conception that God invariably controls history to the benefit of his people was significantly challenged and so demanded reconsideration.

God Suffers along with the People

The Bible understands the ills that befall the people of Israel to result from the purposeful actions of God, who uses defeat at the hands of foreigners to punish the sinful nation. Just as the previous passage did not deny God's power in history, so the present one does not overtly dispute God's ability to punish the people in this way. Nor does it argue that such suffering has no place in God's larger plans. But in stating that God suffers along with his nation, the passage hints at a conception that all is not as God wishes it to be. At a minimum, such thinking assures an agonized people that, whatever the cause of its condition, God shares its distress, hence remains involved with and concerned for its fate (B. Ber. 59a):

A   What are earthquakes?

B   Said R. Qattina, "Rumbling."

C   R. Qattina was going along the way. When he got to the gate of the house of a necromancer, there was a rumbling in the deep.

D   He said, "Can this necromancer possibly know what causes this rumbling in the deep?"

E   [The necromancer] raised a voice after him, "Qattina, Qattina, why should I not know?

F   "When the Holy One, blessed be he, reflects that his children are plunged in distress among the nations of the world, he drops two tears into the Great Sea, and the sound is heard from one end of the world to the other, and that is the rumbling."

Just as this passage leaves open the question of whether or not, if God so desired, he could alter the circumstance of the Jews, so it leaves open the issue of whether it was God's intervention in history that created the current circumstances in the first place. One way or the other, the message of this passage is clear and poignant: that God suffers with the people means that, even if God indeed authors history, he also experiences history, feels it just as his people does, through the human emotions of pain and sorrow. Perhaps God will not – or cannot – change the people's fate. But the people must know that, despite this fact, God has not deserted or ceased to care about them.

The Law is in Human Hands

Associated with the shift in attitudes toward God's place and power in the world is a new notion of the source of truth, that is, a rethinking of Scripture's theory of God's exclusive right to determine the nature and content of the laws to which his people are subject. Axiomatic within the Hebrew Bible's theological construct is the idea that knowledge of God's qualities and demands on Israel can be acquired only insofar as God takes the initiative in revealing them. God controls knowledge as well as history. For the rabbis, by contrast, as we saw above in the story of Aqiba's interpreting of the crowns on the letters of the Torah, knowledge of the divine is left up to people to discover.

The well-known passage at B. B.M. 59b strikingly rejects the biblical concept that, in Sarna's words, quoted above, "knowledge of God's qualities and of his demands on Israel can be acquired only insofar as God takes the initiative in revealing them." This passage indeed challenges the idea that God's intervention into the activities of the study house is acceptable at all. Of interest here is the conception of the sages' capacity not only to determine the content of Torah – which means the nature of revelation – but even to bind God himself to their decision:

A   On that day, R. Eliezer brought forward all of the arguments in the world, but they [that is, the other Rabbis] did not accept them from him.

B   Said he to them, "If the law agrees with me, let this carob-tree prove it!" The carob-tree was torn a hundred cubits out of its place.

C   They said to him, "No proof can be brought from a carob-tree."

D   He said to them, "If the law agrees with me, let the stream of water prove it!" The stream of water flowed backward.

E   Again they said to him, "No proof can be brought from a stream of water."

F   Again he said to them, "If the law agrees with me, let the walls of this house of study prove it!" The walls tilted, about to fall.

G   R. Joshua rebuked the walls, saying, "When disciples of sages are engaged in a legal dispute, what role do you walls play?"

H   Hence, they did not fall, in honor of R. Joshua; but nor did they resume the upright, in honor of R. Eliezer.

I   Again [Eliezer] said to them, "If the law agrees with me let it be proved from heaven!" An echo came forth [from heaven] and said, "Why do you dispute with R. Eliezer? For in all matters, the law agrees with him!"

J   But R. Joshua arose and exclaimed [citing Deut. 30:12], *"It [the law] is not in heaven!"*

K   [Later] R. Nathan met Elijah [the prophet] and asked him, "What did the holy one, blessed be he, do at that time?"

L   [Elijah] replied, "He laughed, saying, 'My sons have defeated me! My sons have defeated me!"

The story asserts that the law is defined by a vote of the majority of sages, who determine proper conduct based upon their wisdom and knowledge and who give no heed to supernatural interference. Miracles, the story asserts, can occur. But, contrary to what the Exodus and, especially, the Sinai narrative would have us believe, they are irrelevant to the emergence of human knowledge and faith, just as, as I–J asserts, the commanding voice of God no longer holds sway. In the Rabbinic academy, rabbis, not God, determine the law.

What is the nature of the "defeat" about which God laughs? Surely, on the one hand, God chuckles over the unexpected result of his own success as a parent. God has created and nurtured children, imbued them with such a sense of responsibility and intellectual cunning that they insist on living in a world of their own making. In their original setting in the book of Deuteronomy, God's words, *"It is not in heaven,"* mean only that people cannot deny that they know the law and are able to follow it. Now these words have a new significance. If the Torah is on earth and not in heaven, if it is in the people's mouth and heart, then God may no longer interfere in its interpretation. The law is among the sages, who are empowered to engage in reasoned debate and then to vote. In this way, they take over the role of God in revealing Torah.

But there is an even more significant way in which God's children have defeated him. This is in the fact that God, as much as the people, is bound by the rules of Torah. God, just like the people, must accept and follow the logically decided view of the sages on earth. That which they deem holy and right becomes, even in God's mind, holy and right. The human mind and intellect thus determine the content of God's mind and intellect. People, and not God, are the source of revelation, their minds producing that which is understood to have been in God's mind from the beginning of time.[4]

Miracles are an Inappropriate Foundation for Faith

In the following example, sages reflect upon the Exodus story's conception of the appropriate foundation for faith in God and acceptance of God's will. The book of Exodus, we recall, presents God's miraculous redemption of the Israelite nation as the sole foundation for the people's faith. Rabbinic sages, by contrast, reject this idea, explicitly calling God's actions against the Egyptians an unsuitable grounds for the covenant relationship. The problem is that God's miracles did more than to aid the Israelites in recognizing God's power and sovereignty. They created a circumstance of compulsion, in which the nation had no choice but to accept the Torah (B. Shab. 88a):

A   "And they [that is, the people of Israel, after the Exodus, camped at Sinai] stood below the mount" (Exod. 19:17):

B   Actually underneath the mountain.

C   Said R. Abdimi bar Hama bar Hasa, "This teaches that the Holy One, blessed be he, held the mountain over Israel like a cask and said to them, 'If you accept the Torah, well and good, and if not, then there is where your grave will be.'"

D   Said R. Aha bar Jacob, "On this basis there is ground for a powerful protest against the Torah [since it was imposed by force]."

E   Said Raba, "Nonetheless, the generation of the time of Ahasuerus accepted it, as it is written, 'The Jews ordained and took it upon themselves'[5] (Esth. 9:27) – they confirmed what the others [at the time of Sinai] had already accepted."

In the rabbis' reading, the Sinai event is too overt, too coercive to be meaningful. God's actions were inappropriate, since people cannot legitimately be forced to accept the obligations of faith. The nation thus has grounds for a protest against the Torah, indeed, for a rejection of God, a circumstance to which the rabbis respond by proposing a different model of faith, exemplified by what happened in the period of Esther and Mordecai. In the Purim story, referred to here, the Jews faced a very real enemy whom they fought through their own power and will. God is never mentioned in the book of Esther, and yet, in the

Rabbinic reading of this event, the people saw in their own victory evidence of God's presence. And hence, as the Talmudic sages read Esth. 9:27, cited at E, they chose of their own volition to confirm the covenant.[6]

The rabbis thus recognize the new imperative of a situation in which the face of God is hidden, in which God does not perform great miracles on behalf of his people. In this circumstance, represented by the rabbis' own period, the people are in a new position *vis-à-vis* God. They must find and support their faith of their own accord, locating God's presence and power in their own conduct, in their own strength, whether in the big things they accomplish or in their day-to-day acts of righteousness. The rabbis thus begin here to define a true partnership between the people and God, in which the people find God despite God's silence. This is, of course, a striking shift from the Exodus narrative's God of history.

A New Perception of God's Actions in History

While the passage just discussed criticizes the God of the Hebrew Bible for using power over history coercively, it does not reject the Bible's central notion that God has the power and ability to act in this way and so purposefully to shape history. Yet even as the rabbis recognized God's might, still, in the Rabbinic period, the weakness of this theology became increasingly apparent. The problem is not only that the perspective of the book of Exodus and the historical narrative of Scripture as a whole does not explain apparently unearned suffering – this was treated already by Job – but that it did not seem to account for the experiences of the nation as a whole and over a long period of time.

On the one hand, to respond to such problems, the rabbis developed the already emergent conceptions of immortality and afterlife, which posited final retribution and reward in a world-to-come. But, within the Rabbinic period, even this theory of suffering is not uniformly applied to explain what the people experienced. Rather, alongside its view of a coming messianic age, period of retribution, and triumph of the Israelite nation, the Talmudic literature introduced the quite radical perceptions of God and God's relationship to history that we have seen: undeserved suffering may have no explanation; God's miraculous intervention in history in all events is undesirable.

But what, then, happened to God in the Judaism of the rabbis? If God is no longer to be experienced in miracles and if God's commanding voice – now depicted as a whisper – is not necessarily to be heeded, then what power does God have and what purpose does God serve? The answer that emerges from the midst of the rabbis' radical changes in conception is that God still is there, to be worshiped and trusted eventually to fulfill the terms of the covenant created at Sinai. All that has changed is the foundation of this faith and basis of the people's comprehension of the terms of the covenant.

The biblical system cherished God's brilliant acts in history, the signs and miracles that show the people God's power and that comfort them, even when they are punished, by assuring them of the absolute logic and justice in the world. Living in a period in which such logic was elusive and in which the punishments received by the Jewish people fit no known sin, the rabbis rejected the old approach, not simply as flawed but, moreover, as an inappropriate path to piety. The rabbis thus rejected the notion that it is appropriate for God to control people or force them into obedience through voices from heaven, miracles, divine messengers, or even by descending to earth personally to fight their battles. Instead, in the Rabbinic view, it is up to individual Jews to find the otherwise hidden God. This they are to do by acting responsibly in pursuing justice, promoting what is good, observing the law and even, when times demand it, by fighting their own battles to save themselves, as happened in the time of Esther and Mordecai. In everyday acts of goodness and self-protection – whether they seem to change the world or not – the people are to appreciate the presence of God and to find strength in the knowledge that they are following God's path.

The rabbis reject the coercion implicit in a system in which God forces belief and conformity to his will through displays of power. Central to Rabbinic faith, instead, is the individual's coming to find God through contact with the compelling divine word – that is, Torah. In this system, the individual is brought into the world of faith and worship by his or her own initiative. This is not in response to God's spectacular show of power but as an aspect of a spiritual and national awakening in which people recognize the presence of God in their own human abilities and intellect.

Indeed, this appears to be perhaps the most striking shift from the biblical to the Rabbinic perspective. I noted above that axiomatic to the perspective of the book of Exodus is that knowledge of God and of God's demands on Israel can be acquired only insofar as God takes the initiative to reveal these things. This idea is at the heart of the Bible's image of the revelation at Sinai and also explains why, at Exod. 18:14–26, when Moses sets up of a system of judges, he explicitly tells the leaders of the people that they may pass judgment only on cases in which the rule to be followed already is known. To deal with any new circumstance – the hard cases – they must come to Moses, who will inquire directly of God regarding the law. As Exod. 18:19, 22, and 26 make clear, this commission of judges thus would not in any way impinge upon God's absolute authority. How different is the Rabbinic picture, which even rejects God's attempts to participate directly in the working out of revelation, seen now to be in human hands alone.

But, in an odd way, exactly by placing the power to define Torah in human hands, the rabbis in fact make the powerful point that, despite the way the events of history made things seem, God still exists, still rules over the people and land of Israel, and still can be depended upon to bring redemption. It is only for these reasons that the Torah still matters at all, still must be explicated, still must be followed. But, in the Rabbinic system, the God who had been understood to make and destroy nations, to show his will through splendid and miraculous deeds, is pictured as moving rather in response to the intentions and perceptions of everyday Jews who engage in the study of, and therefore the creation of, revelation; who lead their daily lives in accordance with divine precepts; who eat their food as though their home-tables were the Temple altar; and who live their lives as though they were a kingdom of priests.

In this way, the rabbis put the individual – not God – at the center of creation, ascribing to the everyday Jew the power to impart to the world order and meaning. This Rabbinic ideology is, of course, poignant. For in the period of the emergence of Rabbinic Judaism, with the Temple destroyed and the land defiled, the deeds of common Jews were all that remained to deny the events of history and to affirm God's Lordship.

At the heart of the Rabbinic approach is the notion that knowledge of God results not primarily from God's self-revelation in history. It depends rather upon humanity's proper grasp of the Torah, requiring the Jews' active engagement with the details of revelation, through sagacity, erudition, and human intelligence. According to Rabbinic Judaism, by thinking about Torah, the Jew asks the deeper question of what can be known about God. Thinking about Torah, the rabbis hold, reveals God's thought in God's own words.[7] With this human participation in revelation comes the possibility of returning the world to the way God meant it to be when, on the seventh day of creation, God saw that what he had created was good.

Often viewed as a rather odd mixture of arcane rules and incoherent documents, united by a penchant for needlessly detailed study, Rabbinic Judaism, we see, is not so unintelligible at all. It is, at base, a very reasonable response to a real world Jews faced that had ceased to make sense, ceased to conform to the image of justice, fairness, and freedom for which all people hope. The Rabbinic response was not to accept the new world order and forget the nation's previous aspirations. Nor was it to retreat into a solitary life in caves and small enclaves to await God's saving actions.

The sages' response, rather, was to fight for the desired end, to declare that the promised world can and will exist, if only people will imagine it, if only they will shape it with their minds, if only they will impose that imagined model of perfection upon their everyday lives. In this way, Rabbinic Judaism faced the world in which Jews lived by answering the questions of what comprises the order in the world, of how people can know that they have power and importance, and of how a nation can actualize the revelation given to its ancestors, creating the perfected world of which all people dream.

The rabbis responded to the devastating events of their day by rejecting the simplistic biblical view that all history attests to God's will. But they did not therefore withdraw from that history into a world of ritual or cultic action. Rather, Jews came increasingly to insist that the individual has the power and the obligation to use his or her intellect to define and then to work to create a new and better world, a world of holiness and sanctification, a world as we know it should be, wish it to be, and, if we only imagine intently enough and work hard enough, will assure that it someday will be. In confrontation with the real world in which people lived, the biblical image of God's power in history yielded the belief that *people themselves have and must use their power to transform the world.* Despite a continued recognition of God's power, it becomes clear that all in fact is in human hands.

Notes

1 On this and the following, see Nahum Sarna, "Exodus, Book of," in D. N. Freedman, ed., *The Anchor Bible Dictionary* (New York, 1992), vol. 2, pp. 698–9.

2 Sean Freyne, *The World of the New Testament* (Wilmington, 1985), pp. 122–3. See also my "Judaism Without the Temple: The Mishnah," in Harold W. Attridge and Gohei Hata, eds., *Eusebius, Christianity, and Judaism* (Detroit, 1992), pp. 409–31.

3 While it is not the focus of this chapter, we shall see in the following other affinities between Rabbinic thinking and Wisdom. Leaving aside the pessimism of Ecclesiastes, viewed as a whole the Wisdom approach is in many regards close to Rabbinic thinking. This is especially the case insofar as the rabbis raised to the highest level of human endeavor those same attributes of mind and activity glorified within the Wisdom literature. Beginning with the Mishnah, human cognition, behaviors appropriate within their societal context, and moral activity in general are made the highest goals of all human endeavor.

4 On the continuation of this Talmudic story and its implications for our understanding of the ideology of Rabbinic Judaism, see Robert M. Price, "Mishnah and Messiah: The Problem of the Jesus-Attributed Saying," in Jacob Neusner, ed., *Approaches to Ancient Judaism XIV* (Atlanta, 1998).

5 The verse continues: "and their descendants and all who joined them, that without fail they would keep these two days according to what was written and at the time appointed every year."

6 On this passage, see Irving Greenberg, *The Jewish Way: Living the Holidays* (New York, 1988), p. 250.

7 I paraphrase Jacob Neusner, "God: How, in Judaism, Do We Know God," in *Formative Judaism, Seventh Series* (Atlanta, 1993), p. 209.

CHAPTER 14
The Doctrine of Israel

Jacob Neusner

In every Judaic religious system, "Israel" stands for the holy people whom God has called into being through Abraham and Sarah and their descendants, to whom the prophetic promises were made, and with whom the covenants were entered. In every Judaism, "Israel" is a theological category, not a fact of sociology or ethnic culture or secular politics. The "Israel" of every Judaism forms a supernatural social entity, "chosen," "holy," subject to God's special love and concern. That "Israel" is not to be confused with the Jewish people, an ethnic group, the people of Israel in a this-worldly framework, let alone the State of Israel, a modern nation-state. "Israel" in Judaism compares to "the Torah," in that, just as the latter is not just another book, so the former is not just another social entity. Just as the story of the Torah speaks of transcendent matters, so the tale of Israel, in Judaism, tells of God's relationship with humanity through the instrument God has chosen for self-manifestation: "You alone have I singled out of all the families of the earth – that is why I will call you to account for all your iniquities," as the prophet Amos put it (Amos 3:2).

Every Judaism uses the word "Israel" to refer to the social entity that it proposes to define, and all Judaisms deem their "Israels" to stand in continuity with the Israel of whom the Hebrew Scriptures speak. Commonly, each Judaism regards its "Israel" as the unique continuator of that of Scripture. Some deem the connection to be genealogical and fundamentally ethnic, putting forth a secular definition of their "Israel." Rabbinic Judaism defines its Israel in supernatural terms, deeming the social entity to form a transcendental community, by faith.

To Rabbinic Judaism, "Israel" does not speak of a merely-ethnic, this-worldly people, but of a social entity defined by matters of supernatural genealogy, on the one side, and religious conversion, on the other. That is shown by the simple fact that a gentile of any origin or status, slave or free, Greek or barbarian, may enter its "Israel" on equal terms with those born into the community, becoming children of Abraham and Sarah. The children of converts become Israelite without qualification. No distinction is made between the child of a convert and the child of a native-born Israelite. Since that fact bears concrete and material consequences, e.g., in the right to marry any other Israelite without distinction by reason of familial origin, it follows that the "Israel" of Rabbinic Judaism must be understood in a wholly theological framework. This Judaism knows no distinction between children of the flesh and children of the promise and therefore cannot address a merely-ethnic "Israel," because, for Rabbinic Judaism, "Israel" is always and only defined by the Torah received and represented by "our sages of blessed memory" as the word of God, never by the happenstance of secular history.

That does not mean that Rabbinic Judaism's Israel ignored this-worldly facts of the life of everyday Israel after the flesh. The fundamental social unit in Israelite society was the household, encompassing the large-scale economic unit of the farmer, his wife and children, slaves, dependent craftsmen and artisans, reaching outward to other such households to form a neatly-composed social unit, the village – and like villages. But Rabbinic Judaism's systemic social entity transformed the extended family into a representation, in the here-and-now, of mythic "Israel." In that way, the social unit adopted for itself and adapted for its purposes the social entity of Scripture and identified itself with the whole life and destiny of that entity. Clearly, therefore, Rabbinic Judaism set forth a theory of the ethnic entity that invoked a metaphor in order to explain the group and identify it. That fundamental act of metaphorization, from which all else follows, was the comparison of persons – Jews – of the here-and-now to the "Israel" of which the Hebrew Scriptures – "the Torah" – speak, and the identification of those Jews with that "Israel." Treating the social group – two or more persons – as other than they actually are in the present, as more than a (mere) given, means that the group is something else than what it appears to be.

To explain what is at stake in the category, "Israel," we have to recognize that the raw materials of definition are not the facts of the social order – how things are in practical terms – but the imagination of the system-builders. An "Israel" – that is, a theory of what Israel is and who is counted as part of Israel or is himself or herself Israel – in any Judaic system finds its shape and structure within that system. That "Israel" takes shape out of materials selected by the framers from a miscellaneous, received or invented repertoire of possibilities. It goes without saying that, in the context of the description of the structure of a Judaism, its "Israel" is the sole Israel (whether social group, whether caste, whether family, whether class or "population," and whether any of the many social entities admirably identified by sociology) defined by that "Judaism." The best systemic indicator is a system's definition of its Israel; and Judaisms, or Judaic systems, from the priests' Pentateuchal system onward, made their statement principally through their response to the question framed in contemporary Judaic and Jewish-ethnic discourse as "who is a Jew?"

But the systemic component, Israel, finds its definition within the systemic imagination, not out of the raw materials of the social world beyond the system.

For a system never accommodates the givens of politics and a sheltering society. The notion that society gives birth to religion is systemically beside the point. Systems do not recapitulate a given social order, they define one, and their framers, if they can, then go about realizing their fantasy. An "Israel" within a given Judaic system forms the invention of the system's builders and presents traits that they deem self-evidently true. That is quite without regard to realities beyond the range of systemic control. All that the context presents is a reper-toire of possibilities. The framers of the contents then make their choices among those possibilities, and, outside of the framework of the system, there is no predicting the shape and structure of those choices. The system unfolds within its own inner logic, making things up as it goes along – because it knows precisely how to do so.

The Doctrine of Israel in the Formative Period of Rabbinic Judaism

The writings produced by sages, or rabbis, of late antiquity in the land of Israel ("Palestine") and Babylonia fall into two groups, each with its own plan and program. The first set of canonical writings begins with the Mishnah, a philo-sophical law book brought to closure at ca. 200 CE, later on called the first statement of the oral Torah. In its wake, the Mishnah drew tractate Abot, ca. 250 CE, a statement on the standing of the authorities of the Mishnah; Tosefta, ca. 300 CE, a compilation of supplements of various kinds to the statements in the Mishnah; and three systematic exegeses of books of Scripture or the written Torah, Sifra, to Leviticus, Sifre to Numbers, and another Sifre, to Deuteronomy, of indeterminate date but possibly concluded by 300 CE. These books form one stage in the unfolding of the Judaism of the dual Torah. Here emphasis is laid on issues of sanctification of the life of Israel, the people, in the aftermath of the destruction of the Temple of Jerusalem in 70 CE, in which, it was commonly held, Israel's sanctification came to full realization in the bloody rites of sacrifice to God on high. I call this system a Judaism without Christianity, because the issues found urgent in the documents representative of this phase address questions not pertinent to the Christian definition of Israel at all.

The second set of the same writings begins with the Talmud of the Land of Israel, or Yerushalmi, generally supposed to have come to a conclusion at ca. 400 CE, Genesis Rabbah, assigned to about the next half century, Leviticus Rabbah, ca. 450 CE, Pesiqta deRab Kahana, ca. 450–500 CE, and, finally, the Talmud of Babylonia or Babli, assigned to the late sixth or early seventh century, ca. 600 CE. The two Talmuds systematically interpret passages of the Mishnah, and the other documents do the same for books of the written Torah. Some other treatments of biblical books important in synagogue liturgy, particularly the Five Scrolls, e.g., Lamentations Rabbati, Esther Rabbah, and the like, are supposed also to have reached closure at this time. This second set of writings introduces, alongside the paramount issue of Israel's sanctification, the matter of Israel's salvation, and give prominence to doctrines of history, on the one side, and the Messiah, on the other.

The first of the two stages in the formation of the Judaism of the dual Torah exhibits no sign of interest in, or response to, the advent of Christianity. The second, from the Yerushalmi forward, lays points of stress and emphasis that, in retrospect, appear to respond to, and to counter, the challenge of Christianity. The point of difference, of course, is that from the beginning of the legalization of Christianity in the early fourth century, to the establishment of Christianity at the end of that same century, Jews in the land of Israel found themselves facing a challenge that, prior to Constantine, they had found no compelling reason to consider. The specific crisis came when the Christians pointed to the success of the Church in the politics of the Roman state as evidence that Jesus Christ was king of the world and that his claim to be Messiah and King of Israel had now found vindication. When the Emperor Julian, 361–363, apostatized and renewed state patronage of paganism, he permitted the Jews to begin to rebuild the Temple as part of his large plan of humiliating Christianity. His prompt death on an Iranian battlefield supplied further evidence for heaven's choice of the Church and the truth of the Church's allegations about the standing and authority of Jesus as the Christ.

The Judaic documents that reached closure in the century after these events attended to those questions of salvation, e.g., doctrine of history and of the messiah, authority of the sages' reading of Scripture as against the Christians' interpretation, and the like, that had earlier not enjoyed extensive consideration. In all, this second Judaism, which I characterize as a Judaism despite Christianity, met the challenge of the events of the fourth century. The Judaic system of the dual Torah, expressed in its main outlines in the Yerushalmi and associated compilations of biblical exegeses concerning Genesis, Leviticus, and some other scriptural books, culminated in the Babli, which emerged as the authoritative document of the Judaism of the dual Torah from then to now.

The Doctrine of Israel without regard to Christianity

The Mishnah's "Israel" bears two identical meanings: the "Israel" of (all) the Jews now and here, but also the "Israel" of which Scripture spoke. And that encompassed both the individual and the group, without linguistic differentiation of any kind. Thus, in the Mishnah, "Israel" may refer to an individual Jew (always male) or to "all Jews," that is, the collectivity of Jews. The individual woman is nearly always called *bat yisrael*, daughter of (an) Israel(ite). Sages in the Mishnah did not assemble facts and define the social entity as a matter of mere description of the given. Rather, they portrayed it as they wished to. They imputed to the social group, Jews, the status of a systemic entity, "Israel." To others within Jewry it was not at all self-evident that "all Jews" constituted one

"Israel," and that that one "Israel" formed the direct and immediate continuation, in the here and now, of the "Israel" of holy writ and revelation. The community at Qumran did not come to that conclusion, and the sense and meaning of "Israel" proposed by the authorships of the Mishnah and related writings did not strike Philo as the main point at all. Paul, for his part, reflected on "Israel" within categories not at all symmetrical with those of the Mishnah.

The Mishnaic identification of Jewry in the here and now with the "Israel" of Scripture therefore constituted an act of metaphor, comparison, contrast, identification, and analogy. It is that Judaism's most daring social metaphor. Implicitly, moreover, the metaphor excluded a broad range of candidates from the status of (an) "Israel," the Samaritans for one example, the scheduled castes of Mishnah-tractate Qiddushin Chapter Four, for another. Calling (some) Jews "Israel" established the comprehensive and generative metaphor that gives the Mishnaic system its energy. From that metaphor all else derived momentum.

The Mishnah defines "Israel" in antonymic relationships of two sorts, first, "Israel" as against "not-Israel," gentile, and, second, "Israel" as against "priest" or "Levite."[1] "Israel" serves as a taxonomic indicator, specifically part of a more encompassing system of hierarchization; "Israel" defined the frontiers, on the outer side of society, on the one hand, and the social boundaries within, on the other. To understand the meaning of "Israel" as the Mishnah and its associated documents of the second and third centuries sort matters out, we consider the sense of "gentile." The authorship of the Mishnah does not distinguish among gentiles, who represent an undifferentiated mass. To the system of the Mishnah, whether a gentile is a Roman, Aramaean, Syrian, or Briton does not matter. That is to say, differentiation among gentiles rarely, if ever, makes a difference in systemic decision-making. And it is also the fact, to the system of the Mishnah, that in the relationship at hand, "Israel" is not differentiated either. The upshot is that just as "gentile" is an abstract category, so is "Israel." "Kohen" is a category, and so is "Israel." For the purposes for which Israel/priest are defined, no further differentiation is undertaken. That is where for the Mishnaic system matters end. But to the Judaic system represented by the Yerushalmi and its associated writings, "gentile" may be Roman or other-than-Roman, for instance, Babylonian, Median, or Greek. That act of further differentiation – we may call it "speciation" – makes a considerable difference in the appreciation of "gentile." In the Mishnah's authorship's "Israel," therefore, we confront an abstraction in a system of philosophy.

If we measure the definition against the social facts in the world beyond, we see a curious contrast. The Mishnah's systemic categories within "Israel" did not encompass the social facts that required explanation. The Mishnah could explain village and "all Israel," just as its system used the word "Israel" for individual and entire social entity. But the region and its counterparts, the "we" composed of regions, the corporate society of the Jews of a given country, language-group, and the like, the real-life world of communities that transcended particular locations – these social facts of the middle distance did not constitute subdivisions of the "Israel" that knew all and each, but nothing in between. The omitted entity, I see, was the family itself, which played no important role in the Mishnah's system, except as one of the taxonomic indicators. By contrast "Israel" as family imparted to the details an autonomy and a meaning of their own, so that each complex component of the whole formed a microcosm of the whole: family to village to "Israel" as one large family.

The village then comprised "Israel," as much as did the region, the neighborhood, the corporate society people could empirically identify, the theoretical social entity they could only imagine – all formed "all Israel," viewed under the aspect of Heaven, and, of still greater consequence, each household – that is, each building block of the village community – constituted in itself a model of, the model for, "Israel." The utter abstraction of the Mishnah had left "Israel" as individual or as "all Israel," thus without articulated linkage to the concrete middle range of the Jews' everyday social life. Dealing with exquisite detail and the intangible whole, the Mishnah's system had left that realm of the society of Jews in the workaday household and village outside the metaphorical frame of "Israel," and "Israel" viewed in the image, after the likeness, of family made up that omitted middle range. In the Mishnah's authorship's "Israel" we confront an abstraction in a system of philosophy, one centered upon issues of sanctification.

"Israel" in the Judaism despite Christianity

Two metaphors, rarely present and scarcely explored in the writings of the first stage (ca. 70–300) in the formation of the Judaism of the dual Torah, came to prominence in the second stage (ca. 400–600). These were, first, the view of "Israel" as a family, the children and heirs of the man, Israel; second, the conception of Israel as sui generis. While "Israel" in the first phase of the formation of Judaism perpetually finds definition in relationship to its opposite, "Israel" in the second phase constituted an intransitive entity, defined in its own terms and not solely or mainly in relationship to other comparable entities. The enormous investment in the conception of "Israel" as sui generis makes that point blatantly. But "Israel" as family bears that same trait of autonomy and self-evident definition. The "Israel" in the second stratum of the canon of the Judaism of the dual Torah bears a socially vivid sense. Now "Israel" forms a family, and an encompassing theory of society, built upon that conception of "Israel," permits us to describe the proportions and balances of the social entity at hand, showing how each component both is an "Israel" and contributes to the larger composite as well. "Israel" as sui generis carried in its wake a substantial doctrine of definition, a weighty collection of general laws of social history governing the particular traits and events of the social group. In comparing transitive to intransitive "Israel," we move from "Israel" as not-gentile and "Israel" as not-priest to powerful statements of what "Israel" is. Now to specify in concrete terms the reasons I adduce to explain the rather striking shift before us. I see two important changes to account for the metaphorical revolution at hand, one out at the borders, the other within, the Jews' group.

Between 200 and 300, the approximate and rough dates for the closure of the Mishnah and its initial exegetical writings, thus the first statement of the Judaism of the dual Torah, and 400 and 500, the approximate dates for the Talmud of the Land of Israel, Genesis Rabbah, and Leviticus Rabbah, hence the counterpart dates for the second, two decisive changes in the Jews' political life took place. One was in the political context of the world beyond, the other, the political circumstance of the world within "Israel." The political control of the world at large in the fourth and fifth centuries, first, lay in Christian, not pagan, hands. Second, the picture we have of the position of sages in the fourth and fifth centuries points to a group of lawyer–philosophers who now exercised practical authority and carried out the everyday administration of the life of the communities in which they lived. Nothing in the Mishnah and related writings portrays the authorships of those documents in a comparable position. Indeed, the very theoretical character of the Mishnah's political conceptions suggests that the sage as administrator lay beyond the imagination of the authorship of the Mishnah.

By claiming that "Israel" constituted "Israel after the flesh," the actual, living, present family of Abraham and Sarah, Isaac and Rebecca, Jacob and Leah and Rachel, sages met head-on the Christian claim that there was – or could ever be – some other "Israel," of a lineage not defined by the family connection at all, and that the existing Jews no longer constituted "Israel." By representing "Israel" as sui generis, sages moreover focused upon the systemic teleology, with its definition of salvation, in response to the Christian claim that salvation is not of Israel but of the Church, now enthroned in this world as in heaven. The sage, model for Israel, in the model of Moses, our rabbi, represented on earth the Torah that had come from heaven. Like Christ, in earth as in heaven, like the Church, the body of Christ, ruler of earth (through the emperor) as of heaven, the sage embodied what Israel was and was to be. So Israel as family in the model of the sage, like Moses our rabbi, corresponded in its social definition to the Church of Jesus Christ, the New Israel, the source of salvation of the savior of humanity. The metaphors given prominence in the late fourth- and fifth-century sages' writings formed a remarkable counterpoint to the social metaphors important in the mind of significant Christian theologians, as both parties reflected on the political revolution that had taken place.

In response to the challenge of Christianity, sages' thought about "Israel" centered on the issues of history and salvation, issues made not merely chronic but acute by the political triumph. That accounts for the unprecedented reading of the outsider as differentiated, a reading contained in the two propositions concerning Rome, first, as Esau or Edom or Ishmael, that is, as part of the family, second, of Rome as the pig. Differentiating Rome from other gentiles represented a striking concession indeed, without counterpart in the Mishnah. Rome is represented as only Christian Rome can have been represented: it looks kosher but it is unkosher. Pagan Rome cannot ever have looked kosher, but Christian

Rome, with its appeal to ancient Israel, could and did and moreover claimed to. It bore some traits that validate, but lacked others that validate.

The metaphor of the family proved equally pointed. Sages framed their political ideas within the metaphor of genealogy, because to begin with they appealed to the fleshly connection, the family, as the rationale for Israel's social existence. A family beginning with Abraham, Isaac, and Jacob, Israel could best sort out its relationships by drawing into the family other social entities with which it found it had to relate. So Rome became the brother. That affinity came to light only when Rome had turned Christian, and that point marked the need for the extension of the genealogical net. But the conversion to Christianity also justified sages' extending membership in the family to Rome, for Christian Rome shared with Israel the common patrimony of Scripture – and said so. The character of sages' thought on Israel therefore proved remarkably congruent to the conditions of public discourse that confronted them.

The Metaphor of the Family, "Israel"

When sages wished to know what (an) "Israel" was, in the fourth century they reread the scriptural story of Scripture's "Israel"'s origins. To begin with, as Scripture told them the story, "Israel" was a man, Jacob, and his children are "the children of Jacob." That man's name was also "Israel," and, it followed, "the children of Israel" comprised the extended family of that man. By extension, "Israel" formed the family of Abraham and Sarah, Isaac and Rebecca, Jacob and Leah and Rachel. "Israel" therefore invoked the metaphor of genealogy to explain the bonds that linked persons unseen into a single social entity; the shared traits were imputed, not empirical. That social metaphor of "Israel" – a simple one, really, and easily grasped – bore consequences in two ways. First, children in general are admonished to follow the good example of their parents. The deeds of the patriarchs and matriarchs therefore taught lessons on how the children were to act. Of greater interest in an account of "Israel" as a social metaphor, "Israel" lived twice, once in the patriarchs and matriarchs, a second time in the life of the heirs as the descendants relived those earlier lives. The stories of the family were carefully reread to provide a picture of the meaning of the latter-day events of the descendants of that same family. Accordingly, the lives of the patriarchs signaled the history of Israel.

The polemical purpose of the claim that the abstraction, "Israel," was to be compared to the family of the mythic ancestor lies right at the surface. With another "Israel," the Christian Church, now claiming to constitute the true one, sages found it possible to confront that claim and to turn it against the other side. "You claim to form 'Israel after the spirit.' Fine, and we are Israel after the flesh – and genealogy forms the link, that alone." (Converts did not present an anomaly, of course, since they were held to be children of Abraham and Sarah, who had "made souls," that is, converts, in Haran, a point repeated in the documents of the period.) That fleshly continuity formed of all of "us" a single family, rendering spurious the notion that "Israel" could be other than genealogically defined. But that polemic seems to me adventitious and not primary for the metaphor provided a quite separate component to sages' larger system.

The metaphor of Israel as family supplied an encompassing theory of society. It not only explained who "Israel" as a whole was but also set forth the responsibilities of Israel's social entity, its society. The metaphor defined the character of that entity; it explained who owes what to whom and why, and it accounted for the inner structure and interplay of relationship within the community, here and now, constituted by Jews in their villages and neighborhoods of towns. Accordingly, "Israel" as family bridged the gap between an account of the entirety of the social group, "Israel," and a picture of the components of that social group as they lived out their lives in their households and villages. An encompassing theory of society, covering all components from least to greatest, holding the whole together in correct order and proportion, derived from "Israel" viewed as extended family.

That theory of "Israel" as a society made up of persons who, because they constituted a family, stood in a clear relationship of obligation and responsibility to one another corresponded to what people much later would call the social contract, a kind of compact that in palpable ways told families and households how in the aggregate they formed something larger and tangible. The web of interaction spun out of concrete interchange now was spun out of not the gossamer thread of abstraction and theory but the tough hemp of family ties. "Israel" formed a society because "Israel" was compared to an extended family. That, sum and substance, supplied to the Jews in their households (themselves a made-up category that, in the end, transformed the relationship of the nuclear family into an abstraction capable of holding together quite unrelated persons) an account of the tie from household to household, from village to village, encompassing ultimately "all Israel."

The power of the metaphor of "Israel" as family hardly requires specification. If "we" form a family, then we know full well what links us, the common ancestry, the obligations imposed by common ancestry upon the cousins who make up the family today. The link between the commonplace interactions and relationships that make "us" into a community, on the one side, and that encompassing entity, "Israel," "all Israel," now is drawn. The large comprehends the little, the abstraction of "us" overall gains concrete reality in the "us" of the here and now of home and village, all together, all forming a "family." In that fundamental way, the metaphor of "Israel" as family therefore provided the field-theory of "Israel" linking the most abstract component, the entirety of the social group, to the most mundane, the specificity of the household. One theory, framed in that metaphor of such surpassing simplicity, now held the whole together. That is what I mean when I propose that the metaphor of family provided an encompassing theory of society, an account of the social contract encompassing all social entities, Jews' and gentiles' as well, that, so far as I can see, no other metaphor accomplished.

The Doctrine of "Israel" and the Social Rules of Judaisms: The systemic context

The shape and meaning imputed to the social component, "Israel," will conform to the larger interests of the system and in detail express the system's main point. That is shown when we take up the case of the apostle Paul and his "Israel" after the Spirit. In his representation of his "Israel," Paul presents us with a metaphor for which, in the documents of the Judaism of the dual Torah, I can find no counterpart in this context. "Israel" compared to an olive tree, standing for "Israel" encompassing gentiles who believe but also Jews by birth who do not believe, "Israel" standing for the elect and those saved by faith and therefore by grace – these complex and somewhat disjointed metaphors and definitions form a coherent and simple picture when we see them not in detail but as part of the larger whole of Paul's entire system. For the issue of "Israel" for Paul forms a detail of a system centered upon a case in favor of salvation through Christ and faith in him alone, even without keeping the rules of the Torah. The consensus of the familiar and rich corpus of scholarship on Paul presents matters this way, and I take the results as definitive.

The generative problematic that tells Paul what he wishes to know about "Israel" derives from the larger concerns of the Christian system Paul proposes to work out. That problematic was framed in the need, in general, to explain the difference, as to salvific condition, between those who believed and those who did not believe in Christ. But it focused, specifically, upon the matter of "Israel," and how those who believed in Christ but did not derive from "Israel" related to both those who believed and also derived from "Israel" and those who did not believe but derived from "Israel." Do the first-named have to keep the Torah? Are the non-believing Jews subject to justification? Since, had Paul been a "gentile" and not an "Israel," the issue cannot have proved critical in the working out of an individual system (but only in the address to the world at large), we may take for granted that Paul's own Jewish origin made the question at hand important, if not critical. What transformed the matter from a chronic into an acute question – the matter of salvation through keeping the Torah – encompassed, also, the matter of who is "Israel."

For his part, Paul appeals, for his taxic indicator of "Israel," to a consideration we have not found commonplace at all, namely, circumcision. For the Mishnah's system, circumcision forms a premise, not a presence, a datum, but not a decisive taxic indicator. But Paul, by contrast, can have called "Israel" all those who are circumcised, and "not-Israel" all those who are not circumcised – pure and simple. Jonathan Z. Smith states:[2]

> The strongest and most persistent use of circumcision as a taxic indicator is found in Paul and the deutero-Pauline literature. Paul's self-description is framed in terms of the two most fundamental halakhic definitions of the Jewish male: circumcision and birth from a Jewish mother. . . . "Circumcised" is consistently used in the Pauline literature as a technical term for the Jew, "uncircumcised," for the gentile.

It must follow, as I said, that for Paul, "Israel" is "the circumcised nation," and an "Israel" is a circumcised male. The reason for the meaning attached to "Israel" is spelled out by Smith:

> What is at issue . . . is the attempt to establish a new taxon: "where there cannot be Greek and Jew, circumcised and uncircumcised, barbarian and Scythian" (Col. 3:11), "for neither circumcision counts for anything nor uncircumcision but a new creation" (Gal. 6:15).

It follows that for Paul, the matter of "Israel" and its definition forms part of a larger project of reclassifying Christians in terms not defined by the received categories, now a third race, a new race, a new man, in a new story. Smith proceeds to make the matter entirely explicit to Paul's larger system:

> Paul's theological arguments with respect to circumcision have their own internal logic and situation: that in the case of Abraham, it was posterior to faith (Rom. 4:9–12); that spiritual things are superior to physical things (Col. 3:11–14); that the Christian is the "true circumcision" as opposed to the Jew (Phil. 3:3) . . . But these appear secondary to the fundamental taxonomic premise, the Christian is a member of a new taxon.

In this same context, Paul's Letter to the Romans presents a consistent picture. In Chapters Nine through Eleven, he presents his reflections on what and who is (an) "Israel." Having specified that the family of Abraham will inherit the world not through the law but through the righteousness of faith (Rom. 4:13), Paul confronts "Israel" as family and redefines the matter in a way coherent with his larger program. Then the children of Abraham will be those who "believe in him that raised from the dead Jesus our Lord, who was put to death for our trespasses and raised for our justification" (Rom. 4:24–25). For us the critical issue is whether or not Paul sees these children of Abraham as "Israel." The answer is in his address to "my kinsmen by race. They are Israelites, and to them belong the sonship, the glory, the covenants, the giving of the law, the worship, and the promises; to them belong the patriarchs, and of their race, according to the flesh, is the Christ. God who is over all be blessed for ever" (Rom. 9:3–4). "Israel" then is the holy people, the people of God. But Paul proceeds to invoke a fresh metaphor (commonplace in the Rabbinic writings later on, to be sure), of "Israel" as olive tree, and so to reframe the doctrine of "Israel" in a radical way: Not all who are descended from Israel belong to Israel, and not all are children of Abraham because they are his descendants . . . it is not the children of the flesh who are the children of God, but the children of the promise are reckoned as descendants (Rom. 9:6–7).

Here we have an explicit definition of "Israel," now not after the flesh but after the promise. "Israel" then is no longer a family in the concrete sense in which, in earlier materials, we have seen the notion. "Israel after the flesh" who pursued righteousness which is based on law did not succeed in fulfilling that law because they did not pursue it through faith (Rom. 9:31), "and gentiles who did not pursue righteousness have attained it, that is, righteousness through faith" (Rom. 9:30). Now there is an "Israel" after the flesh but also "a remnant chosen by grace . . . the elect obtained it . . ." (Rom. 11:5–6), with the consequence that the fleshly "Israel" remains, but gentiles ("a wild olive shoot") have been grafted "to share the richness of the olive tree" (Rom. 11:17). Do these constitute "Israel"? Yes and no. They share in the promise. They are "Israel" in the earlier definition of the children of Abraham. There remains an "Israel" after the flesh, which has its place as well. And that place remains with God: "As regards election they are beloved for the sake of their forefathers. For the gifts and the call of God are irrevocable" (Rom. 11:28–29).

The Philosophical Israel: The case of Philo

By philosopher in the present context I mean an intellectual who attempts to state as a coherent whole, within a single system of thought and (implicit) explanation, diverse categories and classifications of data. For Philo, Israel forms a paradigmatic metaphor, bearing three meanings. The first is ontological, which signifies the places of "Israel" in God's creation. The second is epistemological. This signifies the knowledge of God that Israel possesses. The third is political, referring to the polity that "Israel" possesses and projects in light of its ontological place and epistemological access to God.

For Philo, "Israel" formed a category within a larger theory of how humanity knows divinity, an aspect of ontology and epistemology. What makes an "Israel" into "Israel" for Philo is a set of essentially philosophical considerations, concerning adherence to or perception of God. In the philosophical system of Philo, "Israel" constitutes a philosophical category, not a social entity in an everyday sense. That is not to suggest that Philo does not see Jews as a living social entity, a community. The opposite is the case. His *Embassy to Gaius* is perfectly clear that the Jews form a political group. But that fact makes no difference to Philo's philosophical "Israel." For when he constructs his philosophical statement, the importance of "Israel" derives from its singular capacity to gain knowledge of God that other categories of the system cannot have. When writing about the Jews in a political context, Philo does not appeal to their singular knowledge of God, and when writing about the Jews as "Israel" in the philosophical context, he does not appeal to their forming a this-worldly community. That again illustrates my claim that it is within the discipline of its own logic that the system invents its "Israel," without responding in any important way to social facts out there, in the larger world.

Seeing "Israel" as "the people which is dedicated to his service," Philo holds that "Israel" is the best of races and is capable of seeing God, and this capability of seeing God is based upon the habit of his service to God.[3] The upshot is the capacity to receive a type of prophecy that comes directly from God, and one must be descended from "Israel" to receive that type of prophecy. An Egyptian, Hagar, cannot see the Supreme Cause.[4] The notion of inherited "merit" (in this context an inappropriate metaphor) bears more than a single burden; here "merit" or inherited capacity involves a more clear perception of God than is attained by those without the same inheritance – a far cry indeed from the "merit of the ancestors" as the fourth-century sages would interpret it. Mere moral and intellectual qualifications, however, do not suffice. One has to enjoy divine grace, which Moses had, and which, on account of the merit of the patriarchs, the people have.

The Political "Israel:" The case of the Qumran documents

In defining a systemic component such as "Israel," what matters to begin with is dictated by the traits of the one to whom the subject is important, not by the objective and indicative characteristics of the subject itself; second, is that the importance of a topic derives from the character of the system that takes up that topic. By "Israel," the authorships of the documents of the library of Qumran mean "us" – and no one else. Stated simply, what our authorships meant by "us" was simply "Israel" or "the true Israel." The group did not recognize other Jews as "Israel." That is why the group organized itself as a replication of "all Israel," as they read about "Israel" in those passages of Scripture that impressed them. They structured their group – in Geza Vermes's language, "so that it corresponded faithfully to that of Israel itself, dividing it into priests and laity, the priests being described as the 'sons of Zadok' – Zadok was High Priest in David's time – and the laity grouped after the biblical model into twelve tribes."[5] This particular Israel then divided itself into units of thousands, hundreds, fifties, and tens. The Community Rule further knows divisions within the larger group, specifically, "the men of holiness," and "the men of perfect holiness," within a larger "Community." The corporate being of the community came to realization in common meals, prayers, and deliberations. Vermes says, "Perfectly obedient to each and every one of the laws of Moses and to all that was commanded by the prophets, they were to love one another and to share with one another their knowledge, powers, and possessions."[6] The description of the inner life of the group presents us with a division of a larger society. But – among many probative ones – one detail tells us that this group implicitly conceived of itself as "Israel."

The group lived apart from the Temple of Jerusalem and had its liturgical life worked out in utter isolation from that central cult. They had their own calendar, which differed from the one people take for granted was observed in general, for their calendar was reckoned not by the moon but by the sun. This yielded different dates for the holy days and effectively marked the group as utterly out of touch with other Jews.[7] The solar calendar followed by the community at Qumran meant that holy days for that group were working days for others and vice versa. The group furthermore had its own designation for various parts of the year. The year was divided into seven fifty-day periods, as Vermes says, each marked by an agricultural festival, e.g., the Feast of New Wine, Oil, and so on.[8] On the Pentecost, treated as the Feast of the Renewal of the Covenant, the group would assemble in hierarchical order: "the priests first, ranked in order of status, after them the Levites, and lastly 'all the people one after another in their Thousands, Hundreds, Fifties, and Tens, that every Israelite may know his place in the community of God according to the everlasting design.'"[9] There can be no doubt from this passage – and a vast array of counterparts can be assembled – that the documents at hand address "Israel."

The System's Generative Problematic defines its "Israel"

The systemic importance of the category "Israel" depends on the generative problematic – the urgent question – of the system-builders, and not on their social circumstance. The place of "Israel" within the self-evidently true response offered by the system will prove congruent to the logic of the system – that alone. The proposed hypothesis is that the systemic question – the precipitating crisis that leads several generations of intellectuals to rethink the grounds of social being and to reconsider all fundamental questions in a new way – determines the importance of any category within the system. The paramount character of a category in the social facts-out-there, in the streets and households (in the case of the social entity), has slight bearing upon the proportions and order of the system. Stated in the positive, the rule is that the systemic logic-in-here dictates all issues of proportion, balance, and order. We therefore ask ourselves how on objective grounds and by appealing to data, we may assess the relative importance of a given systemic structural category when we compare one system with another.

Whether or not "Israel" takes an important place in a system is decided by the system and its logic, not the circumstance of the Jews in the here and now. System-building is a symbolic transaction worked out in imagination, not a sifting and sorting of facts. But how do we know whether or not any systemic component plays a more, or a less, important role? A judgment on the importance of a given entity or category in one system by comparison with the importance of that same entity or category in another need not rely on subjective criteria. A reasonably objective measure of the matter lends hope to test the stated hypothesis. That criterion is whether or not the system remains cogent without consideration of its "Israel." Philo's does, the Mishnah's does, Paul's does not, the Essenes' does not, and the second stage in Judaism's does not.

The criterion of importance therefore does not derive from merely counting up references to "Israel." What we must do is to assess the role and place of the social entity in a system by asking a simple question. Were the entity or trait "Israel" to be removed from a given system, would that system radically change in character or would it merely lose a detail? What is required is a mental experiment, but not a very difficult one. What we do is simply present a reprise of our systemic description.

First, without an "Israel," Paul would have had no system. The generative question of his system required him to focus attention on the definition of the social entity, "Israel." Paul originated among Jews but addressed both Jews and gentiles, seeking to form the lot into a single social entity "in Christ Jesus." The social dimension of his system formed the generative question with which he proposed to contend. Second, without an "Israel," Philo, by contrast, can have done very well indeed. For Philo, "Israel" was a detail of a theory of knowledge of God, not the generative problematic even of the treatment of the knowledge of God, let alone of the system as a whole (which we scarcely approached and had no reason to approach!). We may therefore say that "Israel" formed an important category for Paul and not for Philo. Accordingly, the judgment of the matter rests on more than mere word-counts, on the one side, or exercises of impression and taste, on the other. It forms part of a larger interpretation of the system as a whole and what constitutes the system's generative problematic.

If, moreover, we ask whether "Israel" is critical to the library of Qumran, a simple fact answers our question. Were we to remove "Israel" in general and in detail from the topical program at hand, we should lose, if not the entirety of the library, then nearly the whole of some documents and the larger part of many of them. The library of Qumran constitutes a vast collection of writings about "Israel," its definition and conduct, history and destiny. We cannot make an equivalent statement of the entire corpus of Philo's writings, even though Philo obviously concerned himself with the life and welfare of the "Israel" of which, in Alexandria as well as the world-over, he saw himself a part. The reason for the systemic importance among the Essenes of Qumran of "Israel," furthermore, derives from the meanings imputed to that category. The library stands for a social group that conceives of itself as "Israel," and that wishes, in these documents, to spell out what that "Israel" is and must do. The system as a whole forms an exercise in the definition of "Israel" as against that "non-Israel" composed not of gentiles but of erring (former) Israelites. The saving remnant is all that is left: "Israel."

Our survey of four Judaisms yields a single rule. If we wish to know whether "Israel" will constitute an important component in a Judaism, we ask about the categorical imperative and describe, as a matter of mere fact, the consequent categorical composition of that system, stated as a corpus of authoritative documents. A system in which "Israel" – the social entity to which the system's builders imagine they address themselves – plays an important role will treat "Israel" as part of its definitive structure. The reason is that the system's categorical imperative will find important consequences in the definition of its "Israel." A system in which the system's builders work on other questions entirely than social ones, explore the logic of issues different from those addressing a social entity, also will not yield tractates on "Israel" and will not accord to the topic of "Israel" that categorical and systemic importance that we have identified in some Judaisms but not in others. Discourse on "Israel," in general (as in the second phase of the Judaism of the dual Torah) or in acute detail concerning internal structure (as in the writings of Qumran), comes about because of the fundamental question addressed by the system viewed whole.

Paul's context told him that "Israel" constituted a categorical imperative, and it also told him what, about "Israel," he had to discover in his thought on the encounter with Christ. Those who collected the library at Qumran by choice isolated themselves and in that context determined upon the generative issue of describing an "Israel" that, all by itself in the wilderness, would survive and form the saving remnant. Paul – all scholarship concurs – faced a social entity ("church" or "Christian community") made up of Jews but also gentiles, and (some) Jews expected people to obey the law, e.g., to circumcise their sons. Given the natural course of lives, that was not a question to be long postponed, which imparts to it the acute, not merely chronic, character that it clearly displayed even in the earliest decade beyond Paul's vision. And that fact explains why, for Paul, circumcision formed a critical taxic indicator in a way in which, for Philo, for the Mishnah, and other Judaic systems, it did not. The sages of the dual Torah made their documentary statements in reply to two critical questions, the one concerning sanctification, presented by the final failure of efforts to regain Jerusalem and restore the temple cult, the other concerning salvation, precipitated by the now-unavoidable fact of Christianity's political triumph.

To state matters in general terms, the system comes before the texts – in our case, the systemic problem comes before its definition of its "Israel" – and defines the canon of the texts. The exegesis of the canon then forms that ongoing social action that sustains the whole. A system does not recapitulate its texts, it selects and orders them, imputes to them as a whole a cogency, one to the next, that their original authorships have not expressed in and through the parts. A system expresses through the composition formed of the documents its deepest logic, and it also frames that just fit that, we have observed, joins system to circumstance. The whole works its way out through exegesis, and the history of any religious system – that is to say, the history of religion writ small – is the exegesis of its exegesis. And the first rule of the exegesis of systems is the simplest, and the one with which I conclude: the system does not recapitulate the canon. The canon recapitulates the system.

Notes

1   In my *"Israel": Judaism and its Social Metaphors* (New York, 1988), I provide the data to back up these statements.
2   Jonathan Z. Smith, "Fences and Neighbors," in W. S. Green, ed., *Approaches to Ancient Judaism* (Missoula, 1978), vol. 2, pp. 1–25; reprinted in: Jonathan Z. Smith, *Imagining Religion. From Babylon to Jonestown* (Chicago, 1982), pp. 1–18.

3   Harry A. Wolfson, *Philo: Foundations of Religious Philosophy in Judaism, Christianity and Islam* (Cambridge, MA, 1962), vol. 1, pp. 51–1.
4   Ibid., p. 51.
5   Geza Vermes, *The Dead Sea Scrolls in English: Qumran in Perspective* (New York, 1981), p. 88.
6   Ibid., p. 89.
7   Ibid., p. 176.
8   Ibid., p. 177.
9   Ibid., p. 178.

CHAPTER 15

The Doctrine of the Messiah

William Scott Green and Jed Silverstein

Probably no religious idea seems more fundamental to Judaism or more essentially Jewish than that of the messiah, Israel's eschatological redeemer. It is widely supposed that Judaism is a messianic religion and that hope for the messiah's appearance is the major focus of, and driving force behind, Jewish religious belief and behavior. Indeed, two commonplaces of western history are that, in first-century Palestine, enhanced Jewish anticipation of the messiah's arrival was the backdrop for the emergence of Christianity and that conflicting opinions about the messiah's appearance, identity, activity, and implications caused the division between Judaism and Christianity. The idea of the messiah thus appears fundamental to the structure and character of Judaism and therefore to the emergence of Christianity.

But recent research suggests that these assumptions need qualification. Judaism's scripture, the Hebrew Bible, contains no doctrine of an eschatological redeemer and does not use the term "messiah" to refer to one. Post-biblical Jewish texts – the Apocrypha, Pseudepigrapha, Dead Sea Scrolls, the writings of Philo and Josephus – use the term "messiah" infrequently and inconsistently. On their basis, there is no reason to think that the Jews of first-century Palestine were anticipating a messiah. The idea of the messiah is barely present in the Mishnah, the foundational document of Rabbinic Judaism. A key reason for the unclarity about the messiah in these texts is that the Temple-centered religion practiced in Jerusalem and described in Scripture, which dominated ancient Judaism and is the basis of all other forms of Judaism, provides no religious role for a savior. God alone is Israel's – and therefore humanity's – redeemer. In this religion, living according to God's design – ethically and ritually – maintains Israel's relationship with God, including the forgiveness of sin. "Levitical religion," as we might call it, offers no religious function for a messiah that is not already covered in some other way.

Of all the Jewish writings of the Second Temple and immediate post-destruction periods, only the New Testament – which became Christianity's scripture – offers the rudiments of a coherent doctrine of the messiah. Early Christian teaching about Jesus (though perhaps not Jesus' own teaching about himself) ultimately shifted the focus of redemption from God to the messiah. This shift, which made the messiah the medium of humanity's salvation, altered Judaism's structure and produced a new religion.

Ancient and medieval Rabbinic writings as well as the synagogue liturgy contain the category of "messiah." But, as in earlier writings, the pictures in these varied literatures are not consistent. In the Talmuds, "the messiah" is a secondary category, subordinate to the generative and more central components of the Rabbinic religious system. In Jacob Neusner's words, in Rabbinic literature, the messiah

> does not define a categorical imperative in the way that Israel and the gentiles, . . . sin and atonement, resurrection and the world to come, all do. . . . The Messiah-theme forms a subset of several categories and by itself does not take up an autonomous presence in the theology of the Oral Torah. The Messiah-theme fits into the primary categories but is itself divisible among them.

In this sense, for most forms of Judaism in ancient and medieval times, the messiah is present in, but not essential to, the workings of the Jewish religion.

There is one important exception and one significant qualification to this generalization. The career of Shabbetai Zevi (1626–76), Judaism's most famous false messiah (and the movements that flowed from his messianic claims) is the exception. In 1666, Shabbetai Zevi, a charismatic figure born in Smyrna, was regarded as the messiah by substantial portions of the Jewish world. In an unprecedented act, he converted to Islam. Shabbetai Zevi's principal spokesman and interpreter, Nathan of Gaza, employed the doctrines of Lurianic Kabbalah to explain this conversion as a redemptive act that brought the world closer to salvation. Sabbateanism shifts the focus of Israel's redemption from God to the messiah and thereby alters Judaism's fundamental morphology.

The significant qualification concerns the matter of exile. For most of its history, Judaism has existed without a native center. Its scripture, theology, liturgy, practices, and most of its writings assume that Judaism's adherents are living as aliens, away from their native territory. The figure of the messiah emerges from the loss of the Davidic dynasty and of Israel's political autonomy. The messiah-theme, therefore, is inextricably bound up with the notion of exile, and the Jews' recovery of the land they regard as theirs inevitably has messianic overtones. By realizing the ancient promise of restoration, the contemporary establishment of a Jewish polity in the land of Israel raises unprecedented questions about the religious meaning of return from exile in terms of classic Jewish ideas of the messiah.

The following describes the main contours of the idea of the messiah in Judaism, with particular attention to the ancient period and to the interactions between the traditional Jewish messianism and Zionism. Its focus is on the place of the messiah-theme in the structure of Jewish religion rather than on messianism as the broad ideology of Jewish redemption. The so-called "messianic" movements that appeared in nearly every century sought – but failed – to ameliorate the position of the Jews, and they did not foster major changes in the workings of Judaism itself.

Israelite Antecedents

The term "messiah" means "anointed" or "anointed one." In ancient Israel, as in other Near Eastern cultures, the smearing or pouring of oil conferred leadership status on an individual, usually a priest, prophet, or king. The shift from the conception of the "messiah" as simply a current leader – a duly anointed king or judge, for instance – to the idea of a future redeemer for Israel is a function of both the nature of the Davidic monarchy and its dissolution after the destruction of the First Temple in 586/587 BCE. The conception of kingship represented by the divine promise that David's house will rule Israel in perpetuity – for example, in 2 Sam. 7 – lays a foundation for the Israelite belief in an ideal future king, whose appearance fulfills that promise. Such a figure is the object of both hope and speculation in the writings of Israel's exilic and post-exilic prophets. The loss of the monarchy, political sovereignty, and the land of Israel itself constituted a cultural trauma that was written deep into Israel's national literature. The transformation of that literature into Judaism's scripture and the land of Israel's continued subjugation to foreign powers (save for a century of Hasmonean rule) institutionalized the trauma and made an ideal Davidic monarch and the exiles' return to the land conventional components of Jewish views of redemption. These hopes persist to varying degrees and in various forms throughout the history and literature of Judaism.

Jewish texts from biblical through the post-70 periods illustrate a progressive idealization of the future "anointed" king. Their speculations about the future king's rule range from restorative (an idealized but this-worldly Davidic kingdom) to utopian (an almost magical age of idyllic perfection). This development seems to be the basis of the idea of a divinely ordained figure who will redeem Israel at the end of time or the end of the age. As we shall see below, such figures, most of whom are not called "messiah," appear in Jewish literature from the Second Temple period. The wish for a new or ideal Davidic king retained its currency in several Jewish circles during the Second Temple period.

Jewish expectation of a restored Davidic monarchy intensified with the return from the Babylonian exile and ultimate rebuilding of the Temple during the Persian period, 540–330 BCE. However, the colonial context generated an important modification in ideas about Israel's redeemer. Persian rule allowed the Jews autonomy in "ritual and sacred institutions," which valorized the priesthood at the expense of the Davidic monarchy. Zechariah's claim (Zech. 3) that post-exilic Israel would be ruled by a diarchy – a king and a priest – responds to colonial policy by diminishing Israelite political claims in the face of non-Jewish rule.[1]

Continued foreign domination of the Jews in the land of Israel generated a *de facto* distinction between religion and politics that effectively removed the king from the realm of religion. For example, in the Bible, the Israelite king has no role in divine worship and is not responsible for the fall of rain. Moreover the cult is developed in the desert, not in a state. This literary strategy keeps the cult far from royalty and separates the issue of holiness from the question of Israel's sovereignty. A people rather than a polity, the Bible's Israel is bound together by its relationship to the cult, not to the throne. This clearly is an effort by the priestly authorities to focus Israel's relation to God around the cult rather than the state. Nothing in the cultic structure or narrative encourages the development of either monarchy or sovereignty.

Though the king was central in the period of the First Temple, in the Second Temple period the priests were the dominant cultural and religious figures. Their vision of the nature and maintenance of Israel's relationship to God is spelled out in their editing of the Pentateuch. The religion they advocated – "levitical religion" – constitutes the background against which most of the relevant early Jewish texts about the messiah were written and shapes the contours of the messiah in later Judaism.

Levitical Religion and the Messiah

Judaism in the ancient Mediterranean was highly diverse, but its varieties were neither equally distributed nor uniformly influential and important. Between the Persian period and 70 CE, the dominant form of Judaism was the Jerusalem Temple and its cult. The religion represented by the Temple and its priestly personnel conceived of the life of Israel as a comprehensive and integrated system of disciplined engagement with God. That engagement largely took the form of prescribed and repeated behaviors, directed by a caste of priests, that revolved around and focused on a sacred center, a stable reference point – the Holy of Holies – where access to God was certain to occur. Before the Holy of Holies stood the altar, on which the priests offered animal and other sacrifices daily to maintain Israel's relationship with God and to secure God's forgiveness of sin, both individual and collective.

A religion of cult and sacrifice, as levitical religion was, is extremely powerful and difficult to abandon because it guarantees that one is in the presence of God. The Temple is the *Domus Dei*, the house of the god, and the priestly rituals maintain God's presence there. The life and death drama of the sacrifices graphically illustrates what is at stake in being right with God, and the rising smoke is tangible evidence that the relationship with God remains solid. Levitical religion is appealing and effective because it is immediate and concrete. Its interests and traits explain why it provides little place for a future messianic redeemer.

Levitical religion is a religion of distinctions. It maps out a system of categories – usually binary opposites such as clean/unclean, fit/unfit, holy/profane – in which everything that matters has its place. A major distinction is the absolute distinction between the living and the dead. The two states must not be confused or conjoined. The priests have no funerary responsibilities and are forbidden to come in contact with dead human bodies, which are regarded as a source of uncleanness. But, in levitical religion human death is religiously insignificant. It is a fact, and there is no effort to transcend it or triumph over it.

Levitical religion emphasizes the integration of mind and body. It maintains order through acts of conscious labor: proper moral actions and attitudes; correct offering of sacrifices; observance of food and sexual taboos; tithing of produce; celebration of Sabbaths and festivals; and so forth. In levitical religion, there is no categorical difference between what we now call ethics and ritual. Telling the truth, honoring one's parents, observing the Sabbath, and eating permitted food are all important and equally obligatory. Levitical religion is a religion of sanctification. Through conscious action Israel becomes a holy people and repairs any ruptures in its relationship with God.

Because it is centered around the Temple, levitical religion conceives of time cyclically. Every year is conceived as a repetition of every other year. The priestly writers thought paradigmatically rather than diachronically. Their ultimate interest was in nurturing and maintaining the already established relationship between God and Israel. Their preferred literary form was the list – for instance, the genealogies and series of rules of the Pentateuch's P document – rather than narrative.

The goal of levitical religion is not to escape the world but to preserve the present. There is no attempt to do away with the current social structure. Rather, everything in levitical religion reinforces the priestly vision of the cosmic order. For example, the festivals described in Leviticus – Passover, Booths, Pentecost, the New Year – are all intimately tied in to the cycle of the seasons. The Sabbath, which seems unique in the ancient Near East, illustrates how levitical religion celebrates the received order of creation. The Sabbath commemorates the creation of the world. Israel rests as God rested at the end of the seventh day. This powerfully reinforces the idea that the order of creation is good, to be celebrated, and to be preserved.

In its ritual and its writing, levitical religion promulgated a synchronic vision of a centered, structured, hierarchical, and orderly reality. Its practitioners celebrated precision, lineage, precedent, and concreteness and had an exceedingly low tolerance for uncertainty, confusion, and ambiguity.

A religion of having what you want and keeping it, levitical religion in principle has no religious need for a redeemer, savior, or messiah. The consistent message of the priestly editing of Scripture is that so long as the altar is effective, Israel's relationship with God is secure. In levitical religion, there is nothing religious a messiah can do that the altar cannot do. A redeemer is religiously unnecessary.

Rabbinic Judaism is the primary heir and continuator of the levitical religion represented in Scripture. Emerging from the destruction of the Second Temple in 70 CE, its aim, in the absence of the altar, was to preserve Scripture's priestly ideals largely undisturbed. Rabbinic Judaism substituted piety, good deeds, and study of Torah for the altar, and it replaced the Holy of Holies with the sacred Torah scroll. Halakhah, Rabbinic religious praxis, derives from, and shares the values of, the levitical religion outlined in Scripture. Living rabbinically is comprised of a host of behaviors – ethical acts, good deeds, charity; food, purity, and kinship taboos; observance of Sabbaths, holy days, festivals, and prayer – that depend on and promulgate levitical categories. Hence, in Rabbinic Judaism and the forms of Judaism that follow it, the messiah will play an ancillary role and have little impact on religious practice.

Although the levitical worldview dominated and shaped the development of the messiah-theme in Judaism, it did not and could not extinguish the vision of redemption associated with a future or ideal Davidic king. So long as the Jews regard themselves as in exile, the wish for an heir of David who would lead the people back to its land remains a persistent leitmotif. In this sense, despite the levitical effort to limit redemption to the realm of religion, the messiah-theme always had the potential to be political.

The Messiah in Second Temple Literature

Any notion of a messianic belief or idea in ancient Judaism necessarily presupposes that "messiah" was a focal and evocative native category for ancient Jews. But a review of Israelite and early Judaic literature, the textual record produced and initially preserved by Jews, makes such a conclusion dubious at best. The noun *mashiah* ("anointed" or "anointed one") occurs thirty-eight times in the Hebrew Bible, where it applies twice to the patriarchs, six times to the high priest, once to Cyrus, and twenty-nine times to the Israelite king, primarily Saul and secondarily David or an unnamed Davidic monarch. In these contexts the term denotes one invested, usually by God, with power and leadership, but never an eschatological figure. Ironically, in the apocalyptic book of Daniel (9:25f), where an eschatological messiah would be appropriate, the term refers to a murdered high priest.

The term "messiah" has scant and inconsistent use in early Jewish texts. Most of the Dead Sea Scrolls and the Pseudepigrapha, and the entire Apocrypha, contain no reference to "the messiah." Moreover, a messiah is neither essential to the apocalyptic genre nor a prominent feature of ancient apocalyptic writings. A rapid survey of the most pertinent materials helps to justify these generalizations.

The Maccabean documents, which disdain the revival of the Davidic dynasty, ignore the term. There is no messiah in Jubilees, nor in Enoch 1–36 and 91–104, nor in the Assumption of Moses, nor in 2 Enoch, nor in the Sibylline Oracles. The messiah is absent from Josephus' description of Judaism in both *Antiquities* and *Against Apion*, and also from the writings of Philo.

In Ben Sira, which has no interest in a future redeemer, the "anointed one" or "messiah" is the Israelite king – a this-worldly, political leader. The Qumran scrolls report two messiahs, one Davidic and one priestly, who are not necessarily eschatological figures. The scrolls also apply the term to the prophets. In Psalms of Solomon 17, which is neither apocalyptic nor eschatological, the messiah is an idealized, future Davidic king who also exhibits traits of sage and teacher. The term appears only twice in the Similitudes of Enoch (1 Enoch 37–71), where it denotes not a king but a transcendent, heavenly figure. In any case, its use in Enoch is dwarfed by other titles, such as "the Chosen One" and "the Son of Man." The half-dozen references in the first-century text 4 Ezra offer conflicting pictures of the messiah. In 7:28ff the messiah dies an unredeeming death before the eschaton, but later chapters portray him as announcing and executing the final judgment. In 2 Baruch, which contains five references, the term applies primarily to a warrior, the slayer of Israel's enemies. In the Mishnah's legal contexts, messiah refers to an anointed priest, and the messiah as redeemer is negligible.

These texts offer little evidence of sustained thought or evolving Judaic reflection about the messiah. Thus, in early Jewish literature, the term "messiah" is notable primarily for its indeterminacy.

The Messiah and Early Christian Writing

In light of its insignificance in these texts, it is legitimate to ask why the category "the messiah" came to be seen as a fundamental and generative component of Israelite religion and early Judaism and why it persists as a major religious category in the West. It is fair to ask how so much has come to be written about an allegedly Jewish conception in which so many ancient Jewish texts manifest such little interest.

The hegemony of Christianity in the western world answers this question. The primacy of "the messiah" as a religious category and subject of academic study derives directly from early Christian word choice, theology, and apologetics. In contrast to the relatively infrequent references to the term "messiah" in Jewish literature cited above, the New Testament uses the term three hundred and fifty times, two hundred and seventy of them in Paul's epistles. In particular, two aspects of New Testament writing were determinative for the western conception of the messiah.

First, early Christian writers attached the word *christos*, the Greek for *mashiah*, to Jesus' name, as either a title or a surname. This usage valorizes *christos* and thereby makes "messiah" seem a revealing and important category and thus a subject to be studied. To be persuaded that this use of the word *christos* itself was pivotal in shaping later understanding, one need simply imagine the consequences for western history, religion, and theology had, for example, "lord," "son of man," or "rabbi" prevailed instead as Jesus' cognomen.

Second, New Testament authors, particularly of the gospels of Matthew and Luke, made the Hebrew scriptures into a harbinger of Jesus' career, suffering, and death. The "promise-fulfillment" motif, which casts Jesus as a foreseen figure, is perhaps the major achievement of New Testament apologetics. Apparently a later development of early Christian writing, the motif is a major focus of neither Paul's letters, the Q source, nor the Gospel of Mark.

It is richly articulated and elaborated in the Gospel of Matthew, particularly in Matthew's distinctive use of fulfillment formulas ("All this happened in order to fulfill what the Lord declared through the prophet . . .") to make various prophetic statements into predictions of Jesus' birth and career. Nearly half of those statements are not predictions about the future but the prophets' comments about Israel's past or their own present. This suggests that the fulfillment formulas and their attached verses are the results of *post facto* choice rather than remnants of an exegetical heritage. As in the *pesher* commentaries in the Dead Sea Scrolls, early Christians sought to ground their current experience in scripture and so read the present into the text.

The ideology for the motif is explicit at Luke 24:13–27. On the road to Emmaeus, two disciples unknowingly encounter the risen Jesus and express their disbelief at his death, which seems to disconfirm their early supposition about him ("But we had been hoping that he was the man to liberate Israel"). Jesus rebukes their lack of perception and claims that his death was predicted in the Hebrew scriptures ("Then he began with Moses and all the prophets and explained to them the passages which referred to himself in every part of the scriptures"). The Hebrew scriptures are thus classified as anterior literature, the messiah's textual antecedent.

The "promise-fulfillment" motif, along with the (conflicting) genealogies devised by Matthew and Luke (Matt. 1:1–17; Luke 3:23–38) embed Jesus in the Hebrew scriptures and forge an indelible continuity between him (and thus the early Christians) and Israel. By naming Jesus *christos*, giving him an Israelite pedigree, and depicting him and his death as foretold and pre-determined, early Christian writers gave the figure of the messiah a diachronic dimension. They situated the messiah's origin not in the present but in Israelite antiquity and thus established the Hebrew scriptures as a sequence of auguries. Reading Scripture became, and to a large extent has remained, an exercise in deciphering and tracing a linear progression of portents. It was not simply, as Paul claimed, that the messiah exhibited a typological similarity to important biblical characters such as Adam. Rather, the messiah was rooted in Israel's past and his appearance could be tracked and plotted, perhaps even calculated, through time. On the model provided by Matthew and Luke, the messiah emerges not as an abrupt response to a contemporary crisis, but as the ultimate fulfillment of centuries of accumulated hope and intensifying expectation, the culmination and completion of an ancient Israelite tradition.

This strategy of representation established an enduring convention of western discourse about the messiah. The model limned by an apologetic use of Scripture was accepted by later scholarship as a literary fact and a historical reality, not only of Scripture itself but also of Israelite and Jewish religion.

The Messiah in Rabbinic Judaism

In contrast to the New Testament, Rabbinic literature did not develop a consistent doctrine of the messiah or his role. The Rabbinic picture of the messiah and his activity varies according to document, time, and Rabbinic authority. In general, Rabbinic literature depicts the messiah as secondary to the major and generative categories of the Rabbinic system.

According to Jacob Neusner, the Mishnah develops a religion of sanctification that has a "teleology without eschatology." Consequently, it lacks a doctrine of "the Messiah":

> In the system of the Mishnah – vast and encompassing as it is – we look in vain for a doctrine of the Messiah. There "messiah" serves as a taxonomic indicator, e.g., distinguishing one type of priest or general from some other. There is no doctrine of the Messiah, coming at the end of time; in the Mishnah's system, matters focus on other issues entirely. Although the figure of a Messiah does appear, when the framers of the Mishnah spoke of "the Messiah," they meant a high priest designated and consecrated to office in a certain way, and not in some other way. The reference to "days of the Messiah" constitutes a conventional division of history at the end time but before the ultimate end. But that category of time plays no consequential role in the teleological framework established within the Mishnah. Accordingly, the Mishnah's framers constructed a system of Judaism in which the entire teleological dimension reached full exposure while hardly invoking the person or functions of a messianic figure of any kind. . . . For the purpose of our inquiry, the main thing is a simple fact, namely, that salvation comes through sanctification. The salvific figure, then, becomes an instrument of consecration and so fits into an ahistorical system quite different from the one built around the Messiah.[2]

As the primary heir of levitical religion, the Mishnah offers neither a picture of "the Messiah" nor an articulated religious role for one. Its ahistorical vision does not conceive of a dramatic redemption at the end of time. Rather, through the life of piety and the performance of commandments, Israel restores and enacts the ideal conditions of creation and the Garden of Eden. Since Israel's destiny is to be a "holy people," she fulfills her teleology through sanctification. In the Mishnah, therefore, the performance of commandments does not – and cannot – produce the messiah or cause the messiah to come. The commandments are effective in their own terms and not because of some additional consequence that they generate. The Mishnah's worldview makes the messiah virtually irrelevant to the practice of Judaism, and any notion of the messiah as redeemer must stand essentially outside of the Mishnaic system.

The logic of any religious system disciplines the thought and imagination that take place within it. But it cannot restrain thinking that goes on outside it. Since the Mishnah contains no doctrine or description of the messiah, it could neither shape nor block messianic speculation in later Rabbinic Judaism. Hence, post-Mishnaic Rabbinic texts exhibit a wide range of thinking about the messiah. At one end of the spectrum of opinion is the view that severs the messiah completely from the exercise of religion. It holds that the messiah will come unexpectedly, when God, not Israel, determines it. Nothing Israel can do will make the messiah appear. A related view is the Rabbinic posture of messianic quietism, which explicitly warns Israel against trying to "force" God's hand in bringing redemption. The following text illustrates (Song of Songs Rabbah 2:7; Neusner, trans. [see also B. Ket. 111a]):

> R. Helbo says, ". . . He imposed an oath on Israel not to rebel against the kingdoms and not to force the end, not to reveal its mysteries to the nations of the world, and not to go up from the exile by force."

This passage suggests that God actually imposed on Israel four "oaths" concerning the end, each one requiring Israel to be patient and passive, to await God's decision. It reflects both the desire for redemption and the concern that something fundamental will be violated if Israel tries to generate it herself. Both of these positions seem to accord with the Mishnah's worldview.

By contrast, a virtual connection between piety and redemption occurs for the first time at Y. Taanit 1:1:

A   "The oracle concerning Dumah. One is calling to me from Seir, 'Watchman, what of the night? Watchman, what of the night?'" (Is. 21:11).

B   The Israelites said to Isaiah, "O our Rabbi, Isaiah, what will come for us out of this night?"

C   He said to them, "Wait for me, until I can present the question."

D   Once he had asked the question, he came back to them.

E   They said to him, "Watchman, what of the night? What did the Guardian of the ages tell you?"

F   He said to them, "The watchman says, 'Morning comes; and also the night. If you will inquire, inquire; come back again' (Is. 21:12)."

G   They said to him, "Also the night?"

H   He said to them, "It is not what you are thinking. But there will be morning for the righteous, and night for the wicked, morning for Israel, and night for idolaters."

I   They said to him, "When?"

J   He said to them, "Whenever you want, he too wants [it to be] – if you want it, he wants it."

K   They said to him, "What is standing in the way?"

L   He said to them, "Repentance: 'Come back again' (Is. 21:12)."

M   R. Aha in the name of R. Tanhum b. R. Hiyya, "If Israel repents for one day, forthwith the son of David will come."

N   "What is the Scriptural basis? 'O that today you would hearken to his voice!' (Ps. 95:7)."

O   Said R. Levi, "If Israel would keep a single Sabbath in the proper way, forthwith the son of David will come."

P   "What is the Scriptural basis for this view? 'Moses said, Eat it today, for today is a Sabbath to the Lord; today you will not find it in the field' (Exod. 16:25)."

Q   "And it says, 'For thus said the Lord God, the Holy One of Israel, "In returning and rest you shall be saved; in quietness and in trust shall be your strength." And you would not' (Is. 30:15)."

As Neusner observes:

> First, the system of religious observance, including study of Torah, is explicitly invoked as having salvific power. Second, the persistent hope of the people for the coming of the Messiah is linked to the system of Rabbinic observance and belief. In this way, the austere program of the Mishnah, with no trace of a promise that the Messiah will come if and when the system is fully realized, finds a new development. A teleology lacking all eschatological dimension here gives way to an explicitly messianic statement that the purpose of the law is to attain Israel's salvation: "If you want it, God wants it too." The one thing Israel commands is its own heart; the power it yet exercises is the power to repent. These suffice. The entire history of humanity will respond to Israel's will, to what happens in Israel's heart and soul. And, with Temple in ruins, repentance can take place only within the heart and mind.[3]

But even this view, which marks a shift from the Mishnah's position, does not give the messiah a role in religious practice. In all Rabbinic texts, the messiah remains subordinate to Torah. He leads Israel to redemption and so is a precursor, but not the redeemer himself. The messiah gathers Israel from exile and leads Israel to judgment, but the judgment itself is performed by God. The subordination of the messiah to God is evident in the varied roles the Talmuds assign to the messiah and the sometimes conflicting description of his tasks. Again, Neusner's research makes the point:

> Like Elijah, the Messiah is forerunner and precursor, but he is hardly an enduring player in the eschatological drama. Only God is. Time and again we shall see that the Messiah refers back to God for instructions on what he is to do. A mark of categorical subordination of the Messiah-theme is the diversity of Messiahs, each with his own story. One Messiah comes out of the line of Joseph, another out of the line of David. Both Messiahs (and others in that same classification, for example, the Messiah who is anointed to be high priest in charge of the army [Deut. 20:2–7, Mishnah-tractate Sotah Chapter Eight]), are mortal and subject to the human condition. One Messiah is murdered, replaced by another. The Messiah, moreover, is subject to the impulse to do evil, like any other man. The Messiah plays a transient role in the eschatological drama. People want the Messiah to come – that is the premise of the stories told in connection with repentance – but that is only because he will inaugurate the eschatological drama, not because, on his own, he will bring the drama to its conclusion. Only God will.[4]

The diversity in Rabbinic messianic thought underscores the persistence of the Mishnaic view: the messiah is not integral to the practice of Judaism.

The essential unrelatedness of the messiah to Judaic piety also is evident in ancient rabbis' inability to craft a consistent position on the messiah's impact on the performance of the halakhah. The following passage illustrates (B. Shab. 151a):

A   R. Simeon b. Eleazar says, " '. . . and the years draw nigh when you shall say, I have no pleasure in them' (Ec. 12:1) – this refers to the days of the messiah, in which there is neither merit nor guilt."

B   This differs from what Samuel said, for said Samuel, "The only difference between this world and the days of the messiah is Israel's servitude to the nations of the world. As it is said, 'For the poor will never cease out of the Land' (Deut. 15:11)."

The position ascribed to Simeon b. Eleazar can be understood to mean that in the time of the messiah, the commandments will no longer apply. By contrast, the view attributed to Samuel suggests that religious life after the messiah's arrival will be indentical to that before it. Other Rabbinic passages suggest that the days of the messiah will signal the performance of more religious acts, particularly those of the sacrificial cult, than are practiced in this world. The more prevalent view accords with Samuel, and it appears throughout the Judaic literature of antiquity. W. D. Davies' classic study shows that:

> we found in the Old Testament, the Apocrypha and Pseudepigrapha and in the Rabbinical sources the profound conviction that obedience to the Torah would be a dominant mark of the Messianic age. . . . Generally, our sources revealed the expectation that the Torah in its existing form would persist into the Messianic age when its obscurities would be made plain, and when there would be certain natural adaptations and changes. . . .[5]

That the coming of the messiah does not automatically affect religious practice suggests that there is little systemic relationship between the two in the structure of Judaism.

The diversity in the messiah-theme persisted through the Middle Ages. Medieval Jewish thinkers held different views about Israel's redemption. Maimonides held a restorative view and envisioned a messiah who, without miracles or wonders, would signal the end of foreign domination of Israel. Nahmanides made the separation between Judaic piety and redemption explicit: "Our Law and Truth and Justice are not dependent upon a Messiah."[6] Alongside these views, however, a series of apocalyptic works appeared, such as *The Book of Zerubbabel*, which offered fantastic visions of the end, including a cosmic battle between a satanic figure named Armilus, who defeats the Messiah ben Joseph but is then defeated by the Messiah ben David. H. H. Ben Sasson observes that Jewish medieval apocalyptic literature is notable for the

> complete absence from it of any doctrinal religious or ideological elements. In these works the future is described as an inevitable end of the world as known and

the beginning of a new one. In none of these works is there any explanation as to why anything is going to happen or what a Jew should do to help in the great task of bringing about redemption.[7]

The disconnect between religion and redemption described by Ben Sasson conforms to the basic position of levitical religion.

The Messianic Religion of Shabbetai Zevi

A definitive change from the position of levitical religion occurs in the case of Shabbetai Zevi. His career and the movements that follow him have been described in detail by G. Scholem and only a brief recapitulation is given here.

Shabbetai Zevi is the most famous false messiah in Judaism. Born in Smyrna, educated in Egypt and Jerusalem, he was both brilliant and delusional. He had a strange early career, replete with instances of violating various rules of halakhic behavior. In 1665, he connected with a figure named Nathan of Gaza, who proclaimed him to be the messiah. Nathan was to become the principal interpreter – the Paul – of Shabbateanism.

In the mid-seventeenth century, Lurianic Kabbalah became a powerful ideology that deeply affected the worldview of Jews across Europe and the Mediterranean. It held that there had been a dislocation within the Godhead and that "sparks" of divinity had become lodged in the evil, material world. The performance of commandments released the dislocated sparks to their proper place and moved the cosmos closer to redemption. Unlike Levitical religion, Lurianism thus attributed redemptive power to discrete acts of halakhic conformity. It moreover taught that the process of cosmic restoration was nearly complete and that the final redemption was on the verge of occurring.

Nathan of Gaza shared the Lurianic position and, in May 1665, declared that Shabbetai Zevi would soon inaugurate the final redemption. At that time, Shabbetai Zevi went to Smyrna and proclaimed himself to be messiah. The announcement created an enormous stir in the Jewish world, and in February 1666 Shabbetai Zevi was arrested by the Turkish authorities. On September 16 he was brought to the Turkish Sultan, who was staying in Adrianople, and offered the choice of converting to Islam or being beheaded. Shabbetai Zevi chose to convert, for which he received a pension from the Turks.

Nathan of Gaza used Lurianic teaching to make this unprecedented move seem plausible. He claimed that by converting to Islam, Shabbetai Zevi had entered the realm of evil to release the last trapped sparks of divinity and to begin the redemption of the world. The conversion, he insisted, was a subterfuge. It looked like apostasy, but it was really redemption. Although most of the Jewish world rejected this teaching, some groups continued to believe in Shabbetai Zevi after his death in 1676. They developed practices in imitation of him, on the argument that the best way to fulfill the Torah was to violate it. In Europe, a figure named Jacob Frank (1726–91) formed a Sabbatean group that converted to Roman Catholicism. Another group converted to Islam.

Lurianic Kabbalah and the Sabbatean movement represent a break with the structure of levitical religion in the claim that the performance of commandments is redemptive and can move Israel closer to redemption. In effect, it shifts responsibility for Israel's redemption from God to Israel. Aspects of this ideology, as we shall see below, appear in modern Lubavitch Hasidism.

The Messiah, "Messianism," and Zionism

With the exception of the Sabbatean movement and some smaller messianic outbreaks, the Rabbinic prohibition against "forcing" the End dominated Jewish thinking about the messiah until the modern period. On this view, the Jewish people was to remain passively in exile and not agitate for redemption. The messiah's arrival was promised, and the Jews were not to doubt the divine plan by their own impatience. This idea of passivity did not preclude the necessity of individual repentance as a precondition to redemption, but it did prohibit the possibility that human political initiative could have a legitimate role in hastening redemption. Throughout the history of Judaism, the "oaths" against forcing the end cited above evoke the abyss between the human, historical and the divine, metaphysical spheres that can only be crossed with the messiah's appearance.

In premodern Judaism, the "oaths" were deemed non-binding. In modern Hasidic and western Orthodox thought, however, they appear as a central motif. Aviezer Ravitzky argues that this can be explained by the emergence of Jewish nationalism and Zionism, which challenged Judaism's established posture of passivity in exile.[8]

As we have seen, Judaism is a quintessential religion of exile. Return to the land of Israel, therefore, signaled a systemic change, a decisive alteration in Israel's condition. That is why in the modern age the messianic question acquires a unique urgency in the history of Judaism. New trends in European thought and emerging historical realities – both of which influenced Judaism – exposed the ideological tensions inherent in the history of Jewish thinking about the messiah. The physical return to the land of Israel may have been redemption for secular Jews, but it was a problem for many Jewish – particularly Orthodox – religious thinkers.

Modern European Nationalism and the Beginnings of Zionism

Influenced by nineteenth-century European struggles for national sovereignty and "receptiveness to innovation," two Orthodox thinkers argued for a significant reassessment of classical Jewish passivity. Rabbi Judah Alkalai (Serbia, d. 1878) and Rabbi Zvi Hirsch Kalischer (Prussia, d. 1874) developed an activist and worldly idea of redemption. Known as the "Harbingers of Zionism," these rabbis and their followers imagined redemption to be a utopian process of gradual realization, rather than the sudden, complete realization of their contemporaries. Thus, they advocated gradual immigration and agricultural settlement of the land of Israel as a "necessary and organic step toward full redemption."

The Harbingers derived textual support from a distinctive reading of classical Jewish literature. They distinguished between the "messianic process" and the "messianic goal": the former to be made manifest in worldly, historical terms; the latter to burst forth in the sudden, miraculous coming of the messiah. This imagery is based on classical sources in which the redemptive, metaphysical messiah – the Messiah ben David – is thought to follow the appearance of an historical messiah – the Messiah ben Joseph – associated with the last great, apocalyptic battles. Thus the Harbingers focused on a classical tension between history and redemption using the figure of Messiah ben Joseph as proof that historical initiative has a legitimate role in collective redemption. The Harbingers were among the first representatives of a new activist conception of redemption in which human initiative and political, historical developments could have real implications for the coming of the messiah.

The Harbingers provoked criticism from contemporary Jewish thinkers for breaking with the traditional commitment to Jewish quietism. Many Orthodox thinkers found problematic the idea that the Jews' political and social activism could be ways of advancing what previously had been seen as a plan for the world in God's hands alone, and therefore religiously meaningful. Rabbi Isaac Jacob Reines (who laid down the ideological foundations of the Mizrachi [religious-Zionist] movement) developed the most articulate arguments against the ideology of the Harbingers. Reines objected to the Harbingers' distinction between "messianic process" and "messianic goal" on the grounds that redemption was to be achieved solely though supernatural means. He acknowledges the religious value of settling the land, because it seeks to improve the living circumstances of the Jewish community. But it must not be confused with actual metaphysical redemption, which he understood in its traditional utopian mold. Reines cautiously affirms the settlement of the land, but denies that such historical developments have anything to do with the Jewish people's redemption. Still, even his moderate stance in certain respects would have facilitated the emergence of a contemporary Zionist messianism, since it allows religious settlers to cooperate with secular pioneers. These religious traditionalists thus could participate in a utopian social and political movement without fear of violating the traditional prohibition against forcing the End.

The possibility of maintaining such a moderate ideology, however, was doomed to failure. The agent of this failure was the explosive confrontation between traditional understandings of Jewish messianism and the emergence of organized Zionism. Zionism sought to achieve partial salvation in the present through human, political initiative. Moreover, Zionist leaders aimed to reconstitute Jewish nationhood under a secular banner. Both Zionism and traditional messianism sought to end the exile from the land of Israel, cultivate the land, and achieve the social reform of the Jewish people. Transcending these commonalties were irreducible differences of opinion about the meaning of these goals. Ultimately, a moderate stance was too fragile to survive the volatile mix of ideological similarities and differences. Over time, extreme schools of Jewish religious thought developed in direct response to the Zionist challenge. Reines' moderate ideology was replaced by radical anti-Zionism and religious Zionism. Both movements employ a utopian model of redemption, but they interpret the meaning of the Zionist endeavor (and the Holocaust) in radically different ways.

The majority of Orthodox leaders condemned Zionism from its beginnings. At first, their critique focused mainly on the secular character of the movement and its leaders and on the unrealistic, impractical nature of the endeavor. But the challenge Zionism presented to traditional ideas about the nature of collective Jewish redemption became the central motif in anti-Zionist criticism. In 1899, the Lubavitcher Rebbe, Rabbi Shalom Dov Baer Schneersohn, laid the ideological ground of this ultra-Orthodox critique of Zionism. He argued that Zionism was essentially opposed to the classical Jewish messianism because it sought to bring about the redemption of the Jewish people through ordinary human political initiative rather than through the supernatural and miraculous arrival of the messiah. Instead of attempting to force the end of history through impatient and arrogant politics, the Jewish people ought to remain in exile, passively waiting for the eschaton to arrive by metaphysical means.

Schneersohn argued that redemption must be sudden and complete (the utopian model). But secularization is comprehensive and therefore blocks a precondition of the messiah's arrival: the total realization of a repentant world. Jewish identity is intrinsically bound up with a traditional messianic commitment to passivity. To achieve a Jewish nation, the Zionists must erode Jewish identity. Thus Schneersohn conceives of Zionism as unavoidably opposed to authentic Jewish religion. Within this ideological context the passivity in exile is transformed from a persistent Rabbinic theme into a normative article of faith. Only in confrontation with Zionism – a modern ideology – does the fear of forcing the End achieve normative stature and centrality. After Schneersohn, this theological critique becomes the primary theme in the radical critique of Zionism.

Schneersohn may have been the first to articulate an anti-Zionist ideology, but Rabbi Moshe Teitelbaum, the Satmar Rebbe, produced a comprehensive theory of anti-Zionism. For Teitelbaum, Zionism is the anti-messianic work of Satan himself. Indeed the improbable success of Zionism is proof of its satanic assistance, for only with the aid of Satan could the anti-messianic Zionists overcome the inherent holiness of the land of Israel. In this view, the state is *de facto* destructive. The very fact of its existence, and not its policies, is the problem. Not even the passage of religious laws ("Torah legislation") can ameliorate the secular nature of the state, such that any active participation or influence in Israeli government indirectly legitimates a corrupt, heretical entity. The only proper response to the fact of the state is criticism and protest from a distance.

But not all Orthodox thinkers cleaved to the theology of passivity. Some were able to completely rethink the inherited messianic ideal to create a sort of messianism that makes sense of their own experiences and desires, particularly in the settling of the land. This competing school of thought sees the Zionist project as a legitimate first step in the divine *process* of redemption. The ideological founder of religious Zionism, Rabbi Abraham Isaac Kook, interpreted Zionism not as a manifestation of human arrogance and impatience but as the latest symbol of God's concern for the Jewish people and the beginning of a new, post-exilic phase in Jewish history devoid of historical passivity. Religious Zionism attempts to close the gap set up between historical and messianic reality in traditional Jewish imagination. It positions the state of Israel within the ongoing march toward collective redemption and interprets the Zionist project in the traditional religious categories of sin, repentance, and redemption.

Religious Zionist ideology is essentially messianism in the temporal absence of a personal savior. It is "messianism without a messiah." It holds that human collective action begins the process of redemption, and the messiah will appear to conclude and mature this process. Thus redemption is a process, a series of steps leading to eventual redemption conceived in traditional utopian terms, but in which human action has a legitimate role to play.

The question of human initiative in the advent of the messianic age has classical origins. The Kabbalistic teachers "taught the messianic redemption was the collective responsibility of the fellowship or community as a whole." These mystics understood the messiah's arrival as the culmination of a process of collective repentance. Human spiritual purification was the precondition of the messiah's arrival. The religious Zionists added to this classical understanding by seeing religious meaning in political, historical developments. Thus, their ideology attempts to fuse the political and the theological; the image of the Jewish state is that of a fully integrated "theopolitical whole." As it reshapes classical Jewish thinking about the messiah, religious Zionism creates a modern Jewish messianism that works in categories foreign to the Christian ideologies that constitute the established western perception of what the messiah is about.

Due to their dialectical understanding of history and progress, Kook and his followers are able to maintain their optimism even in the face of what may appear to be national disappointment. The religious Zionists – grounded in Kook's dialectic – interpret social, political, military, and cultural upheaval and revolution as integral elements of the determined march towards redemption. Kook's son and ideological heir, Rabbi Zvi Yehudah Kook (1891–1981), voices this interpretative tendency in his treatment of the Holocaust. He sees the destruction of European Jewry as the necessary expurgation of a wretched, Jewish culture of exile. The Holocaust proves to be a "kind of shattering, the destruction of a rotten culture (that of exile) for the sake of national rebirth and the fulfillment of the vision of the revealed End."

The elder Kook interprets the actions of secular Zionist pioneers through his dialectic perspective. They represent an unconscious movement toward repentance, and the return to the land – even for apparently secular reasons – can be affirmed as the beginning of a process in which eventually all Jews in the land will realize their inner, religious nature and live according to the dictates of the Torah and the halakhah. Utopian redemption will ultimately arrive in the form of the messiah when the secularists consciously turn to a purification of their ways and affirm the relevance and authority of traditional Torah Judaism.[9] This interpretation allows Kook and his ideological brethren to assimilate seemingly objectionable elements of the state. What might be construed as apostasy becomes in the hands of the religious Zionists one more integral and necessary challenge on the inevitable road to messianic redemption.

It should be noted that messianic determinism – the belief that redemption is the inevitable end of human history – does not necessarily preclude human responsibility. Although the elder Kook finds religious and messianic significance in the objective historical development of the state, he nevertheless affirms that redemption is not possible until the Jewish people take full responsibility for their own spiritual repentance. Thus, Kook maintains a seemingly delicate position: The End is inevitably on hand, but ultimate redemption does not annul human responsibility, it requires it.[10]

Religious determinism in both the radical anti-Zionist and religious Zionist camps reveals that the fundamental conflict revolves around the "essence" of the Zionist enterprise. Neither school of thought believes in partial redemption. The redemption of the Jewish people will be utopian: sudden and complete. The legitimacy of Zionism does not depend on Israeli social and political reality. For the anti-Zionists and religious Zionists, the question of Zionism ultimately rests on their distinctive understandings of the relationship between human initiative and divine revelation.

The Lubavitch Hasidic Movement – A contemporary case of acute messianism

The Hasidic sect known as Habad Lubavitch maintains an extraordinarily public image in the Jewish world. This is largely due to its ability to harness the cultural and technological elements of modernity for the propagation of its traditional religious message.[11] Apart from this extraordinary feature, the Habad movement also presents a cogent illustration of the effect the Zionist movement has had on traditional messianic ideologies.

Earlier generations of Habad leadership refrained from speaking on the possibility of collective messianic redemption and chose instead to focus on the nature of individual redemption.[12] Yet today, the Habad movement is characterized by extraordinarily explicit messianic discourse and fervor. The key historical factor in this transformation has been the emergence and relative success of Zionism.

That Zionism should have transformed the self-understanding of Habad so significantly is ironic if we recall that a Habad Rebbe, Shalom Dov Baer

Schneersohn, was among the most virulent opponents of Zionism, rejecting outright its legitimacy and authority on traditional theological grounds. Yet the pending destruction of European Jewry prompted a later Habad Rebbe, Joseph Isaac Schneersohn, to publicly yearn for the coming of the messiah. His declaration that redemption was approaching was derived from the collective experience of his followers, the suffering brought on by the systematic destruction of the Holocaust. Rabbi Joseph Isaac, amid the reality of the Holocaust, did not interpret it as punishment for Zionist agitation or as the divine removal of an accursed exile culture. He drew on classical Jewish sources and saw the Holocaust as the "birth pangs" of redemption, the advent of unendurable suffering thought to precede the messianic age.[13]

Under the leadership of the most recent Lubavitcher Rebbe, Menachem Mendel Schneersohn, this messianic fervor reached its most fevered pitch. Unlike Joseph Isaac, who called out for redemption in the wake of profound suffering, Menachem Mendel affirmed a "messianism of prosperity." He interpreted historical events such as the collapse of the Soviet Union and the end of the cold war as explicit indications that the world was moving closer to full observance of the Noachide laws and thus cosmic redemption was approaching.[14]

Yet this messianism of prosperity obviously requires constant stimuli to maintain its optimism, and the history of contemporary Habad shows that this is precisely what has occurred. At the end of Passover in April 1991, Menachem Mendel confessed to his followers that he had expended all of his spiritual energy and that the arrival of the coming messiah rested on their individual repentance. On Shabbat Pinhas, July 6, 1991, the Rebbe aroused even greater emotional fervor when he discussed the coming messiah more explicitly than ever before. Lastly, to further elevate the emotional frenzy, Habad followers began to speak of their Rebbe in terms traditionally reserved for the messiah.[15] After the death of the Lubavitcher Rebbe in July 1994, some of his followers began to assert that he was the messiah. In the fall, 1996, the Israeli Weekly *Sihat HaGeullah* revised the standard messianist slogan to read: "May our Master, Teacher, and Creator (instead of "Rabbi"), the King Messiah live forever." A number of other Lubavitch publications suggested that the Rebbe should be the focus of prayers.

While the belief that the Rebbe is the messiah seems limited to particular circles within Lubavitch Hasidism and cannot be said to reflect the ideology of the entire movement, the messianism associated with Habad has been criticized as a new form of Zionist activism. Fixating on the messianic question and engaging in prayer and repentance with the explicit expectation of bringing about the messiah appeared to some in the Haredi community as an example of forcing the End.[16] The new and dramatic claim that the Rebbe is the Messiah also has generated charges of heresy, because the focus on the Rebbe as, for example, "our Creator," seems to alter the form and basis of Judaism. However, despite some controversy over this issue, Lubavitch Hasidism retains its legitimacy within the larger Judaic world. The radical messianic declarations of some of its members have not been seen to push Habad beyond the pale.

Conclusion

Judaism is grounded in the experience of exile. Ancient Jews, certain that they were God's people always, drew creatively on their Israelite culture and heritage to develop two major responses to the twin challenges of national dislocation and chronic political oppression. The first was the hope for an ideal national leader – often, but not always, from the royal Davidic dynasty – whose work could range from leading the people home to an ideal kingdom to the establishment of a new cosmic order. The idea of "the messiah," an individual savior or redeemer of Israel, derives from this conception. The second response was the establishment of levitical religion, a system of ethics and piety that both maintained and manifested the distinctive relationship between Israel and God. Although initially centered around the Temple and its cult, levitical religion – particularly as adapted and transformed by Rabbinic Judaism – could be performed anywhere.

These two responses are not mutually exclusive, but they are systemically independent of one another. Neither requires the other. Judaism is an extension of levitical religion. The idea of an individual messiah existed alongside, but was never fully integrated into, the levitical system of ethics and piety that constituted the core of Rabbinic Judaism. Structurally, Judaism does not require a messiah to justify fulfilling the commandments. Indeed, a persistent strain of Rabbinic teaching holds that the commandments will apply after the messiah appears. Despite references to the restored Jerusalem and future heir of David, the synagogue liturgy celebrates God, not the messiah, as Israel's redeemer and looks forward to the restoration of the Temple cult. Except for Sabbateanism and the forms of religion that emerge from it, there is no assumption that the commandments are performed to make the messiah arrive.

Because the category of the messiah is extrinsic to the system of Jewish religious practice, it is subject to speculation. In the varied forms Judaism has taken over time, there was and remains a wide range of opinions about what the messiah will be and do. These opinions in themselves do not constitute grounds for separation from Judaism. The figure of the messiah surely is present in Jewish religious imagination, but hope for the messiah's arrival is not the driving force of Jewish religious life. Modern and contemporary developments in Zionism and the State of Israel have posed fresh questions to the classical view. How these will be answered still remains to be seen.

Notes

1   This analysis relies on Shemaryahu Talmon, "The Concepts of Masiah and Messianism in Early Judaism," in J. H. Charlesworth, ed., *The Messiah* (Minneapolis, 1992), pp. 79–115. The cited words are on p. 106.
2   William Scott Green and Jacob Neusner, *The Messiah in Ancient Judaism* (Atlanta, 1999).

3   Ibid.

4   Ibid.

5   W. D. Davies, *Torah in the Messianic Age and/or the Age to Come* (Philadelphia, 1952), pp. 64–6, 84.

6   H. H. Ben Sasson, "Messianic Movements," in *Encyclopedia Judaica*, vol. 11, col. 1263.

7   Ibid., vol. 11, col. 1413.

8   Aviezer Ravitzky, *Messianism, Zionism, and Jewish Religious Radicalism* (Chicago, 1996). This section is based on Ravitzky's research.

9   Ibid., pp. 112–13.

10   Ibid., p. 130.

11   Ibid., p. 182.

12   Ibid., pp. 193–4.

13   Ibid., p. 195.

14   Ibid., p. 197.

15   Ibid., p. 197.

16   Ibid., p. 201.

he Doctrine of Hebrew Language Usage

David H. Aaron

Language is a thing which brings to actuality,
what is imprinted in the soul in potentia.[1]

Although Hebrew ceased functioning as a vernacular at some point during the Roman era, both secular and religious literature have been composed in Hebrew consistently since biblical times.[2] Jews not only continued to use Hebrew as their choice language of prayer but also wrote philosophical and legal tracts, poetry and business records, biblical commentaries, incantations and recipes, all in the tongue of their biblical ancestors. All of these uses of Hebrew were made despite the official endorsement of translations and the explicit permission to use one's colloquial language in virtually all walks of Jewish life. Still, controversies over Hebrew usage occurred and were often deeply embedded in political and social conflicts. One's perspective on Hebrew usage might serve as an emblem of religious or social identity, an indicator of piety, or a symbol of allegiance. Whatever a community's position regarding Hebrew usage, the fact remains that no one has ever been excluded from a Jewish community for not knowing Hebrew. Nonetheless, the notion that Hebrew is a *holy language* is found among Jews of every era and in every locus from the period of classical Rabbinic literature and on.

This chapter explores the religious significance of Hebrew usage in the Judaisms of antiquity. Unlike the many available histories of the Hebrew language,[3] we are not concerned with linguistics or philology, though these disciplines inform our inquiry. Rather, we hope to uncover the roots and social purpose of Hebrew's status as a holy language. Our survey is limited to three broad eras, loosely defined on the basis of their literary corpora: the periods associated with the writings of the Hebrew Bible (tenth to fifth centuries, BCE), the literature of the Second Temple Period (250 BCE–70 CE), and the classical period of Rabbinic Judaism (third to eighth centuries CE). There have been, of course, many subsequent developments, but these all derive in one way or another from notions developed by the eighth century.

By relating to their language as holy, Jews transformed Hebrew into a kind of ritual object, parallel, in many ways, to the Torah scroll itself. In this sense, Hebrew is part of a religious system. The transformation of a mundane object into a holy one entails a mythology that defines the object's broader cultural connotations. By uncovering the origins of that mythology, we place in historical context the transformation of Hebrew's religious status.

Language Consciousness and the Early Evidence

Two obvious factors contribute to the prominence of Hebrew in Jewish history. First, Hebrew was the vernacular of that group of Canaanites identified in the earliest documents of the religion, those of the Tanakh, as both Hebrews and Israelites. The antiquity of the connection between the Jews – originally called "Hebrews" – and this language contributed to the group's *linguacentrism*. A second factor is equally important: Hebrew remained a vernacular from biblical times well into the Hellenistic era (in the land of Israel). This fact undoubtedly influenced the language choices of early Rabbinic literature (especially the Mishnah), all of which is composed in Hebrew. It is precisely at this juncture in history – the emergence of Rabbinic Judaism during the Roman era – that the doctrine of Hebrew's holiness crystallized to become what we now think of when we hear Hebrew referred to as "the holy tongue."

The books that comprise the Jewish Bible, the Tanakh, are all written in Hebrew, save for brief Aramaic sections in Ezra and Daniel. Still, nowhere in the Tanakh is the language of composition ever referred to as Hebrew, or any other name, for that matter. Despite some general observations that concern language consciousness – to be distinguished from Hebrew consciousness – the Tanakh is essentially devoid of the notion that Hebrew usage had religious meaning.

Some biblical writers distinguished clearly between their language and that of other Canaanites. A passage in 2 Kgs. 18, for instance, contrasts the use of *yehudit* with Aramaic, the official language of the Assyrian Empire. The term *yehudit* also occurs when Nehemiah differentiates the Jewish language from that of other Canaanites. In Neh. 13, he criticizes the populace for having taken wives from the Ashdodites, Ammonites, and Moabites, "half of whose offspring speak [only] Ashdodite, while not being able to speak *yehudit*. . . ." It is unclear whether Nehemiah is commenting on a contrast in languages or perhaps denigrating what was judged an inferior dialect. Judg. 12:6 contrasts the pronunciation of distinct dialects: an Ephraimite could be distinguished from a Gileadite by how he pronounced the Hebrew word for "flowing stream": *shibbolet* vs. *sibbolet*. But beyond these brief allusions we lack evidence, biblical or extrabiblical, for establishing the precise differences between northern and southern Hebrew dialects.

The Ancestral Language versus the Patriarchal Language

In Gen. 31, the Jacob–Laban Treaty exemplifies how language was used to differentiate stages in the people's history. When Jacob and his uncle Laban establish a land treaty, the text very consciously differentiates their oaths on the basis of language and their patron gods. Both men participated in creating a stone mound as "witness" to their pact. "Laban named it *yegar-sahaduta*, but Jacob named it *gal-ed*" (Gen. 31:47). Laban's term is Aramaic, Jacob's is Hebrew, but both are identical in meaning. This differentiation by language serves as the climax of an ever-increasing concern for clan divisions. The story's redactor made sure that Laban is repeatedly described as "the Aramean," thereby emphasizing his foreignness (see Gen. 25:20, 28:5, 31:20, 31:24). The irony of this stigmatization derives from the fact that Abraham and Isaac specifically arranged for their sons to take wives from distant Paddan-Aram rather than the indigenous Canaanite population, since the former were considered closest of kin. This endogamous pattern is drawn to a close with Jacob, who is the last to seek a wife in the land of Abraham's origins.

In the Tanakh, Hebrew thus served as a marker of tribal allegiance but lacked the religious connotation that typifies post-biblical documents. One is particularly struck by the lack of language consciousness in the books of Ruth and Esther, both of which focus on the relationship between Jews and indigenous populations *outside* of the land of Israel. We thus find a remarkable degree of uniformity even among radically different genres and eras. Throughout the early literature, there is no discrete notion that Hebrew had a unique value or purpose. Hebrew during the biblical era is not yet the language of Judaism, let alone, a holy tongue.

The Septuagint, Philo, and Josephus

The emergence of a biblical canon and the elevation of Hebrew's status are related but not entirely interdependent solutions to a common set of ideological challenges. The development of a canon was long in coming. Most scholars believe the Pentateuch reached its final state by the middle of the fifth century BCE. The second and third divisions of the Hebrew Bible, the histories, prophets, and other works known as the Writings, were only collected and given holy status after the rise of Hellenism. For Alexandrian Jews, canon and language were rather separate issues. The origins of the Greek translation of the Bible, the Septuagint (LXX), are mired in obscurity. Most likely, the Pentateuch was translated by the Egyptian Jewish community during the third century BCE. Greek versions of the remaining books of the canon were included in the LXX by the first century CE.

While the LXX highlights Greek's importance in the synagogues of Egypt, knowledge and use of Greek by Jewish writers was surely not confined to diaspora contexts. The earliest reference to the Jewish language as "Hebrew" occurred in the Greek version of Ben Sira, translated by the author's grandson, himself a native of Jerusalem. Similarly, there is evidence to suggest that I Esdras, Greek Daniel, and Greek Esther were also penned in Jerusalem. The writings of numerous historians and books that would eventually be called non-canonical were clearly the Greek products of Jews in Jerusalem during the early Hellenistic and Roman eras.[4]

The role of the LXX is highlighted in the writings of Philo and Josephus. Although writing as Jews, the former from within the Alexandrian Jewish community and the latter for a primarily Roman audience, their writings exhibit minimal concern with the status of Hebrew. Philo, the first individual to write exegetical scholarship in his own name, conveys no cognizance of Hebrew's role within religious contexts. Given that Philo might not have known any Hebrew at all, this may not prove terribly surprising. The exegete worked exclusively from the Greek translations prominent in his Egyptian community. As it turns out, the same appears to be true of Josephus. Although many scholars assume Josephus must have had access to the biblical canon in its original, the evidence suggests the contrary. Josephus places great emphasis on retelling the legend of the Septuagint's origins, using the tradition in the *Letter of Aristeas* as his base (*Antiquities of the Jews* XII, 11–118). This has led some scholars to believe he had a great deal invested in the value of the Septuagint as an authentic rendering of Scriptures, perhaps for the purpose of convincing his gentile audience of its importance as a translation. But it may also be the case that this was Josephus' main source for retelling the biblical narratives and that, like Philo, the Hebrew original was thought to be unimportant (perhaps even inaccessible).

What We Learn from the New Testament

The New Testament proves to be a very problematic source when it comes to establishing language consciousness. This is partially because its few references to Hebrew are programmatically motivated. Early Christianity, unlike early Rabbinic Judaism, was not interested in consolidating a long extant, but diverse community via language. Hebrew in the New Testament has a historical significance as the language of the Jews and the "old" Hebrew Scriptures, the New Church's roots. But references to Hebrew are quite limited in scope and fall into three categories: (1) the identification of places with Hebrew names, (2) the utterance of Hebrew phrases by key characters, and (3) the use of Hebrew as a way of identifying one's original religious allegiance.

Whether the New Testament suggests that Jesus, Mary Magdalene, and the Jews in the synagogues actually spoke Hebrew rather than Aramaic is difficult to evaluate. But the question of history aside, there was clearly value in identifying Jesus and Paul, and strangely enough, Mary Magdalene, as Jews who spoke Hebrew. In Acts, the narrator frequently seizes the opportunity to portray Paul as a Hebrew speaker. In contrast, Paul's own use of the word "Hebrew" is exclusively gentilic (Phil. 3:5) and never self-referential. Luke, however, portrays Paul as addressing his audience "in the Hebrew language" (Acts 21:40, 22:2). Acts enhances the reader's impression of Paul's (supposed) intimate knowledge of Judaism and his original identity as a Jew by emphasizing his knowledge of Hebrew. Similarly, Paul's knowledge of Hebrew factors into the portrayal of his vision on the road to Damascus, described in the first person to King Agrippa (Acts 26). When Paul hears Jesus' voice call out to him in the wilderness, the text specifies that Jesus' speech was in "Hebrew" (26:14). Even the insistence that Paul's name was changed from the Hebrew "Saul" may be nothing other than a literary ploy to emphasize just how Jewish Paul was prior to his conversion.[5] Thus, despite the ambiguities in the New Testament's references to Hebrew and Aramaic, some of the writers clearly had the sense that Hebrew was uniquely linked to Jewish identity.

Precursors to the Rabbinic Concept of *Lashon HaQodesh* ("Holy Language")

During the post-biblical period, Hebrew attains religious significance unknown in earlier epochs. The most dramatic developments can be traced to the Hellenistic era, following Alexander the Great's conquest of the Middle East at the end of the fourth century BCE. Even prior to the writings of Philo, Josephus, and the New Testament, other literary documents began to relate to language choices as a central component in Jewish theological discourse. We can attribute various social and religious tensions between traditionalists and assimilationists to the introduction of Greek culture and language. The inevitable cultural syncretism evoked ever more energetic attempts at self-definition. Linguacentrism would emerge as just one symptom of the internal strife brought on by these cultural and political struggles.

In the texts we now consider – all deriving from the two centuries prior to the fall of the Second Temple – five distinct, but surely related, attitudes toward Hebrew are discernable. Each notion of the Hebrew language represents a concrete response to overt political and social conflicts with Greek pagans. But, at a more subtle level, each constitutes an attempt to confront the pressures of syncretistic tendencies within the Jewish community as well. The five notions are: (1) allegiance to language as a form of allegiance to one's ancestors; (2) language as a unifying factor in the people's politic; (3) Hebrew as the original language of all human beings; (4) Hebrew as the forgotten language of civilization, re-taught to Abram by God; (5) Hebrew as a holy language.

No pre-Rabbinic text contains all of these ideas together, but they eventually merged into broader traditions and clustered as a single conceptualization of Hebrew as *the* holy tongue. Whether these ideas coalesced prior to the Rabbinic era cannot be firmly established, due to scant literary evidence. Still, we may safely assume that the ideology of language that emerges explicitly in third- or fifth-century literature was not the result of an individual author's reflections on the problems of assimilation and self-identity. That is to say, rather than viewing the concept of a holy language found in midrashic literature as a new invention, we should see it as the continuation of a long-developing cultural standard the roots of which are found in Second Temple period literature.

The Language of the Ancestors

Chapter seven of 2 Maccabees contains a martyrology of seven brothers and their mother. Having been arrested they are brought before the king, who commands them to eat swine's flesh, forbidden to Jews. Each brother refuses to acquiesce, and each suffers a brutal, martyr's death, witnessed by his remaining brothers and mother. The tormentors – Greek Seleucids – address their victims in Greek, but the narrator informs us that the second brother replies in "the language of their ancestors" (7:8). This phrase is paralleled by the first son's proclamation that they were all ready to die "rather than transgress the laws of [their] ancestors." These two idioms, separated for the sake of clarity and emphasis, serve as a single overarching principle, "the language and laws of our ancestors." It is reiterated at the conclusion of the narrative as well with regard to the youngest son and his mother.

The central core of the story is the notion that the *language* and *laws* of the ancestors constitute the motivating principle behind the martyrdom of the children and their mother. While the mythology of Moses' law is the creation of the biblical writers, who consciously sought to place their legal and social traditions in antiquity, there previously had been no reason to include language under the umbrella of ancestral inheritance. Confronted by the prospect of a strong cultural challenge to their national identity – perhaps in a way never previously encountered – those responding to the pressures of cultural assimilation under the Seleucids augmented the biblical notion of ancestral inheritance (as Torah) with the notion of language.

Language as a Unifying Factor

In the work known as the *Testaments of the Twelve Patriarchs* (second century BCE), the concept of the End of Days includes the notion that the tribes of Jacob will become "one people of the Lord, with one language."[6] The conceptualization of the End of Days, or the Future Redemption, is far more nationalistically conceived in this part of *The Testaments* than it is in other parts of the same document or in other literatures of this genre. The salvation will result in the restoration of a kingship without the yoke of foreign powers. The social circumstances during Israel's state of kinglessness have the commoners pursuing all sorts of "revolting gentile affairs" (23:2). The emphasis throughout this passage is on the factionalism and moral deterioration of the people that result from assimilationist tendencies. Those who "call on the Lord" will be saved, whether they originate with Israel or not. But the key to the "eschatology" in this context is the reunification of Israel under its own, independent sovereignty, coupled with the abandonment of foreign cultural practices.

The Language of Humanity – its loss and revival

The book of *Jubilees* (ca. 150 BCE) includes the earliest known reference to Hebrew as God's language and also establishes Hebrew as the original tongue of the world. In *Jubilees* 12:25–27, we learn that Abram was taught Hebrew by God (or an angel) after the language had been lost for centuries. He thereupon began studying Hebrew books from antiquity, all of which were previously incomprehensible. Hebrew was lost, according to *Jubilees*, on the day of "the Fall" (12:25). On account of Adam and Eve's misdeeds, "all the beasts and cattle and birds and whatever walked or moved was stopped from speaking because all of them used to speak with one another with one speech and one language" (3:28). Despite the fact that *Jubilees* contains a Tower of Babel myth (10:18–26), the author introduced this yet more primeval event of Hebrew-loss to serve etiologically for two distinct events: (1) it provides an explanation for why the animals no longer speak, and (2) it establishes why Hebrew had disappeared. The disappearance of Hebrew also provides a context for its miraculous renaissance: God himself teaches Abram the language he used to create the world.

The Torah does not contain a myth telling of the loss of Hebrew as a spoken tongue. While preserving the more traditional function of Babel – the dispersion of the civilized world and the confusion of tongues – the legend of the loss of Hebrew allows *Jubilees* to focus on the Jews' language as emblematic of God's covenant with Abraham. By having God teach the patriarch of Israel Hebrew, chosenness is extended beyond the person to the culture, a concept not even implicit in the Torah's version of God's first contact with Abram. Moreover, this myth allows for the *rediscovery* of wisdom long lost – a common motif in Second Temple period literature, though also not unknown to former biblical writers (e.g., 2 Kgs. 22). By also introducing the notion that Hebrew was "the tongue of creation," adumbrating the Rabbinic midrashim that would employ this image half a millennium later, *Jubilees* situates Israel's chosenness and their language in God's plan for the world. Incidentally, the notion that Hebrew, as God's language, was the original language of humanity was accepted by the Church Fathers from Origen to Augustine, undoubtedly on the basis of this myth that long predates the Rabbinic midrashic corpus.

The Holy Tongue

The idiom *lashon haqodesh*, "the holy tongue," occurs frequently in the Rabbinic corpus. Some scholars have suggested that its early occurrences derive from the

Second Temple period, when it most likely meant, "the language of the Temple" (with "*haqodesh*" understood as "the Holy of Holies" – or the inner chambers of the Sanctuary). Yet others speculate that the phrase connoted "God's language," with the second part of the phrase, "*the* Holy" serving as an abbreviated form of "the Holy One," a common Rabbinic euphemism for God.

A badly damaged manuscript from the Dead Sea Scrolls (4Q464) contains the earliest known use of the idiom. Unfortunately, the fragmentary nature of this column isolates the two words, making it impossible to reconstruct what came immediately before or after them. But as it happens, the phrase in the Qumran fragment occurs one line above an idiom derived from Zeph. 3:9 that is clearly represented: "For then I will change the speech of the peoples to *a pure speech*." If *pure speech* and *holy language* are parallel in this context (which is a safe bet), then we may surmise that the author used the Zephaniah verse as a proof-text for the destiny of *the holy language*. Esther Eshel and Michael Stone speculate that the Qumran writer was leaning upon the Zephaniah verse to convey that the End of Days involved the restoration of Hebrew to its once primal status, ubiquity among the civilizations. Thus, the Qumran fragment represents the earliest known use of this phrase with the connotations (1) Hebrew is the holy tongue, and, perhaps, (2) Hebrew would be the universal language in the End of Days. Eshel and Stone also contend that Hebrew was the choice of the Qumran writers specifically because, "they believed that they lived on the eve of the End of Days," when Hebrew would again become the only linguistic option.[7]

Unfortunately, the fragmentary nature of this manuscript and the singular appearance of the idiom "holy tongue" among the scrolls found in the Judean Desert make it impossible to establish the broader conceptual framework in which this idiom functioned. Even so, we see clearly that the five ideas introduced above were all in place prior to the emergence of Rabbinic Judaism and its literatures. Their evolution will be one of consolidation and refinement in a world that shared many of the social concerns that emerged during the early Hellenistic period but that were invariably intensified when Christianity became the official religion of Rome.

Rabbinic Judaism: Culture and diglossia

Continuing scholarly debate over when Hebrew ceased serving as a vernacular in the land of Israel means that we have no way to establish with certainty how pervasive Hebrew was as a spoken tongue or what level of Hebrew literacy existed in any particular era. Our suppositions regarding the later Rabbinic periods are hardly more secure. While some texts suggest that even well-known sages were incapable of signing their names in Hebrew on official documents,[8] it may turn out that the literature artificially reflects the linguistic preferences of a redactor and suggests nothing of the reality of a specific moment in the Rabbinic scholastic discourse.

By the first century CE, Greek was a widespread vernacular, perhaps equal to Aramaic, not only for Jews of the diaspora but in the land of Israel as well. As a reaction to the inroads made by Greek culture – often metonymically represented by references to the "Greek language" or "Greek wisdom [philosophy]" – the Mishnah instructs that the war with Vespasian (67–70 CE) prompted the rabbis to forbid the teaching of Greek: "Cursed be a man who rears pigs and cursed be a man who teaches his son Greek wisdom."[9]

But this can hardly be taken as a dominant cultural attitude. The power of cultural syncretism with Greek and later Roman culture made escaping Hellenistic influence impossible and fighting it futile. We learn that in Gamaliel's house there were a thousand disciples, five hundred of whom studied Torah while the other five hundred were steeped in Greek philosophy (B. Sot. 49b). Whether the legend has any basis in historical reality is irrelevant. The important implication from the redactor's perspective is that a renowned Rabbinic scholar was as encouraging of Greek learning as he was of Torah study. Indeed, legends of Gamaliel's comfort in both worlds are recorded in numerous texts (see, e.g., M. A.Z. 3:4.).

Other sages appear to have preferred Greek over Aramaic, perhaps leading Judah to comment: "Why use Syriac [i.e., Aramaic] in the land of Israel? Use either the Holy Tongue or Greek" (B. B.Q. 83a). Thus, there remain these two counter-paradigms: one that condemns anyone who exposes his child to Greek language and thought and one that elevates Greek (i.e., secular) learning to the status of Torah learning, or, at least, above the common usage of Aramaic. In part, this is the classic tension between religion and secular learning, and the fear that the latter results in the loss of the former. It may also reflect an internal cultural clash between the connotations of Aramaic and Greek with regard to class and education.

Rather than framing the issue as *whether or not* Hebrew gave way to Aramaic and Greek as vernaculars in Roman Palestine, some scholars have defined the polyglot character of Jewish society in Hellenistic times with the term *diglossia*.[10] This is when distinct social functions command the usage of varying languages, each understood by the user, but each used discretely in the context society recognized as appropriate.[11] Thus, even though Hebrew in the post-biblical world would not again serve as the exclusive language of any Jewish community until the twentieth century, its status as the Jews' religious language remained relatively constant. The shift away from Hebrew as a vernacular – or, the growth of diglossia – established a dynamic between the language spoken and the language inherited from tradition, and this, in turn, reshaped the meaning of the idiom "the holy tongue," first in the land of Israel but then most prominently in diaspora contexts.[12]

This is *not* to say that, without a contrasting "secular language," the notion of a "holy tongue" would not have developed beyond its connotations at Qumran and in early Rabbinic literature.[13] It is to recognize, however, that the Greek and subsequent Roman conquests of the Middle East, and the ever growing dispersion of Jews beyond the borders of ancient Israel, compelled the emergence of an ever clearer philosophical and spiritual dichotomy between a Jew's vernacular and a Jew's religious language. If one's vernacular is also one's "holy tongue," then there never need arise questions about the spiritual implications of using other than the "holy tongue" in religious contexts. With the demise of Hebrew as a vernacular, reconstruing the relevance of language in the past became essential to preparations for the future.

Liturgy and Scripture Readings

Much of the Rabbinic debate regarding the use of language in public worship responds to the question, What if someone does not understand the language of Hebrew prayers or Scriptural readings used in the synagogue?[14] M. Sot. 7:1–2 lists passages of Scripture and the liturgy that can be recited in any language while noting other passages that can only be read in the "holy tongue." As it turns out, the content of the former list is far more substantive than the latter when it comes to a Jew's daily liturgical observances. One may recite the *Shema* and *Amidah* in any language as well as grace after meals and a variety of oaths.[15] Those passages that can only be read in Hebrew amount to specific passages in Scripture, mostly involving ritual acts limited to Levites. While the *Shema* is essentially a collection of biblical verses along with accompanying benedictions, the other liturgical selections mentioned in the Mishnah – the *Amidah*, grace after meals, and oaths – are Rabbinic compositions in Rabbinic Hebrew.

Translations are approved for use in other contexts as well. M. Meg. 2:1, for instance, states that, on Purim, one should read the scroll of Esther "in Coptic to the Copts, in Hebrew to the Hebrews, in Elamean to the Elameans, in Greek to the Greeks, and he has performed his obligation."[16] In the adjoining passages in the Gemara, it is clear that the Book of Esther serves metonymically for all Scriptural readings. Most Mishnaic passages that touch upon the question of translation are presented in rather theoretical terms. Consider the teaching of M. Shab. 16:1, that Holy Scriptures are to be saved from a fire even if the copies in question are in other than Hebrew.[17] The point is that the sanctity of the scroll depends upon its substantive content regardless of its language. Thus we find that Torah is not conceptualized exclusively as the *Hebrew* Torah – at least not in this discussion. Torah in any language, whether it be "Egyptian, Median, Aramaic, Elamitic or Greek," maintains its sanctity.[18]

The Mishnah's favorable attitude toward the use of translation in worship was apparently implemented in some places. The Jerusalem Talmud records that in a synagogue in the port city of Caesaria, it was customary to recite the *Shema* in Greek.[19] Whether this was a common practice in other synagogues in the land of Israel, or unique to this locus, cannot be determined; but surely it was not an isolated phenomenon in the context of the Hellenistic Judaism of the diaspora. In this sense, the Mishnaic passages that approve use of translations may constitute sanctions for what was already commonly in practice rather than ground-breaking positions. Scriptural readings in the Alexandrian Jewish community were apparently done exclusively in Greek. While there is considerable evidence of Greek liturgies, there is no evidence of a Hebrew liturgy in the Egyptian–Jewish community.[20] There is also no basis for determining that Hebrew ever played a part in any curriculum of the Alexandrian Jewish community.

A positive attitude toward Torah in translation does surface regularly in early Rabbinic literature. The early midrashic anthology on the book of Deuteronomy, Sifre Deuteronomy (§343), suggests that the revelation of the written Torah took place in four languages simultaneously: Hebrew, Latin (Roman), Arabic, and Aramaic. Although Sifre Deuteronomy presents a universalistic approach to Torah's language, it frequently refers to Hebrew as *the holy tongue*, in contrast to the other languages of the world. We learn elsewhere within this same anthology (§46) that a father must teach his child both Hebrew and Torah (apparently, as separate endeavors) and that if he does not do these *two* things, it is as if he were shortening his son's life! As we have noted, the attitude toward translations and the daily use of "foreign" languages leans toward inclusion rather than exclusion. But Sifre Deuteronomy hints at the underlying zealousness for the exclusive use of Hebrew, despite the more formal sanctioning of non-Hebrew prayer and Torah readings.

The Exclusive Use of Hebrew

The legal dispensation for the use of the vernacular in liturgical settings has dominated all discussions of liturgical rites throughout Jewish history.[21] Despite this consistent sanctioning of translation, synagogue liturgies developed almost exclusively in Hebrew. Moreover, even the most prominent home-ceremony, the Passover Seder contained in the Pesah Haggadah, developed exclusively in Hebrew. This is particularly noteworthy because this ceremony, developed over many years, was written for a home service, not the synagogue. While the bulk of the narrative draws from the Torah, the most prominent liturgical element of the Haggadah is the *Hallel* (a cluster of Pslams recited on festive occasions). But what holds everything together is composed in Rabbinic Hebrew. Except for the benedictions related to food and the sanctification of the holy day (Qiddush), the passages written in Rabbinic Hebrew are not, formally speaking, liturgical. Thus, no matter what the attitude toward language usage in a liturgical context was, the Passover Haggadah represented potentially fertile ground for use of one's vernacular. The fact that the rabbis held this composition so close to the language preferences of their other genres supports the impression that Rabbinic Judaism functioned with two sets of values simultaneously: an official sanctioning of vernaculars and an overt, unofficial preference for Hebrew ritual.[22]

The tension between those supporting a fixed Hebrew worship and those advocating prayers in the vernacular, especially Aramaic, may have led to the polemically charged proclamation that "when one petitions for his needs in

Aramaic, the ministering angels do not heed him, for they do not understand Aramaic" (see B. Shab. 12b and Y. Sotah 7:1). Hebrew prayer, according to the purveyors of this mythology, is superior to prayer uttered in Aramaic (and presumably other languages as well) – regardless of whether they are written and recited from memory (i.e., "fixed") or spontaneous. Obviously this sentiment contradicts those passages of the Mishnah that sanction vernacular prayer. Of course, the harshness of this dictum was mitigated by compromising contingencies in numerous Talmudic passages (in times of duress, for instance, it was declared that prayers went directly to God without the angelic intermediaries), but ultimately, its attitude must be seen as that which will dominate the history of Jewish worship.

What the Talmud and Midrash Teach about Language

It is not surprising to find in the Jerusalem Talmud much that emphasizes the importance of the land of Israel and Hebrew, while the Babylonian Talmud quite regularly sheds a positive light on Aramaic and the use of translations in general. For instance, the Jerusalem Talmud states that "whoever is situated in the land of Israel . . . and speaks the Holy Tongue, and recites the *Shema* in the morning and in the evening is promised life in the world to come" (Y. Shab. 1:3, 3c). In contrast, the Babylonian Talmud contains the dictum that "God only exiled Israel to Babylonia because their language was close to the language of Torah" (B. Pes. 77b). The sages were keenly aware of the differences between the two languages. More than just recognizing that Hebrew and Aramaic were not the same language, the redactors of the Babylonian Talmud, on a macro level, were keenly aware of the potential meaning in language choices. A study by Jacob Neusner suggests that a statement's language is usually determined on the basis of a set of intellectually consistent criteria employed by the redactor.[23]

Neusner maintains that while "Aramaic is the language of the Talmud . . . the use of Hebrew serves a purpose dictated by the document and bears significance within the norms of thought that the framers of the document have defined."[24] The redactors chose to convey something in Hebrew when they wished "to signal that a thought forms a normative statement." A "normative statement" in this context, connotes a "fact formulated as generalization, authoritative proposition, or rule."[25] Aramaic, in contrast, was the language of analysis. Essential to such a query into language usage is the underlying question of why this structure and not another. Surely one could write a highly rhetorical composite document in one language exclusively, making perfectly clear that some statements represented analysis while others were conclusive and authoritative. The linguistic frames of reference must have already been built into the cultural milieu out of which the documents were born. In order for the connotations of language usage in the Talmud to have been meaningful, the writer and his audience (certainly, scholars exclusively) needed to be equally attuned to the distinct languages and their connotative roles. Thus, we should not view the talmudic choices regarding language as having paved new ground, but, rather, as reflecting and preserving a set of cultural values already well entrenched.

Neusner's study deals exclusively with the Babylonian Talmud, and, to date, no comprehensive consideration of language usage in the midrashim or the Yerushalmi has been done. Nonetheless, it is clear that the use of Aramaic and Hebrew in the midrashim from the classical period does not exhibit the same structural or rhetorical choices as are detected by Neusner in the Babylonian Talmud. The so-called Tannaitic Midrashim are in Hebrew almost exclusively; and the earliest "Amoraic" midrashim, while containing passages in Aramaic (often those that parallel texts in the Talmud), are, nonetheless, dominated by Hebrew. For the most part, there is no division between authoritative statements and analytic discourse in these works (their rhetorical structure does not demand such a division).

The midrashim do not employ the same stratification of analysis as found in the Talmud. This is nowhere more evident than when we find parallels between a midrashic anthology and a passage in the Talmud. When there are differences, they invariably relate to the rhetorical devices employed in structuring a pericope. In other words, the very same passages will frequently look one way in the Talmud and another way in the Midrash. In a Midrash, scriptural elucidation does not enter the text by way of explaining a Mishnaic passage (as it does in the Talmud). Instead, it starts with the Torah text – which sees itself as the word of God dictated to Moses in Hebrew – and, in that sense, it is an extension thereof. Once again, we should not surmise that every sage ostensibly recorded in the midrashic anthologies taught, spoke, or wrote in Hebrew, or Aramaic, for that matter. But the more or less uniform Hebraization of the early midrashic anthologies can only be the result of a focus on the underlying connotations of Hebrew usage in a world that had long incorporated Aramaic and Greek.

The Conceptualization of Language in Genesis Rabbah

The second chapter of Genesis tells us that the first woman was created from a rib of the first man. This organic link is echoed in their names: *this one shall be called Woman* ('isha), *because out of man* ('ish) *was she taken*" (Gen. 2:23). The sages conclude from the assonance of these two words that "the Torah was given in the Holy Language" (Genesis Rabbah 18§4; Theodore–Albeck edition, p. 164, l. 8). The reasoning is transparent enough. The phonological tie between 'isha and 'ish could only be possible if the language containing those two words was original to the creation process. Since other languages do not exhibit such a link between the words for man and woman, it was concluded that the meanings and sounds of Hebrew words must be integral to the natural order of the universe.[26] Hebrew's origins are expounded yet further: "Just as Torah was given in the Holy Language, so was the world created with the Holy Language."

A similar passage occurs later in Genesis Rabbah (31§8). There too, the assonance shared by two words (*nehash* and *nehoshet*) is understood to prove that the Torah was given in Hebrew and that the world was created with Hebrew, for otherwise the words themselves could not have such a dynamic structural (and phonemic) inter-dependency.

Numerous other passages in Genesis Rabbah illustrate this unique bond between Hebrew and the world order. This very theme serves as the building block for a great array of mystical speculations, in both standard and esoteric works. The letters not only served God in the act of creation, but they serve humans in the context of magic and ancient medicine. The power of Hebrew was ultimately placed in the hands of humanity in the form of Torah. Torah, by virtue of its language, constitutes the very blueprint by which God *creates* the world. But the midrash goes even further: Torah precedes the creation and in some sense has independent existence. Consequently, the language of Torah is itself independent of the physical act of creation.

Other midrashic passages employing the letters in various allegorical guises are not uncommon. In Lamentations Rabbah (§24.1), for instance, the twenty-two letters of the alphabet testify concerning Israel's transgressions against the Torah. In B. Ned. 32b, the connotation of the letter "hey," which is added to the name Abram to make it Abraham, is said to provide the patriarch with greater powers over the body. Thus it is that by the end of the sixth century the implications of Hebrew's holiness both as a language within the normal rules of semantics and according to a newly devised metasemantics has been fully developed in standard literary contexts. Contemporaneous to these developments, and, in many senses, parallel to the standard midrashic and talmudic literatures, there developed variations on these themes in esoteric (mystical) literatures. To these developments we now turn.

Mysticism, Magic, and the Alphabet

In the earliest mystical tracts known to us, we find a virtual obsession with names and their letters. Surely we can see similarities between the atomization of language that occurred in the midrashic and talmudic literatures with what took place in mysticism. Nonetheless, there are differences, albeit, often subtle. Ironically, the mystical concern for the atomization of language may have had its most profound impact in the area of liturgy. It is admittedly very difficult to establish the direction of influence when considering the exchange of ideas between the esoteric and the exoteric in religion. It is perhaps best to think of the lines between the two as ever shifting rather than clearly defined. Scholars have long recognized the liturgical character of much of the *Hekhalot* literature (perhaps contemporaneous with the later stages of the Babylonian Talmud), and the conceptualization of language there is often similar if not identical to the midrashic corpus.

One finds among the *Hekhalot* passages the declaration that the mere use of a divine name could assure well-being and progeny: "For each one who makes use [of the divine name and its letters] in fear, in awe, in purity, in holiness, in humility, [his] seed will be multiplied and he shall be successful in all his endeavors and his days shall be long."[27] While it is difficult to establish whether this outcome was planned, it turns out that the emphasis on the power of discrete names and even letters – all outside of the normal rubrics of syntax and semantics – empowered the person who may have been ignorant of the Hebrew language beyond being able to recite phrases of the liturgy by rote. By pointing to a meaning that was beyond the words, one could tap into a power that was not dependent upon knowledge of Hebrew or any common semantic rubric. In any event, many of the "sentences" and formulae involve clusters of phonemes that amount to nothing more than nonsense. Consequently, even the person possessing a profound understanding of the language does not engage this material with a normal sense of language usage. Two effects result simultaneously: (1) the sense that Hebrew is holy is intensified, and (2) the notion that certain effects could only be achieved by using Hebrew exclusively is enhanced. Neither concept is dependent upon normal language usage.

This is the theological context that allows a sage to teach that one should "pronounce the three names that the angels of glory pronounce[28] . . . and the three letters that the *galgalim* of the Merkavah pronounce . . . [in order to] acquire wisdom, for whoever pronounces them acquires eternal wisdom."[29] Emphasis is on pronunciation of the language, not as a sensible strings of words, but as discrete phonemes. No single letter can have a meaning in any regular semantic sense; and as it turns out, the names of angels themselves are often equally empty of clear connotations. What the mystic seeks is the creation of a vehicle that is intellectually neutral – mere letters – upon which anyone can contemplate, regardless of one's knowledge of the language. Hebrew, the holy tongue, becomes a vehicle of religiosity, with or without what we normally view as semantic value, but, nonetheless, loaded as a semiotic vehicle, especially in the context of worship.

The earliest document containing an extended explication of the Hebrew letters is the obscure tract known as *The Book of Creation* (*Sefer Yetzirah*).[30] Here we read of the "foundational letters" of the universe (*otiyot yesod*), which serve as the fundamental elements for all creatures. The twenty-two consonants of the Hebrew alphabet are divided into three groups, corresponding to the three realms of existence (the world, time, and the human body). Combinations of the letters in pairs resulted in the acts of creation. The algorithms prescribed for the various combinations share much in common with ancient astrology and numerology.[31] Other non-mystical sources reflect similar legends of letter-magic. A frequently cited passage at B. Ber. 55a attributes to Bezalel, master artisan of the tabernacle's holy utensils, knowledge of "how to combine letters by which heaven and earth were created." Bezalel was imbued with the divine spirit (*ruah elohim*), wisdom, understanding and knowledge (Exod. 31:3). According to Rabbinic mythology, this translated into creative forces harnessed by humans through mastery of the alphabet's mysteries. Although these talmudic images share much with the ideas behind the *Book of Creation*, this work still stands very much on its own in the history of Rabbinic writing on language, in terms of both content and genre.

Numerous other texts, including those known as the *Lesser* and *Greater Hekhaloth* literatures, ascribe to the letters, as well as those who know how to combine them, powers of creation.[32] The difficult-to-date *Hebrew Book of Enoch* readily moves back and forth between expositions on the letters, numerological speculation on the heavenly bodies, the roles of angels in natural and supernatural phenomena, and speculation on future worlds. *Enoch* makes very clear that the letters themselves are derived from God and emanate from his domain in the Holy of Holies, where they are "engraved with a pen of flame upon the throne of glory."[33]

Both mysticism and midrashic literature developed ideas of Hebrew's holiness in the context of a language theory founded upon a metasemantics. The long-term implications for the use of Hebrew exclusively in worship should now be apparent. The emphasis on Hebrew's characteristics independent of the standard theories of semantics furthered the objectification of language into a ritual object. In modern terms, we might see this objectification as having had a democratizing impact on the conceptualization of ritual and religiosity. Knowledge of Hebrew in the normal semantic sense carried by any language might otherwise have separated the scholar and the mystic from the common person. But once language is atomized, objectified into a ritual object, and deemed meaningful according to a metasemantics, the gap between the knowledgeable and the ignorant is partially neutralized. In the recitation of a benediction, all are equal, the scholar and the commoner, simply by virtue of their ability to intone the liturgical formulae required to make one's plea heard on high.

Conclusion

During the Rabbinic period, despite relatively low levels of Hebrew literacy among common Jews, Hebrew began serving as Judaism's language in ritual contexts. The success of this ritualization of language was part of a conceptualization of language that sought to transcend the common level of semantics we normally ascribe to simple utterances. Any history of the concept *lashon haqodesh* must reflect the ambivalence so many generations of Jews have felt toward issues of language usage. It could not be denied that, in order for Torah and prayer to be meaningful, Jews had to understand what was being said. Moreover, in order to perpetuate its heritage, beliefs, aspirations, and values, everything had to be transferred from one generation to another by means of a sensible medium, a language easily understood. The ritualization of language usage brought about a transformation of the common notions of semantics. With ritualization, meaning could be found not only in the semantic values of the words read but also in the *act of recitation* itself. Jews had to recognize the legitimacy of relating to Torah for its literal content. But ultimately they framed their unique relationship to the text and its language by transcending the literal meanings of the written words. The whole Rabbinic enterprise is founded upon a metasemantics of sorts, one that holds that meaning is at once rooted in the words of Torah but not identical to their common connotations. This same principle came to function in the realm of liturgy. Ultimately, a Jew's relationship to the Hebrew language was to be defined in spiritual terms. The mere recitation of the holy words of Torah constituted a visceral religious experience, for the words themselves were said to be "as sweet to my palate as apples from the Garden of Eden."[34]

This survey stops with the close of the Rabbinic period. We have traced the history of an idea without considering in a comprehensive manner the social, political, or interreligious causes relevant to its evolution. And, thus, we fall short of allowing the meaning of Hebrew's holiness to be understood in the grander context of a theory of social organization. We should also recognize that the story of how Hebrew was conceptualized in Judaism became increasingly complex with the ever greater dispersion of Jews in the European diaspora. The medieval world introduced into Jewish circles theories of language usage developed by Christians and Muslims that would frequently factor into a continual reassessment of Hebrew's place in Jewish theology and practice. The rise of "Jewish languages" such as Yiddish, Ladino, Judeo-Arabic, etc., introduced issues that had not previously been germane to daily Jewish life. In each of these cases, Jews were writing their colloquial modes of expression in the letters of their holy tongue. Rather than allowing this process to diminish their esteem for Hebrew, Jews sanctified their use of their vernacular, composing in it liturgy, philosophy, and eventually sermons.

Despite the ever changing intellectual and spiritual landscape of history, Hebrew remained with few exceptions a central component in the self-definition and religious sentiments of Jews throughout the world. Ironically, with the establishment of the State of Israel in 1948 (where Hebrew is the vernacular), questions of Hebrew usage have been transformed considerably. Secular Israelis, largely detached from and often unknowledgeable of religious traditions, relate to their vernacular in a manner not unsimilar to what we found in our survey of biblical attitudes toward language usage. Just as secular Hebrew literature written today bears the resonances of sacred writ, religious discourse cannot escape the influence of an ever modernizing Hebrew syntax and vocabulary bound to serve secular interests.

The influence of the modern Jewish state on the religious ideologies of Jews in the diaspora may, in the end, manifest itself more poignantly in a transformed attitude toward Hebrew than in any other mode of religious expression. One cannot help but sense irony in the fact that it was the ritualization of Hebrew usage that made it integral to Jewish identity during the Rabbinic period, but it will be the secularization of Hebrew usage in the modern world that may reinvigorate its religious meaning for Jews living outside of the State of Israel.

And so it may be that the conviction expressed in the Talmud, that secular things can be said in the Holy Tongue, but holy things cannot be said in a secular tongue (B. Shab. 40b),[35] will find new meaning in the land of Israel and in the diaspora, but in ways never envisioned by the rabbis who first struggled with the implications of Judaism's holy language.

Notes

1   Abraham Abulafia, from his *Sefer ha-Melammed*, cited and translated in Moshe Idel, *Language, Torah, and Hermeneutics in Abraham Abulafia* (Albany, 1989), p. 22.

2   For a fuller consideration of this subject, including extensive references to primary and secondary literatures, see my "Judaism's Holy Language," in Jacob Neusner, ed., *Approaches to Ancient Judaism* XVI (Atlanta, 1999), pp. 49–108.

3   See, e.g., W. Chomsky, *Hebrew, the Eternal Language* (Philadelphia, 1969); E. Y. Kutscher, *A History of the Hebrew Language* (Jerusalem, 1982); Angel Sáenz-Badillos, *A History of the Hebrew Language* (Cambridge, 1993).

4   See Wacholder, *Eupolemus*, ch. 11. Also Lester L. Grabbe, *Judaism from Cyrus to Hadrian* (Minneapolis, 1992), vol. 1, pp. 236–45.

5   See Acts 9 and then 13:9, where his identification as "Paul" is first presented. My thanks to Professor Michael Cook for pointing out how the name change from Hebrew to Greek may be part of a larger set of literary strategies for emphasizing Paul's authenticity as a Jew. There is, otherwise, no natural link between the Hebrew *Shaul* and the Greek *Paulos*.

6   See 25:3, in Charlesworth, *Old Testament Pseudepigrapha* (Garden City, 1983), vol. 1, pp. 801–2 (henceforth, *OTP*).

7   E. Eshel and M. E. Stone, "The Holy Language at the End of Days in Light of a New Fragment Found at Qumran," in *Tarbiz* 62.2 (1993) [in Hebrew].

8   See B. Git. 36a and, also, Genesis Rabbah 79§7 (Theodore–Albeck edition, 946–948), about sages who were uncertain of the meaning of certain biblical words. On this and similar texts, see S. Fraade, "Rabbinic Views on the Practice of Targum," in L. Levine (ed.), *The Galilee in Late Antiquity* (New York, 1992), p. 272.

9   Cf., M. Sot. 9:14, which cites the "war of Titus," who is Vespasian's son. Other manuscripts read Quietus, who was governor of Judea in 117 CE. Elucidations occur in B. Sot. 49b, B. B.Q. 82b–83a, B. Men. 64b.

10   The term was first used by C. A. Ferguson, "Diglossia," in *Word* 15 (1959), pp. 325–40.

11   See Eric M. Meyers, "Roman Sepphoris in Light of New Archaeological Evidence," in Levine, *The Galilee*, p. 330, who argues regarding Sepphoris that the "mixture of Hebrew, Greek, and Aramaic was symbiotic." Sepphoris was at once an important center of Rabbinic learning and emblematic of fine Greco-Roman architectural paradigms.

12   See B. Spolsky, "Jewish Multilingualism in the First Century: An Essay in Historical Sociolinguistics," in J. A. Fishman, ed., *Readings in the Sociology of Jewish Languages* (Leiden, 1985), vol. 1, pp. 35–50.

13   Counter-examples are numerous, with Islam's attitude toward Arabic as God's tongue being an example of a vernacular language that was imbued with holiness by virtue of God's usage. But the point here is that the notion of Hebrew as a "holy

language" is absent from the Tanakh and most Second Temple literature (Ben Sirah, for instance). In contrast, Islam is born into a world of multiple languages, where the Muslim's relationship to the Qur'an – in Arabic – is a tension built into the culture's origins.

14   This particular issue was not limited to liturgical contexts. In various legal domains, the question of language was particularly important, such as regarding contracts, marriage and divorce documents, etc. See, for instance, questions regarding the language of a document and that of its signatories in M. Git. 9:6, 8 and B. Git. 87a-b.

15   Deut. 6:4–6, 11:13–21, and Num. 15:37–41 stand at the core of a larger liturgical rubric known as "the Shema and its blessings," recited every morning and evening. The "*Tefillah*," or "*Amidah*," is the central core of every morning, *musaf*, afternoon, and evening worship service. The composition is altogether in Rabbinic Hebrew, save for a few biblical verses that are part of the third benediction.

16   See Y. Meg. 4:1, 17a–21a; B. Meg. 18b.

17   The underlying concern is the prohibition against transporting things on Shabbat. So the issue is not simply, which books do you save, but for what kind of books do you violate the Sabbath law?

18   This is the list proposed by Huna in the name of the Tannaim, B. Shab. 115b. Similarly, see T. Shab. 13.2.

19   See Y. Sot. 7:1, 21b, and Levine's discussion in "The Sages and the Synagogue in Late Antiquity," in Levine, *The Galilee*, pp. 201–22.

20   See J. H. Charlesworth, "Jewish Liturgies, Hymns and Prayers (ca. 167 BCE–135 CE)," in R. A. Kraft and G. W. E. Nickelsburg, eds., *Early Post-Biblical Judaism and Its Modern Interpreters* (Chico, 1985); "Hellensitic Synagogal Prayers," in *The Pseudepigrapha and Modern Research with a Supplement* (Society of Biblical Literature, 1981); and *OTP*, vol. 2, pp. 671–97, "Hellenistic Synagogal Prayers," with an introduction by D. A. Fiensy. See also Pieter W. Van Der Horst, "Neglected Greek Evidence for Early Jewish Liturgical Prayer," in *Journal for the Study of Judaism* 29.3 (1998), pp. 278–96.

21   See Maimonides, *Mishneh Torah, Hilkhot Berakhot* 1:6; *Sepher Hasidim*, §1590; *Shulhan Arukh, Orah Hayyim* 101:4.

22   The Haggadah does contain some Aramaic passages, e.g., the opening paragraph ("This is the bread of affliction"), and vernacular songs were regularly appended at the conclusion of the home ritual. In some regions it became custom to recite the highly imaginative (Aramaic) Targum to the Song of Songs on the intervening nights of the holiday.

23   Jacob Neusner, *Language as Taxonomy: The Rules for Using Hebrew and Aramaic in the Babylonian Talmud* (Atlanta, 1990). For a perspective quite antithetical to Neusner's, see David Weiss Halivni, *Midrash, Mishnah and Gemara* (Cambridge, MA, 1986).

24   Ibid., p. 7.

25   Ibid., p. 25.

26   Ironically, English does. A brief (Aramaic) passage appended to this pericope further expounds how other languages don't work this way. Greek uses *gyne* and *anthropos* for woman and man, respectively; and, similarly, Aramaic uses *'itᵉta* and *gavra*.

27   Peter Schäfer, *Synopse zur Hekhalot-Literatur* (Tübingen, 1981), §337.

28   The names themselves include nonsense words and sounds, as do the formulae prescribed in other parts of this passage.

29 Schäfer, *Synopse*, §564. The *galgalim* in this context appear to be another group of angels, perhaps the wheels of the *Merkavah* personified. See also Gershom Scholem, "The Name of God and the Linguistics of the Kabbalah," in *Diogenes* 79 (1972), pp. 59–80; 80 (1973), pp. 164–94.

30 Gershom Scholem, *Kabbalah* (Jerusalem, 1974), pp. 23–30, suggests that the work derives from between the third and sixth centuries. Two versions exist, with the longer form not exceeding two thousand words. See also Moshe Idel, *Golem: Jewish Magical and Mystical Traditions on the Artificial Anthropoid* (Albany, 1990), ch. 2.

31 Scholem draws attention to similarities in the neo-Pythagorean "mystical arithmology" of Nikomachos of Gerasa, who lived during the middle of the second century.

32 See Gershom Scholem, *Jewish Gnosticism, Merkabah Mysticism and Talmudic Tradition* (New York, 1960), pp. 75–83.

33 *Hebrew Book of Enoch*, 41:3, in *OTP*, I, translated by P. Alexander. The whole chapter elucidates the role of the letters in creation. See also ch. 13.

34 From the Targum to Song of Songs, 2:5, here as translated by Isaac Jerusalmi, *The Song of Songs in the Targumic Tradition* (Cincinnati, 1993), p. 53.

35 I am using the dictum somewhat out of context, as its original connotation concerned where and when one could discuss verses of Torah. Spelled out, the passage would read as follows: Secular concerns can be discussed even in a bath house in the Holy Tongue, but it is forbidden to speak of holy matters in a bath house even in the (non-Hebrew) vernacular.

PART III
Modern and Contemporary Judaisms

CHAPTER 17
Reform Judaism

Dana Evan Kaplan

Reform Judaism, sometimes called Progressive Judaism or Liberal Judaism, adapts its beliefs and practices to the norms of modern society. In the late 1990s, there were about 1.5 million Reform Jews worldwide. More than one million of those live in the United States and Canada; the rest live in a variety of countries, including France, Great Britain, Australia, South Africa, South America, and Asia. The international umbrella organization for Reform Jews around the world is the World Union for Progressive Judaism (WUPJ). The largest constituent organization of the WUPJ is the Union of American Hebrew Congregations (UAHC), with about 875 organizations.

Founded in London in 1926 and subsequently located in New York and then Jerusalem, where it is housed today, the World Union for Progressive Judaism promotes Reform Judaism, its practices, ideas, and organizations, around the world. It includes not only the American Reform movement but the American Reconstructionist one as well and also encompasses movements in countries in which the word "reform" is not used or is even looked down upon, often replaced with the term Progressive. The World Union works to maintain and strengthen existing Progressive congregations and to build new ones. It supports the Israeli movement for Progressive Judaism and ARZENU, the international federation of Reform and Progressive religious Zionists.

Reform Judaism around the World

The WUPJ has affiliates in about thirty-five countries on six continents.[1] In Great Britain there is both the Reform movement, which is somewhat more traditional and larger, and the Liberal movement, which was traditionally closer to Classical Reform in the United States. In recent years, the two movements have become much more similar. They share a rabbinical school, Leo Baeck College, which trains rabbis not only for Great Britain but for all of Europe and beyond.

Despite the dramatic decline in the Jewish population of Great Britain over the last generation due to assimilation, intermarriage, and emigration, the Liberal movement and to an even greater degree the Reform movement have managed to keep their strength. While their numbers are not growing, their influence in and percentage of the community are increasing. Indeed, a number of congregations are moving ahead with major development plans, including Radlett and Bushey, Maidenhead, Wimbledon, and South West Essex Settlement.[2] Two new Progressive day schools are opening, and the Sternberg Centre provides a focus for Progressive religious and cultural activities, including an active interfaith dialogue program.

In Australia as in England, the predominant mentality regards Orthodoxy as the only authentic form of Judaism, despite the fact that many of those who belong to Orthodox synagogues do not observe the mitzvot in a halakhic fashion. This is a problem for the Progressive movement, because it is difficult to convince people to view Reform as religiously authentic. Many if not most of those who do join do so because a problem in personal status – a question regarding whether or not they are Jewish by traditional standards – prevents them from joining an Orthodox synagogue. In Australia in 1999, there were fifteen Progressive congregations belonging to the Australian and New Zealand Union for Progressive Judaism, which represented eight thousand adult members. They had two day schools, a Reform Zionist youth movement called Netzer, and a Reform Zionist movement called Arzi. They are changing the name of their Union to reflect the increasing participation of a number of congregations in Asia, in such places as Hong Kong and Singapore.

In South Africa, the number of congregations is decreasing because of, the continued emigration from that country of whites in general and Jews in particular. Congregation Bet David in Sandton, an affluent northern suburb of Johannesburg; Temple Emanuel in Parktown, Johannesburg; and Temple Israel in Cape Town are viable congregations. Many of the other Reform congregations in Pretoria, Durban, Port Elizabeth, and East London are declining dramatically, and several others in smaller towns have closed completely. South African Jews, like the Australians, tend to prefer non-observant Orthodoxy and to view Reform as lacking religious legitimacy and authenticity. Unlike in Australia, however, the Reform movement in South Africa never established day schools, which is perhaps the single most important factor in the precipitous decline in what was once a very significant movement. At its peak the Reform movement may have represented 20 percent of the 118,000 Jews in South Africa. Today Reform represents less than 10 percent of the approximately 80,000 Jews left.

The two biggest growth regions for the WUPJ are the former Soviet Union and Germany. In the former Soviet Union, numerous congregations have been established in such countries as Russia, Ukraine, Belarus, and Estonia. Russia alone now has fifteen congregations in places such as Moscow and St. Petersburg as well as lesser-known places such as Saltykovka and Bryansk. In the Ukraine there are ten congregations, one in Kiev and the others in smaller cities. The first Russian rabbi, Misha Tillman, graduated from Hebrew Union College–Jewish Institute of Religion (HUC–JIR) in Cincinnati but decided to stay in the United States and is serving a Russian-speaking congregation in the Chicago area. A number of other Russians are being trained for the rabbinate at the Leo Baeck College and at HUC–JIR in Jerusalem. A recent American graduate, David Wilfond, has volunteered to serve in Russia for a two-year period and has done a great deal of work in building up congregations throughout the former Soviet Union.

This is in many ways pioneer work, because it involves developing not only religious congregations but entire Jewish communities, which, under Communism, were not allowed to function freely. Of course, there is much emigration from the former Soviet Union, and this has a tremendous impact on the ability of the Reform movement as well as every other Jewish organization to build institutions as well as programming.

The other country in which there has been a dramatic rise in the number of Reform congregations is Germany. Today there are thirteen congregations in cities such as Berlin, Cologne, Munich, and Frankfurt, as well as smaller cities. In Germany, as elsewhere in Europe, the Orthodox establishment is dominant, which has made it difficult for the Progressive movement. However, in recent years, increasing numbers of people have turned to the Reform movement for two reasons: their increasingly assimilated life-styles make Orthodoxy more distant from their mentality, and the resulting intermarriage has put many in a situation in which they are not recognized by the Orthodox authorities. Many of the Jews in these congregations are from the former Soviet Union, which has been the major source of the increase in the Jewish community of Germany.

The revival of Jewish life in Germany is an emotionally charged trend for Jews throughout the world. Before World War II, of course, Germany had a distinguished Jewish community of about 500,000, including a very strong and intellectually vibrant Reform community. After the Holocaust, it was felt by many that Jewish life in Germany was untenable. With the passage of time and the arrival of tens of thousands of refugees from the former Soviet Union, Jewish life in Germany is growing again, and the Reform movement has been able to develop despite the sometimes vicious opposition of the Orthodox establishment. There are also Reform communities in other German-speaking countries such as Switzerland and Austria. These communities contain a mixture of people who lived in these countries before World War II, or their descendants, and people who have moved to those countries from the United States or elsewhere for business or personal reasons.

France has the largest Jewish community in all of Europe, with estimates ranging between 600,000 and 700,000. Until recently it was completely dominated by the Orthodox, despite very high levels of assimilation and intermarriage. The two main Reform congregations in Paris were, because of religious and political differences, unable or unwilling to work together. Recently there has been growth, and there are now eight congregations in the country and others in French-speaking Switzerland. Movement leaders have expressed the conviction that with additional French-speaking rabbis the movement could grow exponentially. This may be the next big growth area for the Reform movement.

There are Reform congregations in South America, particularly in Brazil, but in countries such as Mexico and Argentina the Conservative movement was first to establish a non-Orthodox presence and has successfully built networks of congregations. Therefore, there are no Reform congregations in Mexico and only one very new one, Emanuel, in Buenos Aires, Argentina. There are, however, Reform congregations in Costa Rica, Guatemala, Curaçao, and Panama.

It should be pointed out that, with the exception of Great Britain, these are small movements. None is of sufficient size to support a rabbinical school, and in most of the countries they represent a minority of the established Jewish community. It is in the United States and to a lesser degree in Canada that Reform Judaism has developed most extensively.

The Origins of Reform Judaism

Reform Judaism was the first of the modern responses to the emancipation of the Jews and the intellectual atmosphere of enlightenment that developed in eighteenth-century central Europe. Because of its stress on autonomy, both of the individual and of the congregation, Reform Judaism has manifested itself differently in different places, and yet there are certain characteristics that all Reform communities share in common. At base, Reform believes in the legitimacy of change, rejecting the idea that the written and oral Torah were given by God word for word, letter for letter, and belief by belief, which would preclude conscious changes of any sort. Rather, Reform accepts that human conceptions of the divine are, in fact, human, so that both belief and practice legitimately may evolve in the face of scientific, social, ethical, and other human developments.

The first Reform Jews were Germans seeking to find a middle course between conversion to Christianity, on the one hand, and the inherited halakhic Judaism, on the other. They hoped that by introducing an atmosphere of modern aesthetics and much stricter decorum, they could make worship services far more attractive to apathetic German Jews, who may have even contemplated conversion to Christianity. The liturgy was abbreviated, and a vernacular sermon was added. A mixed male–female chorus sang, accompanied by the organ, and German prayers were introduced alongside the Hebrew ones. Israel Jacobson, regarded by many as the founder of Reform Judaism, introduced a Reform service in his school chapel in Seesen in 1810 and later in his home in Berlin in 1815.[3] The Hamburg Temple, which was founded in 1818, was the first Reform synagogue with a full-service calendar.

Most of the early German reformers hoped that they could justify their mainly aesthetic reforms on the basis of halakhic analysis. They therefore made great efforts to write responsa trying to show that the halakhah in fact permitted such things as reciting prayers in English, the use of an organ, and similar changes.

By the early 1840s, a trained Rabbinic leadership began to assert itself in central Europe. Abraham Geiger was called to the Breslau Jewish community in 1839 and developed into the most distinguished intellectual defender of Reform Judaism. In 1844, 1845, and 1846, Reform rabbinical conferences were held in Brunswick, Frankfurt, and Breslau, respectively. At the 1845 conference, a debate on the use of Hebrew in the service led Rabbi Zacharias Frankel to walk out. This is seen as the origin of the historical school, which later became known as the Conservative movement. Despite the fact that most of the rabbis at these conferences were quite a bit more Reform than Frankel, they understood that they had to operate within the broader Jewish community and thus maintained a strong connection with traditional rituals and observances. On the other hand, perhaps because of this need to compromise on a great many practices, a number of radical Reform rabbis, in particular Samuel Holdheim, made anti-traditional statements; even Geiger himself has been quoted over and over again as appearing to have a strong emotional aversion to circumcision. Still, their practice, on the whole, remained far more traditional than their rhetoric, and the vast majority of Reform rabbis worked to remain a part of the broader Jewish community, not fully accepting the Radical Reform groups in Berlin and Frankfurt.[4]

Reform comes to the United States[5]

The Reform movement was the first Jewish religious movement in the United States to organize itself on a denominational basis, pioneering what Lance Sussman refers to as a "tripartite polity" that was subsequently adopted by the other major denominations of American Judaism.[6] That is, within Reform Judaism, there are three types of organizations, each with its own "turf": the congregational organization, today represented nationally by the Union of American Hebrew congregations (UAHC); the rabbinical schools, represented by the Hebrew Union College–Jewish Institute of Religion (HUC–JIR); and the rabbinate, represented by the Central Conference of American Rabbis (CCAR).

Sussman further says that American Reform Judaism can be divided into six periods: its early development, 1824–65; Classical Reform, 1865–1900; the period of Progressivism, 1900–20; the period of reorientation in response to anti-Semitism and Zionism, 1920–45; Reform during the suburbanization period, 1945–65; and contemporary Reform, 1965 to the present.[7]

The first attempt at Reform Judaism in the United States began in 1824, when forty-seven members of Congregation Beth Elohim in Charleston, South Carolina, requested that their congregation consider a number of minor ritual reforms, including the introduction of some English prayers during Sabbath worship. The congregational board rejected the request, and, on November 21, 1824, a small group of members founded a new congregation, called the

Reformed Society of Israelites. This attempt at building a Reform congregation failed, in part due to the death of its leader, an interesting Sephardic intellectual named Isaac Harby,[8] and the original Reform group disbanded in 1833. Despite this setback, Congregation Beth Elohim itself soon after moved toward Reform, under the leadership of its *hazzan*, Gustavus Poznanski.[9]

Whereas the Charleston Reform community was an isolated phenomenon, by the 1830s large numbers of central European Jews were arriving in the United States. These were referred to as German Jews, although their geographic origins were quite a bit wider.[10] This emigration increased the Jewish population of the United States from around 3,000 in 1820 to about 15,000 in 1840 and to 150,000 in 1860. Although earlier historians have assumed that these "German Jews" brought Reform Judaism with them from Germany, Leon Jick has demonstrated that mostly Jews from small towns far removed from Reform's influence in Germany emigrated to the United States. Rather than bringing Reform with them, in response to the American social and religious environment, these traditional Jews slowly developed their own version of what became known as Reform Judaism.[11]

A number of intellectually oriented Reform *verein* (a small religious group) were ideologically committed to Reform Judaism, such as the Har Sinai Verein, which was founded in 1842 in Baltimore, and Emanu-El, which was founded in New York in 1845. These groups were committed to Reform Judaism in an ideological manner and were very much in contact with their Reform co-religionists in Germany.[12] The vast majority of what became Reform synagogues, however, were far more concerned than the *verein* with the realities of everyday life in America and adjusting to that life while maintaining some sort of attachment to their traditional religion.

Isaac Mayer Wise and Other Early Leaders

Isaac Mayer Wise, who arrived from Bohemia in 1846, became the most important leader of nineteenth-century American Reform Judaism.[13] Although advised to become a peddler, Wise was encouraged by Rabbi Max Lilienthal to consider the pulpit rabbinate. Lilienthal sent Wise in his stead to dedicate a number of synagogues, which led to an opportunity for Wise to begin serving as rabbi in Albany, New York.[14]

Wise was offered a life contract to become the rabbi of Congregation Bnei Jeshurun in Cincinnati, which became his base for building what became the American Reform movement. It bears noting that, from the beginning, Wise did not intend to build a new denomination. At every opportunity he strove, rather, for unity, hoping and believing that through compromise and sheer charisma he could unify all or almost all American Jews under the banner of American Judaism. This would be a moderate form of Judaism, with some ritual reforms but a good deal of tradition as well.[15] Wise established a newspaper, *The*

Israelite, which later became *The American Israelite*; edited a Siddur called *Minhag America*; and eventually founded the Hebrew Union College in 1875 and the Central Conference of American Rabbis in 1889. He was also instrumental in inspiring one of his lay leaders, Moritz Loth, to establish the Union of American Hebrew Congregations in July 1873,[16] which thirty-four congregations joined, most of which were from the Midwest or the South. By the end of the 1870s, one hundred and eighteen congregations belonged to the UAHC, more than half of all identified synagogues in the United States.

Wise represented a pragmatic and moderate stream of American Reform Judaism. Although some scholars have pointed to the numerous inconsistencies in his written positions,[17] what must be emphasized is that Wise was primarily an institution builder who used ideology as a tool for compromise and consensus. To take his words at face value and to express shock and dismay at the inconsistencies and outright contradictions is really to miss the brilliance of his activities as an institutional leader who succeeded in building an entire American religious movement under very difficult circumstances.

Despite this brilliance, Wise was considered an uneducated and unworthy colleague by some of the German Reform rabbis who arrived in the 1850s and 1860s with Ph.D.s from prestigious central European universities. Primary among them was David Einhorn, who arrived shortly before the 1855 Cleveland Conference. At that conference, Wise attempted to build a coalition with Isaac Leeser and other traditionalists by agreeing to two principles that accepted the validity of the Talmud and its applicability to American Jewish practice and belief. Einhorn wrote a number of scathing attacks on Wise for abrogating Reform theology and turning a consistent and principled approach to modern Judaism into a jumble of beliefs that made no sense. Einhorn served Har Sinai in Baltimore from 1855 until he was forced to flee because of his brave and principled stand against slavery. He went on to serve congregations in Philadelphia and New York. His sons-in-law, Kaufmann Kohler and Emil Hirsch, carried on his tradition of principled radical reform, although Kohler and Hirsch differed from each other as well in a number of significant ways.

Classical Reform

From the late 1860s or 1870s, the Reform movement matured and developed into a much more Americanized form of worship and religion. This was due to the fact that Americanization proceeded very quickly among second- and later third-generation German Jews. These Americanized children of German Jewish emigrants saw the tremendous influence that liberal religion had on their Protestant neighbors and wanted to develop a form of Judaism that would serve as a Jewish equivalent to Presbyterianism, Episcopalianism, and, especially, Unitarianism.

The best known statement of what Classical Reform Judaism believed appears in the Pittsburgh Platform.[18] The platform attempted, on the one hand, to define Reform Judaism as a more rational and modern religion than the much more traditional Judaism being expounded by Alexander Kohut, whose series of debates with Kohler earlier in 1885 had attracted wide attention in synagogues and the press. Kohler wanted to write down in a more formal manner what, in his mind, distinguished Reform from traditional Judaism.

On the other hand, Kohler felt it essential to explain what was Jewish about Reform Judaism; this was a reaction against the Society for Ethical Culture, founded by Felix Adler, the son of Samuel Adler, the rabbi at Congregation Emanu-El in New York.[19] Adler had returned from Rabbinic studies in Germany advocating a form of ethics placed in a universalistic framework. This Society was very attractive to many formerly Reform Jews who were looking for a way to express their conviction that ethics were important and yet were interested in loosening or breaking their particularistic ties with Jewish ethnic identity. In this case, particularism means an approach that concentrates on the Jews as a coherent group, in contrast to universalism, in which the primary emphasis is on humanity as a whole. Kohler responded aggressively to Adler and his fledgling movement, finding it essential to reaffirm Reform's commitment to Jewish particularism, expressed in the religious idea of the mission of Israel.

Classical Reform stressed that Jews no longer lived in ghettoes but in a free society. Because this equality was so new, the dream of working, living, and striving together with Christian neighbors to help to make the world a better place, a place of justice and peace, was a central part of the Reform vision. The prophetic mandate to work tirelessly for the rights of the downtrodden was emphasized, and the term "prophetic Judaism" was used to describe a Reform vision of following the dictates of the prophets to make the world a better place.[20] Reform rabbis spoke often of ethical monotheism, in which the Jewish belief in one God was combined with rational thought and modern innovations in scientific knowledge. The "Mission of Israel" was to help spread ethical monotheism throughout the world.

Reform in the Twentieth Century

A steady trickle of immigration of Eastern European Jews turned into a flood beginning around 1881, and the American Jewish population had increased from 250,000 in 1880 to one million by 1900 to 3.5 million by 1920. Since these immigrants were almost all from eastern Europe, where there had been no full emancipation and almost no Reform movement, very few joined the Reform movement. This was partly a matter of the newcomers' not liking the Reform service and also due to the fact that many Reform Jews maintained a haughty and sometimes arrogant attitude toward the immigrants, preferring not to remember that their own parents or grandparents had arrived in the United States only forty to sixty years earlier in almost the exact same circumstances.

During those years, the Reform movement grew very slowly relative to the increase in the American Jewish population. There were only ninety-nine congregations consisting of 9,800 units in 1900 and two hundred congregations with 23,000 units in 1920. Thus, the Reform movement went from being the single most important voice of the Jewish American community to being a small minority. Although the elite nature of many Reform Jews meant that they retained a high profile, they were swamped by the huge number of eastern European organizations and ideologies.

Under the influence of the immigrant Jewish masses, the Reform movement began very slowly to move back toward a more traditional approach to Jewish thought and practice. By the 1920s and especially the 1930s, this trend became very clear with the rise of Adolph Hitler in Germany and the dramatic increase in anti-Semitism in the United States itself. Policies that had seemed rational and level-headed just a few decades earlier appeared naive and foolhardy. The Pittsburgh Platform, for example, argued that Jews should remain together solely as a religious group in order to fulfill their mission of bringing ethical monotheism to the world. By the 1930s, with the rise in anti-Semitism, it was clear that many perceived Jews as an alien group and that Jewish physical survival was much more the issue than theology or ideology. In 1937, the CCAR thus adopted the Columbus Platform, which was openly Zionistic and the culmination of a revolutionary shift in the ideology of the American Reform movement that would encourage a greater diversity of opinion and a multiplicity of approaches.[21] The platform urged Jews to rededicate themselves to the "timeless aims and ideals of our faith," it placed greater stress on tradition, and it encouraged the use of Hebrew as well as other traditions that "possess inspirational value." In the context of the political events of the 1930s and the increasingly serious crisis facing European Jewry, the movement thus encouraged a feeling of solidarity with Jews around the world.

Abba Hillel Silver, one of the most important rabbis during the inter-war period, was a significant leader of American Zionism. After serving as a rabbi in Wheeling, West Virginia, he became rabbi of the Temple in Cleveland, Ohio; from this pulpit he worked tirelessly for Zionism and the hope of establishing a Jewish state. With Stephen S. Wise, Silver formed the American Zionist Emergency Council, which lobbied the US Congress on behalf of the cause of Zionism. Silver was the leader who announced to the United Nations that Israel had declared itself an independent state. He was a candidate to become the first president of Israel, a position given to Chaim Weizmann.

In 1922, Stephen Wise established the Jewish Institute of Religion (JIR) in New York City. He felt a new rabbinical seminary was necessary because Hebrew Union College was not sufficiently Zionistic. JIR was to serve *Klal Yisrael*, the totality of the Jewish people. Despite this philosophy, worship services at JIR were very non-traditional. Partially as a result of this, upon graduating, the majority of its students took Reform pulpits, with some going to Conservative congregations, and almost none becoming Orthodox rabbis. In 1950, JIR merged with HUC.

Following World War II, a large number of American Jews abandoned city centers for the burgeoning suburbs.[22] The Conservative movement benefited most from this suburbanization, for it appealed to the now-Americanized eastern European emigrants and their children, being substantially more traditional than the Reform movement while allowing far greater flexibility than Orthodoxy. But Reform benefited from suburbanization as well. In 1940, there were 265 congregations with 59,000 units in the UAHC; by 1955, there were 520 congregations and 255,000 units.

During this time, the American Reform movement was led by Maurice Eisendrath,[23] who became executive director of the UAHC in 1943 and its president in 1946, and by Nelson Glueck, who became head of the HUC in 1947. Eisendrath moved the national headquarters of the UAHC from Cincinnati to New York, where he built an entire building on Fifth Avenue across the street from Central Park and next to Congregation Emanu-El, which he called the House of Living Judaism. This was the headquarters of the Reform movement until it was sold under the presidency of Rabbi Eric H. Yoffie in 1998. Glueck, a world-famous archeologist who appeared on the cover of *Time* magazine, was able to oversee the merger of HUC with the Jewish Institute of Religion. Glueck also established a third Reform branch in Los Angeles in 1954 and a fourth campus, in Jerusalem, in 1963.

In the 1960s, many American Reform Jews became involved in the US civil rights struggles as well as in opposition to the war in Viet Nam. The Six-Day War of 1967 in Israel galvanized all of American Jewry and increased the loyalty of Reform Jews to the Jewish state, as did the 1973 Yom Kippur War, in which Israel's survival was in doubt for a short time. This new period in American Jewish life and attitudes called for a rethinking of the ideologies expressed in the Reform liturgy. In response, in 1971, under its new executive vice president, Rabbi Joseph Glaser, the CCAR began a campaign to develop a new liturgy, which culminated in 1975 with the publication of *Gates of Prayer*. This was the first completely rewritten prayer book used in American Reform synagogues since the publication of the earliest version of the Union Prayer Book in the late nineteenth century. In 1978, *Gates of Repentance*, a completely reworked high holiday prayer book, was published.

Alexander M. Schindler, who succeeded Maurice Eisendrath, served as UAHC president from 1973 to 1995, becoming the most recognized Reform leader and perhaps the leading spokesman for all of American Jewry. He was known for his assertive support of the movement's social action and social justice agenda and became identified with the full liberal agenda of the 1970s and 1980s, including civil rights, world peace, nuclear disarmament, a "Marshall Plan" for the poor, opposition to the death penalty, and women's and gay rights. During Schindler's presidency, the UAHC grew from 400 congregations in 1973 to about 875 in 1995.

Outreach

Schindler is perhaps best remembered for two issues, his outreach to intermarried couples and his advocacy of patrilineal descent. At a meeting of the UAHC's board of trustees in Houston in December 1978, Schindler issued a public call to the Reform movement to reach out to the non-Jewish spouses of Jewish partners in interfaith marriages. Even more surprising, he urged that the Jewish religion be made available to unchurched gentiles. This call passively to proselytize those with no connections to the Jewish community was controversial, as it appeared to be a dramatic departure from two thousand years of Jewish religious policy. Some of his critics argued that this might encourage Christian groups to launch opposing campaigns within the Jewish community. Despite the attention this suggestion garnered, little was done in the succeeding years actually to proselytize unchurched gentiles, though much was done to develop outreach programs to interfaith couples. In this same period, Reform adopted the controversial policy that children of intermarriages, even if the mother was not Jewish, would be considered Jewish so long as they were raised as Jews, including involvement in the synagogue and participation in life-cycle events. In the late 1990s, even as this approach remains a consensus position in the Reform movement, there is increasing belief that the so-called patrilineal descent resolution was adopted too hastily and that its wording has led to considerable misunderstanding.

The 1990s: American Reform in Transition

Eric H. Yoffie was installed as president of the UAHC on June 8, 1996. He inherited a movement that had grown in numbers and yet was viewed as having fundamental weaknesses that had to be addressed. In particular, he recognized that the level of knowledge among most of the laity was extremely low, and he therefore initiated a Jewish literacy campaign that encouraged synagogue board members to read four books on Jewish concerns a year, books that were selected for their content and variety. Soon this program was expanded to the entire movement, with each quarterly edition of the movement's magazine, *Reform Judaism*, featuring two books recommended for reading.

Another weak area was the youth movement. Yoffie, admitting that the movement was a shadow of what it had been in earlier decades, proposed appointing full-time youth coordinators to each of the UAHC's thirteen regions to oversee the rebuilding of the National Federation of Temple Youth (NFTY) youth group system. Yoffie is a strong and energetic leader who has done much to confront the weaknesses of the movement and to develop initiatives to meet the many challenges facing American Reform Judaism today.

Current Issues

Reform in Israel

The position of Reform Judaism in Israel had always been tenuous. Even before the Mandate period in Palestine, there was an Orthodox rabbinate that controlled much of Jewish religious life in the Holy Land. From the establishment of the state, the government of Israel accepted the "status quo" concerning religious authority and practice and avoided transforming the relationship between religion and state. Adding to the problem, most of the emigrants to Israel had come from countries without a pluralistic and democratic societal background and therefore had no experience or awareness of pluralistic approaches to Judaism. There were only a few Reform congregations founded before the rise of the state in 1948, and the Israeli movement for Progressive Judaism was slow to develop congregations even in comparison to the Conservative movement. By the end of the 1980s, about eighteen Reform congregations existed in the entire state, as opposed to forty Conservative and hundreds and hundreds of traditional ones. Orthodoxy remains the official state religion. Orthodox rabbis are supported by the ministry of Religious Affairs; Orthodox synagogues are built and maintained by that same body. Local religious councils are run almost exclusively by Orthodox representatives, who distribute huge sums of money.

During the 1990s, the Reform movement's Israel Religious Action Center, headed by Rabbi Uri Regev, led a sustained legal battle to gain recognition for the Reform movement in Israel. Two key issues were the right of non-Orthodox and specifically Reform candidates to run for and be seated on local religious councils and the right of Reform rabbis to perform conversions in Israel that are recognized at least by the state if not by the Chief Rabbinate. The world Reform and Conservative movements, and especially American Reform and Conservative Jews, began to place far greater pressure on the State of Israel than ever before.

Partially in response to this, the Ne'eman Commission was established. It attempted to bring together representatives of the different movements to devise a workable solution to the conversion crisis, giving the Reform and Conservative movements much greater input in the conversion process without compromising the halakhic standards that the Orthodox deem sacrosanct. The Commission was unable to achieve a workable solution, although, despite the lack of agreement, a jointly taught conversion school was created. What is significant, however, is that, for the first time, the world's non-Orthodox communities were able and willing to use their influence to push for the religious rights of their movements in the State of Israel. This is a battle that will continue into the next decade and probably beyond.

The role of women, the ordination of women, and gender roles

Women have been taking on a far greater role in American religious life over the past 30 years than they were allowed to in previous generations. This trend has been a direct consequence of the Feminist movement and has had a dramatic impact on every aspect of American life. Reform Judaism has been able to respond quickly and actively to the changing sex role expectations and has allowed women to assume responsibility for all aspects of the religious and communal life of individual congregations and the movement as a whole.

In 1972, Sally J. Priesand became the first woman to be ordained a Reform rabbi at HUC–JIR. This was a highly revolutionary breakthrough, because even though Reform had been committed to egalitarianism essentially from its origins, in practical terms it had always found reasons to maintain a male-only policy in the rabbinate. Since Priesand's ordination, a great many women have entered the rabbinate, with close to 50 percent of Reform rabbinical classes now comprised of women. Despite the fact that so many women are becoming rabbis, it is as yet unclear whether they will be accepted at the higher ranks of the movement and whether they will be willing to make the sacrifices necessary to rise through the movement's hierarchy.

Gay and lesbian marriages

One of the most controversial areas the Reform movement has considered in the 1990s is the role of gays and lesbians in the synagogue. In 1987, the UAHC passed a resolution affirming its commitment to welcoming gay and lesbian Jews into its congregations and encouraging gay and lesbian involvement and participation in all aspects of synagogue life. In 1990, the CCAR adopted a position paper encouraging rabbis to treat gays and lesbians with full respect and to integrate everyone into their congregations regardless of sexual orientation.

The CCAR position paper acknowledged, however, the need to continue a dialogue regarding the religious status of monogamous gay and lesbian relationships. Specifically, the CCAR was still grappling with what type of ceremony is appropriate and what the religious meaning of that rite would be. There was the possibility of having a commitment ceremony, but there was also the potential for sanctioning a full marriage ceremony involving *kiddushin*, completely equivalent to the marriage ceremony performed for heterosexual couples.

In April 1996 the CCAR passed a resolution supporting the rights of gay and lesbian couples to a civil marriage. Much attention was focused on Hawaii, which appeared at the time to be the first state that might pass a law allowing gay and lesbian civil marriage. At the UAHC biennial, October 29 to November 2, 1997, in Dallas, Texas, the UAHC passed a resolution supporting secular efforts to promote legislation that would provide through civil marriage equal opportunity for gays and lesbians and encouraged the UAHC constituent congregations to honor monogamous gay and lesbian domestic relationships.

The 1999 Pittsburgh Platform

Since the Pittsburgh Platform of 1885 and Columbus Platform of 1937, discussed above, and until the late 1990s, only one other American Reform platform was prepared, a centenary perspective, written by Eugene Borowitz and adopted in San Francisco in 1976. This statement moved Reform closer to tradition as well as to Jewish peoplehood even as it stressed the movement's tremendous diversity.

Borowitz is one of the most seminal thinkers in the Reform movement, regarded as its leading theologian in the United States. Interestingly, he uses the term *Liberal Judaism* as the title of one of his more influential books, thus connecting contemporary Reform thought to its German origins.[24] He describes Judaism by drawing an analogy to personal relationships rather in terms of universal ethics, peoplehood, or law. Borowitz identifies the "root Jewish religious experiences of our time as the absoluteness of value and Jewish particularity, with God as their ground." He then creates a theory on non-Orthodox Jewish duty based on the Jewish self's intimate involvement with God, with the Jewish people today, its tradition, and its messianic hope, and thus with a self fully individual, yet primarily shaped by its Jewish relationships covenant."[25]

Borowitz and the others working on the 1976 document agreed that if a statement could not make affirmations of what it was that the Reform movement stood for, then it was better to abandon the whole effort rather than issue a paper that was hopelessly equivocal. Nevertheless, the resulting document stresses the movement's diversity. It is a strong statement of support by the Reform movement for the State of Israel and for the first time talks about Reform Jews' religious obligations, although it does not use the word *mitzvah*. The San Francisco centenary perspective does talk in much greater detail than ever before about the tension between Reform Jews' commitment to the Jewish people and their responsibilities to humanity as a whole.

In 1998, the CCAR President Richard Levy proposed a new platform to be voted on at the Pittsburgh Conference in May 1999, justifying the need for such a statement on the grounds that the religious world of the Reform Jew had changed so much since the 1976 statement. The cover story of the Winter, 1998, issue of *Reform Judaism* was titled, "Is It Time to Chart a New Course for Reform Judaism?" There Levy explained that it had been more than one hundred and ten years since the publication of the original Pittsburgh platform and that it was time to "chart a new course for our movement in the twenty-first century, just as the first Pittsburgh meeting defined Reform for much of the twentieth century. Strange as it might seem, despite the moderating influences of Columbus and the centenary perspective, the Pittsburgh platform of the nineteenth century continues to influence how we Reform Jews relate to Jewish tradition." The magazine also printed a draft of Levy's ten principles, which had also been sent to all the rabbis in the CCAR for their comments.[26]

Levy further argued that whereas the 1885 Pittsburgh Platform had argued that "the views and habits of modern civilization" should determine which

Jewish ceremonies are appropriate for the Reform Jew to observe, today there is a much greater desire on the part of many Reform Jews to "build more and more *mitzvot* into their lives." This was really the key theme of the new platform, especially in its first draft. Levy encouraged Reform Jews to consider observing more and more *mitzvot*, including those that had long been considered completely outside of the spectrum of normative Reform practice, such as *mikvah* and *tefillin*.

When *Reform Judaism* published the third draft of what was then called the "Ten Principles for Reform Judaism," along with a photo of Richard Levy wearing *tallit* and yarmulke, it unleashed a torrent of emotions. On the one hand, many people applauded the tone and substance of the proposed platform; on the other, many were distressed and saddened by what they felt was an abrogation of the historical positions of the Reform movement. In response to the large volume of comments, Levy, working with other CCAR leaders, produced a fourth draft, discussed at the December 1998, UAHC board meeting. At that meeting the feeling developed that it might indeed be possible to reach consensus on a new platform, based on the much more moderate tone of the fourth draft. A number of issues still caused certain members difficulty, among them the "challenge and practicality of urging the reading and speaking of Hebrew," the fact that the platform encouraged American Jewish immigration to Israel, and so forth.

Some of the responses to the article were quite harsh. As one woman from Mequon, Wisconsin, wrote, "Abandonment, hurt, outrage, violation, betrayal. These are just a few of the first words that came to mind after I read Rabbi Richard Levy's proposal. I ask Rabbi Levy: How much further does the Reform movement want to take the religion and faith away from their congregants?"[27] Another reader stated sarcastically, "It was quite a surprise to read the contents of Rabbi Levy's article. . . . I did have to check the cover to make sure it said winter 1998 and not winter 1698."[28] Others were very enthusiastic and, at the CCAR conference in Pittsburgh, "A Statement of Principles for Reform Judaism" was adopted in a majority vote by the rabbis present. Rabbi Paul J. Menitoff, executive vice president of the CCAR, stated, "On the eve of a new century, when so many individuals are striving for religious meaning, moral purpose and a sense of community, it is important that we have a modern set of principles that define and invite commentary on Reform Jewish belief and practice."[29]

Religious standards and the movement toward tradition

Reform Judaism today faces the same problem that has been both its strength and its weakness since its origins about two hundred years ago, the question of how a liberal religious movement sets standards, if indeed it can at all. Standards would give Reform Judaism more structure and allow people a clear vision of what being a Reform Jew means. Yet the movement has been very careful not to do anything that might indicate that it is moving toward fixed halakhic standards, even as it wants to move much more in the direction of tradition.

Rabbi Walter Jacob, the rabbi emeritus of Rodef Shalom Congregation in Pittsburgh, Pennsylvania, and a former president of the CCAR, writes in favor of standards. He argues that in many cases the richness and fullness of Jewish religious life has been lost in the Reform context because people have used the ideal of autonomy as an excuse to neglect an active involvement in their religion. Jacob argues that the theory of Reform Judaism was very noble in that it intended for people to exercise their autonomy in selecting the most uplifting elements of the Reform religious tradition: "No one can fault this ideal, but it has not worked. We need direction, standards – a system of mitzvot (ethical observances) – and halacha as we go beyond guidance to governance."

Indeed, the Reform movement over the last number of years has made an amazing turnabout in terms of embracing a much greater degree of tradition than would have been thought possible just a generation ago. Many classical Reform congregations that prohibited men from wearing yarmulkes now allow it and find an increasing percentage choosing to do so; many of the newer suburban Reform congregations find it the norm rather than the exception. The amount of Hebrew used in the service has increased dramatically, and many congregations are now observing two days of Rosh Hashanah instead of one. Many congregations are holding Saturday-morning services for the first time and almost all are marking bar and bat mitzvahs in addition to confirmation. Even the study of Talmud has become far more popular. Many other formerly abandoned rituals, such as ritual immersion in a *mikvah*, have been brought back with new religious or spiritual justifications. Although by no means all Reform Jews are practicing these rituals, substantial numbers of the elite and significant numbers of congregants, particularly in more progressive locations, are starting to investigate previously abandoned practices.

Parallel to the move toward tradition has been a move away from formalism and decorum toward informality and warmth. This has created a more "spiritual" religious ambience that contrasts dramatically with the "awe inspiring" atmosphere of classical Reform worship. Balfour Brickner, the rabbi emeritus at the Stephen Wise Free Synagogue in New York, said, "We are no longer God's most frozen people. Orderliness and strict dramatic decorum have finally given way to warmth."

Looking to the future

In a speech to Reform leaders at the Stephen Wise Free Synagogue in New York in April 1999, Eric Yoffie, President of the UAHC, admitted that the Reform Movement's twenty-year outreach program had not yet reached its potential. "We have not accomplished all that we should have," he said. "Let me say one final time to all those who ask that we change our direction: There will be no retreat in the Reform Movement from the principles or practice of outreach. North American Jews of all stripes want energetic outreach to intermarried Jews and Jews-by-choice in order to save them for the Jewish people."[30]

Yoffie is responding to the inreach–outreach debate in which a number of other community leaders have called on all segments of the Jewish community to devote the community's resources to inreach, that is, to reinforcing Jewish identity among those already moderately committed. Yoffie argues the reverse, that the Reform Movement intends to continue devoting substantial resources to trying to reach out to those already unaffiliated.

Among other things, Yoffie spoke of how many in the Reform movement had failed to urge non-Jewish spouses in Reform-affiliated intermarried couples to convert. He also admitted that the movement had failed to help Reform synagogue nursery school programs develop as much Jewish content as possible. "We provide no curricular assistance, no teacher training, no forum for exchange of ideas and problems. Incredibly, we have ignored an institution which . . . is best positioned to serve the young intermarried and unaffiliated population." Yoffie also stated that the Reform movement continued to be plagued by the problem of how to set standards for intermarried couples and their participation in Reform congregations. He argued that ". . . some Reform Jews still find it difficult to acknowledge that any limitation is consistent with Reform belief. A lowest-common-denominator/no-one-must-ever-be-hurt Judaism is not and has never been what outreach is about." On the other hand, Yoffie stated, "If the need for boundaries is our primary message, and if confronting others with endless demands is the thrust of our program, then we are lost and Judaism is doomed."

Notes

1   For historical background on the World Union for Progressive Judaism, see Michael A. Meyer, *Response to Modernity: A History of the Reform Movement in Judaism* (New York and Oxford, 1988), pp. 335–52.
2   *Reform Judaism News*, Spring 1999, no. 12, pp. 1–2.
3   See Jacob R. Marcus, *Israel Jacobson: The Founder of the Reform Movement in Judaism* (Cincinnati, 1971).
4   On the Frankfurt group, see Michael A. Meyer, "Alienated Intellectuals in the Camp of Religious Reform: The Frankfort Reform Freunde, 1842–1845," in *AJS Review*, vol. 6 (1981), pp. 61–86.
5   For background on American Judaism, see Jacob Neusner, *Introduction to American Judaism: What the Books Say, What the People Do* (Minneapolis, 1994); Marc Lee Raphael, *Profiles in American Judaism: The Reform, Conservative, Orthodox, and Reconstructionist Traditions in Historical Perspective* (San Francisco, 1986); and Jack Wertheimer, *A People Divided: Judaism in Contemporary America* (Hanover and London, 1997).
6   Lance J. Sussman, "Introduction," in Kerry M. Olitzky, Lance J. Sussman, and Malcolm H. Stern, eds., *Reform Judaism in America: A Biographical Dictionary and Sourcebook* (Westport, 1993), p. xv.
7   Ibid., p. xix.
8   On Congregation Beth Elohim, see Robert Liberles, "Conflict Over Reforms: The Case of Congregation Beth Elohim, Charleston, South Carolina," in Jack Wertheimer,

ed., *The American Synagogue: A Sanctuary Transformed* (Hanover and London, 1989), pp. 274–96.

9   Gary Phillip Zola, *Isaac Harby of Charleston, 1788–1828: Jewish Reformer and Intellectual* (Tuscaloosa and London, 1994).

10 This argument has been made by Hasia R. Diner, *A Time for Gathering: The Second Migration 1820–1880* (Baltimore and London, 1992), pp. 49–56.

11 Leon Jick, *The Americanization of the Synagogue, 1820–1870* (Hanover and London, 1992).

12 On German Jewish immigration to America, see Avraham Barkai, *Branching Out: German-Jewish Immigration to the United States, 1820–1914* (New York and London, 1994).

13 On Wise, see James G. Heller, *Isaac M. Wise: His Life, Work and Thought* (New York, 1965); and Sefton D. Temkin, *Isaac Mayer Wise: Shaping American Judaism* (Oxford, 1992).

14 Wise and Lilienthal both led congregations in Cincinnati, where they worked together closely. On Lilienthal's congregation, see Jonathan D. Sarna and Karla Goldman, "From Synagogue-Community to Citadel of Reform: The History of K. K. Bene Israel (Rockdale Temple) in Cincinnati, Ohio," in James P. Wind and James W. Lewis, eds., *American Congregations* (Chicago and London, 1994), vol. 1, pp. 159–220; see also Karla Goldman, "In Search of an American Judaism: Rivalry and Reform in the Growth of Two Cincinnati Synagogues," in Jeffrey S. Gurock and Marc Lee Raphael, eds., *An Inventory of Promises: Essays on American Jewish History in Honor of Moses Rischin* (Brooklyn, 1995), pp. 137–50.

15 On liturgical developments in American Reform, see Eric L. Friedland, *Were Our Mouths Filled with Song* (Cincinnati, 1997).

16 Michael A. Meyer, "Thank You, Moritz Loth: A 125-Year UAHC Retrospective," in *Reform Judaism*, Fall 1998, pp. 30–9.

17 See, for example, Aryeh Rubinstein, "Isaac Mayer Wise: A New Appraisal," in *Jewish Social Studies* (Winter–Spring 1977), vol. 39, nos. 1–2, pp. 53–74. Rubinstein concludes that "Wise's conservative pronouncements were only lip-service, while his rationalist, Deist-like statements represented his true opinions.... What makes Wise so complex is that his opportunism impelled him to cover his tracks" (p. 74).

18 Walter Jacob, ed., *The Changing World of Reform Judaism: The Pittsburgh Platform in Retrospect* (Pittsburgh, 1985). The Proceedings of the Conference appear on pp. 91–123.

19 On Felix Adler, see Benny Kraut, *From Reform Judaism to Ethical Culture: The Religious Evolution of Felix Adler* (Cincinnati, 1979).

20 Walter Jacob, "Prophetic Judaism: The History of a Term," in *Journal of Reform Judaism*, Spring 1979, pp. 33–46.

21 For an overview of this period, see Henry L. Feingold, *A Time for Searching: Entering the Mainstream 1920–1945* (Baltimore and London, 1992).

22 For a survey of this period, see Edward S. Shapiro, *A Time for Healing: American Jews since World War II* (Baltimore and London, 1992).

23 See Maurice N. Eisendrath, *Can Faith Survive? The Thoughts and Afterthoughts of an American Rabbi* (New York, 1964).

24 Eugene B. Borowitz, *Liberal Judaism* (New York, 1984).

25 Olitzky, Sussman and Stern eds., *Reform Judaism in America*, p. 23.

26   Aron Hirt-Manheimer, "Interview – Is It Time to Chart a New Course for Reform Judaism? Interview of Rabbi Richard Levy," in *Reform Judaism*, Winter 1998, pp. 10–22, 54.
27   Beth Sampson Bauer, letter to the editor, "Is It Time to Chart a New Course for Reform Judaism? Reactions," p. 4.
28   Henry A. Fribourg, "Is It Time to Chart a new Course for Reform Judaism? Reactions," p. 8.
29   CCAR press release, "North America's Reform Rabbis Adopt New Statement of Principles for Reform Judaism," May 26, 1999.
30   Eric J. Greenberg, "Yoffie Renews Call for Outreach," in *New York Jewish Week*, April 23, 1999, p. 23.

Bibliography

Barkai, Avraham, *Branching Out: German–Jewish Immigration to the United States, 1820–1914* (New York and London, 1994).

Borowitz, Eugene B., *Liberal Judaism* (New York, 1984).

Diner, Hasia R., *A Time for Gathering: The Second Migration 1820–1880* (Baltimore and London, 1992).

Eisendrath, Maurice N., *Can Faith Survive? The Thoughts and Afterthoughts of an American Rabbi* (New York, 1964).

Feingold, Henry L., *A Time for Searching: Entering the Mainstream 1920–1945* (Baltimore and London, 1992).

Friedland, Eric L., *Were Our Mouths Filled with Song* (Cincinnati, 1997).

Goldman, Karla, "In Search of an American Judaism: Rivalry and Reform in the Growth of Two Cincinnati Synagogues," in Jeffrey S. Gurock and Marc Lee Raphael, eds., *An Inventory of Promises: Essays on American Jewish History in Honor of Moses Rischin* (Brooklyn, 1995), pp. 137–50.

Heller, James G., *Isaac M. Wise: His Life, Work and Thought* (New York, 1965).

Jacob, Walter, ed., *The Changing World of Reform Judaism: The Pittsburgh Platform in Retrospect* (Pittsburgh, 1985).

Jacob, Walter, "Prophetic Judaism: The History of a Term," in *Journal of Reform Judaism*, Spring 1979, pp. 33–46.

Jick, Leon, *The Americanization of the Synagogue, 1820–1870* (Hanover and London, 1992).

Kraut, Benny, *From Reform Judaism to Ethical Culture: The Religious Evolution of Felix Adler* (Cincinnati, 1979).

Liberles, Robert, "Conflict Over Reforms: The Case of Congregation Beth Elohim, Charleston, South Carolina," in Jack Wertheimer, ed., *The American Synagogue: A Sanctuary Transformed* (Hanover and London, 1989), pp. 274–96.

Marcus, Jacob R., *Israel Jacobson: The Founder of the Reform Movement in Judaism* (Cincinnati, 1971).

Meyer, Michael A., "Alienated Intellectuals in the Camp of Religious Reform: The Frankfort Reform Freunde, 1842–1845," in *AJS Review*, vol. 6 (1981), pp. 61–86.

Meyer, Michael A., *Response to Modernity: A History of the Reform Movement in Judaism* (New York and Oxford, 1988).

Meyer, Michael A., "Thank You, Moritz Loth: A 125-Year UAHC Retrospective," in *Reform Judaism*, Fall 1998, pp. 30–9.

Neusner, Jacob, *Introduction to American Judaism: What the Books Say, What the People Do* (Minneapolis, 1994).

Raphael, Marc Lee, *Profiles in American Judaism: The Reform, Conservative, Orthodox, and Reconstructionist Traditions in Historical Perspective* (San Francisco, 1986).

Rubinstein, Aryeh, "Isaac Mayer Wise: A New Appraisal," in *Jewish Social Studies* (Winter–Spring 1977), vol. 39, nos. 1–2, pp. 53–74.

Sarna, Jonathan D., and Karla Goldman, "From Synagogue-Community to Citadel of Reform: The History of K. K. Bene Israel (Rockdale Temple) in Cincinnati, Ohio," in James P. Wind and James W. Lewis, eds., *American Congregations* (Chicago and London, 1994), vol. 1, pp. 159–220.

Shapiro, Edward S., *A Time for Healing: American Jews since World War II* (Baltimore and London, 1992).

Temkin, Sefton D., *Isaac Mayer Wise: Shaping American Judaism* (Oxford, 1992).

Wertheimer, Jack, *A People Divided: Judaism in Contemporary America* (Hanover and London, 1997).

Zola, Gary Phillip, *Isaac Harby of Charleston, 1788–1828: Jewish Reformer and Intellectual* (Tuscaloosa and London, 1994).

CHAPTER 18
Orthodox Judaism

Benjamin Brown

Orthodoxy (Greek: "true opinion") is a Jewish religious movement that advocates the full observance of Jewish religious law (the halakhah), interpreted in traditional ways, and is critical of modernity and its values. In its adherence to the laws, customs, and beliefs of the ancestors, Orthodoxy portrays itself as the faithful continuation of traditional Jewish society. In many ways, though, Orthodoxy should be regarded as a movement of the modern era, whose birth occurred toward the end of the eighteenth century, in reaction to the challenges posed by Reform, secularization, and assimilation in western and central Europe. In this setting, one sector of the Jewish population struggled to maintain the supremacy of halakhah in Jewish life. As the endeavor to preserve the society as a whole was doomed to fail, the efforts were focused on the protection of their own sector, yielding what now is called Orthodoxy.

Orthodox theology accepts the literal interpretation of traditional doctrines, such as the election of Israel, divine providence, reward and punishment in the world-to-come, and the future coming of the messiah. However, more than any specific dogma, it is the commitment to the full observance of the halakhah that has guided the creation of a separate Orthodox identity.

Orthodoxy asserts the divine source of the Torah and the eternal, unchanging nature of its laws. Seeing the law as a direct expression of God's will, Orthodox Judaism refuses to reduce the halakhah to historical, sociological, or psychological grounds. Unlike Conservative Judaism, Orthodoxy does not accept halakhic rulings based on such considerations. Orthodox theologians understand changes and developments in the halakhah not as new norms but rather as elaboration and realization of the existing ones. Accordingly, halakhic ruling is authoritative only when based on specific texts (i.e., the Talmud and traditional halakhic codes and commentaries) and issued by an authorized rabbi. The qualities required of the latter are thorough learning of the traditional texts, a deep conviction in the divine source of the Torah, and a sincere attempt to reach a true understanding of the law.

The Term "Orthodox"

The title "Orthodox" first appears in a Jewish context in the first half of the nineteenth century, in western Europe. It was coined by opponents of Orthodoxy who compared Jewish traditionalism to a parallel phenomenon in the Christian world. Only later did Orthodox Jews themselves adopt the term. Later in the nineteenth century, the term Neo-Orthodoxy was created to denote the moderate wing of Orthodoxy, which by then had emerged in Germany. In Hebrew texts up to the second half of the twentieth century the Orthodox refer to themselves as *Haredim* ("Men of Awe"), *Yereim* ("God-fearers"), or *Shlomei Emunei Israel* ("Israelites of Wholehearted Faith"). By the second half of the twentieth century, the latter two titles no longer denote a specific social group, while the term Haredim refers to the more extreme trend of Orthodoxy, sometimes titled Ultra-Orthodoxy. In the State of Israel, the designation *Datiyim* ("religious") denotes the Orthodox but recently is often used in reference to a specific trend of Orthodoxy, the Zionist-Religious (or: Modern-Orthodox), which is the contemporary moderate wing of the movement. Although some of the non-Orthodox, such as Reform and Conservative Jews, identify themselves as "religious," in colloquial Israeli speech the term *Datiyim* is almost synonymous with Orthodox.

History

Roughly speaking, Orthodoxy has experienced three main stages of development since the late eighteenth century. These reflect Orthodoxy's changing attitude toward competing forces in the larger Jewish society as well as the dynamic relations within its own wings.

The first stage: From the end of the eighteenth century to the end of the nineteenth century Orthodoxy is formed, first in Hungary and Germany and later in eastern Europe, each region responding differently to the challenges of modernity.

The second stage: From the late nineteenth century until the Holocaust, Orthodoxy moves toward uniformity in some religious practices but splits on the political question of Zionism.

The third stage: Following the establishment of the State of Israel in 1948, the attitude to Zionism becomes more than a political issue and engenders a deep social and religious schism, which splits Orthodoxy to two main trends: the Zionist-Religious (or Modern Orthodox) and the Haredi.

The First Stage

The end of the eighteenth century marks the beginning of a new age in the history of the Jewish people: the age of emancipation in western and central Europe. If in the preceding decades Jewish traditional society had begun to show signs of a forthcoming crisis, now, as the gates of the ghetto opened and Jews turned to take advantage of new professional, social, and intellectual opportunities, it seemed that traditional Jewish society had come to an end. Many Jews in western Europe converted to Christianity, others assimilated without any formal religious ceremony, while others sought a reformed Judaism that would adapt to contemporary values. These processes were often so rapid and sweeping that Rabbinic authorities found it almost hopeless to respond to those viewed as already lost to the community. Feeling that the preservation of Jewish traditional society as a whole was out of their reach, they focused on building a protective wall around the core of traditional Judaism – observance of the halakhah.

While in western and central Europe the process of modernization took rapid and radical forms, in Russia, where anti-Jewish laws prevailed until the Russian Revolution of February 1917, it emerged later and was more gradual and less oriented toward non-Jewish culture. The Orthodox reaction varied accordingly. Their common purpose notwithstanding, the rabbis of each geographical region adopted their own strategy in the fight to preserve the halakhah. We must, therefore, distinguish no fewer than three major Orthodox patterns of response to modernity: the Hungarian, the German, and, later, the eastern European.

Hungarian Jewry's most prominent rabbinical leader in the age of the crisis, Moshe Sofer, better known as the Hatam Sofer (1762–1839), led the first clear-cut Orthodox response to the challenges of modernity. Using the phrase a few times in his letters and responsa, he coined the motto that later became the banner of radical Orthodoxy: "*Haddash Asur min ha-Torah*" ("The new is forbidden by the Torah"). A paraphrase of M. Orlah 3:9, the statement expresses the conviction that the halakhah's protection demands more than mere observance of the law's positive norms. Rather, additional "fences" and stringencies are required, coupled with a prohibition against anything with a modern flavor. The Hatam Sofer rigorously opposed any change or reform and rejected involvement in western society and culture. He stressed the religious value of the Hebrew language and land of Israel, themes Reform circles pushed aside.

In comparison with Hungarian extremism, German Orthodoxy's response to modernity is conspicuously moderate. Already in the first third of the nineteenth century, German rabbis were prepared to accept the challenges of emancipation and welcome general culture, so long as observance of the halakhah was not disrupted. Rabbi Samson Raphael Hirsch (1808–88), leader of the Frankfurt Orthodox congregation, and Rabbi Esriel Hildesheimer (1820–99), leader of the Berlin Orthodox congregation, best represent this response to modernity. Their religious trend, known as Neo-Orthodoxy, adopted the motto "*Torah im Derekh-Eretz*" (approximately: "Torah and civilization," from M. Abot 2:2) and sought an ideal integration of religious and secular achievements. Hirsch's writings in particular advocate the belief that observant Judaism is entirely consistent with humanist values (see below).

This openness to modernity notwithstanding, Hirsch shared Hungarian Orthodoxy's unhesitating and uncompromising fight against the Reform movement. Orthodox leadership in both Hungary and Germany viewed Reform as undermining traditional Judaism and as a short and easy bridge to full assimilation. When German Reform Jews won power over important communal institutions, Orthodox leaders created a "separate community" (*Austrittsgemeinde*). Prominent leaders of Orthodoxy called their followers to break off with the general community and establish an independent community, based on a commitment to halakhah. Appropriate legislation on the part of the secular authorities, which had been achieved both in Hungary (1871) and in Germany (1876), facilitated this move. The policy of separation achieved a greater measure of success in Hungary, as many German Orthodox Jews continued to belong to the general community.

Modernity reached eastern Europe later than it did the West. Since the late eighteenth century and still in the first half of the nineteenth century, the primary conflict within eastern European Jewry was not between Orthodoxy and modernity but between the Hasidim and Mitnagdim. Both groups shared the values of traditional Judaism but differed over how to attain them. Beginning in the middle of the eighteenth century, Hasidism called for greater emphasis on spiritual and mystical experience among even common Jews, placing the mystical and charismatic master – the *Tzaddik* or *Rebbe* – in a central leadership position. The Mitnagdic reaction insisted that mysticism be pursued in an esoteric framework alone and maintained the traditional hierarchy of values, in which the study and observance of the halakhic texts are paramount. To promote Torah study, the Mitnagdim established the Volozhin Yeshiva (1802–92), the first yeshiva of the Lithuanian type, which soon became a stronghold of Mitnagdic scholarship and a model for later similar institutions. The conflict between Hasidim and Mitnagdim had significant social aspects: early Hasidism attracted many of the lower social and economic strata, while the Mitnagdim enjoyed the support of the elite segments of Jewish society.

Even before the appearance of modernity, the gaps between Hasidim and Mitnagdim had begun to diminish. In a rapid but thorough process, beginning in the early nineteenth century, Hasidism was gradually institutionalized, mystical experience was removed from its practical program, and mystical terminology was invested with more traditional significance. Hasidic leadership, originally attained through mystical and charismatic qualities, now passed on dynastically. By the end of the nineteenth century, the first Hasidic yeshivot were founded, largely following the model of Volozhin. Conversely, the Mitnagdim – called *Litvaks* (Lithuanians) – began to encourage a greater and richer expression of emotion and experience in religious life.

In the second half of the nineteenth century, Rabbi Israel Salanter (Lipkin) (1810–83) initiated a new movement within Mitnagdic Lithuanian society: the Musar movement, which championed the moral emendation of man's personality in addition to the traditional ideals of Torah study and the observance of the halakhah. Although it evoked some opposition, Musar affected the majority of Lithuanian yeshivot, and the debate over its ideas remained, in most cases, at a low level of intensity.

The struggle between Hasidim and Mitnagdim dominated eastern European Jewry for decades. Yet, as modernity advanced, the parties found themselves working together in the battle against the common adversary. Both parties developed a unique Orthodox response to modernity. Its uniqueness was not in what it was but rather in what it was not: The rabbis and rebbes of eastern Europe did not have an overall strategy, but an *ad hoc* approach, and, thus, they adopted neither the open Judaism of "Torah and civilization" nor the policy of "The new is forbidden by the Torah." They rejected even the concept of "separate community" common to both German and Hungarian Orthodox Jewries. Several prominent eastern European Orthodox leaders, such as the Head of the Volozhin Yeshiva, Rabbi Naphtali Tzvi Yehuda Berlin (1817–93), expressed their explicit opposition to the policy of separation, and a few Hasidic rebbes took a similar stand. However, the Hasidim, previously marked with an anti-establishment spirit and revolutionary ardor, now adopted the more conservative approach, sticking to the warm communities of *Anshei Shlomenu* (approximately: "Our men").

At the end of the nineteenth century, Orthodox Judaism was far from being religiously uniform. Only in the last decade of that century did the challenge of Zionism succeed in unifying Orthodox forces in several important matters, even as it set the stage for the great split of the next stage in the history of Orthodoxy.

The Second Stage

From the last decades of the nineteenth century until the Holocaust, Orthodox Judaism in both eastern and western Europe suffered a deepening crisis. Increasing numbers of Jewish youth abandoned religion for a secular way of life, many of them also joining secular political movements, the presence of which quickly dominated Jewish society. Many of them perceived Orthodoxy as an archaic remnant of the past and scorned adherence to an anachronistic way of life. The rapid deterioration caused a trauma that influenced the Orthodox experience for generations.

Toward the end of the nineteenth century, Orthodoxy developed increasingly uniform religious patterns and sought social and political structures that would unite its various groups. With time, this tendency toward relative internal conformity and unification increased its hold in Orthodox life. In eastern Europe, Rabbi Israel Meir Ha-Cohen, known as the Hafetz Hayyim (1839[?]–1933), was recognized by almost all Orthodox groups as a paragon religious figure. He, in return, viewed the different Orthodox groups with favor: Himself a Litvak, the Hafetz Hayyim appreciated Hasidism; not a member of the Musar movement, he sympathized with the latter's goals, but also was respectful of some of its opponents. No less than his scholarship, it was possibly the Hafetz Hayyim's personality that made his book, the *Mishnah Brurah*, on the laws of everyday life, the major halakhic source for most Orthodox Jews.

While Orthodox Judaism moved only gradually toward uniformity, the fact that a single text gained such wide acceptance reflects the search for greater uniformity and unity among the various groups. On a political level as well, Orthodox Jewry sought a single framework that would unite it. Some of these attempts (such as the *Mahzikei Ha-Dat* party, founded in 1878) achieved partial success. A more complete success, however, was achieved only later, in the face of the challenge of Zionism.

Zionism, the most influential and significant of Jewish nationalist movements in modern times, officially focused on the fight for a Jewish national home. Behind the political idea, however, no few Jews (both partisans and opponents of the movement) discerned in Zionism a new basis for Jewish identity, an identity based on national – i.e., secular – components like land, language, and culture. In this respect, Zionism, though claiming indifference to religion, was conceived as a threat to Judaism. Indeed, it facilitated some Jews' break with Judaism even as it was a path that kept others within the community.

Two important Orthodox political frameworks were created in response to Zionism, one partisan, the other in opposition, and both presumed to cross the boundaries of group distinctions within Orthodoxy. In 1902, Rabbi Isaac Jacob Reines (1840–1915) founded the Mizrachi movement, a Zionist-religious party that was integrated into the greater Zionist organization and participated in its activity. Except for its early stages, the Mizrahi movement failed to gain the support of influential rabbis and spiritual leaders, most of whom remained suspicious of Zionism. In 1912, Agudat Israel, another all-Orthodox political framework, was founded, this time in order to counter Zionism.

Although German–Jewish laymen (the most active of whom was Jacob Rosenheim [1870–1965] of Frankfurt), and not rabbis, established Agudat Israel, the movement drew to its ranks some of the foremost east European religious personalities. The Hafetz Hayyim and rabbi Avraham Mordechai Alter (1866–1948), the third rebbe of Gur, the largest Hasidic group, both expressed their support for Agudat Israel. The bulk of the Hungarian Orthodox leaders, though, remained suspicious of this "new" phenomenon.

Several important Hungarian Hasidic rebbes argued that Agudat Israel was both too moderate and too innovative. The extremists' criticism could be harsh. One of them, Rabbi Hayyim Elazor Shapiro (1872–1937), the rebbe of Munkacs, for example, saw Agudat Israel as one with secular Zionism and Mizrahi, both of which he detested. But despite the resistance it faced, Agudat Israel offered an Orthodox common denominator that contributed to the consolidation of Orthodoxy. In need of a supervising spiritual body, Agudat Israel established

Moetzet Gedolei ha-Torah ("The Council of Great Torah Masters"), recognizing the authority of leading rabbis even on issues that were not explicitly halakhic. This was explained by the doctrine that the rabbis of the Council were credited with great personal virtues and an ability to internalize not only the words of the Torah but also its spirit (*Da'at Torah*). In addition to the political struggle, Agudat Israel took several significant initiatives in Orthodox literature, and press. Despite these achievements, it was unable to suggest a concrete, definite solution for the problems at stake (growing anti-Semitism etc.), thus failing to present a real alternative to the Zionist program.

Agudat Israel viewed the Zionist program as a danger: Its leaders saw the proposed Jewish state as merely an instrument of the Zionists' aspiration to secularize Jewish identity. This shift in the foundation of identity meant – as some Haredi leaders asserted – the creation of a "new Jew," whose Jewishness was detached from religion. Indeed, the intention to create such a "new Jew" arose from the writings of several Zionist ideologists. The fact that the Zionist leadership was secular lent great weight to this argument. Some rabbis added another justification for the anti-Zionistic stance, the notion that Judaism forbids the establishment of a Jewish sovereign state before the coming of the messiah. This latter argument reached its full intensity only later, after the Holocaust, in the teachings of Satmar Hasidism (see below).

Because of these reasons, Haredi leaders did not encourage their adherents to move to the land of Israel, and some even firmly objected to emigration. No less did they discourage emigration to the United States, a country in which the full observance of the halakhah was rare and difficult.

The early twentieth century also witnessed the evolution of the Zionist-religious movement. In the land of Israel, the chief rabbinate was founded in 1921, under the auspices of the British Mandate, and contemporary Zionist-religious leaders expected the new body to play an important role in the antici-pated Jewish state. Rabbi Abraham Isaac Kook (1865–1935), appointed the first chief rabbi, believed that the Zionist enterprise of settling and rebuilding the Holy Land constituted *At'halta di-Geula* ("The Commencement of Redemp-tion"). He perceived the secular Zionist pioneers' rebellious atheism as part of a complex dialectical process of history, destined to purge traditional Judaism of defects it acquired during the exile and to prepare it for its ultimate messianic purpose (more on this below). These views of Rabbi Kook were considered very eccentric at the time. Extremist Haredim, members of the Old Yishuv (the Jewish population that preceded the Zionist immigrations), accused him of subverting their struggle against the Zionist secularization of the Holy Land and opposed him bitterly.

The Old Yishuv was now the main pillar of Haredi anti-Zionism. During the 1920s, its members collaborated with Agudat Israel. By 1927, however, they organized the Jerusalem *Eidah Haredit*, "the Haredi Community," an independent social and political framework inspired by the separate communities in Hungary. During the 1930s, relations between the *Eidah Haredit* and Agudat Israel deteri-orated and precipitated a crisis within the Haredi ranks. Following the death of the Hafetz Hayyim (1933), Agudat Israel was characterized by a growing ambivalence. On the one hand, party functionaries were increasingly bound to take a pragmatic line towards Zionism, and their policy was spiritually backed by Rabbi Hayyim Ozer Grodzhensky (1863–1940), the head of *Moetzet Gedolei ha-Torah*. On the other hand, the influential Rabbi Elhanan B. Wassermann (1875–1941) wrathfully preached for a dogmatic hard line.

Considering themselves the spearhead of the anti-Zionist struggle and feeling betrayed by Agudat Israel, the *Eidah Haredit* increasingly relied on its alliance with extremist Hungarian rabbis. In about 1936, several young militant members of the Jerusalem *Eidah Haredit* founded a group of *Kano'im* ("Zealots") with a particularly radical line, including use of moderate violence in the fight against the Zionist political establishment. This group was later named *Neturei Karta* ("Guardians of the City"). In spite of its meager membership, it attracted considerable public attention. Through demonstrations against the violation of the Sabbath in Jerusalem and other acts of protest, it exercised influence on other Haredi circles, who were now emboldened in their opposition to the secular state.

Orthodoxy of this period, then, was marked by two parallel, opposing trends. As *religious* differences between its various groups were put aside (though preserved), mainly in order to maintain a unified front against the Zionist enterprise, the *political* question of Zionism increasingly divided the Orthodox ranks. It is important to emphasize that at this stage, the controversy within Orthodoxy over Zionism was chiefly political and had not yet developed into a deeper split with religious and social implications, as occurs in the next period.

The Third Stage

World War II and the Holocaust devastated Orthodox Judaism along with the rest of European Jewry. Along with the physical destruction, the Nazi occupation of eastern Europe eradicated the great Orthodox centers, yeshivas, and Hasidic rebbe-courts, and, with few exceptions, Orthodoxy's spiritual leadership perished. The Holocaust also presented Orthodox theology with especially painful and difficult questions.

The anti-Zionist Orthodox, the Haredim, additionally had to face their own unique ideological crisis. Zionists reminded Haredim of their prewar objection to emigration to Palestine, and some even accused Haredi leaders of responsibility for the deaths of their followers. Haredi leaders who had fled Europe in time were condemned for abandoning their followers. Zionist politicians, religious and secular alike, further claimed repeatedly that the destruction of European Jewry provided hard proof that the diaspora had never been a viable option for the Jews. The fact that the Nazis did not conquer the land of Israel was seen as evidence that Zionism had the right diagnosis. The propaganda was effective, even as it ignored the facts that Nazi troops had been very close to conquering Palestine and that their failure to do so had nothing to do with Zionism.

Accusations were made in both directions, however, and following the Holocaust some Haredi leaders – such as Rabbi Jacob Israel Kanievsky (1899–1985) and Rabbi Yekutiel Yehuda Halberstamm, the rebbe of Zans-Klausenburg (1904–94), attributed indirect responsibility for the Holocaust to the "lawless," that is, assimilated, Reform and secular Jews. The drive to imitate the gentiles, they claimed, only increased anti-Semitism. Germany, the birthplace of Jewish enlightenment and Reform, they pointed out, served also as the home of Nazism, and not coincidentally.

Still, Haredi anti-Zionist doctrine suffered a further blow in 1947, when the United Nations accepted the resolution on the Partition of Palestine, recognizing Jews' right to establish their independent state in the land of Israel. Half a year later, the state of Israel was declared, and Zionism appeared to have won the battle against all its opponents. Following these developments, Orthodoxy divided into two opposing camps. A new Zionist Orthodoxy interpreted the birth of the State as a realization of a divine promise. The great immigrations to the new State and the surprising military victories in the War of Independence (1948–9) strengthened this messianic view of the period. One prominent political leader of this camp, Rabbi Yehuda Leib Maimon (Fischmann) (1875–1962), even called for a renewal of the Sanhedrin, and many Orthodox Zionists believed that the dawn of redemption had arrived. Thus Zionist Orthodoxy joined secular authorities in building the fledgling state. A military draft, efforts to settle the land, and the promotion of the new *Sabra* identity took on a religious significance and were incorporated into a Zionist Orthodox theology, which took shape in a new religious group, known as "Zionist-Religious" (*Dati-Tzioni*) or "National-Religious" (*Dati-Le'umi*).

In the United States, too, a new "Modern Orthodoxy," in many ways similar to its Israeli counterpart, emerged after the Holocaust. Beginning in the early fifties, Modern Orthodoxy accepted the guidance of Rabbi Joseph Baer Soloveitchik (1903–93). Following the Holocaust, Rabbi Soloveitchik, previously a member of the Agudat Israel spiritual leadership, crossed the lines to Modern Orthodoxy. Introducing existentialist motifs into his theology (see below), he portrayed a new ideal of Jewish believer. Rabbi Soloveitchik attributed the foundation of the state of Israel, right after the Holocaust, to providence and interpreted it as God's call to the people to reaffirm the covenant. Even several moderate non-Zionists in Agudat Israel circles spoke about the events of the time in messianic terms, but their voices were quite sparse.

In Israel, non-Zionist Orthodox Jews, now called Haredim, followed the leadership of Rabbi Avraham Yeshayahu Karelitz, known as the Hazon Ish (1878–1954). The Hazon Ish found dialogue with the secular society useless. "How can we ever talk to them" – he is alleged to have said – "if we don't even have a common language? – what they call 'love' we call *Karet* (approximately: 'That soul shall be cut off from God's people')." Objecting to the new State's image as the defender of Jewish existence, the Hazon Ish was skeptical of Israel's chances at survival and feared that Zionism aimed to root out Jewish religion. According to him and his doctrinal partners, the Torah alone had preserved the

Jewish people during two thousand years in exile, and the Torah alone could guarantee survival in the future. Putting one's confidence in a fragile and perilous human experiment was a terrible mistake. Some of his co-believers, among them the head of the Ponivezh Yeshiva in Bnei-Brak, Rabbi Wassermann (who perished in the Holocaust), and Rabbi Eleazar Menahem M. Shach (born 1898[?]), even labeled Zionism a modern form of idolatry (see below).

The Hazon Ish held that the destruction of East European Jewry required that Haredi Judaism devote all its efforts and resources to a single goal, rebuilding the world of Torah in the land of Israel. "We have no other remnant but this Torah," Haredi leaders quoted from the penitential liturgy. In order to realize the Hazon Ish's vision, Agudat Israel in Israel worked tirelessly to secure State support for their educational projects, especially for new yeshivot, and secured an arrangement that exempted yeshiva students from military service. Haredi society adopted study in a *kolel*, a Torah institution for married men, as the single preferred occupation for adult males, and the institutions proliferated. Haredi educators encouraged women to prefer marriage to a full-time Torah scholar over a man who worked for a living. In addition to accepting the traditional responsibilities of a Jewish wife, Haredi women now were expected to enter the workforce to enable their husbands to continue learning.

Unlike the Ashkenazim, Sepharadic Jews had lived in traditional Jewish societies until the 1940s. The modernization in these areas was moderate and unideological, so no Orthodox reaction was needed. Only in Israel were Sepharadic Jews abruptly exposed to anti-religious sentiment and rapid secularization, as young Sepharadic immigrants were sent to Kibbutzim and immigrant-camps. In response, in the early 1950s, Israeli Lithuanian yeshivot began to open their doors – though in allotted numbers – to sons of Sepharadic immigrants. Coming from such a different cultural and religious background, Sepharadic youth did not always adapt well to these institutions and often were not treated equally. Despite this difficulty, these young men would decades later provide rabbinical and political leadership of the Sepharadic Haredi Judaism, which now forms a distinct and significant group within Israeli Orthodoxy.

While mainstream Haredi Orthodoxy, politically represented by Agudat Israel, made the pragmatic decision to work with the state, extremist Haredi groups still refused even to accept the State's existence. Beginning in the 1950s, the Satmar Hasidim, who have since grown into the largest Hasidic community in the world, provided the leadership for extreme anti-Zionism. Satmar's rebbe, Joel Teitelbaum (1886–1979), preached that the very foundation of the Jewish state – regardless of the state's nature – constituted a revolt against the kingdom of God (see below). His community in the United States, large and wealthy, provided both economical and moral-ideological support for the Jerusalem *Eidah Haredit*. These anti-Zionist groups refused to participate in any of the State's institutions.

By the early 1950s, the Haredi Orthodoxy and the Zionist-Religious Orthodoxy had evolved into two separate movements. At this stage they not only differed on political issues but followed different, often contradictory, religious worldviews and ways of life. Haredim and religious Zionists differed in almost every facet of life: in the choice of clothing, language, place of residence, educational institutions, attitude toward secular culture, depth and scope of Torah learning, readiness to obtain secular learning and university education, approach to military service, age of marriage, size of the family, woman's status in family and society, vocation and sources of living, identity of rabbinical leaders and their status in society, degree of preserving interior distinctions based in traditional Jewish society, political parties, and a long list of other factors. In all of these, Zionist-Religious Orthodoxy adopted elements of modern culture and expressed a strong desire to integrate into Israeli society, while the Haredim harbored a growing hostility toward western culture and its ideas.

But the most outstanding difference between the Religious Zionists and the Haredim lay in the diverging attitudes towards halakhic observance: While many of the former adopted a lenient, sometimes heedless, approach to the precepts, especially to ritual ones, the latter followed them punctiliously, and their rabbis produced increasingly stringent halakhic decisions. The difference is manifested in the two groups' dress codes. Haredim have preserved the traditional dress of their European ancestors, while Zionist-Religious Jews wear more or less the same clothes as secular Israelis. Haredi men generally wear a white shirt, long black trousers, black upper-coat (a long garment for most of the Hasidim; a short jacket for most of the Lithuanians), black hat, and bearded face. Conversely, the crocheted skullcap for men has become a symbol of Zionist-Religious Judaism, and relatively few Modern Orthodox Jews grow beards. Haredi women refrain from trousers, wear modest dresses, and, after marriage, cover their head with a tightly fitting cloth or wig. Zionist-Religious women observe a more lenient standard of modesty.

Additionally, Zionist-Religious Judaism has suffered fewer internal divisions than the Haredim. While the vast array of Haredi splinter groups mirrors the diversities of pre-Holocaust diaspora Jewry, the Modern Orthodox differ primarily on how best to apply the Zionist-Religious ideology to the particular problems of the present.

In the United States, as in Israel, Orthodoxy defied those who predicted its decline and grew to become a significant (though minority) force in postwar American Jewry. The divisions between the Modern and Haredi Orthodox in America were more elusive and less bitter than those in Israel. American Orthodoxy, too, established yeshivot. The largest of these, the Lakewood Yeshiva, was established by Rabbi Aharon Kotler (1892–1962) and became the world's largest Torah institution. But relatively few young men pursued full-time yeshiva-studies after marriage. This is probably one of the reasons American Haredi Judaism remained relatively open to the surrounding society. Moderate American halakhic scholars, such as Rabbi Moshe Feinstein (1895–1986), moved their followers away from the stringencies of their Israeli colleagues. Besides, in America, the ideological debate over Zionism and the State was less divisive and more theoretical. Only in the eighties did the American Orthodox community polarize along Israeli lines.

The generation following the Six-Day War (1967) witnessed the development of three new forces in Orthodox Jewry: the worldwide Habad (Lubavitch) Hasidism, the Israeli Gush Emunim party, and the Israeli Shas movement, which represents Sepharadic Haredi Judaism.

Habad Hasidism was established in the late eighteenth century but remained relatively small until the twentieth century, when, under the leadership of Rebbe Menahem Mendel Schneersohn (1902–94), it took on a new form. Schneersohn developed a strategy of relative openness towards the modern secular world and dedicated great resources to the dissemination of the Hasidic message. Habad recruited to its ranks large numbers of Ba'alei Teshuvah ("repentant Jews"), and, unlike other Hasidic groups, exerted an influence on Jewish consciousness far beyond its own membership. The messianic tension that had characterized this movement since the Holocaust, exploded in the late 1980s with the claim that Schneersohn himself was to be revealed as the messiah. Habad's messianic fervor, combined with its populist and open approach, brought the movement into conflict with other Haredi circles. Rabbi E. M. M. Shach, the leader of Lithuanian Orthodoxy, led the opposition to Habad. Schneersohn's death in 1994 brought a debate between those who accepted his death and those who clung to a messianic faith that he would return.

The Zionist-Religious Gush Emunim follow the doctrine of Rabbi Zvi Yehudah Kook, Rabbi A. I. Kook's son, and interpret Israel's victory in the Six-Day War as realization of his father's messianic expectations. Opposing concession of the territories occupied in the war, Gush Emunim built new settlements in the controversial areas of Judea and Samaria and exerted political influence, pushing Religious-Zionist Orthodoxy to the right on the Israeli political map.

The third group, of utmost significance, that has started to play a role since the eighties is Sepharadic Haredi Judaism, politically represented by the Shas party. Shas was created to improve the status of Sephardim within Haredi society, heretofore dominated by Ashkenazim. While, when founded, Shas received the blessings of both the Ashkenazic and Sepharadic leading rabbis, a dispute between the two was only a matter of time, leaving Shas to turn away from the Ashkenazic Rabbi Shach to prefer the spiritual guidance of the Sepharadic halakhic genius, Rabbi Ovadiah Yosef (b. 1920). This move tore Shas away from the Haredi Ashkenazic world but enabled it to earn unprecedented popular support as an ethnic-traditionalist movement. In the nineties, apart from the growth of its parliamentary power, Shas has become a major factor in the growing process of *hitkarvut* (return) to religion among Sepharadic Israelis.

The fluctuations in Israeli society affected some of the developments in both Orthodox camps, including the relationship between the two. The traumatic Yom Kippur War (1973) caused a change in the Israelis' self-image and cooled the ideological passion of secular Zionism. This, as well as the economic growth, made Israeli society adopt many of the "normal" goals it perceived in its western counterparts. The Israel–Egypt peace treaty (1978), in which Israel undertook to evacuate and rip down settlements in the Sinai, the opposition to the Lebanon War (1982), and the Israeli-Palestinian Oslo talks initiated by the

Rabin government in 1992, in which Israel agreed to withdraw from great parts of Judea and Samaria, increased Religious-Zionists' disappointment with secular Zionism. Their bitter ideological wing interpreted the change as a betrayal of a common "holy" cause, and has begun a revision of several sections of its ideology. The messianic rhetoric of its founders was mitigated, and the objection to withdrawal was now defended through pragmatic arguments of national security. The debate escalated in 1995, when a Zionist-Religious university student assassinated Prime Minister Rabin, an unprecedented event in Israeli history. Despite overall Orthodox condemnation of the act, it caused a strong anti-Orthodox wave in Israeli secular society.

The new generation of the Haredim, on the other hand, was already born into a situation in which the Zionist state is not only an existing fact, but a place of thriving Haredi religious life and education. Many of them could no longer be indifferent to Israel's fate, and felt a part of it in their hearts if not in their official ideology. The feelings of solidarity were strengthened as the Haredim entered the government coalition (1977), after two and a half decades of refraining from such a step. These moves have begun to cause a tendency of relative openness in the Haredi camp, but the growing tensions between them and secular Israelis have kept them constantly on the defensive, which has balanced this tendency. The secularists' accusations have focused mainly on the fact that most of the Haredi men are not drafted to the army and do not take an active part in the national workforce, while accepting state handouts for their educational institutions, thus increasing the Israeli taxpayer's burden. The Haredim, on their part, argue that their Torah learning guarantees Jewish continuity no less, and even more, than the secularists' corporeal activities, and therefore the secularists also benefit from it, even if they don't recognize its importance (see below). Taking active part in these corporeal activities, most of the Zionist-Religious share the secular criticism.

The deterioration in the relationship between religious and secular Jews in Israel was a defeat for the Zionist-Religious way and shook their self-confidence. The Haredim, on the other hand, lacking any messianic expectations of the state of Israel and harboring no illusions about a partnership with the secular Israelis, strengthened their self-confidence. Another fact contributed to these feelings. The Zionist Orthodoxy values its ability to function as a bridge between religious and secular Israelis. Their openness to secular society had a cost, as many Zionist-Religious young people abandoned religious observance. Conversely, the Haredim could proudly note that they almost totally blocked such losses, even as they attracted *Ba'alei Teshuva* (= "repentants") to their ranks. Haredim have always mocked Zionist Orthodoxy's self-definition, and often quote the sarcastic remark misattributed to the Hazon Ish and actually stated by rabbi E. B. Wassermann: "A real bridge is used both for those who come back and those who go forth. Yet this one [= the Zionist-Religious] serves only those who go forth" (a pun in Hebrew: come back = repent; go forth = transgress, sin).

The relative moderation in the Haredi camp and the embracing of stricter standards of halakhic observance and Torah scholarship in the Zionist-Religious camp could pave the road for reunification of the two. Actually, a very limited rapprochement has been felt in recent years, most of it during the Rabin government period, when the Zionist-Religious Israelis' disappointment with secular Zionism was at its peak. However, in spite of crises, the Religious-Zionists are deeply involved with the secular Israeli society, from which the Haredim so incisively isolated themselves, and the two camps' common commitment to halakhah does not seem to be a sufficient platform on which the cultural and religious gaps could be bridged. Today Haredi and Zionist-Religious Jews view each other with growing respect, and in both camps there are some who wish to strengthen the ties, but the voices of those who oppose the alliance seem to be stronger. The relationship between the two is, therefore, unstable, and a full unification remains remote.

While most Orthodox Jews live in either Israel or America, every large Jewish center in the world today includes a sizeable Orthodox contingent. Although there are no hard statistics on Orthodox numbers in the worldwide Jewish population, recent (1999) assessments based on surveys from the early 1990s place the number of American Orthodox Jews above 400,000 of a total Jewish population of about 5,800,000. Of the approximately 4,600,000 Jews living in Israel, more than 20 percent identify as Orthodox, a third of them Haredim. Yet, these numbers are unreliable, as many Jews fall between the conventional categories of religious identity. The recent emergence of Shas in particular has clouded the boundaries between "traditional," religious, and Haredi Israelis. An additional 500,000 Orthodox Jews live dispersed around the world in Jewish centers such as France, Britain, Belgium, and Australia.

The flight from Orthodoxy to a more secular life-style, which devastated the movement in the first half of the century, has been checked and in some cases reversed. As the birth rate among Orthodox Jews (especially Haredim) is significantly higher than among other sectors of the Jewish population, and as non-Orthodox Jewish populations are diminished by assimilation, the percentage of Jews who identify as Orthodox is assumed to be growing.

Halakhah and Religious Practice

The observance of religious law, the halakhah, has generally been the main indicator of Orthodox identity. Although Orthodoxy has produced a rich literature in several religious fields (theology and biblical commentary, religious ethics, etc.), the study of halakhah (including talmudic novellae) has remained the field on which the Orthodox religious elite focuses most of its intellectual resources.

The fundamental Orthodox tenet sees the halakhah as eternally valid and forever unchanging. This commitment notwithstanding, during the nineteenth and twentieth centuries, Orthodoxy initiated several changes in the interpretation of the law. It is noteworthy that interest in questions of civil law (*Hoshen*

Mishpat) declined over the years and was addressed mainly in theoretical discussions. Instead, questions regarding daily ritual (*Orah Hayyim*) dominated Jewish legal discussion.

Orthodoxy has reshuffled its priorities regarding halakhic decision making. Preserving the legal system's stability has become a primary component of Rabbinic rulings, pushing aside almost any competing value. In the Hungarian Orthodox Halakhic tradition, the struggle for the very survival of the halakhic system has led to far-reaching *humras* ("stringent rulings"), while in the German tradition of Neo-Orthodoxy (in which prominent halakhists were few), the same concern has had an opposite effect, resulting in significant *kulas* ("lenient rulings"). Prewar eastern European halakhic tradition – definitely the richest and most impressive in Orthodoxy – succeeded in preserving both trends, side by side. The formation of the new Haredism in the third stage of Orthodox history emphatically advanced the tendency towards stringency, especially due to the Hazon Ish's strong influence. He wrote explicitly that in any case of doubt, one should prefer the *Humra*.

The question of the status of custom (*minhag*) as a source of law provides an illuminating example of the different approaches to halakhah within Orthodoxy. Custom has always functioned as one of the law's recognized normative sources ("*Minhag Israel Toran*," that is, "the custom of Israel is law"), but, over the generations, halakhic masters have disagreed regarding the significance of *minhag* in relation to other normative sources of law. Neo-Orthodox halakhah expressed willingness to abandon some customs not firmly anchored in the halakhic literature, if these hindered Jewish participation in modern social and economic life. Even Neo-Orthodox rabbis, though, firmly defended customs that had been attacked by Reform movements. Hungarian Orthodox halakhah, on the other hand, treated customs – insofar as they embodied *humras* – as a foremost halakhic source. Lithuanian halakhists evaluated each custom individually. In principle, the view of *minhag* was favorable, but since many popular conventions ceased to reflect an *opinio juris* of religious observance, only customs anchored in the legal literature and expressing an authorized rabbinical opinion were accepted as normatively binding.

Zionist settlement activity raised new halakhic problems for Orthodoxy, and the response to individual questions often reflected the attitude of a specific halakhic master to the Zionist enterprise as a whole. The question of halakhic authority – largely a moot question in the diaspora, as each community adopted its own authority without state intervention – thus rose to the forefront of halakhic dispute. Immediately after the establishment of the Palestine Chief Rabbinate in 1921, Zionist-Religious Jews hailed the chief rabbis as the supreme Jewish religious authority in the land. Members of the Old Yishuv, however, perceived it as an "Official Rabbinate" and refused to obey the new body; no few Haredi immigrants to Palestine followed the same path.

Another contested halakhic issue concerned the laws of the Sabbatical year, the principle that every seventh year the land must be left uncultivated (Lev. 25:1–7; Deut. 15:1–6). The prohibition, if observed, could have caused the economic collapse of religious settlements. Rabbi A. I. Kook, chief rabbi of Palestine and the paramount pro-Zionist halakhic thinker in the first decades of the twentieth century, accepted a halakhic construction known as *Heter ha-Mekhirah* ("Permission to Sell"). In cases of necessity, Kook suggested, Jews could formally "sell" their land to non-Jews (while continuing to work it themselves), thus avoiding the Sabbatical restrictions, which apply to Jewish-owned land alone. Haredi rabbis, later headed by the Hazon Ish, attacked this as a transparent and unacceptable legal fiction. The controversy continues today, each seven years, as the chief rabbinate extends the permissive ruling. Haredi Jews buy agricultural goods from Jewish farmers only if they were grown in areas outside the territory of (ancient) Israel. Similar disputes arose regarding the prohibition of milking cows on the Sabbath (where Rabbi Kook took a surprisingly stringent stand) and other agricultural issues.

Haredi and Zionist-Religious rabbis clashed over the halakhic authority of the state, its laws and institutions. Although the Talmud affirms that *Dina de-Malkhuta Dina* ("the law of the kingdom is law"), extremist Haredi rabbis, such as the rebbe of Satmar, vehemently objected to the application of this principle to "the Kingdom of Heresy." More moderate Haredi rabbis acknowledged partial authority of the State, not so much in recognition of the halakhic status of the "Kingdom" but because some of Israel's laws attained the status of "custom." Zionist-Religious rabbis, on the other hand, apply the Talmudic injunction almost indiscriminately. Attempts made by Zionist-Religious rabbis, such as Chief Rabbi Yitzhak Isaac Herzog (1889–1959), to legislate new halakhic regulations (*Takkanot*) and reconcile the halakhah with the State's laws were firmly rejected by the Hazon Ish and other conservative halakhists.

Whatever their original intent, in both Modern and Haredi Orthodoxy, certain fragments of western legal doctrine penetrated the halakhah. In ancient halakhah, for example, there were no legal persons other than human beings. When modern company law recognized corporations as legal persons, rabbis had to determine whether these are also recognized by the halakhah. Most of the rabbis responded negatively, perceiving an incorporeal legal body as a means for frauds and deceptions, but some did recognize it to a limited extent and for specific purposes. The question as a whole has not yet been conclusively determined.

The question of military service also presented religious thinkers with several controversial halakhic issues. Regarding women, almost all halakhic masters agreed that the State's attempt to draft them into military service contradicts the halakhah. Some Haredi rabbis (including the Hazon Ish) went so far as to rule that such a law, if accepted, would constitute a *Gzeirat Shmad* ("an ordinance of forceful transgression"), in response to which the halakhah commands: "One should be killed rather than transgress." Zionist-Religious politicians suggested a compromise, that Orthodox women be drafted into a non-military "national service." While some Zionist-Religious rabbis accepted the arrangement, the Haredim insisted that all Orthodox women be fully exempted from any form of service. Similarly, with almost no precedent in the classic halakhic literature, the military service of men raised halakhic questions. On the whole, the Zionist-Religious camp has adopted a creative, sometimes impressive, approach. In particular, Rabbi Shlomo Goren (1917–95), chief rabbi of the military and later of Israel, adopted a systematic approach to solving such purely modern halakhic questions. Haredi rabbis, by contrast, have virtually ignored these issues, in part due to their ideological opposition to the State, and, in part, because the issues rarely arise within their community, as most of the Haredim are exempted from draft.

Orthodox rabbis of both movements (Haredim even more than their Modern Orthodox counterparts) have written authoritative responsa on issues of modern technology, especially in the field of medicine, regarding such matters as artificial insemination, limb transplants, and euthanasia. Some, like Rabbi Moshe Feinstein, have exhibited a consistent willingness to accept the advantages of technology. Among the Sepharadic halakhic masters, Rabbi Ovadiah Yosef's rulings also are conspicuously lenient in everyday-life questions. However, when problems raise social and value-ridden issues, most Haredi rabbis rule stringently, casting themselves as guardians against fissures in the wall of resistance to modernity. Deep differences broke out, for instance, regarding the halakhic status of the secular Jew. Most Orthodox rabbis identify non-observant Jews as *Tinok she-Nishba* ("a captured infant"), that is, as Jews uprooted from Judaism since early childhood, who cannot be held fully responsible for transgressing the precepts. Haredi halakhists, however, still tend to deprive secular Jews of certain halakhic rights, while Zionist-Religious rabbis try to treat them with more equality.

The changing status of women in the western world has affected Orthodox Jews of almost all circles. In Zionist-Religious society, many women no longer focus exclusively on the household and child-rearing but pursue university education and professional careers. Even Haredi women join the workforce, but, while Zionist-Religious rabbis sometimes champion the recent changes in the status of women, Haredi rabbis merely tolerate them given the circumstances.

In light of the changes, not only secular spheres, but also religious ones, have become open to women. The most important is Torah-learning. In recent decades, the medieval halakhic prohibition against women's studying Torah has been abrogated. In Haredi institutions, women study primarily theological, ethical, and practical texts, avoiding thorough Talmudic discussions, while, in the Zionist-Religious community, an increasing number of institutions have attained rabbinical approval to teach women Talmud.

In summary, although they accept the same basic texts and principles for the halakhic process, in many fields, Haredi and Modern Orthodox rabbis arrive at different conclusions. In matters of ritual observance, Haredi rabbis often adopt a stricter line than their Zionist-Religious counterparts, and in issues of social or ideological concern the views in the two camps often contradict one another. It is noteworthy that the Haredi world seems to have produced the bulk of the great halakhic masters of the recent decades. Zionist-Religious rabbis make great use of halakhic material from the Haredi camp, while Haredi rabbis generally refrain from halakhic works of the Zionist-Religious camp. The ideological differences between the wings of Orthodoxy thus also leave their marks on halakhic decision making. The main question that has concerned Orthodox leaders since the late eighteenth century – where to locate the limits of resistance to modern values – continues to be the dividing line between the camps today.

Theology and Religious Worldview

While all Orthodox groups agree on the central importance of the study of halakhah, disagreement remains over the need for similar systematic discussions of faith and theology. Hungarian Orthodoxy is traditionally suspicious of theological discussions, and the Hatam Sofer once implied that anyone who neglected Talmud and halakhah for theology should be suspected of reformist tendencies and shunned. Nevertheless, Hungarian Orthodox rabbis address questions of theology in Sabbath and holiday sermons as well as in their biblical interpretation. While, generally speaking, very little innovative theological work has emerged from these sources, a notable exception is a disciple of the Hatam Sofer, Rabbi Moshe (Maharam) Schick (1807–79), whose sermons and interpretations of both Torah and Pirke Abot provide an eloquent, if not systematic, expression of traditional beliefs, sometimes in confrontation with those of modernity.

In German Neo-Orthodoxy, theological creativity occupies a place of honor within the hierarchy of Jewish values. Rabbi Samson Raphael Hirsch, the preeminent representative of German Neo-Orthodoxy, made extensive efforts to demonstrate that Judaism not only complies with modern humanistic values (especially those of German romanticism), but embodies them. According to Hirsch, Judaism aims to produce an ideal human type, the *Mensch-Jisroel* ("Israelite Man"). He understood emancipation as an opportunity for Jews to realize this ideal and present it to the gentiles. His assumptions about Judaism's higher goals encouraged him to discuss the rationale behind individual precepts (*Ta'amei ha-Mitzvot*), a field that many generations of Jewish thinkers perceived as dangerous.

Since the doctrines of Neo-Orthodox thinkers were primarily apologetic, some scholars question the movement's lasting value and see its main achievement in the field of education rather than theology. An important exception is Rabbi Hirsch's grandson, Dr. Isaac Breuer (1883–1946). With both a Talmudic and university education, Breuer created an impressive and original doctrine on which he based a political theology. He accepts the idea of Jewish nationalism but rejects Zionism. Jewish national identity is not based on territory, language, culture, and race (as according to Zionism) but on law. It was its law, the Torah, that created it, formed its nationhood, and preserved it throughout the generations. The Jewish people is, therefore, "the Nation of the Torah," and any new basis of identity creates a new, different nation. In contrast to Herzl's secular *Judenstaat* ("State of the Jews"), Breuer aspired to establish the Jewish state as the "State of the Torah," a task he failed to convince his Haredi colleagues in Agudat Israel to undertake.

The most impressive Orthodox theological achievement in the second half of the nineteenth century and first half of the twentieth is that of the Lithuanian Musar Movement. Commencing with Rabbi Israel Salanter, Musar thinkers, who saw themselves more as educators than theologians, focused their discussions on man, the powers acting within him, and his stance before God. Like other nineteenth-century philosophical and scientific trends, many Musar thinkers sought to expose the dark side of man and the unconscious factors that motivate him. They emphasized the power of drives and instincts in human activity and exhorted action according to Reason. The way of Reason, they believed, is the way of Torah and Musar.

Different Musar thinkers interpreted the core premise in very different ways. The radical Novardok school stressed the "savage" nature of man and the strength of his instincts. Novardok postulated the "annihilation of Will" as a way to impose Reason (namely, the Torah) on man's behavior. The Slobodka school, on the other hand, stressed the "Loftiness of Man" (or "Greatness of Man") and his quasi-divine supremacy. It portrayed the Evil Drive as an element essentially alien to man's true nature, which was created only to enable him to reveal his free choice (which is, of course, a part of his loftiness). Slobodka Musar instructs man to overcome his drives through a sober and rational consciousness of his own greatness, bringing this capacity into action. Most Musar thinkers came from a third school. The Kelm Musar adopted a position stressing the variety of man's mental forces, and advocated a strict discipline to keep them in order. Some integrated Kabbalistic concepts, transforming mystical senses into psychologistic ones. The Musar movement's view of man has had an overriding influence on postwar Haredi thinkers.

Late nineteenth- and early twentieth-century Hasidic thought gradually neutralized the mystical elements of early Hasidism. Rebbes continued to use the essential terminology of early Hasidic doctrine but neutralized their original dimension of mystical experience and rendered them traditional, "harmless" denotations. A similar transformation occurred in the bodies of Hasidic theology, as the strong monistic emphasis of early Hasidism has given way to more dualistic metaphysical models, in which the notion of the world's absolute unity in God is less emphasized. The very influential theology of the second rebbe of Gur, Yehuda Leib Alter (1847–1905), known as the Sfat-Emet, is a typical example of this trend. Actually, most of the Hasidic rebbes rejected theological discussion altogether and preached the ideal of *Emuna Tmima* (approximately: "Simple Faith"), which became the leading ideal of Haredi doctrine in the second and third stages.

Influenced by early Hasidic thought, Rabbi Abraham Isaac Kook's thought is immersed in mystical and monistic elements. He was convinced that the Supreme Holiness, identified with the Perfect Good, cannot be fully grasped by human beings and therefore descends to our reality as an only partial appearance of the Good. One of the places we can witness this is in the aspirations of social movements. Each movement seeks to attain another "partial" good, and, as the movements clash with one another, they sharpen, discern, and expose the good hidden within them. The resulting synthesis brings them all closer to the Perfect Good. Thus, according to Kook, everyone, including secularists, is actually aspiring to Supreme Holiness. Positive religion is only one, partial search for this, though the highest one. Rabbi Kook identifies attainment of the Perfect Good with redemption, the ideal of Judaism. The whole course of history is nothing but the gradual ascent of humanity towards this achievement. Kook maintains, however, that the main thing is not the objective but the process. This philosophy adopts the modern idea of progress and contradicts the traditional concept of *Yeridat ha-Dorot* ("the Degradation of the Generations"), which Haredi thinkers have developed into a predominant theology of history. Rabbi Kook's theology supported his tolerant approach to both secular Zionism and Haredi opponents (including the extremists of the Old Yishuv), enabling him to interpret the struggles between them as a stage in the self-emendation of diaspora Judaism and its preparation for its messianic goal.

The thought of Rabbi Joseph Baer Soloveitchik, the most prominent post-Holocaust Zionist-Religious thinker, evolves from different premises. His basic point of view is not metaphysical but existential. In his early essay "The Halakhic Man," he portrays two human "types" with fundamentally different approaches to the world: Scientific Man strives for a formal and generalized explanation of reality, while the *Homo Religiosus* seeks to enrich his world with a direct experience of the divine. Each of these types misses something of reality. Science misses the touch with the transcendent, while religious experience is subjective and elusive. Soloveitchik's ideal, the Halakhic Man, reaches the two goals. The halakhah, he claims, is the "objectification" of religious consciousness. Halakhic Man aspires to the divine but is aware that the chasm separating the creator and the created cannot be bridged. His desire to come closer to God is satisfied through his analysis of the Lord's commandments, the halakhah, with the same logical accuracy with which the scientist approaches nature. Soloveitchik basically refers to an analytic–conceptual method of Torah study, such as the one developed by his renowned grandfather, Rabbi Hayyim Soloveitchik of Brisk. The halakhah, he asserts, provides a system of *a priori* categories, through which the Halakhic Man perceives reality.

In his later essay "The Lonely Man of Faith," Rabbi Soloveitchik offers a similar typology, though this time not in the intellectual sphere but, rather, the social one. Majestic Man wishes to imitate God: he wishes to be active, creative, to rule the world. The Man of Faith, conversely, seeks complete submission to God. The former lives and works in a community, while the latter stands alone before God, contemplating his own self. Both paths are problematic: The Majestic Man is afflicted with "anxiety and neurotic complexes," a result of the machinery he has built, while the Man of Faith feels loneliness and lack of confidence. Consequently, the Man of Faith grasps that he, too, must act in a community, but, unlike the Majestic Community based on ambition, his community, the Covenant Community, is based on obligation. The common experience of its members enables them to continue the dialogue with God, himself a "member" of the Community, through common prayer and observance of the law. Saved from his loneliness, the Man of Faith turns to dialogue with the Majestic Man. This dialogue, especially in the modern age, might make him feel again the desire to withdraw to his loneliness, but this, says Soloveitchik, is the challenge of the modern Man of Faith: to return to the community, act within it, and influence it, as a believing man. It seems that this view shaped Soloveitchik's attitude to Zionism. The establishment of the State and the following events are God's call to reaffirm the covenant. Believing Jews must accept the call by active involvement in the entire society's efforts, but as believing Jews.

Another Orthodox thinker, eccentric in many respects, is Yeshayahu Leibowitz (1903–94), who based his doctrine on the distinction between facts and values. Facts are discovered through cognitive capacities. Once a fact is discovered, it is imposed on one's mind. Conversely, values are chosen to guide practical behavior. Judaism, according to Leibowitz, demands that we choose as a supreme value the worship of God *lishmah* ("for its own sake"). This choice expresses itself in the fulfillment of the practical precepts of halakhah without seeking any reward or utility. Therefore, Leibowitz asserts, any attempt to read the Torah as a source of facts – whether metaphysical (such as the world-to-come, the messiah, and the resurrection), historical (such as the creation or the revelation), or scientific – is an abuse of the divine text. The Torah must not serve as a human tool but as a source for divine imperatives. Leibowitz did not accept much of Judaism's traditional dogma and argued that Judaism never demanded – and could not demand – belief. At most, he concedes, Judaism could recognize dogmatic belief as a compromise for those who could not meet the ideal of worship of God *lishmah*. In this, Leibowitz sees the difference between Judaism, a religion of demands, and Christianity, a religion that endows mankind.

Leibowitz's distinction also provides him with a solution to the conflict between religion and science (the problem that, apparently, generated the whole doctrine): Science gives us information, it serves us; religion (Judaism) elaborates our duties – the norms of halakhah – and demands submission. The two cannot, therefore, contradict. Leibowitz offers a similar description of the relationship between religion and state: state norms are made to tend human needs and interests, while religion's precepts demand that we transcend them. Therefore, any attempt to incorporate religious norms into the state's laws (as desired by many Orthodox Israelis) degrades religion. This is why Leibowitz, especially in his later years, keenly opposed conceptions that attributed a religious value to the state of Israel, demanding instead separation between religion and the State.

Haredi Judaism's approach to theological discussions resembles that of nineteenth-century Hungarian Orthodoxy. Haredi thinkers shy from doctrinal creativity and deny the existence of "Haredi thought." Nevertheless, Haredi theology does exist. Forced into existence by the confrontation with modernity, it has yielded an insightful critique of its values and achievements. It disputes the ideals of freedom, equality, and nationality; the idea of progress, so dominant in early modern thinking; modern ideologies such as communism and nationalism, but also liberalism and democracy; and modern technology, which gave ideologies the power to reach their destructive goals. A disciple of the Musar school of Kelm, Rabbi Eliahu Eliezer Dessler (1891–1954), one of the most influential thinkers of postwar Haredi society, built his critique of modernity on the premises of Musar theology, coping with novel ideological problems through the use of traditional concepts. It seems that the critique of modernity and its ramifications is Haredi thought's main contribution to contemporary Jewish theology. Its discussions on classical questions – such as providence and free will, nature and miracles, reason and revelation – contains but modest innovations.

Unlike Rabbis Kook and Soloveitchik, who seek to learn the divine will from historical processes, some Haredi thinkers believe that we are unable to read God's will from history. It is expressed first and foremost in the Torah and only through the Torah can one decipher the meaning of events. Rabbi Joel Teitelbaum of Satmar, for instance, could never accept the argument that the successes of the Zionist state reflect divine support for its existence. According to his interpretation of a famous passage at B. Ket. 111a, founding an independent Jewish state before the coming of the messiah constitutes an open revolt against the sovereignty of God; it is a breach of the "Three Oaths" the Lord imposed on the Israelites. Creation of the State thus invited a horrendous punishment, which he finds in the Holocaust. All the successes of the State, further, are only divine tests of the faithfulness of the Lord's few worshipers in the last hour before the true redemption.

Some Haredi personalities, such as Rabbi E. M. M. Shach (greatly influenced by Rabbi E. B. Wassermann) and Rabbi Y. Y. Halberstamm of Zans-Klausenburg, adopted a more moderate position on these questions. Their point of view is clearly historical. Both describe the premodern world as more or less stable, being based on a fixed tradition that passed the test of time. The modern era, they argue, is characterized by chaos. People began to believe in their own understanding and presumed to take God's place. They created new societies, based on new values. For these utopias' sake, millions lost their lives, other millions were outraged, and the outcome was but disappointment and agony. Not only the suffering cries out, but the absurdity does as well, for the move to elevate humankind ultimately lowered people more than ever. According to these thinkers, Zionism is one with the rest of the twentieth century's ideologies, even if it seems unusually successful. A state is in adjecto a transient thing, and the Jewish state is no different. Neither a political institution nor military forces saved the Jewish people in exile: the power of the Torah alone preserved Jewish identity. The role of Haredi Judaism, these leaders argue, is to refrain by all means from entering the wild game of the twentieth century and to focus on the growth and fortification of the Torah world (i.e., Yeshivot and kolelim) as the best guarantee for Jewish continuity.

Rabbi Shach's doctrine underlies the basic nature of Haredi Orthodoxy, which differentiates it so much from Modern Orthodoxy: Zionist-Religious thinkers wish to create a versatile Jewish existence, risking exposure to the dangers and challenges of modern civilization. As part of this enterprise, they incorporate into their doctrines western ideas and modes of thinking. Haredi thinkers, by contrast, reject any such involvement with modern civilization. They seek to present their followers a pure, uncompromising Judaism that rejects the tempting glamor of modernity.

It seems that, unlike accusations sometimes heard from its critics, the wells of Orthodoxy have not dried up. Whether it chooses or not, Orthodox Judaism faces the challenges it meets and, consequently, new dilemmas arise and an alert inward discourse develops upon them. This discourse might sometimes be estranged to external observers but, for those who can understand it, Orthodoxy today presents an interesting and colorful rainbow of ideas, a variety of social groups, and an impressive display of religious creativity.

CHAPTER 19

Conservative Judaism: The Struggle between Ideology and Popularity

Daniel Gordis

In the spectrum of American Jewish life, Conservative Judaism is the "middle position." Members of Conservative synagogues have historically been perceived as more traditional than members of Reform congregations and less traditional than their Orthodox counterparts. A thumbnail sketch of Conservative ideology also places it at the center. Unlike Reform, Conservative Judaism insists on the ongoing authority of the system of Jewish law, known as halakhah. By the same token, Conservative Judaism is perceived as being more liberal than Orthodoxy to its right, because unlike Orthodoxy, which shares its commitment to Jewish law, Conservative Judaism stresses the historical development of Judaism. As a result, the movement believes that Jewish law can, and at times must, change.

Of all the major denominations in American Jewish life, Conservative Judaism is also the most uniquely American. Though scholars trace its intellectual roots to nineteenth-century Germany, Conservative Judaism – unlike Reform or Orthodoxy – became a popular movement only in the United States. In the more than one hundred years that it has been a force on the American scene, Conservative Judaism has at times been the predominant presence in American Jewish life, and, despite many challenges currently facing the movement, it promises to remain a major force for the foreseeable future.

Unlike the other movements, it is primarily in the United States and in Canada that Conservative Judaism has thrived. In the United States, there are approximately 1,800,000 people who identify themselves as Conservative Jews, and Conservative Jews account for approximately 36 percent of the American Jewish community.[1] Only Reform is larger, and even *that* phenomenon is relatively recent. The story of American Judaism, quite simply, cannot be told without Conservative Judaism as part of the drama.

The same cannot be said, however, for Conservative Judaism in other Jewish communities throughout the world. There is a growing, but still very small, Conservative movement in Israel; though that movement is aggressively staking out a position of "traditional Judaism coupled with modernity and religious tolerance," most Israelis are basically unfamiliar with it, and very few among even the intellectuals could thoughtfully answer even the most basic questions about what the movement represents. In 1999, there were approximately forty congregations affiliated with the movement in Israel, consisting of about 3,500 members in a population of 5,000,000 Jews.

In Europe, there are a few Conservative congregations, but, for the most part, the Jewish community tends to be at least formally split between Orthodoxy and Liberal Judaism, a variety of Judaism that is similar to traditional Reform in the United States. Since the 1960s, there has also been a noteworthy presence of Conservative Judaism in Argentina, particularly in Buenos Aires. Ultimately, however, Conservative Judaism is an American phenomenon, and when it has appeared in other places, it has typically done so as an "American export." In order to best understand Conservative Judaism, therefore, we must focus on its North American manifestation.

A Brief History of the Conservative Movement

Despite its very mainstream appearance, Conservative Judaism was the latest of the three major movements (Orthodox, Conservative, and Reform) to appear.[2] Orthodox leaders, of course, claim that their Judaism is simply a continuation of the past and that "Orthodoxy" began with God's revelation of the Torah at Sinai. While that view is historically simplistic, it is nonetheless reasonably fair to say that forms of Jewish religious practice that closely resemble contemporary Orthodoxy have existed for hundreds of years.

Reform developed essentially as a response to the social and political emancipation of the Jews in nineteenth-century Europe. Given unprecedented opportunities for participation in the economic, cultural, and political life of countries such as Germany, many Jews came to believe that a commitment to the ancient religious forms of Jewish life – distinctive eating practices, particular ways of dress, observance of the Sabbath that precluded participation in the culture of the surrounding community, worship and liturgy that were neither aesthetically appealing nor comprehensible to their non-Jewish neighbors and acquaintances – would impede Jews' acceptance by the Christian communities in which they lived. Gradually, several prominent German Jewish leaders determined that the time had come to "reform" Judaism. The history of this process is the history of Reform Judaism.

To best understand the origins of Conservative Judaism, it is important to note that the social and political emancipation of the Jews was not the only driving force behind Reform. There was an academic–intellectual drive as well, known today as *die Wissenschaft des Judentums*, the "scientific study" of Judaism. *Wissenschaft* scholars propounded the view that Judaism – like almost any other cultural phenomenon – could and should be studied as a historical phenomenon, influenced and changed by the ideas, people, and events that confronted

Judaism throughout its history. The leaders of Reform Judaism, in contrast to the leaders of Orthodoxy, who claimed that Judaism was divinely revealed and therefore not subject to change, enthusiastically embraced this new perspective and undertook intensive studies of Jewish life that reflected this new orientation.

As the Reformers moved ever more rapidly toward change, however, there emerged a cadre of scholars who embraced at least some of the principles of *Wissenschaft* but who remained wholly opposed to what they saw as the whole-sale and unjustifiable reform of Jewish practice. The best known of these scholars in Europe was Zacharias Frankel (1801–75), a man who is in many ways regarded as the European intellectual "forefather" of Conservative Judaism. Frankel, a noted scholar, had at first been associated with the traditionalists among Reform but ultimately broke with that movement. In response to a vote of Reform leaders that worship in Hebrew should not be considered "objectively necessary," Frankel walked out and later wrote that he could not participate in a movement that "eliminates the historical element which has weight and power in every religion."[3] In language that would ultimately become critical for the Conservative movement, he asserted that the decision to permit worship in a language other than Hebrew was "not [in] the spirit of preserving but of destroying positive historical Judaism."[4]

In framing his departure from Reform this way, Frankel set up what would become both the defining characteristic and the fundamental internal struggle of Conservative Judaism; he was committed not only to the "permissibility" but indeed the desirability of the academic study of Judaism, but, at the same time, he was unwilling to let the theological or historical questions that arose from this study undermine a commitment to the value of tradition for its own sake. For this reason, the Conservative Judaism that ultimately grew out of Frankel's work would be beset by a fundamental tension that did not afflict the other large movements. Orthodoxy insists on the divinely revealed nature of the Torah and, as a result, can understandably claim that Jewish tradition is essentially unalterable. Reform, on the other hand, committed as it is to studying Judaism as a historical phenomenon, is perfectly consistent in claiming that, if Judaism was the product of historical forces, it can, should, and will continue to change. Conservative Judaism, by contrast, open to the questions of the "critical school" but opposed to radical change, created for itself an ongoing tension – the need to explain how Judaism can be both a historical product and also one that Jews today have no right dramatically to change. Put otherwise, Conservative Judaism shared one important characteristic with Reform and one with Orthodoxy. With Reform, it shared an openness to study Judaism as a historical phenomenon that has changed continuously throughout the ages. With Orthodoxy, however, Conservative Judaism shared a commitment to the ongoing authority of Jewish law, or halakhah.

But this set of views has led to questions that Conservative Judaism has never successfully answered, at least in the minds of many of its members. If the Torah – and Judaism's other sacred texts – can be studied like any other documents, what makes this tradition and these works sacred? If human beings had a role in the development of Jewish law, by virtue of what is it still authoritative in our own age? If we know that Judaism has continuously evolved over the course of centuries, why does the movement pose such strict limits on change today? Leaders of the movement, of course, have well articulated responses to these questions; but as we will see below, one of the salient features of Conservative Judaism as a living form of Jewish life is that most of those responses have essentially eluded most of the movement's laity.

While the "positive-historical school" associated with Zachariah Frankel and others continued to develop in Germany, it was only in America that it became associated with a large population of followers. This popularization of what had been an elitist, academic school in Germany was the product of the massive waves of Jewish immigration to the United States at the end of the 1800s. It was during this period that many of the institutions that now characterize American Jewish life were founded – among them the Jewish Theological Seminary, which remains to this day the intellectual fountainhead of Conservative Judaism.

Though founded in 1887, the Seminary did not get off to an auspicious beginning, so that its importance for our purposes begins only in 1901, when several prominent New York lay people brought it back from the brink of bankruptcy and convinced Dr. Solomon Schechter, an internationally acclaimed scholar, to take its helm. Schechter was by no means a radical or committed reformer. On the contrary, his commitment to the Jewish Theological Seminary and the Conservative Judaism that it espoused stemmed primarily from the belief that the newly established American Jewish community needed "American" rabbis – not European ones – to serve its members. Indeed, describing his vision for the rabbinate that would emerge from the Seminary, he spoke of three critical characteristics: they would be able to deliver sermons in English (as opposed to Yiddish), they would conduct services characterized by aesthetic awareness and decorum, and they would employ "modern methods" in the education of both children and adults. Speaking to the very nature of Conservative Judaism, he wrote that contemporary American Jews "accept all the ancient ideas, but they want modern methods, and this, on the whole, may be the definition of Conservative Judaism."[5]

But Schechter's notion that the Jews who made up the nascent Conservative community "accept all the ancient ideas" may have been one of the gravest miscalculations of his career and of the movement's founders in general. Much evidence suggests that the members of Conservative communities had for the most part grown up in distinctly and intensively Jewish neighborhoods, communities, and families and that Jewishness was an undeniable part of their lives. But they did not accept or deny the "ancient ideas" – indeed, they differed from Schechter and his colleagues in that the world of ideas was simply not what animated their Jewish lives. These Jews were put off by Reform, but they did not in any significant way espouse the theory behind the rigor of practice endorsed by the movement's leaders.

The leaders of the movement seem to have intuited this tension early in the movement's history. Whether consciously or not, they assiduously avoided articulating with clarity what they meant by "Catholic Israel," a phrase that Solomon Schechter had introduced when he wrote that "the centre of authority is actually removed from the Bible and placed in some living body . . . the collective consciousness of Catholic Israel. . . ."[6] This implicit decision left open the possibility that a largely non-halakhically committed community could still be a legitimate partner in the emerging project called Conservative Judaism.

What drew people to Conservative Judaism was not history or theology. Rather, Conservative communities provided a comfortable environment that felt Jewishly legitimate and authentic. Prior to the emergence of Conservative Judaism, these people found little that was appealing in American Jewish life. The still largely European world of Orthodoxy did not fit, as its lack of decorum, use of Yiddish, and other characteristics smacked of the "old-world." Furthermore, this Orthodoxy insisted on practices (such as the strict observance of the Sabbath) that were difficult for a generation of Jews just starting out in business.

At the same time, American Reform had moved far beyond anything these traditionally inclined Jews found comfortable. In Reform synagogues, men no longer covered their heads. Many Reform congregations used an organ on the Sabbath, a violation of Jewish law that reminded many traditionally inclined Jews of churches. Some congregations even moved the Sabbath to Sunday. Radical changes had been made in the prayer book and, in general, much of the service had been altered to emulate the style and feel of American Protestant churches. All of this was far too much for "middle of the road Jews" who felt they lacked an appropriate modern option that still seemed religiously authentic.

With time, a seemingly natural match was made between the Seminary that Schechter was guiding and the growing number of Jews searching for a new alternative. It was a natural match because these Jews needed rabbis, and Schechter's rabbis needed lay people. It *appeared* that these two groups could build a movement together, and, in many ways, they have. Conservative Judaism, as we noted above, has become an enormous movement, with approximately seven hundred and fifty active Conservative rabbis in the United States associated with many hundreds of congregations. There is an active organization of rabbis (the Rabbinical Assembly), a large group of affiliated congregations (the United Synagogue), a youth movement (United Synagogue Youth), two rabbinical schools (the original school at the Jewish Theological Seminary and the newer Ziegler School of Rabbinic Studies at the University of Judaism in Los Angeles, founded in 1996), and several lay support organizations including the Women's League for Conservative Judaism and the Federation of Jewish Men's Clubs. It is an enormous operation; on the surface, the fledgling movement that Solomon Schechter founded in the early 1900s has become a major success, one of the very defining elements of American Jewish life.

But despite its success, this was a problematic marriage from the start. The underlying tensions in the early relationship between Schechter's intellectuals and the more viscerally motivated lay people have never disappeared. Schechter and his community of scholars were essentially Orthodox leaders committed to a certain openness in study and approach. The lay people, by contrast, were not theologically motivated; their interests were aesthetic, not intellectual.

In many regards, these are ongoing tensions that lie at the core of the challenges Conservative Judaism must confront as it charts its future in the early part of the twenty-first century. In order to understand the challenges facing Conservative Judaism, we need first to describe in greater detail how the movement defines itself and the principles to which it subscribes.

The Principles and Theology of Conservative Judaism

Where does the Conservative movement lie on the continuum of important issues in American Judaism? In matters touching on the authority of Jewish law, the movement approximates certain important elements of Orthodoxy, while in terms of its members' religious practices and its belief that Jewish law can and should change, Conservative Judaism is more aligned with Reform. In a graphic fashion, we might illustrate the Conservative movement's ambiguous place in the religious spectrum of American Jewish life (see box). While

The "Liberal" Position	The "Tradition" Position	
Jewish law is binding and authoritative, and Jews are obliged to live up to its standards		
NO: Reform and Reconstructionist	YES: CONSERVATIVE and Orthodox	
Hebrew ought to be maintained as the primary language of prayer, and the structure of the liturgy should remain largely (or completely) intact		
NO: Reform and Reconstructionist	YES: CONSERVATIVE and Orthodox (though Conservative liturgy is a bit more flexible than its Orthodox counterpart)	
Like all legal systems, *halakhah* develops with time, and change is possible even in contemporary times		
YES: Reform, Reconstructionist and CONSERVATIVE	NO: Orthodox	
The role of women ought to be changed to permit women to take major roles in leading services, being Ordained as rabbis, etc.		
YES: Reform, Reconstructionist and CONSERVATIVE	NO: Orthodox	
Traditional Jewish law ought to be modified to validate and celebrate monogamous and committed homosexual relationships		
YES: Reform and Reconstructionist	SPLIT: CONSERVATIVE leaders are split on this issue	NO: Orthodox

Orthodoxy consistently finds itself on the "traditional" side of the divide, and Reform and Reconstructionism invariably take the "liberal" position, the Conservative movement is not as easy to categorize. It not only occupies a "middle position"; it actually constitutes a rather internally conflicted one. The fundamental nature of this conflict is evident in the actual practices of the Conservative laity, to which we will return, and in the theoretical statements of the movement, to which we turn now.

The most important source for describing the principles of contemporary Conservative Judaism is a booklet known as *Emet Ve-Emunah* (Truth and Belief).[7] *Emet Ve-Emunah* was a product of a specially convened Commission on the Philosophy of Conservative Judaism, designed to address the movement's lack of self-definition, which can be traced directly to the uneasy partnership initiated almost a century earlier in Schechter's time. In fact, the document itself acknowledges the long-standing lack of definition and admits that, at the time of its writing, that characteristic had become a problem. Rabbi Kassel Abelson, then President of the Rabbinical Assembly, wrote as follows in his introduction:

> Rabbis [are] confronted frequently with the question "What does Conservative Judaism stand for?" Implied in the question [is] a suspicion that Conservative Judaism is simply a vague, indefinite middle ground between Orthodoxy and Reform.
>
> For almost a century, it could be argued, this lack of definition was useful since the majority of American Jews wished to be neither Orthodox nor Reform, and therefore joined Conservative organizations. But the situation has radically changed. Orthodoxy, which has [sic] been widely considered moribund a few generations ago, has assertively come back to life, and is generally characterized by an aggressive ideology which denies the legitimacy of non-Orthodox approaches to Judaism. On the other hand, the Reform movement is also growing in size, and has been seeking to spell out its philosophy. In our day, it is no longer sufficient to define Conservative Judaism by what it is not. It is now clear that our avoidance of self-definition has resulted in a lack of self-confidence on the part of Conservative Jews, who are unable to tell others, let alone themselves, what Conservative Judaism stands for. Our goal, then, [is] to teach members of Conservative congregations to become Conservative Jews.

Emet Ve-Emunah proceeds to define the Conservative position on a variety of important religious and theological issues, including God, revelation, Jewish law, the "Election of Israel," and the State of Israel. In many respects, these statements are extraordinarily clear and offer simple and articulate definitions of what Conservative Judaism believes. At the very same time, the movement's discomfort with theological axioms remains, resulting periodically in competing viewpoints being expressed in the very same section.

Consider, for example, the section on God. *Emet Ve-Emunah* begins with a classic theistic claim, with which most Orthodox authorities would have no disagreement (p. 17):

> We believe in God. Indeed, Judaism cannot be detached from belief in, or beliefs about God. . . . God permeates our language, our law, our conscience, and our

lore. From the opening words of Genesis, our Torah and tradition assert that God is One, that He is the Creator, and that His Providence extends through human history.

Soon after, however, the differences of opinion so characteristic of Conservative Judaism begin to surface. At first continuing to proclaim that "for many of us, belief in God means faith that a supreme supernatural being exists and has the power to command and control the world through His will" (p. 18), just several sentences later, the document offers a much less classically theistic alternative: "some view the reality of God differently. For them . . . God is . . . a presence and a power that transcends us, but His nature is not completely independent of our beliefs and experiences" (p. 18). Perhaps most instructively, the passage on God concludes by remarking that (p. 19):

> God's elusive nature has always given us many options in deciding how we shall conceive of Him and how that will affect our lives. . . . In our own fragile world, the tenacious belief in God that has characterized our history since Abraham and Sarah stands as instruction and inspiration, and continues to call us to pattern our lives after the God in whom we believe.

That *Emet Ve-Emunah* both claims that God's nature is "elusive" and asks the Conservative Jew to pattern his or her life "after the God in whom we believe" is probably the best possible example of the difficulty the movement faces in inculcating in its members a filial devotion to Jewish law. The move from religious life as a human construct to a commitment to a rigorous way of life is not an easy one, and though some theologians in the movement *have* written extensively on how this move can be made, that work has not reached most of the lay people, who, as a result, simply do not find themselves able to make the move.

This is not the only section of *Emet Ve-Emunah* that evinces clear internal conflict; the same is true of the portion of the document dedicated to the topic of revelation. Revelation is a critical issue in traditional Jewish life, for the claim that God revealed the Torah to the Jewish people, either shortly after the Exodus from Egypt atop Mount Sinai or at some other point, has long served as the basis of the community's claim that the dictates of Jewish law are binding and authoritative. In a legal culture, which Judaism has classically been, the origins of the Bible are of more than mere theological interest; these origins are in many ways the foundation upon which much of the legal system which defines traditional Judaism has been built.

Like the discussion of God, *Emet Ve-Emunah*'s section on revelation begins with a broad statement of faith, though this time articulating one of the primary differences between Conservative Judaism and Orthodoxy: "Conservative Judaism affirms its belief in revelation, the uncovering of an external source of truth emanating from God. This affirmation emphasizes that although truths are transmitted by humans, they are not a human invention" (p. 20). Note how this definition of revelation differs from the classic religious view. In most religious circles, revelation is a matter of God's revealing God's will to human beings. In *Emet Ve-Emunah*, however, revelation suddenly becomes "the uncovering of an external source of truth emanating from God." The actor here is not God who reveals, but the human being who discovers.

This shift, though subtle, has profound implications. Now the role of the Jew is not to conform to the revealed word of God but first to discover the "real intent" of that amorphous revelation and only subsequently to conform to the expectations of that understanding. For contemporary Americans, raised and educated in a world in which acceptance of the classic notion of divine author- ship of the Torah has become difficult or even impossible, this shift in emphasis is understandably very liberating and has undoubtedly been one of the main attractions of Conservative Judaism to both its professional elite and the more sophisticated and committed laity. At the same time, one of the critical ques- tions facing the Conservative movement is whether the vast majority of its lay people has ever gotten beyond the first stage to the second.

A similar tension between a traditional worldview and an attempt to grapple with the implications of modernity surfaces in the discussion of halakhah. Sentence after sentence in *Emet Ve-Emunah* seeks to assert the traditional role of halakhah but, at the same time, to read halakhah in a modern light. *Emet Ve-Emunah* avers both that "Halakhah consists of the norms taught by the Jewish tradition" and that "Halakhah is an ongoing process" (p. 21). The docu- ment claims that "Halakhah in its developing form is an indispensable element of a *traditional* Judaism which is vital and *modern*" (p. 22, emphasis added). Apparently seeking to explain how the halakhic enterprise can be sacred at the same time that the Conservative movement makes so many changes in issues such as the role of women, attitudes to non-Jews, and the like, the authors write that "the sanctity and authority of Halakhah attaches to the body of the law, not to each law separately, for throughout Jewish history Halakhah has been subject to change" (p. 22).

To American Jews seeking a Judaism that is both traditional in its orientation and open to what they perceive as the moral progress of modernity, this delicate balancing act has proven a major attraction. Most committed and involved Conservative Jews readily assert that Jewish law is important (in a recent study, 62 percent agreed with the statement that "Conservative Jews are obligated to obey Halakhah"),[8] but these lay people also invariably point to changes in the law, particularly those having to do with the roles of women, as one of the elements of Conservative Judaism that most attracts them.

But here, too, the implicit tension in these beliefs should not be overlooked. What does it mean to assert that "the sanctity and authority of Halakhah attaches to the body of the law, not to each law separately"? What would we say of a religious tradition that asserted that all human beings are created in the image of God but that we act out this belief only with regard to humanity in general, not with respect to each and every individual? Would we sense that the divinity of humanity is something that this tradition took seriously, or would we argue that the failure to actualize this belief in every human encounter somehow undermined the urgency of the belief itself?

That conundrum is precisely the challenge that faces Conservative Judaism. Most Conservative Jews understand that their rabbi genuinely believes in the sanctity of the halakhic system. Somehow, however, their knowledge that in critical areas the movement has made profound changes in the law seems to undermine their ability to internalize the notion that this law is sacred, authoritative, commanding. For many lay people, the attraction of the movement has been its traditional aesthetic coupled with its elasticity and openness to change, its traditional orientation without a burdensome sense of obligation to live according to traditional standards. These people see Orthodoxy either as too demanding or as intellectually indefensible in a post-*Wissenschaft* age, but consider Reform and Reconstructionism insufficiently rooted in the past.

In many ways, it seems, the intellectual and theological "tightrope" that the leadership of the movement has sought to walk may well have proven too subtle for the typical lay member of the average Conservative congregation. As we shall now see, Conservative lay people express a deep admiration for and commitment to Jewish tradition in principle, while, in the realm of practice, their own behaviors often belie those theoretical commitments.

The Religious Lives of Conservative Jews

In many ways, the religious behavior of today's Conservative Jews is rather traditional, beginning with synagogue membership itself. Even though Conservative Judaism lags a bit behind Reform in terms of absolute numbers of adherents, for example, the absolute numbers of non-Orthodox Jews who belong to synagogues are disproportionately Conservative. Of those American Jews who belong to synagogues, 47 percent are Conservative, while only 36 percent are Reform.[9]

In general, anecdotal evidence as well as statistical surveys suggest that what draws people to Conservative Judaism is a desire for a synagogue experience more traditional than what they would find within Reform. Not surprisingly, therefore, Conservative services tend to use more Hebrew than Reform (though less than Orthodox services, which are often conducted almost exclusively in Hebrew),[10] and Conservative worship tends to maintain more of the traditional structure of the liturgy. The Torah-reading is more commonly done from a scroll in the traditional fashion and some elements of (or even the entire) Musaf service continue to be recited.[11]

In Conservative congregations, the popular expectation is that the rabbi and cantor will be much more traditional than their counterparts in the Reform community. Even Conservative Jews who do not themselves maintain the standards of kashrut (the Jewish dietary laws) would be aghast at the notion that their rabbi or cantor does not, a concern not found among Reform or

Reconstructionist Jews. Beyond their expectations of their clergy, Conservative Jews in fact are more likely than their Reform counterparts to maintain traditional Jewish practices. According to the 1990 National Jewish Population Survey (NJPS), 24 percent of members of Conservative synagogues keep kosher homes, 37 percent light Sabbath candles, and no less than 90 percent attend a Passover seder. Similarly, the taboo against intermarriage is apparently reasonably strong among members of Conservative congregations. The NJPS found that, among synagogue members, the rate of intermarriage was 3 percent in the Orthodox community, 6 percent in the Conservative community and 17 percent in Reform. In this regard, as well, Conservative Judaism seems to reflect the traditional sentiments of its creators much more than the drive to liberalism reflected in the work and vocabulary of early Reform leaders.

Formal education is also a priority among today's Conservative Jews. Despite the general concern among leaders of the American Jewish community about declining levels of Jewish education across the American Jewish spectrum, Conservative Jews seem to be getting a better exposure to Jewish education than their parents or grandparents did. Of those in the 18–24-year-old age bracket, 63 percent received six or more years of Jewish education. By contrast, the rates for 25–44-year-olds was 56 percent, for 45–64-year-olds it was 45 percent and for those 65 and over, it was 30 percent.[12] Similarly, the rates of those who received no formal Jewish education whatsoever have dropped appreciably. Among those 65 and older, that rate was 26 percent, while for those 18–24, it was a mere 3 percent.

All of this points to the deeply ingrained traditional aesthetic of many Conservative Jews. What, then, distinguishes this variety of Judaism from Orthodoxy, the denomination to the right of Conservativism? As we noted above, one of the defining elements of Conservative Judaism has been that, although it stresses the abiding authority of the halakhic system, it also insists that gradual change in the system of Jewish law is not only permissible but occasionally even necessary. *Emet Ve-Emunah* addresses this issue head on:

> We in the Conservative community are committed to carrying on the rabbinic tradition of preserving and enhancing Halakhah by making appropriate changes in it through rabbinic decision. This flows from our conviction that Halakhah is indispensable for each age. As in the past, the nature and number of adjustments of the law will vary with the degree of change in the environment in which Jews live. The rapid technological and social change of our time, as well as new ethical insights and goals, have required new interpretations and applications of Halakhah to keep it vital for our lives; more adjustments will undoubtedly be necessary in the future.[13]

At the same time, the authors of *Emet Ve-Emunah* make clear that their fundamental loyalty is to tradition; that the pace of change in the movement ought to be gradual, if not glacial; and that their goal is to steer away from the rapid rate of change that made Reform unacceptable to their intellectual and spiritual forebears. *Emet Ve-Emunah* again: "While change is both a traditional and a necessary part of Halakhah, we, like our ancestors, are not committed to change for its own sake. Hence, the thrust of the Jewish tradition and the Conservative community is to maintain the law and practices of the past as much as possible, and the burden of proof is on the one who wants to alter them."[14]

This perspective on change in the halakhah is evident from many of the decisions that the movement has rendered in the past several decades. As suggested by the above passage from *Emet Ve-Emunah*, many of the changes instituted by the movement, usually through its Committee on Jewish Law and Standards, have been motivated by the perceived need to address ethical shortcomings in the halakhah as it currently stood. The most important example of this has been in the role of women. While a variety of traditional Jewish texts restrict the role of women in reading from the Torah in public, in reciting the worship service on behalf of the congregation, and in counting toward the minimum quorum of ten (the *minyan*) required for a public prayer service, the Conservative movement has made modifications in all these areas.

In the vast majority of Conservative synagogues, women may read from the Torah and be called up to the Torah for an *aliyah*. Except for Canadian congregations, in which Conservative Judaism is much more traditional than in the United States, particularly with regard to the role of women, it is now the norm for women to be permitted to lead the service as well. Moreover, in over 85 percent of Conservative congregations in the United States, women are now counted in the *minyan*. The Bat Mitzvah ceremony for girls has become virtually as common as the Bar Mitzvah for boys, and women have served as president of the vast majority of American Conservative congregations (and of about 50 percent of Canadian ones). The most momentous change in the movement took place in 1984, when the faculty of the Jewish Theological Seminary voted to admit women to the Seminary's Rabbinical School and to ordain them as rabbis.[15] As of this writing, approximately 40 percent of the rabbinical students in New York and a full 50 percent of the rabbinic students in Los Angeles are women. Changes that fifty years ago would have been considered unthinkable have now become the norm.

The movement's leadership has instituted other changes, also animated by a concern for the ethical standards of the halakhah. Traditional Jewish law does not permit a *kohen* (a male of priestly descent) to marry a convert or a divorcee, because these statuses were deemed to raise questions about the woman's sexual history or character; the Conservative movement has rejected that reasoning and permits both of these marriages. Similarly, in some congregations, the use of the titles *kohen* and *levi* (priest and Levite) has been discarded entirely, either because this "caste" system seems irrelevant and contrary to Judaism's egalitarian and democratic spirit or because these titles and roles were never granted to women.

As *Emet Ve-Emunah* clearly notes, however, not all the changes made by the Conservative movement are motivated by ethical concerns. Some are animated by what the document calls "the rapid technological and social change of our time."[16] In this category of change, the best known innovation has been the granting of permission to drive to Sabbath services. As the Torah prohibits the use of fire on the Sabbath (Exod. 35:3), classic Jewish law had always prohibited the use of automobiles, which produce energy through combustion, on the Sabbath. Even so, in an attempt to revitalize Conservative celebration of the Sabbath and to encourage suburban Jews who no longer lived within walking distance of their synagogues to attend services, the movement issued a very controversial ruling permitting driving to synagogue on the Sabbath.[17]

Supporters of the measure argued that anything short of this change would prevent people from joining with their religious community on the Sabbath. Opponents argued, and continue to argue, that the decision is unjustifiable within the parameters of even a Conservative approach to Jewish law, that it is inevitably misconstrued to permit driving *anywhere* on the Sabbath, and that the result is to undermine, rather than strengthen, the celebration of Shabbat. While the decision remains controversial (and is the ruling to which Orthodox authorities most often point when illustrating what they perceive as the lack of halakhic seriousness in the Conservative movement), its acceptance has become widespread. The vast majority of Conservative lay people now ride to the synagogue on Sabbath, as do a substantial portion of Conservative rabbis.

Other modifications of Jewish law have been made on the basis of "scientific" evidence. The Conservative movement permits the use of electricity on the Sabbath, arguing that it is not "fire" and therefore not subject to any Sabbath prohibition.[18] With regard to kashrut, the movement has permitted the use of gelatin, claiming that it undergoes such a profound chemical change as to render it no longer in the category of a derivative of the non-kosher animal from which it came, and swordfish, which was shown to fulfill the requirement that fish have scales to be considered kosher (Lev. 11:9–12), albeit only when it is young.[19] Many other changes of this sort could be adduced, but these are by far among the best known of such decisions.

At the same time, as suggested by *Emet Ve-Emunah*, change in the Conservative movement has not been without limit. Unlike in the Reform movement, Conservative Judaism continues to oppose interfaith marriage, and Conservative rabbis are prohibited from participating in such a ceremony. The Conservative movement has also resisted several attempts by a minority group of the Rabbinical Assembly to consider adoption of the "patrilineal principle" accepted by the Reform movement in 1983, by which a child would be considered Jewish if *either* parent were Jewish (under current Jewish law, the religion of the mother determines the religion of the child). Proponents of such a change, mostly the liberal segment of Conservative rabbis, argue that the matter is one both of ethics and of reaching out to intermarried couples. Opponents argue that it is unjustifiable in Jewish law, that it would undermine Conservative opposition to intermarriage, and that no ethical issue is involved, since the Jewish partner *decided* to marry a non-Jewish person in full knowledge of the movement's principles, and since both the non-Jewish spouse and the children of the union can become Jewish through conversion. Though the matter has temporarily receded from the agenda of the movement, with continuing increases in inter-marriage, it will, in all likelihood, become an issue again in the future.

The issue of homosexuality has become extremely controversial in the Con-servative movement. Though the book of Leviticus and subsequent rabbinic texts explicitly prohibit homosexual behavior, a not insignificant portion of the Rabbinical Assembly now advocates a variety of changes in Conservative standards, among them sanctioning loving homosexual unions, performing "commitment ceremonies" for gay and lesbian couples, and admitting gays and lesbians to the movement's rabbinical schools, all changes that have already been adopted in the Reform and Reconstructionist movements. Conservative proponents of these changes construct arguments on a combination of moral and scientific grounds. They insist that we now know enough about the etiology of sexual orientation to understand that it is not a "choice" that people make; since gays and lesbians are as "naturally" homosexual as heterosexuals are heterosexual, the Torah's use of the term "abomination" for homosexual prac-tice is simply inexcusable. Opponents of change argue that while the movement has made a variety of changes in Jewish law it always has tried to stay away from altering rules that are explicit in the Torah, that our knowledge about the etiology of sexual orientation is still in its infancy, and that the movement should not rush to make such a momentous change before the scientific and cultural understanding of homosexual orientation progresses much further.

Unlike the issue of patrilineality, which has subsided for the time being, the issue of homosexuality continues to elicit strong feelings on both sides of the divide. No changes of the sort listed above have yet been formally instituted, but individual Conservative rabbis *have* begun to permit "commitment ceremonies," and vocal groups at both of the rabbinical schools continue to advocate change in admissions policies. The issue is likely to remain a prominent and contentious one among the Conservative leadership for the foreseeable future.

In all, the picture that emerges of mainstream Conservative Jews depicts people with a strong desire for Jewish education and involvement, a tendency towards tradition greater than that of Reform lay people, and an aversion to the rigor and theology of Orthodoxy. The leadership, we have seen, is even more deeply committed to tradition, but, at the same time, wrestles with many of the implications of its openness to change. The desire to balance "halakhic serious-ness" with legal flexibility has produced an entire literature of its own;[20] indeed, the nature of the parameters of legal change within the Conservative move-ment are among the most important intellectual issues that the movement still addresses on an ongoing basis.

But in what many consider an ominous indicator about the future vitality of Conservative Judaism, many of these debates are lost on the vast majority of Conservative Jews. Indeed, the implications of the movement's commitment to halakhah have clearly been lost on a wide swathe of the laity. In a recent study, 62 percent of Conservative Jews agreed with the statement that "Conservative Jews are obligated to observe Halakhah (Jewish Law),"[21] but as part of a differ-ent series of questions in the same survey, 64 percent agreed with the view that "[Conservative Judaism] lets you choose parts of Judaism you find mean-ingful."[22] Obviously, the coexistence of those two statistics is difficult to explain unless one argues that Conservative Jews have not thought about their ideo-logical commitments in any meaningful way. Similarly, while 62 percent agree that Conservative Jews are obliged to observe halakhah, 69 percent also agreed with the statement "Anyone who was raised Jewish – even if their mother was Gentile and their father was Jewish – I would regard as a Jew." But traditional halakhah does not deem such people Jews. While it is quite possible that some of the respondents to the survey were giving a sociological response rather than a "halakhic" one, it is more likely that many Conservative Jews have simply not been sufficiently prompted to think through the implications of their ideological commitments.

The proclivity of Conservative lay people to live their lives as "cultural" Jews rather than as rigorously committed to an ideology of Jewish tradition, Jewish law, or some other related postulate is further evidenced by other statistics from the Wertheimer study. In response to questions about their religious practice, 90 percent of the members of Conservative synagogues polled stated that they attend a Passover seder.[23] While that is an impressive number, the Passover seder has become a major Jewish cultural event, and even many people who are not religiously inclined attend such a celebration. In this vein, when asked whether they light Sabbath candles, only 37 percent of the members of Con-servative synagogues responded affirmatively. As there are many people who light Sabbath candles but then do not observe the Sabbath in a way at all in accord with Conservative guidelines, it is clear that the percentage of actual Sabbath observers must be much lower than 37 percent. Similarly, although we saw that 62 percent of those polled agreed with the statement that Con-servative Jews are obligated to observe halakhah, the Wertheimer study showed that only 24 percent of members (and 6 percent of non-members who still defined themselves as Conservative Jews) said that they kept kosher.

This disparity between theory and practice is noteworthy. Conservative Jews are largely culturally driven; they are not ideologues in any real sense. In the Wertheimer study, 48 percent of those polled said that Reform is "too much influenced by non-Jewish culture and ideas," and 62 percent said that they did not believe they could ever be Reform.[24] But, at the same time, it is clear that the majority of these people do not subscribe to Conservative practice either. They are drawn to Conservative Judaism by its tone, its aura of authenticity, its commitment to Jewish education. What does not interest them is the halakhic dimension of Conservative Jewish life, the very dimension of the movement that was its original *raison d'être*.

The Challenges that Lie Ahead

It is this vast discrepancy between what one scholar has called the "elite" and the "folk" of the movement[25] that is the greatest challenge Conservative Judaism will have to address in the coming generation. Though there is naturally some appreciable difference between the commitments of clergy and lay people in almost all religious communities, the nature of that difference is profoundly different in Conservative Judaism. Reform rabbis may well wish that their congregants were better educated or more devoted to Jewish life, but their theology does not suggest that what their communities do is in any way improper. Similarly, most Orthodox congregants might well acknowledge a gap between their current behavior and what it *ought* to be; but for the most part, they understand the demands and dictates of Orthodoxy and, particularly among the younger generation, strive to bring their personal practice ever closer to the guidelines set by their rabbi and by halakhah.

The situation in the Conservative movement is different. The laity does not understand the movement, and, for all intents and purposes, congregants and their rabbis live in two different denominations. The future of Conservative Judaism will depend on whether this gap can be narrowed or bridged. If it cannot be bridged, the differences between Conservative and Reform lay people, which are already virtually non-existent in some West Coast communities, will disappear almost entirely throughout the United States. The movement's leaders are keenly aware that this process is likely to accelerate as Reform becomes increasingly traditional.

This awareness is not new. As Rabbi Abelson's introduction to *Emet Ve-Emunah* makes clear, Conservative leaders have begun publicly to acknowledge this challenge. Perhaps most tellingly, even scholars outside the movement are aware of the malaise affecting Conservative Judaism. The final volume of a recently published five-volume social and cultural history of American Jews[26] notes that in the years after World War II many observers believed that Conservative Judaism represented the wave of the future, but this optimism, the study suggests, gradually gave way to what it calls Conservative Judaism's enduring "plagu[e] of self-doubt, disquiet and gloom."[27] Marshall Sklare, the preeminent scholar of Conservative Judaism, echoes this notion. The second edition of his book referred to a "crisis" in Conservative Judaism and opined that "the belief among Conservative leaders that the movement's approach to halakhah had the power to maintain observance, as well as to inspire its renewal . . . proved illusory."[28] A more recent, much discussed essay suggested that "until very recently . . . most American Jews affiliated with synagogues have . . . found their home in this movement . . . [but] now the movement is in trouble."[29]

Is the crisis real? To an extent, the answer depends on what one hopes to preserve when speaking of the future of Conservative Judaism. For the vast majority of the almost two million American Conservative Jews, there is no crisis. Conservative congregations, schools, and other organizations afford these people a meaningful way to be involved in Jewish life. They cherish the movement's respectful attitude to tradition and appreciate the fact that despite its theoretical commitment to halakhah, the ethos of the movement as it actually exists does not conflict with the profound individualism and sense of autonomy they have internalized as Americans. These people derive deep cultural and religious satisfaction from participating in a movement in which the standard of kashrut is respected and even enforced in public settings, but in which what they do in their own home is not carefully scrutinized. They value the fact that their sons are taught to use phylacteries even if they do not intend to wear them every weekday morning as Jewish tradition mandates. They appreciate a community in which the traditional standards of Shabbat are respected and taught, even if they do not live according to those standards in their own lives.

But for those who had hoped that Conservative Judaism could represent a unique form of commitment to halakhah and an openness to critical study at the same time, the history of Conservative Judaism tells a story that has been at best frustrating, and, at worst, a failure. There is an ever greater recognition in some branches of the movement that "business as usual" is not working and that a new educational paradigm is necessary. What the movement needs, perhaps more than anything else, is a new vocabulary for teaching its students – both children and adults – that people can take the historical dimension of the Jewish people seriously without undermining their sense of reverence and awe for the tradition, without compromising their sense that despite the potential human role in creating this tradition, its dictates still have the capacity to speak as commandments rather than suggestions.

This is an ever greater challenge for the movement now that the baby-boomer generation has come of age. For the Conservative Jews of the 1940s and 1950s, the decades when the movement grew most rapidly, the value of tradition was self-evident. Even if many of these people did not worry about the details of halakhic rituals, they had a natural reverence for tradition. Many had grown up in the homes of traditional immigrant families and had internalized those neighborhoods' love for Jewish tradition; what they were seeking in Conservative Judaism was a "modern" way gradually to alter the nature of the tradition with which they were so familiar and to which they were profoundly committed. For them, the "tradition" in the movement's motto "Tradition and Change" was a given; what was new and exciting was the "change."

To respond to this generation's need, and in keeping with their own sense of excitement at what *Wissenschaft* had bequeathed them, Conservative leaders fashioned a vocabulary designed to justify the notion of tradition as a living entity, to focus attention on the element of "change."[30] But shifting sands soon made this "tool-chest" problematic. For the baby-boomer generation, the element of change is self-evident. This generation is highly educated and understands quite naturally the evolving nature of most society and religious institutions. What is new – and sometimes problematic – for this generation is the "tradition" in "Tradition and Change." But this generation has inherited a vocabulary ill-suited to pressing the need for tradition, for framing conversations in terms of awe and reverence rather than change and history.

The future of Conservative Judaism depends on whether the movement can respond to the need for a new vocabulary. At present, the vast majority of Conservative Jews continues, quite content, in a variety of Judaism that is traditional without being rigorous, that stresses communal standards without infringing on personal autonomy. With Reform moving steadily to the right, the boundaries on Conservative Judaism's left are becoming ever more blurred. And on the right, for the few (often elite) lay members who seek something more intensive, increasingly demanding and characterized by a sense of deeper reverence, the liberal end of Orthodoxy has become ever more appealing.

On the eve of the twenty-first century, Conservative Jewish leaders must decide if they will accept this *de facto*, amorphous brand of Conservative Judaism as the next stage of their movement or whether they will toil to create the vocabulary, the educational paradigms, and an ideology that can both maintain Conservative Judaism's intellectual and academic rigor and restore its sense of reverence and submission to tradition. Creating this new ideology will not be easy. For to Conservative Judaism, ideology is an ally and a danger at the same time. It is the ally of a Conservative Judaism that seeks a *raison d'être* because it is in *ideology* that Conservative Judaism has always been unique, and through which it has made a profound contribution to the intellectual currents of American Judaism. But ideology is also a risk for the movement, because it raises the possibility that if most Conservative Jews came to understand what the movement genuinely stands for, they might decide that it is not for them.

Ambiguity, sometimes intentional and sometimes not, has long been one of the Conservative movement's hallmarks, and it has also been one of the keys to its enormous success. The movement's leadership must now decide whether that ambiguity – with both its advantages and dangers – should be allowed to persist or whether the time has come to bring the ideology of the movement to the masses of people who are its members.

Notes

1   Jack Wertheimer, *Conservative Synagogues and Their Members: Highlights of the North American Survey of 1995–96* (New York, 1996), p. 7.

2   A fourth movement, Reconstructionist Judaism, developed later but is statistically not a significant presence in American Judaism, comprising approximately 1 percent of American Jews. The *ideas* of Reconstructionist Judaism, however, are far more prevalent and have influenced all walks of Jewish life, particularly Conservative Judaism. Indeed, the founder of Reconstructionist Judaism, Rabbi Mordecai Kaplan, hailed from the Conservative movement and was a long time faculty member at its academic center, the Jewish Theological Seminary of America.

3   Neil Gillman, *Conservative Judaism: The New Century* (New York, 1993), p. 20. This volume is an excellent introductory reader on the history of the Conservative movement.

4   What "positive-historical Judaism" actually means has been the subject of significant discussion. *Emet Ve-Emunah*, discussed below, defines the word "positive" as a belief that "Judaism is the result of a historical process and that its adherents are called upon to take a *positive* attitude toward the product of this development as we encounter it today" (emphasis added). For an alternate suggestion, which

associates positive-historical Judaism with the movement of legal positivism, see Ismar Schorsch, "Zacharias Frankel and the European Origins of Conservative Judaism," in *Judaism*, vol. XXX (Summer 1981), pp. 344–54.

5   Solomon Schechter, "Report of the First Annual Meeting of the United Synagogue" (New York, 1913), pp. 16–19.

6   Solomon Schechter, *Studies in Judaism* [First Series] (Philadelphia, 1896), p. xviii. This passage is cited in David J. Fine, "The Meaning of Catholic Israel," in *Conservative Judaism*, vol. 50, no. 4 (Summer 1998), p. 29. Fine presents an excellent summary of the confusion surrounding what Schechter and later Conservative leaders meant by the phrase "Catholic Israel" and where they located the authority for shifts in Jewish law.

7   Robert Gordis, ed., *Emet Ve-Emunah: Statement of Principles of Conservative Judaism* [hereinafter *Emet Ve-Emunah*] (New York, 1988). Page references in the following are to this work.

8   Wertheimer, *Conservative Synagogues and Their Members*, p. 10.

9   Ibid., p. 7.

10   These are generalizations, of course. Furthermore, many Reform congregations are in the process of restoring traditional elements of their liturgy and worship. As a whole, nonetheless, the generalization remains true at this point in the vast majority of cases.

11   The *Musaf* service is considered problematic because its central theme is the sacrificial cult of the ancient Temple in Jerusalem, an idea that many liberal Jews find objectionable. The traditional *Musaf* liturgy not only celebrates this ancient rite but prays for its restoration; that fact has accounted for many liberal communities dropping it altogether.

12   Wertheimer, *Conservative Synagogues and Their Members*, p. 36.

13   *Emet Ve-Emunah*, p. 23.

14   Ibid., p. 23.

15   A collection of the various papers written by faculty members both in favor of and against this decision can be found in Simon Greenberg, ed., *On the Ordination of Women as Rabbis: Studies and Responsa* (New York, 1988).

16   *Emet Ve-Emunah*, p. 23.

17   See "Two Views of Sabbath Observance," in Mordechai Waxman, *Tradition and Change* (New York, 1958), pp. 351ff.

18   Cf., esp., Arthur Neulander, "The Use of Electricity on Shabbat," in Waxman, *Tradition and Change*, pp. 401–7.

19   Isaac Klein, *Responsa and Halakhic Studies* (New York, 1975), pp. 75–8.

20   The literature is enormous. For a summary of many of the issues that it has raised, cf., *inter alia*, Daniel Gordis, "Precedent, Rules and Ethics in Halakhic Jurisprudence," in *Conservative Judaism*, vol. XLVI, no. 1 (Fall 1993), pp. 80–94. For classic examples of the centrist camp in the Conservative movement, cf., e.g., Robert Gordis, "A Dynamic Halakhah: Principles and Procedures of Jewish Law," in *Judaism: A Quarterly Journal*, 28, no. 3 (March 1979), pp. 263–82; Robert Gordis, *The Dynamics of Judaism: A Study in Jewish Law* (Bloomington, 1990); and Seymour Siegel, *Conservative Judaism and Jewish Law* (New York, 1977).

21   Wertheimer, *Conservative Synagogues and Their Members*, p. 10.

22   Ibid., p. 9.

23   Ibid., p. 35, for this and future statistics.

24   Ibid., p. 9.

25 The classic discussion of this notion is Marshall Sklare, *Conservative Judaism: An American Religious Movement* (Glencoe, 1955).

26 Edward S. Shapiro, ed., *The Jewish People in America* (Baltimore and London, 1992). The volume discussed below is vol. V, *A Time For Healing: American Jewry Since World War II*, and is authored by Shapiro. The project was sponsored by the American Jewish Historical Society.

27 Shapiro attributes that phrase to Lawrence J. Kaplan, a faculty member at McGill University.

28 Sklare, *Conservative Judaism*. The second edition, referred to here, was published by the Jewish Publication Society of America, 1972.

29 Clifford Librach, "Does Conservative Judaism Have a Future," in *Commentary Magazine*, vol. 106, no. 3 (Summer 1998), p. 28.

30 I have examined this issue at greater length in "Positive-Historical Judaism Exhausted: Reflections on a Movement's Future," published first in *Conservative Judaism*, vol. XLVII, no. 1 (Fall 1994), pp. 3–18. The paper was republished in Jacob Neusner, ed., *Signposts on the Way of Torah* (Belmont, 1998), pp. 166–82.

Bibliography

Gillman, Neil, *Conservative Judaism: The New Century* (New York, 1993).

Gordis, Daniel, "Positive-Historical Judaism Exhausted: Reflections on a Movement's Future," *Conservative Judaism*, vol. XLVII, no. 1 (Fall 1994), pp. 3–18.

Gordis, Daniel, "Precedent, Rules and Ethics in Halakhic Jurisprudence," in *Conservative Judaism*, vol. XLVI, no. 1 (Fall 1993), pp. 80–94.

Gordis, Robert, "A Dynamic Halakhah: Principles and Procedures of Jewish Law," in *Judaism: A Quarterly Journal*, 28, no. 3 (March 1979), pp. 263–82.

Gordis, Robert, ed., *Emet Ve-Emunah: Statement of Principles of Conservative Judaism* (New York, 1988).

Gordis, Robert, *The Dynamics of Judaism: A Study in Jewish Law* (Bloomington, 1990).

Greenberg, Simon, ed., *On the Ordination of Women as Rabbis: Studies and Responsa* (New York, 1988).

Klein, Isaac, *Responsa and Halakhic Studies* (New York, 1975).

Librach, Clifford, "Does Conservative Judaism Have a Future," in *Commentary Magazine*, vol. 106, no. 3 (Summer 1998), p. 28.

Schorsch, Ismar, "Zacharias Frankel and the European Origins of Conservative Judaism," in *Judaism*, vol. XXX (Summer 1981), pp. 344–54.

Shapiro, Edward S., ed., *The Jewish People in America* (Baltimore and London, 1992).

Siegel, Seymour, *Conservative Judaism and Jewish Law* (New York, 1977).

Sklare, Marshall, *Conservative Judaism: An American Religious Movement* (Glencoe, 1955).

Wertheimer, Jack, *Conservative Synagogues and Their Members: Highlights of the North American Survey of 1995–96* (New York, 1996).

CHAPTER 20
New Age Judaism

Jeffrey K. Salkin

New Age Judaism refers to a style of Jewish thought and practice within American non-Orthodox Judaism. The most basic unifying factor among the various New Age Judaisms is that each one has sought to bring a sense of spiritual renewal into Contemporary American Judaism.

Why has American Judaism needed this sense of renewal? American Judaism grew massively after World War II. Jewish veterans and their families flooded the suburbs, building new synagogues and institutions. But as the Jewish children of those suburbs began to grow into maturity, they began to sense that American middle-class Judaism was spiritually empty. In the 1950s, the modern theologian–activist Abraham Joshua Heschel wrote: "The modern temple suffers from a severe cold. The services are prim, the voice is dry, the temple is clean and tidy. . . . No one will cry, the words are still-born."

By the late 1960s, American Judaism was ready for a spiritual revival, and we can thank the 1960s for making it possible. America had become more pluralistic. The black revolution had made ethnicity and a search for roots acceptable. Just as 1960s culture was a kind of counter-culture, with its own music, arts, and literature, so American religion was becoming more exotic, no longer confined to the standard Jewish/Catholic/Protestant suburban model. People became interested in Eastern religion, meditation, and different kinds of therapies. Increasingly, Americans wanted a sense of community. As Jews had all those hungers as well, they would find ways to meet their needs.

The Havurah Movement: Community lost and found

As many Jews searched for a new sense of intense community, the late 1960s saw the rise of the havurah (pl.: havurot), literally, a fellowship group. These were self-contained spiritual communities that functioned in place of the synagogues that seemed to have bred the spiritual emptiness from which young people were fleeing.

Havurot typically consist of ten to fifty Jews who meet regularly for Torah study, worship, and doing mitzvot (the primary obligations of Jewish life). The first independent havurah in America was *Havurat Shalom*, in Somerville, Massachusetts. It was founded in 1968, and it started as an alternative rabbinical seminary with a faculty that included Rabbi Zalman Schachter (now Schachter-Shalomi; see below).

Havurat Shalom was a place for serious and intense prayer and study. Teachers and students were equals. They spent the Sabbath together and shared communal meals. A typical service would be in the round and would often feature Hasidic chanting and meditation, especially *niggunim* (wordless chant). It could include the singing of one prayer for fifteen minutes. Some meditations could go on for two hours.

The second classic example of the havurah was the New York *Havurah*, located on the Upper West Side of Manhattan during the 1970s. Some participants lived in the large, rambling apartment that housed it; others "commuted" to the havurah. The New York *Havurah* pioneered Jewish family education when its religious school required parental participation. Yet a third havurah was the *Aquarian Minyan*, founded by Zalman Schachter in Berkeley, and a fourth notable institution is the *Havurah* of South Florida, a network of independent havurot founded in 1980 by a Reform rabbi, Mitchell Chefitz. Various havurot were formed in the Miami area, some based on geographic location, others based on interests. Chefitz has emphasized the need for people to feel empowered to perform various holy, primary Jewish tasks. There has also been a national network of havurah resources and leadership, the National Havurah Committee, that has sponsored various gatherings, including week-long summer institutes devoted to intensive study and prayer.

What were some of the common characteristics of havurot?

An emphasis on intimacy. Smaller was deemed better. Learning and leadership were decentralized. People could not join havurot in name only; one had to be actively, passionately involved.

Egalitarianism between men and women became a basic cardinal of faith and practice and would have a far-reaching impact on American Judaism.

"Do it yourself" Judaism. American Judaism had become a "surrogate Judaism," in which rabbis, cantors, and professional teachers "did" Judaism before the eyes of passive spectators. Havurah members preferred to do it their own way, even creating their own ritual objects.

A counter-culture style. Worship was spontaneous, disorderly, and informal. Instead of Psalms, worshipers would sing a Paul Simon or Bob Dylan song. A poem by Allen Ginsberg could become a responsive reading.

A comfort with doubt and ambiguity. The havurot were places of theological creativity and struggle. Creative textual interpretation flourished in the form of poetry, short story, drama, and modern midrashim. The new attitude towards traditional Jewish law was indebted to Mordecai Kaplan, founder of Reconstructionism: Halakhah should inform, set guidelines, raise questions, offer solutions, provide inspiration – but not dictate behavior.

Finally, havurot were *post-denominational*. Havurah Jews were increasingly impatient with divisions like Reform, Conservative, Reconstructionist, and Orthodox, so that the havurah movement became a stew of pieces of every modern Jewish movement. Conservative Judaism contributed its emphasis on scholarship. Reform gave its social activism and its liberalization of Jewish theology. Reconstructionism offered a democratic perspective and its emphasis on the Jewish people as a historical and cultural force. Orthodoxy threw in its sense of text, tradition, and authenticity.

Which Jewish denomination would have the most to offer the havurah movement? As it turned out, Hasidism. Hasidism had begun among eastern European Jews after the massacres of 1648, when the old answers were not working any more. Miracle workers and charismatic teachers emerged. People needed joy. The havurah movement was truly a modern Hasidism, coming into fruition after the Holocaust, and it borrowed many Hasidic practices, especially ecstatic prayer, meditation, and *niggunim*.

The havurah movement's basic text was the three-volume work *The Jewish Catalog*, edited by Michael and Sharon Strassfeld and Richard Siegel (Siegel departed after the first volume). The first volume was published by the Jewish Publication Society in 1973, with subsequent volumes in 1976 and 1980. By the early 1980s, *The Jewish Catalog* had sold more than 200,000 copies, more than any other Jewish Publication Society book other than the Hebrew Bible.

The Jewish Catalog was a combination of the *Shulhan Arukh*, the classic code of Jewish law, written by Joseph Caro in the sixteenth century, and the "do-it-yourself" style of the 1960s *Whole Earth Catalogue*. It brought a rebellious, counter-cultural style to its description of ritual, synagogue, Israel, charity, communal life, etc. Later, Michael Strassfeld would expand the *Catalog* approach into a book on the Jewish holidays, treating each holiday the way Jews traditionally looked at sacred texts, with layers of interpretation and insights.

Synagogue Havurot: Turning up the heat

Considering its small size, the havurah movement has had a major impact on contemporary American Jewish life. Many veterans of the movement ultimately found places in synagogues as rabbis, cantors, educators, Jewish scholars, communal professionals, and lay leaders. The movement had a massive impact on Conservative, Reconstructionist, and Reform Judaism, and on the college campus. As a conscious *rejection* and *re-invention* of the synagogue, the havurot would eventually have an impact on synagogues themselves, in the process transforming synagogue Judaism.

The major pioneer in the area of synagogue-based havurot has been Rabbi Harold Schulweis of Temple Valley Beth Shalom, a large Conservative synagogue in Encino, California. Soon after he arrived at Valley Beth Shalom in 1970, Schulweis sensed that he was dealing with a new kind of Jew – "psychological Jews" who regarded community with as much suspicion as they regarded religion. His answer was the creation of a network of havurot. Each was comprised of ten families and contained social, cultural, and celebratory ingredients. By autumn 1984, there were more than sixty such havurot, involving about one-third of the congregation's families.

Different synagogues had different styles of havurah organization. Sometimes these became neighborhood groups or interest groups revolving around a particular religious task. Some groups studied Judaism together, worshiped together, or attended synagogue functions together as a group. Some havurot became involved in family retreat weekends, social action concerns, *tzedakah* (charity), or writing a prayer book. As with the independent havurot, the styles of liturgy and study were largely informal, with many synagogues debating the role of their professional leaders within those groups. Some of these groups became extensions of the rabbi's personality and functioned as barely independent of professional leadership. Others fostered true lay leadership and growth, leading to the growth of a genuine American Jewish spirituality.

By the early 1980s, Charles Silberman estimated the number of synagogue havurot at about three thousand. Another estimate suggested that fully one-quarter of all congregations in the United States had havurot.

New Kinds of Synagogues

Synagogues thus began to transform themselves along havurah models, and several examples of such synagogues began to flourish in the 1960s through 1990s. Congregation Solel, in Highland Park, Illinois, was one of the first. Led by Rabbi Arnold Jacob Wolf, the new community was, in Wolf's words, "intellectual, political, and exceedingly innovative and radical in its expectations." It would be a synagogue that would pioneer egalitarianism and would focus on study, prayer, and action.

Rabbi Wolf's assistant at Solel was a young rabbi named Lawrence Kushner (see below). In 1971, Kushner moved to Congregation Beth El of the Sudbury River Valley in Sudbury, Massachusetts. There he created a synagogue that would carry the Solel model into the next generation. Indeed, few congregations have adapted the havurah model as effectively as Beth El.

Soon after his arrival at Beth El, Kushner helped the congregation write its own *mahzor* (prayer book for the High Holy Days). That was soon followed by the congregation's creation of its own Sabbath prayer book, *Vetaher Libenu*. Kushner created a style of "Neo-Hasidic" Reform Judaism. The worship style consisted of chairs gathered around a table that holds candles, *hallah*, and wine. Kushner rejected the role of the rabbi as standing above the people and therefore led services from the same level as the congregation. Anita Diamant remarked, "We greet the Sabbath by looking not at the backs of heads, but by meeting each other's eyes across a table." There is a certain lightness and informality.

Kushner organized family retreats, encouraged families to form havurot, and insisted that parents of bar/bat mitzvah candidates participate in his weekly Torah class. Evoking the havurah principle that "smaller is better," the congregation experimented with limiting the size of its membership. Beth El became one of the few Reform synagogues with a *hevra kaddisha* (lit.: "the holy society," a group who prepares the dead for burial).

The havurah model has inspired some synagogues to create *intentional communities*, which members cannot join without a commitment to continuing involvement. For example, Congregation Mishkan Shalom, a Reconstructionist synagogue in Haverford, Pennsylvania, was founded on the principle that Judaism requires social and political action, and members must make a covenant with the synagogue that they will help fulfill the congregation's vision. So, too, Ohr HaTorah in Los Angeles, a post-denominational though nominally Reform synagogue in which the Sabbath service has been lengthened into a massive teaching experience.

An important facet of this spiritual renewal is the revitalization of moribund, mostly urban congregations. The two best examples are on the Upper West Side of Manhattan, New York. Long a Jewish neighborhood, the Upper West Side underwent a Jewish renaissance, at least partially because of the Jewish Theological Seminary and the New York *Havurah*. This Jewish renaissance had a major impact on the restoration of Congregation Anshe Hesed, an old, established synagogue on the Upper West Side that had fallen by the wayside. It was entirely recreated by havurah veterans (especially the co-authors of *The Jewish Catalog*; Michael Strassfeld serves as the rabbi of that congregation) and has become a major communal and worship center.

Consider too B'nai Jeshurun, the oldest Ashkenazic Conservative synagogue in New York. In 1985, B'nai Jeshurun called the late Rabbi Marshall Meyer to be its spiritual leader. Meyer had already distinguished himself through selfless duty during the *junta* in Argentina, where his activism and left-wing politics earned him the nickname *El Royo Rabbino*, "the Red rabbi." When he arrived at B'nai Jeshurun, he found a once-proud synagogue with severe structural and spiritual problems, unable even to muster a *minyan* (a quorum of ten Jews for communal worship). Meyer created a vigorous outreach to the homeless, AIDS patients, and the spiritually hungry. He assembled a worshiping community that sometimes numbered close to one thousand on a Friday night. After his untimely death in 1993, his assistant, Rolando Matalon, became the congregation's senior rabbi. Friday night services are jubilant, with music, chanting, and dance, so popular that people line up as early as five o'clock to get a seat for services.

Finally, we can credit the havurah movement for creating an atmosphere in which people feel comfortable criticizing conventional synagogue life and for producing Jewish professionals willing to change the culture. The most ambitious of such attempts is the "Synagogue 2000" project, funded by the Cummings Foundation and directed by Lawrence Hoffman and Conservative educator Ron Wolfson. They know that the synagogue must be reinvented for the twenty-first century, because, as they have written in their promotional material: "Beyond the coldness of the corporate–consumer culture lies the spiritual ambiance of the synagogue as community and home, a place where people feel welcome, connected, and intellectually alive – partners on a sacred odyssey of a sacred people, completing creation and thereby themselves."

New Kinds of Jewish Education

The transformation of the American synagogue ultimately affected the process and content of Jewish education. That transformation began with a mass protest by student activists at the Council of Jewish Federations General Assembly in Boston in 1969. These activists, many of whom became the founders of the havurah movement, protested that Jewish education was woefully under-funded and inadequate. They initiated a process by which the organized Jewish community would confront its own funding policies and ask hard questions about the distribution of money to Israel and the amount of money that would be used for domestic needs. Intensive and meaningful education was the most pressing domestic need of the American Jewish community.

A new generation of creative Jewish educators began experimenting with new techniques, curricula, and technologies. A major, and hitherto unheralded, contribution to this process was the Rocky Mountain Curriculum Planning Workshops, founded in 1971 by educator Audrey Friedman (Marcus). Friedman took Jewish college students, rabbinical students, and teachers away on retreats where they would brain-storm new curricula and techniques. Friedman's efforts led her to found Alternatives in Religious Education, Inc., an independent publishing house for Jewish educational materials that specialized in new forms of education and paths into traditional material. Her efforts would be followed, years later, by other such companies, including Torah Aura Productions in Los Angeles, California, founded by Joel Grishaver.

Here we must consider CAJE (the Coalition for Advancement of Jewish Education), founded in 1976. CAJE became the major activist Jewish educational organization, raising consciousness about the need for creativity, better curricula, and more communal funding for Jewish education. It began out of a sense that Jewish educational change was imperative; its name had originally been the Coalition for *Alternatives* in Jewish Education.

Like most of the institutions of New Age Judaism, CAJE is consciously trans-denominational and post-denominational. Bringing together Jewish educators, rabbis, cantors, youth workers, academics, social workers, writers, and artists from all sectors of Jewish life, it is actively involved in the creation of innovative curricula, curriculum banks, and resources. Like many of the new institutions American Jewry has created in the last decades of the twentieth century, CAJE, which started out as a radical critique of American Jewish apathy regarding both Jewish education and the career needs and goals of Jewish educators, has become mainstream.

New Kinds of Jewish Music

Even with music, to quote Bob Dylan, the times they were a-changing. An earlier generation of Reform Jews had preferred synagogue music in the form of organ and choirs. An earlier generation of Conservative Jews preferred traditional *hazzanut* (cantorial chant). Now, as a result of the Reform and Conservative camping movements, the counter-culture, and the havurah style, a new Jewish musical style emerged. Using guitars and other informal instruments, with new tunes written to engage the soul and to create community, it combined contemporary pop and folk idioms with Hasidic and eastern European traditions as well as Israeli folk music.

This new tradition began with Rabbi Shlomo Carlebach (1926–95), the popular singer and story-teller. His neo-Hasidic style blended traditional *niggunim*, Israeli song, and American folk style. His concerts in the United States and Israel were popular in both religious and nonreligious circles. But the greatest center of musical activity proved to be the Reform camping and youth movement, which gave birth to Kol B'Seder (Rabbi Daniel Freelander and Cantor Jeffrey Klepper), who adapted classic and modern Jewish texts for guitar and voice. Debbie Friedman is regarded as the master Jewish songstress of her generation, inheriting Carlebach's mantle and producing a body of spiritually moving work that has galvanized audiences. Ms. Friedman is the principal voice of a new Jewish feminist sensibility and aesthetic, and she has become involved in the healing movement as well (see below).

The New Spirituality

These elements together point to a resurgence of Jewish spirituality parallel to the spiritual journey that for many baby boomers has been a continuation of the 1960s counter-culture. In the case of Judaism, this new spirituality has led to increased Jewish observance, including some return to Orthodoxy among young people. But even when heightened spirituality has not involved increased halakhic observance, it *has* led to a deepened sense of ultimacy, a recapturing of the inner-life, the intuitive, and the non-rational, in daily Jewish life.

The roots of the new Jewish spirituality are in the growing interest in alternative religion, especially mysticism and Eastern religion and meditation, that has existed since the 1960s. Alongside this interest, Jewish mysticism (kabbalah) became popular for a number of reasons. The great scholar of mysticism,

Gershom Scholem, demonstrated that Jewish mysticism has been a constant theme within historical Judaism. There was the massive outreach success of Lubavitcher Hasidism, which saw kabbalah as the "salt" that flavors the basic "meat" of Judaism. Finally, there was the new popularity of Jewish meditation as a method for achieving spirituality. Kabbalah in particular has retained, and even increased, its popularity, becoming a Jewish cottage industry and yielding an avalanche of popular books – of uneven intellectual depth – and celebrities like Madonna and Sandra Bernhard who flock to study it at Rabbi Philip Berg's Kabbalah Learning Center. The major figures of this mysticism-based spiritual revival have been:

Arthur Green (b. 1941), the founder of *Havurat Shalom*, is the major academic voice of Jewish spiritual revival. He is the author of a biography of the charismatic and troubled Hasidic teacher, Nahman of Bratslav (*Tormented Master: The Life and Spiritual Quest of Rabbi Nahman of Bratslav*), which, in ways that resonate with modern people struggling with their own inner lives, demonstrates the depth of both the sage's teachings and his personal pain. Green also collaborated with Barry Holtz on *Your Word Is Fire: Hasidic Masters on Contemplative Prayer*, which presented a selection of Hasidic prayer and meditation texts, thus helping to redeem some of the classics of Jewish spirituality.

Green has clearly articulated the meaning of Jewish spirituality as "seeking the face of God; striving to live in His (*sic*) presence and to fashion the life of holiness appropriate to God's presence." In "Judaism for the Post-Modern Era," he paints a deep, often humorous portrait of the contemporary Jewish spiritual seeker as someone who describes herself (*sic*) in a personals ad as "spiritual, not religious." His major academic statement is *Seek My Face, Speak My Name: A Contemporary Jewish Theology*, which is an extended meditation on the mysterious four-letter name of God. Green teaches that the goal of spiritual striving is unity with God – that we can find a way to connect with God especially in Jewish practices. The book is organized according to traditional Jewish theological categories: creation, revelation, and redemption. *Creation* teaches Green about the necessity of radical awareness (for him, it is the first mitzvah); the ethical dimension of seeing people as being made in God's image; the observance of Shabbat, ecological caution, and vegetarianism. *Revelation* leads Green to confront the complicated Sinai story in Exod. 19–20. Green argues that we find God not only through vertical ascent up a mountain but through inner journeying as well. He believes that Jews should perform mitzvot in response to the transcendent and the demands made by it. *Redemption*, for Green (as it was for the Hasidic masters), is nothing less than spiritual homecoming from exile, repairing the world, and the heralding of Messiah.

Lawrence Kushner (b. 1943) is a rabbi in Sudbury, Massachusetts (see above) and a widely published author and prolific teacher, perhaps the American congregational rabbi most responsible for the recapturing of Jewish spirituality. His work is best known for its elegant use of stories in which he restates Hasidic and mystical truths in a contemporary idiom. *Honey from the Rock*, for instance, is written in the style of a traditional Jewish *sefer* (holy text). In short chapters, it describes how the individual can become linked to the holy and transcendent. Kushner deftly combines his own experiences, midrash, and modern cosmology.

Two of Kushner's works use biblical narrative as their point of departure. *The River of Light: Spirituality, Judaism, Consciousness* is a super-*midrash*. It ostensibly begins with the angels visiting Abraham and Sarah (Gen. 18) to announce the birth of Isaac, and Abraham's running to the flock to fetch food for the visitors. The Zohar (the cardinal work of Jewish mysticism) teaches that on that errand Abraham discovers the Cave of Machpelah, which was to become the burial place of the patriarchs, and discovers that the cave is also, in fact, the burial place of Adam and Eve. That insight, interwoven with references to both Torah and modern science, allows Kushner to meditate on the origins of consciousness, mortality, and immortality.

God Was In This Place and I, I Did Not Know: Finding Self, Spirituality, and Ultimate Meaning is an extended midrash on Jacob's vision of the ladder of angels (Gen. 28) and its meaning for personal and communal spirituality. Through several different readings of the verse "God was in this place . . ." Kushner invites the reader into a thorough exploration of the spiritual possibilities inherent within the text. In *Invisible Lines of Connection: Sacred Stories of the Ordinary*, Kushner uses personal narrative as a starting point, showing the "Aha!" factor in daily life and discerning the holy in everyday encounters. His principal thesis is that there are levels and layers of reality of which the individual is unaware.

Finally, *The Book of Letters* and *The Book of Words* start with the smallest units of Jewish meaning – in the former, meditating on the shape and interconnection of the Hebrew alphabet; and, in the second, offering mischievous translations of basic Hebrew value terms.

Jeffrey K. Salkin. This author's own work is concerned with how to find spirituality in areas of Jewish life where it had been abandoned or ignored, i.e., the modern celebration of bar and bat mitzvah and the spirituality of the workplace. In *Putting God on the Guest List: How to Reclaim the Spiritual Meaning of Your Child's Bar or Bat Mitzvah*, the author notes that American secularism has depleted bar and bat mitzvah of its spiritual meaning and presents a way of reshaping and re-interpreting this tradition. In *Being God's Partner: How to Find the Hidden Link between Spirituality and Your Work*, the author essentially invents a theology of the workplace, demonstrating how religious values can infuse one's work; how work can reflect a sense of divine obligation and spiritual uplift; and how one can achieve balance in life. In this sense, the work reflects the sense, expressed earlier, that secular life has become bifurcated into competing realms of holy and profane and that there can be glimpses of holiness even and especially in the midst of the mundane realities of this world.

Holy from Profane

The growth of Jewish spirituality led to a revolution in Jewish ritual life. In the last twenty-five years, for instance, the *havdalah* ("separation") ceremony that ends the Sabbath has returned to non-Orthodox Judaism, largely a result of Jewish summer camps, where the sensuousness of the ceremony's candles and spices entranced a generation. Other reclaimed ceremonies include *tashlich*, the ceremony held on Rosh HaShanah in which sins are symbolically thrown into a body of water, and the mystical *Tu B'shevat seder*, held on the Jewish New Year of Trees, a celebration of the various kinds of fruits in the world.

There has also been a reclamation of *mikvah* – ritual immersion – as a rite of welcome for converts to Judaism and prior to marriage, but far less so as an expression of traditional norms of family purity and sexual separation during menstruation. As Rachel Adler interpreted it in *The Jewish Catalog*, *mikveh* now represented "the original living water, the primal sea from which all life comes, the womb of the world, forcing participants to confront life and death and resurrection."

By increasing the individual's search for Jewish meaning, the new Jewish spirituality has created as the dominant theme for this generation *t'shuvah* ("return to Judaism"). Thousands of young Jews have become *baalei t'shuvah* (newly Orthodox). But even among those who have not become Orthodox, there has been an increased return to Jewish practice and norms, reflected in part in a new Jewish confessional autobiographical form, in which previously estranged Jews have spoken about their spiritual journeys back to Judaism. The most prominent of these books have been Paul Cowan's *An Orphan in History* and Anne Roiphe's *Generation Without Memory: A Jewish Journey in Christian America*. In both books, prominent Jews speak of their return either from being Jewish "WASPs" or from Jewish apathy.

The new spirituality also has made Jews more comfortable with the subject of conversion to Judaism. The Reform movement has taken massive leadership in this regard, especially since Rabbi Alexander Schindler's 1978 call for a new, assertive receptivity to those who would enter the Jewish people. Such calls for understanding and acceptance have been renewed perennially. In most cases, the candidates for conversion to Judaism are non-Jews entering Jewish families through marriage. Increasingly, however, non-Jews unconnected to Jewish families have converted to Judaism, sometimes after reclaiming a long-buried Jewish family legacy. Here the model is the life story of the black activist and academic Julius Lester, told in his autobiography *Lovesong: Becoming a Jew*. A more recent work on this theme is Stephen Dubner's *Turbulent Souls*, in which a young Catholic confronts the fact that his parents had converted to Catholicism from Judaism and in which he chronicles his road "home" to Judaism.

Gender Issues and Prayer

Jews have become increasingly uncomfortable referring to God as "He," "Father," "King," and "Lord." Feminist Judith Plaskow suggests that language not only *mirrors* reality but *creates* it, and that religious symbols express a people's sensibility and moral character. In response to this concern, contemporary forms of Judaism have developed inclusive attitudes both in their language and through the development of new and reclaiming of old rituals. The last two decades, for instance, have seen a growth in the celebration of *Rosh Hodesh* (the first day of the Jewish month) as a woman's festival as well as in women's Passover seders, which focus on the role of women in the Exodus story.

A major figure in feminist ritual is Lynn Gottlieb, a rabbi in Albuquerque, New Mexico, who has been creating a feminist Judaism for more than two decades. Her poetry and ritual feature the *Shechina*, the mystical sense of God's feminine presence, and her search for the female face of divinity has led her even into a celebration of ancient Near Eastern goddesses. Gottlieb has also pioneered the reclamation of women's stories: Lilith, Adam's first wife; Eve; the matriarchs; Hagar; Shifra and Puah, the Egyptian midwives; Yocheved, the mother of Moses; Miriam, the sister of Moses – all find their places in her poetry and ritual inventions. She has been particularly successful in bringing a feminist consciousness into the creation of community, stressing openness and hospitality.

The creation of gender-conscious liturgies has become standard in all liberal Jewish movements. Sometimes the language is truly neutral, with God portrayed as "Loving Parent," "Ruler," etc. Other feminists have experimented with the reclamation of Jewish female terms for the divinity, i.e., *Shekinah*. Perhaps most radical has been the solution by Marcia Falk in *The Book of Blessings*. Instead of the traditional opening of Jewish blessings – "Blessed are you, Lord our God . . ." – Falk has invented a whole new blessing formula: *Nevarekh et eyn hahayim*, "Let us bless the wellspring of life."

New life-cycle ceremonies also have emerged, including the growth of baby-namings for girls, often with new rituals such as feet-washing (an evocation of an ancient Middle Eastern form of greeting) and even, a (rarely done) ceremony, invented by Mary Gendler, in which the hymen is broken, as a conscious imitation of the power and pain of the *brit milah*, ritual circumcision ceremony for boys. The growing sense that ritual can heal in life's moments of vulnerability further has led Jewish feminists to create rituals for mourning for infertility, healing after abortion or miscarriage, and recovery from rape.

Healing

Through the pioneering work of the National Center for Jewish Healing and its branches (now more than twenty), healing in general has been a new focus of synagogue programming and worship. This is not only a return to faith but also an acknowledgment of what modern science has discovered. In *Healing Words: The Power of Prayer and the Practice of Medicine*, Dr. Larry Dossey shows that the body and soul are intimately connected and that prayer, when combined with modern medical treatments, sometimes bridges the gap between illness and recovery. Many Reform, Conservative, and Reconstructionist synagogues now have healing services, which include psalms, singing, and meditations. Names of those who need healing are mentioned aloud.

Another development is the recent increased willingness of Jews to talk about addictions. As Jews have found spirituality in Twelve Steps groups, ways for them to confront addiction as Jews also have been created. Much of the Jewish material on addiction seeks to establish theological links between Twelve Steps therapy and Jewish wisdom, so that, for instance, the "Higher Power" of Twelve Steps becomes the God of Judaism. The pioneer in this field is the Orthodox rabbi–therapist Dr. Abraham Twerski, while much of the creative work in linking Twelve Steps and Judaism has been done by Dr. Kerry Olitsky, who has created an entire literature of recovery, much of it based on daily meditations, affirmations, and texts linked to the weekly Torah portions. He has been particularly adept at using the lectionary and festival cycle to help those in recovery.

Gay and Lesbian Inclusiveness

Starting in the mid-1970s, gay and lesbian Jews began to create their own movement of liberation. The first gay synagogue was Beth Chayim Chadashim ("House of New Life") in Los Angeles, founded in 1972 and affiliated with the Reform movement in 1973. Other gay and lesbian outreach synagogues have been established in such cities as New York (Congregation Beth Simchat Torah, the largest, with some eleven hundred members), San Francisco (Sha'ar Zahav, which has pioneered creative gay/lesbian inclusive liturgy), Philadelphia, Atlanta, Washington, D.C., Chicago, and Miami. There are now many openly gay and lesbian rabbis, ordained by both the Reform and Reconstructionist movements, which also have taken steps to counter overt discrimination in hiring. But liberal Jewish movements continue to struggle with the official place of gay/lesbian weddings and commitment ceremonies, even as a significant number of Reform and Reconstructionist rabbis consent to honor such relationships publicly. There has been a growth of consciousness in this area within the Conservative movement as well, with such prominent rabbis as Harold Schulweis, Stuart Kelman, and Bradley Shavit-Artson pioneering new theological and ethical re-assessments of such unions.

The Jewish Renewal Movement

The Jewish Renewal movement is the institutional successor of the havurah movement. It has a retreat center – Elat Chayyim, near Woodstock, New York – which hosts week-long conferences every summer, renowned Rabbinic leaders and authorities, a dedicated following of several thousand Jews, and various publications. It seeks to nurture communities that are intimate, participatory, and egalitarian, and to assist the spiritual growth and healing of individuals, communities, and society as a whole. Jewish Renewal shares with the earlier havurah movement a deep attachment to the wisdom of Jewish mysticism and hasidism, as well as the prophets and rabbis, infusing these with the insights of contemporary ecology, feminism, and participatory democracy. This Judaism thus blends the styles of human potential movements, therapeutic psychology, and interpretation of ancient texts. While there is some overlap with the trends in Jewish spirituality, Jewish Renewal has added its own unique signature to Judaism:

A use of New Age techniques in worship, including chant, meditation, new music, dance, even yoga techniques. Jewish Renewal has fostered a new intensity regarding prayer, seeking to deepen the *kavvanah* (intentionality, spiritual meaning and direction) of worshipers.

New ways of creating and learning Torah: Poets, especially David Curzon and Joel Rosenberg, and scholar/translators, such as Everett Fox, have actively "rewritten" Torah for this generation. Psychotherapist Peter Pitzele has pioneered the use of "bibliodrama" and role playing as ways of getting into the inner life of sacred texts. Closely related are scholars and authors who integrate family dynamics into their textual studies, for instance, Norman J. Cohen's *Self, Struggle and Change: Family Conflict Stories in Genesis and Their Healing Insights for Our Live* and his *Voices from Genesis: Guiding Us through the Stages of Life.*

Reclamation of previously ignored theological options. A rebirth of interest in angels in Jewish lore has occurred, just as in non-Jewish circles. Similarly, a serious new interest in issues of life after death has emerged, so that Jewish Renewal has recaptured traditional Jewish views of immortality of the soul, reincarnation, and even flirted with the issue of the messianic resurrection of the dead.

A maximalism about Judaism's reach and voice. Jewish Renewal rejects the earlier bifurcation of the world into the categories "relevant to Judaism"/ "irrelevant to Judaism." It applies Jewish teachings to food, money, sex, health, and politics, rather than restricting Judaism to prayer or Torah study. Indeed, Jewish Renewal takes everything a Jew does – kashrut, Shabbat, festivals, daily prayer – and lifts it to a higher level. In this way, it resembles the hasidic masters, who inserted meditations for spiritual direction into the pages of their prayer books.

Within this setting, even sexuality at its most intimate has been sanctified. A course title from the 1997 Elat Chayyim brochure is telling: "Menstruation, Birth and Sexuality as Individual States of Sacredness." In recent years, Jewish men too have been asking how Judaism views masculinity and men's life issues. Among the thinkers in this area are Daniel Boyarin and the current author, whose *Searching for My Brothers* is a history of Jewish masculinity and an examination of how Judaism responds to the inner needs of men.

The encounter with other religions. Jewish Renewal respects and learns from other spiritual paths. In the words of Rabbi Jeff Roth of Elat Chayyim, it has "mined other traditions for vitamins and minerals that we need in our own community." There has been a certain syncretism, too, between Kabbalah and Eastern faiths, especially in the case of the encounter with Buddhism, particularly Tibetan Buddhism. That encounter finds its classic expression in Rodger Kamenetz's theological travelogue, *The Jew in the Lotus*, which describes the journey of American Jewish intellectuals and teachers to India to meet with the Dalai Lama. He had requested this remarkable meeting because he sensed that Jewish wisdom and history could counsel him on how to maintain a nation in exile from its homeland.

While the book is mostly an account of the dialogue between the Dalai Lama and the Jews, it also revealed the existence of numerous "Jubus" in India and elsewhere – Jews who had integrated Buddhism into their life-styles and philosophy. Kamenetz's work was followed by Sylvia Boorstein's *Funny, You Don't Look Buddhist!*, a memoir of a Jewish life enriched and even defined by Buddhist insights. Indeed, considerable interest has arisen in how Buddhist practices – in particular, silent retreats – can enhance Judaism. New Age Jews like Buddhism's body-based activities because they don't require learning a new language, vocabulary, or ideas. To many, it is enticing simply because it is *not* Judaism. There is no Jewish cultural baggage to shed.

Jewish Renewal has not only conversed with and borrowed from Buddhism. It has also begun a process of intellectual cross-pollination with Hinduism and Sufism (Islamic mysticism). Jewish Renewal often teaches the implicit message that all spiritual paths are similar and that all spiritual wisdom is interchangeable, even to the point of flirting with syncretism. Speaking of his experiences praying with Trappists, Native Americans, and Sufi mystics, Zalman Schachter-Shalomi has said, "I see myself as a Jewish practitioner of generic religion."[1] To some extent, the renewed interest in Jewish mysticism has provided a Jewish alternative to other religions, showing that Judaism has its own exotic elements that are conducive to personal, intense involvement.

Principal Teachers of Jewish Renewal

Zalman Schachter-Shalomi was born in Poland in 1924. "Reb Zalman," as he is affectionately known, grew up in Vienna and then fled to Antwerp. He attended both a Zionist gymnasium and a Lubavitcher yeshiva. He became a passionate missionary for Habad and was ordained a rabbi in 1947.

Schachter-Shalomi has a fertile imagination and a creative intellect. He became interested in psychology (writing his doctoral dissertation on hasidic modes of counseling) and psychedelic drugs, which he used for the enhancement of religious experience. Schachter-Shalomi was active in the inception of the havurah movement. He created P'nai Or Religious Fellowship, which is now ALEPH: The Alliance for Jewish Renewal. His publications include *The First Step*, which translated Jewish mysticism into a popular, practical idiom; and

Paradigm Shift, a collection of his Jewish Renewal writings. While he has written relatively few books, in the style of a true rebbe, his impact has come from his charismatic leadership.

Arthur Waskow has long been a powerful voice in the Jewish Renewal movement. A veteran of 1960s activism, he returned to Judaism in the aftermath of the assassination of Martin Luther King in 1968. Witnessing the riots in Washington, D.C., Waskow believed that King was the Moses of his people, and the armed policemen in the streets were Pharaoh's soldiers. This insight led to the creation of an interreligious Freedom Seder, incorporating universal themes of freedom – for blacks, Vietnamese, and all oppressed peoples.

Waskow's political and spiritual activism in the Jewish community has been a constant over the past thirty years. He was a founder of *Farbrengen* in Washington, D.C.; *Breira*, which actively criticized Israeli policies; and the Shalom Center, the Jewish address for the anti-nuclear movement. He began editing "Menorah: Sparks of Jewish Renewal" in 1978 (now "New Menorah," published by ALEPH: Alliance for Jewish Renewal). Waskow's major books all emphasize the integration of Jewish truths with social justice and transformation.

Michael Lerner is the editor of *Tikkun* magazine, a left-wing Jewish intellectual journal. His philosophy is "the politics of meaning," the notion that politics and public life should speak to the inner anguish of the contemporary individual. Lerner believes that the secular Left has failed because it only addresses economic issues and not spiritual ones. The Right gained ascendancy because it willingly engaged those issues. Lerner's "politics of meaning" is centrally concerned with human values that are anchored in spirituality. His message is that through our efforts we can rediscover authentic Jewish teaching and make it come alive in our lives and in our institutions.

Conclusion

New Age Judaism continues to struggle with massive issues. How can one construct a Jewish identity that is rooted in the past and yet creative and individualistic? How can a movement be authentically Jewish and yet be nourished by many non-Jewish intellectual and theological streams? Will this movement prove to be fertile, replicating itself into the next generation?

There is much to criticize in New Age Judaism. Much of the new American Jewish spirituality is anti-intellectual, relying more on feelings than connection to texts. It is highly personalistic, often at the expense of community. New Age Judaism may become ever more syncretistic, borrowing from New Age religions and also from Buddhism, Hinduism, Sufism, ancient paganism, and even Christianity. Judaism needs to be careful about "generic" religion of any kind. Its flirtation with mysticism can be dangerous, bordering on the cult-like and exposing people to doctrines that are essentially meaningless without a firm rooting in Judaism.

Still, New Age Judaism has brought many people back from the peripheries to a deepened sense of Judaism. It is the classic late twentieth-century illustration of an ongoing principle in Jewish history: All historic Judaisms have borrowed from the majority culture and have wrestled with that culture. In the words of Ecclesiastes, they have known that there is "a time to embrace, and a time to refrain from embracing." New Age Judaism now needs to discern exactly what to embrace and what to refrain from embracing. Therein will lie its unique blessing.

Note

1   Schachter-Shalomi, Zalman, *Paradigm Shift* (Northvale, 1993), p. 257.

Bibliography

Boorstin, Sylvia, *Funny, You Don't Look Buddhist!* (New York, 1997).

Cowan, Paul, *An Orphan in History: Retrieving a Lost Jewish Legacy* (Garden City, 1982).

Falk, Marcia, *The Book of Blessings* (New York, 1996).

Gottlieb, Lynn, *She Who Dwells Within: A Feminist Vision of a Renewed Judaism* (New York, 1995).

Green, Arthur, *Tormented Master: The Life and Spiritual Quest of Rabbi Nahman of Bratslav* (Woodstock, 1992).

Green, Arthur, and Barry Holtz, *Your Word Is Fire: Hasidic Masters on Contemplative Prayer* (Woodstock, 1993).

Green, Arthur, *Seek My Face, Speak My Name: A Contemporary Jewish Theology* (Northvale, 1992).

Hoffman, Lawrence A., *The Art of Public Prayer: Not For Clergy Only* (Washington, D.C., 1988).

Kamenetz, Rodger, *The Jew in the Lotus* (New York, 1994).

Kushner, Lawrence, *The Book of Letters* (Woodstock, 1990).

Kushner, Lawrence, *The Book of Words* (Woodstock, 1993).

Kushner, Lawrence, *God Was In This Place and I, I Did Not Know: Finding Self, Spirituality, and Ultimate Meaning* (Woodstock, 1991).

Kushner, Lawrence, *Honey from the Rock* (Woodstock, 1990).

Kushner, Lawrence, *Invisible Lines of Connection: Sacred Stories of the Ordinary* (Woodstock, 1996).

Kushner, Lawrence, *The River of Light: Spirituality, Judaism, Consciousness* (Woodstock, 1990).

Lerner, Michael, *Jewish Renewal: A Path to Healing and Transformation* (New York, 1994).

Olitsky, Kerry M., and Stuart A. Copans, *Twelve Jewish Steps to Recovery: A Personal Guide to Turning from Alcoholism and Other Addictions . . . Drugs, Food, Gambling, Sex* (Woodstock, 1992).

Pitzele, Peter, *Our Fathers' Wells: A Personal Encounter with the Myths of Genesis* (New York, 1995).

Plaskow, Judith, *Standing Again at Sinai: Judaism from a Feminist Perspective* (New York, 1990).

Salkin, Jeffrey K., *Being God's Partner: How to Find the Hidden Link between Spirituality and Your Work* (Woodstock, 1994).

Salkin, Jeffrey K., *Putting God on the Guest List: How to Reclaim the Spiritual Meaning of Your Child's Bar or Bat Mitzvah* (Woodstock, 1996).

Schachter-Shalomi, Zalman, with Donald Gropman, *The First Step: A Guide for the New Jewish Spirit* (New York, 1983).

Schachter-Shalomi, Zalman, *Paradigm Shift* (Northvale, 1993).

Schachter-Shalomi, Zalman, *Spiritual Intimacy: A Study of Counseling in Hasidism* (Northvale, 1991).

Strassfeld, Michael, Sharon Strassfeld, and Richard Siegel, *The Jewish Catalog*, vol. 1 (Philadelphia, 1973).

Strassfeld, Michael, and Sharon Strassfeld, *The Jewish Catalog*, vols. 2–3 (Philadelphia, 1976, 1980).

Strassfeld, Michael, *The Jewish Holidays: A Guide and Commentary* (New York, 1985).

Waskow, Arthur, *Down-to-Earth Judaism: Food, Money, Sex, and the Rest of Life* (New York, 1995).

Waskow, Arthur, *Godwrestling – Round 2: Ancient Wisdom, Future Paths* (Woodstock, 1996).

Waskow, Arthur, *Seasons of Our Joy: A Celebration of Modern Jewish Renewal* (New York, 1982).

Waskow, Arthur, *These Holy Sparks: The Rebirth of the Jewish People* (San Francisco, 1983).

Wertheimer, Jack, *A People Divided: Judaism in Contemporary America* (New York, 1993).

PART IV
Special Topics in Understanding Judaism

CHAPTER 21
Ethics of Judaism

Elliot N. Dorff

The presumption that Judaism can educate and guide us morally is a major source of Jews' interest in Judaism. Morality is certainly not the sum total of the Jewish tradition, nor its only attraction; but the moral sensitivity and instruction that Jewish religion, law, and history can provide are surely an important part of what the Jewish tradition has meant to Jews historically and continues to mean for Jews in our day as well. In the contemporary world, where technology and freedom have produced great gifts but also difficult moral problems, Jews – including those who are not otherwise religious – look ever more to their heritage for guidance in how to think and act.

Jewish Ethics

While the terms "ethical" and "moral" are often used interchangeably in common parlance – or even to reinforce each other, as in, "He is unquestionably a moral and ethical person" – in philosophy the two terms denote different things. "Morals" refers to the concrete norms of what is good or bad, right or wrong, in a given situation. Thus the extent to which life-support mechanisms should be used on dying patients, the degree to which an employee's privacy must be maintained, and the norms that should govern sexual relations among unmarried people are all moral questions.

"Ethics," in contrast, refers to the *theory* of morals. Ethics, in other words, is one level of abstraction higher than moral discussions. That does not mean that ethical questions are more important than moral ones; they just occupy a different level of thought. Thus in a university course in Ethics one would examine *questions of meaning, knowledge, justification, and comparison* such as these: How should you *define* the terms "good" and "bad," "right" and "wrong,"

and why should you define them that way? How are judgments of "good" different from judgments of "right"? Are there universal, absolute standards of moral
norms, or do they extend only to given societies (or perhaps only to individuals)?
Whatever the scope of moral norms, how do you *know* what is right or wrong,
good or bad? (Do you, for example, take a vote, ask an authority figure, decide
what pleases you, use your conscience, seek God's will in some way, or do
something else?) How do you know that this is the proper method to determine
what is moral? To what factors do you appeal in *justifying* your moral judgments?
(Some possible answers: the act designated as good provides the most happiness
for the greatest number of people; it fits the requirements of conscience; it follows
from some previously justified principles or decisions; it obeys an authority figure,
whether divine or human; it is what most people in my community think is
right; it is what the law requires; or, it is what pleases you personally.) And how
is morality *related* to law? to religion? to custom? to politics? to police or military
power? to economics? to art? to education? etc. While all of these ethical questions have been addressed from a distinctly Jewish point of view, two particular
issues have occupied Jewish thinkers up to our own day: Why should I carry
out Judaism's moral demands, and how can I define and know what is moral?

The variety of rationales that have been suggested may be surprising to
some contemporary readers who, motivated perhaps by the biblical depiction of
the revelation of the Torah at Mount Sinai amidst thunder, lightning, and earthquakes, are used to thinking that there is really only one reason to obey: God
will punish you if you do not and reward you if you do. A mere forty days after
that revelation, though, the very people who experienced it were worshiping
the Golden Calf, and so it became clear early on that divine reward and punishment alone would not suffice as rationales for obedience. As a result, the Torah
itself provides an immensely sophisticated list beyond reward or punishment
at the hands of God or human beings of why people should obey laws and act
morally. That list includes the inherent wisdom of doing so; the Covenant, with
its inherent morality of promise-keeping and the duties of the relationship it
establishes; gratitude to God; the responsibility we have to preserve and enhance
God's reputation, and our own; the aspiration for holiness; and, ultimately, the
love between us and God.[1] Rabbinic literature adds a few more rationales –
including, for example, the fact that the commandments create a separate,
national identity, have aesthetic value, and make us more humane. Medieval
Jewish literature specifies additional rationales, in particular the rationalist
philosophers' insistence that the commandments accord with, and are demanded
by, reason, and the mystics' affirmation that Jewish norms bridge the gap
between us and God, enabling us to know God – not just intellectually, but
intimately – and, in some later versions of Jewish mysticism, actually to become
part of God. Modern Jewish thought adds yet further rationales, for example,
Franz Rosenzweig's assertion that the commandments create a personal relationship between us and God.[2]

Even if we are convinced that we should adhere to Jewish moral norms, how
do we know what they are? Classical Judaism defines the moral in terms of

God's will as articulated in God's commandments. Some modern theorists, however, have challenged the nexus between God's will and Jewish law, and some humanistic Jews have even denied that we should look to God's will in any form to define the right and the good. Even those who believe that Jewish moral norms are to be defined in terms of God's will and that Jewish law is the proper vehicle for knowing what God wants of us cannot rest with Jewish law alone, for the Talmud itself declares that the law is not fully sufficient to define morality, that there are morals "beyond the letter of the law" (*lifnim m'shurat ha-din*).[3] Beginning, then, with Abraham's challenge to God, "Shall the judge of all the earth not do justice?" (Gen. 18:25), one ethical question addressed throughout Jewish history has been the relationship between moral norms and God's word.

Another, more modern question, is this: if we assume that God's will defines that which is morally right and good, how shall we discern what God wants us to do now? Reform theories, such as that of Eugene Borowitz,[4] maintain that individual Jews should make that decision. They should inform themselves as much as possible about the relevant factors in the case and about the Jewish sources that apply, but ultimately individual Jews, rather than rabbis, should determine what God wants of us on the basis of their knowledge and conscience.

This Reform methodology raises major questions about how to identify any Jew's decision as being recognizably Jewish. Indeed, it makes it possible and even likely that there will be multiple, conflicting moral decisions, all claiming to be Jewish, for each and every Jew has the right to articulate the "Jewish" position on a given issue. This challenges the coherence and intelligibility of the Jewish moral message. Moreover, Borowitz's methodology depends crucially upon the assumption that individual Jews know enough about the Jewish tradition and how to apply it to carry out this task, an assumption that regrettably does not comply with reality.

Positively, though, Reform methodology empowers individual Jews to wrestle with the Jewish tradition themselves, and it encourages – even demands – that Jews learn more about their tradition in order to carry out this task. By making the decision depend on a specifically *Jewish* self, rather than an isolated, undifferentiated self, Borowitz also goes some way in the direction of explaining how such choices can be identified as specifically Jewish: Jewish choices come from self-identified and self-consciously Jewish people.

At the other end of the spectrum, most Orthodox theorists claim that Jewish law as it has come down to us should serve as our authoritative source for knowing God's will, and the more straightforwardly and literally we can read those sources, the more assured we can be that we have discovered God's will. No change is necessary or possible, for God has proclaimed these moral norms through the Written Torah (the Five Books of Moses) and the Oral Torah that, Orthodox Jews believe, was given to Moses at Mount Sinai simultaneously with the Written Torah.

For those who affirm these beliefs, this methodology imparts a sense of assuredness that one knows how to identify God's will and why one should obey it: God demands that of you. On the other hand, this methodology rests, first, on the assumption that God's will is literally expressed in the Torah and in later Rabbinic literature; that is a conviction of faith that one either affirms or denies. Beyond that, to adopt the Orthodox approach one must believe that we have the exact expression of the divine will in hand in the texts that have come down to us. That assertion is undermined by the overwhelming evidence that biblical and Rabbinic literature – including the Torah itself – were written at a variety of times and places. Moreover, even if one believes in the literal, divine authority of the Torah and Rabbinic literature, one still needs to interpret and apply those sources, and that leaves plenty of room for human controversy and error. Thus this methodology does not deliver the certainty it promises to inform us what God demands. Finally, as some left-wing Orthodox rabbis have themselves noted,[5] we still have to ask whether the law defines the entirety of our moral duty – and, I would add, whether the law might actually conflict with what morality demands.

Conservative theorists and rabbis (and a few Orthodox ones) use Jewish law as much as possible to know God's will (and hence the right and the good), and they pay attention also to Jewish theological convictions and Jewish stories.[6] They combine this broader use of Jewish sources with an historical understanding of them. Thus when it comes time to apply them to contemporary circumstances, Conservative theorists look carefully at the ways in which a given contemporary setting is similar to, or different from, the historical one in which a given source was written in order to be able to judge the degree to which it should guide us today. They also look to the sources not so much for specific directions as for the principles that underlie past applications of Jewish law so that we can intelligently apply them to the modern context. For that matter, an historical understanding of the Jewish tradition requires that even past ethical principles themselves be subject to recurrent evaluation. Both past principles and past applications of them, however, are assessed with a bias toward conserving the tradition (and hence the name "Conservative"), such that the burden of proof rests on the one who wants to change a particular moral or ethical stance rather than the one who wants to maintain what has come down to us.

This Conservative approach does not present a neat, clearly identifiable lesson on all moral matters in our day; on the contrary, it invites discussion and controversy. Moreover, it requires judgment; no source may be taken at face value, none is immune from evaluation. This is clearly not a methodology for the anal compulsive! Unlike the Reform approach, though, the Conservative methodology requires that such evaluation be done not just by individuals but by the community, thus preserving a greater degree of coherence and Jewish identity. It makes such decisions primarily through its Rabbinic leaders, since they are the most likely to know what the tradition says and how to apply it to modern circumstances.[7] This way of discerning what God wants thus does not depend on knowledge and skills that most Jews lack. In contrast to the Orthodox approach, the Conservative one has the distinct advantage of historical awareness and authenticity, for it interprets sources in their historical context and, like generations past, combines received Jewish law with an openness to the moral sensitivities and needs of the time. It thus has a greater balance of the traditional with the modern, greater openness to learning from others, and greater flexibility.

Yet a fourth way of discerning God's will is that pioneered by Martin Buber, developed further by Emanuel Levinas, and articulated in a contemporary feminist version by Laurie Zoloth-Dorfman.[8] In this approach we discover Jewish moral norms through our encounters with other human beings in one-to-one, direct interactions.

This approach, sometimes called "personalist" or even "feminist," suffers from the same problems that Reform individualism has: it is weak on Jewish identity, continuity, coherence, and authority. At the same time, it locates moral decisions where they in fact lie, in the interaction among human beings. Moreover, it invokes the inherent authority another human being has for us simply by virtue of being another human being who faces us directly.

Jewish Morals

Why should Jews use any of these methodologies to determine what is moral? Why, in other words, should we expect that Judaism has anything to teach us about morality? The reason is inherent in the word "religion," which comes from the Latin root meaning bonds or linkages, the same root from which we get the word "ligament." Religions describe the ties that we have to our families, our community, the rest of humanity, the environment, and the transcendent. In so doing, religions give us conceptual eyeglasses, as it were, through which we look at the world. Secular philosophies like liberalism, Marxism, or existentialism do that too, but philosophies, *qua* philosophies, are purely intellectual. Religions, on the other hand, by their very nature embody their views of life in myths and rituals and thereby form communities of people connected to each other and to their shared vision of what is and what ought to be. Such religious communities provide comradery, strength, and meaning in the ongoing aspects of life – the life-cycle, the seasonal cycle, and, indeed, the progress of each day and week; they furnish moral education in a variety of formats; and they also work together toward realizing their ideals. Religions, then, are related to morality because they depict the way the world is, offer visions of what it ought to be, and define communities to teach morality and work toward moral goals.

Religions do not all present the same moral view however. Some norms, of course, are virtually universal – prohibitions against murder and theft, for instance, and demands to help others. Even widespread norms, though, vary in definition; so, for example, for some pacifist religions, all killing of human beings constitutes murder, while for others killing an enemy in war or in self-defense is not only permissible but mandatory. Furthermore, even when a norm is defined in the same way by two religions, each of them may give a different degree of emphasis to it. Finally, some positive duties or prohibitions are affirmed by some religions but not by others.

As a result of these variations, each religion presents a picture of reality and of the ideal that is distinctive in degree or kind. Each religion also inculcates its version of morality in its youth and adults in varying ways. To understand Jewish morality, then, we shall describe some important elements of Judaism's vision of the real and the ideal. Because Jews often think that the entire world thinks as Jews do, it will be helpful along the way to compare the Jewish norm with Christian norms and with western norms as embodied in secular culture.

The human being

We begin with several Jewish convictions about the individual:

(a) *The body belongs to God.* For Judaism, God, as creator of the world, owns everything in it, including our bodies.[9] God loans our bodies to us for the duration of our lives, and we return them to God when we die. Consequently, neither men nor women have the right to govern their bodies as they will; God, as creator and owner, asserts the right to restrict how we use our bodies in ways articulated in Jewish law.

Some of God's rules require us to take reasonable care of our bodies, just as we would be obliged to protect and clean an apartment on loan to us. Rules of good hygiene, sleep, exercise, and diet in Jewish sources are therefore not just words to the wise designed for our comfort and longevity, as they are in American thinking; they are, rather, commanded acts that we owe God. So, for example, Hillel regards bathing as a commandment (Lev. Rabbah 34:3), and Maimonides includes his directives for good health in his code of law, considering them just as obligatory as other positive duties such as caring for the poor.[10]

Just as we are commanded to maintain good health, so we are obligated to avoid danger and injury.[11] Indeed, Jewish law views endangering one's health as worse than violating a ritual prohibition.[12] So, for example, anyone who can survive only by taking charity but refuses to do so out of pride is, according to the tradition, shedding his or her own blood and is guilty of a mortal offense.[13] Conservative, Reform, and some Orthodox authorities additionally have prohibited smoking as an unacceptable risk to our God-owned bodies.[14] Judaism similarly teaches that human beings do not have the right to dispose of their bodies at will (i.e., commit suicide), for doing so obliterates something that belongs not to us but to God.[15] In contrast, the laws of most American states permit suicide (although most prohibit aiding and abetting a suicide).[16]

(b) *Being created in God's image imparts value to life, regardless of the individual's level of capacity or incapacity.* The American way of thinking is thoroughly pragmatic: a person's value is a function of what that person can *do* for others. This view, so deeply ingrained in American culture, prompts Americans to value those who have unusual abilities, who *succeed* – and, conversely, to devalue those who are disabled in some way. In sharp contrast, the Torah declares that God created each of us in the divine image: "God created the human being in his image, in the image of God he created him; male and female God created them" (Gen. 1:27; see also Gen. 5:1). Exactly which feature of the human being reflects this divine image is a matter of debate within the tradition. The Torah itself seems to tie it to humanity's ability to make moral judgments, that is, to distinguish good from bad and right from wrong, to behave accordingly, and to judge one's own actions and those of others on the basis of this moral knowledge (see Gen. 1:26–27; 3:1–7, 22–24). Another human faculty connected by the Torah and later tradition to divinity is the ability to speak.[17] Locating the divine image within us may also be the Torah's way of acknowledging that we can love, just as God does,[18] or that we are at least partially spiritual and thus share God's spiritual nature.[19]

Not only does this doctrine *describe* aspects of our nature; it also *prescribes* behavior. Specifically, because human beings are created in God's image, we affront God when we insult another person.[20] On the contrary, we must treat people with respect, recognizing each individual's uniqueness and divine worth because all human beings embody the image of God:

> For this reason Adam was created as a single person, to teach you that anyone who destroys one soul is described in Scripture as if he destroyed an entire world, and anyone who sustains one soul is described in Scripture as if he sustained an entire world. . . . And to declare the greatness of the Holy One, praised be he, for a person uses a mold to cast a number of coins, and they are all similar to each other, while the Sovereign of all sovereigns, the Holy One, praised be he, cast each person in the mold of the first human being and none of them is similar to any other. Therefore each and every person must say: "For me the world was created."[21]

Consider also the traditional blessing recited when seeing someone with a disability: "Praised are you, Lord our God, who makes different creatures" or "who created us with differences" (*meshaneh ha-briyyot*). Precisely when we might recoil from a deformed or incapacitated person, or thank God for not making us like that, the tradition instead bids us to embrace the divine image in such people – indeed, to bless God for creating some of us so.[22]

(c) The human being is an integrated whole, combining all aspects of our being. Western philosophical thought and Christianity have been heavily influenced by the Greek and Gnostic bifurcation of body and mind (or soul). In these systems of thought, the body is seen as the inferior part of human beings, either because it is what we share with animals, in contrast to the mind, which is distinctively human (Aristotle), or because the body is the seat of our passions and hence our sins (Paul in Romans and Galatians[23]). Even though the Greeks glorified the body in their art and sculpture, it was only because developing the body was seen as a means to an end, a necessary prerequisite to cultivating the mind (as, for example, in Plato's pedagogic program in *The Republic*). Similarly, Paul regarded the body as "the temple of the Holy Spirit" (1 Cor. 6:19), but only because it serves to sustain the soul so that it can accept faith in Jesus; the body *per se* "makes me a prisoner of that law of sin which lives inside my body" (Rom. 7:23).

Such classical views have shaped western and Christian traditions from ancient times to our own. In Christianity, Augustine, Luther, and Calvin follow the lead of Paul and maintain that the body's needs are to be suppressed as much as possible; indeed, asceticism and monasticism have been important themes in Christian ideology and history. In secular philosophic thought, "the mind–body problem" continues to be a stock issue in philosophic literature, which asks how the two, presumed to be so different and separate, are related in some ways to each other.

While some Jews (in particular, Philo and Maimonides[24]) were heavily influenced by these doctrines of the people living around them, biblical and talmudic literature does not share in this divided understanding of the human being. In the Talmud and midrash, our soul is, in some senses, separable from our body. For example, when the Torah describes God as breathing life into Adam's body, Rabbinic sources understand that to mean not only physical life but consciousness. God repeats that process each day by taking our souls away during sleep and returning them again when we awake. Moreover, at death, the soul leaves the body only to be united with it again at the time of resurrection.[25] Rabbinic sources conflict, however, as to whether the soul can exist apart from the body, and even those who say it can, depict the soul in physical terms, capable of performing many of the functions of the body.[26]

In any case, in sharp contrast to the Greek and Christian traditions, classical Rabbinic sources maintain that the soul is definitely not superior to the body. Indeed, one Rabbinic source speaks of the soul as a guest in the body here on earth: one's host must accordingly be respected and well treated (Lev. Rabbah 34:3). Moreover, since the rabbis regarded the human being as an integrated whole, the body and the soul are to be judged as one:

> Antoninus said to Rabbi [Judah, the President, or "Prince," of the Sanhedrin], "The body and soul could exonerate themselves from judgment. How is this so? The body could say, 'The soul sinned, for from the day that it separated from me, lo, I am like a silent stone in the grave!' And the soul could say, 'The body is the sinner, for from the day that I separated from it, lo, I fly like a bird.'"
>
> Rabbi [Judah] answered him, "I will tell you a parable. What is the matter like? It is like a king of flesh and blood who had a beautiful orchard, and there were in it lovely ripe fruit. He placed two guardians over it, one a cripple and the other blind. Said the cripple to the blind man, 'I see beautiful ripe fruit in the orchard. Come and carry me, and we will bring and eat them.' The cripple rode on the back of the blind man and they brought and ate them. After a while the owner of the orchard came and said to them, 'Where is my lovely fruit?' The cripple answered, 'Do I have legs to go?' The blind man answered, 'Do I have eyes to see?' What did the owner do? He placed the cripple on the back of the blind man and judged them as one. So also the Holy Blessed One brings the soul and throws it into the body and judges them as one."[27]

Not only is this concept of the human being as fundamentally integrated manifest in God's ultimate, divine judgment of each of us; it is also the rabbis' recipe for life and their method for moral education. Although the rabbis emphasized the importance of studying and following the Torah, even placing it on a par with all the rest of the commandments (M. Pe. 1:1; B. Qid. 40b), they nonetheless believed that the life of the soul or mind by itself is not good, that it can, indeed, be the source of sin:

> An excellent thing is the study of Torah combined with some worldly occupation, for the labor demanded by both of them causes sinful inclinations to be forgotten. All study of Torah without work must, in the end, be futile and become the cause of sin.[28]

Thus, while the rabbis considered it a privilege to be able to study Torah, they themselves – or at least most of them – earned their livelihood through bodily work, and they also valued the hard labor of the field worker who spends little time in the study of Torah:

> A favorite saying of the rabbis of Yavneh was: I am God's creature, and my fellow [who works in the field and is not a student] is God's creature. My work is in the town, and his work is in the country. I rise early for my work, and he rises early for his work. Just as he does not presume to do my work, so I do not presume to do his work. Will you say, I do much [in the study of Torah] and he does little? We have learned: One may do much or one may do little; it is all one, provided that the person directs his heart to Heaven.[29]

(d) The body is morally neutral and potentially good. The body is neither bad nor good. Rather, its energies, like those of our mind, will, and emotions, are morally neutral. All our faculties can and should be used for divine purposes as defined by Jewish law and tradition. Within these constraints, the body's pleasures are God-given and are not to be shunned, for to do so would be an act of ingratitude toward our creator. The body, in other words, can and should give us pleasure to the extent that such pleasure enables us to live a life of holiness.

Here Judaism differs markedly both from the American secular view of the body, on the one hand, and from Christianity, on the other. In the American media, the body is portrayed as a virtual pleasure machine. In contemporary films, commercials, and music, we are encouraged to derive as much pleasure as possible from the body, for that is its primary purpose. The only restriction inherent in this ethic is that I may not deprive you of pleasure in the process of getting it for myself. Yet even this limitation is not absolute. Characters in American popular culture, such as James Bond, are "cool" precisely because they do not care about whether they injure others. In contrast, Judaism teaches that the body's pleasures are indeed to be enjoyed, but only when experienced within the framework of holiness delineated by Jewish law and theology.

At the other end of the spectrum is Christianity, which depicts the body as a negative part of us to be suppressed as much as possible. Thus in Catholic and many Protestant sources, the ideal Christian is the ascetic who as much as possible denies him or herself the pleasures of sex, food, and possessions. Of course, not all forms of contemporary Christianity embrace this ascetic way of thinking in its entirety, but Roman Catholicism, by far the most populous Christian faith, still does, and in some degree so do many Protestant sects.

The closest Judaism comes to this attitude are the rules governing Yom Kippur and historical fast days like Tisha B'Av, on which Jews "afflict our souls" through fasting, sexual abstinence, and other forms of physical self-denial. But in each case such abstinence is restricted to that day alone and is designed to call attention to the spiritual theme of the day; deprivation itself is not expected to effect atonement or historical memory.

The Jewish mode for attaining holiness is thus not to endure pain but to use all of our faculties, including our bodily energies, to perform God's commandments. For example, though we eat as all animals do, our eating takes on a divine dimension when we observe Jewish dietary restrictions and surround our meals with the appropriate blessings. Some bodily pleasures are even commanded. Thus, with the exception of Yom Kippur, we may not fast on the Sabbath, and we must eat three meals to celebrate it. We should also bathe and wear clean clothes in honor of the day.[30] Furthermore, as we shall see, the ideal in Judaism is marriage, where sex can bring not only children but joy and companionship. In all, the rabbis deem it a sin to deny ourselves the pleasures God's law allows. Just as the Nazirite (Num. 6:11) was to bring a sin offering after denying himself the permitted delight of wine, so we will be called to account in the world-to-come for the ingratitude and haughtiness of denying ourselves the pleasures God has provided (B. Ta. 11a).[31]

According to Maimonides, bodily pleasures are most appropriately enjoyed when we have the specific intent to enhance our ability to do God's will:

> He who regulates his life in accordance with the laws of medicine with the sole motive of maintaining a sound and vigorous physique and begetting children to do his work and labor for his benefit is not following the right course. A man should aim to maintain physical health and vigor in order that his soul may be upright, in a condition to know God. . . . Whoever throughout his life follows this course will be continually serving God, even while engaged in business and even during cohabitation, because his purpose in all that he does will be to satisfy his needs so as to have a sound body with which to serve God. Even when he sleeps and seeks repose to calm his mind and rest his body so as not to fall sick and be incapacitated from serving God, his sleep is service of the Almighty.[32]

The family

The family is a critical unit in Jewish ideology and practice, for it serves several purposes:

(a) *Provides for adult needs*. Ever since the Torah's story about the creation of Eve out of Adam's side, the Jewish tradition has considered it to be God's plan that "a man leaves his father and mother and clings to his wife and they become one flesh" (Gen. 2:24). They do not "become one flesh" in the ontological way of becoming one being, never to be rent asunder through divorce, for divorce, while often sad, is both permissible, as Deut. 24 makes clear, and sometimes the right thing to do. They instead "become one flesh" in several other important ways.

Physically, they become one flesh when they have sexual relations together; marriage and family are designed, in part, to satisfy the sexual needs of both spouses. Most other traditions in both the Occident and Orient – and in American law as well until recently – assume that men have sexual drives, women do not, but women acquiesce to the sexual advances of their husbands because they want economic security and children. Judaism, by contrast, from its earliest sources, assumes that women have sexual needs just as much as men do. Thus Exod. 21:10 stipulates that even a man who marries a slave "must not withhold from her her food, her clothing, or her conjugal rights," and the rabbis reasoned that this holds even more obviously for a man marrying a free woman. Thus, while a husband may never force himself upon his wife, the Mishnah stipulates the number of times each week he must offer to have sexual relations with her, making that depend upon the frequency that his job enables him to be home. Conversely, he has rights to sex within marriage too, and if his wife consistently refuses to have sex with him, he may gradually reduce the amount of money he would have to pay her in a divorce settlement until he does not have to pay her anything (M. Ket. 5:6–7). Both parties may agree to have sexual relations according to a different schedule, but these provisions in Jewish law establish clearly that both partners to a marriage are entitled to have their sexual needs satisfied.

The spouses "become one flesh" psychologically as well. Thus the rabbis declare that "although a man may have many children, he must not remain without a wife," for, as God declares in the Garden of Eden story, "it is not good for a person to live alone" (Gen. 2:18; B. Yeb. 61b). Moreover, the rabbis affirm, "a man without a wife lives without blessing, without life, without joy, without help, and without peace."[33] Conversely, they denigrate bachelorhood (B. Qid. 29b–30a), a far cry from the ideal of asceticism in other cultures. Marriage, in the Jewish view, thus is the optimal context for human development and for meeting adult needs.

Since a major objective of marriage and family is mutual love and support, spousal, parental, or child abuse, aside from being violations of Judaism's laws prohibiting assault and battery, are a total undermining of what family relations should be. Abuse is also a desecration of the divine image inherent in each of us and a failure to respect those so created. Such acts are therefore condemned and punished in Jewish law.

(b) Creates, educates, and supports the next generation. Sex within marriage has two distinct purposes: companionship and procreation. Thus, on the one hand, sexual relations are valued as a form of human love even when the couple cannot, or is not planning to, have children. On the other hand, procreation is an important activity, so important, in fact, that it is the very first commandment

mentioned in the Torah: "God blessed them [the first man and woman] and God said to them: 'Be fruitful and multiply . . .' " (Gen. 1:28). The rabbis later define that obligation as the duty to have minimally two children – although this does not apply to those who cannot comply because of problems of infertility – and the ideal is to have as many children as one can.[34]

Marriage not only provides the venue for having children; it is also, in the Jewish view, the context in which they are educated. Parents have the duty to educate their children in Judaism, including its moral components.[35] Parents may use schools to help them fulfill that duty, but they must periodically check to make sure that their children are in fact learning what they should, because ultimately the duty to educate children remains theirs. Moreover, much of the Jewish tradition can only be taught at home, for this is a tradition that is not restricted to the synagogue or school: it intends to influence virtually every detail of life.

Education

Education is not only for children; it is a life-long activity in Judaism. Thus already in the Torah "Moses summoned all the Israelites and said to them: Hear, O Israel, the laws and rules that I proclaim to you this day! Study them and observe them faithfully!" (Deut. 5:1). Moreover, the Torah requires that once every seven years all Israelites – "men, women, and children" – gather to hear the entire Torah read (Deut. 31:10–13). Later Jewish tradition would make this instead a weekly reading from the Torah on each Sabbath, with smaller sections read on Mondays and Thursdays, the market days, as well. From the very beginning, then, this was not to be an esoteric tradition, kept a secret for the few privileged to know; it was, rather, to be an open, public tradition, studied and interpreted by Jews of both genders and all ages. One striking indication of the depth of this Jewish value is that while the Bible calls Moses a "prophet" and describes him as a military leader and an intermediary between God and the Israelites, the rabbis call him "Moses, our teacher."[36]

Jews for generations identified this commandment with studying the Jewish tradition, convinced that one should "turn it over, and turn it over again, for everything is included in it" (M. Abot 5:24). As Jews interacted with other cultures that were making progress in science, medicine, law, and other fields, however, a number of them learned those lessons and integrated their new knowledge into their practice and understanding of Judaism. This trend became considerably more pronounced after the Enlightenment, so much so that even a nineteenth-century Orthodox thinker like Samson Raphael Hirsch could affirm that Jews should learn other fields, for God's revelation is contained not only in traditional Jewish literature, but also in the world that God created. One's study of the world in fields like science and philosophy must, in his view, be evaluated by what one learns in the Torah, for that was given by God while the topics taught in universities were developed by fallible human beings; but one must study the results of human inquiry nevertheless.[37] Not all Orthodox Jews then or now agree with this approach, but many do, and certainly the vast majority of Jews, who are not Orthodox, take general education seriously.

The community

If the family is the primary unit in Jewish life, the community follows close behind. Communities are necessary, in part, for practical purposes, for only through living in a community can one have what one needs to live life as a Jew – synagogues, schools, kosher food, a person skilled in circumcision, a cemetery, and more. Furthermore, only in a community can all the duties of Judaism be fulfilled, for justice, care for the poor, education, and many other Jewish demands require other people. Thus Jewish life is organized around the community.

The community is not only important for practical purposes, though; it also has theological import. Israel stood at Sinai as a community, and it was as a group that they made the covenant with God. From then on, each Jew, as the Passover ritual powerfully states, is to see himself or herself "as if he himself left Egypt" and stood at Sinai, thereby sharing in God's work of liberation and God's covenant with all other Jews in all generations. Judaism, contrary to Enlightenment ideology, does not see us as isolated individuals with rights; it sees us rather as members of a community, with duties to each other and to God.

This sense of community is much stronger than the kinds of communities we are used to in modern, post-Enlightenment societies. In the United States, for example, all communities are voluntary: I may join a group or leave it at any time. I may even choose to give up my citizenship as an American. In Jewish law, though, once I am Jewish by either being born to a Jewish woman or converting to Judaism, I am Jewish for life. If I convert to another religion, I am an apostate, and I lose the privileges of being Jewish (such as being married or buried as a Jew, being counted as part of the prayer quorum, etc.), but I retain all the obligations of being Jewish! This is, then, not a voluntary sense of community but a corporate one, in which I am literally part of the body of the Jewish community and cannot be severed from it.[38]

This sense of community in covenant with God is symbolized by the *minyan*, the prayer quorum consisting of ten Jewish adults. Jews may pray or study individually, but some parts of the liturgy may only be recited, and the official Torah reading may only be accomplished, in the presence of ten Jewish adults, the minimum number deemed a community. Only in that setting may we bless and sanctify God fully, and only there may we hear and study God's word adequately. A talmudic list of facilities and people that must be part of any Jewish community fit for a rabbi to reside in reveals what a community is for the Jewish tradition (B. San. 17b):

> It has been taught: A scholar should not reside in a city where [any] of the following ten things is missing: (1) a court of justice that can impose flagellation and

monetary penalties; (2) a charity fund, collected by two people and distributed by three [to ensure honesty and wise policies of distribution]; (3) a synagogue; (4) public baths; (5) toilet facilities; (6) a circumciser; (7) a doctor; (8) a notary [for writing official documents]; (9) a slaughterer [of kosher meat]; and (10) a schoolmaster. Rabbi Aqiba is quoted [as including in the list] also several kinds of fruit, because they are beneficial for eyesight.

The community must provide facilities and people necessary for (1) justice (a court and notary); (2) Jewish religious life (a synagogue, a circumciser, and a kosher slaughterer); (3) Jewish education (a rabbi and schoolmaster); (4) charity; and (5) health care, including public baths and toilets (remember that this was written before the advent in the past century of indoor plumbing), a doctor, and, according to Rabbi Aqiba, even the foods necessary for health.

If the Jewish community of talmudic times did not live under foreign rule, this list would undoubtedly also include other functions that the rulers supplied – defense, roads and bridges, etc. Still, in many times and places, Jewish communities had semi-autonomy, with the powers of taxation and policing that that implied. The Jewish court would, for example, appoint inspectors of the weights and measures used by merchants to insure honesty in business.[39]

Social action and the messianic future

All of these elements of Jewish life – the individual, the family, education, and the community – are necessary for the ongoing life of Jews, but they are also intended to enable Jews to carry out the Jewish mission. Jews believe that the messiah has not yet come, that the world is still broken and fragmented by war, disease, poverty, meanness, and the like. Only God can ultimately bring the messiah; the *Aleinu*, the prayer that ends every Jewish service, expresses the hope that God will "utterly destroy false gods and fix the world through the reign of the Almighty."[40] Nevertheless, we human beings are to help God in that task as God's agents and partners in the ongoing repair of the world. This includes research into preventing or curing disease, political steps to avoid war and reinforce peace, political and economic measures to stop hunger, legal methods to assure justice, and educational efforts to teach morality and understanding. Jews have been and continue to be heavily involved in social action; indeed, they overwhelmingly see it as the most important factor in their Jewish identity.[41] This commitment to repair the world stems from the conviction that the world is not now redeemed, that we must act in order to help God bring about the messianic hope for the future.

Epilogue

In the end, both Jewish ethics and morality shape the Jew. Jewish theoretical convictions about the divine source of morality and the ways to discern God's will give Jews a sense of why they should be moral and how, even in the radically changed world of today. Jewish moral beliefs about the nature of the human being, the family, education, the community, and the future define what is important in life and motivate Jews to try to achieve those moral goals. Together they pose a distinct challenge to Jews to know God's will and to do it, just as it was in the time of the Torah (Deut. 30:11–14):

> Surely, this instruction which I enjoin upon you this day is not too baffling for you, nor is it beyond reach. It is not in the heavens, that you should say, "Who among us can go up to the heavens and get it for us and impart it to us, that we may observe it?" Neither is it beyond the sea, that you should say, "Who among us can cross to the other side of the sea and get it for us and impart it to us, that we may observe it?" No, the thing is very close to you, in your mouth and in your heart, to observe it.

Notes

1   For a more detailed analysis of the biblical and Rabbinic rationales for abiding by Jewish moral norms, see my *Mitzvah Means Commandment* (New York, 1989).
2   Franz Rosenzweig, "The Builders," in Nahum Glatzer, ed., *On Jewish Learning* (New York, 1955), pp. 72–92.
3   E.g., B. B.M. 30b. To explore the relationship between Jewish law and morality further, see my *Matters of Life and Death: A Jewish Approach to Modern Medical Ethics* (Philadelphia, 1998), pp. 395–417. For other Conservative views, see Robert Gordis, *The Dynamics of Judaism: A Study in Jewish Law* (Bloomington, 1990), pp. 50–68; and Simon Greenberg, *The Ethical in the Jewish and American Heritage* (New York, 1977), pp. 157–218.

   For unusual, but thoughtful, left-wing Orthodox approaches to this issue, see David Hartman, *A Living Covenant: The Innovative Spirit in Traditional Judaism* (Woodstock, 1997), pp. 89–108; and Shubert Spero, *Morality, Halakha, and the Jewish Tradition* (New York, 1983), pp. 166–200. Since, for Reform Judaism, Jewish law is, in Rabbi Solomon Freehof's words, "not directive, but advisory," "our guidance, but not our governance," moral norms, however they are construed, always take precedence over Jewish law, for moral norms are binding but Jewish law is not. See Solomon Freehof, *Reform Responsa* (Cincinnati, 1960), pp. 3–23; the citations are on p. 22. The Reform platform, *A Centenary Perspective*, issued in 1976, says: "Our founders stressed that the Jewish ethical responsibilities, personal and social, are enjoined by God. The past century has taught us that the claims made upon us may begin with our ethical obligations, but they extend to many other aspects of Jewish living. . . ." Reform Jews are therefore "to confront the claims of Jewish tradition, however differently perceived, and to exercise their individual autonomy, choosing and creating on the basis of commitment and knowledge." This represents a wider commitment to Jewish practice, but not a conviction that Jewish law *per se* is binding, and so the relationship between Jewish law and morality does not bother Reform thinkers nearly as much as it does those in the Conservative and Orthodox movements, who hold that Jewish law is binding. See Eugene B. Borowitz, *Reform Judaism Today* (New York, 1983), pp. xxii–xxiii.

4   Eugene Borowitz, *Renewing the Covenant* (Philadelphia, 1991), pp. 284–99; reprinted in Elliot N. Dorff and Louis E. Newman, eds., *Contemporary Jewish Ethics and Morality: A Reader* (New York, 1995), pp. 106–17. See also the exchange between Rabbi Borowitz and myself on the extent to which his theory is indeed Reform, beginning with my review of his book in *Conservative Judaism* 48:2 (Winter 1996), pp. 64–8, and our exchange of letters in *Conservative Judaism* 50:1 (Fall 1997), pp. 61–71.

5   See note 3 above.

6   See Dorff, *Matters of Life and Death*, pp. 7–13, 395–423; and Aaron L. Mackler, "Cases and Principles in Jewish Bioethics: Toward a Holistic Model," in Dorff and Newman, *Contemporary Jewish Ethics and Morality*, pp. 177–93.

7   This goes back to the idea of Solomon Schechter, one of the founders of Conservative Judaism, of "catholic Israel." For more on Conservative theories of Jewish law, including the communal aspect of it, see my *Conservative Judaism: Our Ancestors to Our Descendants* (New York, 1996).

8   Martin Buber, *I And Thou* (New York, 1958). Emanuel Levinas, *Ethics and Infinity*, Richard A. Cohen, trans. (Pittsburgh, 1985) is one good source, among his many works, for his ethical views. Laurie Zoloth-Dorfman, "An Ethics of Encounter: Public Choices and Private Acts," in Dorff and Newman, *Contemporary Jewish Ethics and Morality*, pp. 219–45.

9   See, for example, Exod. 19:5; Deut. 10:14; Ps. 24:1. See also Gen. 14:19, 22 (where the Hebrew word for "creator" [*koneh*] also means "possessor," and where "heaven and earth" is a merism for those and everything in between) and Ps. 104:24, where the same word is used with the same meaning. The following verses have the same theme, although not quite as explicitly or as expansively: Exod. 20:11; Lev. 25:23, 42, 55; Deut. 4:35, 39; 32:6.

10   *Mishneh Torah*, *Laws of Ethics (De'ot)*, chs. 3–5. He spells out there in remarkable clarity that the purpose of the positive duties to maintain health is not to feel good and live a long life but to have a healthy body so that one can serve God.

11   B. Shab. 32a; B. B.Q. 15b, 80a, 91b; *Mishneh Torah Laws of Murder* 11:4–5; *Shulhan Arukh Yoreh De'ah* 116:5 gloss; *Shulhan Arukh Hoshen Mishpat* 427:8–10.

12   B. Hul. 10a; *Shulhan Arukh Orah Hayyim* 173:2; *Shulhan Arukh Yoreh De'ah* 116:5 gloss.

13   *Shulhan Arukh Yoreh De'ah* 255:2.

14   J. David Bleich, "Smoking," in *Tradition* 16:4 (Summer 1977), pp. 130–33; Solomon Freehof, *Reform Responsa for Our Time* (Cincinnati, 1977), ch. 11; *Proceedings of the Rabbinical Assembly*, 44 (1983), p. 182. All of the above are reprinted in Elliot N. Dorff and Arthur Rosett, *A Living Tree: The Roots and Growth of Jewish Law* (Albany, 1988), pp. 337–62.

15   Gen. 9:5; M. Sem. 2:2; B. B.Q. 91b; Gen. Rabbah 34:19 states that the ban against suicide includes not only cases in which blood is shed but also self-inflicted death through strangulation and the like; *Mishneh Torah Laws of Murder* 2:3; *Mishneh Torah Laws of Injury and Damage* 5:1; *Shulhan Arukh Yoreh De'ah* 345:1–3.

This reasoning extends to inanimate property as well: we may use what we need, but we may not destroy any more of God's world than we need to in order to accomplish our purposes. This is the prohibition of *ba'al tashhit*, "Do not destroy," based on Deut. 20:19–20 and amplified in the tradition to prohibit any unnecessary destruction: M. B.Q. 8:6, 7; B. B.Q. 92a, 93a; Mishneh Torah *Laws of Murder* 1:4, where Maimonides specifically invokes this theological basis for the law against suicide; Mishneh Torah *Laws of Injury and Damage* 5:5; *Sefer Ha-Hinnukh*, Commandment 529; Shulhan Arukh *Hoshen Mishpat* 420:1, 31.

16 Forty-four states currently deem aiding a person to commit suicide a felony. See David G. Savage, "Supreme Court to Decide Issue of Right to Die," in *Los Angeles Times*, October 2, 1996, p. A-16. Oregon is the only state that specifically permits such aid.

17 See Gen. 2:18–24; Num. 12:1–16; Deut. 22:13–19. Note also that *"ha-middaber,"* "the speaker," is a synonym for the human being (in comparison with animals) in medieval Jewish philosophy.

18 See Deut. 6:5; Lev. 19:18, 33–4, and note that the traditional prayer book juxtaposes the paragraph just before the Shema, which speaks of God's love for us, with the first paragraph of the Shema, which commands us to love God.

19 Consider the prayer in the traditional, early morning weekday service, *"Elohai neshamah she-natata bi,"* "My God, the soul (or life-breath) that you have imparted to me is pure. You created it, You formed it, You breathed it into me; You guard it within me . . ." in Jules Harlow, ed., *Siddur Sim Shalom* (New York, 1985), pp. 8–11. Similarly, the rabbis describe the human being as part divine and part animal, the latter consisting of the material aspects of the human being and the former consisting of that which we share with God; see Sifre Deut., par. 306; 132a. Or consider this Rabbinic statement in Gen. Rabbah 8:11: "In four respects man resembles the creatures above, and in four respects the creatures below. Like the animals he eats and drinks, propagates his species, relieves himself, and dies. Like the ministering angels he stands erect, speaks, possesses intellect, and sees [in front of him and not on the side as an animal does]."

20 Gen. Rabbah 24:7. Consider also: "Great is human dignity, for it overrides a negative prohibition of the Torah" (B. Ber. 19b, etc.). "The Holy One, blessed be he, has concern for the honor of all his creatures, including non-Jews and even wicked people like Balaam" (Num. Rabbah 20:14). "All the Holy One, blessed be he, created, he created for his own honor" (B. Yom. 38a, based on Is. 43:7).

21 M. San. 4:5. Some manuscripts are less universalistic; they read: ". . . anyone who destroys one *Israelite* soul is described in Scripture as if he destroyed an entire world, and anyone who sustains one *Israelite* soul is described in Scripture as if he sustained an entire world." A Hasidic *bon mot* (from Martin Buber, *Tales of the Hasidim* (New York, 1961), vol. 2, pp. 249–50) reminds us that we must balance this recognition of our divine worth with a proper dose of humility:

> Rabbi Bunam said: A person should always have two pieces of paper, one in each pocket. On one should be written, "For me the world was created." On the other should be written, "I am but dust and ashes" (Gen. 18:27).

22 For a thorough discussion of this blessing and concept in the Jewish tradition, see Carl Astor, . . . *Who Makes People Different* (New York, 1985).

The Torah requires that the body of a person who was executed for a capital crime must be removed from the place of hanging by morning out of respect for the divine image inherent even in such a human being, and the rabbis thus require us to respect the divine image even within a criminal whose past actions we detest and punish. See Deut. 21:22–23; B. M.Q. 16a; Y. Qid. 4:1; Y. Naz. 7:5.

23   Rom. 6–8, especially 6:12; 7:14–24; 8:3, 10, 12–13; Gal. 5:16–24; see also 1 Cor. 7:2, 9, 36–38.

24   The Greek side of Maimonides is most in evidence in his *Guide for the Perplexed*, where he states flatly that:

> It is also the object of the perfect Law to make man reject, despise, and reduce his desires as much as is in his power. He should only give way to them when absolutely necessary. It is well known that it is intemperance in eating, drinking, and sexual intercourse that people mostly rave and indulge in; and these very things counteract the ulterior perfection of man, impede at the same time the development of his first perfection [i.e., bodily health], and generally disturb the social order of the country and the economy of the family. For by following entirely the guidance of lust, in the manner of fools, man loses his intellectual energy, injures his body, and perishes before his natural time; sighs and cares multiply; and there is an increase of envy, hatred, and warfare for the purpose of taking what another possesses. The cause of all this is the circumstance that the ignorant considers physical enjoyment as an object to be sought for its own sake. God in His wisdom has therefore given us such commandments as would counteract that object, and prevent us altogether from directing our attention to it . . . For the chief object of the Law is to [teach man to] diminish his desires . . ." (part III, ch. 33)

Philo's views can be found, in part, in the selections from his writings in Hans Lewy, Alexander Altmann, and Isaak Heinemann, eds., *Three Jewish Philosophers* (Philadelphia, 1960), esp. pp. 42–51, 54–5, and 71–5. He calls the body a "prison house," p. 72.

25   Gen. 2:7; B. Ta. 22b; Gen. Rabbah 14:9; B. Nid. 31a. The departure of the soul and its return upon waking is articulated in the first words one is supposed to say upon awaking: "I am grateful to you, living, enduring sovereign, for restoring my soul (life-breath, *nishmati*) to me in compassion. You are faithful (trustworthy) beyond measure." It is also articulated in the previously mentioned *Elohai neshamah she-natata bi*, with roots in Lev. Rabbah 18:1 (toward the end) and Midrash Shahar Tov, ch. 25. The blessing at its conclusion most probably refers not to resurrection after death but, also, to the return of consciousness after sleep.

26   The predominant view seems to be that it can (cf., B. Ber. 18b–19a; B. Hag. 12b; B. Ket. 77b), but even such sources depict the soul in terms of physical imagery, thereby enabling it to perform many of the functions of the body. Some sources, in the meantime, assert that the soul cannot exist without the body, nor the body without the soul (e.g., Tanhuma, Vayikra, 11).

27   B. San. 91a–91b. See also Mekhilta, Beshalah, Shirah, ch. 2 (edited Horowitz-Rabin, 1960, p. 125); Lev. Rabbah 4:5; Yalkut Shimoni on Lev. 4:2 (# 464); Tanhuma, Vayikra 6. The very development of the term *neshamah* from meaning physical breath to meaning one's inner being bespeaks Judaism's view that the physical and the spiritual are integrated.

28   M. Abot 2:1. See B. Ber. 35b, especially the comment of Abayye there in responding to the earlier theories of Ishmael and Simeon bar Yohai.

29   B. Ber. 17a; the earlier Rabbinic teaching cited at the end as what we have learned appears in B. Men. 110a. While a few of the classical rabbis belonged to wealthy families, most were menial laborers and studied when they could. Hillel was so poor that he became the symbol of the poor man who nevertheless found the time and money to study Torah (B. Yom. 35b); Aqiba was a shepherd before devoting himself to study at age forty, subsisting on the price he received for the bundle of

wood he collected each day (Abot d'Rabbi Natan, ch. 6); Joshua was a charcoal burner (B. Ber. 28a); Yose bar Halafta worked in leather (B. Shab. 49b); Yohanan was a sandal maker (M. Abot 4:11); Judah was a baker (Y. Hag. 77b); and Abba Saul kneaded dough (B. Pes. 34a) and had been a grave digger (B. Nid. 24b).

30   Cf., Mishneh Torah *Laws of the Sabbath*, ch. 30.

31   Cf., Mishneh Torah *Laws of Ethics (De'ot)* 3:1.

32   Mishneh Torah *Laws of Ethics (De'ot)* 3:3.

33   Gen. Rabbah 17:2; B. Yeb. 62b–63a; Midrash Psalms on Ps. 59:2.

34   The minimum of two: M. Yeb. 6:6; Mishneh Torah *Laws of Marriage* 15:4; Shulhan Arukh *Even Ha'ezer* 1:5. The ideal of having more: B. Yeb. 62b, based on Is. 45:18 and Eccl. 11:6; Mishneh Torah *Laws of Marriage* 15:16.

35   Deut. 6:7, 20–25; 11:19. This was already one of Abraham's duties: Gen. 18:19.

36   Moses as a prophet: Deut. 34:10. The phrase, "Moses, our teacher," appears fifty-six times in the Babylonian Talmud! For example, see B. Ber. 3b, 12b, 33b, 55a, 55b; B. Shab. 30a, 92a.

37   Samson Raphael Hirsch, *Judaism Eternal*, Isidor Grunfeld, trans. (London, 1956), vol. II, pp. 245–50.

38   For more on this, see my essay, "Training Rabbis in the Land of the Free," in Nina Beth Cardin and David Wolf Silverman, eds., *The Seminary at 100* (New York, 1987), pp. 11–28, esp. 12–19; and Milton R. Konvitz, *Judaism and the American Idea* (New York, 1978), ch. 5.

39   B. B.B. 89a; Mishneh Torah *Laws of Theft* 8:20; Shulhan Arukh *Hoshen Mishpat* 231:2.

40   This prayer is found in the prayer books of all Jewish denominations, but see, for example, Jules Harlow, *Siddur Sim Shalom* (New York, 1985), pp. 162f.

41   Half of American Jews polled across the nation by the *Los Angeles Times* listed a commitment to social equality as the factor most important to their sense of Jewish identity, whereas only 17 percent cited religious observance and another 17 percent cited support for Israel. See Robert Scheer, "Jews in U.S. Committed to Equality," in *Los Angeles Times*, April 13, 1988, section I, pp. 1, 14–15.

Bibliography

Bleich, J. David, "Smoking," in *Tradition* 16:4 (Summer 1977), pp. 130–33.

Borowitz, Eugene B., *Reform Judaism Today* (New York, 1983).

Borowitz, Eugene B., *Renewing the Covenant* (Philadelphia, 1991).

Dorff, Elliot N., "Training Rabbis in the Land of the Free," in Nina Beth Cardin, and David Wolf Silverman, eds., *The Seminary at 100* (New York, 1987), pp. 11–28.

Dorff, Elliot N., and Louis E. Newman, eds., *Contemporary Jewish Ethics and Morality: A Reader* (New York, 1995).

Dorff, Elliot N., *Conservative Judaism: Our Ancestors to Our Descendants* (New York, 1996).

Dorff, Elliot N., *Matters of Life and Death: A Jewish Approach to Modern Medical Ethics* (Philadelphia, 1998).

Dorff, Elliot N., *Mitzvah Means Commandment* (New York, 1989).

Freehof, Solomon, *Reform Responsa* (Cincinnati, 1960).

Gordis, Robert, *The Dynamics of Judaism: A Study in Jewish Law* (Bloomington, 1990).

Greenberg, Simon, *The Ethical in the Jewish and American Heritage* (New York, 1977).

Harlow, Jules, *Siddur Sim Shalom* (New York, 1985).

Hartman, David, *A Living Covenant: The Innovative Spirit in Traditional Judaism* (Woodstock, 1997).

Konvitz, Milton R., *Judaism and the American Idea* (New York, 1978).

Rosenzweig, Franz, "The Builders," in Nahum Glatzer, ed., *On Jewish Learning* (New York, 1955), pp. 72–92.

Spero, Shubert, *Morality, Halakha, and the Jewish Tradition* (New York, 1983).

CHAPTER 22

Women in Contemporary Judaism

Judith R. Baskin

Women play a variety of roles in the diverse forms of Judaism that characterize the contemporary world Jewish community. All of their modes of Jewish identity and practice, however, are shaped by history and tradition as well as in response to recent trends in the larger world. This essay delineates the activities of Jewish women in contemporary forms of Judaism under the following rubrics: women in traditional Jewish societies, the impact of *Haskalah* (Jewish Enlightenment), women in pre-state and post-1948 Israel, the impact of feminism on contemporary forms of Jewish life and practice, and feminist theology in Judaism.

Women's Roles in Traditional Jewish Societies

Traditional Jewish societies are organized according to the principles of Rabbinic Judaism, which mandate separate roles and responsibilities for women and men. On the basis of belief in the divine origin of the halakhah, the evolved Jewish legal precepts and practices codified in the Babylonian Talmud and associated texts, Rabbinic Judaism provided shared religious principles, institutions, and modes of governance for Jews spread throughout an often hostile and dangerous diaspora. While this patriarchal system protected and honored women who complied with its customs, its framers portrayed females as essentially other than males and connected to the realm of nature as opposed to culture. Rabbinic social policy preferred to situate women's activities in the private sphere of home, husband, children, and family economic endeavors, while men occupied the public domains of worship, study, community leadership, and judicial authority. Thus, B. Ber. 17a remarks that women earn merit "By sending their sons to learn in the synagogue and their husbands to study in the schools of the rabbis." In this spiritual equation, a woman's exertion in the private domain to enable the males of her family to participate in culturally valued activities in the public sphere becomes a paradigm of female nobility and a sufficient religious act in itself.

Rabbinic Judaism exempts women from most commandments which must be performed at set times, including communal worship. Women who attend synagogue sit apart from men, often separated by a physical barrier (*mehitzah*). They do not count in the group of ten adult Jewish males (*minyan*) essential for full communal worship, including the *minyan* required for communal recitation of the mourner's prayer (*kaddish*), from which bereaved women often find themselves excluded in traditional Jewish practice. It is generally understood, as well, that in most instances women may not receive the honor of reciting the blessings that precede and follow reading from the Torah scroll, nor read from the Torah scroll itself in public worship. While women are certainly enjoined to pray, their prayers are private: they may be spontaneous, in any language, and need not follow a set liturgy. Historically this has meant that regularized religious education in sacred language, texts, or legal traditions was not provided for most girls in traditional Jewish societies.

What was incumbent upon women and what they did have to be taught was to observe the three specific women's commandments, summarized as *hallah*, *niddah*, and *hadlaqah*. *Hallah* refers specifically to reserving and burning some of the dough used for baking the Sabbath loaves (or other bread); this is in remembrance of the dough offering that, in Temple times, was given to the priest (Num. 15:17–21). *Hallah* may also be understood more broadly to stand for a woman's knowledge of all of the Jewish dietary laws concerned with permissible foods and food combinations (*Kashrut*), essential for running her home according to Rabbinic ritual law. *Niddah*, the word for the menstruating woman, refers in this context to punctilious obedience to the regulations ordaining physical separation between a menstruating, post-menstrual, or post-partum woman and her husband prior to her ritual cleansing at a specified time, a central aspect of marital life in traditional Jewish practice. *Hadlaqah*, "kindling," alludes to the ritual kindling of the lights marking the advent of the Sabbath, and, more generally, to women's participation in domestic rituals connected with the festivals and holy days of the Jewish calendar. In fact, both *hallah* and *hadlaqah* may also be performed by men in the absence of a woman.

Among those contemporary Jews who continue to follow traditional modes of Rabbinic Judaism, particularly in ultra-Orthodox (*haredi*) Jewish communities, these practices are still the central religious actions that define Jewish women's lives. Tamar Frankiel, a contemporary Jewish woman who assumed the practices of traditional Judaism as an adult, has written of the spiritual benefits of the woman's role in Rabbinic Judaism, beginning with the premise that there are profound and inherent male–female differences in perception, abilities, and contributions that traditional Judaism has always recognized and celebrated. In Frankiel's view, traditional Judaism nurtures these gender-based distinctions by prescribing domestic roles for women. Through the bearing and nurturing of children, the preparation and serving of food, the creation and preservation of *shalom bayit* (household harmony), and their special affinity to the Sabbath, New Moons, and other Jewish festivals, she believes that women fulfill their distinctive roles in a cycle of Jewish life "richly interwoven with feminine themes."[1] Frankiel speaks in exalted terms of the special benefits of family purity rituals, finding in monthly immersion an experience of renewal, and in enforced marital separation a safeguard for the spirituality of sexual expression.

Frankiel draws on Jewish literature to present a number of biblical and post-biblical heroines as models of various desirable female qualities; however, she self-consciously omits any citations or argumentation from Jewish legal traditions, apparently because Frankiel accepts the view that most women do not find "abstract learning," such as Talmud study, satisfying, "since it does not call forth [their] capacities for relationship or involvement" (p. 47). Still, Frankiel is not immune to influences from the contemporary world: she admits that examples of admirable females are scant in post-biblical Jewish texts, and she advocates changes in the system to give Orthodox Jewish women the models they need. She insists that there is no justification for forbidding women to study Torah, although she notes that "we must also recognize more deeply what is at stake behind male defensiveness, namely, [fear of] a disturbance of the balance of male and female forces in the Jewish spiritual universe" (p. 47). While Frankiel is convinced that halakhic tradition is to be accepted with faith and trust, she also looks toward a future in which women's Jewish education will be of the same quality as men's, and in which their spiritual impact on Jewish law, ritual, and custom will be recognized and appreciated.

The anthropologist Susan Sered has documented another contemporary Jewish community that continues the traditions of the past in her study of the Judaism of elderly Middle Eastern women, primarily impoverished widows originally from Kurdistan, who frequent a senior day center in Jerusalem.[2] Sered portrays her illiterate subjects as part of a female-oriented Jewish tradition that, over the course of centuries, has developed ways to sacralize and enrich women's lives religiously, even though women were excluded from participation in synagogue ritual and Jewish learning. This "women's" Judaism, which she calls the "little" tradition, as opposed to the "great" tradition of normative, male-centered Judaism, is primarily oriented to human relationships rather than adherence to the ritual details of halakhah. Sered suggests that the women she studied have redefined normative Judaism in their own terms, emphasizing those aspects of the tradition which affirm and make sense of their lives. Thus, they understand a religious woman as someone who cares for her family and neighbors and who engages in ritual to petition divine protection on their behalf; such a woman prepares traditional kosher foods appropriate to the Sabbath and holidays, donates to charity, and visits and tends the tombs of kin and saints. Even though this woman is excluded from significant public or formal male-oriented religious activities, she is able to become expert at filling her everyday female sphere with sacred meaning. And, ironically, as their Israeli children and grandchildren become secularized, these women have increasingly become the primary bearers of religious culture for their progeny. Yet at the same time, as Sered documents, the long tradition of rituals these elderly Middle Eastern Jewish women have preserved is now rapidly being destroyed by the pressures of both modernity and a male-oriented religious establishment.

The Role of Haskalah

The historical trend that has shaped and determined the status of women in most contemporary forms of Judaism is Haskalah, the Jewish Enlightenment movement. Originating in late eighteenth-century Germany, Haskalah laid the foundations of modern Jewish religious, political, and social life in western and central Europe and in North America. Open to modernity and European culture, Haskalah insisted that Jewish acculturation to the mainstream mores and customs of the public sphere was not incompatible with adherence to Jewish tradition and rituals in the private domain of home and synagogue. While the goals of Jewish political emancipation and achievement of full civil rights, with their accompanying economic benefits, were central to this movement, some of its supporters also championed religious change within the Jewish community. Most contemporary forms of Jewish religious practice: Reform Judaism, Conservative Judaism, and Modern Orthodoxy, were shaped in this milieu. Moses Mendelssohn, the founder of Haskalah in central Europe, and others of his circle also advocated social change in gender relations, opposing arranged marriages and advocating love matches.

While Haskalah set in motion the processes of Jewish accommodation, acculturation, and assimilation to the larger culture that continue to the present day, scholars like Marion A. Kaplan and Paula E. Hyman have shown that Jewish women in central and western Europe and in North America prior to World War II experienced the intersection of Judaism and modernity quite differently from men. Kaplan[3] demonstrates that in Germany, gender, which limited women's educational and occupational opportunities, also tended to slow the assimilation of Jewish women into mainstream society, rendering their progress to integration halting and incomplete in comparison with Jewish men. Confined to the domestic scene by the bourgeois values of their milieu, restricted in their instructional opportunities, and prevented from participating in the public realms of economic and civic life, Jewish women had far fewer contacts with the non-Jewish world than their husbands. Rather, women were encouraged to cultivate a home-based Judaism in which spirituality was expressed in domestic activities.

Hyman points out that nineteenth-century domestic Judaism not only reflected traditional Judaism's preferred positioning of women in the private realm of husband and family but was also a form of Jewish conformity to the Christian bourgeois model of female domesticity that put religion in the female sphere. Jewish literature and the Jewish press of the late nineteenth century, both in Europe and in the United States (where the Jewish community prior to 1881 was overwhelmingly from German-speaking Europe), described the Jewish woman as the "guardian angel of the house," "mother in Israel," and "priestess of the Jewish ideal," and assigned to her the primary responsibility for the Jewish identity and education of her children.[4] This was a significant indication of acculturation in an ethnic group in which men had historically fulfilled most religious obligations, including the Jewish education of their sons. Moreover, this shifting of responsibility for inculcating Jewish identity and practices to women led rapidly from praise to denigration, as commentators began to blame mothers for their children's assimilation. Such criticisms not only allowed men to ignore the implications of their own assimilationist behavior but also revealed central tensions in the project of acculturation itself, including a communal inability to prevent individual defections into the larger society.

Reform Judaism, which sought to offer nineteenth-century western and central European Jews a modernized form of Jewish belief and practice emphasizing personal faith and ethical behavior rather than ritual observance, proclaimed that women were entitled to the same religious rights and subject to the same religious duties as men in both home and synagogue. Emphasis on religious education for girls and boys, including the introduction of a confirmation ceremony for young people of both sexes, and an accessible worship service in the vernacular also made the new movement attractive to many women. Pressure from young women may have prompted the Reform rabbinate to adopt the innovation of double ring wedding ceremonies in which not only men but women made a statement of marital commitment. In fact, however, European Reform Judaism made few substantive changes in women's actual synagogue status, offering no extension to women of ritual participation in worship and maintaining separate synagogue seating for men and women well into the twentieth century.[5]

As Riv-Ellen Prell has pointed out, by making Jewish women "honorary men" without equal rights, Reform Judaism not only failed to enhance women's role in Judaism but made women even less Jewishly visible than before by eliminating women's traditional personal and domestic rituals and obligations.[6] This was not so much the case in the United States where mixed seating was the norm and where women were afforded increasing opportunities to assume some synagogue leadership roles as the nineteenth century progressed.[7] However, in North America, too, the Reform movement was only prepared to go so far; despite a few young women who undertook and even completed Rabbinic training during the first half of the twentieth century in both Germany and the United States, American Reform Judaism did not ordain its first female rabbi, Sally Priesand, until 1972.[8]

One significant religious innovation in the early decades of the twentieth century that ultimately affected significant numbers of American Jewish women was the Bat Mitzvah ceremony, first introduced in 1922 by Mordecai Kaplan, the founder of Reconstructionist Judaism, to celebrate his daughter Judith's religious coming of age. This ceremony for twelve- and thirteen-year-old girls became widespread in the decades following World War II in

Reconstructionist and Reform congregations, where it is now fully equivalent to the Bar Mitzvah ceremony for boys. Bat Mitzvah ceremonies are also frequent in Conservative synagogues, although the details of what girls may and may not do ritually vary. Some Orthodox congregations also offer girls an opportunity to publicly affirm their Jewish knowledge and commitment, although generally not in a format parallel to male Bar Mitzvah.[9]

Ellen Umansky has argued that the establishment of service and social welfare organizations in the nineteenth and early twentieth centuries by middle-class Jewish women in Germany, England, and North America should be seen as religiously inspired. While emulation of Christian models of female philanthropy and religious activism certainly played a significant motivating role, Jewish women understood their philanthropic and communal activities as appropriate extensions of their traditional Jewish domestic roles. Organizations such as the Jüdischer Frauenbund in Germany (founded in 1904 by Bertha Pappenheim), the Union of Jewish Women in Great Britain (founded in 1902), and the National Council of Jewish Women in the United States (founded in 1893 under the leadership of Hannah Greenbaum Solomon and Sadie American) cooperated in the international campaign against coercion of poor women into prostitution and argued for greater recognition of women within their respective Jewish communities as "sustainers of Jewish communal life and guardians against defection from Judaism." In the process, their members blurred the boundaries between traditional male and female spheres as women acquired administrative expertise and assumed authoritative and responsible public roles. Women's organizational activism directly affected the Jewish community in such areas as social welfare services, feminist trade unionism, support for women's suffrage, and agitation for religious change.[10]

In the United States, the proliferation of Jewish women's organizations has also included synagogue sisterhoods that devoted themselves to the "domestic management" of the synagogue, decorating the sanctuary for festivals, catering for synagogue events, and performing many other housekeeping functions. National organizations of sisterhoods, separated by denomination, encouraged local groups in their activities and provided a forum for public female leadership. While the Reform National Federation of Temple Sisterhoods provided a platform for women to demand greater synagogue participation, including the ordination of women rabbis, the Conservative movement's Women's League emphasized the role of women in enhancing the Jewishness of their homes. Sisterhoods of all denominations, however, recognized that females must be Jewishly educated in order to strengthen Jewish observance at home and instill Jewish values in their children, and encouraged expanded educational opportunities for women of all ages.[11] Similarly, as they had throughout American Jewish history, Jewish women played a central role in establishing, supervising, and teaching in Jewish religious schools.[12] Through these activities, as well as in their involvement with other Jewish women's groups, such as the Zionist organization Hadassah (founded by Henrietta Szold in 1912), middle-class American Jewish women found opportunities to articulate through service and philanthropy their understandings of the religious and spiritual obligations of the Jewish woman.[13]

The Jewish Enlightenment movement in eastern Europe, which began in the last few decades of the nineteenth century, was very different from Haskalah in the West, lacking both the emphasis on Jewish achievement of political rights and civic equality and the impetus for religious reform, objectives that were unlikely in the politically oppressive and religiously conservative eastern European environment. Nor was the impoverished and predominantly rural Jewish population an appropriate constituency for the middle-class norms and values of the West. Rather, Haskalah in eastern Europe was a secularizing process that led to a discontinuation of religious observance among its exponents, who tended to adopt a Jewish national/ethnic identity, often linked to idealistic socialist political goals.

Eastern European women were frequently in the forefront of this movement of cultural transformation. This was partly educational: as a result of the customary exclusion of girls from substantive Jewish educations, prosperous parents often provided their daughters with secular instruction. The Orthodox community did not begin to provide vehicles for female religious education until after World War I. Moreover, girls and women in eastern European Jewish society, where the strong capable woman shrewdly interacting with the outside world was the dominant cultural ideal, were also secularized by their active participation in public economic life. In many ways, late nineteenth-century eastern European women were far more involved in the process of Jewish assimilation than women in western Europe or the United States. This is evident in the large numbers of eastern European Jewish women who sought higher education in western Europe, a significantly higher percentage of female conversions to Christianity, and particularly in female involvement in a wide range of political movements including Zionism and the socialist Bund, which offered women opportunities for activism and leadership unavailable in traditional Jewish society.[14]

Of the almost two million eastern European Jewish immigrants to arrive in the United States between 1880 and 1914, 43 percent were women, a far higher proportion than among other immigrant groups. The values these immigrants brought with them, even as they were gradually transformed by America, permitted women to play a complex role in helping their families adjust to their new environment. Thus, most women contributed to the family income in one way or another. A significant number sought the benefits of higher education, while others participated in a variety of progressive activities. Women such as Rose Schneiderman (d. 1972), many of whom began their working careers in the garment industry, devoted their considerable energies and abilities to workers' rights and left-wing movements for social justice and political change.[15] As eastern European Jewish immigrants and their children became increasingly successful economically and began to enter the middle class, particularly in the period after World War II, they tended to follow the educational, occupational, residential, and religious patterns of previous waves of Jewish settlers in North America. This often included affiliation with Conservative and Reform synagogues and a preference that women should not work outside the home. Many women from this group, who now had leisure for volunteer activities, became members of the national Jewish women's organizations founded earlier in the American Jewish experience or became involved in synagogue sisterhood activities.

Jewish Women in pre-State and post-1948 Israel

Inequality in the treatment of the sexes has been a reality in the modern Jewish settlement of the land of Israel since the first pioneers, inspired by the fervor of Labor Zionism, began arriving as settlers from eastern Europe at the end of the nineteenth century. As many scholars have pointed out, Zionist ideology was gendered from the start. Late nineteenth-century anti-Semites frequently equated Jewishness with perceived feminine qualities such as physical softness, moral weakness, and a tendency to hysteria. One Jewish response was the Zionist construction of the masculine and muscular new Jew who symbolized the Zionist possibility for the physical and spiritual rebirth of diaspora Jewry. Zionist writers appealed to women, on the other hand, to play their part in Jewish redemption by returning to the home and instilling Jewish pride in their husbands and children.[16]

   This orientation toward maintaining separate gender roles was reinforced by everyday conditions in Palestine. Although many idealistic young people prepared for emigration in Zionist training schools in Russia that stressed the equality of women and men, upon arrival in the Land, young single women pioneers found their options limited and their choices narrowed. Betrayed by their male comrades who did not support their struggle, and limited by male perceptions of their biological inequality, unmarried women found themselves virtually unemployable as agricultural workers and were forced to survive by providing the men with kitchen and laundry services. Denied membership as single women in most collective settlements, and refused employment as agricultural workers, a few women founded successful female agricultural and urban collectives, and women's training farms. Most, however, were compelled to accept their secondary roles, and take whatever employment they could find, often in urban settings, sacrificing their egalitarian ideals and Labor Zionist fervor to what they saw as the more pressing task of the building up of the state.[17] As Deborah Bernstein has written of pre-state Israel, women's unequal and marginal position in the labor market, and their sole responsibility for family care, created a distinctly different life pattern for women as compared with that experienced by men. Women's secondary and intermittent visibility in the all-important public sphere, and the invisibility of the private sphere where women were central, reinforced female exclusion from power and influence.[18]

   Israel continues to be far from progressive where the status of women is concerned and is, at the end of the twentieth century, despite popular mythology to the contrary, more conservative than most other western democracies on women's issues. The secondary status of Israeli women is a result of generations of past discrimination in many of the traditional Jewish cultures that make up Israeli society as well as of contemporary disadvantages for women in the workplace mandated by paternalistic legislation and the expectation that women will also assume most household responsibilities. Israeli women continue to fulfill the traditional Jewish role of enablers, supporting their husbands and sons, who hold the primary power and powerful jobs, and whose lives are at risk in defending the State. While most Israeli women do fulfill a military service obligation, women in the military are limited to support positions. A small number of contemporary Israeli women reject women's subsidiary possibilities but they also recognize that women will not achieve equality as long as war and conflict is a dominant theme in Israeli society.[19]

Jewish women in Israel are also significantly disadvantaged in personal status issues. The State's Declaration of Independence of May 1948 stated that, "The State of Israel will maintain equal social and political rights for all citizens, irrespective of religion, race, or sex," a sentiment reiterated in 1949 in the basic guidelines of the first government of Israel. Yet in 1953 legislation awarded the Orthodox religious establishment monopolistic control over marriage and divorce for all Jewish citizens, thus legalizing women's substantial legal disadvantages in the halakhah, particularly in areas of family law.[20] There is no civil marriage or divorce in Israel, nor do Reform or Conservative Judaism, with their more egalitarian approaches, have any official standing. The issue of the over ten thousand *agunot*, women who cannot get a divorce because their husbands refuse to grant one or cannot be located, is the best known instance of the inability of the Orthodox rabbinate to deal with real social problems that cause immense pain and suffering to women and their families.

Only recently have women begun to fight back, forming an International Coalition for *Agunah* Rights, reflecting an intensive effort to reform what are perceived as unjust and discriminatory divorce proceedings in rabbinical courts worldwide.[21] Israel's nascent feminist movement has also brought cases to Israel's Supreme Court on issues as diverse as access to abortion, women's right to be elected to and hold seats on municipal religious councils, and the ability of women's prayer groups to convene at the Western Wall, the remains of the ancient center of Jewish worship in Jerusalem. Up to the present, such efforts by "Women of the Wall" and others to hold female or mixed male and female group prayer at this site have met with verbal opposition from Israel's religious leadership and violent physical responses from groups of outraged individuals.

Although Reform and Conservative Judaism are granted no official religious recognition in Israel, both movements have established an institutional presence that has begun to alter Israeli perceptions of women's appropriate roles in Judaism; since 1992, for instance, the Reform movement in Israel has ordained women as rabbis. While the Israeli religious establishment objects to women in the rabbinate as well as to egalitarian worship, it is noteworthy that a program has recently been created in which women are being trained in Talmudic law to serve as advocates for women facing legal issues connected with personal status, apparently with the religious establishment's approval. This increased feminist activity, influenced by the women's movement throughout the western world – and the hostility it has generated – is indicative of the gender and religious tensions that characterize Israeli society at the end of the twentieth century.

Contemporary Jewish Women in North America

The resurgent feminist movement of the early 1970s has brought both religious renewal and bitter controversy to contemporary western Judaism, especially in North America, where affiliation to liberal forms of Judaism predominates. Significant numbers of Jewish women, linking feminism's mandate for female equality in all areas of human endeavor with an explicit commitment to Jewish identification and the Jewish community, are demanding participation in and access to a tradition that has rarely considered women as central figures in its history, thought, religious practice, or communal life. Susannah Heschel and Sylvia Barack Fishman, among many others, have documented how American Jewish feminists are re-visioning their roles within contemporary Judaism and have explored feminist efforts to empower women as full and equal Jews in situations in which they have often been excluded.[22] This movement for change comes at a time when American Jewish women face previously unimagined challenges in the areas of family formation and life-style choices; unprecedented higher education and career paths opportunities; and a wide range of options in religious and spiritual expression, and political and civic activism. Significant transformations in all of these spheres result from revolutionary changes in technology, social attitudes, and economic expectations over the half-century since World War II. The issue for Jewish feminists, according to Fishman, is how feminism can help the American Jewish community respond meaningfully to a society in a seemingly continuous state of transformation.[23]

The Jewish feminist movement has had a significant impact on Jewish religious practice. At century's end, egalitarian worship, in which women have all the same responsibilities and possibilities of participation as men, is the norm in Reform and in Reconstructionist Judaisms and is generally a feature of Conservative practice, as well. Among the most visible changes for women in the past few decades are their emergence as synagogue lay leaders in all the denominations of contemporary Judaism, as well as the opportunity now offered women in the Reform, Reconstructionist, and Conservative movements to undertake Rabbinic and cantorial studies and to receive Rabbinic ordination. Pamela Nadell has detailed the long battle for female ordination in both Germany and the United States, and the strong resistance to it from constituencies within the Jewish community.[24] It seems clear that only major shifts in public attitudes and female possibilities brought about by the American feminist movement of the 1960s prompted the leadership of the Reform movement to sanction the ordination of Sally Priesand in 1972. Rabbinic pioneers in the other liberal movements of American Judaism include Sandy Eisenberg Sasso, ordained by the Reconstructionist Rabbinical College in 1974, and Amy Eilberg, who received ordination from the Conservative movement's Jewish Theological Seminary in 1984. As the twentieth century ends, several hundred women have now been ordained as rabbis, and at least half of Rabbinic students in Reform, Reconstructionist and Conservative seminaries are female. Over one hundred women have also been ordained as cantors, and scores of others function in synagogues as lay cantors.

Women's paths in the rabbinate, however, have not been free of obstacles. Fishman has discussed the challenges encountered by women rabbis in pulpit positions in balancing their demanding professional and personal lives, noting that thus far few women have scaled the higher rungs of the rabbinical ladder in assuming senior positions in large and prestigious congregations. This reality reflects both persistent cultural and prestige-oriented prejudices as well as the short time in which women have been in the rabbinate. However, it is also indicative of many women's choices of Rabbinic options, such as teaching, chaplaincy, or youth and communal work, that allow them time for home and family.[25] On the other hand, as increasing numbers of women become rabbis, some in the Jewish community have expressed fears that an imminent "feminization of the rabbinate" will diminish the respect in which the rabbi and the rabbi's functions are held, and that "men will relegate religious life to women and cease being active in the synagogue."[26]

Another example of the significant impact of feminism on Jewish religious life in North America is alterations in liturgical language and liturgical practice. The traditional *siddur*, the Jewish prayer book, portrays communal worship as a prerogative for men and understands the congregation of worshipers to be wholly male. Liturgical translations into English have until recently been couched in solely masculine terms, while women have tended to be portrayed as objects of prayer rather than as participating in prayer themselves.[27] Among areas of concern and controversy for liturgical change have been the broadening of references to the congregation of worshipers to include women as well as men, gender-sensitive language about God, inclusion of references to Jewish foremothers together with forefathers in prayer language, alterations of the Hebrew as well as the vernacular liturgy, and reflections of women's experiences in liturgical contexts.

The 1972 Reform movement Task Force on Equality recommended the elimination of unnecessary and inaccurate masculine references in prayer, whether referring to humanity in general or to God, suggesting that such language misleads worshipers about the nature of both human beings and the divine. Thus, "Sovereign" or "Ruler" might replace "Lord" or "King," while "God of our Fathers" could give way either to "God of our Fathers and Mothers," "God of our ancestors," or "God of Israel." Changes in both the Hebrew and English liturgies reflecting some of these guidelines have appeared in a number of recent liturgical works, including the Reform movement's 1975 *Gates of Prayer* series. In further innovations planned for a complete revision of *Gates of Prayer*, to appear in the early twenty-first century, all English references to God will be gender-neutral and the mothers of Israel will be included appropriately in both Hebrew and English prayers. Similar, if less far-reaching, English formulations characterize the Conservative movement's 1985 *Sim Shalom* prayer book and, especially, that prayer book's entirely rewritten 1997 edition, which includes references to the biblical matriarchs as an option in English and Hebrew and which addresses the congregation inclusively. The Reconstructionist movement, significantly smaller than Reform, Conservative, and Orthodoxy in the United States, has been particularly receptive to issues raised by Jewish feminism, both in its liturgical texts such as *Kol Haneshamah: Shabbat Vehagim* (1994) and in its general policies.

Some feminist advocates of liturgical changes have added references to a variety of Jewish women of the past and have developed imagery that conceives God in female as well as male terms – as, for example, a nurturing mother – in addition to creating new prayers and blessings that delineate women's experiences and describe their search for spirituality.[28] Religious leaders such as Lynn Gottlieb have also experimented with references to God as "Shekinah" or "She who Dwells Within." Gottlieb writes that her invocation of Judaism's term for the nurturing feminine aspect of God is based on her exploration of three traditional images of the Shekinah from a feminist perspective: "Shekinah as the Being who Connects All Life, Shekinah as the Longing for Wholeness, and Shekinah as the Cry for Justice."[29] Some liturgists have alternated between using masculine and feminine forms in divine address, while others suggest that gender issues can be obviated by only addressing God in the second person as "You." Among contemporary liturgists are Marcia Falk, whose many new blessings in Hebrew and English stressing the connectedness of all beings are being incorporated into communal worship across a wide spectrum of the Jewish community.[30]

Falk, whose liturgical innovations have a strong theological foundation, believes that all personal images of God are limited; she attempts to move beyond anthropomorphic images of deity to a multiplicity of divine images affirming the unity of all creation. By invoking God as "Source of Life," "Flow of Life," "Breath of All Living Things," Falk underscores her vision of the divine as an immanent force or power that is neither apart from nor above creation. Committed to *tikkun olam*, repair of a fragmented world, Falk replaces the traditional liturgical epithet "Blessed are You, Lord our God, King of the Universe" with the simple Hebrew *N'varech*, "Let us bless"; by claiming for the community the power to bless she not only eliminates images of God as male and as the one who hierarchically dominates the world but also asserts for the Jewish people a more active role in the creation and redemption of the world.[31]

Side by side with liturgical changes has been women's adopting the prayer accoutrements that in traditional settings are a part of men's worship. For some women, particularly in Conservative Judaism, these include wearing a head covering (*kipah*) and prayer shawl (*tallit*) during communal worship; for others it also includes praying with phylacteries (*tefillin*).[32]

Another instance of contemporary spiritual creativity is the proliferation of religious observances directed specifically at women and addressing particular aspects of women's experiences. These include the recovery of the traditional observance of Rosh Hodesh, the New Moon, as a day for Jewish women's study and prayer,[33] as well as versions of the Passover Seder that focus on the female experience.[34] New rituals also mark milestone events in women's biological and personal lives. As Debra Orenstein has documented, feminist Jews have expanded life-cycle events in four different ways. The first is the establishment of rituals for women that parallel those long established for men, for instance, the already discussed Bat Mitzvah as well as ceremonies welcoming baby girls into the covenant of Israel (*Simhat Bat*), which are becoming increasingly common. A second category of ritual change is altering, supplementing, or reinterpreting traditional rituals related to life-cycle events in ways that include women as equals. Such innovations include marriage contracts that emphasize mutuality and supplemental divorce rituals that give a woman a role in acknowledging the final dissolution of her marriage. Inclusion of women as recognized mourners whose obligations, including recitation of the *kaddish* prayer, are the same as those of men also falls into this category.[35] A third category of modernization recognizes the sacred nature of events of a woman's biological cycle and ritualizes such milestone events as menarche, menses, childbirth, miscarriage, and menopause. Finally, rituals have been developed to sacralize passages not previously considered in Jewish tradition, including ceremonies celebrating elder wisdom or healing from rape or sexual abuse.[36] It is impossible to know which of these rituals will ultimately become part of normative Jewish practice, but their wide variety is testimony to the inventive impact of feminist spirituality on contemporary Judaism.

Although feminist efforts at expanding women's roles have prompted unyieldingly hostile reactions in many sectors of the Orthodox community, where they are perceived as contrary to centuries of Jewish tradition and as undermining women's customary roles, there can be no doubt of feminism's profound impact even on contemporary Orthodoxy. As the dissonance between possibilities for women in the secular and traditional worlds has become more obvious, quality Jewish education for girls has become a central priority in a number of traditional Jewish communities; some Modern Orthodox leaders are working with women, through Halakhah, to increase their scope in such areas as participation in Torah study and female prayer groups. While Orthodox feminists often feel psychologically split as they simultaneously champion and attempt to reconcile both the spiritual equality of women and a fundamentally androcentric Jewish tradition,[37] rapid social change in the Modern Orthodox feminist community is ongoing. The first newsletter of the recently formed Jewish Orthodox Feminist Alliance, issued in late 1998, listed a wide range of worldwide conferences on Orthodox feminism while articles addressed, among other topics, enhancing education for traditional Jewish women, rediscovering

Jewish women of the past, the problem of *agunot* (bound wives), and the growth and challenges of women's prayer groups.

The issues of whether women may gather in single-sex prayer groups and whether such groups may read from a Torah scroll are extremely controversial in Orthodox circles, where a number of influential rabbis have expressed firm opposition to such practices.[38] Modern Orthodox rabbi Avraham Weiss, on the other hand, has concluded that, while women cannot be counted in a prayer *minyan*, since they are not obligated to participate in communal prayer, they may pray together in a private group so long as they omit prayers that can only be recited when a *minyan* is present. Similarly, Weiss holds that women should be taught Torah "on the same quantitative and qualitative level as men,"[39] and he allows women with the requisite skills to read from a Torah scroll in private prayer groups. However, since women are not obligated to participate in public Torah reading, and since they are excluded from the *minyan*, they cannot recite the blessings that accompany Torah reading in the communal setting. Weiss believes that women who wish to increase their involvement in Jewish ritual should be encouraged and given educational and institutional support.[40] While his approach seems tame to many outside the Orthodox community, from within it is welcomed by many Orthodox women as compassionate and courageous.

Debra Kaufman has studied contemporary Jewish women who have chosen to become Orthodox Jews. For most of her college-educated subjects, this so-called "return" represented a conscious rejection of a secular culture devoid of the coherent and timeless moral values they believe they found in Orthodoxy. Kaufman suggests that her subjects, whose opportunities to effect significant change within the Orthodox hierarchy are extremely limited, find female solidarity and worth in mandated women's roles and rituals. In an analysis of the uniformly positive ways in which her subjects understand traditional family purity regulations, for example, Kaufman illustrates the ways in which sexual intimacy is "placed in a sacred and communal context" that allows women to transcend the self and connect to the "public Orthodox community of timeless truths" (p. 70). Most of these *baalot teshuvah*, who are convinced that in Orthodoxy "the female and the feminine are central,"[41] also bring secular skills and concerns to their new communities, including the belief that girls should receive educations commensurate with boys, that daughters should be able to pursue advanced studies, and the hope expressed by some that eventually there will be changes in the structure of gender-related roles connected with communal prayer.[42]

Feminism has brought alterations to all sectors of Jewish communal life as many women have given up the hours they once devoted to volunteer activities for full-time employment. Moreover, many women who continue to volunteer prefer to divert their energies to causes beyond the Jewish community, particularly those that support and further gender equality. The significant decline in female volunteers in Jewish women's organizations and synagogue sisterhoods at century's end has grave consequences for the future of these enterprises and those they serve.[43]

Although an increasing number of qualified women professionals are employed in Jewish communal agencies, several observers have noted that the Jewish communal sphere has proved particularly reluctant to recognize and encourage female leadership potential.[44] According to Hyman, this resistance to women in positions of authority is indicative of the sexual politics of contemporary Jewish identity in general.[45] While some men will continue to resist what they perceive as female encroachment on male hegemony in the public domain, others may simply abandon Jewish communal institutions and Judaism to women altogether. As Fishman cautions, for North America the stakes are significant, since, "The American Jewish community not only shares in all the human consequences of feminism but also carries with it the additional responsibility of preserving three thousand years of Jewish history and culture and confronting the problems of a numerically challenged population as well."[46] However, if the past is any indication, forces from outside the Jewish community will be as influential as any from within in determining the future roles of women in Judaism and in Jewish life.

Contemporaneous and in many ways linked with the growth and development of Jewish feminism is the visibility of identified gay and lesbian Jews,[47] as well as single Jews regardless of sexual orientation, as active participants within the Jewish community. While Jewish domestic life has historically been almost wholly centered around family units consisting of a male and a female parent and their children, delayed age of marriage and growing numbers of unmarried Jews, as well as contemporary openness regarding homosexuality, have changed the demographic makeup of many Jewish communities. Those who believe that definitions of Jewish community must be broadened to include and value formerly marginalized individuals and groups agree with theologian Judith Plaskow that, "The creation of Jewish communities in which differences are valued as necessary parts of a greater whole is the institutional and experiential foundation for the recovery of the fullness of Torah."[48]

However, acceptance of homosexual couples for synagogue membership remains a controversial issue in many communities, as does admitting openly gay or lesbian individuals to Rabbinic study in most of Judaism's religious denominations. While all wings of Orthodox Judaism are adamant in their refusal to appear to condone homosexual activity through communal recognition of identified homosexuals or homosexual couples, the more liberal forms of contemporary Judaism vary in their approaches. While Reconstructionism is fully accepting of gays and lesbians as congregants and as lay and Rabbinic leaders, Reform Judaism has struggled with its position, recently moving towards increasing recognition that homophobia is a serious societal problem and that education and dialogue within the Jewish community are essential. As Ellen Umansky has written, this shift reflects an awareness, "largely brought to American consciousness through feminist writings, that religious and societal attitudes towards homosexuality, like religious and societal attitudes towards women and the construction of gender, are culturally based . . . rather than reflecting the will of God."[49] In 1990, a majority of Reform rabbis present at the movement's annual meeting declared that "homosexuality can be a legitimate expression of Jewish and human personhood" and that the Reform movement should accept and evaluate homosexuals [including Rabbinic applicants] "as they are and not as we [those of us who are heterosexual] would want them to be."[50] Conservative Judaism in the late 1990s remains deeply conflicted over this issue in all of its ramifications.

Feminist Theology in Judaism

Jewish feminism at the beginning of the twenty-first century also has its theoretical aspect that looks beyond issues of ritual innovation and egalitarian practice. As Ellen Umansky has noted, Jewish feminist theologies challenge theories of Judaism that view male experience as universal. Based on a hermeneutics of suspicion, feminist theologians assume that Judaism's traditional texts and their interpretations are androcentric and that women's experiences were included mostly to reinforce male power or justify the traditional roles to which women have been assigned by men. Thus, the feminist theologian understands Judaism's received visions as incomplete: to hear her own voice and feel her own presence within sources of Jewish tradition, she must rediscover women's religious experiences, even if this requires reading between the lines, filling in stories, writing new ones, or making guesses about the past. While God, Torah, and Israel remain the fundamental categories of Judaism, Jewish feminist theologians view them through the lens of their own contextualized experiences as women and as Jews. Thus, feminist theology privileges the personal by inviting individuals to understand and interpret the details of their own lives as located within a larger Jewish experience.[51]

For Judith Plaskow, the central figure in the development of Jewish feminist theology, ordination of women as rabbis and cantors is not a sufficient response to normative Judaism's inherent androcentrism. She believes feminists must move beyond their delineation of women's status in Jewish law and their demands for legal and institutional equality in Judaism to expose the origins of women's oppression in the core of Judaism itself. For Plaskow, the future of Judaism demands profound transformations that recognize the full and equal humanity of all Jews, that reflect and voice the female experience, and that reintegrate the female aspects of the divine into Jewish conceptions of the Godhead.[52] In *Standing Again at Sinai*, Plaskow insists that women are not only peripheral to biblical and Rabbinic texts; they are in fact perceived as "other" than normative (male) Jews. Theologians must reconstruct Jewish memory by recovering women's previously hidden voices; Judaism will be transformed as women reshape Torah, God, and Israel into a system that recognizes and respects the full humanity of women.

The greatest barrier Plaskow perceives to a feminist reconceptualization of the Jewish community is Judaism's hierarchical structure, which separates God from human being, Jew from gentile, and men from women, and which defines recognition of these separations as essential to holiness. She writes that Jewish feminists cannot recast the place of women's difference within the people of Israel without addressing the larger system of separations and constant creations of "others" in which it is embedded. Similarly, Plaskow believes that Judaism's vision of God must also reflect the experiences of women, noting that exclusively masculine images of God continue to legitimate male political, social, and economic power. While she explores a variety of female images of divinity, she is also aware that reimaging the divine as female may perpetuate similar images of hierarchical domination (p. 168). Rather, she writes of the necessity of affirming a "broad and changing variety of metaphors" to teach that God is known in myriad ways, none of which are final (pp. 154–5). Yet most important to Plaskow's view of the divine and to what it means to be a Jew is the recognition of the presence of God in an empowered, egalitarian community. She writes, "Whether the substance of our cause be our lives as women, the fate of the earth, the pursuit of justice in human community, or some more narrowly religious purpose, it is through the struggle with others to act responsibly in history that we come to know our own actions as encompassed and empowered by a wider universe of action and thus come to know God in a profound and significant way" (p. 157).

A central component of Plaskow's theology is her vision of a model of Jewish sexuality that includes gay and lesbian relationships as well as heterosexual marriages. Judaism must recognize the power of sexuality not only to overturn rules and threaten boundaries in both positive and negative ways, but also to connect the human being and the human community with God, the "sustaining source of energy and power in the universe." Thus, the Song of Songs, for Plaskow, offers the finest Jewish vision of what our sexual relationships can be because it unifies sensuality, spirituality, and profound mutuality, while also providing for many people "the closest we can come in this life to experiencing the embracing wholeness of God" (p. 210).

The theological writings of Rachel Adler combine a deep knowledge of Jewish law and traditional texts with a passionate commitment to justice. Unable to define herself as Orthodox, since she believes traditional understandings of halakhah address the Jewish people solely as a community of men, Adler emphasizes the need to reimagine the divine in female and male ways, and she stresses the importance of expanding God-language to include masculine and feminine metaphors and words. Committed to a vision of God as a personal being commanding and revealing religious teachings, she insists on the reality of an ongoing human–divine relationship rooted in personal and communal experience as well as in sacred texts. In *Engendering Judaism: An Inclusive Theology and Ethics*, Adler advocates retaining practices that remain central to the progressive Jewish community while adding new traditions that emerge out of female and male interpretation and insight; Halakhah must be a dynamic process, evolving cooperatively, communally, and covenantally rather than being externally imposed and passively obeyed. Adler's redemptive focus is on how

Jews themselves can create *tzedek* (justice or righteousness) and in so doing "regenerate a world of legal meaning that fully, complexly, and inclusively integrates the stories and revelations, the duties and commitments of Jewish women and men."[53]

Ellen Umansky, a historian, Jewish theologian, and interpreter of the impact of feminism on contemporary Judaism, works within Reform Judaism to bring about transformations that reflect feminist insights and values. Particularly committed to creating a theology of peoplehood rooted in the experiences of American Reform Jews, she understands the Jewish self as existing in relationship to others and the wider world. Umansky believes that God is both immanent and transcendent; she works to create new images of divinity that will encourage herself and others to work with God rather than under God's authority.[54] Like many other contemporary Jewish feminists, Umansky encourages the creation of new midrashim as a way to re-vision traditional literature through the lens of female experience. In this way women are re-interpreted from "objectified Others" to "normative Jews whose experiences of God, Torah, and Israel can add to, challenge, and transform previously held theological convictions."[55]

The impact of Jewish feminism on contemporary Jewish women is also evident in the outpouring of scholarship about women in Judaism and about Jewish women and their roles, activities, and creative contributions, past and present. The growth of women's studies as a field of scholarly endeavor, and the increasing number of women who are undertaking academic careers in Judaic Studies has led to impressive scholarly activity that often illuminates contemporary dilemmas and concerns through gender analyses of the lives and texts of Jews of previous eras.[56]

Notes

1   Tamar Frankiel, *The Voice of Sarah: Feminine Spirituality and Traditional Judaism* (San Francisco, 1990), p. 58. References in the text in the following are to this book.

2   Susan Starr Sered, *Women as Ritual Experts: The Religious Lives of Elderly Jewish Women in Jerusalem* (New York, 1992).

3   Marion A. Kaplan, *The Making of the Jewish Middle Class: Women, Family, and Identity in Imperial Germany* (New York, 1991).

4   Paula E. Hyman, *Gender and Assimilation in Modern Jewish History: The Roles and Representation of Women* (Seattle, 1995), pp. 25–30, 46–9; Kaplan, *The Making of the Jewish Middle Class*, p. 64.

5   Kaplan, *The Making of the Jewish Middle Class*, pp. 67–8.

6   Riv-Ellen Prell, "The Vision of Women in Classical Reform Judaism," in *Journal of the American Academy of Religion* 50:4 (December 1982), pp. 575–89.

7   Ellen M. Umansky, "Piety, Persuasion and Friendship: A History of Jewish Women's Spirituality," in Ellen M. Umansky and Dianne Ashton, eds., *Four Centuries of Jewish Women's Spirituality: A Sourcebook* (Boston, 1992), p. 9.

8   Pamela Nadell, *Women Who Would Be Rabbis: A History of Women's Ordination, 1889–1985* (Boston, 1998).

9   Umansky, "Piety, Persuasion and Friendship," p. 22.

10 Kaplan, *The Making of the Jewish Middle Class*, pp. 211–19; Hyman, *Gender and Assimilation in Modern Jewish History*, pp. 40–1; Umansky, ibid., pp. 17–18; see also Linda Gordon Kuzmack, *Women's Cause: The Jewish Woman's Movement in England and the United States, 1881–1933* (Columbus, 1990).

11 Hyman, ibid., pp. 42–4; Umansky, ibid., pp. 15–17.

12 Hyman, ibid., pp. 31–2; Ellen M. Umansky, "Spiritual Expressions: Jewish Women's Religious Lives in the United States in the Nineteenth and Twentieth Centuries," in Judith R. Baskin, ed., *Jewish Women in Historical Perspective*, second edition (Detroit, 1998), pp. 341–3.

13 Umansky, "Piety, Persuasion and Friendship," p. 108.

14 Hyman, *Gender and Assimilation in Modern Jewish History*, pp. 71–81.

15 Joyce Antler, *The Journey Home: Jewish Women and the American Century* (New York, 1997).

16 Hyman, *Gender and Assimilation in Modern Jewish History*.

17 Leslie Hazeleton, "Israeli Women: Three Myths," in Susannah Heschel, ed., *On Being a Jewish Feminist* (New York, 1983, 1995), pp. 65–9.

18 Deborah S. Bernstein, "Daughters of the Nation: Between the Public and Private Spheres in Pre-State Israel," in Baskin, ed., *Jewish Women in Historical Perspective*, p. 288.

19 Hazeleton, "Israeli Women", pp. 77–8; cf., B. Swirski and M. Safir, eds., *Calling the Equality Bluff: Women in Israel* (New York, 1991).

20 Hazeleton, "Israeli Women," pp. 71–2.

21 Rivka Haut, "Women's Prayer Groups and the Orthodox Synagogue," in Susan Grossman and Rivka Haut, eds., *Daughters of the King: Women and the Synagogue* (Philadelphia, 1992), pp. 135–58; Sylvia Barack Fishman, *A Breath of Life: Feminism in the American Jewish Community* (New York, 1993), pp. 35–7.

22 Susannah Heschel, ed., *On Being a Jewish Feminist* (New York, 1983, 1995); Fishman, *A Breath of Life*.

23 Fishman, ibid., pp. 14–15.

24 Nadell, *Women Who Would Be Rabbis*.

25 Fishman, *A Breath of Life*, pp. 216–18.

26 Laura Geller, "Reactions to a Woman Rabbi," in Heschel, ed., *On Being a Jewish Feminist*, pp. 210–11.

27 Rela Geffen Monson, "The Impact of the Jewish Women's Movement on the American Synagogue: 1972–85," in Grossman and Haut, eds., *Daughters of the King*, p. 229.

28 Annette Daum, "Language and Liturgy," in Grossman and Haut, eds., *Daughters of the King*, p. 201.

29 Lynn Gottlieb, *She Who Dwells Within: A Feminist Vision of a Renewed Judaism* (San Francisco, 1995).

30 Marcia Falk, *The Book of Blessings: New Jewish Prayers for Daily Life, the Sabbath, and the New Moon Festival* (San Francisco, 1996).

31 Ellen M. Umansky, "Jewish Feminist Theology," in Eugene B. Borowitz, *Choices in Modern Jewish Thought: A Partisan Guide* (West Orange, 1995), p. 331.

32 Susan Grossman, "On *Tefillin*," in Umansky and Ashton, eds., *Four Centuries of Jewish Women's Spirituality*, pp. 279–82; Aliza Berger, "Wrapped Attention: May

Women Wear *Tefillin?*" in Micah D. Halpern and Chana Safrai, eds., *Jewish Legal Writings by Women* (Jerusalem, 1998), pp. 75–118.

33 Cf., Penina V. Adelman, *Miriam's Well: Rituals for Jewish Women Around the Year* (New York, 1990).

34 E. M. Broner, *The Telling* (New York, 1993), and E. M. Broner, with Naomi Nimrod, *The Women's Haggadah* (New York, 1994).

35 Rochelle L. Millen, "The Female Voice of Kaddish," in Halpern and Safrai, eds., *Jewish Legal Writings by Women*, pp. 179–201.

36 Debra Orenstein, ed., *Lifecycles: Jewish Women on Life Passages and Personal Milestones*, Volume One (Woodstock, 1994), p. xviii.

37 Fishman, *A Breath of Life*, pp. 158–9.

38 Haut, "Women's Prayer Groups and the Orthodox Synagogue."

39 Avraham Weiss, *Women at Prayer: A Halakhic Analysis of Women's Prayer Groups* (Hoboken, 1990), p. 66.

40 Ibid., pp. 123–4.

41 Debra Renée Kaufman, *Rachel's Daughters: Newly Orthodox Jewish Women* (New Brunswick, 1991), p. 56.

42 Ibid., p. 58; cf., Lynn Davidman, *Tradition in a Rootless World: Women Turn to Orthodox Judaism* (Berkeley, 1991).

43 Fishman, *A Breath of Life*, pp. 72–8, 222–4.

44 Ibid., p. 229.

45 Hyman, *Gender and Assimilation in Modern Jewish History*, pp. 168–9.

46 Fishman, *A Breath of Life*, p. 247.

47 Christie Balka and Andy Rose, eds., *Twice Blessed: On Being Lesbian or Gay and Jewish* (Boston, 1989).

48 Judith Plaskow, *Standing Again at Sinai: Judaism from a Feminist Perspective* (San Francisco, 1990), p. 106.

49 Ellen M. Umansky, "Feminism in Judaism," in Arvind Sharma and Katherine K. Young, eds., *Feminism and World Religions* (Albany, 1999), p. 201.

50 Ibid.

51 Umansky, "Jewish Feminist Theology," p. 314.

52 Plaskow, *Standing Again at Sinai*, p. 10. Page references in the following are to this work.

53 Rachel Adler, *Engendering Judaism: An Inclusive Theology and Ethics* (Philadelphia, 1998), p. 59.

54 Umansky, "Jewish Feminist Theology," p. 336.

55 Umanksy, "Jewish Feminist Theology," p. 338. Among other contemporary authors who have undertaken midrashic reinterpretations of biblical characters and events from a feminist stance are Norma Rosen, *Biblical Women Unbound: Counter-Tales* (Philadelphia, 1996), and Ellen Frankel, *The Five Books of Miriam: A Woman's Commentary on the Torah* (San Francisco, 1996).

56 See, for example, essay collections edited by Baskin, *Women of the Word: Jewish Women and Jewish Writing* (Detroit, 1994) and *Jewish Women in Historical Perspective*, second edition (Detroit, 1998); and Peskowitz and Levitt, *Judaism since Gender* (New York, 1997). An anthology of essays documenting the impact of this ongoing phenomenon on various fields within Jewish Studies was edited by Lynn Davidman and Shelly Tenenbaum, *Feminist Perspectives on Jewish Studies* (New Haven, 1994).

Bibliography

Adelman, Penina V., *Miriam's Well: Rituals for Jewish Women Around the Year* (New York, 1990).

Adler, Rachel, *Engendering Judaism: An Inclusive Theology and Ethics* (Philadelphia, 1998).

Antler, Joyce, *The Journey Home: Jewish Women and the American Century* (New York, 1997).

Balka, Christie, and Andy Rose, eds., *Twice Blessed: On Being Lesbian or Gay and Jewish* (Boston, 1989).

Baskin, Judith R., ed., *Jewish Women in Historical Perspective*, second edition (Detroit, 1998).

Baskin, Judith R., ed., *Women of the Word: Jewish Women and Jewish Writing* (Detroit, 1994).

Berger, Aliza, "Wrapped Attention: May Women Wear *Tefillin?*" in Micah D. Halpern and Chana Safrai, eds., *Jewish Legal Writings by Women* (Jerusalem, 1998), pp. 75–118.

Bernstein, Deborah S., "Daughters of the Nation: Between the Public and Private Spheres in Pre-State Israel," in Judith R. Baskin, ed., *Jewish Women in Historical Perspective*, second edition (Detroit, 1998), pp. 287–311.

Broner, E. M., *The Telling* (New York, 1993).

Broner, E. M., with Naomi Nimrod, *The Women's Haggadah* (New York, 1994).

Daum, Annette, "Language and Liturgy," in Susan Grossman and Rivka Haut, eds., *Daughters of the King: Women and the Synagogue* (Philadelphia, 1992), pp. 183–202.

Davidman, Lynn, and Shelly Tenenbaum, eds., *Feminist Perspectives on Jewish Studies* (New Haven, 1994).

Davidman, Lynn, *Tradition in a Rootless World: Women Turn to Orthodox Judaism* (Berkeley, 1991).

Falk, Marcia, *The Book of Blessings: New Jewish Prayers for Daily Life, the Sabbath, and the New Moon Festival* (San Francisco, 1996).

Fishman, Sylvia Barack, *A Breath of Life: Feminism in the American Jewish Community* (New York, 1993).

Frankel, Ellen, *The Five Books of Miriam: A Woman's Commentary on the Torah* (San Francisco, 1996).

Frankiel, Tamar, *The Voice of Sarah: Feminine Spirituality and Traditional Judaism* (San Francisco, 1990).

Geller, Laura, "Reactions to a Woman Rabbi," in Susannah Heschel, ed., *On Being a Jewish Feminist* (New York, 1983, 1995), pp. 210–13.

Gottlieb, Lynn, *She Who Dwells Within: A Feminist Vision of A Renewed Judaism* (San Francisco, 1995).

Grossman, Susan, "On *Tefillin*," in Ellen M. Umansky and Dianne Ashton, eds., *Four Centuries of Jewish Women's Spirituality: A Sourcebook* (Boston, 1992), pp. 279–82.

Haut, Rivka, "The Agunah and Divorce," in Debra Orenstein, ed., *Lifecycles: Jewish Women on Life Passages and Personal Milestones*, Volume One (Woodstock, 1994), pp. 188–200.

Haut, Rivka, "Women's Prayer Groups and the Orthodox Synagogue," in Susan Grossman and Rivka Haut, eds., *Daughters of the King: Women and the Synagogue* (Philadelphia, 1992), pp. 135–58.

Hazeleton, Leslie, "Israeli Women: Three Myths," in Susannah Heschel, ed., *On Being a Jewish Feminist* (New York, 1983, 1995), pp. 65–87.

Heschel, Susannah, ed., *On Being a Jewish Feminist* (New York, 1983, 1995).

Hyman, Paula E., *Gender and Assimilation in Modern Jewish History: The Roles and Representation of Women* (Seattle, 1995).

Kaplan, Marion A., *The Making of the Jewish Middle Class: Women, Family, and Identity in Imperial Germany* (New York, 1991).

Kaufman, Debra Renée, *Rachel's Daughters: Newly Orthodox Jewish Women* (New Brunswick, 1991).

Kuzmack, Linda Gordon, *Women's Cause: The Jewish Woman's Movement in England and the United States, 1881–1933* (Columbus, 1990).

Millen, Rochelle L., "The Female Voice of Kaddish," in Micah D. Halpern and Chana Safrai, eds., *Jewish Legal Writings by Women* (Jerusalem, 1998), pp. 179–201.

Monson, Rela Geffen, "The Impact of the Jewish Women's Movement on the American Synagogue: 1972–1985," in Susan Grossman and Rivka Haut, eds., *Daughters of the King: Women and the Synagogue* (Philadelphia, 1992), pp. 227–36.

Nadell, Pamela, *Women Who Would Be Rabbis: A History of Women's Ordination, 1889–1985* (Boston, 1998).

Orenstein, Debra, ed., *Lifecycles: Jewish Women on Life Passages and Personal Milestones, Volume One* (Woodstock, 1994).

Peskowitz, Miriam, and Laura Levitt, eds., *Judaism since Gender* (New York, 1997).

Plaskow, Judith, *Standing Again at Sinai: Judaism from a Feminist Perspective* (San Francisco, 1990).

Prell, Riv-Ellen, "The Vision of Women in Classical Reform Judaism," in *Journal of the American Academy of Religion* 50:4 (December 1982), pp. 575–89.

Rosen, Norma, *Biblical Women Unbound: Counter-Tales* (Philadelphia, 1996).

Sered, Susan Starr, *Women as Ritual Experts: The Religious Lives of Elderly Jewish Women in Jerusalem* (New York, 1992).

Swirski, B., and M. Safir, eds., *Calling the Equality Bluff: Women in Israel* (New York, 1991).

Umansky, Ellen M., "Feminism in Judaism," in Arvind Sharma and Katherine K. Young, eds., *Feminism and World Religions* (Albany, 1999), pp. 179–213.

Umansky, Ellen M., "Jewish Feminist Theology," in Eugene B. Borowitz, *Choices in Modern Jewish Thought: A Partisan Guide* (West Orange, 1995), pp. 313–40.

Umansky, Ellen M., "Piety, Persuasion and Friendship: A History of Jewish Women's Spirituality," in Ellen M. Umansky and Dianne Ashton, eds., *Four Centuries of Jewish Women's Spirituality: A Sourcebook* (Boston, 1992), pp. 1–30.

Umansky, Ellen M., "Spiritual Expressions: Jewish Women's Religious Lives in the Twentieth-Century United States," in Judith R. Baskin, ed., *Jewish Women in Historical Perspective*, second edition (Detroit, 1998), pp. 337–63.

Weiss, Avraham, *Women at Prayer: A Halakhic Analysis of Women's Prayer Groups* (Hoboken, 1990).

CHAPTER 23

Judaism as a Theopolitical Phenomenon

Daniel J. Elazar

Jews can be fully understood only when they are recognized as members of a polity – a covenantal community linked by a shared destiny, a promised land, and a common pattern of communications whose essential community of interest and purpose and whose ability to consent together in matters of common interest have been repeatedly demonstrated.[1] In traditional terms, *Judaism* is essentially a theopolitical phenomenon, a means of seeking salvation by constructing God's polity, the proverbial "city upon a hill," through which the covenantal community takes on meaning and fulfills its purpose in the divine scheme of things.[2] *Jewish peoplehood* has been the motivating force for communal life and creativity throughout the long history of the Jewish people. The power and pervasiveness of this force has certainly been demonstrated in our own time.

The Jewish polity has some special characteristics. It is worldwide in scope but territorial only in a limited sense. It is not a state, although a state is an essential part of it.[3] It is authoritative but only for those who accept citizenship within it. It does not demand the exclusive loyalty of those attached to it, because many of its members share multiple loyalties.[4] And, finally, it exists by virtue of a mystique, and orientation toward a future that looks to the redemption of humanity.

Preeminently, the Jewish polity survives because of the will of its citizens and their active application of that will to carve out an area of autonomous existence in the midst of peoples who would absorb or eliminate them.[5] As it turns out, this is as true of the modern state of Israel as it has been of the diaspora Jewish communities, just as it was true of all the earlier Jewish commonwealths.

It is always a mistake to underestimate the continuity of culture. Individuals are formed early in their lives by the cultures into which they are born. So, too, is a people. The seeds of whatever Jews are today were planted at the very birth of the Jewish people. Certain key characteristics visible then and deriving from those original conditions have persisted over time despite all the subsequent changes in the Jewish situation.

The Jewish polity is a product of a unique blend of kinship and consent. The blend is already reflected in the biblical account of its origins: a family of tribes that becomes a nation by consenting to God's covenant, thereby retaining its federal character.[6] (It should be noted that the term *federal* is derived from the Latin *foedus* meaning covenant.) That federal character continues to be reflected in one way or another throughout Jewish history.[7]

Post-biblical Jewish history gave the blend a new meaning. That Jews were born Jewish puts them in a special position to begin with, one which more often than not has forced them together for self-protection. Yet sufficient opportunities for conversion, assimilation, or the adoption of a posture of simple apathy toward any active effort to maintain Jewish life were almost always available as options. The survival of organized and creative Jewish life, then, can only be understood in the light of the active will of many Jews to function as a community, in itself a form of consent ratified by repeated consensual acts over the millennia.

Beyond the sheer fact of communal survival, consent has remained the normal basis for organizing the Jewish polity. Jews in different localities consented (and consent) together to form congregations and communities – in Hebrew the terms are synonymous.[8] They did (and do) this formally through articles of agreement, charters, covenants, and constitutions. The traditional Sephardic term for such articles of congregational–communal agreement, *askamot*, conveys this meaning exactly. The local communities were (and are) then tied together by additional consensual arrangements, ranging from formal federations to the tacit recognition of a particular *halakhic* authority, *shtadlan*, or supralocal body as authoritative.[9] When conditions were propitious, the *de facto* confederation of Jewish communities extended to wherever Jews lived. When this level of political existence was impossible, the binding force of Jewish law served to keep the federal bonds from being severed.

Covenantal Foundations

Jews have traditionally organized their communities into coherent bodies politic on a constitutional basis. In Jewish law, every Jewish community is a partnership of its members. There is no such thing as "the state" existing independently of the people in Halakhah or Jewish tradition. The ultimate constitutional basis of that partnership is the original covenant establishing the Jewish people, the covenant that tradition records as having been made between God and the twelve tribes of Israel at Sinai. From that covenant came the Torah, the traditional constitution of the Jewish people. When Jews speak of Torah, they do not refer to the five books of Moses alone but to the Torah as it has grown, with the Talmud, interpretations, and commentaries added to it. Until modern times, nobody disputed the traditional constitution. Jews accepted the Torah. They may have argued over its interpretation, but they accepted it. And out of that acceptance the Jewish polity was given constitutional form.

A covenant is a morally informed agreement or pact between parties having an independent and sufficiently equal status based upon voluntary consent and established by mutual oaths or promises involving or witnessed by a transcendent authority. A covenant provides for joint action to achieve defined ends, limited or comprehensive, under conditions of mutual respect in a way that protects the respective integrities of all the parties to it. Every covenant involves consenting, promising, and agreeing. Most are meant to be of unlimited duration, if not perpetual. Covenants can bind any number of partners for a variety of purposes, but in essence they are political in that their bonds are used principally to create relationships best understood in political terms.

As much as covenant is a theological and political concept, it is also informed by a moral or ethical perspective that treats political relationships in the classical manner. That is, covenants link *power* and *justice* – the two faces of politics – and preserve the classic and ancient links between ethics and politics. The emphasis is on relationships rather than structures as the key to political justice. Structures are always important, but, ultimately, no matter how finely tuned the structures, they come alive (or fail to) only through the human relationships that inform and shape them.

Covenant is tied in an ambiguous relationship to two related terms, *compact* and *contract*. On one hand, both compacts and contracts are closely related to covenant, and sometimes the terms are even used interchangeably. Moreover, covenantal societies tend to emphasize contractual arrangements at every level of human affairs. However, there are real differences between the three terms. Covenants and compacts differ from contracts in that the first two are constitutional or public and the last private. As such, covenantal or compactual obligation is broadly reciprocal; those bound by one or the other are obligated to respond to one another beyond the letter of the law rather than to limit their obligations to the narrowest contractual requirements. Hence, covenants and compacts are inherently designed to be flexible in some respects and firm in others. As expressions of private law, contracts tend to be interpreted as narrowly as possible as to what the contract explicitly mandates.

A covenant differs from a compact in that its morally binding dimension takes precedence over its legal dimension. In its heart of hearts, a covenant is an agreement in which a higher moral force, traditionally God, is either a direct party to or guarantor of a particular relationship. A compact, based as it is on mutual pledges rather than guarantees by or before a higher authority, rests more heavily on legal as well as moral grounding for its politics. In other words, compact is a secular phenomenon.

This is historically verifiable by examining the shift in terminology that took place in the seventeenth and eighteenth centuries. Although those who saw the hand of God in political affairs as a rule continued to use the term *covenant*, those who sought a secular grounding for politics turned to the term *compact*. Though the distinction was not always used with strict clarity, it does appear consistently. The issue was further complicated by Rousseau and his followers, who talk about the social contract, a highly secularized concept, which, even

Table 23.1   Epochs, covenants, and constitutions in Ancient Israel

Epoch	Covenant	Constitution
1 Ha-Avot	Brit Bein ha-Betarim (Abraham's Covenant)	
2 Avudut Mizrayim		Maserot he-Avot (Patriarchal Tradition)
3 Adat Bnei Yisrael	Brit Sinai (Sinai Covenant)	Torat Moshe (Mosaic Law)
4 Brit ha-Melukhah	Brit between David and Am before God	Torat Moshe and Mishpat ha-Melekh (Law of Kinship)
5 Malkhut Yehudah	Covenant renewed on Pesach of Hezekiah	Torat Moshe and Mishpat ha-Melekh (Prophetic works)
6 Knesset haGedolah	Amanah (Covenant) of Ezra and Nehemiah	Torat Moshe and Takkanot Ezra vehaSoferim (Ordinances of Ezra and the Scribes)
7 Hever haYehudim	Brit between Simon the Hasmonean, the Zekenim and the Am	Torat Moshe and Torah she-ba'al Peh (Oral Torah)

when applied for public purposes, never develops the same moral obligation as either covenant or compact.

In its original biblical form, covenant embodies the idea that relationships between God and humans are based on morally sustained compacts of mutual promise and obligation. God's covenant with Noah (Gen. 9), which came after Noah had hearkened fully to God's commands in what was, to say the least, an extremely difficult situation, is the first of many examples. Table 23.1 lists others. In its political form, covenant expresses the idea that people can freely create communities and polities, peoples and publics, and civil society itself through such morally grounded and sustained compacts (whether religious or otherwise in impetus), establishing thereby enduring partnerships.[10]

The covenantal approach is closely connected with constitutionalism. A covenant is the constitutionalization of a set of relationships of a particular kind. As such, it provides the basis for the institutionalization of those relationships; but it would be wrong to confuse the order of precedence. Again, the biblical model whereby a covenant provides the basis for constitutional government by first establishing a people or civil society that then proceeds to adopt a constitution of government for itself is paradigmatic. Here the constitution involves the translation of a prior covenant into an actual frame or structure of government. Sometimes the constitution includes the covenant within it, serving both purposes simultaneously.

The US Declaration of Independence is an excellent example of a political covenant. The diverse inhabitants of the thirteen colonies reaffirmed that they consented to become a people. It was not without reason, therefore, that Abraham Lincoln fondly described the union created by that act as "a regular marriage."[11] The partners do not unquestionably live happily ever after, but they are bound by covenant to struggle toward such an end, a commitment well understood and made explicit by Lincoln during the Civil War.

The covenantal approach not only informs and animates the Jewish polity but represents the greatest Jewish contribution to political life and thought. It is possible that covenant ideas emerged spontaneously in different parts of the world. If covenant thinking is rooted in human nature as well as nurture, it is to be expected that some people everywhere would be oriented toward the idea somehow. However, it is not sufficient for random individuals to be disposed to it for an idea to take root and spread. Somehow a culture or civilization must emerge that embodies and reflects that idea. The first such civilization or culture was that of ancient Israel, whose people transformed and perfected a device originally developed among the west Asian peoples who inhabited the area. The first known uses of covenant were the vassal treaties through which the empire builders of west Asia secured the fealty of lesser peoples and their domains through pacts secured by oath before their respective deities.[12] These international or intra-imperial pacts laid out the form that covenants have taken ever since, which include five elements: a prologue indicating the parties involved, a preamble stating the general purposes of the covenant and the principles behind it, a body of conditions and operative clauses, an oath to make the covenant morally binding, and stipulated sanctions to be applied if the covenant is violated.

Either parallel to or derived from these ancient vassal covenants there emerged domestic political and religious usages of covenant. The two were connected in the bible to form the classic foundation of the covenant tradition.[13] God's covenant with Israel established the Jewish people and founded it as a body politic, while at the same time creating the religious framework that gave that polity its *raison d'être*, its norms, and its constitution, as well as the guidelines for developing a political order based on proper, that is, covenantal, relationships.

Biblical adaptation of the forms of the vassal covenants involved a transformation of the purpose and content so great as to mean a difference in kind, not merely degree. A covenant was used to found a people, making their moral commitment to one another far stronger and more enduring than that of a vassal to an imperial overlord. The Bible draws a distinction between "sons of the covenant," *bnei brit* in Hebrew, and "masters of the covenant," *ba'alei brit*. *Bnei brit* is used where the covenant has created a new entity whose partners are bound together as siblings in a family. The covenant that unites and forms the Jewish people in the biblical account and in all later Jewish history makes all Jews *bnei brit*. However, where the term used is *ba'alei brit* the covenant is essentially an international treaty. It does not create a new entity but establishes a relationship of peace and mutual ties between entities that remain separate for all purposes outside the limited-purpose pact.

This new form of covenant was understood not simply to be witnessed by Heaven, but as bringing God in as a partner, thus informing it with religious value and implication for the Israelites, who saw no distinction between its religious and political dimensions. The covenant remained a theopolitical document with as heavy an emphasis on the political as could be. The strong political dimension reflected God's purpose in choosing one people to be the builders of a holy commonwealth that would be a model for all others.

It was only later with the rise of Christianity and the beginning of the long exile of the Jews from their land that covenant took on a more strictly religious character for some, in which the political dimension was downplayed, if not downright ignored by Christian theologians on the one hand and diminished by Jewish legists on the other. Christianity embraced the covenant idea as one of its foundations but reinterpreted the old biblical covenant establishing a people and polity to be a covenant of grace between God and individual humans, created unilaterally and mediated by Jesus.[14] Jewish legists simply took the basic covenantal framework of Judaism for granted and concentrated on the fine points of the law as applied to daily living or the expected messianic redemption.[15]

In the Jewish world, the political dimension of covenanting received new impetus in the eleventh through fourteenth centuries to provide a basis for constituting local Jewish communities throughout Europe. That effort ran parallel to the establishment of municipal corporations throughout the continent, which were legitimized by royal charter, usually negotiated between the municipality and the throne.[16]

All this is well documented in Jewish sources. Because Jews were always moving, either by choice or necessity, when they came to new places they had to organize communities, for Jews cannot fully function Jewishly without organized communities. It was to ease the process that model covenants for setting up communities and communal institutions came into existence. Thus *Sefer HaShtarot* ("The Book of Contracts"), a late eleventh- or early twelfth-century compendium of model laws (significantly, in the form of contracts) by Rabbi Judah HaBarceloni, a Spanish Jew, includes model laws for every contingency, all of which are in accord with the Torah, that is, constitutional.[17] It is the first such compendium that we know of in Jewish history. Perhaps it is the first in history. It includes model covenants or contracts for establishing welfare societies, for organizing synagogues, for organizing assistance to widows and orphans, for establishing schools, and many others. Most especially, it includes a model covenant for establishing a *kehal kadosh*, a local community.

The principles of community enunciated in the foregoing document are clear. For the actions of a community to be legally binding in Jewish law, it had to be duly constituted by its prospective members, preferably through a constituent assembly and a constitutional document. They must be able to say that "we have met together as the elders," that "we have discussed the matter," that "we have agreed in assembly of the entire community." If these patterns were not followed the action would not be valid.

Covenant and the Origins of the Polity

Since its beginnings, political science has identified three basic ways in which polities come into existence: conquest, organic development, and covenant.[18] These questions of origins are not abstract; the mode of founding of a polity does much to determine the framework for its later political life.

Conquest can be understood to include not only its most direct manifestation, a conqueror gaining control of a land or a people, but also such subsidiary ways as a revolutionary conquest of an existing state, a coup d'état, or even an entrepreneur's conquering a market and institutionalizing control through corporate means. Conquest tends to produce hierarchically organized regimes ruled in an authoritarian manner: power pyramids with the conqueror on top, his agents in the middle, and the people underneath the entire structure. The original expression of this kind of polity was the pharaonic state of ancient Egypt. It was hardly an accident that those rulers who brought the pharaonic state to its fullest development had pyramids built as their tombs. Although the pharaonic model has been judged illegitimate in western society, modern totalitarian theories, particularly fascism and nazism, represent an attempt to give it theoretical legitimacy.

Organic evolution involves the development of political life from its beginnings in families, tribes, and villages to large polities in such a way that institutions, constitutional relationships, and power alignments emerge in response to the interaction between past precedent and changing circumstances with the minimum of deliberate constitutional choice. The result is a polity with a single center of power, dominated by an accepted political elite, controlling the periphery, which may or may not have influence at the center. Classic Greek political thought emphasized the organic evolution of the polity and rejected any other means of polity-building as deficient or improper. The organic model is closely related to the concept of natural law in the political order. Natural law informs the world and, when undisturbed, leads to a kind of organic development, which, in turn, results in this model of the polity.

The organic model has proved most attractive to political philosophers precisely because, at its best, it seems to reflect the natural order of things. Thus it has received the most intellectual and academic attention. However, just as conquest produces hierarchically organized regimes ruled in an authoritarian manner, organic evolution produces oligarchic regimes, which, at their best, have an aristocratic flavor and, at their worst, are simply the rule of the many by the few. In the first, the goal is to control the top of the pyramid; in the second, the goal is to control the center of power.

Covenantal foundings emphasize the deliberate coming together of humans as equals to establish bodies politic so that all reaffirm their fundamental equality and retain their basic liberties. Polities whose origins are covenantal reflect the exercise of constitutional choice and broad-based participation in constitutional design. Polities founded by covenant are essentially federal in the original meaning of the term – whether they are federal in structure or not. That is, each polity is a matrix compounded of equal confederates who come together freely and retain their respective integrities even as they are bound in a common whole. Such polities are republican by definition, and power in them must be diffused among many centers or the cells within the matrix.

Recurring expressions of the covenant model are found among the Jews, whose people started out as rebels against pharaonic Egypt; the Swiss, whose people started out as rebels against the Holy Roman Empire; and the Dutch, Scots, and Puritans who rebelled against the Roman Catholic hierarchy in the Reformation era. In the modern epoch, republicans who were rebels against either hierarchical or organic theories of the state adopted the covenant model in one version or another. Frontiersmen – people who have chosen to settle in new areas where there are no established patterns of governance in which to fit and who, therefore, have had to compact with one another to create governing institutions – are to be found among the most active covenanters.

What is common to all political societies rooted in the covenant idea is that they have drawn their inspiration proximately or ultimately from its biblical source. There is evidence of other contractual or oath-bound societies, and, of course, constitutionalism of various kinds exists outside the biblical tradition. But there is no evidence of any developed covenantal tradition that is not derived from the Bible.

The biblical grand design for humankind is federal in three ways.

1   It is based on a network of covenants beginning with those between God and humankind, which weave the web of human, especially political, relationships in a federal way – through pact, association and consent.

2   The classical biblical commonwealth was a fully articulated federation of tribes instituted and reaffirmed by covenant to function under a common constitution and laws. Any and all constitutional changes in the Israelite polity were introduced through covenanting, and, even after the introduction of the monarchy, the federal element was maintained until most of the tribal structures were destroyed by external forces. The biblical version of the restored commonwealth in the messianic era envisages the reconstitution of the tribal federation.

3   The biblical vision for the "end of days" – the messianic era – sees not only a restoration of Israel's tribal federation, but what is, for all intents and purposes, a world confederation of nations, each preserving its own integrity while accepting a common divine covenant and constitutional order. This order will establish appropriate covenantal relationships for the entire world. Although it shares many of the same positive ends, it is the antithesis of the ecumenical world state envisaged by the Roman and Christian traditions, which see the merging of everyone into a single entity. The biblical–covenantal–Jewish view sees peoples preserving their own integrities within a shared whole.

Covenant theory emphasizes human freedom because only free people can enter into agreements with one another. It also presupposes the need for government and the need to organize civil society on principles that assure the maintenance of those rights and the exercise of power in a cooperative or partnership-like way.

Covenantal (or federal) liberty, however, is not simply the right to do as one pleases within broad boundaries. Federal liberty emphasizes liberty to pursue the moral purposes for which the covenant was made. This latter kind of liberty requires that moral distinctions be drawn and that human actions be judged according to the terms of the covenant. This does not preclude changes in social norms, but the principles of judgment remain constant. Consequently, covenantal societies, founded as they are on covenantal choice, emphasize constitutional design and choice as a continuing process.

The *Edah* as a Classic Republic

The Jewish polity has followed the covenant model since its inception, adapting it to variegated circumstances in which Jews have found themselves over the millennia – as a tribal federation, a federal monarchy, a state with a diaspora, a congress of covenantal communities, a network of regional federations or confederations, or a set of voluntary associations.

The classic Hebrew name for this kind of polity is *edah*. The *edah* is the assembly of all the people constituted as a body politic. *Edah* is often translated as congregation; that term has a religious connotation today that it did not have when introduced in sixteenth- and seventeenth-century biblical translations. Then it had a civil meaning as well. It was a "congregation – an institutionalized gathering of people who congregate (come together) that meets at regular times or frequently for common action and decision making."[19]

In Mosaic times *edah* became the Hebrew equivalent of "commonwealth" or "republic," with strong democratic overtones. The idea of the Jewish people as an *edah* has persisted ever since and the term has been used to describe the Jewish body politic in every period to the present. In this respect, the term parallels (and historically precedes) similar phenomena such as the *landesgemeinde* in Switzerland, the Icelandic *althing*, and the town meeting in the United States.

The characteristics of the original *edah* can be summarized as follows:

1 The Torah is the constitution of the *edah*.
2 All members of the *edah*, men, women, and children, participate in constitutional decisions.
3 Political equality exists for those capable of taking full responsibility for Jewish survival.
4 Decisions are made by an assembly that determines its own leaders within the parameters of divine mandate.

5   The *edah* is portable and transcends geography.
6   Nevertheless, for it to function completely, the *edah* needs Eretz Israel.

These basic characteristics have been preserved with such modifications as were necessary over the centuries. Thus, in biblical times, taking full responsibility for Jewish survival meant being able to bear arms. Subsequently, the arms-bearing measure of political equality gave way to one of Torah study. Today the diaspora measure is contributing to the support of Israel, while arms-bearing is again the measure in Israel. The principles of assembly, leadership, and decision making have remained the same although modes of assembling, leadership recruitment, and leaders' roles and responsibilities have changed from time to time. The portability of the desert-born *edah* is as notable a characteristic as is its attachment to Zion. The Torah has persisted as the *edah*'s constitution albeit with changing interpretations.

Jewish republicanism is rooted in a democratic foundation based on the equality of all Jews as citizens of the Jewish people. All Jews must participate in the establishment and maintenance of their polity, as demonstrated in the Bible – at Sinai, on the plain of Moab, before Shechem, and elsewhere – in *Sefer HaShtarot*, and in many other sources. Nor is that foundation merely theoretical; even where power may not be exercised on a strictly democratic basis, it is generally exercised in light of democratic norms.

There are problems associated with the use of these terms, but they do help us understand that the Jewish polity often has been governed by a kind of trusteeship. It is a trusteeship because the community is republican, because it is a *res publica*, a public thing or a commonwealth – a body politic that belongs to its members. The Jewish people is a *res publica* with a commitment to a teaching and law, which its members are not free simply to alter as they wish but which must be maintained to be faithful to principles.

The western world today takes the republican revolution for granted. Yet the republican revolution was one of the great revolutions of modernity, the foundation of modern democracy. The Jews were among the first pioneers of republicanism many centuries ago. Then came the Greeks and the early Romans. Except for a few outposts, including the Jewish *kehillah*, republicanism died under the realities of imperial Rome and medieval feudalism, to be replaced by absolutism. In modern times, a revolution was needed to restore the democratic republican principle. Before the republican revolution, the prevailing view was that the state was the private preserve of its governors. When Louis XIV said "I am the state," he was articulating a classic anti-republican position.

The history of governance in the Jewish community has been one of swinging between the two poles of aristocratic republican trusteeship and oligarchy. Though this is a perennial problem, the basic republicanism of the Jewish polity has worked equally well to prevent absolutism or autocracy. The Jewish people rarely has had anything like dictatorship and then only locally and *de facto* under unique circumstances. Jews are notably intractable people, even under conditions of statehood where coercion theoretically has been possible; hence, dictatorship has not been an acceptable regime for Jews.

Nor have Jews in the past had anything like the open society of the kind envisaged by many contemporary westerners, in which every individual is free to chose his or her own "life-style." One of the reasons for this is that being Jewish and maintaining the Jewish polity has not been simply a matter of survival. It has also been a matter of living up to specific norms based on divine teaching and law, which establish the expectation that private and public life is to be shaped according to that teaching and law. John Winthrop, the Puritan leader in seventeenth-century Massachusetts, referred to this as "federal liberty," emphasizing its covenantal basis.

The Three Arenas of Jewish Political Organization

From earliest times, the Jewish polity has been organized in three arenas. Besides the *edah*, or national, arena, there are country-wide (or regional) and local arenas of organization. The immediately local arena comprises local Jewish communities around the world of varying sizes, under varying forms of communal organization. Whether we are speaking of Yavneh or Saragossa, Mottel or Chicago, the local community remains the basic cell of Jewish communal life. Here the institutions that serve the Jewish community are organized and function.

Beyond the local arena, there is a larger, country-wide arena in which the Jews in particular regions, countries, or states organize for common purposes. The organizational expressions of that arena have included such phenomena as the *Resh Galuta* (exilarch) and yeshivot of Babylonia, the *Vaad Arba Aratzot* (Council of the Four Lands) of late medieval Poland, the State of Israel, the Board of Deputies of British Jewry, and the congeries of "national" (meaning country-wide) organizations of American Jewry framed by the Council of Jewish Federations. Fund-raising for Israel, for example, depends on work in local communities but is generally organized in this second arena on a country-by-country basis.

Beyond the second arena, there is the third, that of the Jewish people as a whole: the *edah*. This arena was extremely weak for nearly a millennium but has been given new institutional form within the last century, most particularly in our time. The *edah* is the main focus of the reconstitution of the Jewish people in our time.

This threefold division into separate arenas of governance, once formulated in early Israelite history, has remained a permanent feature of Jewish political life. This is so despite frequent changes in the forms of organization of the several arenas and in the terminology used to describe them.

The Bible delineates the first form in which these three arenas were constituted. The *edah* was constituted by the *shevatim* (tribes), each with its own governmental institutions. Each *shevet* was, in turn, a union of *batei av* (extended households). After the Israelite settlement in Canaan, the most prominent form of local organization was the *ir* (city or township) with its own assembly (*ha'ir*) and council (*sha'ar ha'ir* or *ziknai ha'ir*).

Subsequently, in the local arena, just as the *bet av* gave way to the *ir*, the *ir* gave way to the *kehillah* (local community) wherever the Jewish population was a minority. The *kehillah* became the molecular unit of organization for all post-biblical Jewry, especially because new *kehillot* could be established anywhere by any ten adult Jewish males who so constituted themselves. Although the *kehillah* survives in the diaspora, in contemporary Israel, the local arena is once again governed by comprehensive municipal units – cities or villages.

Similarly, the breakdown of the traditional tribal system (a phenomenon that long preceded the first exile) resulted in the replacement of the *shevet* by the *medinah* (properly rendered as autonomous jurisdiction or province in its original meaning), a regional framework, which embraces a congeries of *kehillot* that it unites in an organizational structure, as in *Medinat Yehud* (Judea in the Persian Empire). In the diaspora, the term *medinah* became almost interchangeable with *eretz* (country) to describe the intermediate arena, as in Medinat Polin (the organized Jewish community in Poland) or Eretz Lita (the organized Jewish community in late medieval Lithuania). In modern times, the term came to mean a politically sovereign state and is now used only in connection with Medinat Yisrael (the State of Israel).

The term *edah*, as an expression of the widest form of Jewish political association, retained its original usage unimpaired until transformed in colloquial modern Hebrew usage, where it came to denote a country-of-origin group in Israel. Occasionally, it was replaced by such synonyms as *Knesset Yisrael*. In antiquity, the *edah* managed to survive the division of Israel into two kingdoms, the Babylonian exile, and the Roman conquest of Judea by developing new forms of comprehensive organization. During the period of the second commonwealth (ca. 440 BCE–140 CE) and again from the second to the eleventh centuries, it was particularly successful in constructing a fully-articulated institutional framework that embraced both Israel and the diaspora. The breakdown of the universal Muslim empire and the consequent demise of the *edah*-wide institutions of the Resh Galuta (exilarchate) and Geonate in the middle of the eleventh century left world Jewry bereft of comprehensive institutions other than the Halakhah itself. From then until the mid-nineteenth century, the *edah* was held together principally by its common Torah and laws as manifested in a worldwide network of rabbinical authorities linked by their communications (responsa) on halakhic matters.[20]

The Three *Ketarim*

Classically, leadership in the Jewish polity has been divided and shared among three domains known in Hebrew as the three *ketarim* (crowns): the *keter torah*, the domain of the Torah; the *keter kehunah*, the domain of the priesthood; and the *keter malkhut*, literally, the crown of kingship but more correctly understood as the domain of governance. Each of these *ketarim* has functions it must perform if Jewish life is to be complete; hence, all are necessary for the survival and development of the *edah*.[21] There has never been a time when the *edah* has not in some way functioned through some kind of division of authority and powers among the three *ketarim*. This is not separation of powers in the modern sense. The *ketaric* division is for comprehensive polities involving more than the organs of government. It concerns itself with every aspect of the body politic, civil and religious. Hence it comes prior to the executive–legislative–judicial division that falls primarily within the *keter malkhut*. Each *keter* combines a range of functions, institutions, and roles within its domain and shares some of them with the other domains.

The *keter torah* embraces those who are responsible for the maintenance and application of the Torah, its laws, principles, and spirit in the life of the Jewish people and governance of the *edah*. Its roots go back to Moses, the first *navi* (prophet) and, as such, the first to bear that *keter*. It passed to the prophets and, after the age of prophecy, it passed to the *soferim* (scribes), and then to the Sanhedrin with its *hakhamim* (sages) and rabbis. In the traditional Jewish polity, its bearers functioned primarily as teachers and judges.

The *keter kehunah* embraces those who are responsible for the ritual and sacerdotal expressions of Jewish being, designed to bring Jews closer to Heaven individually and collectively (and hence to each other as Jews). From a public perspective, the functions of this crown play a major role in determining the fact and character of citizenship in the *edah*. Originally granted in the Torah to Aaron and his heirs, it is principally identified with the *cohanim*, but after the destruction of the Second Temple, its functions passed to other religious functionaries, principally *hazzanim* and, more recently, congregational rabbis, and generally it was confined to the most local arena of Jewish organization.

The *keter malkhut* embraces those who are responsible for conducting the civil business of the *edah*: to establish and manage its organized framework, its political and social institutions, to raise and expend the money needed for the functioning of the *edah*, and to handle its political and civic affairs. Although, like the others, it is bound by the Torah-as-constitution, this *keter* is described in the Torah as originally granted to Abraham through God's covenant with him. It has existed as a separate source of authority since the beginning of the *edah*, with its own institutions, responsibilities, and tasks. It is the oldest of the *ketarim*, emerging out of the patriarchal leadership of the original Israelite families. Later, it passed to the *nesi'im* (magistrates), *shofetim* (judges), and *zekenim* (elders), and then to the *melekh* (king). After the end of Jewish political independence in the land of Israel, it was carried on by the *Nasi* (patriarch) there and the *Resh Galuta* (exilarch) in Babylonia, the *negidim* of Spain, and the *parnassim* of the *kehillot*.

Constitutional Structure of the *Edah*

Thus, one of the ways in which Jews attempted to prevent the corruption of their leaders and governing bodies was through the division of powers in the polity. The legitimacy of the division is made explicit in many texts. For example, Bereshit Rabbah, the Midrashic commentary on Genesis, comments on the verse: "The scepter shall not depart from Judah, nor the ruler's staff from between his legs" (Gen. 49:10). According to the Midrash, the "scepter" is interpreted as the exilarchs in Babylon, who rule the people, Israel, with the stick; the "ruler's staff" is the patriarchs of the family of Rav, who teach Torah to the populace in the land of Israel.

Another explanation of the verse is offered: "The scepter is the messiah, son of David (*mashiah ben David*) who will rule over the kingdom, that is to say, Rome, with a stick. And the ruler's staff is those who teach halakhah to Israel." Even after the messiah comes there will have to be a separation of powers, for even he is not to be trusted with all the powers alone. Even if he can rule over Rome, there still must be the great Sanhedrin to teach Halakhah to Israel.

This traditional pattern underwent many changes in the modern epoch but continued to be the basic model for the *edah* and its *kehillot*, if only out of necessity because the classic division persisted in new forms. In the western world in the nineteenth century, the institutions of the *keter kehunah* became stronger at the expense of the others as Jewish life was redefined under modernity to be primarily "religious," even as Jews ceased to rely on the Torah as binding law. The synagogues became elaborate institutions and their rabbis the principal instrumentalities of the *keter kehunah*. Today, however, the Jewish polity is in the midst of a resurgence of the *keter malkhut*. This is principally because of the re-establishment of a Jewish state in the land of Israel, but it also reflects changes in the orientation of Jews in the diaspora.

The increasing narrowness of approach of the traditional bearers of the *keter torah*, coupled with the growing secularization of Jews that made that sphere and the sphere of *keter kehunah* less attractive to them, all contributed to this power shift. In the political world, the domain with the key to political power obviously had an advantage. In addition, as the other two domains were fragmented among different movements, each claiming to be authoritative, the *keter malkhut* became the only domain in which all groups would meet together, at least for limited political purposes, further strengthening the latter's position in the *edah*. These shifts in power are only several of many in the history of the *edah*, part of the continuing and dynamic tension among the *ketarim*.

The Constitutional Periodization of Jewish History

Implicit in the foregoing discussion and otherwise a matter of commonsense knowledge is that the *edah* has gone through periodic regime changes in the course of Jewish history. The key to understanding those changes is to be found in the patterns of constitutional development of the Jewish people and its polity. Indeed, it is possible to suggest that Jewish history can be read as the progression of the generations through a series of historical epochs, each marked by the unfolding and subsequent undoing of its own constitutional synthesis within the overall framework of the Torah, leading in turn to a new epoch and the necessity for a new constitutional synthesis.

It has been the genius of the Jews as *am* and *edah* to keep the flow of generations intact via those periodic reconstitutions, through exile and dispersion. Hence the issue of constitutionalism and constitutional change is central to the study of Jewish political history in its entirety and provides a base for its periodization. Basically, this is because the Jewish constitution has differed from modern constitutions, most significantly because of its all-embracing character. It is not confined to the delineation of the political power of a secular state, but extends into nearly all phases of life by virtue of its religious as well as political character.

A study of constitutionalism in Jewish history, accordingly, must embrace far more than the record of specific fundamental political laws. A reconstruction of the communal constitution of any particular period of Jewish history must come to terms with the entire range of communal living during that time and thereby provide a framework that can encompass virtually all aspects of Jewish civilization.[22] The Torah is, in this respect, both an exemplar and a touchstone. It contains all the characteristics of organic and all-embracing law; it has also (for the vast majority of Jewish history and by the vast majority of the Jewish people) been perceived to be of divine origin.

On both counts, the Torah must be regarded as the basic and foremost constitutional document of Jewish history. Its subsequent modifications and/or amplifications must, therefore, be considered to be necessitated by overwhelming pressures for constitutional change. All subsequent constitutional referents claim, whether explicitly or implicitly, to maintain the traditions embodied in the Torah; but all nevertheless do so in a manner that supplements and redirects the original in line with the pressures of contemporary conditions. The Mishnah, Gemara, and the subsequent great halakhic codes (to cite only a few such documents) thus constitute indices for the identification and analysis of such adjustments and an explanatory device for relating the change from one epoch to another. Indeed, the Torah-as-constitution can be understood as a kind of nucleus to whose original core have been added layers of additional material, each of which becomes compacted onto the original to the point at which it is bonded to it permanently and no operational difference exists between earlier and later materials even where it is possible to distinguish between them.

At the same time, the Torah is a uniquely Jewish constitution in that it is first and foremost a teaching, as the word Torah itself indicates. Although binding on Jews through the Sinai covenant, as a teaching it is based on the recognition that, in a covenantal system, its binding character still requires consent. Jews must hearken to their constitutional teaching, and since hearkening begins with hearing, they must be rendered open to hearing. In Jewish tradition, this openness comes as a result of learning, not by nature or grace. This characteristic of the Jewish constitution is reflected, inter alia, in the use of

terms that refer to teaching to describe the most important constitutional referents, e.g., Torah, Mishneh Torah (Deuteronomy), Mishnah, Gemara, Talmud.

The idea of Jewish history as constitutional history is not new, just as explicit
reference to the Torah as the fundamental constitution of the *edah* is at least as
old as Philo and Josephus.[23] Applying this idea in the special way in which the
constitution of the Jewish people embraces more than fundamental political
law, it is possible to discuss meaningfully constitutions and constitutionalism
in Jewish history. Indeed, the principal value of the constitutional approach to
the study of Jewish history lies in its ability to provide a framework that can
embrace virtually every aspect of Jewish life without either de-emphasizing or
over-emphasizing the political dimension.

Distinctive in this approach is its deliberate emphasis on the political facet of
Jewish history. Accordingly, it is not bound by conventional historiographical
categories. Most conspicuously is this so in the thorny matter of chronological
divisions. The traditional breakdown into "ancient," "medieval," and "modern"
periods is superseded by a more refined typology based on the rhythm of political life; so, too, is the less obtuse (but hardly more helpful) division into standard
subperiods: "biblical," "post-biblical;" "talmudic," "post-talmudic;" "premodern,"
"modern," and the like.

Patterns of Constitutional Development

We may distinguish periods of constitution-making and constitutional change
in the course of Jewish history on the basis of the Jewish response, or series of
connected responses, to challenges from within or without the *edah*. In doing
so, we can rely first on recognized constitutional texts and the benchmarks of
Jewish political history and constitutional development, noting how they relate
to one another. Out of those relationships temporal patterns emerge, with each
period representing a particular rhythm of challenge and response. Once that
rhythm is identified, the framework within which it moves – and which it
modifies – can be identified as well. Each epoch is characterized not only by its
constitutional synthesis but also by particular institutional expressions of that
synthesis. Each is set off by founding, climactic, and culminating events which
set its constitutional agenda, bring that agenda to whatever degree of fruition
is achieved, and tie off the epoch's loose ends in such a way as to start the
movement toward a new constitutional agenda for a new epoch.

Constitutions are changed or modified only as the necessity for change
becomes overwhelming. In the Jewish polity this is particularly true because of
the traditionally divine nature of Jewish fundamental law. Hence these epochal
transitions occur relatively infrequently. By tracing the subsequent constitutional modifications of the Torah that supplemented and redirected the original
Torah in line with the demands of later ages, we posit that Jewish history can
be divided into fourteen constitutional epochs, each of approximately three

centuries' duration and each of which can be seen to possess a distinct political character of its own.

Table 23. 2 (p. 432) lists the fourteen constitutional epochs of Jewish history as delineated in accordance with the above criteria, also supplying the dates of each epoch, its principal constitutional referents, and dominant events of political significance.

The thirteen epochs that have been completed were remarkably uniform in duration. Each epoch extended over nine historical generations (the years available to mature humans for participation in public affairs), between twenty-five and forty years in length. The shortest epochs were approximately 280 years in length and the longest 320. This seems to indicate rise and decline of historical epochs within a similar general pattern. Each of these epochs corresponds to parallel periods of general history that had their impact on the Jewish people. But what is of the essence in this scheme is the Jewish response to whatever challenges are posed, external as well as internal. Indeed, its emphasis on the internal Jewish rhythm of events is one of the marks of its authenticity. Significantly, the pattern itself is suggested in the Torah, which marks off epochs on a similar basis, i.e., ten generations from Adam to Noah (nine pre-flood and then the generation of the new founding), ten more from Noah to Abraham, 322 years from the birth of Abraham to the death of Jacob, ten generations in Egyptian bondage, and ten more from Moses to David.

During each epoch, a body of interpretations of the Torah, as understood through the constitutional framework established at the epoch's beginning, is developed, reaching its apogee in the climactic generations and thereafter. Then, after some three hundred years, new challenges of time and place demand a more thorough revision of the framework. Utilizing the body of interpretations developed since the preceding constitutional revision (some of which already set forth guidelines for the new era), a revision emerges that provides a basis for meeting the new conditions. Then the process begins again. In the course of the epoch, each new revision becomes universal in its application, not confined to the part of the world in which it originated. So far as the local differences need to be considered, they are provided for in the interpretative process, but within the constitutional framework of time.

Beginning a New Epoch

World War II marked the culmination of all the trends and tendencies of the modern epoch and the end of the epoch itself for all peoples. Sometime between 1946 and 1949, the postmodern epoch began. For the Jewish people, the Holocaust and the establishment of the State of Israel provided the pair of decisive events that marked the crossing of the watershed into the postmodern world. In the process, the entire basis of the Jewish polity was radically changed, the locus of Jewish life shifted, and virtually every organized Jewish community

Table 23.2 The constitutional periodization of Jewish history

Period	Dates	Constitution	Founding Events	Climactic Events	Culminating Events
1 *Ha-Aavot* (The Forefathers)	ca. 850 BCE–1570 BCE	Abraham's Covenant	Abraham leaves Haran	Jacob becomes Israel	Descent to Egypt
2 *Avut Mizrayim* (Egyptian Bondage)	1570–1280	Patriarchal covenant is reaffirmed	Settlement in Goshen	Egyptian slavery	Exodus
3 *Adat Bnei Yisrael* (The Congregation of Israelites)	1280–1004	Mosaic Torah	Sinai	Gideon rejects kinship	David accepted as king
4 *Brit HaMelukhah* (The Covenant of Kingship)	1004–721	Covenants of Kingship	David's kinship	Division of kingdom	Destruction of Israel
5 *Malkhut Yehuda* (The Kingdom of Judah)	721–440	Deuteronomy	Judean rule consolidated	Josianic reform	Abortive restoration of monarchy
6 *Knesset HaGedolah* (The Great Assembly)	440–145	Ezra/Nehemiah Covenant	Ezra restoration	Shift to Helenistic world	Hasmonean revolt
7 *Hever HaYehudim* (The Jewish Commonwealth)	145 BCE–140 CE	Oral Tradition (Torah)	Hasmonean kinship	Destruction of Temple	Bar Kokhba Rebellion
8 *Sanhedrin ve-Nesi'ut* (The Sanhedrin and Patriarchate)	CE 140–429	Mishnah	Organization of Mishnah/Renewal of exilarchate	Christian ascendancy established anti-Jewish policy	End of Patriarchate

9	*Yeshivot ve-Rashei* (The Yeshivot & Exilarch)	429–748	Gemara	Completion of Gemara	Jews come under Islam	Reunification of Jews under Islamic rule
10	*Yeshivot ve-Geonim* (The Yeshivot and the Geonim)	749–1038	Talmud and Codes	Geonim and first codes	Last Israel–Babylonian controversy	End of Geonate
11	*HaKehillot* (The Communities)	1038–1348	Sefer HaHalakhot	Passage of hegemony to Europe	Kabbalah in Spain. Re-establishment of Jewish settlement in Jerusalem	Black Death massacres
12	*Vaadei Kehillot* (Community Federations)	1348–1648	Arba'ah Turim	Polish Jewry's charters. Council of Aragonese community	Spanish expulsion and aftermath	Sabbatean movement
13	*Hitagduyot* (Voluntary Associations)	1648–1948	Shulhan Akrukh	Rose of Modernism	Emancipation	The Holocaust
14	*Medinah ve-Am* (State and People)	1948–	?	Establishment of Israel	?	?

was reconstituted in some way. Central to the reconstitution was the re-establishment of a politically independent Jewish commonwealth in Israel. The restoration of the Jewish state added a new factor to the *edah*, creating a new focus of Jewish energy and concern precisely at the moment when the older foci had reached the end of their ability to attract most Jews. As the 1967 crisis demonstrated decisively, Israel was not simply another Jewish community in the constellation but the center of the world for Jews.

The Jewry that greeted the new state was no longer an expanding one, gaining population even in the face of the attrition of intermarriage and assimilation. On the contrary, it was a decimated one (even worse, for decimated means the loss of one in ten; the Jews lost one in three), a Jewry whose very physical survival had been in grave jeopardy and whose rate of loss from defections came close to equaling its birthrate. Moreover, the traditional strongholds of Jewish communal life in Europe (which were also areas with a high Jewish reproduction rate) were those that had been wiped out.

At the end of the 1940s the centers of Jewish life had shifted decisively away from Europe to Israel and North America. By then, continental Europe ranked behind Latin America, North Africa, and Great Britain, as a force in Jewish life. Its Jews were almost entirely dependent on financial and technical assistance from the United States and Israel. Except for those in the Muslim countries that were soon virtually to disappear, the major functioning Jewish communities all had acquired sufficient size to become significant factors on the Jewish scene only within the previous two generations. In many cases, the original shapers of those communities were still alive, and many were still the actual community leaders. The Jewish world had been willy-nilly thrown back to a pioneering stage.

This new epoch is still in its early years, hardly more than a single generation old; hence, its character is still in its formative stages. Nevertheless, with the establishment of the State of Israel in 1948 the Jewish polity began a constitutional change of revolutionary proportions, inaugurating a new epoch in Jewish constitutional history. For the first time in almost two millennia, the Jewish people were presented with the opportunity to attain citizenship in their own state. Israel's very first law (*Hok Ha-Shevut*, the Law of Return) specified that every Jew had a right to settle in Israel and automatically acquire Israeli citizenship.

To date, only a fraction of the *edah* has taken advantage of Israel's availability. Most continue to live in the lands of the diaspora of their own free will. Hence the dominant structural characteristic of the *edah* continues to be the absence of a binding, all-embracing political framework, although it now has a focus. The State of Israel and its various organs have a strong claim to preeminence in fields that touch on every aspect of Jewish communal life. The Israeli leadership have argued consistently that Israel is qualitatively different from the diaspora and hence its centrality must be acknowledged. The American Jewish leadership, in particular, has taken the position that Israel is no more than first among equals. Nevertheless, the re-establishment of a Jewish state has crystallized the *edah* as a polity, restoring a sense of political involvement among Jews and shaping a new institutional framework in which the business of the *edah* is conducted.

The diffusion of authority and influence that continues to characterize the structure of the *edah* and its components has taken various forms in the new epoch. The *keter malkhut* has been transformed into a network of single and multipurpose functional authorities, most of which do not aspire to do more than serve their particular functions, but all of which acknowledge the place of the State of Israel at the fulcrum of the network. The *keter kehunah* has become a conglomeration of synagogue movements and their rabbinates, mainly responsible for ritual and pastoral functions. Each manages – independently – various ritual functions in a manner it deems appropriate to its own traditions, perspectives, and environment. That each of these movements has established a framework with worldwide aspirations, such as the World Union for Progressive Judaism and the World Council of Synagogues, merely underlines the new organizational character of the *edah*.

Sectoral segmentation is most pronounced in the *keter torah*. Contemporary Jews take their cues in this domain from a kaleidoscopic spectrum of authorities. Their range stretches from the Jewish professors and scholars who influence contemporary Jews' understanding of what is expected of them as Jews, to the rabbinical leadership of the Orthodox, Conservative, and Reform camps, who may use the traditional devices for ruling on matters of Torah but often in untraditional ways; to the heads of very traditional yeshivot and the rebbes of various émigré Hasidic communities who have re-established themselves in the principal cities of Israel and the United States, from which they have developed multi-country networks.

The fragmentation of the *keter torah* is both a reflection and an expression of the absence yet of a clear cut, commonly accepted constitutional basis for the entire *edah*. The tendency toward a wide variety of interpretations of the Torah (traditionally referred to in Hebrew as *Torat Moshe*, the teaching of Moses) that emerged during the modern epoch has now become exacerbated. It is a sign of the times that if the Torah is to be included in the definition of the constitution, it has to be reinterpreted for a majority of Jews. The reality is that the norms by which Jews live their lives are interpreted through various prisms, of which the traditional prism is now only one. Still, it seems that most Jews perceive the Torah to be a constitutional referent in some way.

This fragmentation is further reflected in the multiplicity of camps and parties that influence the life of the *edah* and its constituents. Broadly speaking, the principal camps can be termed: the Orthodox and the Masorati (traditional), who see themselves as continuing the ways of the Pharisees, the Liberal religious, and the Neo-Sadducees. The last includes Israelis seeking to express their Judaism through Israeli Jewry's emerging civil religion – Zionists – and those diaspora Jews who find their best means of Jewish expression in the Jewish communal institutions. These camps are separate but not mutually exclusive. Presented diagrammatically, they ought to be viewed as a triangle, a device that stresses their points of overlap as well as their distinctiveness. The Mizrahi Party, for instance, straddles the Zionist and the Orthodox camps, viewing its Zionism as one expression of its Orthodoxy. Increasingly, too, do the Conservative (Masorati) and Reform (Liberal) movements find themselves linked with Zionism. At the same time, the Neturei Karta, the secular Zionists, and the surviving classical Reform elements remain separated in their respective camps.

Whatever its form of organization, the primary fact of Jewish communal life today is its voluntary character. Although there are differences from country to country in the degree of actual freedom to be Jewish or not, the virtual disappearance of the remaining legal and even social or cultural barriers to individual free choice in all but a handful of countries has made free association the dominant characteristic of Jewish life in the postmodern era. Consequently, the first task of each Jewish community is to learn to deal with this freedom. This task is a major factor in determining the direction of the reconstitution of Jewish life in this generation.

The new voluntarism also extends into the internal life of the Jewish community, generating pluralism even in previously free but relatively homogeneous or monolithic community structures. This pluralism is increased by the breakdown of the traditional reasons for being Jewish and the rise of new incentives for Jewish association. This pluralistic Jewish polity can best be described as a communications network of interacting institutions, each of which, while preserving its own structural integrity and filling its own functional role, is connected to the others in a variety of ways. The boundaries of the polity, insofar as it is bounded, are revealed only when the pattern of the network is uncovered. The pattern stands revealed only when both its components are: its institutions and organizations with their respective roles and the way in which communications are passed between them.

The pattern is inevitably dynamic. There is rarely a fixed division of authority and influence but there is, instead, one that varies from time to time and often from issue to issue, with different entities in the network taking on different "loadings" at different times and relative to different issues. Because the polity is voluntary, persuasion rather than compulsion, influence rather than power, are the only tools available for making and executing policies. This, too, works to strengthen its character as a communications network because the character, quality, and relevance of what is communicated and the way in which it is communicated frequently determine the extent of the authority and influence of the parties to the communication.

The reconstitution of the *edah* is only in its beginning stages; its final form for this epoch cannot yet be foreseen. At this writing, the Jewish people is in the buildup period of the second generation of the postmodern epoch and is actively engaged in trying to work through a new constitutional synthesis, both political and religious. It is likely that the constitution for the new epoch will find its source in the traditional Torah as understood and interpreted in traditional and nontraditional ways. The continued reliance on the Torah as a constitutional anchor could not have been forecast during the first generation of the new epoch, when the late modern trend of secularization was still alive. But it is now fair to conclude that, for most Jews, the Torah continues to serve as a con-stitutional foundation even though they no longer feel bound by its command-ments as traditionally understood.

A second element in the new constitutional framework is the commitment to Jewish unity and peoplehood as embodied in the network of institutions serving the *edah*. This commitment is basically founded on a people-wide con-sensus. However, it is also acquiring a documentary base through congeries of quasi-covenantal constitutional documents generated in the new institutions of the *edah*. These may develop into a comprehensive postmodern constitutional supplement to the *edah*'s historic constitution, following the patterns of earlier epochs.

Notes

1   This chapter is based on material originally presented in four publications by the author, "The Reconstitution of Jewish Communities in the Post-War Period," in *Jewish Journal of Sociology*, vol. 11, no. 2 (December 1969), pp. 188–226; "Kinship and Consent in the Jewish Community," in *Tradition*, vol. 14, no. 4 (Fall 1974), pp. 63–79; *Covenant and Freedom in the Jewish Political Tradition*, Annual Sol Feinstone Lecture (Philadelphia: Gratz College, March 1981); and *Participation and Accountability in the American Jewish Community* (New York, 1980).

2   The close connections between the theological and the political are manifest in Jewish literature beginning with the Bible. In our time, Martin Buber has been the foremost expositor of those connections. See, in particular, his *Kinship of God* (London, 1967). See also Hans Kohn, *The Idea of Nationalism* (New York, 1944), ch. 2, and Harold Fisch, *Jerusalem and Albion* (New York, 1964).

3   Jews have always desired an independent territorial state, but they have desired it only as a means to a larger end and not as an end in itself.

4   Robert Pranger, *The Eclipse of Civilization* (following the Bible and Aristotle, among others) provides a useful discussion of citizenship as the creation of official identity, itself a culturally created necessity that enables every person to become fully human. The necessity for citizenship has become universal (p. 10): "In the language of psychology, citizenship supplies an integral segment of one's 'identity pattern,' something taken as second nature." It is in this sense that the concept is used here. See also Benjamin Akzin, *State and Nation*. Relevant to the Jewish situation is D. F. Aberle et al., "The Functional Prerequisites of a Society," in *Ethics*, vol. 60, no. 2 (January 1950), pp. 100–10. On the compatibility of multiple loyalties, see Morton Grodzins, *The Loyal and the Disloyal* (Chicago, 1957).

5   Pranger, *The Eclipse of Civilization*, following Sheldon S. Wolin in *Politics and Vision* (Boston, 1960), defines this phenomenon as the carving out of political space, space "shaped by a dualist structure of tangible objects and subjective perceptions which arranges a system of shared political meanings among citizens and also establishes these meanings in hierarchies of valued priorities." Pranger continues, "Around a nation are drawn a number of physical and non-physical boundaries within which citizens feel at home, outside of which they are foreigners. Such a space is molded by objective factors such as geographical frontiers, an economic system, a legal

system, a common political language . . . , and by the special governmental institutions called offices. But one also discovers certain subjective perceptions and expectations that members share about correct political action, expectations drawn from the members' own individual needs and values and from the social symbolism attributed to boundaries, economics, language, and governments. These symbolic perceptions may not find common agreement throughout a nation. Nevertheless, there are often common relationships between more specialized perceptions which entitle an observer to speak of a 'pattern' for even the heterogeneous political life of a Switzerland or an India. . . . In every political situation, no matter how transient, one can locate such patterns of civic expectations." Pranger defines this as the political culture of a "national state" but with a few modifications it is useful in defining the political space and culture of the Jewish polity. Thus, for example, this concept's being related to the study of Jewish political life, the tangible objects are the patterns of community organization and activity; the subjective perceptions relate to the questions of individual identity and involvement. See also Daniel J. Elazar and Joseph Zikmund, eds., *The Ecology of American Political Culture: Readings* (New York, 1975), Introduction.

6   The biblical understanding of the covenant as a consensual, theopolitical act is discussed in George E. Mendenhall, *The Tenth Generation* (Baltimore, 1973); R. A. F. MacKenzie, *Faith and History in the Old Testament* (Minneapolis, 1963); see ch. 3, "Israel's Covenant with God."

7   The record of the reaffirmation of the covenant in the Bible is easily discernible in the text itself. Buber, *Kinship of God*, deals with this in his textual exegesis. See also the studies of Avraham Malamut, "Organs of Statecraft in the Israelite Monarchy," in *The Biblical Archaeologist*, vol. 28, no. 2 (1965), pp. 34–51; G. E. Mendenhall, "Covenant Forms in Israelite Tradition," in *The Biblical Archaeologist*, vol. 17, no. 3 (1954), pp. 50–76; Hayim Tadmor, "'The People' and the Kingship in Ancient Israel: The Role of Political Institutions in the Biblical Period," in *Journal of World History*, vol. 11, no. 1–2 (1968), pp. 46–68; Moshe Weinfeld, "The Transition from Tribal Republic to Monarchy in Ancient Israel and Its Impression on Jewish Political History," in Daniel J. Elazar, ed., *Kinship and Consent: The Jewish Political Tradition and Its Contemporary Uses* (Ramat Gan, 1981), pp. 151–66.

8   Leo Baeck discusses this phenomenon in *This People Israel: The Meaning of Jewish Existence* (Philadelphia, 1965). The historic evidence is mustered in Daniel J. Elazar and Stuart Cohen, *The Jewish Polity* (Bloomington, 1985).

9   See, for example, Louis Finkelstein, *Jewish Self-Government in the Middle Ages* (New York, 1964); and H. H. Ben-Sasson, *Perakim beToldot haYehudim beYamei haBaynayim* ("Chapters in the History of the Jews in the Middle Ages") (Tel Aviv, 1969).

10 Cf., Daniel J. Elazar and John Kincaid, eds., *Covenant, Polity, and Constitutionalism* (Lanham, 1982), and Daniel J. Elazar, "Covenant as the Basis of the Jewish Political Tradition," in *The Jewish Journal of Sociology*, vol. 20, no. 1 (June 1978), pp. 5–37.

11 Daniel J. Elazar, "The Constitution, the Union, and the Liberties of the People," in *Publius: The Journal of Federalism*, vol. 8, no. 3 (Summer 1973), pp. 141–75.

12 See, for example, Delbart R. Hillers, *Covenant: The History of a Biblical Idea* (Baltimore, 1969).

13 Ibid.

14 Ibid.

15 Cf., Gordon Freeman, "Rabbinic Conceptions of Covenant," in Elazar, *Kinship and Consent*.

16 See I. A. Agus, *The Heroic Age of Franco-German Jewry* (New York, 1969); "On Power and Authority: Halachic Source of the Tradition Community and Its Contemporary Implications," in Elazar, *Kinship and Consent*; Gerald Blidstein, "Individual and Community in the Middle Ages," in Elazar, *Kinship and Consent*; Elazar and Cohen, *The Jewish Polity*, especially Epoch XI.

17 R. Judah HaBarceloni, *Sefer HaShtarot*.

18 In the words of *The Federalist*, force, accident, or choice. See Alexander Hamilton, John Jay, and James Madison, *The Federalist* (1788), No. 1.

19 Elazar and Cohen, *The Jewish Polity*, Introduction; Robert Gordis, "Democratic Origins in Ancient Israel: The Biblical Edah," in *Alexander Marx Jubilee Volume* (New York, 1950); Moshe Weinfeld, "The Transition from Tribal Republic to Monarchy in Ancient Israel and Its Impression on Jewish Political History," in Elazar, *Kinship and Consent*.

20 Elazar and Cohen, *The Jewish Polity*.

21 See Stuart A. Cohen, *The Concept of the Three Ketarim*, Working Paper No. 18 of Workshop in the Covenant Idea and the Jewish Political Tradition (Ramat Gan and Jerusalem: Bar Ilan University Department of Political Studies and Jerusalem Center for Public Affairs, 1982).

22 This discussion draws heavily on the political science literature on constitutionalism. Standard works on the subject include James Bryce, *Constitutions* (New York, 1905); Carl J. Friedrich, *Constitutional Government and Politics: Nature and Development* (Boston, 1937) and "Constitutions and Constitutionalism," in David L. Sills, ed., *International Encyclopedia of the Social Sciences*, vol. 3 (New York, 1968), pp. 318–26; Charles H. McIlwain, *Constitutionalism, Ancient and Modern* (Ithaca, 1947); and M. J. C. Vile, *Constitutionalism and the Separation of Powers* (Oxford, 1967). Although otherwise problematic for a system the origins of which are in a divine covenant, Hans Kelsen's constitutional theory is particularly helpful in this connection, cf., his *General Theory of Law and State* (New York, 1961).

23 Cf., Josephus Flavius, *Antiquities of the Jews*, book IV, ch. 8, especially paragraphs 196–8, and Philo, *De Specialibus Legibus*, book IV, "De Constitutione Principum." For an analysis of Philo's political thought, with frequent references to Josephus and to classical Jewish sources, see Harry Austryn Wolfson, *Philo: Foundations of Religious Philosophy in Judaism, Christianity, and Islam* (Cambridge, 1962), vol. 2, pp. 322–437.

Bibliography

Agus, I. A., *The Heroic Age of Franco-German Jewry* (New York, 1969).

Baeck, Leo, *This People Israel: The Meaning of Jewish Existence* (Philadelphia, 1965).

Ben-Sasson, H. H., *Perakim beToldot haYehudim beYamei haBaynayim* (Tel Aviv, 1969).

Bryce, James, *Constitutions* (New York, 1905).

Cohen, Stuart A., *The Concept of the Three Ketarim* (Ramat Gan and Jerusalem, 1982).

Elazar, Daniel J., "The Constitution, the Union, and the Liberties of the People," in *Publius: The Journal of Federalism*, vol. 8, no. 3 (Summer 1973), pp. 141–75.

Elazar, Daniel J., "Covenant as the Basis of the Jewish Political Tradition," in *The Jewish Journal of Sociology*, vol. 20, no. 1 (June 1978), pp. 5–37.

Elazar, Daniel J., "Kinship and Consent in the Jewish Community," in *Tradition*, vol. 14, no. 4 (Fall 1974), pp. 63–79.

Elazar, Daniel J., "The Reconstitution of Jewish Communities in the Post-War Period," in *Jewish Journal of Sociology*, vol. 11, no. 2 (December 1969), pp. 188–226.

Elazar, Daniel J., and John Kincaid, eds., *Covenant, Polity, and Constitutionalism* (Lanham, 1982).

Elazar, Daniel J., and Joseph Zikmund, eds., *The Ecology of American Political Culture: Readings* (New York, 1975).

Elazar, Daniel J., and Stuart Cohen, *The Jewish Polity* (Bloomington, 1985).

Elazar, Daniel J., ed., *Kinship and Consent: The Jewish Political Tradition and Its Contemporary Uses* (Ramat Gan, 1981).

Elazar, Daniel J., *Participation and Accountability in the American Jewish Community* (New York, 1980).

Finkelstein, Louis, *Jewish Self-Government in the Middle Ages* (New York, 1964).

Fisch, Harold, *Jerusalem and Albion* (New York, 1964).

Friedrich, Carl J., *Constitutional Government and Politics: Nature and Development* (Boston, 1937).

Gordis, Robert, "Democratic Origins in Ancient Israel: The Biblical Edah," in *Alexander Marx Jubilee Volume* (New York, 1950).

Hillers, Delbart R., *Covenant: The History of a Biblical Idea* (Baltimore, 1969).

Kelsen, Hans, *General Theory of Law and State* (New York, 1961).

Kohn, Hans, *The Idea of Nationalism* (New York, 1944).

MacKenzie, R. A .F., *Faith and History in the Old Testament* (Minneapolis, 1963).

Malamut, Avraham, "Organs of Statecraft in the Israelite Monarchy," in *The Biblical Archaeologist*, vol. 28, no. 2 (1965), pp. 34–51.

McIlwain, Charles H., *Constitutionalism, Ancient and Modern* (Ithaca, 1947).

Mendenhall, George E., "Covenant Forms in Israelite Tradition," in *The Biblical Archaeologist*, vol. 17, no. 3 (1954), pp. 50–76.

Mendenhall, George E., *The Tenth Generation* (Baltimore, 1973).

Tadmor, Hayim, "'The People' and the Kingship in Ancient Israel: The Role of Political Institutions in the Biblical Period," in *Journal of World History*, vol. 11, no. 1–2 (1968), pp. 46–68.

Wolfson, Harry Austryn, *Philo: Foundations of Religious Philosophy in Judaism, Christianity, and Islam* (Cambridge, 1962).

CHAPTER 24
Contemporary Jewish Theology

Neil Gillman

The term "contemporary" here designates the period from the mid-point to the end of the twentieth century. While periodizations of this kind are inevitably somewhat arbitrary, in this case, our decision reflects the wish to study Jewish theology as a living process, a work in progress. Further, the mid-point of the twentieth century was marked by two major historical events, the Nazi Holocaust and the establishment of the State of Israel in 1948. Events of this magnitude transform all forms of Jewish expression, its theology as well. While it is impossible to write at length about our contemporaries without reference to their teachers in the first half of the century who continue to have an impact, we will avoid references to the broader past history of Jewish theological inquiry.

Note too that the term "theology" here will be used in the narrow, literal sense of that discipline that views Judaism as (at least) a religion and that deals with questions regarding the existence and nature of God and of God's manifold and varied relationships with human beings. We will then avoid issues raised by the anthropological and phenomenological study of Jewish religion, by Jewish political and social thought, or cultural (i.e. secular) Zionism. These latter issues pertain more to the status of the Jewish people than to its religion.

The Teachers

The first half of our century bequeathed two models for doing Jewish theology: an existentialist model in the work of German thinkers, Martin Buber (1878–1965) and Franz Rosenzweig (1884–1929); and a naturalist model in the work of the American Mordecai Menahem Kaplan (1880–1993). Both models were revolutionary in their own day and remain controversial. But they continue to be studied today, and both have had a significant impact on the thought of their students/successors.

Buber and Rosenzweig, colleagues and collaborators, were influenced by nineteenth-century continental existentialism, particularly by the Danish Protestant thinker Søren Kierkegaard. Buber's *I and Thou* (1923), arguably the most widely read book written by a Jew in centuries, understands religious faith as an immediate, spontaneous, passionate, and totally subjective encounter with God. Buber insists that his I–Thou experience is rooted in the Bible (e.g., in biblical prophecy) and in eighteenth–nineteenth-century hasidism. However, in order to preserve the purity of this encounter as the heart of the religious experience, Buber tends to dismiss as inauthentic much of conventional, institutional Jewish religion, particularly the body of biblical and Rabbinic law (the Halakhah). Buber thus has become the mentor of liberal Jewish theologians and of those Jews who seek a more individualized, personal, spiritual gratification from their Judaism. He is also widely read by liberal Protestant thinkers and by educators and social scientists. But he has alienated those Jews who find enduring value in traditional forms of Jewish expression.

Rosenzweig shares Buber's understanding of the religious experience but departs from him in his claim that God's self-revelation to Israel involved a "commanding" (though not "legislating") voice. In a celebrated exchange of letters with his colleague, "Revelation and Law," Rosenzweig proposes that law (*gesetz*) is third-person, essentialist thinking, while command (*gebodt*) is first-person, existentialist thinking. Thus the I–Thou experience acquires an obligating quality that opens the way for individuals to reappropriate the body of Jewish behavioral prescriptions, albeit in a highly individualized form.[1] For this reason, Rosenzweig is rarely studied by Christians but, together with Buber, remains highly influential among contemporary Jewish existentialists such as Eugene Borowitz, Will Herberg, and Emil Fackenheim.

Mordecai Kaplan, for his part, was probably the first committed Jew to have read widely in the emerging field of the social sciences at the turn of the century, particularly in the social scientific approach to religion. This inquiry led him to a religious and theological naturalism, first propounded in his *Judaism as a Civilization* (first published in 1934), still the most comprehensive expression of his views, which claims that Jewish religion is a function of the Jewish people, this community's discovery of what makes for human fulfillment. Kaplan understands this discovery as the revelation of a God who is a power within nature, history, and people. Since the original authority for what constitutes Judaism was a community of Jews, it remains the right and responsibility of every generation of Jews to reshape its Judaism in the light of its experience of God in order to make identification with the Jewish people possible. Kaplan thus avoids a total secularization of Judaism but opens the door for the frequently radical reconstruction of Jewish belief and practice, a feature of the Reconstructionist movement in American Judaism that he founded.

Though Kaplan's proposals inevitably relativize Jewish religious forms, other themes in his writings, notably the centrality of peoplehood in Judaism, have become mainstream even in the traditionalist camp, though rarely explicitly identified with this author.

A Transitional Figure

It is tempting to classify Abraham Joshua Heschel (1905–72) among the group of early twentieth-century teachers who created new paradigms for their students, but almost all of his theology was written after his arrival in America in 1940 and under the cloud of the Holocaust.

Polish born, educated both in the intense world of Polish hasidism and in philosophy in Berlin, Heschel is primarily concerned with reappropriating biblical and Rabbinic expressions of Jewish theology in a strikingly modern idiom that combines touches of the hasidism of his youth, mysticism, continental phenomenology, and a hint of existentialism. His characterization of God's nature as "pathos," that is, the image of God as caring, reaching out, yet frustrated and vulnerable, is an unconventional but striking appropriation of the biblical image of God.[2] Heschel excels at phenomenological descriptions of Jewish ritual practice, particularly prayer.[3] His *God in Search of Man: A Philosophy of Judaism* (1956), the most comprehensive statement of his beliefs, remains indispensable to any review of Jewish thought to this day. With Buber, Heschel can be viewed as the father of modern Jewish spirituality, though his insistence that Jewish law remains largely binding on the Jew separates him from his more radical contemporary.[4]

The Issue of Theological Language

The contemporary Jewish religious community is riddled with divisiveness. In broad strokes, it is divided between two groups: traditionalists who insist on the sanctity of all classical, i.e., mainly biblical and Rabbinic, doctrines and laws; and liberals, who insist that little in the Jewish past is inherently sacred, though it may be privileged, and that each generation of Jews has the right to reshape the tradition to meet its own distinctive sense of what God commands in its particular cultural context.

There are many ways of accounting for this polarization, but one of them is surely theological. Traditionalists believe that the body of Jewish thinking in matters of doctrine and practice was explicitly revealed by God at Sinai (Exod. 19–24), which they understand as a literal and historically accurate account of an event that occurred centuries ago. Liberals, for their part, question the historicity of that event and certainly reject its characterization of a God who descends on a mountain-top and speaks to Israel. The first group reads Torah (literally, "Instruction," narrowly defined as the Pentateuch, or, more broadly, as the entire body of Jewish teaching), as a literally true account of God's will; the second claims that the Torah's description of God, God's activity, and the content of revelation, involved a substantive human contribution alongside the divine dimension, which these theologians understand in different ways. This divide leads to very different views on the intrinsic authority of Torah in matters of belief and practice.

The modern theological paradigms studied thus far, even to a certain extent that of Heschel,[5] have all been comfortably within the liberal tradition. But it is noteworthy that in the past three decades, a group of philosophically trained traditionalist thinkers has entered the debate. Two factors may account for this development: Orthodoxy's greater sense of security and legitimacy, together with a sense that in this theologically pluralistic age, Jewish traditionalism can and should be defended in a sophisticated way.

The seminal influence on these thinkers is Joseph B. Soloveitchik (1903–93), a towering Rabbinic scholar who trained generations of Orthodox rabbis at Yeshiva University. But he was also schooled in modern continental philosophy during his early years in Berlin and lectured frequently on theological and philosophical issues, synthesizing his Talmudic studies with a Barthian/Kierkegaardian approach to religion. Until a decade ago, Soloveitchik's lectures, typically delivered in Hebrew, remained untranslated and unpublished and were known only among the inner circles of the yeshiva world. But since his death, many of his lectures and writings have been published in translation, notably two extended essays, *The Lonely Man of Faith* (1965 in the periodical *Tradition*, and in book-length form in 1992) and *Halakhic Man* (1983). Both have become widely studied as a significant philosophically-based defense of Jewish traditionalism.

One of Soloveitchik's more articulate students is David Hartman. Trained as an Orthodox rabbi, Hartman now lives in Jerusalem where he teaches Jewish philosophy and is the founder and director of the Shalom Hartman Institute for Advanced Jewish Studies. Hartman's *A Living Covenant: The Innovative Spirit in Traditional Judaism* (1985) is a book-length defense of a moderate traditionalism; indeed the two key terms in the title, "innovative" and "traditional," reflect Hartman's attempt to capture the tension between his two impulses. Hartman locates that tension in the polarity between the human impulses for submission and for self-assertion. The first is manifest in Judaism's insistence that Jews must accept God's revealed, yet inscrutable, will; the second, in the wide-ranging interpretive freedom granted by God in the study of sacred texts. "The autonomy of Rabbinic Judaism was expressed within a framework of divine authority rooted in the revelation at Sinai." [6]

Hartman concedes that "it is a near-impossible task to define the limits of interpretive freedom found in the tradition," but quotes the late historian Jacob Katz to the effect that "the limits are simply what the community is in fact prepared to accept as Torah."[7] This is an astonishing affirmation of the position of liberal theologians. Though Hartman identifies the covenant as a metaphor, he does not systematically deal with the broader issue of theological language, nor, more strikingly, does he deal with how he understands the Sinai revelation.

The most theologically and philosophically rigorous of these defenses of traditionalism is in Michael Wyschogrod's *The Body of Faith: God in the People Israel* (1989). Wyschogrod embraces the traditionalist claim that God explicitly revealed God's law at Sinai and that this law is recorded in Torah (i.e., in the written Torah, though not necessarily in the oral Torah, an extensive commentary on and expansion of the written Torah, which was ultimately recorded in the Talmud and which traditionalists insist was also explicitly revealed to Moses at Sinai). But because biblical injunctions are largely ambiguous, Jews must depend on Rabbinic authorities to discern God's precise will in a concrete situation. Wyschogrod concedes the inherent insecurity of this enterprise; we can never be completely sure that we know what God wills. But we have no alternative, since all we have is not God's direct speech to us but God's will as embodied in a revealed but ambiguous text.[8]

Revelation

At the heart of this issue, then, is the theology of revelation. In a remarkably clear and candid exposition of the traditionalist position, in a Symposium, *The Condition of Jewish Belief* (1966), Norman Lamm, Orthodox rabbi and president of New York's Yeshiva University, insists that he accepts "unapologetically" the notion of "verbal revelation." God communicated with Israel in "discrete words and letters," for if God cared enough to reveal anything to Israel, God would choose the least ambiguous form of communication, namely language. To deny this is to deny God. God's explicit authority rests behind the entire body of biblical and Rabbinic doctrines and laws and the entire package is binding on all Jews to eternity.[9] This absolutist sense of divine authority is understandably comforting to many modern Jews, but it also drastically diminishes the freedom to reshape Jewish beliefs and practices.

Fundamentalists of the Lammian variety tend to polarize their opponents as "secular humanists." But, in fact, there are other models for a Jewish theology of revelation that stake out a position somewhere between fundamentalism and a thoroughgoing secularism. Three of these models nurse from the thought of Buber, Rosenzweig, Kaplan, and Heschel.

The Buber/Rosenzweig model has received its clearest and most rigorous formulation in the work of Eugene Borowitz, who has been singularly responsible for shaping modern Reform ideology in America through his many writings and his role as teacher of generations of Reform rabbis at Reform's Hebrew Union College/Jewish Institute of Religion in New York. Borowitz has long championed the notion of individual autonomy that remains central in Reform thinking to this day. This doctrine claims that individual Jews have the right and responsibility to shape Jewish beliefs and practices in light of our own equally divinely revealed conscience. This radical individualism clearly nurses from Buber and Rosenzweig's existentialist temper and their theory of revelation as interpersonal encounter. But in his most recent and comprehensive statement, *Renewing the Covenant: A Theology for the Postmodern Jew* (1991), Borowitz retreats somewhat from this sharp individualism by conceding that other factors such as the role of tradition, the community past and present, and eschatology all play a significant role in determining the nature of Jewish obligation. True, for Borowitz, it is the individual who refracts all of these other dimensions, but, effectively, the role of individual conscience becomes more muted.[10]

A second model for understanding revelation in a non-fundamentalist way is suggested by Heschel's striking claim: "As a report about revelation, the Bible itself is a *midrash*."[11] The conventional understanding of the term midrash views it as exegesis, interpretation, or extension of some narrative, law, word, or even letter in the biblical text. Thus talmudic literature is an elaborate set of midrashim on the Bible. What Heschel suggests here is that the Bible itself is a midrash. But a midrash on what? Presumably on some more primitive text such as the Torah that emanated from God. What we have is not that primordial Torah but the Torah that has passed through the screen of human thinking and language.

Heschel's daring statement reflects his concern for preserving the majesty of God, which he feels is demeaned by the literalist position. But the effect of the claim is to concede that, whatever God had to do with revelation, the Torah is also a human document, influenced by the cultural conditions of the ages in which it was shaped. The implication is that the generations that follow can also invoke changes in their cultural life to modify some of Torah's claims. Despite this liberal stance on revelation, Heschel takes a strong traditionalist stance on the binding quality of Jewish law. Since he is not a systematic thinker, the relation between these two positions is never made explicit, but it probably stems from his impulse to have his readers take Jewish ritual practices more seriously.

A suggestive extension of Heschel's claim is proposed by one of his students and colleagues, Seymour Siegel (1927–88). In his contribution to *The Condition of Jewish Belief*, Siegel quotes liberally from Heschel and then adds this summary statement: "In a real sense the *halakha* is constantly reevaluated by the *aggadah*. The community reinterprets and changes its structure of obligations in the light of their ability to express our faith and by their power to evoke faith."[12] By *aggada*, in this context, Siegel refers to the sweeping and changing ideological assumptions that serve as the underpinnings of any culture. In one stroke, then, the body of Jewish law loses its independent and absolutist authority and becomes subject to the cultural conditions of the age.

Still a third model reflects Mordecai Kaplan's theological naturalism. As we noted above, Kaplan's model differs from the other two in that he rejects the notion that God is an independent, supernatural entity but says he is, rather, a power or process that works through nature and history. In his contribution to *The Condition of Jewish Belief*, Kaplan's student and disciple, Ira Eisenstein, spells out the implication of this claim that understands divine revelation as human "discovery"; the terms "divine revelation" and "human discovery" are synonymous. Whatever human beings "discover" that advances human fulfillment is by definition divine revelation.[13] Of the three positions, this one accentuates most strongly the human factor in shaping the content of revelation.

Finally, another model that echoes Kaplan's position but in a different idiom is suggested by this author in his *Sacred Fragments: Recovering Theology for the*

Modern Jew, who appropriates Paul Tillich's notion of the symbolic and mythic character of theological language.[14] The term "myth" here represents not a fiction but also not an objectively determined truth. It is rather a structure that ties together the varied experience of a community so that it acquires meaning and becomes coherent. To speak of the Torah as the canonization of the Jewish religious myth is to suggest that it represents one community's way of making sense of the world and of its historical experience. It is "revealed" simply because whatever pattern is "discovered" is out there to be discerned by human beings in their attempt to understand the world and their place in it.[15]

The common denominator of these four models is inevitably a relativization of the contents of Torah. Whatever God's role in the revelation of Torah, its contents are decisively shaped by human beings and are hence subject to ongoing re-evaluation by new generations of Jews. This applies most directly to the body of Jewish behavioral obligations, but it applies to its doctrinal formulations as well. In the traditionalist option, God's original revelation is eternal and absolutely binding. But if no human being knows explicitly what God wills for Israel, there can be multiple understandings of that will, and it can change. The implication of the liberal positions is that there are no intrinsic parameters for delimiting reformulations of Torah, that each community must set its own parameters consensually and accept the authority for its own reading of the tradition.

The Knowledge of God

Of the three classical Jewish pathways to gaining an awareness of the existence and nature of God – rationalism, experientialism, and existentialism – the first, so prominent in the Middle Ages, is largely ignored by contemporary thinkers. The other two are alive and well, the experientialist model inspired by Abraham Heschel, and the existentialist, by Martin Buber and Franz Rosenzweig. Both have roots in the Jewish theological tradition. The experientialist, overwhelmingly the model employed in the Bible and Rabbinic literature, in Judah Halevi among the medievals, and in mystical and hasidic literature, claims that one acquires an awareness of God by an interpretive "seeing" of nature and history. The existentialist, harking back to certain biblical texts such as the binding of Isaac (Gen. 22), and Job, and to the writings of thinkers such as Pascal, Dostoevsky, and Kierkegaard, claims that we meet God in an inner encounter with a reality that both transcends and infuses us. The difference between the two approaches is the subjectivity of faith: in the first, a degree of subjectivity is understood to be inevitable, but a community can devise ways to diminish its impact. In the second, faith at its purest is totally subjective.

The existentialist model is reflected in the works of Will Herberg (1901–77), Eugene Borowitz, and Emil Fackenheim. Herberg's *Judaism and Modern Man* (1951) was the first comprehensive and systematic attempt to reformulate the teachings of Buber and Rosenzweig in English. For Herberg, faith is a "leap" because it has absolutely no basis in reason or experience. It leaps over and beyond the abyss of meaninglessness into a relation with a reality that transcends all things. It is hence, "risk, venture, decision." It is never secure, never a permanent acquisition, but must constantly be renewed. It is not simply a matter of feeling nor of thinking but rather an existential act of the entire person – emotion, thought and will combined in one decision.[16]

Fackenheim, in an essay entitled "On the Eclipse of God," polarizes what he calls "the Buberian man of faith" and "the subjectivist reductionist." The former captures the human sense of living in relation with a "real" God beyond the believer; the latter "reduces" the act of faith to a human projection or wish-fulfillment. Fackenheim concludes that there is no middle ground between these positions, that they represent two faiths that can reject but never disprove each other. Religious faith, then, is unfalsifiable and unverifiable.[17] In a different context, Fackenheim challenges the biblical account of Elijah on the Carmel (1 Kgs. 18). What would have happened, Fackenheim asks, if God had answered the prayers of the priests of Baal instead of Elijah's? Obviously, Elijah would not have begun to worship Baal. He would have simply insisted that experience neither proves nor disproves faith and that he must continue to work for God even in the face of the divine silence, even against God. This is existentialist faith in its purity. Not at all parenthetically, Fackenheim's discussion here constitutes one of the very few attempts by Jewish theologians to challenge the claims of the school of linguistic or analytic philosophers on the epistemological issues involved in religious faith.[18]

The most thorough of our contemporary experientialists is Heschel. One enduring dimension of Heschel's work is his phenomenological description of the religious experience. His avoidance of theological systemization stems from his belief that any attempt to summarize the nature of God in an abstract way misses the main point: the wrestling, on the part of both God and human beings, to relate with each other. For Heschel, the religious experience, the very core of religion, is the moment when a person's faculty of "radical amazement" discerns God's pathos in and through the world. God is discerned through a momentary, fragile, transitory, but emotion-laden act of "seeing" God's presence in history, nature and the human experience.[19]

Heschel's model has been widely influential. It informs the thought of his student Arthur Green, currently at Brandeis University, whose writings reflect an intriguing mix of hasidism and mysticism, on one hand, and Kaplan's naturalism, on the other. In an extended meditation on God's "visibility" in his *Seek My Face, Speak My Name* (1992), Green acknowledges that the biblical God is not generally "seen" by human beings. But, "[t]o be a religious Jew is to walk the tightrope between knowing the invisibility of God and seeing the face of God everywhere." Green calls Judaism "incarnational" religion because "the divine presence is incarnate in all the world." Specifically, Green claims, we see God in ourselves, in intense interpersonal relationships, in nature and history, and in the study of Torah. This formulation inherits the subjectivism of all experiential approaches to religion because such a "seeing" demands that the individual wants to see God in the world and interprets what he literally "sees" to reflect God's presence.[20]

Heschel's thought also informs the work of another of his students, Elliot Dorff, whose *Knowing God: Jewish Journeys to the Unknowable* (1992) begins with the methodological claim that, "We human beings have no unmediated knowledge of God but rather . . . have to construct our conceptions of God on the basis of experiences we have."[21] He then discloses his debt to Heschel by including among his relevant experiences of God, human behavior, Torah as revelation, divine action in history, and prayer – an echo of Heschel's claim that there are three starting points that lead us to God. We sense God's presence in the world, in the Bible, and in sacred deeds.[22]

The Nature of God

Although the notion that all of our images of God are metaphors or analogies should be, at least from the time of Maimonides, commonplace among Jews, in practice that distinction is largely irrelevant. Traditionalists insist that the metaphors themselves are explicitly revealed and hence inherently sacred; contemporary liberal thinkers claim that the metaphors are crafted by human beings, that the classical ones may be privileged but are certainly not sacred, and that they can be replaced. One example is God's maleness: traditionalists would stubbornly resist any attempt by modern Jewish feminists to characterize God as female, all the while acknowledging that God's essence is neither male nor female.

One of the major issues among contemporary thinkers is the tension between viewing God as person or as process. For Buber and his disciples, God is the eternal Thou who enters into intense interpersonal relationships with nature, human beings, and Israel. The core of the I–Thou relation is precisely that it acknowledges the personhood of both parties; both God and people become fully personal only in and through the relationship. In contrast, Kaplan's God is a power in nature. In a telling analogy, Kaplan portrays God's presence as similar to magnetic waves, which are themselves not visible but that are "revealed" when iron filings are exposed to the magnetic force.[23]

> That God is supremely personal is at the heart of Will Herberg's theology. Drawing heavily on the Buberian model, he distinguishes between the "God-idea" and the "living God." The former is the product of Greek metaphysics, medieval scholasticism, and modern rationalism. The latter is biblical. "What do we mean when we speak of God as Person? We mean that we meet God in life and history, not as an object, not as a thing, not as an It . . . but as a Thou, with whom we can enter into personal relations. . . ." He adds, "God . . . can never be expressed; he can only be addressed. . . . This personal encounter with God . . . is not "merely" subjective . . . ;

it is an immediate self-validating encounter which transcends the ordinary distinction between subject and object. . . ."[24]

This insistence that God exists only in the "living" encounter inevitably
downplays the validity of theology as a speculative enterprise. A similar result
emerges out of Heschel's insistence that the core of the biblical image of God is
pathos. That notion is most clearly articulated in his *The Prophets* (1962), a
phenomenological inquiry into the nature of biblical prophecy. For Heschel,
"God does not reveal Himself in an abstract relationship to the world, but . . . in
a personal and intimate relation to the world. . . . God . . . is also moved and
affected by what happens in the world and He reacts accordingly." God then
enjoys the full range of emotions familiar to us: joy, anger, mourning, frustration,
and hope, and the "ground-tone" of all these attitudes is the divine pathos.
Heschel acknowledges the "anthropopathic" nature of this approach but insists
that it best captures the biblical (as opposed to the philosophical) image of God.[25]

Heschel documents this distinction between the biblical and the philosophical images of God through a wide-ranging study of the role of emotion in Greek
philosophy and oriental religions. He recalls these traditions' emphasis on stoi-
cism, apathy, and divine detachment and asks rhetorically, "Is it more compatible with our conception of the grandeur of God to claim that He is emotionally
blind to the misery of man rather than profoundly moved?"[26]

Jewish Feminist Theology

Heschel's notion of the divine pathos informs two comprehensive studies of
Jewish religion by two committed Jewish feminists, Judith Plaskow's *Standing
Again at Sinai* (1990) and Rachel Adler's *Engendering Judaism* (1997). Both of
these volumes subject traditional Jewish doctrines and practices to a scathing
feminist critique and suggest how the tradition can be reshaped to make it more
accessible to Jewish women. For both, theology, specifically beliefs on the nature
of God and our metaphors for God, are at the heart of the issue. Both acknowledge the metaphorical nature of God-language, and both denounce the hierarchical metaphors that view God as male, dominating, punitive and often abusive.

Plaskow insists that a critique of traditional metaphors for God is criticism
not of God but rather of ways of speaking about God, who remains unknowable
by humans. The traditional symbols may be privileged, but they are not binding, and when they "become socially, morally or politically inadequate, they
are also religiously inadequate."[27] Instead of revealing God's presence, for Jewish
feminists, ". . . they block out the possibility of religious experience." In their
place, Plaskow recommends a series of other terms proposed by Jewish feminists,
beyond simply referring to God in the feminine or invoking the more conventional mystical nature of God as *Shekinah* (a feminine term that portrays God as
immanent and present in the world), in favor of images such as "Mother birthing

the world," "the source of life," "fountain," "wellspring," or "friend." What characterizes God-language now is ". . . its sense of fluidity, movement, and multiplicity, its daring interweaving of women's experiences with Jewish, Native American, and Goddess imagery that leaves the reader/hearer with an expanded sense of what is possible in speaking of/to God."[28]

Plaskow is fully conscious that this ensemble of metaphors, particularly those that smack of paganism, is offensive to many Jews, and she quotes extensively from her critics. But she insists that her goal is to enrich the range of God-metaphors, that the traditional ensemble is not sufficiently inclusive, and that worshiping any metaphor constitutes idolatry.

Adler's proposals are similar. She looks for metaphors of relationship rather than power; she finds them in the poetry of Jewish women, and she asks that men and women work together to create a prayer language that is both authentic and inclusive. "Two points are fundamental: prayer is not for lying to God, and prayer is not for hurting or excluding members of our community."[29] Her insistence that liturgical formulations of theological ideas are crucial is undoubtedly accurate. She also echoes Plaskow's methodological claim that there are no firm, rigid, sacred boundaries to define what is or is not Jewish. To this writer's knowledge, there is no rigorous and systematic inquiry into the issue of criteria for determining that a Jewish theological statement is authentically Jewish. But it is easy to discern within the literature of Jewish feminists a hint of Heschel's anthropopathic understanding of God.

All of these thinkers agree in characterizing God as person. The alternative metaphor views God as process. What has come to be called process theology reflects the influence of philosophers such as Alfred North Whitehead and Charles Hartshorn. In Jewish thought, they trace their roots to Mordecai Kaplan, who used to teach Whitehead and Hartshorn in his classes at the Jewish Theological Seminary and whose notion of God as "a power that makes for salvation" echoes this idea.

Kaplan's student and disciple William Kaufman has offered a suggestive interpretation of Kaplan's thought in terms of process theology. The core assumption of all process theologies is that God is not a substantive but rather a verb or adverb, not a being, but a becoming, not a transcendent entity but a pattern that infuses all creation. Kaufman identifies the specific qualities of this divine becoming as an impetus for "order, novelty, and value."[30] Kaplan himself unified these goals under the rubric "salvation," with God the "power" that makes for all of them.

The most serious implications of these assumptions is that God's power is limited, that God is not immutable, but rather changing and growing within and together with creation. God's power is limited because the impetus for order, novelty, and value remains an ideal to be achieved, not a current reality, and because people can frustrate this drive; there are many other powers at work within the world, and this God has no monopoly in controlling reality. The notion of an intrinsically limited God is the core of process theologians' attempts to deal with the issue of theodicy, as we shall see. Clearly, this metaphor constitutes a radical departure from the traditional image of God, but it serves two purposes: first, it provides intellectuals in the community with a more intellectually coherent, acceptable way of thinking about God; and second, it integrates theology with science so that, taken together, they provide a unified reading of reality.

If God is not a being but a becoming, not a substantive but a verb, not an entity but a power, where can God's nature be discerned? Another of Kaplan's students and disciples, Harold Schulweis, approaches this question through the notion of predicate theology. In his *Evil and the Morality of God* (1984), he draws on thinkers such as Ludwig Feuerbach to propose that we should no longer think of God as a being that possesses attributes such as compassion but rather that we should begin by identifying predicates such as compassion as "godly." God then is not an independent being but rather an accumulation of predicates, verbs, and adverbs that describe human and natural behavior. Traditional theology is stood on its head. "The first shall become last and the last first. . . . The predicates are now the proper subject of theology. . . . We look to them to understand the character of divinity."[31]

For Schulweis too, God is intrinsically limited. The divine predicates remain idealizations not actualizations, potentialities not realizations. The non-divine attributes remain an equally powerful dimension of reality. This is at the heart of process theology's approach to theodicy.

Theodicy

There is no obvious single resolution in Jewish classical literature to the challenge to God posed by apparently unjustified and irremediable human suffering, what has come to be called "the problem of evil." In broad strokes, the answers fall into two camps: the first sees evil as coming within the scope of God's power and concern; the other sees it as an independent, chaotic element over which God has no control. Each resolution entails its own problems, and neither is entirely satisfactory. This broad issue has been sharpened considerably by the Nazi Holocaust.

The advocates of an intrinsically limited God opt for the second of these options. To a child who asks, "Why did God make polio?" Kaplan answers, "God did not make polio. God is always helping us humans to make this a better world, but the world cannot at once become the kind of world He would like it to be." God is present in the intelligence of the doctors, the scientific research, the love and care of doctors, nurses, families, and friends. And if the polio is not cured, "it is not because God does not love you. . . . He will find other ways of enabling you to enjoy life."[32] It should be noted, however, that Kaplan never explicitly addresses this issue in the context of the Holocaust.

A more popular version of this approach is in Harold Kushner's *When Bad Things Happen to Good People* (1981). This book, widely read and translated into many languages, is less a theological treatise than a pastoral guide for the suffering and their families. But the theological core of Kushner's argument is thoroughly Kaplanian: "Residual chaos, chance and mischance, things happening for no reason, will continue to be with us. . . . In that case, we will simply have to learn to live with it, sustained and comforted by the knowledge that the earthquake and the accident . . . are not the will of God, but represent that aspect of reality which stands independent of His will, and which angers and saddens God even as it angers and saddens us."[33]

The notion of a limited God who is saddened by human suffering but impotent to conquer it has clear dualistic implications. This has led other thinkers to adopt the first of the cited options. They echo Is. 45:6–7's counter-claim: "I am the Lord and there is none else; I form light and create darkness, I make *shalom* (peace, well-being, harmony, cosmos) and create *ra* (evil, chaos)."

In his *Faith After the Holocaust* (1973), Eliezer Berkovits, Orthodox rabbi and theologian, confronts the ambiguities of God's presence in history and insists that the Jew of faith "knows of the numerous revelations of the divine presence as he knows of the overlong phases of God's absence. Auschwitz does not stand alone."[34] Berkovits cites the many acts of kindness, generosity, and loyalty that occurred throughout the terror, the fact that the Final Solution ultimately failed, and preeminently the establishment of the State of Israel as dramatic revelations of God's lasting power over history and love for Israel. God may weep over the Holocaust, but God's tears are directed at our inhumanity to each other, not over any failure on God's part.

In a similar mode, some thinkers have invoked the image of God's hiding of the face, omnipresent in the Bible. Though, typically, biblical references to this experience of abandonment by God signal God's punishment for Israel's sins, at times (see, e.g., Ps. 13), it denotes the mysterious ebb and flow of God's relatedness to humanity. Emil Fackenheim adopts this notion in a modern idiom in his essay "On the Eclipse of God," referred to above. Using a Buberian model of faith, Fackenheim acknowledges that faith is neither demonstrable nor falsifiable, but the modern believer must remain uncertain "as to whether what is experienced is an eclipse of God, or the final exposure of an illusion."[35] In his more recent writings, Fackenheim, who has settled in Israel, goes beyond theology in insisting that the only possible response to the Holocaust is the simple reaffirmation of daily life as it is lived in the young state.[36]

The notion of God's eclipse is invoked also by Irving Greenberg, who was trained as an Orthodox rabbi but has achieved greater renown as an articulate advocate of Jewish theological and halakhic pluralism. In an early essay, Greenberg uses the Buberian notions of "moment faith" and "moment God." Faith, then, is never a permanent acquisition but rather a momentary achievement, all too easily dispelled. Atheism is a legitimate stage in the dynamic of faith. The only difference between the atheist and the believer is the frequency of the faith moments.[37]

More recently, Greenberg's theology has taken a more radical turn. In his paper "Voluntary Covenant" (1982), he traces the idea of covenantedness through Jewish history as a process of God's progressive self-limitation. In the Bible, the very fact of God's entering into a covenant with people is a decision to limit God's power. After the destruction of the Temple, God's power diminishes even further: Prophecy ceases, God's will is vested in a book, and human authorities (the talmudic rabbis) become the arbiters of God's will. Finally, after the Holocaust, even this minimal power is shattered. "Morally speaking . . . God can have no claims on the Jews by dint of the covenant. . . . [The covenant] can no longer be commanded." Its authority is broken; Jews owe God nothing. In this new historical context, the simple choice by Jews to remain Jews is the sole possible affirmation; by this act, we acquire complete power over how our Jewishness is to be expressed.[38]

Greenberg's radical turn distinguishes his response from the traditionalists such as Berkovits. In broad strokes, the traditionalist views the Holocaust as one more example of God's hiddenness, not intrinsically different from any other such event in the Jewish past. It therefore demands no radical departure from traditional ways of dealing with personal and historical disaster. In contrast, Greenberg suggests that, with the Holocaust, something radically new has entered the picture. The Holocaust is unprecedented in its scope and, as a result, demands equally unprecedented responses.

The most radical of these responses is that of Richard L. Rubenstein, trained as a Conservative rabbi but for many years, serving on the faculty of Florida State University. Rubenstein sparked a major controversy among Jewish thinkers by proposing that Auschwitz marks "the death of God." He thus associates himself with the Christian death of God theologians whose thought was popular during the 1960s. The Christian use of this radical metaphor designated, in a striking way, the basic incompatibility of Christian thinking and the increasing secularization of modern culture. The metaphor also had clear Christian roots because the Christian God did die, though his death was a necessary step in God's redemptive purposes. Rubenstein appropriates the metaphor as the only possible response to Auschwitz. In an early (1966) statement of his position, he acknowledges that

> No man can really say that God is dead. . . . Nevertheless I am compelled to say that we live in the time of the "death of God." This is more a statement about man and his culture than about God. The death of God is a cultural fact . . . the thread uniting God and man, heaven and earth has been broken. We stand in a cold, silent, unfeeling cosmos, unaided by any purposeful power beyond our own resources.[39]

To put this in another idiom that acknowledges Rubenstein's debt to the Protestant theologian Paul Tillich, what has died is the classic Jewish religious myth. It is not "broken" (i.e., exposed as myth), but "dead," no longer capable of finding meaning in human existence or of mobilizing the energy required for Jewish religious identity. But for Rubenstein, the death of God does not mean the death of religion or of Judaism. "I do not believe that a theistic God is necessary for

Jewish religious life." Judaism is "the way we share the decisive times and crises of life through the traditions of our inherited community" and that need is in no way diminished. He concludes that the death of God does not mean the end of all Gods. "I believe in God, the Holy Nothingness, known to mystics of all ages, out of which we have come and to which we shall ultimately return."[40]

Equally radical, but in a different way, is David R. Blumenthal's "Theology of Protest" in his *Facing the Abusing God* (1993). This is a rigorous inquiry into what may be called the "dark side" of the images of God in classical Jewish texts. He builds on the Holocaust and the experiences of a victim of child abuse, closely comments on four psalms, and concludes that "God is an abusing God, but not always" (p. 248). His response to divine abuse is to challenge God, face-to-face, and the most radical dimension of that protest is to translate it into the liturgy. Thus, on the Day of Atonement, during the confessional prayer when Jews acknowledge that "we have sinned against You," Blumenthal adds that we should recite a formula in which we remind God, "You have sinned against us" (pp. 290–1). Whether or not Jews are prepared to actually recite a passage of this kind is very much open to question. But methodologically, Blumenthal's assumption that it is the liturgy that concretizes theological responses is surely on target.

The enterprise of Holocaust theology is clearly a work in progress. But, as of this writing, most thinkers who have dealt with the issue have opted for one of the more traditionalist responses that draws on classical motifs, such as God's hiding of the face or Second Isaiah's suffering servant. In contrast, Rubenstein's proposal has had little impact, probably because of the radical quality of its central metaphor.

Eschatology

Of all the issues on the agenda of Jewish theology, the one that modern thinkers seem most to avoid is eschatology. The universalist prophecies of Isaiah 2 are everywhere accepted but rarely discussed. Though the creation of the modern State of Israel is frequently liturgically understood as the dawning of the messianic age, little effort has been made to specify the relationship between the messianic return of Jews to Zion, one of the central claims of classical Jewish eschatology, and the current reality of a secular state.

But eschatology is very much at the heart of Will Herberg's *Judaism and Modern Man*. Before rediscovering Judaism, Herberg had been a Marxist, and he thoroughly understands the lure of eschatological thinking. He devotes three full chapters of his book to a study of Jewish (i.e., biblical) historiography, which he contrasts with that of Oriental religions, philosophical idealism, materialism, and Greek thought, dubbing all of these idolatrous. Only in the Bible, Herberg claims, was history "linear" (p. 195). It has a purpose, an ultimate goal, brought about by the will and power of a transcendent God, who will redeem and transfigure history as we know it.[41]

Herberg's treatment of the dimension of personal eschatology is equally singular. He reappropriates the "symbol" of the resurrection of the dead over the Greek notion of the immortality of the soul. "The whole point of the doctrine of the resurrection is that the life we live now, the life of the body, the life of empirical existence in society, has some measure of permanent worth in the eyes of God. . . ."[42] In effect, the doctrine affirms the ultimate value of history and society. Herberg's discussion is the basis for this author's book-length treatment of the doctrine in *The Death of Death: Resurrection and Immortality in Jewish Thought* (1997).

Jewish Postmodernism

Within the last decade of the twentieth century, a new sensibility has entered the Jewish theological enterprise. This is a manifestation of a broader cross-cultural phenomenon that seeks to illuminate new approaches to the human experience in a wide variety of fields including art, literature, philosophy and the social sciences, and even the natural sciences as well. The conventional label for this new sensibility is "postmodernism," which Borowitz aptly characterizes as "an intuition seeking self-understanding."[43]

As its name implies, the postmodern impulse can be understood as a distancing from and critique of the age that immediately preceded this new one, the age of "the modern." If modernity exhibited a basic confidence in our ability to understand and control the world, a reliance on science and technology and an unbridled confidence in human reason as the most sublime expression of our humanity, postmodernism implies the very opposite. It emphasizes a new humility about human power, a vision of science as resting on arbitrary foundations, and a recognition of the limits of reason as a resource for dealing with the most significant dimensions of human experience. In more positive terms, the postmodern impulse accentuates the subjectivity of all human experience, the constructive use of the imagination in defining what we know, a certain romantic temper, and a concern for issues that are at the heart of human experience and that science is incapable of addressing: life and death, love, sexuality and the body, pain and grief.

Jewish postmodernism was impelled first by the Holocaust, which is viewed as the most demonic expression of modernity; second, by the failure of the scientific, critical, dispassionate approach to the study of Torah (usually referred to as the *wissenschaft* approach), which was omnipresent in Jewish academic circles since the Jewish enlightenment and which studiously avoided issues of human meaning; and third, by the emergence of a distinctive Jewish feminist voice. This last factor has also led to an outpouring of creative new liturgies and rituals to deal with significant moments in the human life-cycle.

If there is a central figure in Jewish postmodernism, it is Emmanuel Levinas (1906–97). A survivor of Nazi incarceration during the war, Levinas toiled in relative obscurity for most of his subsequent career, teaching in France and writing extensively in French. Within the past decade, however, he has been discovered by the Jewish theological community, much of his work has been translated into English, and scholarly articles and books on his writings trace his relationship to Buber and Rosenzweig as well as to Heidegger and other continental phenomenologists.

The core of Levinas's thinking lies in his postulating that morality supersedes knowledge, that the good supersedes the true, that ethics supersedes theology or epistemology. It is the intersubjective relationship, one's confrontation with "the other," that is the primary datum for philosophy. Levinas pursues this inquiry through a close reading of biblical and Rabbinic texts, illuminating the most minute details of Jewish morality and their ultimate redemptive value.[44] Levinas's writings have enjoyed an ever-growing readership and have spawned an equally growing body of studies that elaborate and extend his basic paradigm.[45]

Conclusion

By almost any criteria, this past half-century has seen a rich outpouring of Jewish theological inquiry by thinkers who span the spectrum from strict traditionalism to radical liberalism. Why this should have occurred at this point in Jewish history is not at all clear. It may have resulted from the twin events that marked the mid-century. Or, it might be the result of an increasing sense of marginalization that has accompanied Judaism's encounter with the aggressive cultures of the western world. Jewish theology has always been written by and for Jews for whom a religious commitment to Judaism is in some way problematic and hence must be justified. Whatever the cause, as of this writing, Jewish theologians and their students can luxuriate in the awareness that Jewish theology is firmly ensconced at the heart of the Jewish agenda and that it will continue to hold that position at least through the dawn of the new millennium.

Notes

1 The distinction appears in his monograph, "The Builders: Concerning the Law," pp. 72–92, and again in the extended exchange of letters with Buber, "Revelation and Law: Martin Buber and Franz Rosenzweig," pp. 109–24, both in *On Jewish Learning* (New York, 1965).

2 The most comprehensive statement of this view is in Abraham Joshua Heschel's *The Prophets*, chs. 12–14.

3 See his *Man's Quest for God: Studies in Prayer and Symbolism*, chs. 1–4.

4 As in *God in Search of Man: A Philosophy of Judaism* (Philadelphia, 1956), part III.

5 See Heschel's *God in Search of Man*, part II, particularly chs. 19 and 27.

6 David Hartman, *A Living Covenant: The Innovative Spirit in Traditional Judaism* (New York, 1985), p. 40.

7 Ibid., p. 8.

8 Michael Wyschogrod, *The Body of Faith: God in the People Israel* (1989), pp. 188–90.

9 Norman Lamm, *The Condition of Jewish Belief: A Symposium Compiled by the Editors of Commentary Magazine* (Northvale, 1989), pp. 124–6.

10 Eugene Borowitz, *Renewing the Covenant: A Theology for the Postmodern Jew* (Philadelphia, 1991), ch. 20.

11 Heschel, *God in Search of Man*, p. 185.

12 Seymour Siegel, in Lamm, *The Condition of Jewish Belief*, pp. 223–5.

13 Ira Eisenstein, in ibid., pp. 45ff.

14 See Paul Tillich's *The Dynamics of Faith* (New York, 1958), ch. 3.

15 Neil Gillman, *Sacred Fragments: Recovering Theology for the Modern Jew* (Philadelphia, 1990), pp. 25–35.

16 Will Herberg, *Judaism and Modern Man* (New York, 1970), ch. 5.

17 The essay is included in Fackenheim's *Quest for Past and Future: Essays in Jewish Theology* (Bloomington, 1973), ch. 15. See, in particular, pp. 242–3.

18 The essay is titled "Elijah and the Empiricists," in Fackenheim's *Encounters Between Judaism and Modern Philosophy* (New York, 1973), ch. 1.

19 Heschel, *God in Search of Man*, part I.

20 Arthur Green, *Seek My Face, Speak My Name: A Contemporary Jewish Theology* (Northvale, 1990), pp. 25–7, 36–7.

21 Elliot Dorff, *Knowing God: Jewish Journeys to the Unknowable* (Northvale, 1992), p. 14.

22 Heschel, *God in Search of Man*, pp. 31–2.

23 In Mordecai Kaplan's discussion of God in his *Questions Jews Ask: Reconstructionist Answers* (New York, 1961), pp. 80–9.

24 Will Herberg, *Judaism and Modern Man* (New York, 1970), p. 60. Emphasis Herberg's.

25 Abraham Joshua Heschel, *The Prophets* (New York, 1975), pp. 223–4.

26 Ibid., p. 257.

27 Judith Plaskow, *Standing Again at Sinai* (San Francisco, 1990), p. 135.

28 Ibid., pp. 141–2.

29 Rachel Adler, *Engendering Judaism: An Inclusive Theology and Ethics* (Philadelphia, 1998), p. 103.

30 William Kaufman, *A Question of Faith: An Atheist and a Rabbi Debate the Existence of God* (Northvale, 1994), p. 82. See also his *The Evolving God in Jewish Process Theology* (Lewiston, 1997).

31 Harold Schulweis, *Evil and the Morality of God* (1984), p. 122.

32 Kaplan, *Questions Jews Ask . . . .*, pp. 119–20.

33 Harold Kushner, *When Bad Things Happen to Good People* (New York, 1981), p. 55.

34 Eliezer Berkovits, *Faith After the Holocaust* (1973), p. 135.

35 Fackenheim, *Quest for Past and Future*, p. 143.

36 See, e.g., in Fackenheim's "Diaspora and Nation: The Contemporary Situation," in *The Jewish Thought of Emil Fackenheim: A Reader*, ch. 30.

37 In Greenberg's essay, "Cloud of Smoke, Pillar of Fire: Judaism, Christianity and Modernity After the Holocaust," in Eva Fleischner, ed., *Auschwitz: Beginning of a New Era?* (New York, 1977), particularly pp. 26–8.

38 See the pamphlet, *Perspectives: A CLAL Thesis*, pp. 32–5. See also the conversation, *Living in the Image of God*, ch. 3.

39   *The Condition of Jewish Belief*, p. 199.
40   Ibid., p. 201.
41   Herberg, *Judaism and Modern Man*, ch. 16, in particular, pp. 211–16.
42   Ibid., p. 229.
43   Borowitz, *Renewing the Covenant*, p. 23.
44   English versions of Levinas's writings are increasingly available. As of this writing, two in particular are useful entrées into his thought: *Difficult Freedom: Essays on Judaism* (1990) and *Nine Talmudic Readings* (Baltimore, 1990).
45   Inter alia, see Robert Gibbs, *Correlations in Rosenzweig and Levinas* (Princeton, 1992); Robert Bernasconi and Simon Critchley, eds., *Re-Reading Levinas* (Bloomington, 1991); Susan A. Handelman, *Fragments of Redemption: Jewish Thought and Literary Theory in Benjamin, Scholem and Levinas* (Bloomington, 1991); and Ira Stone, *Reading Levinas/Reading Talmud: An Introduction* (Philadelphia, 1998).

Bibliography

Adler, Rachel, *Engendering Judaism: An Inclusive Theology and Ethics* (Philadelphia, 1998).

Bernasconi, Robert, and Robert Critchley, *Re-Reading Levinas* (Bloomington, 1991).

Borowitz, Eugene, *Renewing the Covenant: A Theology for the Postmodern Jew* (Philadelphia, 1991).

Buber, Martin, *I and Thou*, A New Translation with a Prologue "I and You" and Notes by Walter Kaufmann (New York, 1970).

The Condition of Jewish Belief: A Symposium Compiled by the Editors of Commentary Magazine (Northvale, 1989).

Dorff, Elliot, *Knowing God: Jewish Journeys to the Unknowable* (Northvale, 1992).

Fackenheim, Emil, *Encounters Between Judaism and Modern Philosophy: A Preface to Future Jewish Thought* (New York, 1973).

Fackenheim, Emil, *Quest for Past and Future: Essays in Jewish Theology* (Bloomington, 1973).

Fleischner, Eva, ed., *Auschwitz: Beginning of a New Era?* (New York, 1977).

Gibbs, Robert, *Correlations in Rosenzweig and Levinas* (Princeton, 1992).

Gillman, Neil, *Sacred Fragments: Recovering Theology for the Modern Jew* (Philadelphia, 1990).

Gillman, Neil, *The Death of Death: Resurrection and Immortality in Jewish Thought* (Woodstock, 1997).

Green, Arthur, *Seek My Face, Speak My Name: A Contemporary Jewish Theology* (Northvale, 1990).

Greenberg, Irving, "Voluntary Covenant," in *Perspectives: A CLAL Thesis* (New York, 1982).

Greenberg, Irving, *Living in the Image of God: Jewish Teachings to Perfect the World: Conversations with Rabbi Irving Greenberg* (Northvale, 1998).

Handelman, Susan A., *Fragments of Redemption: Jewish Thought and Literary Theory in Benjamin, Scholem, and Levinas* (Bloomington, 1991).

Hartman, David, *A Living Covenant: The Innovative Spirit in Traditional Judaism* (New York, 1985).

Herberg, Will, *Judaism and Modern Man* (New York, 1970).

Heschel, Abraham Joshua, *God in Search of Man: A Philosophy of Judaism* (Philadelphia, 1956).

Heschel, Abraham Joshua, *Man's Quest for God: Studies in Prayer and Symbolism* (New York, 1954).

Heschel, Abraham Joshua, *The Prophets* (New York, 1975).

Kaplan, Mordecai M., *Judaism as a Civilization* (Philadelphia, 1981).

Kaplan, Mordecai M., *Questions Jews Ask: Reconstructionist Answers* (New York, 1961).

Kaufman, William, *A Question of Faith: An Atheist and a Rabbi Debate the Existence of God* (Northvale, 1994).

Kaufman, William, *The Evolving God of Jewish Process Theology* (Lewiston, 1997).

Kushner, Harold, *When Bad Things Happen to Good People* (New York, 1981).

Levinas, Emmanuel, *Difficult Freedom: Essays on Judaism*, translated by Sean Hand (Baltimore, 1990).

Levinas, Emmanuel, *Nine Talmudic Readings*, translated and with an Introduction by Annette Aronowicz (Bloomington, 1990).

Plaskow, Judith, *Standing Again at Sinai: Judaism from a Feminist Perspective* (San Francisco, 1990).

Rosenzweig, Franz, *On Jewish Learning*, Nahum N. Glatzer, ed. (New York, 1965).

Schulweis, Harold, *Evil and the Morality of God* (New York, 1984).

Soloveitchick, Joseph B., *Halakhic Man* (Philadelphia, 1983).

Soloveitchick, Joseph B., *The Lonely Man of Faith* (New York, 1992).

Stone, Ira, *Reading Levinas/Reading Talmud: An Introduction* (Philadelphia, 1998).

Tillich, Paul, *Dynamics of Faith* (New York, 1958).

CHAPTER 25
Secular Forms of Jewishness

Paul Mendes-Flohr

Since the Enlightenment and Emancipation, Jewish identity is no longer exclusively defined by loyalty to the Torah and God's commandments. Indeed, formal definitions of identity – membership in the community, acceptance of its norms, teachings, values, aspirations – are no longer the only self-evident criteria of Jewish identity.[1] The eclipse of Jewish tradition as the defining matrix of Jewish self-understanding and affiliation is generally called secularization – a term that since the late nineteenth century entered the lexicon of the West to characterize the attenuation of religion as the ultimate arbiter of meaning and value.[2] Bereft of traditional definitions of Jewish affiliation and practice, secularized Jews are often hard pressed to provide alternative criteria formally determining their abiding "Jewishness." Hence, we witness the multiplicity of frequently competing conceptions of a secular Jewish identity. Indeed, as the novelist and Nobel Prize laureate Elias Canetti observed, "Jews are a people who most widely differ among themselves."[3] The ambiguities of Jewish identity in the modern period are, of course, well documented, indicatively often in fiction[4] and cinema.[5]

The ambiguity of a secular, modern Jewish identity is compounded by the fact that the Jews of modernity are members of numerous communities – residential, vocational, cultural, professional, political, recreational – that are not necessarily coterminous, and hence the sociological parameters establishing one's identity, both formally and phenomenologically, may not be exclusively Jewish. One may, for instance, live in a *Jewish* neighborhood but pursue one's livelihood in a profession whose membership is drawn from any number of ethnic and religious backgrounds; similarly one may have a political orientation and recreational interests that transcend particulars of one's cultural or communal provenance. Moreover, the boundaries of these communities are often fluid. The upshot is that one is no longer exclusively Jewish. The flux is not only sociological, but also phenomenological: it is often within one's self, for, as moderns, secular Jews may continuously reconfigure their identities. No longer bound by primordial fidelities and sentiments, one's world of imagination and affection may constantly shift. As Kafka once ironically queried, "What have I in common with Jews? I have hardly anything in common with myself."[6]

A preoccupation with the meaning of their existence as Jews is not unique to the Jews of modernity. Ever since a seventy-five-year-old Chaldean, Abraham the son of Tirah, received the divine calling and promise of nationhood (Gen. 12:1–5), Jews have reflected on their identity. Buffeted by agonizing decisions and tests of faith, the founding patriarch of the Hebrew nation was recurrently obliged to question the meaning of his life before God; and so it was for his children and his children's children. As the twentieth-century German–Jewish philosopher Franz Rosenzweig observed, "with other nations the birth of self-consciousness is the beginning of the end; with us [Jews] it was the beginning."[7] The problem of identity, Rosenzweig suggested, generally marks for a people the loss of innocence and thus the weakening, if not ultimate dissolution, of its primordial bonds. For Israel it is different, however. From its inception as a people – or rather a people-faith – Israel has "thematized" its own existence. For as the patriarch Abraham already knew, the nation he sired was not simply the anthropological means (as Hermann Cohen once put it) to promote the faith in the One God.[8] Israel's very existence and history were flush with religious meaning. That meaning is suffused in the very substance and rhythms of Israel's temporal life. Nineteenth-century German scholars coined the term *Heilsgeschichte* – salvational history – to capture this fact. Traditional Jewry was wont to refer to the image of Abraham's grandson, Jacob – who was the first to bear the name Israel (Gen. 32:28), a name God bestowed upon him and his descendants after his mysterious struggle with the angel (Gen. 32:28–29).[9] Jacob emerged from the episode blessed with a new name but also "limping on his hip" as a result of an injury acquired in his bout with the angel. The pain and blessing attendant to the struggle are embodied in the name Israel, thus marking Jewish self-understanding throughout the ages. Recurrently tossed between the poles of injury and blessing, the Jews tended to view the trials and tribulations of their journey through mundane time as raising the question of theodicy, the justification – and meaning – of God's rule as reflected in their history. As a mirror of the divine presence, Jewish existence became the focus of sustained metaphysical meditation and scrutiny.[10]

Yet as the Hebrew publicist and Zionist Ahad Ha'am (Hebrew: "one of the people," *nom de plume* of Asher Ginzberg, 1856–1927) noted, prior to their passage into the modern world, it never occurred to Jews to ask why they were Jews. "Such questions would not only have been considered blasphemy, but would have been seen as the highest level of stupidity."[11] Before they crossed the threshold into the realm of secular sensibility, the Jews did not question why they were Jews; despite their preoccupation with the meaning of their collective existence and troubled history, their identity was clear and unambiguous. The parameters of traditional Jewish identity were summarized by Ruth, the Moabite, when upon her conversion to the faith of Israel she declared: "Your people is my people, your God is my God, and where you die I shall die" (Ruth

1:16–17) – being a Jew by birth or by choice entails "membership in a people, a religion, and in a *Schicksalsgemeinschaft*"[12] – a community of a shared fate. The pivotal element in this statement of allegiance is the faith in the God of Israel; remove it and the other elements of traditional Jewish identity begin to totter. For, as an eminent scholar of comparative religion has observed, underscoring what I have already noted, "to describe Judaism as the religion of the Jewish people is . . . slightly misrepresenting the situation. Judaism is the religious dimension of the Jewish people. Israel . . . is a people born of, and with, religion."[13] Accordingly, it is the weakening, if not utter eclipse, of religion that creates the problem of Jewish identity.

Sundered from its religious dimension, the peoplehood and shared destiny of the Jews is inherently beset by ambiguity – a situation that, as already noted, is exacerbated by the fact that Jews of modernity are integrated in the cultural and political fabric of various societies among whom they dwell. Indicatively, Jewish self-reflection shifts from theology to sociology and even psychology. Whereas traditional Jews would ask, "What is the theological meaning of Jewish existence?" secularized Jews wonder, "Why am I a Jew?" "Should I identify as a Jew?" "If so, how?" "With the loss of faith and a commitment to fulfill the precepts of the Torah, what is the content of my identity as a Jew?" To be sure, Jewish theologians have not been unemployed, rendered irrelevant by the modern experience; in fact, since the Enlightenment they have been a rather active breed. Their task, however, is decidedly different from that of their predecessors. Philosophers and rabbis have enjoined theology in order to shore-up faith or to revalorize it so that the edifice of Jewish identity will endure.

These rabbis and religious philosophers have had to share the arena of Jewish self-reflection with a battery of secular intellectuals who have offered new paradigms of Jewish identity. Acknowledging the rupture in faith and religious practice brought on by secularization, they have sought to construct a Jewish identity without a belief in God; indeed, much of modern Jewish thought has been devoted to devising strategies to foster a Jewish identity simply as membership in the Jewish people and a *Schicksalsgemeinschaft*. (The two are not synonymous: One can feel oneself as belonging to the Jewish people but not necessarily accept or acknowledge its fate as one's own. The former may be characterized as a sense of ethnic identification, the later as ideological affiliation.) Competing secular ideologies – Zionism, Bundism, Diaspora Nationalism, Yiddishism – have proffered various national and cultural conceptions of Jewish identity.[14] Others have appealed to what Theodor Herzl (1860–1904) called negative pride, in the face of anti-Semitism a defiant affirmation by otherwise assimilated Jews of their Jewish identity – a position that was somewhat ironically called in German *Trotzjudentum*. Jean-Paul Sartre had such a position in mind when he stated that it is "the antisemites who define the Jew."[15] In response to the Holocaust, the philosopher Emil Fackenheim propounded a theologized *Trotzjudentum*. Employing theological language and its apodictic intonations, he spoke of the "revelatory voice of Auschwitz." This voice "commands" contemporary

Jews not to grant Hitler a posthumous victory by assimilating, and undermining Judaism by critical, corrosive questions.[16] Lest Jews help Hitler after his death and the collapse of the Third Reich achieve the objective of not only exterminating their people but also their religion and culture, they are to desist from all actions that might endanger the continued survival of Jewry as a distinctive people and religious culture. Fackenheim also regards the commanding voice of Auschwitz as appertaining to the politics of the State of Israel, especially as pursued by those leaders most jealously concerned with promoting the Jewish state's security, namely – and he is rather explicit – the right-wing parties; should one criticize the policy of a Likud government with respect to the Palestinians and the Arab world, in Fackenheim's judgment, one perforce endangers the State and thus possibly contributes to the work that Hitler began.[17]

By grounding his appeal to Jewish solidarity and defiant pride in quasi-theological constructs, Fackenheim betrays not only what I regard to be profoundly mistaken – indeed, frightening – political judgment. His assignment of absolute, categorical obligations to the survivors of Auschwitz – and all Jews, he argues, are honor-bound to regard themselves as survivors – also discloses a fundamental predicament facing post-traditional Judaism: namely, the difficulty of endowing Jewish identity with a compelling, indeed, obligatory quality in the absence of a prescribed content and formal definition – at least a universally accepted content and definition.[18]

The difficulty of determining the content and definition of a post-traditional, secular Jewish identity is particularly manifest in the State of Israel. Having the legal obligation of providing a juridical definition of who is a Jew, Israel encounters an inevitable antinomy: constitutionally bound to correlate Jewish identity with citizenship, the state must stipulate the formal criteria according to which the law would recognize one as a Jew and *ergo* a citizen; yet, as a secular institution, the state must also acknowledge the diverse and divergent conceptions of Jewish identity that distinguish contemporary Jewish life. It is thus not surprising that since its founding the State of Israel has recurrently failed to provide a satisfactory legal definition of who is a Jew. Although the Orthodox elements who dominate the religious discourse of the State advocate traditional Jewish definitions of who is a Jew – based on Halakhah or talmudic law – these invariably prove problematic, because they fail to accommodate the contemporary social reality of the Jewish people as a community whose members are constituted by individuals whose mothers may not be Jewish (the primordial criterion of Jewishness according to Halakhah), or who may have chosen to join the House of Israel through the auspices of Reform or Conservative Judaism. If one of the founding purposes of the State of Israel – stipulated by its Law of Return – is to provide refuge for anyone who is persecuted as a Jew, then clearly the halakhic definition would exclude the hundreds of thousands of persons of partial Jewish descent who suffered as Jews under the Nuremberg laws, or the hundreds of thousands of immigrants from the former Soviet Union who halakhically are not strictly Jewish. The traditional definition is also incompatible with contemporary Jewish sensibility.

The inadequacy of traditional definitions of Jewish identity are vividly highlighted by the Brother Daniel case[19] and the Shalit case,[20] adjudicated by the Israeli Supreme Court in 1966 and 1970, respectively. A Jew by birth and a former partisan who fought in the forests of Poland against the Nazis, Brother Daniel converted to Christianity during the Holocaust. As a Carmelite monk, he sought Israeli citizenship under the Law of Return. His petition was supported by the Halakhah, which recognizes him as a Jew despite his apostasy. The Supreme Court, however, ruled against Brother Daniel and in effect against the Halakhah, basing its decision on secular and national Jewish sensibilities, arguing that by converting to Christianity he had removed himself from "the history and destiny of the Jewish community." The Shalit case involved an intermarried couple – an Israeli Jew (who had a heroic battle record in defense of the country) and his gentile wife – who, despite the fact they declared themselves non-believers, sought to have their children registered as Jews by nationality. When the Ministry of the Interior balked, the Shalits turned to the Supreme Court, which ruled that, although technically, that is, halakhically, they are non-Jews, the children should be registered as Jews because they were being raised within the Jewish community of the State of Israel and were as such indissolubly bound to its destiny. The Israeli parliament later passed legislation nullifying the Supreme Court decision and reaffirmed the halakhic definition of Jewish identity. The then socialist-dominated legislature argued that, notwithstanding their sympathy for the Shalits and countless others in their situation, the Supreme Court's secular definition of a Jew would endanger the unity of world Jewry, that unity being assured only by the formal, juridical definitions of Halakhah.[21]

This legislation satisfied few but the minority of Orthodox Jews. Moreover, aside from the matter of the juridical definition of personal status under Israeli law, the Halakhah and Jewish tradition have clearly ceased providing the framework by which the vast majority of contemporary Jews in the State of Israel and elsewhere would identify themselves as Jews. Definitions of Jewish identity by other formal criteria, such as cultural and institutional affiliation, also court ambiguity. Some Zionists fancied that the territorial and linguistic coding of Jewish identity would solve the problem. Restored to their ancient patrimony in the land of Israel and speaking Hebrew once again as the language of everyday discourse, it was reasoned, the Jews would be Jews just as the French are French, that is, they would be Hebrew-speaking citizens of the Jewish state, and, as some Zionists emphasized, irrespective of religious belief or disbelief.[22] But this position is likewise buffeted by ambiguity when one considers that hundreds of thousands of Arabs speak Hebrew and are citizens of the Jewish state – ethnic descent being the only distinguishing variable. Within this context, one is reminded of the quip that Israelis are but Hebrew-speaking gentiles. This observation of course is crude for it fails to consider the simple but incontrovertible fact that most Israeli Jews would regard themselves nonetheless as Jews,[23] and the vast majority of Israeli Arabs would uphold their Arab or Palestinian identity.[24] Below the veneer of a shared language and citizenship, Jewish and Arab Israelis are distinguished by ethnic sensibility, and distinctive cultural and historical memories (not to speak of a not too subtle sociological and political divide between these two sectors of Israeli society).

Both in the State of Israel and the diaspora, contemporary efforts to determine formal, concordant definitions of Jewish identity also continuously falter before the fact that as denizens of the modern world Jews share in multiple cultural and social identities. As moderns, contemporary Jews are open to other cultures and contrasting axiological and ideational systems, and as such their cultural and cognitive horizons are no longer exclusively Jewish. This is true in the State of Israel as in the diaspora.

This situation – which may be descriptively labeled cultural pluralism – Jews naturally share with all moderns, especially with the increasing globalization of culture. The specifics of the Jewish experience of modernity, however, have colored Jewish perceptions of the situation, inevitably confounding all efforts to configure a Jewish identity that takes into account the fact that the modern Jew is no longer exclusively Jewish. Since the Enlightenment, Jews have adopted the cultures of their host societies, being particularly drawn to the high cultures of Europe with their universal, cosmopolitan claims. To be an educated European meant to be at home in a variety of ancient and more contemporary cultures; it meant knowing languages, disparate literary and artistic traditions, and to be open to new ideas, perspectives, and aesthetic expressions. The boundaries of high culture thus not only reached back to classical antiquity but also extended wide and far across space and time, much of which still remained uncharted. In German, this conception of high culture was known as *Bildung*, an unending process of intellectual and aesthetic cultivation, and the emancipated Jews of central and western Europe were among its most devoted adherents.[25] Explanations abound as to why the Jews were so taken by this conception of culture; surely, it has much to do with the dynamics of emancipation and the political and social conditions of their acceptance into the evolving liberal order.

What is beyond debate, however, is that their romance with *Bildung* often led to assimilation, to a serious attenuation if not loss of Jewish identity. Hence, it was natural that the acculturation implied by *Bildung* would be regarded with profound suspicion by many guardians of Jewish tradition. Their apprehensions were evoked not necessarily by the secular inflections of *Bildung* – for there were traditional Jews who consciously sought to wed Torah observance with *Bildung*;[26] it was rather the blurring of the boundaries between Jewish and "alien" culture that *Bildung* seemed to promote that aroused an often militant opposition to an openness to the other and non-Jewish cultures. Led by the great Rabbinic sage Hatam Sofer (1762–1839), this sizeable community of traditional Jews was convinced that the obfuscation of cultural boundaries would lead to the demise of Judaism and Jewry. In his "last will and testament," which to this very day is the *vade mecum* of ultra-Orthodox Jewry, Rabbi Sofer beseeches all God-fearing Jews to preserve the integrity of Judaism.[27] He elaborates what he understands by integrity by rendering the Hebrew for the term *shalem*, an acronym: *sh(a)-l-(e)m*. He notes that the first letter, *shin*, stands for *shemot*, names, and comments that Jews are forbidden to have non-Jewish names. One must, then, reject the practice initiated with the Enlightenment of calling one-self and one's children Paul, Anthony, Klaus, Ivan, Gertrude, or Barbara. The second letter, *lamed*, stands for *leshonot*, languages, and indicates that it is forbidden for Jews to learn non-Jewish languages other than for purely instru-mental purposes; to learn the languages of the other's community is to enter his or her cognitive universe. The last letter of the acronym, *mem*, Hatam Sofer says, stands for *malbush*, clothing: Jews are forbidden to dress like non-Jews; they must maintain a distinctively Jewish attire. Although pronounced by a learned rabbi and exegete of God's revealed teachings, this conception of Jewish integ-rity is unabashedly sociological: by screening out the other's culture, Jews will secure the integrity of their national and religious identity. The scandal of assimilation could only be avoided by social and cultural isolation.

Historical experience certainly seems to have vindicated Hatam Sofer. He has hundreds of descendants, whereas Moses Mendelssohn (1729–86) – the first Jew to embrace publicly the challenge of *Bildung*, a distinction that earned for him the unbridled scorn of Hatam Sofer – has no contemporary Jewish descendants. From this perspective, ultra-Orthodox Judaism must be viewed as a modern Jewish identity. Its dialectical twin is Zionism. The movement for Jewish national rebirth was equally obsessed with stemming the tide of assimilation. Rather than the cultural re-ghettoization of the Jews, however, Zionism held that the regathering of the Jews in their ancestral homeland would allow them not only to rejoin the family of nations but also to participate in world culture without courting a loss of ethnic dignity and self-esteem. By creating the sociological conditions – a society in which Jews would constitute the majority population, the revival of Hebrew as a spoken language comprehending secular activity and experience, and the recasting of the sacred sources and memories of Judaism into a national literature and historical memory – for Jewish cultural autonomy, Zionism seeks to sponsor the possibility of the Jews' uninhibited encounter with the other cultures unfettered by the fear of assimilation. Cultural autonomy as envisioned by the Zionists encourages the translation of the works of other cultures into Hebrew and hence their transformation into a Jewish cultural discourse, or at least their integration into the discourse of Jews, such that these expressions of non-Jewish experience are free of the structural antagonism to Jewish culture and identity that prevails in the diaspora where the Jews are a vulnerable cultural minority.

Zionism assumed that cultural autonomy, under the aforementioned con-ditions, would *eo ipso* spare the Jewish community reconstituted in Zion from the scourge of confused identities consequent to participation in various and even contrasting cognitive and axiological systems. The assumption governing the confidence of the Zionists is basically twofold: Social and linguistic autonomy or separation – a position that Hatam Sofer and his ultra-Orthodox followers would endorse – and a proud affirmation of a national Jewish identity would pro-tect the Jews from assimilation, even when open to others and their culture. While this assumption is not utterly wrong, the mechanism allowing – even encouraging – openness to a plurality of cultures and identities is far more complex than contemplated by the Zionists. Typical of other nationalist movements, Zionists sponsored the view that there is one essential Jewish identity – here I should note parenthetically that the term "identity" is somewhat of an anachronism is this context, for as a cultural and social-psychological category it entered both scholarly and popular discourse only after World War II, primarily with the writings of Kurt Lewin[28] and Erik Erikson.[29] Before that, in Zionist discourse one spoke of national consciousness and continuity.[30] Be that as it may, the Zionists held that there was one essential and perduring Jewish identity, into which all one's experiences are gathered and integrated. It was this identity that Zionism came to strengthen and adapt to the secular and political realities of the modern world.[31]

This premise that continues to determine Zionist politics of identity is undermined by the fact, made manifest by the "ingathering of the exiles" to the State of Israel, that, phenomenologically, there are multiple Jewish identities; the Jewish consciousness or identity of Jews from Afghanistan, Ethiopia, Poland, and Germany are not homologous. Indeed, they are often rather disparate.[32] Furthermore, contrary to the essentialist view of identity, the various identities one may acquire need not be continuous. In fact, one's evolving identities – as experiences and social and ideological affiliations – may be radically discontinuous.[33] This fact has often engendered a certain anxiety among Jews who feel that their Jewishness should retain salience, lest it be swallowed up in the whirl of competing identities. Some eighty-five years ago in Berlin, the philosopher and social critic Gustav Landauer published an essay, "Are These Heretical Thoughts?" in which he boldly challenged his fellow Jews who felt that in order to overcome these perplexities it would be best to retreat into a more exclusively Jewish cultural universe. Defending his simultaneous attachment to Judaism and other cultures, he asserted: "I never felt the need to simplify myself or to create an artificial unity by way of denial; I accept my [cultural] complexity and hope to be an even more multifarious unity than I am now aware of."[34] The late Nobel laureate in literature, Elias Canetti echoed similar sentiments, when, during the dark years of the Holocaust, he protested, "should I harden myself against the Russians because they are Jews, against the Chinese because they are far away, against the Germans because they are possessed by the devil? Can't I still belong to all of them, as before, and nevertheless be a Jew?"[35]

As moderns, Jews have adopted, as the American Jewish Indologist Wendy Doniger has noted in an autobiographical essay, "Other Peoples Myths."[36] As she poignantly relates, her own journey into the spiritual world of the Indian continent is not to be construed as a mere act of scholarly empathy, but rather reflects a personal quest to expand her cultural sensibilities *and* humanity. But as Doniger acknowledges, her eager embrace of a multicultural ethic was at the expense of her own primordial culture, which was relegated to ethnic and culinary affections, consciously modulated lest they becloud her "larger" commitments.

The problematics of living with evolving and ever shifting identities, especially of post-traditional Jews, are the subject of Woody Allen's cinematographic satire *Selig* (1986),[37] pronounced with a Yiddish accent, *Zelig*. The hero of the film, Selig, portrayed by Allen himself, is so adept at identifying with others, that he merely need behold an "other" and he instantaneously takes on his or her physiognomy, tonality of voice, and body language. Selig thus becomes a black, Italian, Chinese, and even a Nazi. A cultural chameleon – or as some have punned, a shamielon – Selig has access to all cultures, but, in effect, has none.[38] An allegory on acculturation,[39] Allen's *Selig* points to the predicament of syncretism: the multiplication of cultural identities leads to their amalgamation, and confounding dilution. Here is the possible significance of Allen's counter-hero, Selig – which is Yiddish for blessed, an appellation granted the deceased – which suggests that the film is Allen's eulogy for the Jews of modernity who in their mad rush to be part of other peoples' cultures have lost a firm grounding in their own culture and identity, thus bringing about its spiritual death.[40]

Allen's reflections of course extend beyond the specific plight of the modern Jew; they bear upon the inescapably plural character of contemporary identity in general. The often contradictory and centrifugal thrust of these identities clearly threatens those who wish to secure the integrity of a particular cultural identity, if not also troubling to those who feel a healthy ego; identity should be cohesive, harmonious, and integrative. Postmodern critics of this conception of cultural and personal identity argue that it is not only out of kilter with the temper of the times but is fundamentally flawed, for identities are always multilayered and differentiated. Accordingly, as one critic recently put it, we need a concept of identity that tolerates "not only greater complexity, but confusion, chaos, and non-sense."[41]

From the Jewish perspective (as that of any particularistic culture), the challenge would then be to determine the mechanism that allows Jews to honor a bewildering and chaotic assemblage of ever multiplying (and subtracting) identities while providing a measure of Jewish or culture-specific continuity. Such a mechanism is elucidated by the concept of "cultural memory" (*kulturelles Gedächtnis*) proposed by Aleida and Jan Assmann of the University of Konstanz and University of Heidelberg respectively.[42] Cultural memory, as they conceive it, is a form of knowledge – accumulated across the generations – specific to a particular group, and by means of which the group "bases its consciousness of its unity and specificity," in other words, its self-image and identity. Cultural memory has its *terminus ad quo* in "fateful events in the past" – historical or otherwise conceived – the memory of which is maintained through a variety of mnemonic activities that constitute the cultural life specific to the group. The Assmanns emphasize that these mnemonic expressions are not confined to the written word but also have musical, pictorial, and ritual forms. Hence, cultural memory is embodied in art, architecture, buildings, ceremonies, holidays, historic and sacred landscapes, law, folklore, literature, music, collective narratives, philosophy, poetry, ritual, song, symbols, theology, etc. What is crucial is that all these mnemonic expressions have a canonical or semi-canonical status in a specific society and thus serve "to stabilize its cultural identity across the generations."[43] Creating "memory spaces"[44] within the context of everyday life, these activities and gestures constitute "islands of [transcendent] time"[45] and thus are also the focus of the structures of meaning, values, and norms that determine the conduct and self-understanding of the group.

The Assmanns highlight two moments characteristic of cultural memory that are especially significant for the formation of collective identities in a secularized culture. The first is that the primary impulse that draws members of a particular group to its culture of memory is not a general "theoretical curiosity"[46] to acquire knowledge but the desire to belong, "the need for identity."[47] Second, although canonical knowledge, cultural memory is constantly being reconstructed, re-read in the light of present circumstances and perceptions. Cultural memory is thus not a simple retrieval of knowledge – as in a cybernetic system – stored in the collective archives of a culture; it is, rather, the re-contextualization of that knowledge, or, if you wish, a contemporalization of the past (Vergenwärtigung). As a contemporized past and a re-contextualized knowledge, cultural memory is, in fact, a process, one that is governed by given modes of response. These modes reflect varying attitudes and ideological postures toward the present and other cultures and systems of knowledge.

Following the Assmanns, one may delineate three essential modes[48] of how the bearers of a cultural memory encounter and accommodate ever new configurations of reality, experiences, information, and sources of knowledge and meaning: One is a rigidly conservative posture that seeks to ensure the preeminence of the inherited cultural memory by veiling it in dogmatic garments, resisting all that might threaten its integrity.

A second posture is that which, while still basically defensive, employs a hermeneutic strategy allowing for a constructive response to contemporary reality. This mode of response fosters a dialectic ebb and flow between innovation and continuity. Yet when confronting fundamentally different systems of knowledge, this position invariably falls prey to dogmatic self-enclosure. A third mode of cultural memory is guided by a self-reflective posture, promoting a critical awareness of the culture's presuppositions, prejudices, and blindspots, as it were; most significantly this third mode of cultural memory acknowledges the polyphonic character of its own evolution. By assuming a tolerant attitude toward the plural voices within their own tradition, the guardians of cultural memory are implicitly aware that no culture is utterly insular and untouched by other, "alien" cultures. Indeed, as the Palestinian scholar Edward Said has noted, virtually all cultures, certainly so-called high cultures, evolve in interaction with other cultures. "Far from being unitary or monolithic or autonomous things, cultures actually assume more 'foreign' elements, alterities, differences, than they consciously exclude."[49] A self-reflective, critical mode of cultural memory thus encourages the formation of a collective identity that is undogmatic, pluralistic, and open.

The vectors of identity are many; it projects a society's (and an individual's) "self-image," but it also perforce defines social boundaries, excluding the other who stands beyond those boundaries, both cognitively and actually. Self-image bears in its breast an image of the non-self. This is the antinomy – irresolvable tension – faced by all those who are beholden to a particular cultural memory whose compassion and humanity also alert them to the dangers of a self-insularity and exclusion. In a prescient observation, Hannah Arendt suggests that this danger is particularly pronounced for those whose Jewish identity has been secularized.[50] In contrast to traditional Judaism, which teaches that Israel's election and destiny are dialectically bound to God's *Heilsplan* and universal redemption, secularized Jews cling to the concept of chosenness as an implicit ethnic privilege:

> The most fateful element of Jewish secularization was that the concept of chosenness was . . . separated from the Messianic hope, whereas in Jewish religion these two elements were two aspects of God's redemptory plan for mankind. . . . Out of the belief in chosenness by God grew that fantastic delusion, shared by unbelieving Jews and non-Jews alike, that Jews are by nature more intelligent, better, healthier, more fit for survival – the motor of history and the salt of the earth.[51]

Despite the humanistic and progressive ideals that often sponsored the secularization of the Jews, Arendt concludes, it "engendered a very real Jewish chauvinism. . . . From now on, the old religious concept of chosenness was no longer the essence of Judaism; it became instead the essence of Jewishness."[52] And one may add that whereas Halakhah, the religious code guiding traditional Jewry, allows non-Jews to join the community through conversion – witness Ruth, the Moabite – secular Jews perforce regard membership in the community in restrictedly ethnic terms, as a matter of descent, of birth. Hence, the ironic paradox, that whereas traditional Judaism is in principle universal, secular Jewish identities are inherently prey to tribalism. A critical cultural memory, allowing one to give salience to one's Jewish identity without forfeiting a dedicated membership in other communities of identity, would at least serve to minimize these dangers.

Notes

1 For a nuanced historical survey of the issue, see Michael A. Meyer, *Jewish Identity in the Modern World* (Seattle and London, 1990). Various philosophical questions raised by the question of a *modern* Jewish identity are offered in an excellent collection of essays edited by David Theo Goldberg and Michael Krauz, *Jewish Identity* (Philadelphia, 1990).

2 The literature on secularization is vast. For a judicious review, particularly as it appertains to Judaism, see R. J. Zwi Werblowsky, *Beyond Tradition and Modernity. Changing Religions in a Changing World.* Jordan Lectures 1974 (London, 1976), especially ch. 3: "Secular Particularity: The Jewish Case (with a Digression on Japan)."

3   Elias Canetti, *Crowd and Power*, trans. Carol Stewart (New York, 1989), p. 178.

4   See, e.g., Norman Finkelstein, *The Ritual of New Creation. Jewish Tradition and Contemporary Literature* (Albany, 1992); and Linda Nochlin and Tamar Garb, eds., *The Jew in the Text. Modernity and the Construction of Identity* (London, 1996).

5   See David Dresseer and Lester D. Friedman, *American-Jewish Filmmakers. Traditions and Trends* (Urbana and Chicago, 1993).

6   Kafka, *The Diaries of Franz Kafka*, ed. Max Brod, trans. Martin Greenberg (New York, 1965), vol. 2, entry of January 8, 1914.

7   Letter to parents, December 18, 1917. Cited in Nahum N. Glatzer, *Franz Rosenzweig. His Life and Thought* (New York, 1953), p. 63.

8   See Martin Buber and Hermann Cohen, "A Debate on Zionism and Messianism," in P. Mendes-Flohr and Jehuda Reinharz, *The Jew in the Modern World*, 2nd edn. (New York, 1995), pp. 571–6, esp. p. 576, n. 1.

9   See Arthur Green, *Devotion and Commandment. The Faith of Abraham in the Hasidic Imagination* (Cincinnati, 1989).

10 See Amos Funkenstein, *Perspectives of Jewish History* (Berkeley, 1993).

11 Ahad Ha-am, "Slavery in Freedom," in *Selected Essays of Ahad Ha-'am*, ed. and trans. Leon Simon (Cleveland and New York, 1962), p. 194.

12 Walter Kaufmann, *Existentialism, Religion and Death. Essays* (New York, 1976), p. 167.

13 Werblowsky, *Beyond Tradition and Moderity*, p. 49.

14 For judicious statements on the most prominent twentieth-century secular Jewish ideologies, see Feliks Gross and Balil J. Vlavianos, eds., *Struggle for Tomorrow. Modern Political Ideologies of the Jewish People* (New York, 1954).

15 J. P. Sartre, *Antisemite and Jew*, trans. G. Becker (New York, 1965), p. 1.

16 Emil Fackenheim, *God's Presence in History. Jewish Affirmations and Philosophical Reflections* (New York, 1972), pp. 67–98.

17 In an extended essay, he argues that the Shoah and the establishment of the State are related events, historically and existentially; as they "confer" upon Jews the twin duties of heeding the "Commanding Voice of Auschwitz" and acknowledging the "centrality" of the State of Israel to contemporary Jewish life. Emil Fackenheim, *The Jewish Return into History. Reflections in the Age of a New Jerusalem* (New York, 1978).

18 See Manfred Vogel, "Some Reflections on the Question of Jewish Identity," in *Journal of Reform Judaism*, XXX, no. 1 (Winter 1983), pp. 1–33.

19 See S. Zalman Abramov, *Perpetual Dilemma. Jewish Religion in the State of Israel* (Rutherford, 1976), pp. 285–90, 296, 301f.

20 See ibid., pp. 298–303, 309, 314.

21 For a spectrum of views on the extensive issues raised by the Shalit case, see Baruch Litvin, in S. Hoenig, ed., *Jewish Identity: Modern Responsa and Opinions on the Registration of Children of Mixed Marriages. Ben-Gurion's Query to Leaders of World Jewry. A Documentary Compilation* (Jerusalem and New York, 1970).

22 Jacob Klatzkin, "A Nation Must Have Its Own Land and Language" (circa 1914), in Arthur Hertzberg, ed., *The Zionist Idea. A Historical Analysis and Reader* (New York, 1969), pp. 318–20.

23 Simon Hermann, *Israelis and Jews. The Continuity of an Identity* (Philadelphia, 1970), and Yair Auron, "Jewish-Israeli Identity among Israel's Future Teachers," in *Jerusalem Letter/Viewpoints* (Jerusalem Center for Public Affairs), No. 334 (May 1, 1996), pp. 1–7.

24 Yoav Peled, "Ethnic Democracy and the Legal Construction of Citizenship: Arab Citizens of the State of Israel," in *American Political Science Review*, vol. 86, no. 2 (June 1992), pp. 434–43.

25 Georg Mosse, *German Jews Beyond Judaism* (Bloomington, 1985), ch. 1; Aleida Assmann, *Arbeit am nationalen Gedächtnis. Eine kurze Geschichte der deutschen Bildungsidee* (Frankfurt am Main, 1993).

26 This position is most prominently associated with Rabbi Samson Raphael Hirsch (1808–88), whose followers are most often referred to as Neo-Orthodox. See S. R. Hirsch, "Religion Allied to Progress," in *The Jew in the Modern World*, 2nd rev. edn. (New York, 1996), pp. 197–202.

27 A somewhat abridged version of Hatam Sofer's testament is translated in Jack Riemer and Nathaniel Stampfer, eds., *Ethical Wills. A Modern Jewish Treasury* (New York, 1986), pp. 18–21.

28 Kurt Lewin, "Erhaltung, Identität und Veränderung in Physik und Psychologie," in K. Lewin, *Werkausgabe*, Carl-Friedrich Graumann, ed. (Stuttgart, 1981), vol. 1, pp. 87–110.

29 Erik H. Erikson, "The Problem of Ego Identity (1956)," in M. R. Stein, A. J. Vidich, and D. M. White, eds., *Identity and Anxiety. Survival of the Person in Mass Society* (New York, 1960), pp. 37–87. On the cultural genealogy of the concept of identity, see Lewis D. Wurgaft, "Identity in World History. A Postmodern Perspective," in *History and Theory* 34 (1995), pp. 67–85.

30 For a general discussion of the language of national "identity" *avant la lettre*, see Walter Sulzbach, intro. by Hans Kohn, *National Consciousness* (Washington, DC, 1943).

31 See Meyer, *Jewish Identity in the Modern World*, pp. 72–3.

32 Shmuel Eisenstadt, *The Transformation of Israeli Society. An Essay in Interpretation* (London, 1985); Shmuel Eisenstadt, *Jewish Civilization. The Jewish Historical Experience in a Comparative Perspective* (New York, 1993), pp. 249–85; also Virginia Dominguez, *Peoples as Subject/People as Object: Selfhood and Peoplehood in Contemporary Israel* (Madison, 1989); and Laurence J. Silberstein and Robert L. Cohn, eds., *The Other in Jewish Thought and History. Constructions of Jewish Culture and Identity* (New York and London, 1994). Among contemporary Israeli historians, there is debate, initiated by the late Amos Funkenstein, regarding the applicability of the "master narrative," which has hitherto dominated Jewish historiography, especially as inspired by Zionism, to the various sub-communities of the Jewish people. See Funkenstein, "The History of Israel among the Thorn Bush. History in the Light of Other Disciplines," in *Zion. The Journal of the Israeli Historical Association*, vol. 60, pp. 335–47 (Hebrew); Shulamit Volkov, "The Jews among the Nations. A National Narrative or a Chapter within an Integrated History," in *Zion*, vol. 61, pp. 91–111 (Hebrew); and Dan Diner, "Cumulative Contingency: Historicizing Legitimacy in Israeli Discourse," in *History and Memory*, vol. 7, no. 1, pp. 147–70.

33 Paul Mendes-Flohr, "Jewish Continuity in an Age of Discontinuity. Reflections from the Perspective of Jewish Intellectual History," in Paul Mendes-Flohr, *Divided Passions. Jewish Intellectuals and the Experience of Modernity* (Detroit, 1991), pp. 54–66.

34 Gustav Landauer, "Sind das Ketzergedanken?" in *Vom Judentum. Ein Sammelbuch*, ed. Verein Jüdischer Hochschuler Bar Kochba in Prag (Leipzig, 1913), pp. 250f.

35 Elias Canetti, *The Human Province* (New York, 1978), p. 51.

36 Wendy O'Flattery Doniger, *Other Peoples' Myths: The Cave of Echoes* (New York, 1988), p. 4.

37   See "Woody Allen: The Schlemiel as Modern Philosopher," in Dresser and Friedman, *American-Jewish Filmmakers*, pp. 36–104, esp. 44ff.

38   Cf., "*Zelig* . . . focuses on a man with no personality, no meaning, of his own," ibid., p. 66.

39   "*Zelig*, the clearest expression of Jewish fear and paranoia ever produced in the cinema, reveals a desperate desire to fit in and achieve total assimilation within mainstream society," ibid., p. 88.

40   Among the real-life commentators in the film – each of whom is a high-profile American Jewish intellectual – Irving Howe, a noted authority on Jewish immigrant literature, states before the camera, "When I think about it, it seems to me that his [Zelig's] story reflected a lot of the Jewish experience in America; the great urge to push in, and to find one's place and then to assimilate into the culture" (ibid., p. 73). The text is apparently Howe's own words, but clearly said with Allen's editorial approval.

41   Humphrey Morris, "Introduction," in Joseph H. Smith and Humphrey Morris, eds., *Telling Facts: History and Narration in Psychoanalysis* (Baltimore, 1992), p. xiv. Cited in Wurgaft, "Identity in World History," p. 72.

42   In a series of commonly authored as well as separately penned studies, they have developed this concept from the perspective of their respective fields, Jan – Egyptology; Aleida – comparative literature, although their purview is ultimately universal. See, for instance, Aleida and Jan Assmann, *Schrift und Gedächtnis: Beiträge zur Archäologie der literarischen Kommunikation* (Munich, 1987); and Jan Assmann, *Das kulturelle Gedächtnis. Schrift, Erinnerung und politische Identität in frühren Hochkulturen* (Munich, 1992).

43   J. Assmann, "Collective Memory and Cultural Identity," in *New German Critique*, no. 25 (Summer 1995), p. 132.

44   Ibid., p. 129.

45   Ibid.

46   Ibid., p. 131.

47   Ibid.

48   Assmann, *Das Kulturelle Gedächtnis*, pp. 293–301 and passim.

49   E. Said, *Culture and Imperialism* (New York, 1993), p. 15, cited in Silberstein and Cohn, *The Other in Jewish Thought and History*, pp. 7f.

50   Hannah Arendt, *The Origins of Totalitarianism* (New York, 1951), pp. 73–5.

51   Ibid., p. 75.

52   Ibid.

Bibliography

Abramov, S. Zalman, *Perpetual Dilemma. Jewish Religion in the State of Israel* (Rutherford, 1976).

Assmann, Aleida, *Arbeit am nationalen Gedächtnis. Eine kurze Geschichte der deutschen Bildungsidee* (Frankfurt am Main, 1993).

Assmann, Aleida, and Jan Assmann, *Schrift und Gedächtnis: Beiträge zür Archäologie der literarischen Kommunikation* (Munich, 1987).

Assmann, Jan, "Collective Memory and Cultural Identity," in *New German Critique*, no. 25 (Summer 1995).

Assmann, Jan, *Das kulturelle Gedächtnis. Schrift, Erinnerung und politische Identität in frühren Hochkulturen* (Munich, 1992).

Auron, Yair, "Jewish-Israeli Identity among Israel's Future Teachers," in *Jerusalem Letter/Viewpoints*, no. 334 (May 1, 1996), pp. 1–7.

Canetti, Elias, *The Human Province* (New York, 1978), p. 51.

Canetti, Elias, *Crowd and Power*, trans. Carol Stewart (New York, 1989).

Diner, Dan, "Cumulative Contingency: Historicizing Legitimacy in Israeli Discourse," in *History and Memory*, vol. 7, no. 1, pp. 147–70.

Dominguez, Virginia, *Peoples as Subject/People as Object: Selfhood and Peoplehood in Contemporary Israel* (Madison, 1989).

O'Flattery Doniger, Wendy, *Other Peoples' Myths: The Cave of Echoes* (New York, 1988).

Dresseer, David, and Lester D. Friedman, *American-Jewish Filmmakers. Traditions and Trends* (Urbana and Chicago, 1993).

Eisenstadt, Shmuel, *Jewish Civilization. The Jewish Historical Experience in a Comparative Perspective* (New York, 1993).

Eisenstadt, Shmuel, *The Transformation of Israeli Society. An Essay in Interpretation* (London, 1985).

Erikson, Erik H., "The Problem of Ego Identity (1956)," in M. R. Stein, A. J. Vidich, and D. M. White, eds., *Identity and Anxiety. Survival of the Person in Mass Society* (New York, 1960), pp. 37–87.

Fackenheim, Emil, *God's Presence in History. Jewish Affirmations and Philosophical Reflections* (New York, 1972).

Fackenheim, Emil, *The Jewish Return into History. Reflections in the Age of a New Jerusalem* (New York, 1978).

Finkelstein, Norman, *The Ritual of New Creation. Jewish Tradition and Contemporary Literature* (Albany, 1992).

Funkenstein, Amos, "The History of Israel among the Thorn Bush. History in the Light of Other Disciplines," in *Zion. The Journal of the Israeli Historical Association*, vol. 60, pp. 335–47.

Funkenstein, Amos, *Perspectives of Jewish History* (Berkeley, 1993).

Goldberg, David Theo, and Michael Krauz, *Jewish Identity* (Philadelphia, 1990).

Green, Arthur, *Devotion and Commandment. The Faith of Abraham in the Hasidic Imagination* (Cincinnati, 1989).

Gross, Feliks, and Balil J. Vlavianos, eds., *Struggle for Tomorrow. Modern Political Ideologies of the Jewish People* (New York, 1954).

Hermann, Simon, *Israelis and Jews. The Continuity of an Identity* (Philadelphia, 1970).

Hoenig, S., ed., *Jewish Identity: Modern Responsa and Opinions on the Registration of Children of Mixed Marriages. Ben-Gurion's Query to Leaders of World Jewry. A Documentary Compilation* (Jerusalem and New York, 1970).

Kaufmann, Walter, *Existentialism, Religion and Death. Essays* (New York, 1976), p. 167.

Landauer, Gustav, "Sind das Ketzergedanken?" in *Vom Judentum. Ein Sammelbuch*, ed. Verein Jüdischer Hochschuler Bar Kochba in Prag (Leipzig, 1913), pp. 250f.

Mendes-Flohr, Paul, and Jehuda Reinharz, *The Jew in the Modern World*, 2nd edn. (New York, 1995).

Mendes-Flohr, Paul, *Divided Passions. Jewish Intellectuals and the Experience of Modernity* (Detroit, 1991).

Meyer, Michael A., *Jewish Identity in the Modern World* (Seattle and London, 1990).

Mosse, Georg, *German Jews Beyond Judaism* (Bloomington, 1985).

Nochlin, Linda, and Tamar Garb, eds., *The Jew in the Text. Modernity and the Construction of Identity* (London, 1996).

Peled, Yoav, "Ethnic Democracy and the Legal Construction of Citizenship: Arabs Citizens of the State of Israel," in *American Political Science Review*, vol. 86, no. 2 (June 1992), pp. 434–43.

Said, E., *Culture and Imperialism* (New York, 1993).

Silberstein, Laurence J., and Robert L. Cohn, eds., *The Other in Jewish Thought and History. Constructions of Jewish Culture and Identity* (New York and London, 1994).

Vogel, Manfred, "Some Reflections on the Question of Jewish Identity," in *Journal of Reform Judaism*, XXX, no. 1 (Winter 1983), pp. 1–33.

Volkov, Shulamit, "The Jews among the Nations. A National Narrative or a Chapter within an Integrated History," in *Zion*, vol. 61, pp. 91–111.

Werblowsky, R. J. Zwi, *Beyond Tradition and Modernity. Changing Religions in a Changing World.* Jordan Lectures 1974 (London, 1976).

Wurgaft, Lewis D., "Identity in World History. A Postmodern Perspective," in *History and Theory* 34 (1995), pp. 67–85.

CHAPTER 26
Judaism and Zionism

Yosef Gorny

Zionism as a national movement has changed the political status of the Jewish people more than any other modern religious or secular movement in the last hundred years. Other modern movements, such as the Reform and Conservative religious movements, did contribute to the process of social and cultural integration and normalization in western democratic emancipated societies. The Jewish socialist movement, especially the Marxist party, the Bund, was also an integrating force in bringing together Jewish workers in the general socialist movement. But unlike Zionism, these movements were only partial solutions for the western Jewish middle class or the Jewish proletariat, especially in eastern Europe. Zionism, on the contrary, proposed from its beginning to normalize the political status of the Jewish people by creating a national society in their historic homeland that would become the center of Jewish existence.

Because of its success in normalizing many aspects in Jewish life, Zionism is one of the three historical "nation-building frames" of the Jewish people: The first is *spiritual* – the idea of the chosen people, the bearers of monotheism; the second is *legal* – the establishment of the Rabbinical law as a unique way of continuing their collective existence in spite of dispersion; the third is *political* – the territorial sovereignty in the State of Israel, where a new national form of the Jewish people is being shaped.

In this political aspect – to borrow Lincoln's famous phrase – Zionism is a movement of the Jewish people, by the Jewish people, and for the Jewish people. "Of" because, in spite of the fact that the Zionists represented a minority among Jews, the Zionist movement was and remains the largest modern movement, the most global one, the most pluralistic, and the most democratic. "By" because its effort for the past hundred years has brought all members of the nation to participate in building the national home and because it still continues at the present time (Spring 2000) to involve immigrants from Russia and the independent republics, as well as Ethiopia, to participate in its building. "For" because the State of Israel as a Jewish state by the Law of Return is open to every Jew who needs it for any reason.

But, paradoxically, these achievements – absorbing millions of *olim* (immigrants), sustaining a democratic regime, and maintaining a Jewish character – have brought Zionists to a problematic crossroad. There is a three-fold tension. The first achievement – absorbing Jews from various cultures all over the world – is generating continual cultural and social changes. The second achievement – sustaining a democracy – becomes politically problematic because of the multiplication of political parties. The third achievement – maintaining a Jewish character – involves the special interference of religious parties in politics. And, finally, there is the growing tension concerning the meaning of the ties that bind the Jewish State with the Jews who live in the free diasporas. These tensions belong specifically to the present but are not new at all. The historical truth is that crises and critical situations have been a part of Zionism from its beginning.

Like every long-lived social movement, Zionism has undergone during its century of existence so many crises that its history can be classified accordingly. The Hibbat Zion era ended in a crisis of leadership, which began in the early 1890s. Pinsker died in 1891, disillusioned with the prospects for Jewish settlement in Palestine; the waning of the second wave of immigration in that same year (because of restrictions imposed by the Ottoman authorities) seemed to confirm his pessimism. Herzl's inspiring debut in 1897 ended in bitter polemics on the question of settlement in Uganda, and he died after only seven years of activity within the Zionist movement. The days of glory of Weizmannite Zionism – from the Balfour Declaration in 1917 to the establishment of the Jewish Agency in 1929 – also terminated in a profound political crisis with the British government and in an internal dispute within the Zionist movement, which led eventually to the reluctant resignation of Weizmann from presidency of the movement. The *sturm und drang* of the 1930s, when immigration flowed into Palestine and settlements sprang up all over the country, ended in the partition controversy that threatened to split the Zionist movement and in the 1939 White Paper, which aimed to repudiate Great Britain's commitment to the Zionist movement with the establishment of a Palestinian state. The mass mobilization of American Jewry for the political struggle for statehood and their financial aid to support immigrant absorption came to an end in a spirit of mutual recrimination and estrangement between Israel and the diaspora, which lasted from the mid-1950s until the Six Day War.

The five decades of statehood have also been marked by periodic crises, but there is a fundamental difference between the pre-state and the post-state crises. The former resulted from the weakness of the Zionist movement and political circumstances it was powerless to change; the latter were the result, paradoxically enough, of the Zionist movement's strengths. During the past two generations, Zionism became the greatest collective achievement of the Jewish people throughout their history. At the same time, the Jews of the free world have won individual achievements on a scale unparalleled in diaspora history.

The dual achievements of Zionism and of diaspora Jewry are not necessarily at odds, but in certain historic situations they can give rise to conflict. First of all, the collective achievement of establishing a state and guaranteeing its survival in a troubled region of the world places a heavy burden on its individuals, by forcing on them the economic, political, and military burden of the collective Jewish interests.

Second, the social revolution wrought by a mass immigration that brought Jews from east and west together to form a core of Jewish historical action for the first time in Jewish history has led to a cultural transformation of that society. The new social reality, reflected in lifestyle and quality of life, is of great concern to many of those who have achieved personal success in the West and in Israel. When Jews in search of individual success and prosperity prefer to migrate to the United States instead of to Israel, Zionism's prestige is dimmed and the reputation of the state suffers. But this is so because the Zionist state reflects the collective will of the people by observing the Law of Return. And, finally, the fact that Zionism has succeeded in restoring to the Jewish people their ancient political and spiritual center arouses great expectations in the hearts of successful Jews abroad, expectations that, because of their intensity, can be transformed swiftly into deep disillusionment.

This disillusionment, still confined to a fraction of diaspora Jews, is expressed in the tendency to question the very principle of the centrality of Israel in Jewish life. It is altering the focus of the Jewish collective effort, which was once directed toward Israel and on Israel's behalf, toward the development of other Jewish centers coexisting with Israel and of equal standing. These ideas, although held only by a minority of Jews, should not be dismissed lightly because they enfold a threat.

At the present time, these ideas seem to confirm Dubnow's views on the proliferation of Jewish centers and the shift from place to place throughout history. Yet, in a world in which Jews are integrated and involved in the culture of their countries of residence, this neo-Dubnowianism could develop into a kind of neo-Bundism and to a gradual erosion of the belief in the unity of one Jewish people throughout the world. In other words, this trend may not lead to the flowering of Jewish cultural autonomy in the countries in which Jews live, as Dubnow or the Bund leaders believed, but may cause the total assimilation of Jewish ethnic groups into the pluralistic societies of their countries of residence and a loss of their national common denominator. This trend, essentially anti-Zionist, is still confined, ideologically, to an intellectual minority but is latent and subconscious, in the social sense, among the Jewish masses in the diaspora and in Israel.

In light of this trend, is Zionist ideology still necessary? This query leads us to one of the central issues for understanding the roots and ideology of the Zionist movement. It is worth pondering to what extent this movement is the outcome of necessity and how much it is the product of free ideological choice. In other words, which ephemeral historical elements and which meta-historical elements exist and operate within it?

Zionism was undoubtedly born out of the political and economic predicament of the Jews of eastern Europe, and was greatly influenced by the national and social ideologies prevailing in nineteenth-century Europe. But it was not only necessity or cultural milieu that determined its essence and its destiny: it is a fact that want and persecution led the masses of Jewish immigrants from eastern Europe to the United States and not to Eretz Israel. The awakening of nationalist feeling in Europe aroused other forms of Jewish nationalism apart from Zionism. Jewish territorialism sought to establish a Jewish state in a more congenial territory than Palestine. Autonomism, the brainchild of Dubnow, advocated the establishment of Jewish cultural autonomy in Jewish centers in the diaspora, and even the Bund had its own socialist-national outlook. Zionism was distinctive among these ideologies in that it offered an absolute alternative, based on freedom of choice.

The basic principles of this choice were the following: return to the historic homeland in the land of Israel, settlement on the land and control of all economic spheres, creation of a Jewish majority in the country, and revival of the Hebrew language as the national tongue of the people. All these goals were contradictory to the processes developing objectively throughout the world, namely the flow of migration from the agricultural nations to the industrial ones. Elsewhere, the masses were moving from village to city, and among the Jews the trend was toward increasing socio-cultural integration in their countries of residence or places of migration. From this we may learn that Zionism, in essence, is not only the fruit of reality but also the personification of a rebellion against reality. This revolt was expressed in ideas and in actions.

The "rebels" were the naive settlers of the First Aliyah, who chose the difficult path of founding colonies and rejected the easier path of urban life in the older Jewish urban communities. They were followed by the young activists of the Second Aliyah, who launched a struggle on behalf of "Hebrew labor" in defiance of economic logic. With their inspiration and guidance, the Third Aliyah settlers implemented the idea of "constructive socialism," both by founding the General Federation of Labor, which differed from any other labor federation in the world, and by establishing the cooperative settlement movement. By these actions they rebelled against reality in the name of utopia and created a model of realistic utopianism, which became a driving and constructive social force. These Zionist rebels included the teachers who revived the Hebrew language through protracted efforts as well as the leaders of the Zionist movement who succeeded, by unconventional means, in transforming objective weakness into subjective political force.

This "rebellious" aspect of Zionism brings to light another paradox inherent in the movement. The Zionist movement restored the Jewish people to its history by means of a strong will and by measures that were, to a large extent, super-historical: thus, its fate was determined not by the changes wrought by time and place but, rather, by the strong will and high aspirations of the Jewish people. However, this statement does not answer the cardinal question: Is Zionism necessary to Jews in their present situation? I believe that we can answer this question only after clarifying the basic ideological essence of Zionism.

From the outset – the Hibbat Zion era – Zionism was a pluralistic movement that, based on consensus, succeeded in concentrating within itself various and conflicting ideological currents and political groups: religious and secular, political and practical, socialist and middle-class, liberal and totalitarian. The grounds for consensus agreed upon by most of those participating in the movement were the principles of the Zionist revolt, as follows: the return to the land of Israel, the historic homeland of the Jewish people; creation of a Jewish majority in the land of Israel as the expression and guarantee of change in the historic status of the people; creation of a normal Jewish economy as the condition for independence of the national society; and the revival of the Hebrew language as the supreme stage in cultural renaissance. Beyond these basic tenets, opinions were divided on every ideological and political issue. Even on the question of attitudes toward the *golah* – diaspora – there was no single viewpoint. Ostensibly, Zionism, insofar as it aimed at establishing a society that would be the antithesis of the diaspora, should have negated the diaspora absolutely. But this was not the case. Zionism negated the diaspora in the sense that it denied that it would be able to survive only on the strength of its own powers, as an entity with Jewish identity, but in practice there was no consensus as to its fate, namely that it was destined to disappear.

On this point, Ahad Ha'am and Herzl differed from the outset. Ahad Ha'am sought a way of preserving the Jewish character of the *golah*, because he did not anticipate its physical disappearance, while Herzl, who despaired of the idea of Jewish integration in European society, advocated the exodus of the majority of European Jews. Paradoxically enough, although Herzlian Zionism became the predominant trend in the pre-state movement, it was Ahad Ha'am's views on the future of the diaspora that prevailed. In other words, the various trends in Zionism, from the moderate to the activist and radical, perceived immigration to Eretz Israel to be a practical solution only for part of the Jewish people.

Furthermore, the demand for territorial concentration in Palestine and the creation of a Jewish majority was not perceived as dependent on the immigration of the large part of the Jewish people. Zionism always took a selective view of the diaspora, related primarily to the predicament of eastern European Jewry. The Jews of western Europe, and particularly the United States, were not considered candidates for immigration; and the Jews of Asia and Africa did not constitute a problem at that time. In the 1930s, when the plight of Europe's Jews worsened, Weizmann and Greenbaum anticipated the immigration of one to two million Jews from that continent. Shortly before his death in 1940, Jabotinsky envisioned a Jewish state of five million Jewish citizens and two million Arabs. After the 1942 Biltmore Conference, Ben-Gurion spoke of the immediate immigration of two million Jewish refugees to the future Jewish state. But, by the fifties he was no longer confident that the vision of the ingathering of the exiles would be realized where American Jews were concerned.

At the same time, inherent in Zionism was a qualitative "negation of the *golah*" that stemmed from the fundamental Zionist view of diaspora life and the alternative Zionism hoped to offer. Ahad Ha'am negated cultural assimilation, or what he called "slavery within freedom," the condition of the Jews of the free western countries. Chaim Weizmann condemned the lack of aesthetic sense among eastern European Jews in the widest meaning of the term. Jabotinsky abhorred *galut* life as lacking dignity and self-pride. The labor movement rejected the parasitic element in Jewish life in the diaspora, the total and undignified dependence of the Jews on their surroundings. In short, "negation of the *golah*" in Zionism, with the exclusion of Herzl, was relative and linked to time and place. This being so, one cannot accept the reverse of "negation of *golah*," namely, "negation of Zionism," which is based on the argument that in the light of the fact that the diaspora did not wane after the establishment of Israel, Zionist ideology is no longer valid. This view of the confrontation between the Zionist and diaspora ideologies emphasizes their mutual negation. It should be stressed that this view does not imply opposition to the state or even its depreciation. The reverse is true. The very connection with the state becomes an argument that Zionism is not really necessary.

Since Israel came into being, its ties with diaspora Jews have strengthened, despite problems and upheavals. Israel is still the central public interest of diaspora Jews, a kind of "religion," common to secular and religious Jews. But, together with this profound identification, there is a natural tendency to distinguish between the value of the state and the value of Zionism in the context of Jewish interests. Whereas the distinction between the sovereign State of Israel and the Zionist Organization, whose members are citizens of other countries, is essential for political reasons, the distinction between the Jewish state and Zionist ideology is artificial and spurious.

The Zionist–Jewish combination is built into the essence of the State and finds expression in its everyday life. It constitutes the territorial–national framework, guaranteeing the continuum of Jewish life with its religious and secular aspects. As an open refuge for all Jews in trouble, it maintains in practice the value of mutual responsibility. The centrality of the state in the consciousness of Jews – reflected both in their concern for it and their quarrels with it, their support for it and their reservations – reinforces Jewish unity and identity, which is the basis of Zionism, as laid down by Herzl. Thus, when the Jews of the diaspora define their devotion to the State as a form of Zionism, this view should neither be belittled nor dismissed as hypocritical and self-indulgent.

Ostensibly, it is the almost unconditional support of diaspora Jews for Israel that demonstrates the validity of Zionist ideology for our times as well. One could interpret this identification, against the general background and the objective developments of today, as an inner need. There is an element of truth in this, but it is not the whole truth. This need stems from the unique lives of western Jewry who are preoccupied with the question of their own freedom, but it lacks the element of the conscious rebellion, which was once the symbol of Zionism. In other words, the Jews of the West are living in a society that not only allots respected status to the Jewish religion but also sanctions ethnicity. Ethnic pluralism is the cultural–psychological norm in the free countries. And, as such, it offers a new and different path to assimilation in non-Jewish society.

Henceforth, in order to become part of general society, there is no longer any need to convert to Christianity or to deny Jewish culture. On the contrary, to maintain a degree of ethnic distinctiveness is the respected and accepted way to total assimilation.

The significance of this trend is that, in the final analysis, the traditional-Jewish character, which on principle was separate and distinct, will be forfeited. One might say that the ethnic trend among Jews is an expression of objective processes occurring within the general society. These processes may cause the Jewish sense of unity to deviate from the idea of the center in Israel, towards the Dubnowian theory and thence to the Bundist ideology. Anyone who rejects this possibility must choose Zionism instead.

Because of the need for Zionism, for the preservation of universal Jewishness, it is incumbent on us to clarify its suitability for this task by examining the essence of the Zionist praxis as a movement operating within history. Let it be stated at once: Zionism was never a religious faith or an ideological doctrine, though such elements existed in many of the ideological groups that composed it. In general, however, Zionism was always the reverse of doctrinarian. Its power lay in the ability to adapt its ideals to changing conditions and to select the right means and instruments for their implementation – all this without losing sight of the main goal. Therefore, over three generations – from Hibbat Zion to statehood – it changed its priorities and shifted its trends without deviating from its path. First, political Zionism replaced Hibbat Zion; then constructive Zionism, headed by Weizmann and implemented by the socialist labor movement, dominated it in the 1920s; from the mid-thirties, in the period of national emergency, the main concern was the struggle for the survival of the Yishuv, which developed into the fight for statehood; after the state was established, it became a movement whose overt and proclaimed aim had been achieved and Jewish sovereignty became its main concern. Each period was characterized by its unique mood.

The Hibbat Zion period was colored by the romanticism of intellectuals who "saw the light"; political Zionism by the aspiration for normalization; constructive Zionism by social utopianism; in the time of national emergency, the mood was one of readiness for combat; and in the era of statehood, the desire to consolidate the patterns of life of an independent society. I believe that we are now on the threshold of a new movement – post-sovereignty.

In the year 2000, Jewish life is characterized worldwide by two conflicting features. On the one hand, world Jewry has never been so united in the political sense; and, on the other, Judaism has never before been so divided culturally. Political unity is fostered by concern for Israel, concern for Soviet Jewry, a vigilant stand against neo-Fascist tendencies, etc. But all these are, by nature, transient issues. The cultural dimension, on the other hand, is durable and profound. In effect, Judaism is split up into a number of trends and increasingly divided on questions of conversion, mixed marriages, and the Law of Return; Jews who are an integral part of their countries of residence and those who are citizens of their own sovereign state; Jewish communities speaking different languages, who not only enjoy the culture of their countries but contribute to it as well; and in the last generation the tension between Holocaust and state consciousness.

The present balance between political unity and cultural division may be disrupted some day because of the changing character of the former and the durability and increasing intensity of the latter. In the face of these trends, those Jews who wish to preserve their Jewish identity as a people with its own distinctive character require an ideology of revolt against objective reality. Of all the trends and movements that have struggled in the past to preserve Jewish distinctiveness and continue to do so, Zionism is the most comprehensive. Extreme orthodoxy represents only a small part of the people, and the more fanatic this minority becomes, the more it promotes division. The modern religious trend, Reform and Conservative, has attracted only a part of the Jewish people. Secular Jews are left without guiding ideology apart from their political support for Israel. Zionism as a pluralistic movement succeeded in the past and can in the present embrace various conflicting trends on the basis of a common denominator. But in order to do so it needs to place at the core of Jewish consciousness an idea that has been deeply repressed until now.

In its century of existence, Zionist thought and action have emphasized the trend to national normalization. This was true of the idea of the return to the historic homeland, the return to physical labor and productivization of the masses, the establishment of a socialist society, the political struggle for the right to self-determination, the desire to achieve sovereignty for the Yishuv, etc. The anomalous element was reflected mainly in the measures adopted in order to implement these trends. Thus the return to nature became an ideal, and physical labor became a value ("the religion of labor"), the class struggle was transformed into constructive socialism, the national commitment of the labor movement took the form of an effort to achieve a cooperative utopia, and the migration movement aspired to become an "ingathering of the exiles." The anomalous means maintained normal tendencies and without them the goals could not have been achieved. Without agricultural settlement, "Hebrew labor," the kibbutz movement, and the ideology of ingathering of the exiles, the state could not have come into being and could not have survived. But in the course of history, the anomality of the means has been overwhelmed by the normality of the tendencies, and society in the Jewish state increasingly resembles other societies. Now, in light of the prevailing situation, the time has come to reverse the order of things. The Jewish people should face the challenge of anomalous trends, which should be achieved through normal deeds.

For those diaspora Jews who wish it, the consolidation of the sense of distinctiveness in a society that is becoming increasingly uniform entails elevating ethnic consciousness to the sphere of overall national consciousness. Such consciousness will constitute a kind of declaration that the Jewish people is one, although Jews for the most part are not concentrated in their national territory; are not for the most part religious; speak many languages and live in diverse cultures; and this being so, the Jewish people does not intend to submit to objective development. Just as their forefathers fought in the name of religious injunctions, they now rebel in the name of national principles. Such a revolt demands intensified awareness of *galut*.

Golah, in the political and economic sense, disappeared when the Jews were given a choice between immigrating to their national home or remaining in their countries of birth. For those who chose the diaspora, the sense of *galut* is the condition for their Judaism – *galut* not in the overall social meaning, namely a place where injustice prevails, nor in the traditional-religious sense of exile of the Divine Presence (*Shekhina*) and anticipation of the messianic era, but *galut* as the historic experience of an extraordinary people, who are a minority wherever they live and struggle for collective survival. This sense of *galut* is not universal but distinctively national.

The rebellious desire of the Jews to maintain their national unity leads, by internal logic, to acknowledgment of the State of Israel as their center – a scattered people, without a cultural and territorial framework, needs a focus where its parts can come together. No diaspora can substitute for Israel's historic function. But, according to that same principle of unity, just as the Jews of the diaspora must promote the center, Israel must encourage autonomous, cultural and ideological trends in the diaspora. This will create the abnormal balance between mutual dependence and independence.

Acknowledgment of the centrality of Israel requires that a distinction be drawn between the state as an *etatist* organization with vital normal functions and natural weaknesses, stemming from the very fact of its activity within history, and the state as guarantor and preserver of Jewish values, as an "open refuge," as the guardian of historical tradition, bolstering the unity of the people and demonstrating the change in the status of the Jews.

This discourse on Zionist ideology in the historical process is defined specifically by the relations between two centers: the American Jewry and the State of Israel – relations that are reflecting on the relations with other diasporas – western Europe and Russia today.

The clearest example of this was the American Jewish response to the events of 1967 – twenty years after the political struggle for the founding of the State of Israel. The tension that gripped diaspora Jewry before the war began, and the release of this tension in an eruption of enthusiasm and emotion after the victory, united the Jewish masses around Israel and placed it in the center of their collective consciousness. It is worth noting that the consciousness of Jewish nationhood, unlike that of Jewish religious existence, had begun to strengthen and solidify in the 1930s with the Nazi accession to power in Germany. This consciousness manifested itself in futile, desperate attempts to assist the Jews who were being slaughtered in Europe, and in the comprehensive economic, political, and national effort to create a Jewish state in Palestine. It suffices to note the change in the attitude of the Reform movement and the American Jewish Committee toward Zionism and the establishment of a Jewish state. This process, however, came to its conclusion when Israel was established, and for almost a generation, between 1948 and 1967, centrifugal trends became evident in the interaction between American Jewry and the State of Israel. This is why the Jewish public awakening shortly before and after the Six Day War was so astonishing. It displayed conspicuously national tones, embraced much of the leadership, and opened a new chapter in the history of the Jewish collective's vacillations on the subject of its collective identity.

According to sociologists, the Six Day War gave rise to a kind of civil religion among American Jews: the concern for and almost total identification with the State of Israel. The radical groups that evolved in this period exhibited this phenomenon with particular salience. I am referring to Jewish student organizations that broke away from the general organization – the Students for a Democratic Society – and various groups of intellectuals known as neo-conservatives.

Among the student organizations were groups of Socialist Zionists, Bundists, *havurot* that sought to revitalize the religious culture, liberal activists who wished to democratize the Jewish community institutions, and so on. Although they differed in their social conceptual outlooks and their internal and external politics, they attained a common denominator by reinvigorating and reinforcing the national consciousness. Their modus operandi was an active reference to the historical past, meant to restore historical continuity. This explains their intensive preoccupation with the heritage of eastern European Jewry. In this sense, members of the third generation were unlike their parents of the second generation, who wished to soft-pedal their collective identity.

The innovation in these young people's activism also manifested itself in an integration of nationalist radicalism and social radicalism, based on criticism of American society. Jewish radicals of the preceding generation had denounced the complexion of this society but totally disregarded Jewish nationhood. In contrast, the Jewish youngsters of the 1960s, unlike their peers in the radical student movements, combined Jewish zealotry with social extremism. Paradoxically, they became the most visible advocates of Jewish normalization. Their important contribution to the consciousness of collective identity is their explicit, forceful recognition of the Jewish people as a nation. Their declaration of the existence of a common Jewish national interest in the universal sense prompted them to assert, unequivocally, the legitimacy of the Jewish national interest in the United States.

The perspective of the neo-conservatives, many of whose outstanding exponents had belonged to far-left groupings in the 1940s and 1950s, may be summarized as follows:

1   Jews are regarded as a "normal" people that behaves in history in the conventional manner of other peoples and nations. For example, they see no contradiction between the State of Israel's strong-arm stance *vis-à-vis* the Arabs and the Jewish value system, a contradiction asserted by many young members of the radical wing.
2   The center of Jewry in matters of statehood is the State of Israel, on which the continued existence of Jewry depends.

3   The collective Jewish interest in all social, cultural, and political respects, in the United States and Israel, is legitimized.
4   The lesson of the Holocaust is advanced primarily as a symbol of national identity and secondly as a moral message to the nations.
5   Jewish tradition is important in preserving the nation's unity and ensuring its survival.

Paradoxically, the two groups had a national common denominator despite their political and social differences in outlook. Both preached the legitimacy of Jewish ethnic and national interests. Both recognized the existence of a Jewish national entity with the Jewish state as its center. Both perceived the Holocaust as a commandment to sustain Jewish national life and to maintain military and political power as the modalities that would assure this life. By combining the two perspectives, nationalism and indigenous American patriotism reflect the Jews' integration into American society.

It is worth noting that the Holocaust underscored the massive identification with the fate of the Jewish state as a message for both the masses and the intellectuals. The slogan "Never Again" made vast inroads, and the awareness that the survival and continued welfare of the Jewish people – in its own state and in the diaspora – represents Jewry's great victory over those who sought to annihilate it in the past and those who wish to harm it in the future became dominant in intellectual circles.

The phenomenon recurred in the Yom Kippur War of 1973. This time, however, in view of the progression of events and the aftermath of the war, it was marked by a lack of fervor and a profound concern that clung to the Jewish population for quite some time. This war sharpened the American Jews' sense of the catastrophe of the Holocaust and the possibility of its recurrence. Consequently, there ensued a slow but persistent and significant erosion in their faith in Israel as the last refuge and stronghold of the Jewish people as a national entity.

Here we reach a point that requires special elucidation, because it reveals the complexity of the perspective espoused by the pro-unity Jewish circles that struggled for the integrity of Jewry as a people with its own distinctive features.

Immediately after the establishment of the state, as the War of Independence still raged, two integrative perspectives began to coalesce. The first, which I define as "distinctive normalization," stressed the favorable aspects of Jewish existence in the diaspora. It accepted the State of Israel as the historical Jewish center but not the only center on which diaspora Jews rely. Their example was the Second Temple period. The Alexandria–Jerusalem relationship – or the Babylonia–Palestine relationship after the destruction of the Second Temple – was balanced and mutual, a worthy model for emulation under the new circumstances that had come about after the establishment of the State. They considered this situation normal in view of the cultural and social realities of the United States, where each ethnic group maintained some degree of affiliation with its country of origin. In their opinion, the distinctiveness of this relationship for Jews had a scope and intensity unknown among other ethnic groups.

According to this perspective, the nature of Jewry is purely religious and cultural. One may say that most of the diaspora leadership elite, both Zionist and non-Zionist, particularly in the United States, espoused this viewpoint.

The second integrating perspective may be termed, paradoxically, "Jewish normalization." That is to say, it stressed the particular, aberrant elements of Jewish existence until they became its norm. The advocates of this perspective were the Israeli leadership, most of the Israeli intelligentsia, and a minority of diaspora Zionists. From their point of view, Exile in its conceptual, symbolic, and intellectual aspects is a permanent element in the Jewish identity. They asserted that consciousness of Exile and yearning for redemption are intertwined. They regarded world Jewry primarily as a nation tied to its national center, the State of Israel. They claimed that without this tie, the Jewish collective has no future either in Israel or anywhere in the diaspora.

In the practical sense of political relations, non-Zionist organizations such as the American Jewish Committee feared attempts by Israel to posture internationally as representing the overall interests of world Jewry. Until 1967, when the new generation of American Jews made its advent, the community was concerned about being accused of "dual loyalties." Even the Zionist leaders demanded a measure of restraint and dichotomization of the Jewish state and the Jewish diaspora. In their opinion, the Zionist movement should represent diaspora Jewry, independently of Israel, and the bilateral relationship of the two entities should express and maintain the unity of the people.

The roots of these attitudes were grounded in contrasting doctrines: Palestino-centric Zionism and Dubnow-type nationalism. One sought to focus all Jewish effort on behalf of Israel and in Israel as the dominant – and the only – Jewish center. The other presupposed the existence of various centers throughout history, some successive and others coterminous. In political terms, this controversy ended with the victory of the non-Zionist "diasporist" approach. The State of Israel and the Zionist movement acknowledged that they do not represent diaspora Jewry. In practical terms, a cooperative equilibrium of sorts came into being between the two. Indeed, diaspora Jewry has helped Israel not only politically but also by raising most of the funds needed to absorb the mass immigration during the first post-independence years. As noted above, the Six Day War upset this equilibrium. From 1967 to the early 1980s, Israel stood at the center of the Jewish collective consciousness. Therefore, these years may be termed the "statist" period.

During this period, when Israel was so central in the Jewish collective consciousness that according to several researchers it became the Jewish "civil religion," the surrogate or complement of this consciousness, Holocaust consciousness, had already begun to germinate among Jews. This consciousness, relegated to the fringes of public awareness, originated in the anxious and tense days of the Six Day War and the Yom Kippur War. This is particularly evident during the latter conflict, when, understandably although somewhat unjustifiably, the mythos and ethos of the Six Day War was shattered. The sense of dread during the protracted war turned into profound concern for Israel's future in view of the crisis of confidence that gripped Israeli society *vis-à-vis* its traditional civilian and military leadership, in which it had formerly placed unreserved trust.

This set in motion a dynamic process that lasted approximately a decade, in which Holocaust consciousness supplanted Israel consciousness, to some extent, as the focus of collective attention and the core of the Jewish "civil religion." As noted, this process originated in rapt concern for Israel's future and fear that it would suffer a new Holocaust. The next step was taken in the realm of public thought, i.e. the deliberate attempt by intellectuals to build these feelings into a collective *weltanschauung*. Their opinions, expressed in articles, panel discussions, and in the Jewish press, also reached the national press. The intellectuals' collective thinking – a blend of historico-philosophical meditation, theological ideas, national thinking, and political trends – contributed to the cultural institutionalization of Holocaust consciousness. I refer here to Holocaust studies that were inserted into the curricula of hundreds of Judaic studies programs in American universities. Even more influential on Jewish and non-Jewish public opinion, however, was a television series of questionable quality and content, *Shoah*, which was screened in the late 1970s in the United States and elsewhere. This led to the establishment of Holocaust study centers, particularly the memorial museums that were established in major cities of the United States. The more popular the phenomenon became, the more vigorously it replaced content with symbols. This explains the proliferation of museums, the largest and most important in Washington, D.C., and the expeditions of youth to the extermination camps in Poland.

Since the early 1980s, American intellectuals have been debating the significance of this development for the image, and the self-image, of the Jewish people. This controversy is waged by the advocates of three approaches, each with its vested interest in the aforementioned issue of paths to normalization.

One approach attempts to ascribe absolute universal significance to the Holocaust. According to this view, the Jewish sufferings and catastrophe are no different from the genocide of the Armenians during World War I, the slaughter of the Biafrans, the devastation caused by the atomic bomb in Japan – even the massacres of the Native American Indians by European settlers in various periods of time in North and South America. This approach may be defined as markedly centrifugal.

At the opposite extreme is a clearly centripetal approach, which emphasizes the collective experience that unites the Jewish people, arising from the lessons and uniqueness of the Holocaust and from the world-view that that experience is casting into a national consciousness. Some even try to endow the Holocaust with religious significance. This mindset, typical of right-wing groups in Israel and the United Stated, fosters a mentality of national siege in a world that is socio-culturally open. It believes, for example, that the impending destruction will come not only from the Arabs who encircle Israel but also from the western world, which is as willing today as it was in the past to abandon the Jews to their fate. Thus, the practical inference is to seek military might and political radicalization in Israel and political power for Jews in the United States and elsewhere in the diaspora.

The third basic approach lies halfway between the first two. Favored by moderate liberals and some conservatives, it notes the inherent historical error that the radical liberals make by attempting to cast the Holocaust in a purely universal light, but it also warns against the opposite approach, the ultra-national attitude that effectively tries to drive a wedge of consciousness between Jews and the surrounding society. As stated, they disregard neither the Jewish uniqueness of the Holocaust nor several implications that derive from it, such as the need for a politically and militarily strong Jewish state, but they express concern at the growing tendency to exchange the drive to foster Jewish intellectual endeavor for an effort, which is also growing, to put the Jews' suffering and fate on public display.

Be this as it may, each of the three approaches strives to attain a different kind of normalization based on the lessons of the Holocaust. The first: normalization through integration; the second: normalization through strength; and the third: normalization by incorporating the past into the present.

The contemporary historian, although accustomed to tracing the social and spiritual changes in Jewish history of the past century, some caused by exogenous factors and others endogenous, cannot but marvel at the speed of change in recent generations. The most important change in the last decade has been the shift in the focus of national identification from the State to the Holocaust. Therefore, this transformation deserves an explanation, albeit a partial one, even one based more on impressions than on methodical research.

The fact that the focus on the Holocaust has become a common denominator of diaspora and Israeli Jewry, and even more characteristically and interestingly, as a recent study shows, between Israelis of European and of Asian/African origin, points to the different ways in which the State and the Holocaust are perceived in the Jewish collective consciousness. One may say that it is ideologically, politically, and psychologically more convenient and expedient to identify with the Holocaust than with Israel. Now that the controversy over the expression "like sheep to the slaughter" has ceased, and now that the dust has settled from two internecine battles – between historians and community leaders over the Jewish leadership's attitude during the war, and concerning evaluations of the activities of the Judenrats on the one hand and the underground and resistance on the other – a kind of equilibrium has been established. Because this development includes an equilibrium or reconciliation of the terms "Holocaust" and "heroism," all of Jewry is able to unite around its catastrophe.

Thus the myth of the Jewish masses' silent valor *vis-à-vis* their tragic fate is generated. This myth leaves no room for speculators and profiteers, for those who frequented the nightclubs and the parties of the Warsaw Ghetto – even if they constituted a tiny minority. This myth has no room for Judenrat members who were partial in meting out suffering and death, nor for the Jewish ghetto police who aided the Germans' genocide, nor for the *kapos* in the death camps who helped impose the Nazi reign of terror, whether for personal interest or because their impulses had taken them over. The mortification and rage of the Jewish masses also find their place in the new mythology. Paradoxically, the expressions "like sheep to the slaughter" and "skin and bones" have become weapons to use in castigating the Zionist leadership, the institutionalized Yishuv, and, in particular, the Labor movement. No one has the interest or patience to consider the origin of these terms: they were coined not by those who dwelled securely in Palestine but by Abba Kovner and Emmanuel Ringelblum in the ghettos. Nor is anyone inclined to understand that the term "skin and bones," irrespective of its bad taste at the time, was meant not to disparage the few survivors but to describe the state of deterioration – actual or imaginary and temporary – that the Holocaust had caused. Ben-Gurion thought this definition was also applicable to American Jewry.

These are some of the symbols of the "civil religion": fostering and identifying with the memory of the catastrophe, pilgrimage to murder sites, assiduous study of books and sources that describe what took place, and the adducing of historico-philosophical and even theological lessons.

How did the Holocaust dislodge the State of Israel as the focus of centrality? It happened not only because of the natural and sincere intensity of popular emotion that accompanies the Holocaust consciousness but also because of the inevitable difficulties the State of Israel encountered on the path it has taken. Political life amid history is a continuous process of shattering myths and disillusionment with utopias. This makes the idealization of daily affairs unsustainable, unlike the potency of idealization by mythologizing a past that does not extend into the present.

Unlike Holocaust consciousness, statehood consciousness sows controversy and tension among Jews. The question of Israel's security and image has divided and continues to divide the Jewish people, both in Israel and in the diaspora, into "hawks" and "doves." By its very definition, the Jewish state has exacerbated the schisms among the Jewish religious streams – Orthodox, Conservative, and Reform – in the interpretation and validation of religious law and in questions of the equality of their status in the Jewish state.

Quite paradoxically, it was the success of Zionism and the State that created the internal tensions that beset Israel today. The masses of Jews from Muslim countries have not yet completely integrated into a society whose cultural die had largely been cast before they arrived. They find it hard to blend into the eastern European Zionist tradition, with all this implies: the past in the diaspora, the Palestinian Yishuv, the path to statehood, and the shaping of a sovereign society. Although motivated to integrate, they find it easier to identify with Jewish tradition and the memory of the Holocaust as a pan-Jewish tragedy than with a modern Zionist ideology rooted in countries and cultures that are not theirs. Even the youth – alienated, rightly or wrongly, from the democratic manifestations and ways of life of Israel – find it easier to accept the message of the significance of nationhood through the genuine emotion and profound experience that the death-camp visits afford them. This phenomenon is likely to

recur with the immigrants from the former Soviet Union, for whom the existence of the State is totally alien.

Such an atmosphere no longer leaves room for an even-handed assessment
of Israel's historical achievements and situation. There is no place for the view
that Israel's suffering originates not in its failures but rather in its relative successes, as manifested in an ingathering of exiles that has yet to result in their
fusion, the maintenance of democracy even where a liberal atmosphere is as yet
lacking, and the sane attitude of the majority toward the Arab minority even if
war shows its cruel face time and again. Despite the internal and external problems that buffet this society, which has been living in a state of emergency since
the 1930s and has faced the absorption of immigrants on a scale unprecedented
in human history – despite all this, a culture of sanity is taking shape. All in all,
in comparison with the other radical movements that surfaced in nineteenth-
century Europe, and in comparison with other nations embroiled in existential
national struggles with other cohesive nations, the Jewish state need not feel
itself inferior or accept humiliation.

Consequently, of the two major events that influence the image of the Jewish
people today – the State of Israel and the Holocaust – the disaster, by revealing
a general national impotence, has triumphed over the manifestations of collective audacity and achievement. The consciousness of national renascence seems
to have lost more than the consciousness of the Holocaust has gained. In the
long term, this may present a threat to Jewish unity, a unity that will not
amount to much unless Israel commands centrality in national consciousness
and is recognized as the most reliable representative, among all other Jewish
collectivities, of the people's collective interest. Failing this, despite the Holocaust commemoration that ostensibly unites the Jewish people, a process of
national fragmentation will occur with growing speed, as Ahad Ha'am warned
almost a century ago.

It is memory that fashions the image of a people. Recollection of the Exodus,
the destruction of the Temple, martyrdom, the expulsion from Spain, the
Chmielnicki pogroms – all of these, coupled with yearnings for redemption and
the messianic–utopian perspective, have given the underlying rationale for Jewish nationhood its ethos. These, however, have never progressed from symbols
to the focus of public and educational activity. The Jewish people, as a collective, has existed with them but not by virtue of them. It has survived because it
knew how to learn, because it summoned the wisdom to build a communal
organizational system, and because it founded a national movement that had
the strength, even after the devastating blow dealt to it, to rise up, struggle for
its political independence, and build a Jewish society in Palestine. Without this
constructive action, no commemoration of martyred victims and no educational memorial marches could maintain the Jews as a national collective.

But the important question that concerns us at the present moment is the
ambivalent relationship between Jewish consciousness of the Holocaust and
Jewish consciousness of the State of Israel. The former embodies the impotence
of the Jewish collective will; the latter illustrates the strength of this will. It is

the Holocaust that symbolizes the Jews' pariah status during the war in the ethical consciousness of the nations and in the political considerations and military strategies of the leaders of the free world. The State of Israel, in contrast, was established with the consent and assistance of most of the enlightened world, not only for reasons of politics and self-interest but also because of the wish and pressure to compensate the Jews for their collective suffering and losses. Today in the light of the changes that are sweeping the globe, Israel needs more than ever to integrate into the universal process of shaping new political superstructures. The conceptions of these two major events lead in two different and opposing directions. Emphasizing the uniqueness of the Holocaust drives an unmistakable wedge between Jews and other nations, whereas, on the other hand, Israeli statehood, by underscoring the normal fundamentals of sovereign life, induces a rapprochement between the Jews in Israel and Jews in the diaspora, and also between Jews and non-Jews.

However, the conceptions of these two major events also have common aims that produce opposite results. One may say, on the one hand, that the ethos embodied in Holocaust commemoration reinforces the mythical ethos of the State and strengthens Israel's relations with the diaspora. On the other hand, the amplification of the Holocaust mythos in the diaspora detracts from the centrality of Israel in the Jewish collective consciousness, in two ways: by creating a facile, contradiction-free mythology and by creating an intellectual acknowledgment of the universal nature of the Holocaust. Similarly, the statehood mythos may emphasize the differences between the diaspora and the State of Israel by obfuscating the particular characteristics of the Jewish image and replacing them with universal ones. This ambivalence creates a tension that deserves the mindfulness of thinkers, scholars, and educators.

How does this development in the relations between those two kinds of consciousness reflect on the status of Zionism among the Jewish people in the present and for the future?

Holocaust consciousness is a major part of two ideological propensities: one, a non-Zionist; and the other, an anti-Zionist. The first one is diasporist, which means making the Holocaust instead of the State of Israel the central historical mythos of the Jewish diaspora. The second one is universalistic; it denies the uniqueness of the Holocaust to the Jewish people who were deigned to be annihilated, and as a people with almost complete collective impotence, being a stateless nation without political power. This is what Zionism came to stand for until this very day for the whole Jewish people.

To sum up, Zionism in the present day is the only ideology with an all-embracing idea about the meaning of Jewishness as one entity. It does not belong to any particular version of Judaism, but contains all of them within itself: Orthodox, Conservative, Reform, secular nationalist Jews, as one embracing form of Jewishness. And Jewishness is the most multi-cultural, multi-political, and multi-denominational phenomenon in the modern and even post-modern society yet to come. For those who wish to keep the totality of Jewishness, Zionism is the only answer to this kind of pluralism.

From its beginning, Zionism as a modern ideology was at the same time post-modern as well. First, because it refused to accept completely the great modern perspectives like Marxism and liberalism, which rejected the recognition of the Jews as one people. And, second, because of the extreme multi-cultural nature of Zionism as a political movement and organization. From this point of view, Zionism was a combination of modernism and post-modernism; of ideological principles, and political pragmatism; functioning all together to achieve a common goal, during a period of more than fifty years. As such, Zionism can prove something and be an example for the general society, which is torn to pieces by post-modern cultures and ideologies. And this may be the "new mission" for the Jewish people who live apart, separated by different versions of Judaism, but remaining together with the unifying ethos of Jewishness in the way Zionism conceived it. This means that Zionism arrived at the third stage of its long problematic and ambivalent relations with Judaism and Jewishness. The first one was the organizing of a national movement and building a national society by the minority of the Jewish people. The second one was the shaping of a political and cultural form of the Jewish state with the support of the majority of the Jewish people. Now after a hundred years of Zionism as a national movement and fifty years as a national state, the task is to keep together the Jewish people as a "Klal Israel." At this time of post-modern individualistic ethos, it is more difficult to conceive than it was in the past with its modern collective ethos. But history has proved that the Jewish people were always rebels, and the historian can only hope that they will continue to be the same in the future.

CHAPTER 27

The "Return" to Traditional Judaism at the End of the Twentieth Century: Cross-Cultural Comparisons

M. Herbert Danzger

Almost fifty years ago, Rabbi Menachem Mendel Schneerson became the seventh Lubavitcher Rebbe. Shortly thereafter he issued a call for an effort of outreach to non-Orthodox Jews. The cause was taken up by Rabbis Shlomo Carlebach and Zalman Schachter, two Lubavitcher disciples who became the first outreach workers for what came to be known as the *t'shuva* movement.

A movement of return had begun earlier. Already in the 1930s and 1940s, one could find individuals reared in non-orthodox homes who became Orthodox as adults. One could also find institutions with programs designed to facilitate such change, such as the Young Israel synagogue movement and schools such as Yeshivot Torah Vodaath and Heychal HaTorah. But these early efforts were directed for the most part at providing bridges to observance for those considered to be "lacking background," or, as in the case of the early Lubavitch efforts, at providing outreach to children.

In the 1960s, the effort came to be redirected at adults. It was no longer a matter of simply providing the necessary information or framework for Orthodox observance but, rather, of actually persuading adults to become Orthodox. This marked the real beginning of the *t'shuva* movement and, with it, the redefinition of those who became Orthodox as *baalei t'shuva* (lit., "masters of return," the Hebrew phrase denoting non-Orthodox Jews who choose to become Orthodox) rather than simply as "people lacking background."

Yeshiva University, which had earlier directed its efforts toward teenagers through retreats, summer camps, and its youth organization, NCSY, opened a school aimed at these newly Orthodox. But the movement first came to public notice when, in the early 1970s, following Israel's triumph in the Six-Day War and the recapture of Jerusalem, a number of yeshivot for *baalei t'shuva* opened in Jerusalem. These schools were for Americans and staffed by Americans. Hundreds of young people flocked to them and to charismatic Orthodox personalities in the United States, such as Shlomo Carlebach.

This was the "age of Aquarius" in America, a time when young people were turning toward religion. It was a time of countercultural movements in the wake of the civil rights era, of urban riots and anti-Vietnam War protests, a time of protest against all things "establishment." But even as the religious establishment was rejected, Orthodox Judaism was perceived as countercultural and therefore embraced. During this period, hippies were role models and many *baalei t'shuva* adopted Orthodoxy as a hippie expression of religion. This could be seen in their style of dress, attitudes toward food, styles of prayer, and even in the kinds of yeshivot they favored.[1]

As the hippie countercultural movement faded in the 1980s, the *t'shuvah* movement changed its form. The *baalei t'shuvah* were now yuppies: young, upwardly mobile, urban, professional. Recruitment into this group came mainly through synagogues and marriage between those reared as Orthodox and those new to it. At the same time, the *t'shuvah* movement continued to draw on the strengths of the people who had already entered and begun to change Orthodoxy, on the yeshivot for *baalei t'shuvah* that had been established, and on the new styles of prayer service that already had been developed (havurah styles and beginners' *minyanim*, for instance).

By 1982, survey data demonstrated that one in four Jews in the New York metropolitan area who followed Orthodox practices had not been raised in those practices. This finding, based on a reanalysis of the Greater New York Population Survey,[2] was fully consistent with studies of other denominations in the United States, in which roughly one-fourth of the population switches denominations.[3] Still, the finding is so startling that it has generally been ignored or minimized as inaccurate.

Why do people choose to become involved in traditional Jewish religious practice? It would seem that such behavior in the twentieth century is paradoxical, almost bizarre. Already in the nineteenth century, religion seemed everywhere to be in retreat. The advance of science, the emergence of secular political and national movements, the radical ideas of Marx, Darwin, and Freud seemed to herald the demise of religion. From the beginning of the twentieth century, religion retreated from the public arena in all modern western societies. By mid-century, radical theologians in America and elsewhere were proclaiming the "death of God." For Jews, the seeming absence of God at Auschwitz was deeply troubling. In fact, the high rates of assimilation and religious disaffiliation seem to reflect this. In the face of the many pressures, that Jews raised in secular or non-Orthodox families would as adults choose traditional religious observance is almost incomprehensible.

To explain this phenomenon, I gathered data on "return to tradition" in three societies: the US, Israel, and the Former Soviet Union (FSU). Here we shall draw on data on the return to traditional Judaism of Americans both in the United States and in Israel as well as on the return to tradition of Russians in the FSU. (Discussion of Israelis' return to tradition is omitted.) Much of the data on Americans has been published elsewhere[4] and will be only briefly discussed. Data on Jews in the FSU has been presented and/or published more recently, so that reference will be made to this material and to new data on the return to tradition in the FSU.

The comparative approach used here highlights the impact of the broader culture within which a particular movement of "return" takes place. Failure to use an approach and to examine contextual factors might make one believe that the return to traditional religion is unprecedented, that it is unique to Jews, and, if not miraculous, at least a tribute to Jews, distinctive courage and inner faith or at least to some other factor uniquely related to the Jewish people. But, as we shall see, what is happening to Jews is happening in a context that cannot be ignored if we are accurately and completely to explain this phenomenon.

Fundamentalism in Various Cultural Contexts

In the United States, return to Christianity, often referred to as fundamentalism, developed in the middle of the twentieth century, from roughly 1925 to 1975. In the Arab world, in the last third of this century, there has been a movement away from secular pan-Arabism and communism and from attempts to imitate the West. These separate movements share a common point of origin, the breakdown of value consensus in society, the questioning of assumptions heretofore taken-for-granted, and the retreat of religious life from the public arena, that is, the "secularization of society." When such secularization occurs, society becomes fragmented, and, for many people, religion disappears from daily life or becomes "privatized." A minority of people develop an intensification of religious identity that becomes self-conscious rather than taken-for-granted. Religious commitment becomes a conscious choice made in – or at the cusp of – adulthood.

In their zeal to be fully involved and protected from "worldly," "outside," or "western" influence, those who choose to be deeply committed to religion often go beyond traditional religious behaviors. Often they create "traditionalistic" religious behavior patterns that may never have existed, intensifying and romanticizing the commitment of religious communities of the past.[5] As we shall see below, the black clothes of the Haredi (extremely pious) Orthodox Jewish community are an example.

While the preceding describes what occurs in theoretical terms and on an abstract level, in each society this process takes a different coloration. In the United States, fundamentalism began primarily as a reaction to urbanization and the changes it introduced in the family structure. Thus the growth of fundamentalism slowed in the 1940s and 1950s, just as mainstream religion became more conservative in response to World War II and the Cold War. But with prosperity and the receding of the Cold War toward the end of the 1960s, the counterculture emerged, and established institutions were challenged in many areas.[6] Fundamentalism then re-emerged in the seventies (Roof and McKinney, 1987). It is within this frame that the movement of return to traditional Judaism also began. As I have described elsewhere,[7] this movement was influenced both by the counterculture and by the larger American society's turn to traditionalistic religion.

In the Soviet Union, religion was so forcefully repressed during the communist era that attempts to renew it were almost entirely underground.[8] With the overthrow of the communist regime, these underground groups emerged and re-established a public presence. Again, these contexts influenced the return to Judaism that reflected, in its own unique way, both the underground period and the period of the re-emergence of religion.

In Arab societies, the period of Turkish domination was, characteristically, a time of stability during which religion was taken for granted. Following the defeat of Turkey in World War I, the traditional Arab world began to crumble. At first the young elite viewed western, secular society as the model to be emulated. Over the next half-century, movements of westernization developed in most of these societies except the most isolated. But as movements of westernization did not result in substantial improvement in the lot of ordinary people, religious movements developed in reaction.[9]

Although fundamentalist movements emerged in the Arab world after most of the Jews had left these countries, the Arab context has affected the movement of return in Israel. Its effects, however, are more subtle and complex than in other contexts for two reasons. First, for the last century, Israel (and the "Yishuv" before that) has been involved in a fight against Arab countries for its very survival, making Arab religious life an oppositional model rather than one to be imitated. Second, in Israel, Judaism is the dominant religion, making it difficult to isolate the impact of cultural contexts, as the factor of the dominant or minority status of Judaism is intertwined with it. Nonetheless, the point is that return to Judaism everywhere reflects the context of the larger society in which Judaism is embedded. But "return" does not simply mirror fundamentalism in the larger society. It typically develops in a pattern peculiar to Judaism, in no small measure because Judaism in America and the FSU is a minority religion within the dominant culture.

Despite this fact, all too often, historians and social scientists explain a phenomenon in a given society without testing their generalizations in comparative perspective. An example will illustrate. In a widely hailed analysis, Haym Soloveitchik, professor of history at Yeshiva University, offers an explanation of the "move to the right," the increasingly restrictive ritual practices, of Orthodox Jews in contemporary Orthodoxy. Soloveitchik[10] argues that until the twentieth century, traditional Judaism was transmitted through a process of mimesis or imitation. Since the mid-twentieth century and particularly since the upheaval and destruction of European Jewry, this transmission has come through the written word, a shift that, he argues, has promoted restrictiveness.

But Soloveitchick has looked at only half of the data. While it is true that increased dependence on the written word came at the moment in contemporary history at which there was a turn toward more restrictiveness in the interpretation of the Halakhah, it is also possible to find restrictiveness in the contemporary *mimetic* transmission of the law. The wearing of black clothes by men in the Hasidic and Haredi communities is an example. Goffman[11] notes that such clothes are a device for self-stigmatization, cutting these men off from the larger society. He quotes Poll's statement that Hasidim wear their traditional garments, "so that they may refrain from any possible sin." Within this community, those who reject these styles, choosing, for example, to wear a suit or hat in a light color, clearly lose status in the religious hierarchy. This affects their lives in the community in important ways, including making young men who deviate in dress less desirable as mates. Thus black clothes, a mimetically transmitted custom, represents a severely restricted dress code for those who wish to be a part of this community.[12]

Yet, in Judaism, wearing black is problematic. It is regarded as a sign of mourning and distress (B. Hag. 16a), as a sign of ritual impurity (M. Mid. 5:4), or as a sign that someone is in a state of excommunication (B. B.M. 59b). It is even associated with sin (B. Qid 30a, B. M.Q. 17a). The written word (here, the statements in the Talmud) seems to be liberating, urging the wearing of clothing other than black, contrary to the restrictive dress code of the traditionalistic Orthodox community. Indeed, black was adopted by that community only in the last quarter of the twentieth century. Presently, many yeshivot (Orthodox religious schools) specifically require their students to adhere to this code as something that is befitting a yeshiva student. Clearly, a process of mimesis has brought about the change, not the written word.

Moreover, until the mid-1960s, the written word actually was used by some religious leaders to loosen restrictive customs (minhagim) and to open Orthodoxy to the contemporary world. This can be seen in the decisions of Rabbi Joseph Dov Soloveitchik, Rabbi Moshe Feinstein, and Rabbi Abraham Isaac Kook, among others. Take for example the partition separating men and women in Orthodox synagogues (mehitzah). Rabbi Moses Feinstein, the leading American halakhic decisor, determined that a mehitzah of eighteen handbreadths (about fifty-four inches) is halakhically acceptable.[13] Nonetheless, in the last quarter-century, synagogues that had installed such partitions have raised them to six or eight feet. Some Hasidic synagogues have replaced the semi-transparent curtains once used in the upper part of the mehitzah with opaque plastic sheets or with solid walls.

It is true that the written word was often used in the post-1960s period to define Halakhah restrictively, as Haym Soloveitchik has argued. But it was also used to promote a more liberal and open view, and that view was at times overridden by a restrictive mimetic practice. To find an association between the written word and restrictiveness is not to show that the written word is the cause of the restriction. To reliably determine cause, it is necessary to examine a variety of contexts. Furthermore, the move from mimetic to written religious law does not account for the emergence of fundamentalism within Christianity and Islam during this same period. In these religions, too, restrictive and sectarian communities (albeit called fundamentalist rather than Haredi) emerged at about the same time, and there is little reason in their case to see the shift as a result of the transition from mimetic traditions to written rules.

For this reason, our approach compares different historical periods and cultural contexts. It is nomothetic rather than idiographic. It uses data to develop broad generalizations rather than seeking to learn the specific facts that characterize a phenomenon viewed in isolation. Thus our approach differs from that of historians such as Soloveitchik and Wertheimer, who, excellent as they are, tend to focus on patterns within Judaism alone.

The United States

In earlier work,[14] I identified four periods of return to traditional Judaism, each period related to specific developments in the wider American culture. First is the period until about the third decade of the twentieth century, when Judaism was in retreat, as was religion generally. This period was characterized by an almost unchallenged outflow from Orthodoxy. In the 1930s, a second period was marked by the sprouting of a movement of return. A very few structures were developed to accommodate those new to Orthodoxy, and there was no attempt actively to recruit adults. Those newly interested in Judaism were considered simply to "lack background," as though the shift to Orthodoxy was not a change in religion but only an alteration in religious practices. The third period began in the 1960s and corresponded to the changes taking place in America during this decade. The fourth stage, the growth of the Yuppie return to tradition, corresponds to the growth of Evangelical, Pentecostal, and fundamentalist religion in America and the decline of mainline religious denominations. At each stage of these movements of return, a different type of recruitment process was in place and a different type of recruit was drawn into Orthodoxy.[15]

The unique sociological and historical patterns that characterized the return to traditional Judaism can only be understood in terms of the larger social context defined by each period within American history. For example, Shlomo Carlebach, a major figure in the third period, had unique qualities especially suited to the Hippie era. The yeshivot for *baalei t'shuva* and the havurah movement similarly were well suited to succeed in that era but faded as that time passed. We shall see that a similar "fit" exists between developments in the former Soviet Union (FSU) and the renewal of interest in Judaism there.

Interestingly, study of return to traditional Judaism demonstrates a process of religious commitment best seen in Judaism but characteristic of other religions as well. In this process, ritual acts precede and play a larger role than belief in the transformation of the *baal t'shuva*. This pattern seemed to characterize all the varieties of returnees described above but has not been noticed or explored in the literature of sociology of religion. Still, this pattern is fully consonant with theoretical perspectives of social psychology and particularly with the work of Leon Festinger and C. Wright Mills.[16] In essence, we find that *naaseh v'nishma* ("We will do and we will listen," the Israelite's response to God's revelation at Sinai; Exod. 14:23) is not simply a Jewish response to revelation but a social psychological rule for religious identification. Ritual practice leads to identification and then to belief.[17]

A second theoretical perspective derived from this data is that the accounts of return provided by "returnees" reflect the specific doctrine or beliefs of the group they join.[18] Accounts differing from what is acceptable to that group will be considered inauthentic. For Orthodox Judaism, the account must include something about how one came to learn about its meaning over a period of time. There can be no sudden revelation of the "truth."

The Former Soviet Union prior to 1989

The repression of Judaism in the Soviet Union under communism occurred in the context of the repression of religion generally. In this context, one cannot ignore the underground religion that characterized both Judaism and Orthodox Christianity. Here we cannot examine this factor at any length save to note that, although there was no direct cooperation between the two groups, it is clear that each was aware of and probably learned from the other. Additionally, some Jews were drawn to the Russian Orthodox Church.[19]

While we cannot here explore them in detail, the many differences between political and religious society in the US and in the FSU are important for understanding the different processes of return in the two places. In the USSR prior to 1989, Jews who desired to emigrate to Israel were both refused permission and fired from their jobs, the Soviets contending, most often as nothing more than a pretext, that they had held security-sensitive jobs. These people began the process of identification as Jews by becoming involved with Jewish ethnicity. Only after finding no outlet or means of expression for this Jewishness did some of them become involved in Judaism as a religion. The process of involvement in "return" for a group whose ethnic and religious identity was repressed and persecuted – not simply neglected – was indeed difficult. Many of the returnees of this group began their return when their sense of rejection by Soviet society seemed to overwhelm them. They were usually isolated; there were no portals of return visible at first and certainly no recruiters. These people tended to try to seek out their connection to Jewishness on their own. Typically this was done by reading or by listening to Israeli radio broadcasts.

Furthermore, since these people were not in a framework that permitted communication with co-religionists, the organizational structure of spiritual absorption was quite different from that which developed in the United States or in Israel. Contacts were developed with the utmost care, lest one be betrayed. A secret network was developed with all the implications that secrecy imposes on an organization. While, for many, persecution was a deterrent to further involvement, it only hardened others' resolve. This is not simply a psychological difference. Sociologically, different portals (or opportunity structures) were developed. While probably thousands gave up their Jewish identity, a few become exemplars of return at this stage.

Some of the loneliness and isolation of those seeking to connect with their people and their religious roots is seen in the following excerpt from an interview with Eliyahu Essas, one of the leaders of the refuseniks (those refused the right to emigrate). A mathematician, he taught himself Hebrew, learned about Judaism, and set about teaching others not only to practice but to be teachers themselves. His was an underground school that was hounded and harassed by the Soviet authorities. The excerpt describes his first experience with observance of the Sabbath:

EE: The first time I saw a Shabbat celebrated by someone who grew up with it was at this Jew's house in Riga. I went alone from Moscow where I lived to see this man. Reb Gershon Yakovson was his name. He is not alive already. I was married in 1970. I went to Reb Gershon Yakovson, I think, in 1975.

HD: With your wife?

EE: No. There was no need. In some sense I was a *shaliach mitzvah* [a messenger to do a good deed]. Then I can continue to practice it at home.

HD: What did you see there that impressed you at this Shabbos?

EE: Maybe you will laugh but I never saw a Kiddush [the blessing over wine that ushers in the Sabbath]. I didn't know anything. I read it in *Shulhan Arukh* [Code of Jewish Law] about Shabbos. I knew what it is. But I never saw how to do it. For you, this may be very difficult to understand. It may be so clear to you. But believe me, unless you have seen it before, the first time you are a guest for Shabbos in someone's home, in a family, you don't have confidence that you are not funny. That you are not doing things the wrong way.

   I remember I prepared myself enormously spiritually. I remember I came to him and all this Friday was preparation for me like *Ma'amad Har Sinai* [the revelation at Mount Sinai].

HD: I understand. How were you preparing? What did you do to make yourself feel that you were ready for a holy experience?

EE: It was a trembling of "now I will see it and I want it." It's very difficult to explain because it's somehow your soul is going for something. It was like one of biggest joys, one of the biggest celebrations. This was the first Shabbos. It was the first time I saw someone make Kiddush. Then we went to make a *Motzi* [the blessing over bread], and then we sit together and talk. He was a lonely person.

HD: He was alone?

EE: Yes. He didn't have any family. He was an elderly person and his elderly sister also came for the meal so we could talk and even sing *Zimiros* [Sabbath hymns]. He was crying from joy because from years and years he didn't see a young person who came for him. Now he understood he was needed to help somebody. You understand? He kept all his Jewishness for himself and now somebody came to him. It was a strong experience.

Then I remember we didn't go to the synagogue for Kabbalas Shabbos [Friday evening services] because the synagogue was quite far away. I remember him *davening* [praying] at home. For me this was a familiar experience because I also couldn't go to the synagogue in Moscow. Everything was good for me. For him, too, it was like *Ma'amad Har Sinai* because he was sleeping in the night like before *Matan Torah* [the revelation at Sinai also occurred early in the morning after a night of sleep] and tomorrow morning came. We got up early in the morning and together this elderly person and I went together.

It was quite a long walk for him although not for me; quite a long journey to the synagogue and then back. And during the Shacharis [morning prayer service] he was happy that a young person stands next to him. He said to everybody he trusted, "You see this boy came from Moscow to me." He didn't elaborate too much. Don't forget 1975. There was KGB. But he said this. For him it was a central achievement in his life. Then I remember very well that everybody shook my hand and then we went back. A long journey, a sunny day. It had to be sunny day because nature also had to be sunny that day. Then we came home and made Kiddush at home and once again he opened Rambam [Maimonides' book of religious law] with me. We studied together. He was very happy. I was very happy. We continued until the *Seudah Shalishit* [the last Sabbath meal] and then Havdalah [the ceremony marking the end of the Sabbath]. I had never seen Havdalah. I had to see it. I remember what he did, he explained himself and he was amazed that I knew many things from the Shulhan Arukh that I never saw in my life. He was amazed and I was amazed. Everything was very nice and I remember that after Shabbos this same evening, I went back to Moscow.[20]

Judaism in the Former Soviet Union post-1989

Following the collapse of the USSR in 1989, hundreds of thousands of Jews sought to emigrate to Israel. Many were able to demonstrate their Jewishness openly for the first time. For most, the only way to do this beyond registering to emigrate was to develop connections to the Jewish community. This meant coming to synagogues and Jewish institutions and registering children in Jewish schools and clubs. For some this was an opportunity to identify as Jews. For others this was simply to prepare themselves for their anticipated move to Israel. They would learn Hebrew so as to get along in Israel or learn Jewish history so as to understand the society they were about to enter. Yet, once having started this process, some carried it further to religious commitment, even where there was no material benefit.[21]

Culturally, a significant difference between returnees in the FSU, particularly in the Ukraine, and in the US is the importance of attachment to the dead, to parents and relatives, perhaps especially those annihilated by the Nazis. This is probably related not only to the Jewish experience but to the surrounding cultures that place great emphasis on the dead. Here we summarize some of the important points and indicate how these developments further our understanding of the process of return.

Judaism in Kiev

Kiev, once a thriving center of Jewish religion and culture, fell to the Germans on September 21, 1941. One week later, the Germans began the massacres at Babi Yar, killing 33,771 in two days. During World War II, a total of about 200,000 people were slaughtered in Kiev, probably 100,000 Jews among them. These massacres and the suppression of Jews and Judaism under communism combined to destroy Jewish life and institutions. Throughout the period of Communist domination, Jews in the Ukraine were cut off from contact with Jews of the West and elsewhere.

Following the war, the Communist regime continued to impose restrictions on Judaism. Only the synagogue in the Podol suburb of Kiev was permitted to open. It attracted an overflow crowd of several thousand for Yom Kippur and the Memorial Day of the Babi Yar massacre. But attempts publicly to memorialize the Babi Yar massacre were quashed, and when a memorial was finally erected in early 1976, no mention was made of the slaughter of Jews. Jewish religious and memorial activities were punished, including religious services held in private homes, which, if discovered, led to severe penalties. Jews also were punished for baking Passover matzah in their homes, for performing ritual circumcision (*brit*), and for other religious observances.

In 1989, Mikhail Gorbachev announced a policy of *perestroika*, openness to the world. Restrictions on religion were removed. Jews from America, Israel, and western Europe sought to assist their brethren in the FSU in rebuilding Judaism and sent funds and personnel to assist in this endeavor. Jacob Bleich, a young Hasidic rabbi from Brooklyn, became chief rabbi of Kiev. He brought with him his wife, and they immediately organized religious schools for children and various programs for adults as well as a variety of other institutional structures to provide for the community of Kiev Jews.[22]

The Podol synagogue can accommodate about a thousand worshipers. Its courtyard now houses a newly equipped matzah factory, producing strictly kosher matzah used in the celebration of Passover throughout the Ukraine. The courtyard also houses a small slaughterhouse producing kosher chicken and other fowl. The synagogue compound features a brand new ritual bath, with modern showers and baths, well lit and tiled to meet standards one might find in a middle-class New York neighborhood. The synagogue courtyard also contains a dining room and large kitchen. The building houses a yeshiva and a *kolel* (an academy for advanced students in Talmud), although here the people in these schools appear to have no more than basic skill in reading Hebrew. It also has dormitories to house students, twenty to thirty of whom are enrolled in the yeshiva.

As one would expect of an Orthodox synagogue, daily prayer services are held. But the minyan (prayer quorum) is composed of several people who seem attracted by the free breakfast that follows the service and a number of others who have been sent by Jewish agencies abroad and serve various functions in the community: ritual slaughterer, teacher, youth leader, etc. In a word, this morning minyan is not indigenous; it is imported.

The Construction of Portals of Return

The religious activities and institutional structures described above are a result of the efforts of Jewish communities elsewhere to re-establish the Jewish community of Kiev and many other communities in eastern Europe. With *perestroika*, the once closed Jewish communities of the former USSR could now communicate with their co-religionists.

Perestroika offered an opportunity to revive communities that had suffered the terrible blows of the Holocaust and seventy years of religious repression under the communist regime. To provide a sense of Jewish life, what was constructed might in some sense be called a theater set. Jews had to learn how to celebrate a Jewish wedding or conduct a Jewish funeral. It was not enough simply to know the rules. They had to learn how it was done and what better way than actually to observe it. Up to 1989, efforts had to be underground or at best behind closed doors. Strong-willed individuals, such as Eliyahu Essas, could learn. But they too would not know the public face of Judaism. And what of the children? When and where would they see how Judaism is lived? And if they only saw it when they grew into adults, would it matter to them by that time? What was undertaken in Kiev appears to be nothing less than an attempt to construct the building blocks, the institutional and organizational structures, of the Jewish community that would be necessary for Judaism to be transmitted to the next generation in Kiev. To see how this works, it is perhaps best to view it from the perspective of the children, to whom Rabbi Bleich's first and most sustained efforts were directed. They appear to be the strategic opening in the effort to rebuild Judaism. We turn to Rabbi Bleich's first encounter with Jews in Kiev.

Visiting the graves of *tzadikkim* – the pious – had long been a practice of some hasidim, a practice more than a little likely supported by the non-Jewish practices of the areas in which hasidism had emerged. In any case, Rabbi Bleich described the scene in the cemetery, visited as part of an initial tour, as "packed with people" who swarmed around his group. This ritual activity gave Bleich and others hope that it might be possible to revive Judaism in the Ukraine.[23] When his group returned from their trip and when other reports made clear the opportunities for outreach, the group mobilized to send Rabbi Bleich back.

When he returned in the summer of 1990, however, he did not organize Jewish burial societies or the like. Instead, in perhaps typical Jewish fashion, he organized a Sunday school. The first week, after distributing flyers and advertising, he had twenty-seven students. Within a few weeks, without further advertising, he had 250 boys and girls. It was clear that this effort was tapping into an existing community need that had not been met. A full-time school opened with thirty-seven children, and, soon after, the city of Kiev transferred to Rabbi Bleich's administrative care a school building to be operated as a Jewish "ethnic" school (rather than a religious school *per se*). There was no bar to teaching religious subjects as long as any Jewish child could attend, whether or not the child observed religious practices.

To provide kosher bread for students learning about the laws of kashrut, the school has a bakery, a large operation that also provides bread to the only kosher restaurant in Kiev. The restaurant, a rather elegant establishment, is an important facility for religious Jews from abroad – particularly delegations from philanthropic agencies – and it serves the Kiev community as well. In addition, bread baked at the school is available for purchase. Most important, children bring home kosher bread so that they may continue to eat kosher food at home, including hallah, the special braided loaves traditionally eaten at the Sabbath dinner. Other foods, such as kosher meat or special Passover holiday foods, may also be provided. This brings the religious practice of kashrut into the home, enables the student to maintain the religious practices taught at the school, and allows parents to learn something of kashrut through their children. Certainly, the parents can object, and the student might eat non-kosher foods. But parents do not object, and, at times, themselves share the food made available. At the same time, in Kiev, where food is relatively expensive, the school's contribution to the upkeep of the student and thus indirectly to the household's budget is not insignificant.

From the perspective of those seeking to determine the extent to which Judaism has re-emerged in Kiev, the involvement of outsiders in creating the appearance of a vibrant indigenous Judaism may be a disappointment. But, in fact, it serves a highly useful function. First, of course, it affords an opportunity to people who have never seen synagogue life to observe and participate in communal prayer, to celebrate bar mitzvah and holidays in an appropriate fashion. The three meals offered daily by the schools are not merely intended to provide kosher food, but also teach the customs and prayers surrounding the meals. When the meal is concluded, Grace After Meals is sung aloud in Hebrew by all the participants. The children quickly memorize this prayer. That synagogue life has a long-term impact on some also seems clear from reports of the impact of the Simhat Torah holiday celebrations in Moscow and elsewhere on those who attended them and participated by merely milling in the streets outside the synagogue.

The synagogue was the center of religious life in other respects as well. As mentioned, it provided kosher meat, Passover matzah, and a ritual bath that made it possible for those interested to practice Judaism. Beyond that, it was the base for shipping thousands of packages of food each month to indigent and housebound elderly. "Warm houses," or homes where elderly gathered to eat, talk, and discuss matters of Jewish interest, were also organized with the help of the synagogue. In fact, through the synagogue, the entire range of Jewish communal life was provided for, from a kosher restaurant to Jewish burial.

Another element some may find distressing is the admixture of external constraints and inducements that affect the choice of both adults and children to participate in the Jewish community and its religious life. The plans to emigrate to Israel, the interest in a higher quality education, the small stipends of food seem to sully that choice. Jews have historically shunned coerced conversions and have avoided open attempts at "buying" religious commitment. But such behaviors are part of ordinary religious life for those raised in religious homes and communities. In everyday life, one's community imposes rewards on conformity and sanctions on deviance. Judaism has accepted this as well as the maxim that even actions inspired by improperly directed motivations eventually come to be religiously motivated. Social psychological theory supports this. Herbert Kelman[24] has pointed out that behaviors reflect three motivations: compliance – where behaviors are induced by external rewards and punishments; identification – where behaviors are induced by attachment to others; and internalization – where behaviors reflect one's own deep-seated meaning system. Kelman is concerned to develop a means of distinguishing these three in action. I suggest that the study of conversion or religious participation needs to examine the possibility that these three motives may, rather, reflect different stages in the process of religious involvement.

Conclusions

A number of conclusions can be drawn from our discussion of the return to traditional Judaism in the FSU. In the period prior to 1989, it took heroic effort to identify with religion in general and the Jewish people in particular. If Russian Jews simply followed the lead of ethnic Russians who turned to religion, they would have become Orthodox Christians. But the prevalent pattern was, first, identification with the Jewish people and, as a second step, identification with Judaism. This was the case not only for Eliyahu Essas but for numbers of others as well. The two-step pattern, first identified with regard to American returnees, held for Jews in the FSU. Clearly, minority ethnic status outweighed religion as a factor in shaping the identity of Jewish returnees.

Despite the nomothetic similarity, the portals of return were radically different from those found in the USA in the 1960s and 1970s. Both the path of return and the kind of person motivated to return was necessarily different. At the very least, the early leaders of return in the FSU seem much more secularly and less Jewishly educated, even as they were much more self-directed and driven than their American counterparts. They existed in a world in which great efforts needed to be expended to engage in the slightest of religious practices and in which government agents stood ready to prosecute any open expression of religion. Following their applications to emigrate, many of these early leaders were jailed and suffered job discrimination. They created portals of entry to Judaism in a wasteland in which portals did not exist or were underground.

In the period following 1989, the religious and ethnic landscape changed radically. Suddenly portals of entry to Jewishness were developed with the help of Jewish groups outside the FSU. Those who had struggled underground could now be Jews openly. New kinds of people were drawn to return to Judaism. Some were drawn by the hope of emigrating to Israel; others by the promise of education or the help available through the Jewish community. Certainly, the desire to identify as a Jew was still there. But now the recruits approached a more normal situation, one in which return to tradition was a result of a "mixed motivation."

Examining the development of Judaism in the post-1989 period allows us to change focus from micro-social to macro-social processes. In this later period, we find the building of institutional structures that enabled a full-blown community to emerge, comprised of various pieces that related to each other in ways that supported Jewish identity, especially for Jewish children. Thinking about this, lets us answer another piece of the puzzle: How is it that traditional religion re-emerges in these circumstances? Why is the religion that emerges not a radical or contemporary version of that religion?

Two answers are possible. One is that radical religion emerges in opposition to traditional religion. Where traditional religion has been destroyed, by contrast, it is traditionalism that one seeks to re-establish out of an oppositional framework. On the macro level, a second answer suggests itself. To re-establish a religion, only that religion's existing apparatus can provide the opportunity structures, the portals of return. The traditional religion, that is, has the resources to assist with the re-creation of the religion and, hence, what is re-created takes a traditional form.

But, if this is so, why could not Reform and Conservative Judaism do the same? That is a question that still waits to be answered more fully. Here we can only suggest a conclusion to which the data point. Only traditionalistic religion has the power to make the effort to recruit. Radical, left-wing, and tolerant denominations do not have that energy probably because they do not bind followers as deeply to their community as traditionalistic religions do. It is this power that is likely to make traditionalistic religions an option for many seeking to turn to religion in the next century.

Notes

I wish to acknowledge the Research Foundation of City University of New York, the Lucius N. Littaur Foundation, and the Memorial Foundation for Jewish Culture for support of the research on which this chapter is based.

1   For an extended discussion of the cultural context of the rise of the *t'shuva* movement, see M. Herbert Danzger, *Returning to Tradition: The Contemporary Revival of Orthodox Judaism* (New Haven, 1989), pp. 71–89.

2   Danzger, ibid., pp. 342–3. Note that this statistic makes no claim regarding denominational self-identification, a different matter entirely.

3   Frank Newport, "The Religious Switcher in the U.S.," in *American Sociological Review*, vol. 44, no. 4 (1979), pp. 528–52, and Wade Clark Roof, "Multiple Religious Switching: A Research Note," in *Journal for the Scientific Study of Religion*, vol. 28, no. 4 (1989), pp. 530–5.

4   M. Herbert Danzger, "Toward a Redefinition of 'Sect' and 'Cult': Orthodox Judaism in the United States and Israel," in Richard F. Tomasson, ed., *Comparative Social Research*, vol. 10 (1987), pp. 113–23, and *Returning to Tradition*.

5   Eric Hobsbawm, *The Invention of Tradition* (Cambridge, 1983).

6   Jeffrey Hadden, *The Gathering Storm in the Churches: The Widening Gap between Clergy and Laymen* (Garden City, 1969).

7   See my *Returning to Tradition*.

8   Jerry G. Pankhurst, "Religious Culture," in Dmitri N. Shalin, ed., *Russian Culture at the Crossroads: Paradoxes of Post-Communist Consciousness* (Westview, 1996).

9   The preceding ignores western societies' attempts to westernize the countries as a means of exploiting them and communist attempts to shake that influence. I have here glossed over the importance of the Cold War and its impact on the Middle East.

10 Haym Soloveitchik, "Migration, Acculturation, and the New Role of Texts in the Haredi World," in Martin E. Marty and R. Scott Appleby, eds., *Accounting for Fundamentalisms* (Chicago, 1994). The article was reprinted with minor modifications in *Tradition*. Jack Wertheimer has cited this argument with approval in a recent article in *Commentary* ("The Orthodox Moment," February 1999, pp. 18–24). Wertheimer adds another reason for this tendency, the post-war immigration to America of large numbers of Hungarian Hasidim. Yet both factors to which he ascribes the turn to more traditional religion are found within the Jewish community only. Scores of other essays and research articles similarly seek the causal factors for the turn to traditional observances within the Jewish community only.

11 Erving Goffman, *Stigma: Notes on the Management of Spoiled Identity* (Englewood Cliffs, 1963), p. 101.

12 See Danzger, *Returning to Tradition*, pp. 143–6.

13 Moses Feinstein, *Igroth Moshe*, Orech Haim, vol. 1, section 39–44, written December 1945 (New York, 1959).

14 Ibid., pp. 71–95.

15 I call these "portals of return." In political movements, they are termed "opportunity structures." See Sidney Tarrow, *Power in Movement* (Cambridge, 1994).

16 Leon Festinger, *A Theory of Cognitive Dissonance* (Stanford, 1957); C. Wright Mills, "Situated Actions and Vocabularies of Motive," in *American Journal of Sociology*, vol. 5, pp. 904–13.

17 See Danzger, *Returning to Tradition*, pp. 4–7, 130–3, 222–4.

18 Ibid., pp. 224–50.

19 Father Alexander Men, one of the leaders of the "underground church," was himself a Jewish convert to Russian Orthodoxy; Michael Meerson, "The Life and Work of Father Alexander Men," in Stephen K. Batalden, ed., *Seeking God: The Recovery of Religious Identity in Orthodox Russia, Ukraine and Georgia* (Dekalb, 1993). The father

of Yuri Edelstein, a member of Israel's Knesset and an observant Jew, converted to Christianity and also became a Russian Orthodox priest. The people I interviewed include a woman who, because of her interest in things spiritual, attended the Russian Orthodox Church and almost converted to Christianity. She chanced to meet a man attached to Lubavitch in Moscow and finally married him. The influence of Russian Orthodoxy was so strong that numbers of Russian Jews joined Russian Orthodox churches even after arriving in the United States. This despite the efforts of Jewish outreach organizations to draw them into the Jewish community. It is also clear that "humanitarian" protests in the Soviet Union were connected to the re-emergence of Judaism.

20   Additional materials on the return of Jews from the FSU to traditional Judaism may be found in my articles and papers listed in the bibliography.

21   The portals of return or organizational structures were developed by the Jewish Agency, by international Jewish philanthropies, by Orthodox Jewish outreach groups, and by foundations interested in the rebirth of Judaism in the FSU. I described the patterns for the emergence of these groups and the source of identification in this period in "Missions to the Jews," a paper presented at the Annual Meeting of the Association for the Sociology of Religion, Toronto, Canada, August 8, 1997.

22   Similar patterns developed in other cities. For example, in Moscow, Pinchas Goldschmidt, a young Swiss-born rabbi who had studied in America and Israel, was appointed chief rabbi. He and his wife developed a fine educational program and helped foster the growth of a number of similar institutional structures. Their work is noteworthy in itself and will be described elsewhere. Here we shall focus on Kiev and examine how institutional structures provided portals of return for Jews there.

23   Similarly, when, about a week later, I interviewed Rabbi Goldschmidt about the causes for the reawakened interest in Judaism, he responded, "Judaism in the Soviet Union lives because of the dead."

24   Herbert Kelman, "Process of Opinion Change," in *Public Opinion Quarterly*, vol. 25, 1961, pp. 57–78.

Bibliography

Danzger, M. Herbert, "Toward a Redefinition of 'Sect' and 'Cult': Orthodox Judaism in the United States and Israel," in Richard F. Tomasson, ed., *Comparative Social Research*, vol. 10 (1987), pp. 113–23.

Danzger, M. Herbert, *Returning to Tradition: The Contemporary Revival of Orthodox Judaism* (New Haven, 1989).

Danzger, M. Herbert, "The Organizational Structure of Spiritual Absorption," paper presented at the annual meeting of the Association for the Sociology of Religion, Miami, Florida, August 1993.

Danzger, M. Herbert, "The Impact of Dominant versus Minority Status on Religious Conversion Processes: Comparisons of Jews Returning to Traditional Judaism in Israel, the USA and the USSR," in Anson Shupe and Bronislaw Misztal, eds., *Religion, Mobilization and Social Action* (Westport, 1998).

Danzger, M. Herbert, "The 'Return' to Traditional Judaism in the United States, Russia and Israel: The Impact of Minority and Majority Status on Religious Conversion Processes," in Madelaine Cousineau, ed., *Religion in a Changing World: Comparative Studies in Sociology* (Westport, 1998).

Feinstein, Moses, *Igroth Moshe*, Orech Haim, vol. 1, section 39–44, written December 1945 (New York, 1959).

Festinger, Leon, *A Theory of Cognitive Dissonance* (Stanford, 1957).

Gitelman, Zvi, *A Century of Ambivalence: The Jews of Russia and the Soviet Union, 1881 to the Present* (New York, 1989).

Goffman, Erving, *Stigma: Notes on the Management of Spoiled Identity* (Englewood Cliffs, 1963).

Hadden, Jeffrey, *The Gathering Storm in the Churches: The Widening Gap between Clergy and Laymen* (Garden City, 1969).

Hobsbawm, Eric, *The Invention of Tradition* (Cambridge, 1983).

Kelman, Herbert, "Process of Opinion Change," in *Public Opinion Quarterly* 25 (1961), pp. 57–78.

Meerson, Michael, "The Life and Work of Father Alexander Men," in Stephen K. Batalden, ed., *Seeking God: The Recovery of Religious Identity in Orthodox Russia, Ukraine and Georgia* (Dekalb, 1993).

Mills, C. Wright, "Situated Actions and Vocabularies of Motive," in *American Journal of Sociology*, vol. 5, pp. 904–13.

Newport, Frank, "The Religious Switcher in the U.S.," in *American Sociological Review*, vol. 44, no. 4 (1979), pp. 528–52.

Pankhurst, Jerry G., "Religious Culture," in Dmitri N. Shalin, ed., *Russian Culture at the Crossroads: Paradoxes of Post-Communist Consciousness* (Westview, 1996).

Roof, Wade Clark, "Multiple Religious Switching: A Research Note," in *Journal for the Scientific Study of Religion*, vol. 28, no. 4 (1989), pp. 530–5.

Roof, Wade Clark, and William McKinney, *American Mainline Religion: Its Changing Shape and Future* (New Brunswick, 1987).

Soloveitchik, Haym, "Migration, Acculturation, and the New Role of Texts in the Haredi World," in Martin E. Marty and R. Scott Appleby, eds., *Accounting for Fundamentalisms* (Chicago, 1994) (republished in *Tradition*, 1997).

Tarrow, Sidney, *Power in Movement* (Cambridge, 1994).

Abbreviations

A.Z.	Avodah Zarah
Ah.	Ahilot
Ar.	Arakhin
Aram.	Aramaic
B.	Babli, Babylonian Talmud
b.	*ben*, "son of"
B.B.	Baba Batra
B.M.	Baba Mesia
B.Q.	Baba Qamma
Bek.	Bekhorot
Ber.	Berakhot
Bes.	Besah
Bik.	Bikkurim
Cant.	Canticles (Song of Songs)
ch(s).	chapter(s)
Chr.	Chronicles
Cod. Theod.	Theodossion code
col(s).	column(s)
Cor.	Corinthians
Dan.	Daniel
Dem.	Demai
Deut.	Deuteronomy
Eccl.	Ecclesiastes
Ed.	Eduyyot
Erub.	Erubin
Esdr.	Esdras
Esth.	Esther
Exod.	Exodus

Ezek.	Ezekiel
Gal.	Galatians
Gen.	Genesis
Git.	Gittin
Gk.	Greek
Hab.	Habakuk
Hag.	Haggai
Hag.	Hagigah
Hal.	Hallah
Heb.	Hebrew
Hor.	Horayot
Hos.	Hosea
Hul.	Hullin
Is.	Isaiah
Jer.	Jeremiah
Josh.	Joshua
Judg.	Judges
Kel.	Kelim
Ker.	Keritot
Ket.	Ketuvot
Kgs.	Kings
Kil.	Kilaim
Lat.	Latin
Lev.	Leviticus
M.	Mishnah
M.Q.	Moed Qatan
M.S.	Maaser Sheni
Ma.	Maaserot
Macc.	Maccabees
Mak.	Makkot
Makh.	Makhshirin
Mal.	Malachi
Matt.	Matthew
Me.	Meilah
Meg.	Megillah
Men.	Menahot
Mic.	Micah
Mid.	Middot
Miq.	Miqvaot
MS(S).	Manuscript(s)
Naz.	Nazir
Ned.	Nedarim
Neg.	Negaim
Neh.	Nehemiah
Nid.	Niddah

Num.	Numbers
Obad.	Obadiah
Oh.	Ohalot
Or.	Orlah
Par.	Parah
Pes.	Pesahim
Phil.	Philemonians
Prov.	Proverbs
Ps. (pl.: Pss.)	Psalm(s)
Qid.	Qiddushin
Qin.	Qinnim
R.	Rabbi
R.H.	Rosh Hashanah
Rab.	Rabbah
Rev.	Revelation
Rom.	Romans
Sam.	Samuel
San.	Sanhedrin
Shab.	Shabbat
Shav.	Shavuot
Sheb.	Shebiit
Sheq.	Sheqalim
Sir.	Sirach
Sot.	Sotah
Suk.	Sukkah
T.	Tosefta
T.Y.	Tebul Yom
Ta.	Taanit
Tam.	Tamid
Tan.	Tanhuma
Tem.	Temurah
Ter.	Terumot
Toh.	Toharot
Uqs.	Uqsin
Y.	Yerushalmi, Palestinian Talmud
Y.T.	Yom Tob
Yad.	Yadaim
Yeb.	Yebamot
Yom.	Yoma
Zab.	Zabbim
Zeb.	Zebahim
Zech.	Zechariah
Zeph.	Zepheniah

Index